Survivors

True Tales of Endurance

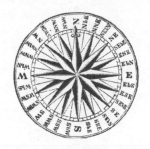

Edited by
John B. Letterman

Simon & Schuster
New York London Toronto Sydney Singapore

SIMON & SCHUSTER
Rockefeller Center
1230 Avenue of the Americas
New York, NY 10020

First published in North America in 2003 by Simon & Schuster, Inc.

For information about special discounts for bulk purchases,
please contact Simon & Schuster Special Sales at
1-800-456-6798 or business@simonandschuster.com

Published by arrangement with Book Creation, LLC New York, NY
Publishing Director: John Kelly

Designed by Anthony Meisel

Manufactured in the United States of America

1 3 5 7 9 10 8 6 4 2

Library of Congress Cataloging-in-Publication Data is available

ISBN 0-7432-4547-4

CONTENTS

INTRODUCTION

There, exhausted, weak and chilled, hanging freely in space and slowly turning round as the rope twisted one way and the other, I felt that I had done my utmost and failed, that I had no more strength to try again and that all was over except the passing...There on the brink of the great Beyond I well remember how I looked forward to the peace of the great release—how almost excited I was at the prospect of the unknown to be unveiled. From those flights of mind I came back to earth, and remembering how Providence had miraculously brought me so far, felt that nothing was impossible and determined to act up to Service's lines:

> "Just have one more try—it's dead easy to die,
> It's the keeping-on-living that's hard."

My strength was fast ebbing; in a few minutes it would be too late. It was the occasion for a supreme attempt. Fired by the passion that burns the blood in the act of strife, new power seemed to come as I applied myself to one last tremendous effort. The struggle occupied some time, but I slowly worked upward to the surface. This time emerging feet first, still clinging to the rope, I pushed myself out extended at full length on the lid and then shuffled safely on to the solid ground at the side. Then came the reaction from the great nerve strain and lying there alongside the sledge my mind faded into a blank.

– Sir Douglas Mawson, Antarctica, 1911

This account of Mawson clawing his way to survival is just one of many truly incredible stories of endurance in this volume, which brings together a selection of the most exciting, moving, and inspiring pieces ever written about human courage and perseverance in the face of mortal danger.

All the stories in this book are true, yet they are as dramatic and astonishing as anything fiction has to offer. My intent has been to cull, from the hundreds of worthy narratives that exist, a truly varied and compelling selection of the literature of survival. The twenty-three accounts in this book surely constitute an honor-role of survival from the dawn of the Age of Discovery to the present day—one that embraces every continent, two vast oceans, the great deserts and mountains of the world, the depths of the sea, and the reaches of outer space; worlds of starvation and thirst, exposure and extremes of heat and cold, the horrors of human cruelty and the nobility of human strength and self-sacrifice.

All but two of the selections are first-hand accounts: Woodes Rogers' narrative of Alexander Selkirk's five solitary years on Juan Fernández Island (Isla Róbinson Crusoe) and Piers Paul Read's striking retelling of the seventy-two day ordeal of the survivors of the crash in the Andes of chartered Uruguayan Air Force Fairchild F-227. These two exceptions satisfy a high standard of truthful and direct testimony. Captain Woodes Rogers, who rescued Selkirk from his island prison, serves well as the spokesman of the castaway's experience; Read, who closely interviewed the survivors of the Andes crash, tells their stories graphically and with scrupulous accuracy.

All the first-hand accounts preserve the exact language, spelling and punctuation of the originals. While I have made every effort to provide introductions with sufficient biographical and historical detail to illuminate the narratives, I have avoided lengthy commentary. The stories are direct and powerful; they speak for themselves. I trust that they will provide you the same degree of astonishment and inspiration, of excitement and admiration that they have brought me.

That being said, I cannot preface this volume without sharing one aspect that I found common to virtually every survival account: that we find our greatest comfort and our greatest support in each other and in our service to each other, and our most bitter suffering in solitude.

These truths of human solidarity were deeply impressed upon John McCain, whose moving account in his memoir *Faith of My Fathers* shows how the suffering he endured as a prisoner of war renewed the values of duty and service that he had been taught in his youth, and made him convinced that we are here "to serve a cause greater than ourselves." This notion that our lives are bound up in the fabric of a larger tapestry is a theme that runs throughout the accounts in this volume, and the literature of survival in general. Saint-Exupéry expresses this in *Prisoner of the Sand*: "Once again we discovered that it was not we who were shipwrecked, not we but those who were waiting for news of us, those who were alarmed by our silence, were already torn with grief by some atrocious and fantastic report. We could not but strive towards them." Primo Levi expresses this human solidarity in his searing *Survival in Auschwitz*, where he finds within himself the strength to speak of his own experiences on behalf of the millions who perished there and on behalf of those few who survived. Black Elk's account is a testament to his struggle to preserve the spiritual strength and resources of his people. Dougal and Lyn Robertson exemplify the power of selfless love in their determined struggle to "get these boys to land." In story after story, each in its unique voice and experience, we observe the quest for survival as a collective endeavor that affirms what John Donne eloquently affirms in his seventeenth meditation: "No man is an *Island*, entire of itself; every man is a piece of the *Continent*, a part of the *main*; . . . any man's *death* diminishes *me*, because I am involved in *Mankind*; And therefore never send to know for whom the *bell* tolls; It tolls for *thee*."

John B. Letterman
New Haven
July, 2003

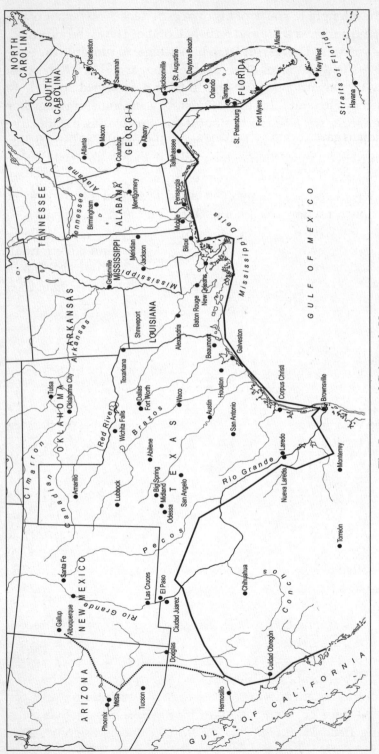

The Journey of Cabeza de Vaca

——— route of Cabeza de Vaca

········· route of Estebanico

1528–1536
THE JOURNEY OF
ÁLVAR NÚÑEZ CABEZA DE VACA

The Indians gave all that talk of theirs little attention. They parleyed among themselves, saying that the Christians lied, for we had come from sunrise, while the others came from where the sun sets; that we cured the sick, while the others killed those who were healthy; that we went naked and shoeless, whereas the others wore clothes and went on horseback and with lances. Also, that we asked for nothing, but gave away all we were presented with, meanwhile the others seemed to have no other aim than to steal what they could, and never gave anything to anybody. In short, they recalled all our deeds, and praised them highly, contrasting them with the conduct of the others.

– Cabeza de Vaca

In June of 1527, barely a generation after Columbus first claimed the Americas for the Spanish Crown, Pánfilo de Narváez set out from Spain with five ships and six hundred men. Álvar Núñez Cabeza de Vaca was his second in command. The conquest of the vast expanse of territory from the river of the Palms in Mexico to the Cape of Florida was the grandiose mission of this ill-fated expedition, which, after making a safe passage across the Atlantic to Santo Domingo, suffered from problems of supply and desertions and the loss of two of its vessels in the blows of a savage hurricane. After laying over during the winter months and again suffering from damaging storms, a refitted expedition finally reached the coast of Florida in April of 1528 and sailed northward along its western coastline until a suitable anchorage was found at the mouth of a large bay in sight of a native settlement.

After proclaiming Spanish sovereignty, Narváez ordered reconnaissance of the surrounding area, finally deciding to move inland and away from the ships, which he ordered north to another harbor, even though the location of the harbor was disputed, grave hazards were likely to be encountered in the unknown interior, and the expedition—once cut off—might altogether lose the lifeline of its supporting fleet. When Cabeza de Vaca counseled against this,

11

Narváez offered him command of the ships. But Cabeza decided to accompany Narváez and his comrades to share with them the very dangers against which he had warned.

On the first of May, Narváez and Cabeza de Vaca headed inland with an expeditionary force of three hundred men, forty of whom were mounted on the expedition's surviving horses. Marching for fifteen days, the expedition had nearly exhausted its supplies when Narváez' men came across an Indian village whose corn stocks they seized, starting a pattern of hunger and pillage that they repeated in their struggle to survive throughout the months of that summer. As the weeks went by, the native population became increasingly hostile to the Spaniards and Narváez' men began to sicken and perish of exhaustion, disease, hunger, and exposure, and by the arrow. With a third of their number stricken, supplies desperately low, and the few remaining horsemen threatening to desert, extreme measures were required to save the expedition. Although there was only one carpenter in their entire company, and no tools at all, Narváez' chief lieutenants decided to construct five rafts by which they hoped to escape the grip of the fatal shore.

It is at this page that we open Cabeza de Vaca's remarkable story of survival, a six-thousand mile, sixteenth-century Odyssey that was to last for close to eight years before Cabeza and three companions— the only surviving members of the Narváez expedition—finally found their way back to Christian civilization. With the rafts finally completed, Narváez and his expeditionary force, which still numbered almost two hundred and fifty men, set out on September 22, 1528. The makeshift flotilla managed to make its way fifteen hundred miles to the mouth of the Mississippi River where the fragile rafts were caught and scattered in a series of storms. Cabeza de Vaca and the surviving crew of his raft were thrown upon an island, which he named the Isle of Misfortunes, where they were greeted by natives who were moved to grief by the miserable condition of the Spaniards and who brought them food. Joined on this island by the crew of another raft, they passed a cruel winter there, naked and nearly starving. By the spring of the following year, only fifteen had survived.

Late that winter Cabeza de Vaca left the island for the mainland, where he fell gravely ill and was rumored to have died. All but two of his companions left the Isle of Misfortunes to try to reach Mexico. After Cabeza recovered he was forced to work for the tribe, with whom he remained for the next few years, entirely isolated from Christian civilization. Eventually, he achieved standing with the natives and was able to move further inland, where, now fully adapted to the ways of aboriginal life, he adopted the role of a trader and quasi-diplomat among native groups who were often in conflict. But, however successful his adaptation to these conditions of life, he still suffered isolation, extreme privation, and exposure.

Finally, in late 1532, Cabeza de Vaca decided to move toward Mexico with don Lope Oviedo, the sole Spanish survivor remaining on the Isle of Misfortune. After a difficult journey brought them to a forbidding coastal inlet and a brutal encounter with the natives on the opposing shore, don Lope insisted that he could not go on and decided to turn back. He was never heard from again. Cabeza de Vaca was enslaved by the local natives, a fate he shared with three former companions with whom he was reunited soon after his capture and with whom he would eventually make his way to Mexico: Andres Dorantes de Carranza, the African Estevanico, and Alonso Castillo Maldonado. During their period of captivity, Cabeza learned the mortal fate of the other members of the expedition and patiently planned his escape. Separated from his three fellow survivors for much of the eighteen months that followed their first astonished and joyful reunion, frustrated in his attempts to flee captivity, threatened several times with death, and tested by further extremes of suffering and privation, Cabeza de Vaca was finally again reunited with his surviving companions and together they made their escape to South Texas in mid-September of 1535.

Their strength and characters tested and tempered in the ordeal of the years of suffering that they had endured, the four castaways were treated favorably by their new hosts. Cabeza de Vaca and Dorantes soon achieved the status of healers, a role which they accepted gingerly at first but in which they steadily grew more confidant. As they made their final journey across the uncharted Southwest to the Pacific coast of Mexico, their renown for healing and justice preceded them wherever they traveled. The castaways finally made contact with their countrymen in the winter of 1535–36. Cabeza de Vaca returned to Spain in 1537 and in late 1540 sailed again for the New World, to assume the position of Governor and Captain General of the Rio de la Plata in South America, where further exploits awaited him, and where his opposition to the enslavement of native populations put him at odds with local powers and eventually led to his overthrow and expulsion in chains for trial in Spain. Never completely vindicated, but granted a pension by the emperor Charles V, Cabeza de Vaca finally died in Spain at an unknown date.

The great American historian, Samuel Eliot Morison, has written: "Álvar Núñez Cabeza de Vaca stands out as a truly noble and humane character. Nowhere in the lurid history of the Conquest does one find such integrity and devotion to Christian principles in the face of envy, malice, treachery, cruelty, lechery, and plain greed." First drafted after his first return to Spain, Cabeza de Vaca's *Relación* has been characterized by some critics as a document written less to provide an honest record of his ordeal than to curry favor. The modesty and lack of self-glorification that Cabeza de Vaca displays in his unique record encourages us to accept it as a valuable and forthright documentation of his experiences in surviving his ordeal of eight years.

The *Relación* provides us with insights into the character that made his survival possible. Although almost forty years old at the beginning of his ordeal, Cabeza de Vaca's sheer physical vitality and resilience, and the moral strength of his will to live, were characteristics unquestionably crucial to his survival. Without doubt his Christian faith sustained him in the times of greatest danger. At least of equal importance to these qualities were his strong common sense and his genius in adapting to his environment. At times utterly dependent on the natives for survival, Cabeza de Vaca had no choice but to survive with them as they survived themselves. He learned from his captors, and grew to respect them as fellow human beings. Ultimately, as trader and diplomat and healer, Cabeza de Vaca transcended the grim subsistence of the existence into which he had been thrust, emerging from his harrowing experiences a man more whole and more enlightened, having achieved among the natives a shamanistic status as a master of survival and as a healer from the east, the "land of the rising sun" from which he emerged.

The Journey of Álvar Núñez Cabeza de Vaca

translated by Fanny Bandelier (1905)

One-third of our people were dangerously ill, getting worse hourly, and we felt sure of meeting the same fate, with death as our only prospect, which in such a country was much worse yet. And considering these and many other inconveniences and that we had tried many expedients, we finally resorted to a very difficult one, which was to build some craft in which to leave the land. It seemed impossible, as none of us knew how to construct ships. We had no tools, no iron, no smithery, no oakum, no pitch, no tackling; finally, nothing of what was indispensable. Neither was there anybody to instruct us in shipbuilding, and, above all, there was nothing to eat, while the work was going on, for those who would have to perform the task. Considering all this, we agreed to think it over. Our parley ceased for that day, and everyone went off, leaving it to God, Our Lord, to put him on the right road according to His pleasure.

The next day God provided that one of the men should come, saying that he would make wooden flues, and bellows of deerskin, and as we were in such a state that anything appearing like relief seemed acceptable, we told him to go to work, and agreed to make of our stirrups, spurs, cross-bows and other iron implements the nails, saws and hatchets and other tools we so greatly needed for our purpose.

In order to obtain food while the work proposed was in progress we determined upon four successive raids into Aute, with all the horses and men that were fit for service, and that on every third day a horse should be killed and the meat distributed among those who worked at the barges and among the sick. The raids were executed with such people and horses as were able, and they brought as many as four hundred *fanegas* [a measure equal to about 1¹/₂ bushels] of maize, although not without armed opposition from the Indians. We gathered plenty of palmettos, using their fibre and husk, twisting and preparing it in place of oakum for the barges. The work on these was done by the only carpenter we had, and progressed so rapidly that, beginning on the fourth day of August, on the twentieth day of the month of September five barges of twenty-two elbow lengths each were ready, caulked with palmetto oakum and tarred with pitch, which a Greek

15

called Don Teodoro made from certain pines. Of the husk of palmettos, and of the tails and manes of the horses we made ropes and tackles, of our shirts sails, and of the junipers that grew there we made the oars, which we thought were necessary, and such was the stress in which our sins had placed us that only with very great trouble could we find stones for ballast and anchors of the barges, for we had not seen a stone in the whole country. We flayed the legs of the horses and tanned the skin to make leather pouches for carrying water.

During that time some of the party went to the coves and inlets for sea-food, and the Indians surprised them twice, killing ten of our men in plain view of the camp, without our being able to prevent it. We found them shot through and through with arrows, for, although several wore good armor, it was not sufficient to protect them, since, as I said before, they shot their arrows with such force and precision. According to the sworn statements of our pilots, we had traveled from the bay, to which we gave the name of the Cross, to this place, two hundred and eighty leagues, more or less.

In all these parts we saw no mountains nor heard of any, and before embarking we had lost over forty men through sickness and hunger, besides those killed by Indians. On the twenty-second day of the month of September we had eaten up all the horses but one. We embarked in the following order: In the barge of the Governor there were forty-nine men, and as many in the one entrusted to the purser and the commissary. The third he placed in charge of Captain Alonso del Castillo and of Andrés Dorantes, with forty-eight men; in another he placed two captains, named Téllez and Peñalosa, with forty-seven men. The last one he gave to the inspector and to me, with forty-nine men, and, after clothing and supplies were put on board, the sides of the barges only rose half a foot above the water. Besides, we were so crowded as to be unable to stir. So great is the power of need that it brought us to venture out into such a troublesome sea in this manner, and without any one among us having the least knowledge of navigation.

... At the end of these thirty days, and when we were in extreme need of water and hugging the coast, we heard one night a canoe approaching. When we saw it we stopped and waited, but it would not come to us, and, although we called out, it would neither turn back nor wait. It being night, we did not follow the canoe, but proceeded. At dawn we saw a small island, where we touched to search for water, but in vain, as there was none. While at anchor a great storm overtook us. We remained there six days without venturing to leave, and it being five days since we had drank anything our thirst was so great as to compel us to drink salt water, and several of us took such an excess of it that we lost suddenly five men.

I tell this briefly, not thinking it necessary to relate in particular all the distress and hardships we bore. Moreover, if one takes into account the place we were in and the slight chances of relief he may imagine what we suffered. Seeing that our thirst was increasing and the water was killing us, while the storm did not abate, we agreed to trust to God, Our Lord, and rather risk the perils of the sea than wait there for certain death from thirst. So we left in the direction we had seen the canoe going on the night we came here. During this day we found ourselves often on the verge of drowning and so forlorn that there was none in our company who did not expect to die at any moment.

It was Our Lord's pleasure, who many a time shows His favor in the hour of greatest distress, that at sunset we turned a point of land and found there shelter and much improvement. Many canoes came and the Indians in them spoke to us, but turned back without waiting. They were tall and well built, and carried neither bows nor arrows. We followed them to their lodges, which were nearly along the inlet, and landed, and in front of the lodges we saw many jars with water, and great quantities of cooked fish. The Chief of that land offered all to the Governor and led him to his abode. The dwellings were of matting and seemed to be permanent. When we entered the home of the chief he gave us plenty of fish, while we gave him of our maize, which they ate in our presence, asking for more. So we gave more to them, and the Governor presented him with some trinkets. While with the cacique at his lodge, half an hour after sunset, the Indians suddenly fell upon us and upon our sick people on the beach.

They also attacked the house of the cacique, where the Governor was, wounding him in the face with a stone. Those who were with him seized the cacique, but as his people were so near he escaped, leaving in our hands a robe of marten-ermine skin, which, I believe, are the finest in the world and give out an odor like amber and musk. A single one can be smelt so far off that it seems as if there were a great many. We saw more of that kind, but none like these.

Those of us who were there, seeing the Governor hurt, placed him aboard the barge and provided that most of the men should follow him to the boats. Some fifty of us remained on land to face the Indians, who attacked thrice that night, and so furiously as to drive us back every time further than a stone's throw.

Not one of us escaped unhurt. I was wounded in the face, and if they had had more arrows (for only a few were found) without any doubt they would have done us great harm. At the last onset the Captains Dorantes, Peñalosa and Téllez, with fifteen men, placed themselves in ambush and attacked them from the rear, causing them to flee and leave us. The next morning I destroyed more than thirty of their canoes, which served to protect us against a northern wind then blowing, on account of which we had to stay there, in the severe cold, not venturing out to sea on account of the heavy storm. After this we again embarked and navigated for three days, having taken along but a small supply of water, the vessels we had for it being few. So we found ourselves in the same plight as before.

Continuing onward, we entered a firth and there saw a canoe with Indians approaching. As we hailed them they came, and the Governor, whose barge they neared first, asked them for water. They offered to get some, provided we gave them something in which to carry it, and a Christian Greek, called Doroteo Teodoro (who has already been mentioned), said he would go with them. The Governor and others vainly tried to dissuade him, but he insisted upon going and went, taking along a Negro, while the Indians left two of their number as hostages. At night the Indians returned and brought back our vessels, but without water; neither did the Christians return with them. Those that had remained as hostages, when their people spoke to them, attempted to throw themselves into the water. But our men in the barge held them back, and so the other Indians forsook their canoe, leaving us very despondent and sad for the loss of those two Christians.

Shortly after the attack, the party set out to sea once more, having to abandon their comrades, and Cabeza de Vaca's barge became separated from the others. Over the next days and weeks, they had several encounters with the natives— some friendly and others not. By November, de Vaca and his men had reached an island where the Indians were initially kind to them, although the extreme cold and lack of food plagued the Europeans and Indians alike.

. . . That same day I saw on one of the Indians a trinket he had not gotten from us, and asking from where they had obtained it they answered, by signs, that other men like ourselves, and who were still in our rear, had given it to them. Hearing this, I sent two Christians with two Indians to guide them to those people. Very near by they met them, and they also were looking for us, as the Indians had told them of our presence in the neighborhood. These were the Captains

Andrés Dorantes and Alonso del Castillo, with all of their crew. When they came near us they were much frightened at our appearance and grieved at being unable to give us anything, since they had nothing but their clothes. And they stayed with us there, telling how, on the fifth of that same month, their barge stranded a league and a half from there, and they escaped without anything being lost.

All together, we agreed upon repairing their barge, and that those who had strength and inclination should proceed in it, while the others should remain until completely restored and then go as best they could along the coast, following it till God would be pleased to get us all together to a land of Christians.

So we set to work, but ere the barge was afloat Tavera, a gentleman in our company, died, while the barge proved not to be seaworthy and soon sank. Now, being in the condition which I have stated—that is, most of us naked and the weather so unfavorable for walking and for swimming across rivers and coves, and we had neither food nor any way to carry it, we determined upon submitting to necessity and upon wintering there, and we also agreed that four men, who were the most able-bodied, should go to Pánuco, which we believed to be nearby, and that, if it was God, Our Lord's will to take them there, they should tell of our remaining on the island and of our distress. One of them was a Portuguese, called Álvaro Fernández, a carpenter and sailor; the second was Mendez; the third, Figueroa, a native of Toledo; the fourth, Astudillo, from Zafra. They were all good swimmers and took with them an Indian from the island.

... A few days after these four Christians had left, the weather became so cold and tempestuous that the Indians could no longer pull roots, and the canebrake in which they used to fish yielded nothing more. As the lodges afforded so little shelter, people began to die, and five Christians, quartered on the coast, were driven to such an extremity that they ate each other up until but one remained, who being left alone, there was nobody to eat him. At this the Indians were so startled, and there was such an uproar among them, that I verily believe if they had seen this at the beginning they would have killed them, and we all would have been in great danger. After a very short time, out of eighty men our two parties only fifteen remained alive.

Then the natives fell sick from the stomach, so that one-half of them died, and they, believing we had killed them, and holding it to be certain, agreed among themselves to kill those of us who survived.

But when they came to execute it an Indian who kept me told

them not to believe we were the cause of their dying, for if we had so much power we would not have suffered so many of our own people to perish without being able to remedy it ourselves. He also told them there remained but very few of us, and none of them did any harm or injury, so that the best was to let us alone. It pleased Our Lord they should listen to his advice and counsel and give up their idea.

To this island we gave the name of the Island of Ill Fate. The people on it are tall and well formed; they have no other weapons than bows and arrows with which they are most dextrous. The men have one of their nipples perforated from side to side and sometimes both; through this hole is thrust a reed as long as two and a half hands and as thick as two fingers; they also have the under lip perforated and a piece of cane in it as thin as the half of a finger. The women do the hard work. People stay on this island from October till the end of February, feeding on the roots I have mentioned, taken from under the water in November and December. They have channels made of reeds and get fish only during that time; afterwards they subsist on roots. At the end of February they remove to other parts in search of food, because the roots begin to sprout and are not good any more. . . .

. . . On the island I have spoken of they wanted to make medicine men of us without any examination or asking for our diplomas, because they cure diseases by breathing on the sick, and with that breath and their hands they drive the ailment away. So they summoned us to do the same in order to be at least of some use. We laughed, taking it for a jest, and said that we did not understand how to cure.

Thereupon they withheld our food to compel us to do what they wanted. Seeing our obstinacy, an Indian told me that I did not know what I said by claiming that what he knew was useless, because stones and things growing out in the field have their virtues, and he, with a heated stone, placing it on the stomach, could cure and take away pain, so that we, who were wiser men, surely had greater power and virtue.

At last we found ourselves in such stress as to have to do it, without risking any punishment. Their manner of curing is as follows: When one is ill they call in a medicine man, and after they are well again not only do they give him all they have, but even things they strive to obtain from their relatives. All the medicine man does is to make a few cuts where the pain is located and then suck the skin around the incisions. They cauterize with fire, thinking it very effective, and I found it to be so by my own experience. Then they breathe on the spot where the pain is and believe that with this the disease goes away.

The way we treated the sick was to make over them the sign of the cross while breathing on them, recite a Pater Noster and Ave Maria, and pray to God, Our Lord, as best we could to give them good health and inspire them to do us some favors. Thanks to His will and the mercy He had upon us, all those for whom we prayed, as soon as we crossed them, told the others that they were cured and felt well again. For this they gave us good cheer, and would rather be without food themselves so as to give it to us, and they gave us hides and other small things. So great was the lack of food then that I often remained without eating anything whatsoever for three days, and they were in the same plight, so that it seemed to me impossible for life to last, although I afterwards suffered still greater privations and much more distress, as I shall tell further on.

The Indians that kept Alonso del Castillo, Andrés Dorantes and the others, who were still alive, being of another language and stock, had gone to feed on oysters at another point of the mainland, where they remained until the first day of April. Then they came back to the island, which was from there nearly two leagues off, where the channel is broadest. The island is half a league wide and five long.

. . . After Dorantes and Castillo had come back to the island, they gathered together all the Christians, who were somewhat scattered, and there were in all fourteen. I, as told, was in another place, on the mainland, whither my Indians had taken me and where I suffered from such a severe illness that, although I might otherwise have entertained some hope for life, this was enough to take it away from me completely. When the Christians learned of it they gave an Indian the robe of marten we had taken from the cacique, as stated, in order that he should guide them to where I was, and so twelve of them came, two having become so feeble that they did not dare to take them.

. . . My sickness prevented me from following or seeing them. I had to remain with those same Indians of the island for more than one year, and as they made me work so much and treated me so badly I determined to flee and go to those who live in the woods on the mainland, and who are called those from (of) Charruco.

I could no longer stand the life I was compelled to lead. Among many other troubles I had to pull the eatable roots out of the water and from among the canes where they were buried in the ground, and from this my fingers had become so tender that the mere touch of a straw caused them to bleed. The reeds would cut me in many places, because many were broken and I had to go in among them with the

clothing I had on, of which I have told. This is why I went to work
and joined the other Indians. Among these I improved my condition
a little by becoming a trader, doing the best in it I could, and they
gave me food and treated me well. They entreated me to go about
from one part to another to get the things they needed, as on account
of constant warfare there is neither travel nor barter in the land.

So, trading along with my wares I penetrated inland as far as I
cared to go and along the coast as much as forty or fifty leagues. My
stock consisted mainly of pieces of seashells and cockles, and shells
with which they cut a fruit which is like a bean, used by them for
healing and in their dances and feasts. This is of greatest value among
them, besides shell-beads and other objects. These things I carried
inland, and in exchange brought back hides and red ochre with which
they rub and dye their faces and hair; flint for arrow points, glue and
hard canes wherewith to make them, and tassels made of the hair of
deer, which they dye red. This trade suited me well because it gave
me liberty to go wherever I pleased; I was not bound to do anything
and no longer a slave. Wherever I went they treated me well, and
gave me to eat for the sake of my wares. My principal object in doing
it, however, was to find out in what manner I might get further away.
I became well known among them; they rejoiced greatly when seeing
me and I would bring them what they needed, and those who did not
know me would endeavor to meet me for the sake of my fame.

My sufferings, while trading thus, it would take long to tell; danger,
hunger, storms and frost overtaking me often in the open field and
alone, and from which through the mercy of God, Our Lord, I escaped.
For this reason I did not go out trading in winter, it being the time
when the Indians themselves remain in their huts and abodes, unable
to go out or assist each other.

Nearly six years I spent thus in the country, alone among them
and naked, as they all were themselves.

The reason for remaining so long was that I wished to take with
me a Christian called Lope de Oviedo, who still lingered on the island.
The other companion, Alaniz, who remained with him after Alonso
del Castillo and Andrés Dorantes and all the others had gone, soon
died, and in order to get him (Oviedo) out of there, I went over to the
island every year, entreating him to leave with me and go in search of
Christians. But year after year he put it off to the year that was to
follow. In the end I got him to come, took him away, and carried him
across the inlets and through four rivers on the coast, since he could
not swim. Thence we proceeded, together with several Indians, to an

inlet one league wide, very deep everywhere and which seemed to us, from what we saw, to be the one called of the Holy Ghost.

On the opposite shore we saw Indians who had come to meet those in our company. They informed us that further on there were three men like ourselves and told us their names. Upon being asked about the rest of the party, they answered that all had died from cold and hunger and that the Indians beyond had killed Diego Dorantes, Valdivieso and Diego de Huelva willfully, only because these had gone from one house to another, and their neighbors with whom was now the Captain Dorantes, had, in consequence of some dream dreamt by these Indians, killed Esquivel and Méndez also. We asked them about those who remained alive, and they said they were in a very sorry condition, as the boys and other Indians, idlers and roughs, kicked them, slapped their faces and beat them with sticks, and such was the life they had to lead.

We inquired about the country further on and the sustenance that might be found in it. They said it was very thinly settled, with nothing to eat, and the people dying from cold, as they had neither hides nor anything else to protect their bodies. They also told us that, if we wished to meet the three Christians about two days hence, the Indians would come to a place about a league from there on the shore of that river to feed on nuts. And to show us that what they said of the ill-treatment of our people was true the Indians with whom we were kicked and beat my companion. Neither did I remain without my share of it. They threw mud at us, and put arrows to our chests, saying they would kill us in the same way as our companions. And fearing this, Lope de Oviedo, my companion, said he preferred to go back, with some women of the Indians in whose company we had forded the cove and who had remained behind. I insisted he should not go and did all I could to prevail upon him to remain, but it was in vain. He went back and I remained alone among these Indians, who are named *Guevenes*, whereas those he went away were called *Deaguanes*.

. . . An Indian told me that the Christians had come and that if I wished to see them I should run away to hide on the edge of a grove to which he pointed, as he and some of his relatives were to visit these Indians and would take me along to the Christians. I confided in them and determined to do it because they spoke a different language from that of my Indians. So the next day they took me along. When I got near the site where they had their lodges, Andrés Dorantes came out to look who it was, because the Indians had informed him also that a Christian was coming, and when he saw me he was much frightened, as for many days they believed me to be dead, the Indians having told them so. We gave many thanks to God for being together again, and that day was one of the happiest we enjoyed in our time, and going to where was Castillo they asked me whither I went. I told him my purpose was to go to a country of Christians and that I followed this direction and trail. Andrés Dorantes said that for many days he had been urging Castillo and Estevanico to go further on, but they did not risk it, being unable to swim and afraid of the rivers and inlets that had to be crossed so often in that country.

Still, as it pleased God, Our Lord, to spare me after all my sufferings and sickness and finally let me rejoin them, they at last determined upon fleeing, as I would take them safely across the rivers and bays we might meet. But they advised me to keep it secret from the Indians (as well as my own departure) lest they would kill me forthwith, and that to avoid this it was necessary to remain with them for six months longer, after which time they would remove to another section in order to eat prickly pears. These are a fruit of the size of eggs, red and black, and taste very good. For three months they subsist upon them exclusively, eating nothing else.

Now, at the time they pluck this fruit, other Indians from beyond come to them with bows for barter and exchange, and when those turn back we thought of joining them and escaping in this way. With this understanding I remained, and they gave me as a slave to an Indian with whom Dorantes stayed. And so, being here with them, they told me that after leaving the Island of Ill Fate they met on the coast the boat in which the purser and the monks were going adrift, and that crossing the rivers, of which there were four, all very large and very swift, the barges in which they crossed were swept out into the sea, where four of their number drowned. Thus they went ahead until they had crossed the inlet, which they did by dint of great efforts. Fifteen leagues from there they met another of our parties, and when they reached there, already two of their companions had died in sixty leagues of travel. The survivors also were very near death. On the whole trip they ate nothing but crawfish and *yerba pedrera* [kelp].

At this, the last cove, they said they saw Indians eating blackberries, who, upon perceiving the Christians, went away to another promontory. While seeking a way to cross the cove an Indian and a Christian came towards them, and they recognized Figueroa, one of the four we had sent ahead from the Island of Ill Fate, who there told them how he and his companions had gotten to that place, where two of their number and one Indian had died from cold and hunger, because they had come and remained in the worst weather known. He also said the Indians took him and Méndez.

While with them Méndez fled, going in the direction of Pánuco as best he might, but the Indians pursued and killed him. So, as he (Figueroa) was with these same Indians he learned (from them) that with the *Mariames* there was a Christian who had come over from the other side and had met him with those called *Guevenes,* and that this Christian was Hernando de Esquivel, from Badajoz, a companion of the commissary. From Esquivel he learned how the Governor, the purser and the others had ended.

The purser, with the friars, had stranded with their barge among the rivers, and, while they were proceeding along the coast, the barge of the Governor and his men came to land also. He (the Governor) then went with his barge as far as the big cove, whence he returned and took his men across to the other side, then came back for the purser, the monks and the rest . . . the Governor revoked the powers he had given to the purser as his lieutenant, giving the office to a captain that was with him called Pantoja.

The Governor did not land that night, but remained on his barge with a pilot and a page who was sick. They had neither water nor anything to eat aboard, and at midnight a northerner set in with such violence that it carried the barge out into the sea, without anybody noticing it. They had for an anchor only a stone, and never more did they hear of him. Thereupon the people who had remained on land proceeded along the coast, and, being much impeded by water, built rafts with great trouble, in which they passed to the other side.

Going ahead, they reached a point of timber on the beach, where they found Indians, who, upon seeing them approach, placed their lodges on the canoes and crossed over to the other side of the coast, and the Christians, in view of the season and weather, since it was in the month of November, remained in this timber, because they found water and firewood, some crawfish and other sea-food, but from cold and hunger they began to die.

Moreover, Pantoja, who remained as lieutenant, ill-treated them. On this Sotomayor, brother of Vasco Porcallo, unable to stand it longer, quarreled with Pantoja and struck him a blow with a stick, of which he died. Thus they perished one after another, the survivors slicing the dead for meat. The last one to die was Sotomayor, and Esquivel cut him up and fed on his body until the first of March, when an Indian, of those who had taken to flight previously, came to look if they were dead and took Esquivel along with him.

Once in the hands of this Indian, Figueroa spoke to Esquivel, learning what we have told here, and he entreated him to go in his company towards Pánuco. But Esquivel refused, saying he had heard from the monks that Pánuco was in their rear, and so he remained, while Figueroa went back to the coast where he formerly had been.

... All this account Figueroa gave after Esquivel's narrative, and thus, from one to the other, it came to me. Through it the fate of the whole fleet will be learned and known, and what happened to every one in particular. And he said furthermore that if the Christians would go about there for some time they might possibly meet Esquivel, because he knew that he had run away from the Indian with whom he was and gone to others called *Mariames,* who were their neighbors. And, as I have just said, he and the Asturian wished to go to other Indians further on, but when those with whom they were found it out, they beat them severely, undressed the Asturian and pierced one of his arms with an arrow.

At last the Christians escaped through flight, and remained with the other Indians, whose slaves they agreed to become. But, although serving them, they were so ill-treated, that no slaves, nor men in any condition of life, were ever so abused. Not content with cuffing and beating them and pulling out their beards for mere pastime, they killed three out of the six only because they went from one lodge to another. These were Diego Dorantes, Valdivieso and Diego de Huelva. The three remaining ones expected to meet the same fate in the end.

To escape from that life Andrés Dorantes fled to the *Mariames,* the ones with whom Esquivel had been. They told him how Esquivel stayed with them and how he fled because a woman dreamt he would kill her son, and the Indians pursued and killed him. They also showed Andrés Dorantes his sword, his rosary, his prayer book and other things of his . . . .

Dorantes remained only a few days with those Indians and then escaped. Castillo and Estevanico went inland to the *Iguaces.* All those people are archers and well built, although not as tall as those we had left behind us, and they have the nipple and lip perforated. Their principal food are two or three kinds of roots, which they hunt for all over the land; they are very unhealthy, inflating, and it takes two days to roast them. Many are very bitter, and with all that they are gathered with difficulty. But those people are so much exposed to starvation that these roots are indispensable and they walk two and three leagues to obtain them. Now and then they kill deer and at times get a fish, but this is so little and their hunger so great that they eat spiders and ant eggs, worms, lizards and salamanders and serpents, also vipers the bite of which is deadly. They swallow earth and wood, and all they can get, the dung of deer and more things I do not mention; and I verily believe, from what I saw, that if there were any stones in the country they would eat them also. They preserve the bones of the fish they eat, of snakes and other animals, to pulverize and eat the powder. . . .

They are a very merry people, and even when famished do not cease to dance and celebrate their feasts and ceremonials. Their best times are when *"tunas"* (prickly pears) are ripe, because then they have plenty to eat and spend the time in dancing and eating day and night. As long as these *tunas* last they squeeze and open them and set them to dry. When dried they are put in baskets like figs and kept to be eaten on the way. The peelings they grind and pulverize.

While with them it happened many times that we were three or four days without food. Then, in order to cheer us, they would tell us not to despair, we would have *tunas* very soon and eat much and drink their juice and get big stomachs and be merry, contented and without hunger. But from the day they said it to the season of the *tunas* there would elapse five or six months, and we had to wait that long.

When the time came, and we went to eat *tunas,* there were a great many mosquitoes of three kinds, all very bad and troublesome, which during most of the summer persecuted us. In order to protect ourselves we built, all around our camps, big fires of damp and rotten wood, that gave no flame but much smoke, and this was the cause of further trouble to us, for the whole night we did not do anything but weep from the smoke that went to our eyes, and the heat from the fires was so insufferable that we would go to the shore for rest. And when, sometimes, we were able to sleep, the Indians roused us again with blows to go and kindle the fires . . . .

. . . When I had been with the Christians for six months, waiting to execute our plans, the Indians went for *tunas,* at a distance of thirty leagues from there, and as we were about to flee the Indians began fighting among themselves over a woman and cuffed and struck and hurt each other, and in great rage each one took his lodge and went his own way. So we Christians had to part, and in no manner could we get together again until the year following. During that time I fared very badly, as well from lack of food as from the abuse the Indians gave me. So badly was I treated that I had to flee three times from my masters, and they all went in my pursuit ready to kill me. But God,

Our Lord, in His infinite goodness, protected and saved my life.

When the time for the *tunas* came we found each other again on the same spot. We had already agreed to escape and appointed a day for it, when on that very day the Indians separated us, sending each one to a different place, and I told my companions that I would wait for them at the *tunas* until full moon. It was the first of September and the first day of the new moon, and I told them that if at the time set they did not appear I would go on alone without them. We parted, each one going off with his Indians.

I remained with mine until the thirteenth of the moon, determined to escape to other Indians as soon as the moon would be full, and on that day there came to where I was Andrés Dorantes and Estevanico. They told me they had left Castillo with other people nearby, called *Anagados*, and how they had suffered many hardships and been lost. On the following day our Indians moved towards where Castillo was and were going to join those who kept him, making friends with them, as until then they had been at war. So we got Castillo also.

All over the land are vast and handsome pastures, with good grass for cattle, and it strikes me the soil would be very fertile were the country inhabited and improved by reasonable people. We saw no mountains as long as we were in this country. These Indians told us that further on there were others called *Camones*, who live nearer the coast, and that they were who killed all the people that came in the barge of Peñalosa and Téllez. They had been so emaciated and feeble that when being killed they offered no resistance. So the Indians finished with all of them, and showed us some of their clothes and weapons and said the barge was still stranded. This is the fifth of the missing ones. That of the Governor had been swept out into the sea, the one of the purser and the monks was seen stranded on the beach and Esquivel told us of their end. Of the two in which Castillo, I and Dorantes were I have told how they sank close to the Isle of Ill Fate.

. . . Two days after moving we recommended ourselves to God, Our Lord, and fled, hoping that, although it was late in the season and the fruits of the *tunas* were giving out, by remaining in the field we might still get over a good portion of the land. As we proceeded that day, in great fear lest the Indians would follow us, we descried smoke, and, going towards it, reached the place after sundown, where we found an Indian who, when he saw us coming, did not wait, but ran away. We sent the Negro after him, and as the Indian saw him approach alone he waited. The Negro told him that we were going in search of the people that had raised the smoke. He answered that the dwellings were nearby and that he would guide us, and we followed. He hurried ahead to tell of our coming. At sunset we came in sight of the lodges, and two crossbow shots before reaching them met four Indians waiting for us, and they received us well. We told them in the language of the *Mariames* that we had come to see them. They appeared to be pleased with our company and took us to their homes. They lodged Dorantes and the Negro at the house of a medicine man, and me and Castillo at that of another. These Indians speak another language and are called *Avavares*. They were those who used to fetch bows to ours and barter with them, and, although of another nation and speech, they understand the idiom of those with whom we formerly were and had arrived there on that very day with their lodges. Forthwith they offered us many *tunas*, because they had heard of us and of how we cured and of the miracles Our Lord worked through us. And surely, even if there had been no other tokens, it was wonderful how He prepared the way for us through a country so scantily inhabited, causing us to meet people where for a long time there had been none, saving us from so many dangers, not permitting us to be killed, maintaining us through starvation and distress and moving the hearts of the people to treat us well, as we shall tell further on.

. . . On the night we arrived there some Indians came to Castillo complaining that their heads felt very sore and begging him for relief. As soon as he had made the sign of the cross over them and recommended them to God, at that very moment the Indians said that all the pain was gone. They went back to their abodes and brought us many *tunas* and a piece of venison, something we did not know any more what it was, and as the news spread that same night there came many other sick people for him to cure, and each brought a piece of venison, and so many there were that we did not know where to store the meat. We thanked God for His daily increasing mercy and kindness, and after they were all well they began to dance and celebrate and feast until sunrise of the day following.

They celebrated our coming for three days, at the end of which we asked them about the land further on, the people and the food that there might be obtained. They replied there were plenty of *tunas* all through that country, but that the season was over and nobody there, because all had gone to their abodes after gathering *tunas;* also that the country was very cold and very few hides in it. Hearing this, and as winter and cold weather were setting in, we determined to spend it with those Indians. Five days after our arrival they left to get more *tunas* at a place where people of a different nation and language lived, and having traveled five days, suffering greatly from hunger, as on the way there were neither *tunas* nor any kind of fruit, we came to a river, where we pitched our lodges.

As soon as we were settled we went out to hunt for the fruit of certain trees, which are like spring bittervetch (orobus), and as through all that country there are no trails, I lost too much time in hunting for them. The people returned without me, and starting to rejoin them that night I went astray and got lost. It pleased God to let me find a burning tree, by the fire of which I spent that very cold night, and in the morning loaded myself with wood, took two burning sticks and continued my journey. Thus I went on for five days, always with my firebrands and load of wood, so that in case the fire went out where there was no timber, as in many parts there is none, I always would have wherewith to make other torches and not be without firewood. It was my only protection against the cold, for I went as naked as a newborn child. For the night I used the following artifice:

I went to the brush in the timber near the rivers and stopped in it every evening before sunset. Then I scratched a hole in the ground and threw in it much firewood from the numerous trees. I also picked up dry wood that had fallen and built around the hole four fires crosswise, being very careful to stir them from time to time. Of the long grass that grows there I made bundles, with which I covered myself in that hole and so was protected from the night cold. But one night fire fell on the straw with which I was covered, and while I was asleep in the hole it began to burn so rapidly that, although I hurried out as quick as possible, I still have marks on my hair from this dangerous accident. During all that time I did not eat a mouthful, nor could I find anything to eat, and my feet, being bare, bled a great deal. God had mercy upon me, that in all this time there was no norther; otherwise I could not have survived.

At the end of five days I reached the shores of a river and there met my Indians. They, as well as the Christians, had given me up for dead, thinking that perhaps some snake had bitten me. They all were greatly pleased to see me, the Christians especially, and told me that thus far they had wandered about famishing, and therefore had not hunted for me, and that night they gave me of their *tunas*. On the next day we left and went where we found a great many of that fruit with which all appeased their hunger, and we gave many thanks to Our Lord, whose help to us never failed.

. . . Early the next day many Indians came and brought five people who were paralyzed and very ill, and they came for Castillo to cure them. Every one of the patients offered him his bow and arrows, which he accepted, and by sunset he made the sign of the cross over each of the sick, recommending them to God, Our Lord, and we all prayed to Him as well as we could to restore them to health. And He, seeing there was no other way of getting those people to help us so that we might be saved from our miserable existence, had mercy upon us, and in the morning all woke up well and hearty and went away in such good health as if they never had had any ailment whatever. This caused them great admiration and moved us to thanks to Our Lord and to greater faith in His goodness and the hope that He would save us, guiding us to where we could serve Him. For myself I may say that I always had full faith in His mercy and in that He would liberate me from captivity, and always told my companions so.

When the Indians had gone and taken along those recently cured, we removed to others that were eating *tunas* also, called *Cultalchuches* and *Maliacones*, which speak a different language, and with them were others, called *Coayos* and *Susolas*, and on another side those called *Atayos*, who were at war with the *Susolas*, and exchanging arrow shots with them every day.

Nothing was talked about in this whole country but of the wonderful cures which God, Our Lord, performed through us, and they came from many places to be cured, and after having been with us two days some Indians of the *Susolas* begged Castillo to go and attend to a man who had been wounded, as well as to others that were sick and among whom, they said, was one on the point of death. Castillo was very timid, especially in difficult and dangerous cases, and always afraid that his sins might interfere and prevent the cures from being effective. Therefore the Indians told me to go and perform the cure. They liked me, remembering that I had relieved them while they were out gathering nuts, for which they had given us nuts and hides. This had happened at the time I was coming to join the Christians. So I had to go, and Dorantes and Estevanico went with me.

When I came close to their ranches I saw that the dying man we had been called to cure was dead, for there were many people around him weeping and his lodge was torn down, which is a sign that the owner has died. I found the Indian with eyes up turned, without pulse and with all the marks of lifelessness. At least so it seemed to me, and Dorantes said the same. I removed a mat with which he was covered, and as best I could prayed to Our Lord to restore his health, as well as that of all the others who might be in need of it, and after having made the sign of the cross and breathed on him many times they brought his bow and presented it to me, and a basket of ground *tunas*, and took me to many others who were suffering from vertigo. They gave me two more baskets of *tunas*, which I left to the Indians that had come with us. Then we returned to our quarters.

Our Indians to whom I had given the *tunas* remained there, and at night returned telling, that the dead man whom I attended to in their presence had resuscitated, rising from his bed, had walked about, eaten and talked to them, and that all those treated by me were well and in very good spirits. This caused great surprise and awe, and all over the land nothing else was spoken of. All who heard it came to us that we might cure them and bless their children, and when the Indians in our company (who were the *Cultalchulches*) had to return to their country, before parting they offered us all the *tunas* they had for their journey, not keeping a single one, and gave us flint stones as long as one and a half palms, with which they cut and that are greatly prized among them. They begged us to remember them and pray to God to keep them always healthy, which we promised to do, and so they left, the happiest people upon earth, having given us the very best they had.

We remained with the Avavares Indians for eight months, according to our reckoning of the moons. During that time they came for us from many places and said that verily we were children of the sun. Until then Dorantes and the Negro had not made any cures, but we found ourselves so pressed by the Indians coming from all sides, that all of us had to become medicine men. I was the most daring and reckless of all in undertaking cures. We never treated anyone that did not afterwards say he was well, and they had such confidence in our skill as to believe that none of them would die as long as we were among them.

And, in Testimony of, that what I have stated in the foregoing narrative is true, I hereunto sign my name:

– Cabeza de Vaca

1552–1554
HANS STADEN: HOSTAGE TO CANNIBALS

I told the savages that this Cario whom they were roasting and eating had always spoken ill of me, saying that while I was among the Portuguese I had shot several of their friends, and that he lied, for he had never seen me before. "Now see," said I, "he had been several years with you and had never been sick, but on account of his lying stories about me, my God was angry with him and smote him with sickness and put it into your minds to kill and eat him. So will my God do to all evil persons who seek or have sought to injure me." And they were greatly terrified at my words, but I thanked God that he had in this wise [way] shown his might and power through me.

– Hans Staden

When the Portuguese discovered and began to colonize Brazil in the early sixteenth century, they did not find the highly developed indigenous civilizations that the Spanish had conquered and enslaved in Mexico, Central America, and Peru. Apart from a few somewhat more advanced groups, mostly concentrated on the Lower Amazon, the aboriginal population of Brazil was composed of widely-dispersed nomadic peoples engaged in fishing, hunting and gathering, in the cultivation of manioc and a few other staples, and in constant warfare upon each other. The Tupinambá Indians, gathered in relatively large communities along the coast, were among the most important of these and among the first with whom Portuguese traders and missionaries had significant dealings. The Tupi language became a *lingua franca* used by the Portuguese, as well as by their Dutch and French rivals, in their dealings with the Indians.

Initial relations between the Portuguese and the Tupinambá, based on mutually beneficial trade, were relatively peaceful, but these relations quickly soured when the Portuguese sought to put the Tupinambá into service as soldiers and to put them to work on sugarcane plantations and elsewhere. Always at war among themselves, and now at odds with the Portuguese, the Tupinambá sometimes enslaved their captives, but as often tortured and ate them. The Indians practiced this cannibalism with little ceremony but with evident relish, the custom supported by their belief that they assumed for themselves the strength of their enemies in consuming their flesh. Into this world came Hans Staden, who left his native Germany at the age of twenty in search of adventure, and, as sailor and soldier of fortune, indeed found adventure enough. After fighting pirates along the Barbary Coast of North Africa, Staden first sailed to Brazil in 1548. During a second voyage there in 1550 with a small Spanish fleet, he was shipwrecked and landed at Itanhaém, some thirty miles south of present-day São Paulo. He served the Portuguese as a gunnery officer at a coastal fort until 1552 when hostile Tupinambá Indians captured him. At the time of his capture, Staden had been in Brazil for almost three years. He already spoke the language of his captors and knew enough of their customs to understand the grave danger that he faced. When Tupinambá women scraped his eyebrows off with glass and were preparing to cut off his beard, Staden knew that he was being made ready for a feast at which he would be dinner rather than guest. But Staden kept his wits about him and managed to survive.

Stripped naked and subjected to torture and constant humiliation, Staden's situation was all the more precarious because his Tupinambá captors identified him as one of their bitter enemies, the Portuguese. Desperately protesting that the Portuguese had forced him into their service, Staden claimed to be a friend of the French, who, in their rivalry with the Portuguese, were allies of the Tupinambá. But when the Tupinambá called a Frenchman from a nearby village to confirm this, the Frenchman, a trader known to the Tupinambá as Karwattuware, told the natives to "kill him and eat him, the good-for-nothing, for he is indeed a Portuguese, your enemy and mine." Staden must have felt that his fate was sealed when tribal chief Konyan Bebe told him that the lies of five other Portuguese, who had claimed to be Frenchmen, had not stopped him from playing his part in killing and eating them. But this was not to be Hans Staden's fate.

Although warrior cannibals, the Tupinambá were also an extremely emotional and sentimental people, inclined to burst into tears when reunited with fellow tribesmen and family members, even after only short separations. Engaged themselves in an unceasing struggle to survive, and not always certain of their own gods, the Tupinamá looked to the alien Europeans with a certain fear and respect and did not hesitate to appeal to them for succor from their God when this might assist them in affronting enemies, natural calamities, or sickness. Through the eight perilous months of his captivity, Staden kept a cool countenance and keenly observed the Tupinambá.

Bolstered by his faith in his own God, he played upon Tupinambá fears of retribution from his God if they harmed him, and responded to their appeals to him to call upon the powers of his God to heal the sick and forestall a variety of natural disasters. As month succeeded month of captivity, Staden's prestige among his captors rose steadily, and the immediate threat of his death receded, as sign after sign proved to them that his God both protected him and could threaten them. Ultimately, although remaining a captive, Staden was transferred to the authority of an important Tupinambá chief into whose household he was accepted with honor and privilege. Not long afterward, through much diplomacy and legerdemain, Staden escaped on a French ship.

Reaching the port of Honfleur in Normandy late in the winter of 1555, Staden returned to Hesse in his native Germany, where he wrote a pioneering ethnographic account of the Tupinambá and his captivity among them. Published in 1557—*Warhaftige Historia und Beschribung eyner Landtschafft der Wilden, Nacketen, Grimmigen Menschfresser, Leuthen in der Neuwenvelt America gelegen* (*The Captivity of Hans Staden of Hesse in A.D. 1547-1555 among the Wild Tribes of Eastern Brazil*)—Staden's *True History* was well received and soon translated into Dutch, French, and Latin, perhaps despite the initial skepticism that some critics may have felt about tall tales from the New World, whose discovery little more than sixty years before had inspired so many fantastic legends. We have confirmation of the truth of Staden's observations from many sources, not least in the writings of the French Huguenot Jean de Lèry, who visited the same territory in Brazil in the few years after Staden's ordeal, so it is with firmest confidence that this passage from Staden's *True History* is offered here, as the remarkable story of a man who, literally, kept his head.

Hostage to Cannibals

from *Hans Staden: The True History of his Captivity*

by Hans Staden

My Capture by the Savages and How It Occurred
I had a savage man for a slave of the tribe called Carios who caught game for me, and it was my custom to make expeditions with him into the forest.

As I was going through the forest I heard loud yells on either side of me, such as savages are accustomed to utter, and immediately a company of savages came running toward me, surrounding me on every side and shooting at me with their bows and arrows. Then I cried out: "Now may God preserve my soul." Scarcely had I uttered the words when they threw me to the ground and shot and stabbed at me. God be praised they only wounded me in the leg, but they tore my clothes from my body, one the jerkin, another the hat, a third the shirt, and so forth. Then they commenced to quarrel over me. One said that he was the first to overtake me, another protested that it was he that caught me, while the rest smote me with their bows. At last two of them seized me and lifted me up, naked as I was, and taking me by the arms, some running in front and some behind, they carried me along with them through the forest at a great pace toward the sea where they had their canoes. As we approached the sea I saw the canoes about a stone's-throw away, which they had dragged out of the water and hidden behind the shrubs, and with the canoes were great multitudes of savages, all decked out with feathers according to their custom. When they saw me they rushed toward me, biting their arms and threatening me, and making gestures as if they would eat me. Then a king approached me carrying the club with which they kill their captives, who spoke saying that having captured me from Perot, that is to say the Portuguese, they would now take vengeance on me for the death of their friends, and so carrying me to the canoes they beat me with their fists. Then they made haste to launch their canoes, for they feared that an alarm might be raised at Brikioka, as indeed was the case.

Before launching the canoes they bound my hands together, but since they were not all from the same place and no one wanted to go

36

home empty-handed, they began to dispute with my two captors, saying that they had all been just as near to me when I was taken, and each one demanding a piece of me and clamoring to have me killed on the spot.

Then I stood and prayed, expecting every moment to be struck down. But at last the king, who desired to keep me, gave orders to carry me back alive so that their women might see me and make merry with me. For they intended to kill me *Kawewi Pepicke*: that is, to prepare a drink and gather together for a feast at which they would eat me. At these words they desisted, but they bound four ropes round my neck, and I was forced to climb into a canoe, while they made fast the ends of the ropes to the boats and then pushed off and commenced the homeward journey.

How My People Came Out When the Savages Were Carrying Me Away, Intending to Recapture Me, And How They Fought with the Savages
There is another island close by the one where I was captured in which nest waterbirds, which are called Uwara (flamingos), and they have red feathers. The savages asked me whether their enemies the Tuppin Ikins had been there that year to take the birds during the nesting season. I told them that the Tuppin Ikins had been there, but they proposed to visit the island to see for themselves if this was so, for they value the feathers of these birds exceedingly since all their adornment depends on them. The savages made for this island, hoping to take the birds, but when they were a distance of some two gun-shots from the place where they had left their canoes, they looked back and saw behind them a number of Tuppin Ikin savages with certain of the Portuguese who had set out to recapture me. For a slave who was with me had escaped when I was taken and had raised an alarm. They cried out to my captors that unless they were cowards they would turn and fight. My captors turned about and those on the land assailed us with blowpipes and arrows while we replied. My captors then unbound my hands leaving the cord still fastened to my neck, and as the king had a gun and a little powder, which a Frenchman had given him in exchange for some Brazilian wood, I was forced to shoot with it towards the land.

After both parties had skirmished for a time my captors, fearing that those on shore might be reinforced with canoes and might give chase, made off with three casualties and passed about a gun-shot distance from the fort at Brikioka where I had been stationed, and as we passed I had to stand up in the canoe so that my companions might see me. They fired two large guns from the fort, but the shot fell short. In the meantime some canoes had set out from Brikioka in pursuit, hoping to overtake us, but my captors rowed too fast, and when my friends saw that they could do nothing they returned to Brikioka.

How They Dealt with Me on the Day on Which They Brought Me
to Their Dwellings
On the same day about Vesper time (reckoning by the sun) we came in sight of their dwellings after we had been journeying for three days. The place to which I had come was thirty miles distant from Brikioka where I had been captured.

When we were near the dwellings I saw that the place was a small village with seven huts, and it was called Uwattibi (Ubat'ba). We landed on a beach close by the sea, and there were the womenfolk in a plantation of mandioca roots. They were going up and down gathering roots, and I was forced to call out to them and say: *A junesche been ermi vramme*, which means: "I your food have come."

As we landed, all the women, young and old, came running out of the huts, which were built on a hill, to stare at me. The men went into their huts with their bows and arrows, leaving me to the pleasure of the women who gathered round and went along with me, some in front and some behind, dancing and singing the songs they are wont to sing to their own people when they are about to eat them.

They then carried me to a kind of fort outside the huts called Ywara, which they defend against their enemies by means of great rails made like a garden fence. When I entered this enclosure the women fell upon me and beat me with their fists, plucking at my beard and crying out in their speech: *Sehe innamme pepikeae*, which is to say: "With this blow I avenge me of my friend, that one who was slain by your people."

After this they took me into the huts where I had to lie in a hammock while the women surrounded me and beat me and pulled at me on all sides, mocking me and offering to eat me. Meanwhile the men had assembled in a hut by themselves, drinking a drink which is known as Kawi, and having their gods, called Tammerka,[1] about them, to whom they sang praises, since these gods, they said, had foretold my capture. I could hear this singing, but for half an hour none of the men came near me, and I was left with the women and children.

[1] Staden later explains that these are hollow gourds filled with pebbles and attached to sticks. The Tuppin Imba pose questions to them, interpreting their sound as answers. The word has entered English from the Spanish *maraca*.

How They Danced with Me before the Huts in Which Their Idols Tammerka Had Been Set Up

After this they carried me from the place where they had cut off my eyebrows to the huts where they kept their idols, Tammerka. Here they made a ring round me, I being with two women in the centre, and tied my leg with strings of objects which rattled. They bound me also with sheaves of feathers arranged in a square, which they fastened behind at my neck so that they stood up above my head. This ornament is called in their language Arasoya. Then the women commenced to sing all together, and I had to keep time with the rattles on my leg by stamping as they sang. But my wounded leg was so painful that I could hardly stand upright, for the wound had not been dressed.

How, After They Had Danced, They Brought Me Home to Ipperu Wasu Who Was to Kill Me

When the dance was ended I was handed over to Ipperu Wasu who guarded me closely. He told me that I had some time to live. And the people brought the idols from the huts and set them up around me, saying that these had prophesied that they would capture a Portuguese. Then I replied that the idols were powerless and could not speak, and that even so they lied, since I was no Portuguese, but a kinsman and friend to the French, and that my native land was called Allemania (Germany). They made answer that it was I who lied, for if I was truly the Frenchmen's friend, how came it that I was among the Portuguese? For they knew well that the French were as much the enemies of the Portuguese as they were, and that they came every year in their boats, bringing knives, axes, mirrors, combs and scissors, and taking in exchange Brazilian wood, cotton, and other goods, such as feathers and pepper. These men were their good friends which the Portuguese were not. For the Portuguese, when they came to the country and settled there, had made friends with their enemies. Moreover, the Portuguese had come to their country, desiring to trade with them, and when they had gone down in all friendship and entered the ships, as they are to this day accustomed to do with the Frenchmen, the Portuguese had waited until sufficient numbers were on board, and had then seized and bound them, carrying them away to their enemies who had killed and eaten them. Others the Portuguese had slain with their guns, committing also many further acts of aggression, and even joining with their enemies and waging frequent war.

How My Captors Made Angry Complaint That the Portuguese Had Slain
Their Father, Which Deed They Desired to Avenge on Me
The savages said, moreover, that the Portuguese had wounded the
father of the two brothers, my captors, and had shot off one of his
arms so that he died of his wounds, and that they intended to take
vengeance on me for his. To which I made answer that they should
not visit this upon me, since I was no Portuguese, but had arrived
some time since with the Castilians, and had been shipwrecked among
the Portuguese, for which reason I remained with them.

Now there was a young man of their tribe who had been a slave
among the Portuguese, for the savages among whom the Portuguese
dwell had waged war on the Tuppin Imbas and had captured a whole
village, killing and eating the grown men. But the young ones had
been carried off and bartered to the Portuguese for goods, and among
them was this young man, who had passed into the hands of a master
in the neighbourhood of Brikioka named Antonio Agudin of Galicia.
My captors had taken this slave some three months before I fell into
their hands, but as he belonged to their tribe they had not killed him.
This young man knew me well and my captors enquired of him what
manner of man I was. He told them that it was true that a ship had
been cast away, and that the people in it were called Castilians, and
that they were friends of the Portuguese. He said also that I was among
them, but knew nothing more of me.

When I heard this and understood that there were Frenchmen
among them who came there in their ships, I persisted in my story
that I was a kinsman and friend to the French, and that they should
leave me alive until the Frenchmen arrived and recognized me. And
they kept me in close confinement, for there were certain Frenchmen
in the district who had been left there to collect pepper.

How a Frenchman Who Had Been Left among the Savages Came to See Me
and Bade Them Eat Me, Saying That I Was Truly a Portuguese
There was a Frenchman four miles distant from the village in which I
was, and when he heard news of me he came and entered one of the
huts opposite to the one in which I was kept. Then the savages came
running to me and said: "Here is a Frenchman. Now we shall see
whether you are in truth a Frenchman or not." At this I rejoiced greatly,
for I told myself that he was at least a Christian and would do his best
for me.

Then they took me to him, naked as I was, and I found him to be
a youth known to the savages by the name Karwattuware. He
commenced to speak to me in French, which I could not well under-

stand, and the savages stood round about and listened. Then, when I was unable to reply to him, he spoke to the savages in their own tongue and said: "Kill him and eat him, the good-for-nothing, for he is indeed a Portuguese, your enemy and mine." This I understood, and I begged him for the love of God to tell them not to eat me, but he replied only: "They will certainly eat you." Whereupon I bethought me of the words of the Prophet Jeremy (chapter 17) when he said: "Cursed be the man that trusteth in man," and I departed from them with a heavy heart. I had on my shoulders a linen cloth which the savages had given me, although I know not where they can have obtained it. This I tore off and flung it at the Frenchman's feet, saying to myself (for the sun had burnt me severely) that it was useless to preserve my flesh for others if I was to die. And they carried me back to the hut which was my prison where I stretched myself in my hammock. God alone knows the misery that I endured, and weeping I commenced to sing the verse: "Let us now beseech the Holy Ghost to save and guard us when death approaches and we pass from sorrows into peace. Kyrioleys." But the savages said only: "He is indeed a true Portuguese. Now he cries. Truly he is afraid to die."

In What Manner They Brought Me to Their Chief Ruler, King Konyan Bebe, and How They Dealt with Me There
A few days later they took me to another village called Arirab, the dwelling place of their chief king who was called Konyan Bebe. Here a great company had assembled, with much rejoicing in the native manner, for the people desired to see me, and he had ordered me to be brought there on that day.

As I arrived at the huts I heard a great noise, with singing and blowing of trumpets, and in front of the huts some fifteen heads had been set up on posts. These were the heads of their enemies, called Markayas, whom they had eaten, and as they took me past them they told me what they were. Then I was afraid, for I could not but consider that they might treat me in the same way. When we entered the huts one of my keepers went forward and spoke, with cruel words, so that all might hear, saying: "Behold I bring you a Portuguese slave," as if it were a fine thing for him to have his adversary in his power, and speaking much else besides according to their custom. He then took me to the place where the king sat, and he and his companions drank together of the drink called Kawawy until they were drunken, and they all regarded me with evil looks, saying: "Is not our enemy now come to us?" And I replied: "I am indeed come to you, but I am not your enemy." Then they gave me to drink.

Now I had heard much of this king Konyan Bebe, how that he was a mighty king and a great tyrant and eater of men's flesh, and when I saw the one among them who looked like a king I went forward and spoke to him, as if I had been of his people. And I said: " Are you king Konyan Bebe, do you still live?" He made answer: "Yes, I am still alive," and I said: "I have heard much of you, how that you are a very mighty man." Upon this he rose up and began to strut about before me with great pomp. He had a round green stone thrust through his lips (as their custom is). These people make also a kind of pater noster of sea-shells, which they use for ornament. This king wore six ropes of them hanging at his neck whereby I saw that he was a great personage.

The king then sat down again and began to question me as to what his enemies the Tuppin Ikins and the Portuguese were about to do; and why I had tried to shoot his people at Brikioka (for he had learnt that I was employed as a gunner against them). I made answer that the Portuguese had placed me there and I had to obey orders. But he said that I was also a Portuguese, for the Frenchman who had seen me, whom he called his son, had told him that I could not speak with him, and that I was a true Portuguese. Whereupon I told him that I had been so long absent from my country that I had forgotten my native tongue. Then said he: "I have already helped to catch and eat five Portuguese who said they were Frenchman, but they all lied."

Then, indeed, I abandoned all hope of life and commended myself to God, for I saw clearly that I must die. But he still questioned me and enquired what the Portuguese reported of him, for they must surely go in fear of him. And I replied that they spoke much of him, and of the mighty wars which he waged against them, but that now they had greatly strengthened Brikioka. Nevertheless he boasted that he would catch them all in time in the forest, as he had caught me. To which I answered that his true enemies the Tuppin Ikins were preparing twenty-five canoes to attack his country, and this indeed fell out as I had said.

While the king was speaking with me the others stood by and listened, for he asked me much and told me much, bragging how many of his enemies, both Portuguese and savages, he had killed. In the meantime, while he spoke thus, the drink in the huts had been consumed, and the people were moving to another hut where more drink had been prepared. With this the king made an end of speaking.

There in the other huts they began to mock me, and the king's son bound my legs in three places, and I was forced to hop thus through the huts on both feet, at which they made merry, saying: "Here comes our food hopping toward us." Then I asked my master whether he had brought me there to be killed, and he said "No," but that it was the people's custom to treat enemy slaves so. They now unbound my legs and began to walk round me, tearing at my flesh, one saying that the skin on my head was his, another claiming the fat on my legs. After this I had to sing to them, and I sang holy songs, and when they asked me what I sang I told them that I was singing of my God. But they replied that my God was no better than dirt, calling him in their tongue Teuire. These words caused me much anguish, and I prayed and said: "O God, thou art long-suffering indeed." When all in the village had seen me and abused me, the king, Konyan Bebe, gave orders on the following day that I was to be closely guarded.

How the Brother of King Jeppipo Wasu Returned from Mambukabe with the News That His Brother and Mother, and All the Company Had Fallen Sick, and Entreated Me to Procure My God to Make Them Well Again
When I was daily expecting the return of the others who, as I have reported, were preparing for my death, I heard one day the sound of howling in the huts of the king who was absent. I was much afraid, for I thought that they had now returned, since it is the custom of the savages, when one of them has been absent for not longer than four days, to cry over him with joy when he returns. Presently one of the savages came to me and reported that the brother of him who owned a share in me had returned with the news that the others were all sick, whereat I greatly rejoiced, for I told myself that now God would show his might. Not long afterward this brother himself came to the hut where I was, and sitting down by me he commenced to cry aloud, saying that his brother, his mother, and his brother's children had all fallen sick, and that his brother had sent him to me with the message that I was to make my God restore them to health; and he added that his brother was persuaded that my God was wrath with them. To which I replied: "My God is indeed angry with you for threatening to eat me, and for going to Mambukabe to prepare the feast, and for falsely accusing me of being a Portuguese." I told him, further, to return to his brother and bid him come back to the huts, and I would intercede with my God to make him well again. He replied that his brother was too ill to come, but that he knew and had observed that if I desired it he would recover. Whereupon I made answer that he must wait until he was strong enough to come home to his huts, and that then he would be restored to health. With this answer he returned to Mambukabe, which is situated four miles from Uwattibi, where I was.

In What Manner the Sick King Jeppipo Wasu Returned Home
After some days the sick persons all came back. Then was I taken to
the king's huts, and he told me how the sickness had come upon them,
and that I must have known of it, for he well remembered my saying
that the moon was wrath with them. When I heard this I told myself
that it was indeed God's doing that I had spoken of the moon on that
evening, and I rejoiced greatly and said: "This day is God with me."

I told the king that this misfortune had befallen him because he
had threatened to eat me, although I was no enemy of his, and he
promised that if he recovered his health no evil should happen to me.
But I was at a loss what to ask of God, for it seemed to me that if the
savages recovered they would kill me at once, and if they died the
others would say: "Let us kill him lest greater misfortunes befall us,"
as indeed they had already begun to say, and I could only submit the
whole matter to God, the king beseeching me anew to make them well
again. I went to and fro laying my hands on their heads as they desired
me to do, but God did not suffer it and they began to die. A child died
first, and then the king's mother, an old woman, whose business it was
to prepare the pots for the drink with which I was to be eaten. Some
days later a brother died, and then again a child, and then another
brother, that one who had first brought me news of their illness.

When the king saw that his children and his mother and brother
were dead he began to fear that he and his wives would die also, and
he begged me to tell my God to make an end of his wrath so that he
might live. I comforted him mightily, telling him not to despair, and
that when he recovered his health he must give up all thoughts of
killing me, which he promised, giving orders to those in his huts to
cease from mocking me and threatening to eat me. He remained sick
for a time, but finally he recovered, as did one of his wives who had
been stricken, but there died of his family some eight persons, besides
others, all of whom had treated me with great cruelty.

When the terror was abated, and one of my masters had recovered,
there was no more talk of eating me, but they guarded me closely and
would not suffer me to go about unattended.

*How the Frenchman Returned Who Had Told the Savages to Eat Me, and
How I Begged Him to Take Me Away, But My Masters Would Not Suffer
Me to Go*
The Frenchman, called Karwattuware, of whom I have reported that
he had abandoned me, had remained with the savages, his friends,
trading with them and collecting pepper and feathers, and when he

was travelling to those parts called Mungu Wappe and Iterroenne, where the ships arrive, he passed by the place where I was. Now when he left me he thought that the savages would certainly eat me, as he had recommended them to do, and having been absent for some time he expected to find me dead.

When, therefore, he entered the huts and saw me he addressed me in the savage tongue, and at that time I was not bound up as previously. He asked me how it came about that I was still alive, and I told him that God in his goodness had protected me until then. It occurred to me that he might have heard from the savages how matters had fallen out, and I drew him aside privately, so that the savages might not hear us, and told him again that God had spared my life, and that I was no Portuguese, but a German who had suffered shipwreck with certain Spaniards and had afterward fallen among the Portuguese. I urged him to tell the savages this, and to make clear to them that I was his kinsman and friend, and to take me away with him when the ships arrived. . . .

Accordingly the Frenchman informed the savages that at our first meeting he had not properly recognized me, that I was from Germany, and was a friend of his nation, and that he proposed to take me to the place where the ships came. But the savages refused to deliver me up, stating that if my own father or brother came with a shipload of axes, mirrors, knives, combs and scissors and gave them these goods, they would not let me go, for they had captured me in the enemy's country and I belonged to them. When the Frenchman heard this he told me that, as I could see, the savages would not part with me. Then I begged him, for the love of God, to send for me and take me back in the first ship sailing for France, and this he promised to do, bidding the savages to care for me and on no account to kill me, for my friends were at hand and would certainly come for me. And with this he departed.

How Once More a Ship Was Sent After Me by the Portuguese
After I had been five months among the savages, another ship came from the island of Sancto Vincente, for it is the custom of the Portuguese from time to time to send ships which are well armed into the country of their enemies to trade with them, giving them knives and sickles in exchange for mandioca meal, which the savages have in great quantities. The Portuguese have many slaves employed in the sugar plantations and require the meal for their food. When the ships come to trade, the savages row out, one or two in a canoe, and keeping as far away as possible, they hand out their goods, and name

what they require in exchange which the Portuguese then give them. All the time that the two men are close to the ship, their companions keep a look out some distance off in their canoes, and when the trading is at an end, the savages often draw near and skirmish with the Portuguese and shoot their arrows at them, after which they return.

The crew of the ship fired a gun so that the savages might know that a ship had arrived, and when the savages rowed out, they inquired of them concerning me, whether I was still alive, and the savages answered "Yes." Then the Portuguese desired to see me, stating that they had a box full of things for me from my brother, also a Frenchman, who was in the ship with them.

Now there was a Frenchman called Claudio Mirando with the Portuguese in the ship who had been my companion. This man I called my brother, and I thought that he might be in the ship inquiring for me, as he had made the voyage before. The savages returned from the ship, and told me that my brother had come back, bringing me a box of goods, and that he desired to see me. Then I said, "Carry me to a place near at hand so I can speak with my brother. The Portuguese will not understand what we say, and I will tell him to ask my father, when he returns home, to send a ship full of goods and take me away." To this they agreed, but they were very much concerned lest the Portuguese should understand what we said, for the savages intended to make war during the month of August in the neighborhood of Brikioka where I was captured, and I knew all their plans, and they were afraid I might disclose them. But I assured the savages that the Portuguese could not understand our speech. Then they carried me to within a stone's throw of the ship, naked as I was and had been all the time of my captivity, and I spoke to those in the ship and said: "The Lord God be with you, my brothers. Let one speak to me alone and do not allow it to be seen that I am otherwise than a Frenchman." Then one spoke who was called Johann Senches, a Biscayan, whom I knew well, and he said: "My dear brother, on your account have we come in the ship, not knowing whether you were dead or alive, for the first ship brought no news of you. Captain Brascupas at Sanctus has ordered us to find out whether you were still alive, and if so to endeavor to buy you back, and if that failed to try and capture some of the savages to exchange for you."

Then I said: "Now may God reward you in eternity, for I am here in great fear and peril, and know not what may befall me. But for God's merciful intervention I should have been eaten." I said further: "They will not sell me to you: they would not even think of it, but do not you in the ship let the savages think of me as otherwise than as a

Frenchman, and give me, for the love of God, knives and fish-hooks."
This they did at once, a man returned to the ship and fetched them.

When I saw that the savages would not suffer me to parley any
longer, I said to the Portuguese: "Look well to it, they are going to
attack Brikioka." They replied that the savages, their allies, were also
preparing for war, and would attack the village where I was, and that
I was to be of good cheer, since God would do what was best, but, as
I could see, they were powerless to help me.

Then I took the knives and fish-hooks and gave them to the savages
saying: "All these my brother, the Frenchman, gave me." And they
inquired what he had spoken about with me. I replied that I had told
my brother to escape from the Portuguese and return to our home,
and bring a ship well stocked with goods to fetch me: "For," said I,
"you are good people and treat me well and I am anxious to reward
you when the ship comes." Thus at all times I had to conciliate them
and they were well pleased.

*How the Savages Went Forth to War Taking Me with Them and What Befell
Me on the Way*
Four days later the canoes began to assemble in the village in readiness
for the expedition, and the chief king Konyan Bebe came also with his
boats. My master announced that he would take me with him, but I
asked to be left behind, and this would have happened if the king,
Konyan Bebe, had not ordered otherwise. I let them see that I went
unwillingly, lest they should think that I intended to escape when
they reached the enemy country, and that they might guard me less
closely. But it had been my intention, if they left me at home, to run
away to the French ship.

However, they took me with them. There were thirty-eight canoes,
each canoe carrying eighteen men more or less. Certain of them had
inquired of their idols by dreams and had committed other follies
concerning their expedition, as is their custom, and they were all much
puffed up. Their intention was to make for the neighbourhood of
Brikioka, where they had captured me, and to conceal themselves in
the forest close by, and take back those who fell into their hands.

It was now about the 14th day of August in the year 1554. At this
time, as I have stated before, it is the custom for the fish which is
called in Portuguese *Doynges*, in Spanish *Liesses*, and in the savage
tongue *Bratti*, to leave the sea for the fresh waters in order to spawn
there, and this season of the year the savages call *Pirakaen*. At this
time the savages go forth to war, both they and their enemies, catching
and eating the fish by the way, and on the journey out they travel

slowly, but on the journey back they travel as speedily as they can.

I hoped that the savages who were friendly to the Portuguese would also then be going to war, for those in the ship had told me that the savages, their allies, intended to attack at this time. My companions inquired of me continually during the voyage whether they would capture any prisoners, and in order not to anger them I said "Yes." I also told them that the enemy would engage them. One night we lay at the place called Uwattibi, where we caught many of the fish called Bratti, which are as large as a good-sized pike. That night the wind blew mightily, and the savages talked much to me and asked me many questions, whereupon I said that the wind was blowing over the bodies of dead men. Now it happened that another party of savages had set out by water to a river called Paraibe, and my companions concluded that this party must have reached the enemy country, and that some of the men were dead. This, as I heard later, had in fact happened. . . .

At daybreak the chiefs gathered round a cauldron of stewed fish, and while they ate they recounted their dreams, insofar as they were propitious; others danced with their idols, and that day they elected to set out for a place called Boywassu Kange, which was close to the enemy's country, where they would rest until evening. When we left the place called Meyenbipe, where we spent the night, the savages inquired of me what was in my mind, and I said at a venture that the enemy would meet us close to Boywassu Kange, but that we had nothing to fear; and it was my intention at Boywassu Kange to make my escape, for it was only six miles from the place I had been captured.

As we were coasting along we saw a number of canoes approaching us from behind an island, and the savages called out: "Here come our enemies the Tuppin Ikins," and we hid ourselves behind a rock so that the others might pass without observing us, but they became aware of us and commenced to row in the direction of their home. We rowed after them as swiftly as we could, and gave chase for four whole hours until we came up with them. There were five canoes full of men, and they all came from Brikioka. I knew them all. In one of the canoes were six mamelukes who had been baptized, and among them were two brothers, one called Diego de Praga, the other Domingus de Praga, who defended themselves stoutly, one with a gun, the other with a bow and arrows. These two alone kept our thirty canoes at bay for two whole hours. But when their arrows were exhausted the Tuppin Imba fell upon them and captured them, and some were knocked on the head at once or shot. The two brothers were unhurt, but two of the six mamelukes were badly wounded, as were also several of the Tuppin Ikin, among whom was one woman.

How the Prisoners Were Disposed of on the Return Voyage
The capture had taken place at sea, two full miles from land, and we hurried back as quickly as we could in order to encamp in the place where we had spent the previous night. When we reached the land called Meyenbipe it was evening and the sun was setting, and each man took his prisoner to his hut. Those that had been badly wounded they carried to the land, where they were killed at once and cut up and roasted. Among those who were roasted that night were two of the mamelukes who were Christians; one was a Portuguese named George Ferrero, the son of a captain by a native woman. The other was called Hieronymus. He had been captured by a native belonging to my hut, whose name was Parwaa, and this man spent the whole night roasting Hieronymus, scarcely a step from the spot where I lay. Hieronymus (God have his soul) was blood relation to Diego de Praga.

That night, when we were encamped, I went into the hut where the two brothers were to talk with them, for they had been my good friends at Brikioka where I was captured. They inquired of me whether they would also be eaten, but I told them that they must trust in our Heavenly Father and in his son Jesus Christ, who was crucified for our sins, and in whose name we were baptized. I said also: "This is my belief. God has watched over me so long here among the savages, and what God decrees must satisfy us."

The two brothers inquired also concerning their cousin Hieronymus, and I told them that he lay by the fire roasting, and that I had seen a piece of Ferrero's son being eaten. Then they commenced to weep, and I comforted them, telling them that I had been eight months or thereabouts among the savages, and that God had been my protector. "So also," I said, "will he protect you, if you trust in him." I told them also that it was harder for me than for them, for I had come from foreign countries, knowing nothing of the dreadful practices of the savages, but, as for them, they had been born in the country and bred there. They replied, however, that I had been hardened by misery and should therefore take less account of it.

As I was discoursing with them, the savages came and ordered me to depart, and they wanted to know what matters I had discussed with them. I was sad at leaving them, and told them to put their whole trust in God, and to remember what sufferings were ours in this vale of sorrows, and they replied that never until then had they realized this, that they owed their lives to God, and that they would die more happily since I was with them. With that I left them and went through the whole camp visiting the prisoners. I went alone and none heeded

me, and I could have escaped then, for the island Meyenbipe was
only some ten miles from Brikioka, but I refrained on account of the
Christian prisoners, of whom four were still alive. I thought that if I
escaped, the savages would kill them at once in their anger. It might
well be that God would still preserve us all, and I resolved to remain
with them and comfort them. The savages were now very favourably
disposed towards me, since I had predicted, by chance, that the enemy
would encounter us, as indeed it fell out. They said also that I was a
better prophet than their prophet Miraka [alt. spelling of Tammaraka].

How They Danced in the Camp on the Following Day with Their Enemies
On the day following we reached a place not far from the country of
my captors, called Occarasu, a great mountain. There we camped for
the night, and I went to the hut of Konyan Bebe, the chief king, and
asked what he intended to do with the two mamelukes. He replied
that they would be eaten, and forbade me to speak with them, for he
was very wrath, saying that they should have stayed at home instead
of going to fight with his enemies. I begged him to spare their lives
and sell them back again to their friends, but he was resolved that
they should be eaten.

This same Konyan Bebe had then a great vessel full of human
flesh in front of him and was eating a leg which he held to my mouth,
asking me to taste it. I replied that even beasts which were without
understanding did not eat their own species, and should a man devour
his fellow creatures? But he took a bite saying *Jau ware sehe*: "I am a
tiger; it tastes well," and with that I left him.

In the evening he gave orders that each man should bring his
prisoner to an open space by the water, and this was done, and the
savages gathered together into a circle with the prisoners in the centre,
and they forced them to sing and rattle the idols which are called
Tammaraka. When the prisoners had finished singing, they
commenced to talk wantonly among themselves, saying: "We set forth
like brave men intending to capture you, our enemies, and to eat you.
Now you have the mastery, and have taken us, but we do not crave
for mercy, for brave men are willing to die in an enemy country. But
our land is wide and there are many waiting to take vengeance for
our deaths."[2] And the others made answer: "You have slain many of
our fellows. Now will we be the avengers." When this speech was
ended the prisoners were taken back to the huts.

[2]Tuppin Imba ritual required the captured warriors to make a show of defiance
to their captors, by speech or song.

Three days later we reached our country and each man took his prisoner to his dwelling. In the village of Uwattibi, where I was, there were eight live savages who were prisoners and three Christian mamelukes, namely Diego and his brother, and another Christian called Antonio, the latter having been captured by my master's son. The two other mamelukes they carried home roasted, ready to be eaten. The journey out and home again had lasted eleven days.

How Shortly After I Had Been Given Away, Another Ship Arrived from France, The Catherine of Vattavilla, Which through God's Providence Was Able to Buy Me, and of the Manner in Which This Fell Out

I remained some fourteen days in the place called Tackwara Sutibi with king Abbati Bossange, and one day it happened that certain of the savages came to me and reported that they had heard the sound of shooting, which must have come from the harbour of Iteronne, or Rio de Janeiro. As I was sure that a ship must have arrived there, I told them to carry me to it, for this was doubtless my brother's ship. They agreed to do this, but detained me for a few days more.

In the meantime it happened that the Frenchmen who had arrived there heard that I was a prisoner among the savages, and the captain sent two of his men, together with certain native kings, their friends, to the place where I was, and they came to a hut, the chief king of which was called Sowarasu. My hut was close at hand, and news was brought to me that the two men had arrived from the ship. At this I rejoiced greatly, and went to them and bade them welcome in the native tongue, and when they saw my misery and nakedness they were full of pity and shared their clothes with me. I asked them why they had come and they said that it was on my account, and that their orders were to take me to the ship and to use force if necessary. Then my heart overflowed with gratitude to God, and I told one of the men, who was called Perot and knew the savage tongue, that he must make believe he was my brother, and that he was to say that he had brought me certain chests full of merchandise and must take me with him to the ship to fetch them. He was to tell the savages also that I would then return to collect pepper and other things and wait until the ship came again next year. Then they took me to the ship, my master going with us, where they received me in all pity and showed me great kindness. After we had been some five days in the ship, the king called Abbati Bossange, to whom I had been given, asked me for the chests which they had brought me, so that we might now return home. I reported this to the ship's captain who told me to put him off until the ship had taken in the full cargo, in case the savages should become angry when they saw that I was kept in the ship and work some mischief, since they were a people in whom no trust could be placed. My master still thought that he would take me back with him, but I held him with empty words, telling him not to hurry, for he knew that when good friends came together they could not part at once, and that when the ship left we would return to the huts.

At last the ship was ready and the Frenchmen were all mustered together and I with them, the king, my master, with his people, being also there. Then the ship's captain spoke to the savages through his interpreter, and said that he was well pleased that they had not killed me when they captured me from among their enemies. He said also, in order to make it easier for him to take me away, that he had ordered me to be brought to the ship so that he might reward them for their care of me. Further, that it was his intention to give me goods and wares, and as I was known to them, to leave me there to collect pepper and other useful commodities until he came again. Meanwhile we had arranged between us that some ten of the crew, who were not unlike me, should gather round and say that they were my brothers and wanted to take me home. And so it fell out. My brothers would not suffer me to land, saying that I must return with them, as my father longed to see me once more before he died. Upon this the captain told the savages that he was captain in the ship and would have preferred that I should return with them, but that he was only one against many and could do nothing. All this was ordained so that we might part from the savages on friendly terms. I told the king, my master, that I should greatly like to return with him, but that, as he could see, my brothers would not allow me to do so. Thereupon he began to howl and cry in the ship, saying that if they took me away I must return with the first boat, for he looked upon me as his son, and was wrath with those of Uwattibi for threatening to eat me. And one of his wives who was in the ship began to cry over me, according to their custom, and I cried also. Then the captain gave them goods, some five ducats' worth in knives, axes, looking-glasses, and combs, and the savages returned with them to their dwellings.

Thus Almighty God, the God of Abraham, Isaac and Jacob, saved me from the hands of these evil men. To him be praise and glory through Jesus Christ, his Son, our Redeemer, Amen.

1675
CAPTIVE:
THE AFFLICTION & REDEMPTION
OF MARY ROWLANDSON

Mary Rowlandson's *The Captive* is a classic of American Literature, the first American bestseller written by a woman, and regarded by many to be the first of the genre of the captivity narrative, the forerunner of the American Western novel. This autobiographical account of a woman's survival of an Indian attack and her three months of captivity, illuminates the mentality and conditions of life of English settlers and Natives on the New England frontier in the second half of the seventeenth century. First printed in 1682, the book subsequently appeared in more than forty editions and was widely read for more than two centuries.

The Captive opens with Mary Rowlandson's heart-wrenching account of an Indian attack in the first light of February 10, 1675 on the Massachusetts frontier settlement of Lancaster. A minister's wife, Mary Rowlandson witnessed the brutal scalping and evisceration of several of her neighbors as her own home came under attack. The defenders of the Rowlandson home held the attackers at bay for two hours before the Indians succeeded in setting fire to the house and forcing the surviving defenders out into the open to be massacred or seized as captives. Herself and her youngest child wounded in the struggle, Mary saw many of her family fall around her, but she survived and was taken into captivity with her children, the youngest of whom died in her arms several days later. So began Mary Rowlandson's *tryal*, which was to last for eleven weeks and five days, until she was finally released for a ransom of twenty pounds, and restored to her husband—who was away at the time of the attack—and their two surviving children restored to them.

King Philip's War was the bloodiest outbreak of violence in the history of seventeenth century New England. More than six hundred settlers were killed, many more were taken into captivity, and dozens of frontier settlements were devastated before the colonial militia, in relentless pursuit of their native foes, and the systematic destruction of their villages and crops, decimated the tribes and broke their power to pose any further threat. The expansion of white settlements into Indian lands was the principle cause of the outbreak of hostilities between white and native populations who had lived in peace for many decades. But the colonial New Englander typically experienced the conflict as God's chastisement for their forgetfulness of Him and of their utter dependence upon Him. It is this spiritual dimension of the conflict, so clearly reflected in Mary Rowlandson's chronicle, that made *The Captive* a bestseller in colonial New England and sustained the popularity of her account well into the nineteenth century.

Some scholars have argued that Mary Rowlandson did not pen the narrative of her captivity and redemption alone. Suggesting that its religious themes are too finely tuned to the Calvinist spiritual polemic of its day, they claim that she had the help of an erudite cleric in writing her account, using it, along with the apt scriptural citations that buttress it, as an argument for man's subjection to God's chastisement and for man's utter dependence on God's grace and redemption. It is certainly true that her story is a perfect illustration of the interpretation of the trauma of King Phillip's War that was preached from the pulpits of churches throughout New England. But the very strength and clarity of voice that the reader may discern throughout *The Captive* affirms—in the view of this editor—Mary Rowlandson's direct, unmediated, and wholly sincere telling of her own story.

The abridgement presented here represents a third of the original text, a full and representative selection from Mary Rowlandson's stirring account of her survival of a brutal Indian raid, her survival of the trauma of loss, of severe deprivation and hunger, of exposure to the harsh conditions of a New England winter, and of winter-long captivity among hostile Indians. Her narrative is an inspiring affirmation of her faith in her God, but it is certainly also a testament of the resilience of an extraordinary woman caught up in a resolute struggle to survive. While Mary Rowlandson's faith was certainly a key element that sustained her in a situation and under conditions in which many others perished, her physical courage, her will and strength of character, her ability to adapt to her captors and show herself useful to them, and ultimately her ability to win their respect, all contributed to her successful passage of a severe trial. In its pious and plainspoken idiom, *The Captive* remains fascinating and inspiring to this day.

The Captive

by Mary Rowlandson

Assault and Capture

On the tenth of February, 1675, came the Indians with great numbers upon Lancaster. Their first coming was about sun-rising. Hearing the noise of some guns, we looked out: several houses were burning, and the smoke ascending to heaven. There were five persons taken in one house. The father, the mother, and a sucking child they knockt on the head, the other two they took and carried away alive. There were two others who, being out of their garrison upon some occasion, were set upon. One was knockt on the head, the other escaped. Another there was who, running along, was shot and wounded, and fell down. He begged of them his life, promising them money (as they told me) but they would not hearken to him, but knockt him in head, and stript him naked, and split open his bowels. Another, seeing many of the Indians about his barn, ventured and went out, but was quickly shot down. There were three others belonging to the same garrison who were killed. The Indians, getting up upon the roof of the barn, had advantage to shoot down upon them over their fortification. Thus these murderous wretches went on, burning and destroying before them.

At length they came and beset our own house, and quickly it was the dolefullest day that ever mine eyes saw. The house stood upon the edge of a hill; some of the Indians got behind the hill, others into the barn, and others behind any thing that could shelter them, from all which places they shot against the house, so that the bullets seemed to fly like hail, and quickly they wounded one man among us, then another, and then a third. About two hours (according to my observation in that amazing time) they had been about the house before they prevailed to fire it (which they did with flax and hemp which they brought out of the barn). There being no defence about the house, only two flankers at two opposite corners, and one of them not finished, they fired it once, and one ventured out and quenched it, but they quickly fired it again, and that took. Now is that dreadfull hour come, that I have often heard of (in time of war, as it was the case of others) but now mine eyes see it. Some in our house were fighting for their lives, others wallowing in their blood, the house on fire over our heads, and the bloody heathen ready to knock us on the head if we stirred out. Now might we hear mothers & children crying out for themselves, and one another, "Lord, what shall we do?"

I took my children (and one of my sisters, hers) to go forth and leave the house, but as soon as we came to the door and appeared, the Indians shot so thick that the bullets rattled against the house, as if one had taken a handful of stones and thrown them, so that we were fain to give back. We had six stout dogs belonging to our garrison, but none of them would stir, though another time, if any Indian had come to the door, they were ready to fly upon him and tear him down. The Lord hereby would make us the more to acknowledge His hand, and to see that our help is always in Him. But out we must go, the fire increasing, and coming along behind us roaring, and the Indians gaping before us with their guns, spears, and hatchets, to devour us.

No sooner were we out of the house, but my brother in law (being before wounded, in defending the house, in or near the throat) fell down dead, whereat the Indians scornfully shouted, and howled, and were presently upon him, stripping off his clothes. The bullets flying thick, one went through my side, and the same (as would seem) through the bowels and hand of my dear child in my arms. One of my elder sister's children, named William had his leg broken, which the Indians perceiving, they knockt him on head. Thus were we butchered by those merciless heathen, standing amazed, with the blood running down to our heels. My eldest sister being yet in the house, and seeing those woeful sights, the infidels hauling mothers one way, and children another, and some wallowing in their blood, and her elder son telling her that her son William was dead, and myself was wounded, she said, "and Lord, let me dy with them," which was no sooner said, but she was struck with a bullet, and fell down dead over the threshold. I hope she is reaping the fruit of her good labours, being faithfull to the service of God in her place. In her younger years she lay under much trouble upon spiritual accounts, till it pleased God to make that precious scripture take hold of her heart, 2 Corinthians 12:9, "And he said unto me, my grace is sufficient for thee." More than twenty years after, I have heard her tell how sweet and comfortable that place was to her. But to return: the Indians laid hold of us, pulling me one way, and the children another, and said, "Come, go along with us." I told them they would kill me; they answered, if I were willing to go along with them, they would not hurt me.

Oh! The dolefull sight that now was to behold at this house! Come, behold the works of the Lord, what desolations he has made in the earth. Of thirty seven persons who were in this one house, none escaped either present death, or a bitter captivity, save only one, who might say as he in Job 1:15: "And I only am escaped to tell the news." There were twelve killed, some shot, some stab'd with their spears, some knock'd down with their hatchets. When we are in prosperity, oh the little that we think of such dreadfull sights, and to see our dear friends and relations ly bleeding out their heart-blood upon the ground. There was one who was chopt into the head with a hatchet, and stript naked, and yet was crawling up and down. It is a solemn sight to see so many Christians lying in their blood, some here, and some there, like a company of sheep torn by wolves, all of them stript naked by a company of hell hounds, roaring, singing, ranting, and insulting, as if they would have torn our very hearts out. Yet the Lord by His almighty power preserved a number of us from death, for there were twenty-four of us taken alive and carried captive.

I had often before this said, that if the Indians should come, I should choose rather to be killed by them, than taken alive, but when it came to the tryal, my mind changed, Their glittering weapons so daunted my spirit, that I chose rather to go along with those (as I may say) ravenous bears, then that moment to end my dayes. And that I may the better declare what happened to me during that grievous captivity, I shall particularly speak of the several removes we had up and down the wilderness.

The First Remove
Now away we must go with those barbarous creatures, with our bodies wounded and bleeding, and our hearts no less than our bodies. About a mile we went that night, up upon a hill within sight of the town where they intended to lodge. There was hard by a vacant house (deserted by the English before, for fear of the Indians). I asked them whither I might not lodge in the house that night, to which they answered, "What, will you love English men still?" This was the dolefullest night that ever my eyes saw. Oh the roaring, and singing, and dancing, and yelling of those black creatures in the night, which made the place a lively resemblance of hell. And as miserable was the waste that was there made, of horses, cattle, sheep, swine, calves, lambs, roasting pigs, and fowl, (which they had plundered in the town) some roasting, some lying and burning, and some boyling, to feed our merciless enemies, who were joyful enough though we were disconsolate. To add to the dolefulness of the former day, and the dismalness of the present night, my thoughts ran upon my losses and sad bereaved condition. All was gone, my husband gone, (at least separated from me, he being in the bay, and to add to my grief, the Indians told me they would kill him as he came homeward) my child-

ren gone, my relations and friends gone, our house and home and all our comforts within door, and without, all was gone, except my life, and I knew not but the next moment that might go too. There remained nothing to me but one poor wounded babe, and it seemed at present worse than death, that it was in such pitiful condition, bespeaking compassion, and I had no refreshing for it, nor suitable things to revive it. Little do many think what is the savageness and brutishness of this barbarous enemy, even those that see to profess more than others among them, when the English have fallen into their hands.

The Third Remove
The morning being come, they prepared to go on their way. One of the Indians got up on a horse and they set me up behind him, with my poor sick babe in my lap. A very wearisome and tedious day I had of it, what with my own wound, and my child being so exceedingly sick, and in a lamentable condition with her wound. It may be easily judged what a poor, feeble condition we were in, there being not the least crumb of refreshing that came within either of our mouths from Wednesday night to Saturday night, except only a little cold water. This day in the afternoon, about an hour by sun, we came to the place where they intended, viz., an Indian town called Wenimesset, northward of Quabaug. When we were come, oh the number of pagans (now merciless enemies) that there came about me that I may say as David, Psalm 27:13. "I had fainted, unless I had believed," etc.

The next day was the Sabbath. I then remembered how careless I had been of God's holy time, how many Sabbaths I had lost and mispent, and how evily I had walked in God's sight, which lay so close unto my spirit that it was easie for me to see how righteous it was with God to cut off the thread of my life, and cast me out of His presence forever. Yet the Lord still shewed mercy to me and upheld me, and as He wounded me with one hand, so He healed me with the other.

This day there came to me one Robert Pepper (a man belonging to Roxbury) who was taken in Captain Beers' fight, and had now been a considerable time with the Indians, and up with them almost as far as Albany to see King Phillip, as he told me, and was now very lately come into these parts. Hearing, I say, that I was in this Indian town, he obtained leave to come and see me. He told me, he himself was wounded in the leg at Captain Beers' fight, and was not able some time to go, but as they carried him, and as he took Oaken leaves and laid to his wound, and through the blessing of God, he was able to travel again. Then I took Oaken leaves and laid them to my side, and with the blessing of God it cured me also.

I sat much alone with a poor wounded child in my lap, which moaned night and day, having nothing to revive her body, or cheer her spirits. But instead of that, sometimes one Indian would come and tell me one hour, that "Your master will knock your child in the head," and then a second, and then a third, "Your master will quickly knock your child in the head." This was all the comfort I had from them, miserable comforters are ye all, as he said.

Thus nine dayes I sat upon my knees, with my babe in my lap, till my flesh was raw again. My child being even ready to depart this sorrowfull world, they bade me carry it out to another wigwam (I suppose because they would not be troubled with such spectacles) whither I went with a very heavy heart, and down I sat with the picture of death in my lap. About two hours in the night my sweet babe, like a lambe, departed this life, on February 18, 1675, it being about six years and five months old. It was nine dayes from the first wounding in this miserable condition, without any refreshing of one nature or other, except a little cold water. I cannot but take notice, how at another time I could not bear to be in the room where any dead person was, but now the case is changed. I must, and could ly down by my dead babe, side by side, all the night after. I have thought since of the wonderfull goodness of God to me, in preserving me in the use of my reason and senses in that distressed time, that I did not use wicked and violent means to end my own miserable life. In the morning when they understood that my child was dead, they sent for me to go to my master's wigwam. (By my master in this writing must be understood Quanopin, who was a Saggamore, and married King Phillip's wife's sister, not that he first took me, I was sold to him by another Narrhaganset Indian, who took me when first I came out of the garrison.) I went to take up my dead child in my arms to carry it with me, but they bid me let it alone. There was no resting, but go I must and leave it. When I had been at my master's wigwam, I took the first opportunity I could get to go look after my dead child. When I came I askt them what they had done with it. Then they told me it was upon the hill. Then they went and shewed me where it was, where I saw the ground was newly digged, and there they told me they had buried it. There I left that child in the wilderness, and must commit it, and my self also, in this wilderness-condition, to Him who is above all.

God having taken away this dear child, I went to see my daughter Mary, who was at this same Indian town at a wigwam not very far off, though we had little liberty or opportunity to see one another. She was about ten years old, & was taken from the door at first by a praying

Indian & afterward sold for a gun. When I came in sight, she would fall a weeping, at which they were provoked, and would not let me come near her, but bade me be gone, which was a heart-cutting word to me. I had one child dead, another in the wilderness I knew not where, the third they would not let me come near to. "Me," as he said, "have ye bereaved of my children. Joseph is not, and Simeon is not, and ye will take Benjamin also; all these things are against me." I could not sit still in this condition, but kept walking from one place to another. And as I was going along, my heart was even overwhelm'd with the thoughts of my condition, that I should have children, and a nation which I knew not ruled over them. Whereupon I earnestly entreated the Lord, that He would consider my low estate, and shew me a token for good, and if it were His blessed will, some sign and hope of some relief.

And indeed quickly the Lord answered, in some measure, my poor prayers, for as I was going up and down mourning and lamenting my condition, my son came to me and asked me how I did. I had not seen him before, since the destruction of the town, and I knew not where he was, till I was informed by himself, that he was amongst a smaller parcel of Indians, whose place was about six miles off. With tears in his eyes, he asked me whether his sister Sarah was dead, and told me he had seen his sister Mary, and prayed me, that I would not be troubled in reference to himself.

The occasion of his coming to see me at this time, was this: There was, as I said, about six miles from us a small plantation of Indians, where it seems he had been during his captivity. And at this time there were some forces of the Indians gathered out of our company, some also from them (among whom was my son's master), to go to the assault and burn Medfield. In this time of the absence of his master, his dame brought him to see me. I took this to be some gracious answer to my earnest and unfeigned desire. The next day, viz. to this, the Indians returned from Medfield. All the company, and those that belonged to the other small company, came through the town that now we were at, but before they came to us, oh! the outrageous roaring and hoping that there was. They began their din about a mile before they came to us. By their noise and hooping they signified how many they had destroyed (which was at that time twenty-three).

I cannot but take notice of the wonderfull mercy of God to me in those afflictions, in sending me a Bible. One of the Indians that come from Medfield fight, had brought some plunder, came to me and asked me if I would have a Bible. He had got one in his basket. I was glad of it, and asked him whether he thought the Indians would let me read.

He answered, yes, so I took the Bible, and in that melancholy time, it came into my mind to read first the 28th Chapter of Deuteronomy, which I did, and when I had read it, my dark heart wrought on this manner, that there was no mercy for me, that the blessings were gone and the curses came in their room, and that I had lost my opportunity. But the Lord helped me still to go on reading till I came to Chapter 30, the seven first verses, where I found, there was mercy promised again, if we would return to Him by repentance, and though we were scattered from one end of the earth to the other, yet the Lord would gather us together, and turn all those curses upon our enemies. I do not desire to live to forget this scripture, and what comfort it was to me.

Now the Indians began to talk of removing from this place, some one way, and some another. There were now, besides myself, nine English captives in this place, all of them children, except one woman. I got an opportunity to go and take my leave of them, they being to go one way, and I another. I asked them whether they were earnest with God for deliverance; they told me they did as they were able, and it was some comfort to me that the Lord stirred up children to look to Him. The woman, viz. Goodwife Joslin told me, she shou'd never see me again, and that she could find in her heart to run away. I wisht her not to run away by any means, for we were near thirty miles from any English town, and she very big with child, and had but one week to reckon, and another child in her arms, two years old. And bad rivers there were to go over, & we were feeble with our poor & coarse entertainment. I had my Bible with me; I pulled it out, and asked her whether she would read. We opened the Bible and lighted on Psalm 27, in which Psalm we especially took notice of that verse, viz. "Wait on the Lord, be of good courage, and He shall strengthen thine heart. Wait, I say, on the Lord."

The Fourth Remove

And now I must part with that little company I had. Here I parted from my daughter Mary (whom I never saw again till I saw her in Dorchester, returned from captivity) and from four little cousins and neighbours, some of which I never saw afterward. The Lord only knows the end of them. Amongst them also was that poor woman before mentioned, who came to a sad end, as some of the company told me in my travel. She having much grief upon her spirit about her miserable condition, being so near her time, would be often asking the Indians to let her go home. They not being willing to do that, yet vexed with her importunity, gathered a great company together about her, and stript her naked, and set her in the midst of them. And when they had sung and danced about her (in their hellish manner) as long as they pleased, they knockt her on head, and the child in her arms with her. When they had done that, they made a fire and put them both into it, and told the other children that were with them, that if they attempted to go home, they would serve them in like manner. The children said she did not shed one tear, but prayed all the while. But to return to my own journey: we traveled about half a day or little more, and came to a desolate place in the wilderness, where there were no wigwams or inhabitants before. We came about the middle of the afternoon to this place, cold and wet, and snowy, and hungry, and weary, and no refreshing for man but the cold ground to sit on and our poor Indian cheer.

   Heart-aking thoughts here I had about my poor children, who were scattered up and down among the wild beasts of the forest. My head was light & dissey (either through hunger or hard lodging, or trouble, or altogether) my knees feeble, my body raw by sitting double night and day, that I cannot express to man the affliction that lay upon my spirit, but the Lord helped me at that time to express it to Himself. I opened my Bible to read, and the Lord brought that precious scripture to me, Jeremiah 31:16. "Thus saith the Lord, refrain thy voice from weeping, and thine eyes from tears, for thy work shall be rewarded, and they shall come again from the land of the enemy." This was a sweet cordial to me when I was ready to faint. Many and many atime have I sat down and wept sweetly over this scripture. At this place we continued about four dayes.

The Eighth Remove
On the morrow morning we must go over the river, i.e. Connecticut, to meet with King Philip. Two canoos full they had carried over; the next turn I myself was to go, but as my foot was upon the canoo to step in, there was a sudden outcry among them, and I must step back. And instead of going over the river, I must go four or five miles up the river farther northward. Some of the Indians ran one way, and some another. The cause of this rout was, as I thought, their espying some English scouts who were thereabout. In this travel up the river, about noon, the company made a stop and sate down, some to eat, and others to rest them.

   But to return, we travelled on till night, and in the morning, we must go over the river to Phillip's crew. When I was in the canoo, I could not but be amazed at the numerous crew of pagans that were on the bank on the other side. When I came ashore, they gathered all about me, I sitting alone in the midst. I observed they asked one another questions, and laughed, and rejoyced over their gains and victories. Then my heart began to fail and I fell a weeping, which was the first time to my remembrance that I wept before them. Although I had met with so much affliction, and my heart was many times ready to break, yet could I not shed one tear in their sight, but rather had been all this while in amaze, and like one astonished. . . .one of them asked me why I wept: I could hardly tell what to say, yet I answered, they would kill me. "No," said he, "none will hurt you." Then came one of them and gave me two spoonfuls of meal to comfort me, and another gave me half a pint of pease, which was worth more than many bushels at another time.

Now the Indians gather their forces to go against North-Hampton. Over-night one went about yelling and hooting to give notice of the design, whereupon they fell to boyling of ground-nuts and parching of corn (as many as had it) for their provision, and in the morning away they went.

During my abode in this place, Phillip spake to me to make a shirt for his boy, which I did, for which he gave me a shilling. I offered the money to my master but he bade me keep it, and with it I bought a piece of horse flesh. Afterwards he asked me to make a cap for his boy, for which he invited me to dinner. I went, and he gave me a pancake, about as big as two fingers. It was made of parched wheat, beaten, and fryed in bear's grease, but I thought I had never tasted pleasanter meat in my life. There was a squaw who spake to me to make a shirt for her sannup, for which she gave me a piece of bear. Another asked me to knit a pair of stockins for which she gave me a quart of pease. I boyled my pease and bear together, and invited my master and mistriss to dinner, but the proud gossip, because I served them both in one dish, would eat nothing, except one bit that he gave her upon the point of his knife.

Hearing that my son was come to this place, I went to see him, and found him lying flat against the ground. I asked him how he could sleep so. He answered me, that he was not asleep, but at prayer, and lay so, that they might not observe what he was doing. I pray God he may remember these things now that he is returned in safety. At this place (the sun now getting higher) what with the beams and heat of the sun and the smoke of the wigwams, I thought I should have been blind, I could scarce discern one wigwam from another. There was here one Mary Thurston of Medfield who seeing how it was with me, lent me a hat to wear, but as soon as I was gone the squaw (who owned that Mary Thurston) came running after me, and got it away again.

Here was the squaw that gave me one spoonful of meal. I put it in my pocket to keep it safe, yet notwithstanding, somebody stole it, but put five Indian corns in the room of it, which corns were the greatest provisions I had in my travel for one day.

The Indians returning from North-Hampton brought with them some horses, and sheep, and other things which they had taken. I desired them, that they would carry me to Albany upon one of those horses, and sell me for powder, for so they had sometimes discoursed. I was utterly hopeless of getting home on foot the way that I came. I could hardly bear to think of the many weary steps I had taken to come to this place.

The Twelfth Remove
It was upon a Sabbath-day morning that they prepared for their travel. This morning I asked my master whither he would sell me to my husband. He answered me, "Nux," which did not much rejoyce my spirit. My mistriss, before we went, was gone to the burial of a papoos, and returning, she found me sitting and reading in my Bible. She snatched it hastily out of my hand, and threw it out of doors. I ran out and catcht it up and put it in my pocket, and never let her see it afterward. They packed up their things to be gone, and gave me my load. I complained it was too heavy, whereupon she gave me a slap in the face, and bade me go; I lifted up my heart to God, hoping that redemption was not far off, and the rather because their insolency grew worse and worse.

The Sixteenth Remove
We began this remove with wading over Baquag river. The water was up to the knees, and the stream very swift, and so cold that I thought it would have cut me in sunder. I was so weak and feeble, that I reeled as I went along and thought there I must end my dayes at last, after my bearing and getting thorough so many difficulties. The Indians stood laughing to see me staggering along, but in my distress the Lord gave me experience of the truth, and goodness of that promise, Isaiah 43:2. "When thou passest thorough the waters, I will be with thee, and through the rivers, they shall not overflow thee." Then I sat down to put on my stockins and shoes, with the tears running down mine eyes, and many sorrowfull thoughts in my heart, but I gat up to go along with them.

Quickly there came up to us an Indian, who informed them, that I must go to Wachusett to my master, for there was a letter come from the Council to the Saggamores about redeeming the captives, and that there would be another in fourteen dayes, and that I must be there ready. My heart was so heavy before that I could scarce speak or go in the path, and yet now so light, that I could run. My strength seemed to come again, and recruit my feeble knees, and aking heart. Yet it pleased them to go but one mile that night, and there we stayed two dayes. In that time came a company of Indians to us, near thirty, all on horseback. My heart skipt within me, thinking they had been English men at the first sight of them, for they were dressed in English apparel, with hats, white neckcloths, and sashes about their waists, and ribbonds upon their shoulders. But when they came near, there was a vast difference between the lovely faces of Christians, and the foul looks of those heathens, which much damped my spirit again.

The Twentieth Remove

It was their usual manner to remove, when they had done any mischief, lest they should be found out, and so they did at this time. We went about three or four miles and there they built a great wigwam, big enough to hold a hundred Indians, which they did in preparation to a great day of dancing. They would say now amongst themselves that the Governour would be so angry for his loss at Sudbury, that they would send no more about the captives, which made me grieve and tremble. My sister, being not far from the place where we now were, and hearing that I was here, desired her master to let her come and see me, and he was willing to it, and would go with her. But she being ready before him, told him she would go before, and was come within a mile or two of the place. Then he overtook her, and began to rant as if he had been mad, and made her go back again in the rain, so that I never saw her till I saw her in Charlestown. But the Lord requited many of their ill doings. For this Indian, her master, was hanged afterward at Boston. The Indians now began to come from all quarters, against their merry dancing day. Among some of them came one Goodwife Kettle. I told her my heart was so heavy it was ready to break. "So is mine too," said she, but yet said, "I hope we shall hear some good news shortly." I could hear how earnestly my sister desired to see me, & I as earnestly desired to see her, and yet neither of us could get an opportunity. My daughter was also now about a mile off, and I had not seen her in nine or ten weeks, as I had not seen my sister since our first taking. I earnestly desired them to let me go and see them. Yea, I intreated, begged, and perswaded them but to let me see my daughter, and yet so hard hearted were they, that they would not suffer it. They made use of their tyrannical power whilst they had it. But through the Lord's wonderfull mercy, their time was now but short.

On a Sabbath-day, the sun being about an hour high in the afternoon, came Mr. John Hoar (the Council permitting him, and his own forward spirit inclining him) together with the two afore mentioned Indians, Tom and Peter, with their third letter from the council. When they came near, I was abroad. Though I saw them not, they presently called me in, and bade me sit down and not stir. Then they catcht up their guns, and away they ran, as if an enemy had been at hand, and the guns went off apace. I manifested some great trouble, and they asked me what was the matter? I told them I thought they had killed the English-man (for they had in the meantime informed me that an English-man was come). They said no. They shot over his horse, and under, and before his horse, and they pusht him this way and that way, at their pleasure, shewing what they could do. Then they let them come to their wigwams. I begged of them to let me see the English-man, but they would not. But there I was fain to sit their pleasure. When they had talked their fill with him, they suffered me to go to him. We asked each other of our welfare, and how my husband did, and all my friends. He told me they were all well, and would be glad to see me. Amongst other things which my husband sent me, there came a pound of tobacco which I sold for nine shillings in money. For many of the Indians, for want of tobacco, smoked hemlock and ground-ivy. It was a great mistake in any, who thought I sent for tobacco, for through the favour of God, that desire was overcome. I now asked them, whither I should go home with Mr. Hoar? They answered no, one and another of them, and it being night we laid down with that answer.

In the morning, Mr. Hoar invited the Saggamores to dinner, but when we went to get it ready, we found they had stolen the greatest part of the provision Mr. Hoar had brought, out of his bags, in the night. And we may see the wonderful power of God, in that one passage, in that when there was such a great number of Indians together, and so greedy of a little good food, and no English there, but Mr. Hoar and myself, that there they did not knock us in the head and take what we had, there being not only some provisions, but trading-cloth and a part of the twenty pounds agreed upon. But instead of doing us any mischief they seemed to be ashamed of the fact, and said, it were some Machit Indians that did it. Oh, that we could believe that there is nothing too hard for God! God shewed his power over the heathen in this, as he did over the hungry lyons when Daniel was cast into the den. Mr. Hoar called them betime to dinner, but they ate very little, they being so busy in dressing themselves, and getting ready for their dance, which was carried on by eight of them; four men and four squaws, my master and mistriss being two.

He was dressed in his Holland shirt with great laces sewed at the tail of it. He had his silver buttons, and his white stockins. His garters were hung round with shillings, and he had girdles of wampum upon his head and shoulders. She had a Kersey coat, and was covered with girdles of wampum from the loins upward. Her arms from her elbows to her hands were covered with bracelets; there were handfuls of neck laces about her neck, and several sorts of jewels in her ears. She had fine red stockins, and white shoes, her hair powdered and face painted red, that was alwayes before black. And all the dancers were after the same manner. There were two others singing and knocking on a kettle for their musick. They kept hopping up and down one after another, with a kettle of water in the midst, standing warm upon some embers, to drink of when they were dry. They held on till it was almost night, throwing out wampum to the standers by. At night I asked them again if I should go home? They all as one said no, except my husband would come for me.

When we were lain down, my master went out of the wigwam, and by and by sent in an Indian called James the Printer, who told Mr. Hoar, that my master would let me go to morrow, if he would let him have one pint of liquors. Then Mr. Hoar called his own Indians, Tom and Peter, and bid them go and see whither he would promise it before them three, and if he would, he should have it, which he did, and he had it. Then Phillip, smelling the business called me to him, and asked me what I would give him, to tell me some good news, and speak a good word for me. I told him, I could not tell what to give him, I would anything I had, and asked him what he would have? He said two coats and twenty shillings in money, and half a bushel of feed corn, and some tobacco. I thanked him for his love, but I knew the good news as well as the crafty fox. My master after he had his drink, quickly came ranting into the wigwam again, and called for Mr. Hoar, drinking to him, and saying he was a good man, and then again he would say, "Hang him, rogue." Being almost drunk, he would drink to him, and yet presently say he should be hanged. Then he called for me, I trembled to hear him, yet I was fain to go to him, and he drank to me, shewing no incivility. He was the first Indian I saw drunk all the while that I was amongst them. At last his squaw ran out, and he after her, round the wigwam, with his money jingling at his knees, but she escaped him. But having an old squaw he ran to her, and lo through the Lord's mercy, we were no more troubled that night.

Yet I had not a comfortable night's rest, for I think I can say, I did not sleep for three nights together. The night before the letter came from the Council, I could not rest, I was so full of fears and troubles, God many times leaving most of us in the dark, when deliverance is nearest. Yea, at this time I could not rest night nor day. The next night I was overjoyed, Mr. Hoar being come, and that with such good tidings. This third night I was even swallowed up with thoughts of things, viz., that ever I should go home again, and that I must go, leaving my children behind me in the wilderness, so that sleep was almost now departed from mine eyes.

On Tuesday morning they called their General Court (as they call it) to consult and determine whether I should go home or no, and they all as one man did seemingly consent to it, that I should go home, except Phillip, who would not come among them.

. . . But to return again to my going home, where we may see a remarkable change of providence: At first they were all against it, except my husband would come for me, but afterwards they assented to it, and seemed much to rejoyce in it. Some asked me to send them some bread, others some tobacco, others shaking me by the hand, offering me a hood and a scarfe to ride in, not one moving hand or tongue against it. Thus hath the Lord answered my poor desire, and the many earnest requests of others put up unto God for me.

In my travels an Indian came to me and told me, if I were willing, he and his squaw would run away and go home along with me. I told him no. I was not willing to run away, but desired to wait God's time, that I might go home quietly, and without fear. And now God hath granted me my desire.

O the wonderful power of God that I have seen, and the experience that I have had! I have been in the midst of those roaring lyons, and savage bears, that feared neither God, nor man, nor the devil, by night and day, alone and in company, sleeping all sorts together. And yet not one of them ever offered me the least abuse of unchastity to me, in word or action. Though some are ready to say I speak this for my own credit, I speak it in the presence of God, and to His glory. God's power is as great now, and as sufficient to save, as when He preserved Daniel in the lyons den, or the three children in the firey furnace. I may well say as His Psalm 107:12, "Oh give thanks unto the Lord for He is good, for His mercy endureth for ever. Let the redeemed of the Lord say so, whom He hath redeemed from the hand of the enemy," especially that I should have come away in the midst of so many hundreds of enemies quietly and peacefully, and not a dog moving his tongue.

So I took my leave of them, and in coming along my heart melted into tears, more than all the while I was with them, and I was almost swallowed up with the thoughts that ever I should go home again. About the sun going down, Mr. Hoar and myself and two Indians came to Lancaster, and a solemn sight it was to me. There had I lived many comfortable years amongst my relations and neighbors, and now not one Christian was to be seen, nor one house left standing. We went on to a farm-house that was yet standing, where we lay all night, and a comfortable lodging we had, though there was nothing but straw to ly on. The Lord preserved us in safety that night, and raised us up again in the morning, and carried us along, that before noon we came to Concord. Now I was full of joy, and yet not without sorrow: joy to see such a lovely sight, so many Christians together, and some of my neighbors. There I met with my brother, and my brother in law, who asked me if I knew where his wife was. Poor heart! He had helped to bury her, and knew it not. She being shot down by the house was partly burnt, so that those who were at Boston at the desolation of the town and came back afterward and buried the dead did not know her. Yet I was not without sorrow, to think how many were looking and longing, and my own children among the rest, to enjoy the deliverance that I had now received. And I did not know whither ever I should see them again.

Being recruited with food and raiment, we went to Boston that day, where I met with my dear husband, but the thoughts of our dear children, one being dead, and the other we could not tell where, abated our comfort each to other. I was not before so much hem'd in with the merciless and cruel heathen, but now as much with pitiful, tender-hearted, and compassionate Christians. In that poor and distressed and beggarly condition I was received in, I was kindly entertained in several houses. So much love I received from several (some of whom I knew, and others I knew not) that I am not capable to declare it. But the Lord knows them all by name. The Lord reward them seven fold into their bosoms of His spirituals for their temporals. The twenty pounds, the price of my redemption, was raised by some Boston gentlemen, and Mr. Usher, whose bounty and religious charity, I would not forget to make mention of. Then Mr. Thomas Shepard of Charlestown received us into his house where we continued eleven weeks. And a father and mother they were to us. And many more tender-hearted friends we met with in that place. We were now in the midst of love, yet not without much and frequent heaviness of heart for our poor children, and other relations, who were still in affliction.

1704–1709
MAROONED:
THE STORY OF ALEXANDER SELKIRK

Alexander Selkirk has left us no reliably direct account of his five years of solitude on the wilderness island of Más a Tierra—now known alternately as Juan Fernández Island or Isla Róbinson Crusoe—some four hundred miles west of Chile. His story was told by a number of early eighteenth-century chroniclers, including essayist Richard Steele (in *The Englishman*, 1713) and Captain Woodes Rogers (in *A Cruising Voyage Round the World*, 1713), the crew of whose privateer, the *Duke*, discovered the castaway on January 31st, 1709. It was Woodes Rogers who took Selkirk away from the island on February 12th of that same year. Daniel Defoe, who is rumored to have met Selkirk, drew inspiration from Selkirk's story for his celebrated *Robinson Crusoe*, which first appeared in 1719, and upon which the Scottish mariner's fame today largely rests. The report of Selkirk's rescuer, Woodes Rogers, is based directly on first contacts with the castaway, and it is this account, flavored with its author's straightforward perceptive character, which is offered here.

Born in 1676 in Largo, Fifeshire, the seventh son of a shoemaker and tanner, unruly Alexander ran off to sea at the age of nineteen. By 1703 he had risen to the rating of sailing master on the British privateer *Cinque Ports,* one of two ships under the command of William Dampier then raiding Spanish shipping off the South American coast.

While the *Cinque Ports* was near Juan Fernández Island, Selkirk bitterly quarreled with its captain, Thomas Stradling, and demanded to be set ashore. Stradling readily acceded. Despite the unseaworthy state of the *Cinque Ports,* which may have played a part in the dispute, Selkirk soon relented his rash demand and pleaded with Stradling to be taken aboard the ship. But Stradling refused to hear the troublesome mariner's pleas and abandoned him to make his way on the island with but a few bare necessities: his Bible and a few other books, a musket with a pound of powder, some mathematical instruments, a hatchet, a knife, and a few utensils. Soon after-wards, the leaking 'Cinque Ports' foundered, with the loss of all but a few of its crew.

Isolated as it was, Juan Fernández Island was known to Spanish, French, and British mariners, who occasionally stopped there to take on fresh water. As an Englishmen, Selkirk feared that the Spaniards would be more likely to kill him or condemn him to slavery in a Peruvian mine than to help him find his way home. During the four years and four months that he was stranded on the island, Selkirk twice narrowly escaped being captured by Spaniards whose ships he had approached hopefully when they came to anchor there.

With a bow to the role of Divine Providence in sustaining Selkirk through five years of solitude, Woodes Rogers also cites the adage "Necessity is the mother of invention" in addressing how Selkirk survived his ordeal. As Rogers' account shows, Selkirk was a man of ability and character, who responded quickly to insure his basic survival; though this was not an insurmountable challenge on Juan Fernández, where food was relatively plentiful and the climate was temperate. The castaway sailor fed on the meat of the goats that populated the island and, after his own clothing had worn to nothing, clothed himself in their hides. He quickly constructed adequate shelter. And he deftly forged an alliance with the cats of the island against the rats, both species having been introduced by visiting European ships. Indeed, when he was finally rescued, though at first barely able to speak for so long not having spoken, Selkirk claimed himself to be stronger and in better health than at any other point in his life.

Our true-life Robinson Crusoe suffered most from his isolation. He told his rescuers he had become a better Christian than he had been or that he was ever likely to become, as he had read his Bible so often to assuage his loneliness. He also took to dancing with his tamed goats and cats. Indeed, through his very success in adapting to his plight, Selkirk grew more and more wild both in behavior and appearance. His rescuers, themselves no courtiers, could barely recognize him as human. But Selkirk never lost his thirst for human companionship. Despite his fear of Spanish capture, he burnt signal fires on an island promontory in the hope of attracting the ships which so rarely passed nearby. And as skillfully as he had adapted to life on the island, Selkirk, upon his rescue, readily resumed the mariner's life.

William Dampier, the commander of the expedition from which Selkirk had been castaway, was serving as Woodes Rogers' pilot at the time of Selkirk's rescue. Dampier commended Selkirk to Rogers, who made him a mate aboard his ship, and entrusted a prize vessel to him less than two months later. In October of 1711 Selkirk sailed into the Thames. Soon afterward he returned to his home in Scotland. Within a few years he was back at sea, where he died, master's mate of H.M.S. Weymouth, on December 12, 1721.

Marooned: The Story of Alexander Selkirk

from *A Cruising Voyage Around the World*

by Woodes Rogers

Feb. 2. We stood on the back side along the South end of the Island, in order to lay in with the first Southerly Wind, which Capt. *Dampier* told us generally blows there all day long. In the Morning, being past the Island, we tack'd to lay it in close aboard the Land; and about ten a clock open'd the South End of the Island, and ran close aboard the Land that begins to make the North-East side. The Flaws (sudden bursts or squalls of wind) came heavy off shore, and we were forc'd to reef our Top-sails when we open'd the middle Bay, where we expected to find our Enemy, but saw all clear, and no Ships in that nor the other Bay next the NW. End. These two Bays are all that Ships ride in which recruit on this Island, but the middle Bay is by much the best. We guess'd there had been Ships there, but that they were gone on sight of us. We sent our Yall ashore about Noon, with Capt. *Dover*, Mr. *Frye*, and six Men, all arm'd; mean while we and the *Dutchess* kept turning to get in, and such heavy Flaws came off the Land, that we were forc'd to let fly our Topsail-Sheet, keeping all Hands to stand by our Sails, for fear of the Wind's carrying 'em away: but when the Flaws were gone, we had little or no Wind. These Flaws proceeded from the Land, which is very high in the middle of the Island. Our Boat did not return, so we sent our Pinnace with the Men armed, to see what was the occasion of the Yall's stay; for we were afraid that the *Spaniards* had a Garrison there, and might have seiz'd 'em. We put out a Signal for our Boat, and the *Dutchess* show'd a *French* Ensign. Immediately our Pinnace return'd from the shore, and brought abundance of Craw-fish, with a Man cloth'd in Goat-Skins, who look'd wilder than the first Owners of them. He had been on the Island four Years and four Months, being left there by Capt. *Stradling* in the *Cinque-Ports*; his name was *Alexander Selkirk* a *Scotch* Man, who had been Master of the *Cinque-Ports*, a Ship that came here last with Capt. *Dampier,* who told me that this was the best Man in her; so I immediately agreed with him to be a Mate on board our Ship. 'Twas he that made the Fire last night when he saw our Ships, which he judg'd to be *English*. During his stay here, he saw several Ships pass by, but only two came in to anchor. As he went to view them, he found 'em to be *Spaniards*, and retir'd from 'em; upon which they shot at him. Had they been *French*, he would have submitted; but chose to risque his dying alone on the Island, rather than fall into the hands of the *Spaniards* in these parts, because he apprehended they would murder him, or make a Slave of him in the Mines, for he fear'd they would spare no Stranger that might be capable of discovering the *South-Sea*. The *Spaniards* had landed, before he knew what they were, and they came so near him that he had much ado to escape; for they not only shot at him but pursued him into the Woods, where he climb'd to the top of a Tree, at the foot of which they made water, and kill'd several Goats just by, but went off again without discovering him. He told us that he was born at *Largo* in the County of *Fife* in *Scotland*, and was bred a Sailor from his Youth. The reason of his being left here was a difference betwixt him and his Captain; which, together with the Ships being leaky, made him willing rather to stay here, than go along with him at first; and when he was at last willing, the Captain would not receive him. He had been in the Island before to wood and water, when two of the Ships Company were left upon it for six Months till the Ship return'd, being chas'd thence by two *French South-Sea* Ships.

He had with him his Clothes and Bedding, with a Firelock, some Powder, Bullets, and Tobacco, a Hatchet, a Knife, a Kettle, a Bible, some practical Pieces, and his Mathematical Instruments and Books. He diverted and provided for himself as well as he could; but for the first eight months had much ado to bear up against Melancholy, and the Terror of being left alone in such a desolate place. He built two Hutts with Piemento Trees, cover'd them with long Grass, and lin'd them with the Skins of Goats, which he kill'd with his Gun as he wanted, so long as his Powder lasted, which was but a pound; and that being near spent, he got fire by rubbing two sticks of Piemento Wood together upon his knee. In the lesser Hutt, at some distance from the other, he dress'd his Victuals, and in the larger he slept, and employed himself in reading, singing Psalms, and praying; so that he said he was a better Christian while in this Solitude than ever he was before, or than, he was afraid, he should ever be again. At first he never eat anything till Hunger constrain'd him, partly for grief and partly for want of Bread and Salt; nor did he go to bed till he could watch no longer: the Piemento Wood, which burnt very clear, serv'd him both for Firing and Candle, and refresh'd him with its fragrant Smell.

He might have had Fish enough, but could not eat 'em for want of Salt, because they occasion'd a Looseness; except Crawfish, which are there as large as our Lobsters, and very good: These he sometimes boil'd, and at times broil'd, as he did his Goats Flesh, of which he made very good Broth, for they are not so rank as ours: he kept an Account of 500 that he kill'd while there, and caught as many more, which he mark'd on the Ear and let go. When his Powder fail'd, he took them by speed of foot; for his way of living and continual Exercise of walking and running, clear'd him of all gross Humours, so that he ran with wonderful Swiftness thro the Woods and up the Rocks and Hills, as we perceiv'd when we employ'd him to catch Goats for us. We had a Bull-Dog, which we sent with several of our nimblest Runners, to help him in catching Goats; but he distanc'd and tir'd both the Dog and the Men, catch'd the Goats, and brought 'em to us on his back. He told us that his Agility in pursuing a Goat had once like to have cost him his Life; he pursu'd it with so much Eagerness that he catch'd hold of it on the brink of a Precipice, of which he was not aware, the Bushes having hid it from him; so that he fell with the Goat down the said precipice a great height, and was so stun'd and bruis'd with the Fall, that he narrowly escap'd with his Life, and when he came to his Senses, found the Goat dead under him. He lay there about 24 hours, and was scarce able to crawl to his Hutt, which was about a mile distant, or to stir abroad again in ten days.

He came at last to relish his Meat well enough without Salt or Bread, and in the Season had plenty of good Turnips, which had been sow'd there by Capt. *Dampier*'s Men, and have now overspread some Acres of Ground. He had enough of good Cabbage from the Cabbage-Trees, and season'd his meat with the Fruit of the Piemento Trees, which is the same as the *Jamaica* Pepper, and smells deliciously. He found there also a black Pepper call'd *Malagita*, which was very good to expel Wind, and against Griping of the Guts.

He soon wore out all his Shoes and Clothes by running thro the Woods; and at last being forc'd to shift without them, his Feet became so hard, that he ran every where without Annoyance: and it was some time before he could wear Shoes after we found him; for not being used to any so long, his Feet swell'd when he came first to wear 'em again.

After he had conquer'd his Melancholy, he diverted himself sometimes by cutting his Name on the Trees, and the Time of his being left and Continuance there. He was at first much pester'd with Cats and Rats, that had bred in great numbers from some of each Species which had got ashore from Ships that put in there to wood and water. The Rats gnaw'd his Feet and Clothes while asleep, which oblig'd him to cherish the Cats with his Goats-flesh; by which many of them became so tame, that they would lie about him in hundreds, and soon deliver'd him from the Rats. He likewise tam'd some Kids, and to divert himself would now and then sing and dance with them and his Cats: so that by the Care of Providence and Vigour of his Youth, being now but about 30 years old, he came at last to conquer all the Inconveniences of his Solitude, and to be very easy. When his Clothes wore out, he made himself a Coat and Cap of Goat-Skins, which he stitch'd together with little Thongs of the same, that he cut with his Knife. He had no other Needle but a Nail; and when his Knife was wore to the back, he made others as well as he could of some Iron Hoops that were left ashore, which he beat thin and ground upon Stones. Having some Linen Cloth by him, he sow'd himself Shirts with a Nail, and stitch'd 'em with the Worsted of his old Stockings, which he pull'd out on purpose. He had his last Shirt on when we found him on the Island.

At his first coming on board us, he had so much forgot his Language for want of Use, that we could scarce understand him, for he seem'd to speak his words by halves. We offer'd him a Dram, but he would not touch it, having drank nothing but water since his being there, and 'twas some time before he could relish our Victuals.

He could give us an account of no other Product of the Island than what we have mention'd, except small black Plums, which are very good, but hard to come at, the Trees which bear 'em growing on high Mountains and Rocks. Piemento Trees are plenty here, and we saw some of 60 foot high, and about two yards thick; and Cotton Trees higher, and near four fathom round in the Stock.

The Climate is so good, that the Trees and Grass are verdant all the Year. The Winter lasts no longer than *June* and *July*, and is not then severe, there being only a small Frost and a little Hail, but sometimes great Rains. The Heat of the Summer is equally moderate, and there's not much Thunder or tempestuous Weather of any sort. He saw no venomous or savage Creature on the Island, nor any other sort of Beast but Goats, *&c.* as above-mention'd; the first of which had been put ashore here on purpose for a Breed by *Juan Fernando* a *Spaniard*, who settled there with some Families for a time; till the Continent of *Chili* began to submit to the *Spaniards*; which being more profitable, tempted them to quit this Island, which is capable of maintaining a good number of People, and of being made so strong that they could not easily be dislodged.

Ringrose in his Account of Capt. *Sharp*'s Voyage and other Buccaneers, mentions one who had escap'd ashore here out of a Ship which was cast away with all the rest of the Company, and says he had lived five years alone before he had the opportunity of another Ship to carry him off. Capt. *Dampier* talks of a *Moskito Indian* that belong'd to Capt. *Watlin,* who being a hunting in the Woods when the Captain left the Island, liv'd here three years alone, and shifted much in the same manner as Mr. *Selkirk* did, till Capt. *Dampier* came hither in 1684, and carry'd him off. The first that went ashore was one of his Countrymen, and they saluted one another first by prostrating themselves by turns on the ground, and then embracing. But whatever there is in these Stories, this of Mr. *Selkirk* I know to be true; and his Behaviour afterwards gives me reason to believe the Account he gave me how he spent his time, and bore up under such an Affliction, in which nothing but the Divine Providence could have supported any Man. By this one may see that Solitude and Retirement from the World is not such an unsufferable State of Life as most Men imagine, especially when People are fairly call'd or thrown into it unavoidably, as this Man was; who in all probability must otherwise have perish'd in the Seas, the Ship which left him being cast away not long after, and few of the Company escap'd. We may perceive by this Story the Truth of the Maxim, That Necessity is the Mother of Invention, since he found means to supply his Wants in a very natural manner, so as to maintain his Life, tho not so conveniently, yet as effectually as we are able to do with the help of all of our Arts and Society. It may likewise instruct us, how much a plain and temperate way of living conduces to the Health of the Body and the Vigour of the Mind, both of which we are apt to destroy by Excess and Plenty, especially of strong Liquor, and the variety as well as the Nature of our Meat and Drink: for this Man, when he came to our ordinary Method of Diet and Life, tho he was sober enough, lost much of his Strength and Agility. But I must quit these Reflections, which are more proper for a Philosopher and Divine than a Mariner, and return to my own subject.

1756
ENSLAVED:
THE ORDEAL OF OLAUDAH EQUIANO

When they come among Europeans, they are ignorant of their language, religion, manners, and customs. Are any pains taken to teach them these? Are they treated as men? Does not slavery itself depress the mind, and extinguish all its fire and every noble sentiment?

    – Olaudah Equiano, Chapter One, *The Interesting Narrative of the Life of Olaudah Equiano, or Gustavus Vassa, the African*

Olaudah Equiano was eleven years old in 1756, when he and his sister were abducted from their home and sold into slavery. The cherished youngest son of a prosperous Ibo village family in the Niger River kingdom of Benin, Olaudah was soon separated from his sister, with whom he was later by chance joyfully, though only briefly, reunited. He was passed from one owner to another, each time further away from his home, until traders finally carried him down river and sold him to European slavers who were riding at anchor off the African coast.

Olaudah was treated almost as an equal by the first of his African masters. Doubtless his well-bred bearing and intelligence recommended him to them as a young man whom they could accept into their homes. It is even evident that the Europeans into whose hands he fell recognized fine qualities in the young man, for it is apparent that they accorded him treatment, however callous and sadistic, that was more favorable than that generally extended to those caught up in their cruel trade. Through four dark centuries of the transatlantic commerce, more than twenty million Africans were enslaved and shipped to the New World, more than half of these to the Caribbean islands. Almost a quarter of those packed into the misery-ridden holds of the slave ships perished in the one to two month ocean crossings. Many more were worked to death on the New World plantations.

This was not the fate of the young man, whose unique and wrenching account of enslavement in Africa and shipment to the New World is offered here. Olaudah was not sold to the sugar planters of Barbados when his ship arrived there. Perhaps he was thought to be too young and too slight to be of value in the cane fields. Perhaps a greater value was placed on his linguistic abilities, which had quickly emerged as a tool for survival when he was first abducted. Whatever the reason, Olaudah was quickly shipped off to Virginia, and was purchased by a lieutenant in the Royal Navy, Michael H. Pascal, in whose service he sailed the world until the conclusion of the Seven Years' War. He was resold to a Philadelphia Quaker, John King, who saw great promise in Olaudah, aided him in extending his education, and eventually allowed him to purchase his own freedom, in 1766, with money that he had accumulated from a variety of employments.

As a free man, Olaudah Equiano moved to England, worked for a time in the West Indies trade, and assiduously continued his education. As assistant to Dr. Charles Irving, he participated in 1773 in an expedition to the Canadian Arctic in search of the Northwest Passage. It was during the time of the American Revolution that Equiano began to speak out against the cruelties of the slave trade. When he returned to Philadelphia in 1785, Equiano's voice was prominent among those calling out for abolition of the heinous institution. He continued his work against slavery, married in 1792, and died in 1797. Equiano's autobiographical account was published in Boston in 1789 and soon after in England where eight separate editions appeared within five years. The book was highly influential in the passionate debate that finally led to the abolition of the English slave trade in 1807.

How was a boy captured into slavery at the age of eleven able to survive and eventually to achieve complete freedom and a full life? We may catch glimpses of the reasons for this in Chapter Two of his *Interesting Narrative* in which we can observe a boy, torn from the happiness of his home, struggling to come to grips with the new condition of his life. Olaudah's intellect and curiosity are never extinguished. From the first moments of his capture, his mind focused on how to make his way home. He carefully observed his surroundings and quickly learned new dialects and languages. Even when completely uncomprehending and disoriented in his first encounter with Europeans, his thoughts were of wonder rather than fear. Allowed to manipulate the quadrant aboard the slave ship, he saw a world overturned with clouds below land that floated above. His intellect and his will to live, despite enormous fear and suffering, could not be suppressed—not with the memory of the love and dignity that he had learned so well at home so alive in his heart. In the end it is certain that Olaudah Equiano's intelligence was never daunted by the dangers and toils of slavery, and that, indeed, he was to grow to master the idiom and manners and religion of his captors and to achieve recognition as a man in the service of other men.

Enslaved: The Ordeal of Olaudah Equiano

from *The Interesting Narrative of the Life of Olaudah Equiano*

Chapter II
The author's birth and parentage—His being kidnapped with his sister—
Their separation—Surprise at meeting again—Are finally separated—
Account of the different places and incidents the author met with till his
arrival on the coast—The effect the sight of a slave-ship had on him—
He sails for the West Indies—Horrors of a slave-ship—Arrives at Barbados,
where the cargo is sold and dispersed.

I hope the reader will not think I have trespassed on his patience in introducing myself to him, with some account of the manners and customs of my country. They have been implanted in me with great care, and made an impression on my mind, which time could not erase, and which all the adversity and variety of fortune I have since experienced, served only to rivet and record: for, whether the love of one's country be real or imaginary, or a lesson of reason, or an instinct of nature, I still look back with pleasure on the first scenes of my life, though that pleasure has been for the most part mingled with sorrow.

I have already acquainted the reader with the time and place of my birth. My father, besides many slaves, had a numerous family, of which seven lived to grow up, including myself and sister, who was the only daughter. As I was the youngest of the sons, I became, of course, the greatest favorite with my mother, and was always with her; and she used to take particular pains to form my mind. I was trained up from my earliest years in the art of war: my daily exercise was shooting and throwing javelins; and my mother adorned me with emblems, after the manner of our greatest warriors. In this way I grew up till I had turned the age of eleven, when an end was put to my happiness in the following manner:—generally, when the grown people in the neighborhood were gone far in the fields to labor, the children assembled together in some of the neighboring premises to play; and commonly some of us used to get up a tree to look out for any assailant or kidnapper, that might come upon us—for they sometimes took those opportunities of our parents' absence, to attack and carry off as many as they could seize. One day as I was watching at the top of a tree in our yard, I saw one of those people come into the yard of our next neighbor but one, to kidnap, there being many stout young people in it. Immediately on this I gave the alarm of the rogue, and he was surrounded by the stoutest of them, who entangled him with cords, so that he could not escape, till some of the grown people came and secured him. But, alas! ere long it was my fate to be thus attacked, and to be carried off, when none of the grown people were nigh. One day, when all our people were gone out to their works as usual, and only I and my dear sister were left to mind the house, two men and a woman got over our walls, and in a moment seized us both, and, without giving us time to cry out, or make resistance, they stopped our mouths, and ran off with us into the nearest wood. Here they tied our hands, and continued to carry us as far as they could, till night came on, when we reached a small house, where the robbers halted for refreshment, and spent the night. We were then unbound, but were unable to take any food; and, being quite overpowered by fatigue and grief, our only relief was some sleep, which allayed our misfortune for a short time. The next morning we left the house, and continued travelling all the day. For a long time we had kept the woods, but at last we came into a road which I believed I knew. I had now some hopes of being delivered; for we had advanced but a little way before I discovered some people at a distance, on which I began to cry out for their assistance; but my cries had no other effect than to make them tie me faster and stop my mouth, and then they put me into a large sack. They also stopped my sister's mouth, and tied her hands; and in this manner we proceeded till we were out of sight of these people. When we went to rest the following night, they offered us some victuals, but we refused it; and the only comfort we had was in being in one another's arms all that night, and bathing each other with our tears. But alas! we were soon deprived of even the small comfort of weeping together. The next day proved a day of greater sorrow than I had yet experienced; for my sister and I were then separated, while we lay clasped in each other's arms. It was in vain that we besought them not to part us; she was torn from me, and immediately carried away, while I was left in a state of distraction not to be described. I cried and grieved continually; and for several days did not eat any thing but what they forced into my mouth. At length, after many days travelling, during which I had often changed masters, I got into the hands of a chieftain, in a very pleasant country. This man had two wives and some children, and they all used me extremely well, and did all they could to comfort me; particularly the first wife, who was something like my mother. Although I was a great many days' journey from my father's house, yet these people spoke exactly the same language with us. This first master of mine, as I may call him, was a smith, and my principal employment was working his bellows, which were the same kind as I had seen in my vicinity. They were in some respects not unlike the stoves here in gentlemen's kitchens, and were covered over with leather; and in the middle of that leather a stick was fixed, and a person stood up, and worked it in the same manner as is done to pump water out of a cask with a hand pump. I believe it was gold he worked, for it was of a lovely bright yellow color, and was worn by the women on their wrists and ankles. I was there I suppose about a month, and they at last used to trust me some little distance from the house. This liberty I used in embracing every opportunity to inquire the way to my own home; and I also sometimes, for the same purpose, went with the maidens, in the cool of the evenings, to bring pitchers of water from the springs for the use of the house. I had also remarked where the sun rose in the morning, and set in the evening, as I had travelled along; and I had observed that my father's house was towards the rising of the sun. I therefore determined to seize the first opportunity of making my escape, and to shape my course for that quarter; for I was quite oppressed and weighed down by grief after my mother and friends; and my love of liberty, ever great, was strengthened by the mortifying circumstances of not daring to eat with the free-born children, although I was mostly their companion. While I was projecting my escape one day, an unlucky event happened, which quite disconcerted my plan, and put an end to my hopes. I used to be sometimes employed in assisting an elderly slave to cook and take care of the poultry; and one morning, while I was feeding some chickens, I happened to toss a small pebble at one of them, which hit it on the middle, and directly killed it. The old slave, having soon after missed the chicken, inquired after it; and on my relating the accident, (for I told her the truth, for my mother would never suffer me to tell a lie,) she flew into a violent passion, and threatened that I should suffer for it; and, my master being out, she immediately went and told her mistress what I had done. This alarmed me very much, and I expected an instant flogging, which to me was uncommonly dreadful, for I had seldom been beaten at home. I therefore resolved to fly; and accordingly I ran into a thicket that was hard by, and hid myself in the bushes. Soon afterwards my mistress and the slave returned, and, not seeing me, they searched all the house, but not finding me, and I not making answer when they

called to me, they thought I had run away, and the whole neighborhood
was raised in pursuit of me. In that part of the country, as in ours, the
houses and villages were skirted with woods, or shrubberies, and the
bushes were so thick that a man could readily conceal himself in them,
so as to elude the strictest search. The neighbors continued the whole
day looking for me, and several times many of them came within a
few yards of the place where I lay hid. I expected every moment, when
I heard a rustling among the trees, to be found out, and punished by
my master; but they never discovered me, though they were often so
near that I even heard their conjectures as they were looking about for
me; and I now learned from them that any attempts to return home
would be hopeless. Most of them supposed I had fled towards home;
but the distance was so great, and the way so intricate, that they
thought I could never reach it, and that I should be lost in the woods.
When I heard this I was seized with a violent panic, and abandoned
myself to despair. Night, too, began to approach, and aggravated all
my fears. I had before entertained hopes of getting home, and had
determined when it should be dark to make the attempt; but I was
now convinced it was fruitless, and began to consider that, if possibly
I could escape all other animals, I could not those of the human kind;
and that, not knowing the way, I must perish in the woods. Thus was
I like the hunted deer—

> —'Every leaf and every whisp'ring breath,
>   Convey'd a foe, and every foe a death.'

I heard frequent rustlings among the leaves, and being pretty sure
they were snakes, I expected every instant to be stung by them. This
increased my anguish, and the horror of my situation became now
quite insupportable. I at length quitted the thicket, very faint and
hungry, for I had not eaten or drank any thing all the day, and crept to
my master's kitchen, from whence I set out at first, which was an
open shed, and laid myself down in the ashes with an anxious wish
for death, to relieve me from all my pains. I was scarcely awake in the
morning, when the old woman slave, who was the first up, came to
light the fire, and saw me in the fireplace. She was very much surprised
to see me, and could scarcely believe her own eyes. She now promised
to intercede for me, and went for her master, who soon after came,
and, having slightly reprimanded me, ordered me to be taken care of,
and not ill treated.

Soon after this, my master's only daughter, and child by his first wife, sickened and died, which affected him so much that for sometime he was almost frantic, and really would have killed himself, had he not been watched and prevented. However, in a short time afterwards he recovered, and I was again sold. I was now carried to the left of the sun's rising, through many dreary wastes and dismal woods, amidst the hideous roarings of wild beasts. The people I was sold to used to carry me very often, when I was tired, either on their shoulders or on their backs. I saw many convenient well built sheds along the road, at proper distances, to accommodate the merchants and travellers, who lay in those buildings along with their wives, who often accompany them; and they always go well armed.

From the time I left my own nation, I always found somebody that understood me till I came to the sea coast. The languages of different nations did not totally differ, nor were they so copious as those of the Europeans, particularly the English. They were therefore, easily learned; and, while I was journeying thus through Africa, I acquired two or three different tongues. In this manner I had been travelling for a considerable time, when, one evening, to my great surprise, whom should I see brought to the house where I was but my dear sister! As soon as she saw me, she gave a loud shriek, and ran into my arms—I was quite overpowered: neither of us could speak; but, for a considerable time, clung to each other in mutual embraces, unable to do any thing but weep. Our meeting affected all who saw us; and, indeed, I must acknowledge, in honor of those sable destroyers of human rights, that I never met with any ill treatment, or saw any offered to their slaves, except tying them, when necessary, to keep them from running away. When these people knew we were brother and sister, they indulged us to be together; and the man, to whom I supposed we belonged, lay with us, he in the middle, while she and I held one another by the hands across his breast all night; and thus for a while we forgot our misfortunes, in the joy of being together; but even this small comfort was soon to have an end; for scarcely had the fatal morning appeared when she was again torn from me forever! I was now more miserable, if possible, than before. The small relief which her presence gave me from pain, was gone, and the wretchedness of my situation was redoubled by my anxiety after her fate, and my apprehensions lest her sufferings should be greater than mine, when I could not be with her to alleviate them.

I did not long remain after my sister. I was again sold, and carried through a number of places, till after travelling a considerable time, I came to a town called Tinmah, in the most beautiful country I had yet seen in Africa. It was extremely rich, and there were many rivulets which flowed through it, and supplied a large pond in the center of town, where the people washed. Here I first saw and tasted cocoa nuts, which I thought superior to any nuts I had ever tasted before; and the trees which were loaded, were also interspersed among the houses, which had commodious shades adjoining, and were in the same manner as ours, the insides being neatly plastered and white-washed. Here I also saw and tasted for the first time, sugar-cane. Their money consisted of little white shells, the size of the finger nail. I was sold here for one hundred and seventy-two of them, by a merchant who lived and brought me there. I had been about two or three days at his house, when a wealthy widow, a neighbor of his, came there one evening, and brought with her an only son, a young gentleman about my own age and size. Here they saw me; and, having taken a fancy to me, I was bought of the merchant, and went home with them. Her house and premises were situated close to one of those rivulets I have mentioned, and were the finest I ever saw in Africa: they were very extensive, and she had a number of slaves to attend her. The next day I was washed and perfumed, and when meal time came, I was led into the presence of my mistress, and ate and drank before her with her son. This filled me with astonishment; and I could scarce help expressing my surprise that the young gentleman should suffer me, who was bound, to eat with him who was free; and not only so, but that he would not at any time either eat or drink till I had taken first, because I was the eldest, which was agreeable to our custom. Indeed, every thing here, and all their treatment of me, made me forget that I was a slave. The language of these people resembled ours so nearly, that we understood each other perfectly. They had also the very same customs as we. There were likewise slaves daily to attend us, while my young master and I, with other boys, sported with our darts and bows and arrows, as I had been used to do at home. In this resemblance to my former happy state, I passed about two months; and I now began to think that I was to be adopted into the family, and was beginning to be reconciled to my situation, and to forget by degrees my misfortunes, when all at once the delusion vanished; for, without the least previous knowledge, one morning early, while my dear master and companion was still asleep, I was awakened out of my reverie to fresh sorrow, and hurried away even amongst the uncircumcised.

Thus, at the very moment I dreamed of the greatest happiness, I found myself most miserable; and it seemed as if fortune wished to give me this taste of joy only to render the reverse more poignant. The change I now experienced, was as painful as it was sudden and unexpected. It was a change indeed, from a state of bliss to a scene which is inexpressible by me, as it discovered to me an element I had never before beheld, and till then had no idea of, and wherein such instances of hardship and cruelty continually occurred, as I can never reflect on but with horror.

All the nations and people I had hitherto passed through, resembled our own in their manners, customs, and language: but I came at length to a country, the inhabitants of which differed from us in all those particulars. I was very much struck with this difference, especially when I came among a people who did not circumcise, and ate without washing their hands. They cooked also in iron pots, and had European cutlasses and cross bows, which were unknown to us, and fought with their fists among themselves. Their women were not so modest as ours, for they ate, and drank, and slept with their men. But above all, I was amazed to see no sacrifices or offerings among them. In some of those places the people ornamented themselves with scars, and likewise filed their teeth very sharp. They wanted sometimes to ornament me in the same manner, but I would not suffer them; hoping that I might some time be among a people who did not thus disfigure themselves, as I thought they did. At last I came to the banks of a large river which was covered with canoes, in which the people appeared to live with their household utensils, and provisions of all kinds. I was beyond measure astonished at this, as I had never before seen any water larger than a pond or a rivulet: and my surprise was mingled with no small fear when I was put into one of these canoes, and we began to paddle and move along the river. We continued going on thus till night, and when we came to land, and made fires on the banks, each family by themselves; some dragged their canoes on shore, others stayed and cooked in theirs, and laid in them all night. Those on the land had mats, of which they made tents, some in the shape of little houses; in these we slept; and after the morning meal, we embarked again and proceeded as before. Thus I continued to travel, sometimes by land, sometimes by water, through different countries and various nations, till, at the end of six or seven months after I had been kidnapped, I arrived at the sea coast. It would be tedious and uninteresting to relate all the incidents which befel me during this journey, and which I have not yet forgotten; of the various hands I passed through, and the manners and customs of all the different people among whom I lived—I shall therefore only observe, that in all the places where I was, the soil was exceedingly rich; the pumpkins, eadas, plantains, yams, &c. &c. were in great abundance, and of incredible size. There were also vast quantities of different gums, though not used for any purpose, and every where a great deal of tobacco. The cotton even grew quite wild, and there was plenty of red-wood. I saw no mechanics whatever in all the way, except such as I have mentioned. The chief employment in all these countries was agriculture, and both the males and females, as with us, were brought up to it, and trained in the arts of war.

The first object which saluted my eyes when I arrived on the coast, was the sea, and a slave ship, which was then riding at anchor, and waiting for its cargo. These filled me with astonishment, which was soon converted into terror, when I was carried on board, I was immediately handled, and tossed up to see if I were sound, by some of the crew; and I was now persuaded that I had gotten into a world of bad spirits, and that they were going to kill me. Their complexions, too, differing so much from ours, their long hair, and the language they spoke, (which was very different from any I had ever heard) united to confirm me in this belief. Indeed, such were the horrors of my views and fears at the moment, that, if ten thousand worlds had been my own, I would have freely parted with them all to have exchanged my condition with that of the meanest slave in my own country. When I looked round the ship too, and saw a large furnace of copper boiling, and a multitude of black people of every description chained together, every one of their countenances expressing dejection and sorrow, I no longer doubted of my fate; and, quite overpowered with horror and anguish, I fell motionless on the deck and fainted. When I recovered a little, I found some black people about me, who I believed were some of those who had brought me on board, and had been receiving their pay; they talked to me in order to cheer me, but all in vain. I asked them if we were not to be eaten by those white men with horrible looks, red faces, and long hair. They told me I was not: and one of the crew brought me a small portion of spirituous liquor in a wine glass, but, being afraid of him, I would not take it out of his hand. One of the blacks, therefore, took it from him and gave it to me, and I took a little down my palate, which, instead of reviving me, as I thought it would, threw me into the greatest consternation at the strange feeling it produced, having never tasted any such liquor before. Soon after this, the blacks who brought me on board went off, and left me abandoned to despair.

I now saw myself deprived of all chance of returning to my native country, or even the least glimpse of hope of gaining the shore, which

I now considered as friendly; and I even wished for my former slavery in preference to my present situation, which was filled with horrors of every kind, still heightened by my ignorance of what I was to undergo. I was not long suffered to indulge my grief; I was soon put down under the decks, and there I received such a salutation in my nostrils as I had never experienced in my life: so that, with the loathsomeness of the stench, and crying together, I became so sick and low that I was not able to eat, nor had I the least desire to taste any thing. I now wished for the last friend, death, to relieve me; but soon, to my grief, two of the white men offered me eatables; and, on my refusing to eat, one of them held me fast by the hands, and laid me across, I think the windlass, and tied my feet, while the other flogged me severely. I had never experienced anything of this kind before, and although not being used to the water, I naturally feared that element the first time I saw it, yet, nevertheless, could I have got over the nettings, I would have jumped over the side, but I could not; and besides, the crew used to watch us very closely who were not chained down to the decks, lest we should leap into the water; and I have seen some of these poor African prisoners most severely cut, for attempting to do so, and hourly whipped for not eating. This indeed was often the case with myself. In a little time after, amongst the poor chained men, I found some of my own nation, which in a small degree gave ease to my mind. I inquired of these what was to be done with us? They gave me to understand, we were to be carried to these white people's country to work for them. I then was a little revived, and thought, if it were no worse than working, my situation was not so desperate; but still I feared I should be put to death, the white people looked and acted, as I thought, in so savage a manner; for I had never seen among any people such instances of brutal cruelty; and this not only shown towards us blacks, but also to some of the whites themselves. One white man in particular I saw, when we were permitted to be on deck, flogged so unmercifully with a large rope near the foremast, that he died in consequence of it; and they tossed him over the side as they would have done a brute. This made me fear these people the more; and I expected nothing less than to be treated in the same manner. I could not help expressing my fears and apprehensions to some of my countrymen; I asked them if these people had no country, but lived in this hollow place? (the ship) they told me they did not, but came from a distant one. 'Then,' said I, 'how comes it in all our country we never heard of them?' They told me because they lived so very far off. I then asked where were their women? Had they any like themselves? I was told they had. 'And why,' said I, 'do we not see them?' They answered, because they were left behind. I asked how the vessel could go? they told me they could not tell; but that there was cloth put upon the masts by the help of the ropes I saw, and then the vessel went on; and the white men had some spell or magic they put in the water when they liked, in order to stop the vessel. I was exceedingly amazed at this account, and really thought they were spirits. I therefore wished much to be among them, for I expected they would sacrifice me; but my wishes were vain—for we were so quartered that it was impossible for any of us to make our escape.

While we stayed on the coast I was mostly on deck; and one day, to my great astonishment, I saw one of these vessels coming in with the sails up. As soon as the whites saw it, they gave a great shout, at which we were amazed; and the more so, as the vessel appeared larger by approaching nearer. At last, she came to an anchor in my sight, and when the anchor was let go, I and my countrymen who saw it, were lost in astonishment to observe the vessel stop—and were now convinced it was done by magic. Soon after this the other ship got her boats out, and they came on board of us, and the people of both ships seemed very glad to see each other.—Several of the strangers also shook hands with us black people, and made motions with their hands, signifying I suppose, we were to go to their country, but we did not understand them.

At last, when the ship we were in, had got in all her cargo, they made ready with many fearful noises, and we were all put under deck, so that we could not see how they managed the vessel. But this disappointment was the least of my sorrow. The stench of the hold while we were on the coast was so intolerably loathsome, that it was dangerous to stay there for any time, and some of us had been permitted to remain on the deck for the fresh air; but now that the whole ship's cargo were confined together, it became absolutely pestilential. The closeness of the place, and the heat of the climate, added to the number in the ship, which was so crowded that each had scarcely room to turn himself, almost suffocated us. This produced copious perspirations, so that the air soon became unfit for respiration, from a variety of loathsome smells, and brought on a sickness among the slaves, of which many died—thus falling victims to the improvident avarice, as I may call it, of their purchasers. This wretched situation was again aggravated by the galling of the chains, now became insupportable; and the filth of the necessary tubs, into which the children often fell, and were almost suffocated. The shrieks of the women, and the groans of the dying, rendered the whole a scene of horror almost inconceivable. Happily perhaps, for myself, I was soon reduced so low here that it was thought necessary to keep me always on deck; and from my extreme youth I was not put in fetters. In this situation I expected every hour to share the fate of my companions, some of whom were almost daily brought upon deck at the point of death, which I began to hope would soon put an end to my miseries. Often did I think many of the inhabitants of the deep much more happy than myself. I envied them the freedom they enjoyed, and as often wished I could change my situation for theirs. Every circumstance I met with, served only to render my state more painful, and heightened my apprehensions, and my opinion of the cruelty of the whites.

One day they had taken a number of fishes; and when they had killed and satisfied themselves with as many as they thought fit, to our astonishment who were on deck, rather than give any of them to us to eat, as we expected, they tossed the remaining fish into the sea again, although we begged and prayed for some as well as we could, but in vain; and some of my countrymen, being pressed by hunger, took an opportunity, when they thought no one saw them, of trying to get a little privately; but they were discovered, and the attempt procured them some very severe floggings. One day, when we had a smooth sea and moderate wind, two of my wearied countrymen who were chained together, (I was near them at the time,) preferring death to such a life of misery, somehow made through the nettings and jumped into the sea: immediately, another quite dejected fellow, who, on account of his illness, was suffered to be out of irons, also followed their example; and I believe many more would very soon have done the same, if they had not been prevented by the ship's crew, who were instantly alarmed. Those of us that were the most active, were in a moment put down under the deck, and there was such a noise and confusion amongst the people of the ship as I never heard before, to stop her, and get the boat out to go after the slaves. However, two of the wretches were drowned, but they got the other, and afterwards flogged him unmercifully, for thus attempting to prefer death to slavery. In this manner we continued to undergo more hardships than I can now relate, hardships which are inseparable from this accursed trade. Many a time we were near suffocation from the want of fresh air, which we were often without for whole days together. This, and the stench of the necessary tubs, carried off many.

During our passage, I first saw flying fishes, which surprised me very much; they used frequently to fly across the ship, and many of them fell on the deck. I also now first saw the use of the quadrant; I had often with astonishment seen the mariners make observations with it, and I could not think what it meant. They at last took notice of my surprise; and one of them, willing to increase it, as well as to gratify my curiosity, made me look one day through it. The clouds appeared to me to be land, which disappeared as they passed along. This heightened my wonder; and I was now more persuaded than ever, that I was in another world, and that every thing about me was magic. At last, we came in sight of the island of Barbadoes, at which the whites on board gave a great shout, and made many signs of joy to us. We did not know what to think of this; but as the vessel drew nearer, we plainly saw the harbor, and other ships of different kinds and sizes, and we soon anchored amongst them, off Bridgetown. Many merchants and planters now came on board, though it was in the evening. They put us in separate parcels, and examined us attentively. They also made us jump, and pointed to the land, signifying we were to go there. We thought by this, we should be eaten by these ugly men, as they appeared to us; and, when soon after we were all put down under the deck again, there was much dread and trembling among us, and nothing but bitter cries to be heard all the night from these apprehensions, insomuch, that at last the white people got some old slaves from the land to pacify us. They told us we were not to be eaten, but to work, and were soon to go on land, where we should see many of our country people. This report eased us much. And sure enough, soon after we were landed, there came to us Africans of all languages.

We were conducted immediately to the merchant's yard, where we were all pent up together, like so many sheep in a fold, without regard to sex or age. As every object was new to me, every thing I saw filled me with surprise. What struck me first, was, that the houses were built with bricks and stories, and in every other respect different from those I had seen in Africa; but I was still more astonished on seeing people on horseback. I did not know what this could mean; and, indeed, I thought these people were full of nothing but magical arts. While I was in this astonishment, one of my fellow-prisoners spoke to a countryman of his, about the horses, who said they were the same kind they had in their country. I understood them, though they were from a distant part of Africa; and I thought it odd I had not seen any horses there; but afterwards, when I came to converse with different Africans, I found they had many horses amongst them, and much larger than those I then saw.

We were not many days in the merchant's custody, before we were sold after their usual manner, which is this:—On a signal given, (as the beat of a drum,) the buyers rush at once into the yard where the slaves are confined, and make choice of that parcel they like best. The noise and clamor with which this is attended, and the eagerness visible in the countenances of the buyers, serve not a little to increase the apprehension of terrified Africans, who may well be supposed to consider them as the ministers of that destruction to which they think themselves devoted. In this manner, without scruple, are relations and friends separated, most of them never to see each other again. I remember, in the vessel in which I was brought over, in the men's apartment, there were several brothers, who, in the sale, were sold in different lots; and it was very moving on this occasion, to see and hear their cries at parting. O, ye nominal Christians! might not an African ask you—Learned you this from your God, who says unto you, Do unto all men as you would men should do unto you? Is it not enough that we are torn from our country and friends, to toil for your luxury and lust of gain? Must every tender feeling be likewise sacrificed to your avarice? Are the dearest friends and relations, now rendered more dear by their separation from their kindred, still to be parted from each other, and thus prevented from cheering the gloom of slavery, with the small comfort of being together, and mingling their sufferings and sorrows? Why are parents to lose their children, brothers their sisters, or husbands their wives? Surely, this is a new refinement in cruelty, which, while it has no advantage to atone for it, thus aggravates distress, and adds fresh horrors even to the wretchedness of slavery.

1816
THE DEATH RAFT OF THE MÉDUSE

Something was absolutely necessary to sustain our miserable existence; and we tremble with horror at being obliged to that of which we made use. We feel our pen fall from our hands; a mortal cold congeals all our members; and our hair bristles erect on our foreheads. Readers! We implore you, feel not indignant towards men already overloaded with misery. Pity their condition, and shed a tear of sorrow for their deplorable fate.

– Correard and Savigny

The fatal grounding in July 1816 of the French frigate *Méduse* off the coast of Africa—and the sequence of hideous events that led to the death of all but ten of the one hundred fifty passengers abandoned by its captain on a makeshift raft—is among the most infamous of nautical tragedies. The horrors of this death raft were memorialized in the vast canvas—measuring sixteen feet in height by twenty-three feet, six inches in width—by Géricault, which was first presented to the Parisian public in 1819. We have no narrative of this disaster more direct than that based directly on the accounts of two of the survivors, Correard and Savigny, which is presented here.

The horror of the tragedy is reinforced by the sequence of degenerate folly, incompetence, and betrayal that led to it. On June 17, 1816, Frigate-Captain Hugues Duroy de Chaumereys set out in command of a French flotilla of four ships—the *Méduse*, the *Argus*, the *Loire*, and the *Echo*—to reclaim the port of St. Louis in Senegal, which the English had restored by treaty to the French crown after the Napoleonic Wars. Having never commanded a ship, and not having been to sea for more than twenty-five years, the effeminate fifty-three year old Chaumereys owed his appointment entirely to his royalist credentials rather than to any competence. He immediately fell under the influence of the most prestigious of his passengers, Colonel Julien-Désiré Schmaltz, the newly appointed Governor of Senegal, who was eager to assume his new post and urged the captain to deliver him there as rapidly as possible.

With a crew of one hundred and sixty and a passenger roster of some two hundred and forty troops and civilians, the *Méduse* was the fastest ship in the small fleet. The *Méduse* soon lost contact with the others as it raced ahead on a dangerous course close to the treacherous reefs and sandbars of the African shoreline. Aboard the ship, concern mounted among passengers and experienced crew alike, as Chaumereys and Schmaltz arrogantly steered the ship toward certain disaster. On July 1st, while he and other notables aboard celebrated crossing into the tropics with drink and revelry, Chaumereys entrusted the navigation of the *Méduse* to a Monsieur Richefort, an inexperienced but vainglorious self-proclaimed African explorer who, in fine weather on the following day, ran the *Méduse* aground on the Arguin Banks.

The sequel to this triumph of bad judgment and irresponsibility compounded the gravity of the situation. Although the *Méduse* had been damaged and was taking on water, it was very much intact. There was even a possibility of freeing the ship and navigating it to safe waters, but Chaumereys, foolishly unwilling to jettison the ship's heavy cannon, instead ordered passengers and crew to abandon ship. The ship's six lifeboats, which could accommodate few more than half of its complement, were reserved for elite passengers and crew. For the others—soldiers and crew and common passengers—Governor Schmaltz conceived the idea of building a raft, which could be towed by the lifeboats to the safety of the shore. A crude raft, measuring some twenty-three by sixty-five feet, was thus quickly constructed of assorted planking, masts, and crossbeams. After the raft was hastily loaded with meager provision—some casks of water and of wine, some flour, and a variety of other supplies—one hundred and fifty people were herded onto it with barely enough room to stand upright, their weight sinking the fragile platform waist-deep into the sea. Seventeen members of the crew decided to remain on the *Méduse*, refusing to board the perilous makeshift craft.

The lifeboats—which had been the first to be loaded—were charged with towing the raft to the safety of shore only four miles away, but these boats were undermanned and came into danger whenever the raft heaved close to them, not least from its desperate passengers seeking safer passage in them. With the security of the lifeboats threatened and their own progress hampered, when the captain's boat lines to the raft parted, the crews of the remaining boats decided to cut the raft loose and abandon it. As its passengers witnessed this betrayal, chaos and despair exploded aboard the raft, and descended into a stormy night of violence and murder. By the following morning, much of the raft's meager provisions had been lost in the tumult, along with twenty lives.

During the twelve days between their abandonment and the ultimate rescue of the few survivors, all but fifteen of the one hundred and fifty souls castaway on the death raft of the *Méduse* perished in a hell of internecine violence, exposure to the elements, extreme thirst, and starvation allayed by cannibalism. The truth of the tragedy emerges clearly through the filter of the ornate Georgian prose of the Correard-Savigny narrative. Desperate soldiers and a few junior officers almost immediately lost their minds and yielded to enraged anarchic fury. A handful of senior officers, workers, and civilian passengers—Correard, Savigny, the head workman Lavigny, Clairet, and Coudin notable among them—struggled to maintain some order and to sustain hope amidst the overwhelming weight of despair. Perhaps no more than twenty, they fought to defend each other and the helpless as much as themselves, day after each worsening day, as lethal attacks, hunger, thirst, exhaustion, and despair diminished them. Defending the high ground in the middle of the raft, desperately clinging to their wits, this group managed to act as a cohesive unit and hold repeated attacks at bay. Ultimately, it emerges that only a few within this group—those with the most resilient minds and the deepest spiritual resources—were able, if only barely, to resist the insanity that threatened everyone on the raft, and survive.

On the thirteenth day the *Argus* fortuitously appeared. Chaumereys had ordered it out more on a mission to salvage gold from the wreck of the *Méduse* than to search for survivors at sea. Fifteen souls were removed from the raft littered with the dismembered and decomposing corpses of the dead. Of these, after extended hospitalization, only ten survived. Among the seventeen who had remained aboard the ship—still intact when it was finally reached fifty-two days after it had grounded—three were discovered piteously close to death. Although all supplies needed for survival had been at hand, the bonds of civilization had snapped and warfare had broken out. Chaumereys was subjected to a court martial, but was acquitted, the politics of the day incapable of acknowledging any wrongdoing.

The Death Raft of the Méduse

from *Narrative of a Voyage to Senegal in 1816*
by J.B. Henri Savigny and Alexandre Correard

The account of the fatal wreck of the *Méduse*, and its concomitant events, furnishes a series of horrors almost unparalleled in human suffering and atrocity. It gives a narrative of men, whose affections, in the day of sympathy, were turned to hatred, and pity converted to envy. They preferred their own destruction to the safety of their fellow sufferers; and crushed to atoms the plank under their feet, which divided them from eternity, rather than allow their companions in misfortune the happiness of ever seeing land again. The following is the substance, abridged from MM. Correard and Savigny, of what took place on the raft during thirteen days before the sufferers were taken up by the brig *Argus*.
– Charles Elims, from the introduction to the 1836 edition

After the boats had disappeared, the consternation became extreme. All the horrors of thirst and famine passed before our imagination; besides, we had to contend with a treacherous element, which already covered the half of our bodies. The deep stupor of the soldiers and sailors instantly changed to despair. All saw their inevitable destruction, and expressed by their moans the dark thoughts which brooded in their minds. Our words were at first unavailing to quiet their fears, which we participated with them, but which a greater strength of mind enabled us to dissemble. At last, an unmoved countenance, and our proffered consolations, quieted them by degrees, but could not entirely dissipate the terror with which they were seized. When tranquility was a little restored, we began to search about the raft for the charts, the compass, and the anchor, which we presumed had been placed upon it, after what we had been told at the time of quitting the frigate.

These things, of the first importance, had not been placed upon our machine. Above all, the want of a compass the most alarmed us, and we gave vent to our rage and vengeance. M. Correard then remembered that he had seen one in the hands of the principal workman under his command. He spoke to the man, who replied, "Yes, yes, I have it with me." This information transported us with joy, and we believed that our safety depended upon this futile resource. It was about the size of a crown-piece, and very incorrect . . . The compass was given to the commander of the raft, but an accident deprived us of it forever. It fell, and disappeared between the pieces of wood which formed our machine. We had kept it but a few hours; and, after its loss, had nothing to guide us but the rising and setting of the sun.

We had all gone afloat without taking any food. Hunger beginning to be imperiously felt, we mixed our paste of sea-biscuit with a little wine, and distributed it thus prepared. Such was our first meal, and the best we had during our stay upon the raft.

An order, according to our numbers, was established for the distribution of our miserable provisions. The ration of wine was fixed at three quarters a day. We will speak no more of the biscuit, it having been entirely consumed at the first distribution. The day passed away sufficiently tranquil. We talked of the means by which we would save ourselves; we spoke of it as a certain circumstance, which reanimated our courage; and we sustained that of the soldiers, by cherishing in them the hope of being able, in a short time, to revenge themselves on those who had abandoned us. This hope of vengeance, it must be avowed, equally animated us all; and we poured out a thousand imprecations against those who had left us a prey to so much misery and danger.

The officer who commanded the raft being unable to move, M. Savigny took upon himself the duty of erecting the mast. He caused them to cut in two one of the poles of the frigate's masts, and fixed it with the rope which had served to tow us, and of which we made stays and shrouds. It was placed on the anterior third of the raft. We put up for a sail the main-top-gallant, which trimmed very well, but was of very little use, except when the wind served from behind; and to keep the raft in this course, we were obliged to trim the sail as if the breeze blew athwart us . . . .

Our consoling thought still soothed our imaginations. We persuaded ourselves that the little division had gone to the isle of Arguin, and that after it had set a part of its people on shore, the rest would return to our assistance. We endeavored to impress this idea on our soldiers and sailors, which quieted them. The night came without our hope being realized; the wind freshened, and the sea was considerably swelled. What a horrible night! The thought of seeing the boats on the morrow, a little consoled our men; the greater part of whom, being unaccustomed to the sea, fell on one another at each movement of the raft. M. Savigny, seconded by some people who still preserved their presence of mind amidst the disorder, stretched cords across the raft, by which the men held, and were better able to resist the swell of the sea. Some were even obliged to fasten themselves. In the middle of the night the weather was very rough; huge waves burst upon us, sometimes overturning us with great violence. The cries of the men, mingled with the flood, whilst the terrible sea raised us at every instant from the raft, and threatened to sweep us away. The scene was rendered still more terrible, by the horrors inspired by the darkness of the night. Suddenly we believed we saw fires in the distance at intervals.

We had had the precaution to hang at the top of the mast, the gunpowder and pistols which we had brought from the frigate. We made signals by burning a large quantity of cartridges. We even fired some pistols; but it seems the fire we saw, was nothing but an error of vision; or, perhaps, nothing more than the sparkling of the waves.

We struggled with death during the whole of the night, holding firmly by the ropes which were made very secure. Tossed by the waves from the back to the front, and from the front to the back, and sometimes precipitated into the sea, floating between life and death, mourning our misfortunes, certain of perishing—we disputed, nevertheless, the remainder of our existence, with that cruel element which threatened to engulf us. Such was our condition till daybreak. At every instant we heard the lamentable cries of the soldiers and sailors. They prepared for death, bidding farewell to one another, imploring the protection of Heaven, and addressing fervent prayers to God. Every one made vows to Him, in spite of the uncertainty of never being able to accomplish them. Frightful situation! How is it possible to have any idea of it, which will not fall far short of the reality!

Towards seven in the morning the sea fell a little, the wind blew with less fury; but what a scene presented itself to our view! Ten or twelve unfortunates, having their inferior extremities fixed in the openings between the pieces of the raft, had perished by being unable to disengage themselves. Several others were swept away by the violence of the sea. At the hour of repast we took the numbers anew. We had lost twenty men. We will not affirm that this was the exact number; for we perceived some soldiers, who, to have more than their share, took rations for two, or even three. We were so huddled together, that we found it absolutely impossible to prevent this abuse.

In the midst of these horrors, a touching scene of filial piety drew our tears. Two young men raised and recognized their father, who had fallen, and was lying insensible among the feet of the people. They believed him at first dead, and their despair was expressed in the most affecting manner. It was perceived, however, that he still breathed, and every assistance was rendered for his recovery in our power. He slowly revived, and was restored to life, and to the prayers of his sons, who supported him closely folded in their arms. Whilst our hearts were softened by this affecting episode in our melancholy adventures, we had soon to witness the sad spectacle of a dark contrast. Two ship boys and a baker feared not to seek death, and threw themselves into the sea, after having bid farewell to their companions in misfortune. Already the minds of our people were singularly altered. Some believed that they saw land; others, ships which were coming to save us. All talked aloud of their fallacious visions.

We lamented the loss of our unfortunate companions. At this moment we were far from anticipating the still more terrible scene which took place on the following night. Far from that, we enjoyed a positive satisfaction, so well were we persuaded that the boats would return to our assistance. The day was fine, and the most perfect tranquility reigned all the while on our raft. The evening came and no boats appeared. Despondency began again to seize our men, and then a spirit of insubordination manifested itself in cries of rage. The voice of the officers was entirely disregarded. Night fell rapidly in; the sky was obscured by dark clouds; the wind which, during the whole day, had blown rather violently, became furious and swelled the sea, which in an instant became very rough. The preceding night had been frightful, but this was more so. Mountains of water covered us at every instant, and burst with fury into the midst of us. Very fortunately we had the wind from behind, and the strongest of the sea was a little broken by the rapidity with which we were driven before it. We were impelled towards the land. The men, from the violence of the sea, were hurried from the back to the front. We were obliged to keep to the centre, the firmest part of the raft; and those who could not get there almost all perished. Before and behind the waves dashed impetuously, and swept away the men in spite of all their resistance. At the center the pressure was such, that some unfortunates were suffocated by the weight of their comrades, who fell upon them at every instant. The officers kept by the foot of the little mast, and were obliged every moment to call to those around them to go to the one or the other side to avoid the waves; for the sea coming nearly athwart us, gave our raft a perpendicular position; to counteract which, they were forced to throw themselves upon the side raised by the sea.

The soldiers and sailors frightened by their danger, seized on casks of wine, and drank till they were void of reason. They now tried to involve all in one common ruin by various acts of destruction, but were prevented by the vigilance of the officers.

One man inspired all of us with terror. This was an Asiatic, and a soldier in a colonial regiment. Of a colossal stature, short hair, a nose extremely large, and enormous mouth and dark complexion, he made a most hideous appearance. At first he placed himself in the middle of the raft, and, at each blow of his fist, knocked down every one who opposed him and none durst approach him. Had there been six such, our destruction would have been certain.

Some men, anxious to prolong their existence, armed and united themselves with those who wished to preserve the raft. Among this number were some subaltern officers and many passengers. The rebels drew their sabres, and those who had none armed themselves with knives. They advanced in a determined manner upon us—we stood on our defence—the attack commenced. Animated by despair, one of them made a stroke at an officer—the rebel instantly fell, pierced with wounds. This firmness awed them for an instant, but diminished nothing of their rage. They ceased to advance, and withdrew, presenting to us a front bristling with sabres and bayonets, to the back part of the raft, to execute their plan. One of them feigned to rest himself on the small railings on the sides of the raft, and with a knife began cutting the cords. Being told by a servant, one of us sprung upon him. A soldier, wishing to defend him, struck at the officer with his knife, which only pierced his coat. The officer wheeled round, seized his adversary, and threw both him and his comrade into the sea.

There had been as yet but partial affairs—the combat became general. Some one cried to lower the sail: a crowd of infuriated mortals threw themselves in an instant upon the haulyards and the shrouds, and cut them. The fall of the mast almost broke the thigh of a captain of infantry, who fell insensible. He was seized by the soldiers, who threw him into the sea. We saved him, and placed him on a barrel; whence he was taken by the rebels, who wished to put out his eyes with a penknife. Exasperated with so much brutality, we no longer restrained ourselves, but pushed in upon them, and charged them with fury. Sword in hand we traversed the line which the soldiers had formed, and many paid with their lives the errors of their revolt. Various passengers, during these cruel moments, evinced the greatest courage and coolness.

M. Correard fell into a sort of swoon; but hearing at every instant the cries, "To arms! with us comrades! we are lost!" joined with the groans and imprecations of the wounded and the dying, was soon roused from his lethargy. All this horrible tumult speedily made him comprehend how necessary it was to be upon his guard. Armed with his sabre, he gathered together some of his workmen on the front of the raft, and there charged them to hurt no one, unless they were attacked. He almost always remained with them; and several times they had to defend themselves against the rebels, who, swimming round to that point of the raft, placed M. Correard and his little troop between two dangers, and made their position very difficult to defend. At every instant he was opposed to men armed with knives, sabres and bayonets. Many had carabines, which they wielded as clubs. Every effort was made to stop them, by holding them off at the point of their swords; but, in spite of the repugnance they experienced in fighting with their wretched countrymen, they were compelled to use their arms without mercy. Many of the mutineers attacked with fury, and they were obliged to repel them in the same manner. Some of the laborers received severe wounds in this action. Their commander could show a great number received in the different engagements. At last their united efforts prevailed in dispersing this mass who had attacked them with such fury.

During this combat, M. Correard was told by one of his workmen who remained faithful, that one of their comrades, named Dominique, had gone over to the rebels, and that they had seized and thrown him into the sea. Immediately forgetting the fault and treason of this man, he threw himself in at the place whence the voice of the wretch was heard calling for assistance, seized him by the hair, and had the good fortune to restore him aboard. Dominique had got several sabre wounds in a charge, one of which had laid open his head.

One of the workmen gave his handkerchief to bind and stop the blood. Our care recovered the wretch; but, when he had collected strength, the ungrateful Dominique, forgetting at once his duty and the signal service which we had rendered him, went and rejoined the rebels. So much baseness did not go unrevenged; and soon after he found, in a fresh assault, that death from which he was not worthy to be saved, but which he might in all probability have avoided, if, true to honor and gratitude, he had remained among us.

Just at the moment we finished dressing the wounds on Dominique, another voice was heard. It was that of the unfortunate female who was with us on the raft, and whom the infuriated beings had thrown into the sea, as well as her husband, who had defended her with courage. M. Correard, in despair at seeing two unfortunates perish, whose pitiful cries, especially the woman's, pierced his heart, took a large rope, which he found on the front of the raft, which he fastened round his middle; and throwing himself a second time into the sea, was again so fortunate as to save the woman, who invoked with all her might the assistance of our Lady of Land. Her husband was rescued at the same time by the head workman, Lavilette. We laid these unfortunates upon the dead bodies, supporting their backs with a barrel. In a short while they recovered their senses. The first thing the woman did, was to acquaint herself with the name of the person who saved her, and to express to him her liveliest gratitude. Finding, doubtless, that her words but ill expressed her feelings, she recollected she had in her pocket a little snuff, and instantly offered it to him; it was all she possessed. Touched with the gift, but unable to use it, M. Correard gave it to a poor sailor, which served him for two or three days. But it is impossible for us to describe a still more affecting scene—the joy this unfortunate couple testified, when they had sufficiently recovered their senses, at finding that they were both saved. The rebels being repulsed, as it has been stated above, left us a little repose. The moon lighted with her melancholy rays this disastrous raft, this narrow space, on which were found united so many torturing anxieties, so many cruel misfortunes, a madness so insensate, a courage so heroic, and the most generous, the most amiable sentiments of nature and humanity.

After this second check, the rage of the soldiers was suddenly appeased, and gave place to the most abject cowardice. Several threw themselves at our feet, and implored our pardon—which was instantly granted. Thinking that order was re-established, we returned to our station on the centre of the raft, only taking the precaution of keeping our arms. We, however, had soon to prove the impossibility of counting on the permanence of any honest sentiment in the hearts of those beings.

It was nearly midnight; and, after an hour of apparent tranquility, the soldiers rose afresh. Their mind was entirely gone—they ran upon us in despair with knives and sabres in their hands. As they yet had all their physical strength, and bedsides were armed, we were obliged again to stand on our defence. Their revolt became still more dangerous, as, in their delirium, they were entirely deaf to the voice of reason. They attacked us: we charged them in our turn, and immediately the raft was strewed with their dead bodies. Those of our adversaries who had no weapons, endeavored to tear us with their sharp teeth. Many of us were cruelly bitten. Many others were wounded, and many cuts were found in our clothes from knives and sabres.

One of our workmen was also seized by four of the rebels, who wished to throw him into the sea. One of them had laid hold of his right leg, and had bit most unmercifully the tendon above the heel. Others were striking him with great slashes of their sabres, and with the butt end of their guns, when his cries made us hasten to his assistance. In this affair, the brave Lavilette, ex-sergeant of the foot artillery of the old guard, behaved with a courage worthy of the greatest praise. He rushed upon the infuriated beings in the manner of M. Correard, and soon snatched the workman from the danger which menaced him. Some short while after, in a fresh attack of the rebels, sub-lieutenant Lozach fell into their hands. In their delirium they had taken him for Lieutenant Danglas, of whom we have formerly spoken, and who had abandoned the raft at the moment when we were quitting the frigate. The troop, to a man, eagerly sought this officer, who had seen little service, and whom they reproached for having used them ill during the time they garrisoned the Isle of Rhe. We believed this officer lost; but hearing this voice, we soon found it still possible to save him. Immediately MM. Clairet, Savigny, L'Heureux, Lavilette, Coudin, Correard, and some workmen, formed themselves into small platoons, and rushed upon the insurgents with great impetuosity, overturning every one in their way, and retook M. Lozach and placed him on the center of the raft.

The preservation of this officer cost us infinite difficulty. Every moment the soldiers demanded he should be delivered to them, designating him always by the name of Danglas. We endeavored to make them comprehend their mistake, and told them that they themselves had seen the person for whom they sought return on board the frigate. They were insensible to every thing we said—every thing before them was Danglas—they saw him perpetually, and furiously and unceasingly demanded his head. It was only by force of arms we succeeded in repressing their rage, and quieting their dreadful cries of death.

We cannot yet comprehend how a handful of men should have been able to resist such a number so monstrously insane. We are sure we were not more than twenty to combat all these madmen. Let it not, however, be imagined, that in the midst of all these dangers we had preserved our reason entire. Fear, anxiety, and the most cruel privations, had greatly changed our intellectual faculties. But being somewhat less insane than the unfortunate soldiers, we energetically opposed their determination of cutting the cords of the raft. Permit us now to make some observations concerning the different sensations with which we were affected. During the first day M. Griffon entirely lost his senses. He threw himself into the sea, but M. Savigny saved him with his own hands. His words were vague and unconnected. A second time he threw himself in; but, by a sort of instinct, kept hold of the cross pieces of the raft, and was again saved.

The following is what M. Savigny experienced in the beginning of the night. His eyes closed in spite of himself, and he felt a general drowsiness. In this condition the most beautiful visions flitted across his imagination. He saw around him a country covered with the most delightful plantations, and found himself in the midst of objects delightful to his senses. Nevertheless, he reasoned concerning his condition, and felt that courage alone could withdraw him from this species of non-existence. He demanded some wine from the master-gunner, who got it for him, and he recovered a little from this stupor. If the unfortunates who were assailed with these primary symptoms, had not strength to withstand them, their death was certain. Some became furious—others threw themselves into the sea, bidding farewell to their comrades with the utmost coolness. Some said, "Fear nothing; I am going to get you assistance, and will return in a short while." In the midst of this general madness, some wretches were seen rushing upon their companions, sword in hand, demanding the wing of a chicken and some bread, to appease the hunger which consumed them. Others asked for their hammocks, to go, they said, between the decks of the frigate, to take a little repose. Many believed they were still on the *Méduse*, surrounded by the same objects they there saw daily. Some saw ships, and called to them for assistance; or a fine harbor, in the distance of which was an elegant city. M. Correard thought he was traveling through the beautiful fields of Italy. An officer said to him, "I recollect we have been abandoned by the boats; but fear nothing. I am going to write to the governor, and in a few hours we shall be saved." M. Correard replied in the same tone, and as if he had been in his ordinary condition, "Have you a pigeon to carry your orders with such celerity?" The cries and the confusion soon roused us from this languor, but when tranquility was somewhat restored, we again fell into the same drowsy condition. On the morrow, we felt as if we had awoke from a painful dream; and asked our companions, if, during their sleep, they had not seen combats and heard cries of despair. Some replied, that the same visions had continually tormented them, and that they were exhausted with fatigue. Every one believed he was deceived by the illusions of a horrible dream.

After these terrible combats, overcome with toil, with want of food and sleep, we laid ourselves down and reposed till the morning dawned, and showed us the horror of the scene. A great number in their delirium had thrown themselves into the sea. We found that sixty or sixty-five had perished during the night. A fourth part at least, we supposed, had drowned themselves in despair. We only lost two of our own number, neither of whom were officers. The deepest objection was seated on every face. Each, having recovered himself, could now feel the horrors of his situation; and some of us, shedding tears of despair, bitterly deplored the rigor of our fate.

A new misfortune was now revealed to us. During the tumult, the rebels had thrown into the sea two barrels of wine, and the only two casks of water which we had upon the raft. Two casks of wine had been consumed the day before, and only one was left. We were more than sixty in number, and we were obliged to put ourselves on half rations.

At break of day the sea calmed, which permitted us again to erect our mast. When it was replaced, we made a distribution of wine. The unhappy soldiers murmured, and blamed us for privations which we equally endured with them. They fell exhausted. We had taken nothing for forty-eight hours, and we had been obliged to struggle continually against a strong sea. We could, like them, hardly support ourselves; courage alone made us still act. We resolved to employ every possible means to catch fish; and, collecting all the hooks and eyes from the soldiers, made fish-hooks of them: but all was of no avail. The currents carried our lines under the raft, where they got entangled. We bent a bayonet to catch sharks: one bit at it, and straightened it; and we abandoned our project. Something was absolutely necessary to sustain our miserable existence; and we tremble with horror at being obliged to tell that of which we made use. We feel our pen fall from our hands; a mortal cold congeals all our members; and our hair bristles erect on our foreheads. Readers! we implore you, feel not indignant towards men already overloaded with misery. Pity their condition, and shed a tear of sorrow for their deplorable fate.

The wretches, whom death had spared during the disastrous night we have described, seized upon the dead bodies with which the raft is covered, cutting them up by slices, which some even instantly devoured. Many nevertheless refrained. Almost all the officers were of this number. Seeing that this monstrous food had revived the strength of those who had used it, it was proposed to dry it, to make it a little more palatable. Those who had firmness to abstain from it took an additional quantity of wine. We endeavored to eat shoulder-belts and cartouch-boxes, and contrived to swallow some small bits of them. Some eat linen; others, the leathers of their hats, on which was a little grease, or rather dirt. We had recourse to many expedients to prolong our miserable existence, to recount which would only disgust the heart of humanity.

The day was calm and beautiful. A ray of hope beamed for a moment to quiet our agitation. We still expected to see the boats or some ships; and addressed our prayers to the Eternal, on whom we placed our trust. The half of our men were extremely feeble, and bore upon their faces the stamp of approaching dissolution. The evening arrived, and brought no help. The darkness of the third night augmented our fears; but the wind was still, and the sea less agitated. The sun of the fourth morning since our departure shone upon our disaster, and showed us ten or twelve of our companions stretched lifeless upon the raft. This sight struck us most forcibly, as it told us we would soon be extended in the same manner in the same place. We gave their bodies to the sea for a grave, reserving only one to feed those who, but the day before, had held his trembling hands, and sworn to him eternal friendship. This day was beautiful. Our souls, anxious for more delightful sensations, were in harmony with the aspect of heavens, and got again a new ray of hope. Towards four in the afternoon, an unlooked for event happened, which gave us some consolation. A shoal of flying fish passed under our raft, and as there was an infinite number of openings between the pieces which composed it, the fish were entangled in great quantities. We threw ourselves upon them, and captured a considerable number. We took about two hundred, and put them in an empty barrel. We opened them as we caught them, and took out what is called their milt. This food seemed delicious; but one man would have required a thousand. Our first emotion was to give to God renewed thanks for this unhoped for favor.

An ounce of gunpowder having been found in the morning, was dried in the sun during the day, which was very fine. A steel, gun-flints, and tinder, made also part of the same parcel. After a good deal of difficulty we set fire to some fragments of dry linen. We made a large opening in the side of an empty cask, and placed at the bottom of it several wet things, and upon this kind of scaffolding we set our fire; all of which we placed on a barrel, that the sea-water might not extinguish it. We cooked some fish, and ate them with extreme avidity; but our hunger was such, and our portion so small, that we added to it some of the sacrilegious viands, which the cooking rendered less revolting. This some of the officers touched for the first time. From this day we continued to eat it; but we could no longer dress it, the means of making a fire having been entirely lost. The barrel having caught fire, we extinguished it without being able to preserve any thing to rekindle it on the morrow. The powder and tinder were entirely gone. This meal gave us all additonal strength to support our fatigues. The night was tolerable, and would have been happy, had it not been signalized by a new massacre.

Some Spaniards, Italians, and negroes, had formed a plot to throw us into the sea. The negroes had told them that they were very near the shore; and that, when there, they would enable them to traverse Africa without danger. We had to take to our arms again, the sailors, who had remained faithful to us, pointing out to us the conspirators. The first signal for battle was given by a Spaniard; who, placing himself behind the mast, holding fast by it, made the sign of the cross with one hand, invoking the name of God, and with the other held a knife. The sailors seized him, and threw him into the sea. An Italian, servant to an officer of the troops, who was in the plot, seeing all was discovered, armed himself with the only boarding axe left on the raft, made his retreat to the front, enveloped himself in a piece of drapery he wore across his breast, and of his own accord threw himself into the sea. The rebels rushed forward to avenge their comrades, and a terrible conflict again commenced. Both sides fought with desperate fury; and soon the fatal raft was strewed with dead bodies and blood, which should have been shed by other hands, and in another cause. In this tumult we heard them again demanding, with horrid rage, the head of Lieutenant Danglas . . . In this terrible night Lavilette failed not to give proofs of the rarest intrepidity. It was to him, and some of those who had survived the sequel of our misfortunes, that we owed our safety. At last, after unheard of efforts, the rebels were once more repulsed, and quiet restored. Having escaped this new danger, we endeavored to get some repose. The day at length dawned upon us for the fifth time. We were now no more than thirty in number. We had lost four or five of our faithful sailors, and those who survived were in the most deplorable condition. The seawater had almost entirely excoriated the skin of our lower extremities; and we were covered with contusions or wounds, which, irritated by the salt water, extorted from us the most piercing cries. About twenty of us only were capable of standing upright or walking. Almost all our fish was exhausted—we had but four days' supply of wine. "In four days," said we, "nothing will be left, and death will be inevitable." Thus came the seventh day of our abandonment. In the course of the day, two soldiers had glided behind the only barrel of wine that was left, pierced it, and were drinking by means of a reed. We had sworn that those who used such means should be punished with death; which law was instantly put in execution, and the two transgressors were thrown into the sea.

There now remained but twenty-seven of us. Fifteen of this number seemed able to live yet some days; the rest, covered with large wounds, had almost entirely lost the use of their reason. They still, however, shared in the distributions; and would, before they died, consume thirty or forty bottles of wine, which to us were inestimable. We deliberated, that by putting the sick on half allowance, was but putting them to death by halves; but after a council, at which presided the most dreadful despair, it was decided they should be thrown into the sea. This means, however repugnant, however horrible it appeared to us, procured the survivors six days' wine. But after the decision was made, who durst execute it? The habit of seeing death ready to devour us; the certainty of our infallible destruction without this monstrous expedient; all, in short, had hardened our hearts to every feeling but that of self-preservation. Three sailors and a soldier took charge of this cruel business. We looked aside, and shed tears of blood at the fate of these unfortunates. Among them were the wretched sutler and her husband. Both had been grievously wounded in the different combats. The woman had a thigh broken between the beams of the raft, and a stroke of a sabre had made a deep wound in the head of her husband. Every thing announced their approaching end. We consoled ourselves with the belief, that our cruel resolution shortened but a brief space the term of their existence. Ye who shudder at the cry of outraged humanity, recollect that it was other men, fellow-countrymen, comrades, who had placed us in this awful situation.

This horrible expedient saved the fifteen who remained; for when we were found by the Argus brig, we had very little wine left, and it was the sixth day after the cruel sacrifice we have described. The victims, we repeat, had not more than forty-eight hours to live; and by keeping them on the raft, we would have been absolutely destitute of the means of existence two days before we were found. Weak as we were, we considered it a certain thing, that it would have been impossible for us to have lived only twenty-four hours more without taking some food. After this catastrophe, we threw our arms into the sea: they inspired us with horror we could not overcome. We only kept one sabre, in case we had to cut some cordage or some piece of wood.

A new event—for every thing was an event to wretches to whom the world was reduced to the narrow space of a few toises [archaic French measurement equal to a fathom, or six feet], and for whom the winds and waves contended in their fury, as they floated across the abyss—an event happened, which diverted our minds from the horrors of our situation. All on a sudden, a white butterfly, of a species common in France, came fluttering above our heads, and settled on our sails. The first thought this little creature suggested was, that it was the harbinger of approaching land; and we clung to the hope with the delirium of joy. It was the ninth day we had been upon the raft; the torments of hunger consumed our entrails; and the soldiers and sailors already devoured with haggard eyes this wretched prey, and seemed ready to dispute about it. Others looking upon it as a messenger from Heaven, declared that they took it under their protection, and would suffer none to do it harm. It is certain we could not be far from land, for the butterflies continued to come on the following days, and flutter about our sail. We had also, on the same day, another indication not less positive, by a Goeland [gull] which flew around our raft. This second visitor left us no doubt that we were fast approaching the African soil; and we persuaded ourselves that we should be speedily thrown upon the coast by the currents.

This same day a new care employed us. Seeing we were reduced to so small a number, we collected all the little strength we had left, detached some planks on the front of the raft, and, with some pretty long pieces of wood, raised on the center a kind of platform, on which we reposed. All the effects we could collect were placed upon it, and tended to make it less hard; which also prevented the sea from passing with such facility through the spaces between the different planks; but the waves came across and sometimes covered us completely. On this new theatre we resolved to meet death in a manner becoming Frenchmen, and with perfect resignation. Our time was almost wholly spent in speaking of our unhappy country. All our wishes, our last prayers, were for the prosperity of France. Thus passed the last days of our abode upon the raft.

Soon after our abandonment, we bore with comparative ease the immersions during the nights, which are very cold in these countries; but latterly, every time the waves washed over us, we felt a most painful sensation, and we uttered painful cries. We employed every means to avoid it. Some supported their heads on pieces of wood, and made with what they could find a sort of little parapet to screen them from the force of the waves; others sheltered themselves behind two empty casks. But these means were very insufficient; it was only when the sea was calm that it did not break over us.

An ardent thirst, redoubled in the day by the beams of burning sun, consumed us. An officer of the army found by chance a small lemon, and it may easily be imagined how valuable such a fruit would be to him. His comrades, in spite of the most urgent entreaties, could not get a bit of it from him. Signs of rage were already manifested, and had he not partly listened to the solicitations of those around him, they would have taken it by force, and he would have perished the victim of his selfishness. We also disputed about thirty cloves of garlic, which were found in the bottom of a sack. These disputes were for the most part accompanied with violent menaces; and if they had been prolonged, we might perhaps have come to the last extremities. There was found also two small phials, in which was a spirituous liquor for cleaning the teeth. He who possessed them kept them with care, and gave with reluctance one or two drops in the palm of the hand. This liquor, which we think was a tincture of guiacum, cinnamon, cloves, and other aromatic substances, produced on our tongues an agreeable feeling, and for a short while removed the thirst which destroyed us. Some of us found some small pieces of powder, which made, when put into the mouth, a kind of coolness. One plan generally employed was to put into a hat a quantity of seawater, with which we washed our faces for a while, repeating it at intervals. We also bathed our hair and held our hands in the water. Misfortune made us ingenious, and each thought of a thousand means to alleviate his sufferings. Emaciated by the most cruel privations, the least agreeable feeling was to us happiness supreme. Thus we sought with avidity a small empty phial which one of us possessed, and in which had once been some essence of roses; and every one, as he got hold of it, respired with delight the odor it exhaled, which imparted to his senses the most soothing impressions. Many of us kept our rations of wine in a small tin cup, and sucked it out with a quill. This manner of taking it was of great benefit to us, and allayed our thirst much better than if we had gulped it off at once.

Three days passed in inexpressible anguish. So much did we despise life, that many of us feared not to bathe in sight of the sharks which surrounded our raft; others placed themselves naked upon the front of our machine, which was under water. These expedients diminished a little the ardor of their thirst. A species of molusca, known to seamen by the name of gatere, was sometimes driven by great numbers on our raft; and when their long arms rested on our naked bodies, they occasioned us the most cruel sufferings. Will it be believed, that amid these terrible scenes, struggling with inevitable death, some of us uttered pleasantries, which made us yet smile, in spite of the horrors of the situation? One, besides others, said jestingly, "If the brig is sent to search for us, pray God it had the eyes of Argus," in allusion to the name of the vessel we presumed would be sent to our assistance. This consolatory idea never left us an instant, and we spoke of it frequently.

On the 16th, reckoning we were very near land, eight of the most determined among us resolved to endeavor to gain the coast. A second raft, of smaller dimensions, was formed for transporting them thither; but it was found insufficient: and they at length determined to await death in their present situation. Meanwhile night came on, and its sombre veil revived in our minds the most afflicting thoughts. We were convinced there were not above a dozen or fifteen bottles of wine in our barrel. We began to have an invincible disgust at the flesh, which had till then scarcely supported us; and we may say, that the sight of it inspired us with feelings of horror, doubtless produced by the idea of our approaching dissolution.

On the morning of the 17th the sun appeared free from clouds. After having addressed our prayers to the Eternal, we divided among us a part of our wine. Each, with delight, was taking his small portion; when a captain of infantry, casting his eyes on the horizon, perceived a ship, and announced it to us by an exclamation of joy. We knew it to be a brig, but it was at a great distance: we could distinguish the masts. The sight of this vessel revived in us emotions difficult to describe. Each believed his deliverance sure, and we have a thousand thanks to God. Fears, however, mingled with our hopes. We straightened some hoops of casks, to the ends of which we fixed handkerchiefs of different colors. A man, with our united assistance, mounted to the top of the mast, and waved these little flags. For more than half an hour, we were tossed between hope and fear. Some thought the vessel grew larger, and others were convinced its course was from us. These last were the only ones whose eyes were not blinded by hope, for the ship disappeared.

From the delirium of joy, we passed to that of despondency and sorrow. We envied the fate of those whom we had seen perish at our sides; and we said to ourselves, "When we shall be in want of every thing, and when our strength begins to forsake us, we will wrap ourselves up as we can; we will stretch ourselves on this platform, the witness of the most cruel sufferings, and there await death with resignation." At length, to calm our despair, we sought for consolation in the arms of sleep. The day before we had been scorched by the beams of a burning sun: today, to avoid the fierceness of his rays, we made a tent with the mainsail of the frigate. As soon as it was finished, we laid ourselves under it: thus all that was passing without was hid from our eyes. We proposed then to write upon a plank an abridgement of our adventures, and to add our names at the bottom of the recital, and fix it to the upper part of the mast, in the hope it would reach the government and our families.

After having passed two hours, a prey to the most cruel reflections, the master gunner of the frigate, wishing to go to the front of the raft, went out from below the tent. Scarcely had he put out his head, when he turned to us, uttering a piercing cry. Joy was painted upon his face— his hands were stretched toward the sea—he breathed with difficulty. All he was able to say was, "Saved! see the brig upon us!" and in fact it was not more than half a league distant, having every sail set, and steering right upon us. We rushed from our tent: even those whom enormous wounds in their inferior extremities had confined for several days, dragged themselves to the back of the raft, to enjoy a sight of the ship which had come to save us from certain death. We embraced one another with a transport which looked much like madness, and tears of joy trickled down our cheeks, withered by the most cruel privations. Each seized handkerchiefs, or some pieces of linen, to make signals to the brig, which was rapidly approaching us. Some fell on their knees, and fervently returned thanks to Providence for this miraculous preservation of their lives. Our joy redoubled when we saw at the top of the foremast a large white flag; and we cried, "Is it then to Frenchmen we will owe our deliverance." We instantly recognized the brig to be the Argus: it was then about two gun shots from us. We were terribly impatient to see her reel her sails, which at last she did; and fresh cries of joy arose from our raft. The Argus came and lay to on our starboard, about half a pistol shot from us. The crew, ranged upon the deck and on the shrouds, announced to us, by the waving of their hands and hats, the pleasure they felt at coming to the assistance of their unfortunate countrymen. In a short time we were all transported on board the brig, where we found the lieutenant of the frigate, and some others who had been wrecked with us. Compassion was painted on every face, and pity drew tears from every eye which beheld us.

We found some excellent broth on board the brig, which they had prepared; and when they had perceived us, they added to it some wine, and thus restored our nearly exhausted strength. They bestowed on us the most generous care and attention: our wounds were dressed, and on the morrow many of our sick began to revive. Some, however, still suffered much; for they were placed between decks, very near the kitchen, which augmented the almost insupportable heat of these latitudes. This want of space arose from the small size of the vessel. The number of the shipwrecked was indeed very considerable. Those who did not belong to the navy were laid upon cables, wrapped in flags, and placed under the fire of the kitchen. Here they had almost perished during the course of the night, fire having broken out between decks about ten in the evening; but timely assistance being rendered, we were saved for the second time. We had scarcely escaped, when some of us became again delirious. An officer of infantry wished to throw himself into the sea, to look for his pocket book; and would have done it had he not been prevented. Others were seized in a manner not less frenzied.

The commander and officers of the brig watched over us, and kindly anticipated our wants. They snatched us from death, by saving us from our raft: their unremitting care revived within us the spark of life. The surgeon of the ship, M. Renaud, distinguished himself for his indefatigable zeal. He was obliged to spend the whole of the day in dressing our wounds; and during the two days we were in the brig, he bestowed on us all the aid of his art, with an attention and gentleness which merits our eternal gratitude.

In truth, it was time we should find an end of our sufferings: they had lasted thirteen days in the most cruel manner. The strongest among us might have lived forty-eight hours or so, longer. M. Correard felt that he must die in the course of the day. He had, however, a presentiment we would be saved. He said, that a series of events so unheard of, would not be buried in oblivion: that Providence would at least preserve some of us to tell to the world the melancholy story of our misfortunes.

Such is the fatal history of those who were left upon the memorable raft. Of one hundred and fifty, fifteen only were saved. Five of that number never recovered from their fatigue, and died at St. Louis. Those who yet live are covered with scars; and the cruel sufferings to which they have been exposed, have materially shaken their constitutions.

1820–1821
THE WRECK OF THE WHALE SHIP ESSEX
A Narrative Account by Owen Chase, First Mate

> It was impossible to prevent ourselves from feeling all the poignancy and bitterness that characterizes the separation of men who have long suffered in each other's company and whose interest and feelings fate had so closely linked together.
>
> – Owen Chase, on being separated from
> the two other whaleboats, January 13, 1821

In the late 18th century the intrepid whalers of Nantucket began rounding the dangerous waters of Cape Horn to reach the warm waters of the South Pacific in pursuit of the coveted sperm whale. This gigantic whale was dangerous prey. Prone to violently attack its attackers, it could smash a whaleboat in its jaws and was capable of staving in a stout ship in a determined charge.

Under the command of young twenty-nine-year-old Captain George Pollard, Jr., the aging whaling ship *Essex* set sail from Nantucket on August 12, 1819, refitted for a voyage of more than two years. At eighty-seven feet and two hundred and thirty-eight tons, the relatively small *Essex* and its crew endured a difficult passage, but survived nearly capsizing in a squall only days after leaving port and the brutal conditions of a five week passage round Cape Horn. Finally reaching the South Pacific in late February, the *Essex* enjoyed month after month of successful whaling, until, on November 20, 1820, an infuriated sperm whale—some eighty-five feet in length—twice rammed the ship and punched a hole below the waterline of its bow.

At the time of the catastrophe, only First Mate Owen Chase and his whaling crew were aboard, making repairs to their boat, which another whale had attacked and damaged that day. Chase and his men quickly abandoned ship, hastily launching their frail whaleboat and salvaging what they could from the ship before it capsized. Joined soon afterward by the other two whaleboats, the crew of twenty gathered what fresh water, provisions, and supplies they could recover from the wreck, and fashioned sailing rigs before setting out two days later on their fatal voyage. The nearest landfall was a thousand miles to the west, but fearing both hostile savages and violent seasonal storms in that direction, the captain and his first and second mates decided to sail with the prevailing winds to the south, where they hoped to catch variable winds that would carry them to the coast of South America. So began the odyssey of survival of the crew of the whaling ship *Essex*.

Over the next four weeks, the desperate flotilla sailed southward from the equator. By December 9th the three whale boats had reached 17° 40' south. Their crews—after almost three weeks on the open sea—were weary, parched with thirst, and barely surviving on meager rations, but they were still disciplined, sound in mind, and in good spirits. Over the next ten days their strength was tested to its limits, but, on December 20th, starving and wracked with thirst, in boats perilously weakened by the strain of continuous service in open seas, the survivors of the *Essex* reached landfall on what they thought to be "Ducie" Island. Here is where we take up our selection from Owen Chase's account. In fact, their island, now known as Henderson Island, was almost two hundred miles to the west of Ducie. The most desperate need upon landing was to locate water, but none was immediately apparent. This need was miraculously supplied, and the men scoured the island for provisions. Soon realizing that the island could not support twenty men for any extended period of time, all but three of them—Thomas Chapple, Seth Weeks, and William Wright—set out to sea again on December—27th—on a horrific voyage that would be fatal for all but five of them.

Had the men of the *Essex* remained on "Ducie" Island, most if not all of them would eventually have starved. The three men who remained were rescued on April 5th—only after the survivors of the final voyage had spoken of their presence on the island and a ship was dispatched for them. Although the men on the three whaleboats that set out from "Ducie" had enough water for an extended voyage, they had not been able to provision the boats adequately. What little food they had was rationed, the meager rations halved and halved again as day after day passed with almost no prospect of rescue and progress toward land was frustrated by storms, contrary winds, and calms. On January 13th, the three boats were separated in a storm, one of the boats never to be seen again, and the crews steadily lost strength and clarity of mind and began to perish. Upon last resort, the men began to eat the flesh of their perished comrades. On February 18th the British brig *Indian* rescued Owen Chase, Benjamin Lawrence, and Thomas Nickerson at the extreme limit of death. Five days later the whaling ship *Dauphin* rescued Captain Pollard and Charles Ramsdell, the sole survivors of the second boat.

The five survivors who managed to endure until the moment of their rescue were simply the most resilient among the seventeen men who cast off from "Ducie" Island. It is not difficult to understand how close these men were to each other. The small crew of the Essex had shared many dangers together. The sorrow that Owen comments upon when the three whaleboats were ultimately separated plainly underscores the loyalty and affection that bound together the men of the *Essex*. Every man shared equally in the meager rations and, with only one exception that we are told of—one that Owen treated with both compassion and firmness—the men maintained discipline even as their situation became extremely dire. The men of the three whaleboats knew that their fates were entirely in the hands of providence. But had they not decided to try to reach the west coast of South America, had they not worked together and treated each other with respect, it is unlikely that any among them would have lived to be rescued. It was the dead who by their very flesh saved the living.

Chase's sober and truthful account of the ordeal was published in New York in 1821 as *Narrative of the Most Extraordinary and Distressing Shipwreck of the Whale-Ship* Essex. A pure archetype of survival narrative, this honest, plainspoken account displays matter-of-fact nobility even in its depiction of horrors, and the fear and desperation, and the resolve, of men on the edge of death. Twenty years after the publication of this American classic, Herman Melville met the author's young son—while both men were whaling on separate ships in the South Pacific—who gave a copy of the book to him. The book deeply moved and impressed Melville, whose great *Moby Dick* would appear a decade later. Who can forget the climax of Melville's great novel, his powerful account of the fury and rage of the great white whale in its attack on the Pequod? Surely Melville never forgot the fury of the whale that rammed and crippled the *Essex*.

George Pollard was given command of another whaling ship, which was wrecked on a coral reef in March of 1823. Returning to Nantucket after this second disaster, he never went to sea again. Benjamin Lawrence successfully captained two whaling voyages but ultimately retired from the sea to live as a farmer. Charles Ramsdell and Thomas Nickerson also captained ships before retiring, as did our author, Owen Chase.

The Wreck of the Whale Ship Essex

A Narrative Account by Owen Chase, First Mate

"There is land!"

December 20th. This was a great day of happiness and joy. After having experienced one of the most distressing nights in the whole catalogue of our sufferings, we awoke to a morning of comparative luxury and pleasure.

About seven o'clock, while we were sitting dispirited, silent, and dejected in our boats, one of our companions suddenly and loudly called out: "There is land!"

We were all aroused in an instant, as if electrified. We cast our eyes to leeward, and there, indeed, was the blessed vision before us, "as plain and palpable" as could be wished for.

A new and extraordinary impulse now took possession of us. We shook off the lethargy of our senses and seemed to take on another and fresh existence. One or two of my companions—whose lagging spirits and worn-out frames had begun to inspire them with an utter indifference to their fate—now immediately brightened up and manifested a surprising alacrity and earnestness to gain, without delay, the much wished for shore.

It appeared at first a low white beach and lay like a basking paradise before our longing eyes. It was discovered nearly at the same time by the other boats, and a general burst of joy and congratulation now passed between us. To divine what the feelings of our hearts were on this occasion is not within the scope of human calculation. Alternate expectation, fear, gratitude, surprise, and exultation swayed our minds and quickened our exertions.

We ran down for the beach, and at eleven o'clock A.M., we were within a quarter of a mile of the shore.

It was an island, to all appearance, about six miles long and three broad, with a very high, rugged shore, and surrounded by rocks. The sides of the mountains were bare, but the tops of them looked freshand green with vegetation. Upon examining our navigators, we found it was Ducie Island, lying in latitude 24° 40' south, longitude 124° 40' west.

A short moment sufficed for reflection, and we then made

immediate arrangements to land. None of us knew whether the island was inhabited or not, nor what it afforded, if anything. If inhabited, it was uncertain whether by beasts or by savages, and a momentary suspense was created by contemplation of the dangers which might possibly arise by proceeding without due preparation and care. Hunger and thirst, however, soon determined us, and having taken the musket and pistols, I, with three others, effected a landing upon some sunken rocks and waded hence to the shore. Upon arriving at the beach, it was necessary to take a little breath and to lie down for a few minutes to rest our weak bodies before we could proceed.

Let the reader judge, if he can, what must have been our feelings now and he will have but a faint idea of the happiness that here fell to our lot! After being bereft of all comfortable hopes of life for the space of thirty days of terrible suffering—with our bodies wasted to mere skeletons by hunger and thirst and with death itself staring us in the face—we were suddenly and unexpectedly conducted to a rich banquet of food and drink, which subsequently we enjoyed for a few days to our full satisfaction.

We now, after a few minutes, separated and went in different directions in search of water, the want of which had been our principal privation and called for immediate relief. I had not proceeded far in my excursion before I discovered a fish, about a foot and a half in length, swimming along in the water close to the shore. I commenced an attack upon him with the breach of my gun and struck him, I believe, once. He ran under a small rock that lay near the store. From there I took him with the aid of my ramrod. I brought him on the beach and immediately fell to eating him. My companions soon joined in the repast, and in less than ten minutes the whole was consumed—bones, skin, scales, and all.

With full stomachs, we imagined we could now attempt the mountains, where we considered water—if on any part of the island—would be most probably obtained. I accordingly clambered with excessive labour, suffering, and pain up among the bushes, roots, and underwood of one of the crags, looking as I went in all directions in vain for every appearance of water that might present itself. There was no indication of the least moisture to be found within the distance to which I had ascended—although my strength did not enable me to get higher than about twenty feet. I was sitting down at the height that I had attained to gather a little breath, and was ruminating there upon the fruitlessness of my search and on the consequent evils and continuation of suffering that it necessarily implied, when I perceived that the tide had risen considerably since our landing. It threatened to cut off our retreat to the rocks—by which alone we should be able to regain our boats. I therefore determined to proceed again to the shore to inform the captain and the rest of our want of success in procuring water and to consult upon the propriety of remaining at the island any longer.

I never for one moment lost sight of the main chance, which I conceived we still had, of either getting to the coast or of meeting some vessel at sea. And I felt that every minute's detention, without some equivalent purpose, was lessening those chances by a consumption of the means of our support.

When I had got down, one of my companions informed me that he had found a place, in a rock some distance off, from which the water exuded in small drops at intervals of about five minutes. He had, by applying his lips to the rock, obtained a few of these drops, which only served to whet his appetite and from which nothing like the least satisfaction had proceeded. Upon this information, I immediately resolved in my own mind to advise remaining until morning in order to endeavour to make a more thorough search the next day, as well as to pick away the rock, which had been discovered, with our hatchets—with the view of increasing, if possible, the run of the water.

We all repaired again to our boats. There we found that the captain had the same impressions as to the propriety of our delay until morning. We therefore landed and, having hauled our boats up on the beach, lay down in them that night. Free from all the anxieties of watching and labour, we gave ourselves up, amid our sufferings of hunger and thirst, to an unreserved forgetfulness and peace of mind that seemed so well to accord with the pleasing anticipations that this day had brought forth.

It was but a short space, however, until the morning broke upon us. Sense and feeling, gnawing hunger, and the raging fever of thirst then made me redouble my wishes and efforts to explore the island again. By traversing the shore a considerable distance that night, we had obtained a few crabs and a few very small fish. But we waited until the next day to begin the labours for which we considered a night of refreshment and undisturbed repose would better qualify us.

December 21st. We had still reserved our common allowance, but it was entirely inadequate for the purpose of supplying the raging demands of the palate. Such an excessive and cruel thirst was created as almost to deprive us of the power of speech. The lips became cracked and swollen, and a sort of glutinous saliva, disagreeable to the taste and intolerable beyond expression, collected in the mouth. Our bodies had wasted away to almost skin and bone and possessed so little strength as often to require each other's assistance in performing some of its weakest functions. Relief, we now felt, must come soon, or nature would sink. The most perfect discipline was still maintained in respect to our provisions, and it now became our whole object—if we should not be able to replenish our subsistence from the island—to obtain, by some other means or other, a sufficient refreshment to enable us to prosecute our voyage.

Our search for water, accordingly, again commenced with the morning; each of us took a different direction and prosecuted the examination of every place where there was the least indication of it. The small leaves of the shrubbery afforded a temporary alleviation by being chewed in the mouth and, but for the peculiarly bitter taste which those of the island possessed, would have been an extremely grateful substitute. In the course of our rambles, too, we would now and then meet with tropic birds of a beautiful figure and plumage. These occupied small holes in the sides of the mountain, from whence we plucked them without the least difficulty. Upon our approaching them, they made no attempts to fly, nor did they appear to notice us at all. These birds served as for a fine repast. Numbers of them were caught in the course of the day, cooked by fires which we made on the shore, and eaten with the utmost avidity.

We found also a plant, in taste not unlike the peppergrass, growing in considerable abundance in the crevices of the rocks, which proved to us a very agreeable food when chewed with the meat of the birds. These, with a few birds' nests—some of them full of young, others of eggs—which we found in the course of the day, served us for food and supplied the place of our bread. During our stay here, we had restricted ourselves from the use of this provision.

But water, the great object of all our anxieties and exertions, was nowhere to be found, and we began to despair of meeting with it on the island. Our state of extreme weakness—and many of us were without shoes or any covering for the feet—prevented us from exploring any great distance, lest, by some sudden faintness or overexertion, we should not be able to return and at night be exposed to attacks of wild beasts, which might inhabit the island. Beyond the reach of feeble assistance that otherwise could be afforded to each, we were alike incapable of resistance.

The whole day was thus consumed in picking up whatever had

the least shape or quality of sustenance. Before us was another night of misery, which was to be passed without a drop of water to cool our parching tongues. In this state of affairs, we would not reconcile it to ourselves to remain longer at this place. A day, an hour lost to us unnecessarily here might cost us our preservation. A drop of the water that we then had in our possession might prove, in the last stages of our debility, the very cordial of life.

After some considerable conversation on this subject, it was finally concluded to spend the succeeding day in the further search for water and, if none should be found, to quit the island the morning after.

December 22nd. We had been employed during the last night in various occupations, according to the feelings or the wants of the men. Some continued to wander about the shore and to short distances in the mountains, still seeking for food and water. Others hung about the beach, near the edge of the sea, endeavouring to take the little fish that came about them. Some slept, insensible to every feeling but rest, while others spent the night in talking of their situation and reasoning upon the probabilities of their deliverance. The dawn of day aroused us again to labour, and each of us pursued his own inclination as to the course taken over the island after water.

My principal hope was founded upon my success in picking the rocks where the moisture had been discovered two days before, and thither I hastened as soon as my strength would enable me to get there. It was about a quarter of a mile from what I may call our encampment. With two men, who had accompanied me, I commenced my labours with a hatchet and an old chisel.

The rock proved to be very soft, and in a very short time I had obtained a considerable hole, but, alas, without the least wished for effect! I watched it for some little time with great anxiety, hoping that, as I increased the depth of the hole, the water would presently flow, but all my hopes and efforts were unavailing. At last I desisted from further labour and sat down near the rock in utter despair.

As I turned my eyes towards the beach, I saw some of the men in the act of carrying a keg along from the boats with, I thought, an extraordinary spirit and activity. The idea suddenly darted across my mind that they had found water and were taking a keg to fill it. I quitted my seat in a moment and made my way towards them with a palpitating heart. Before I came up with them, they gave me the cheering news that they had found a spring of water. I felt, at that moment, as if I could have fallen down and thanked God for this signal act of His mercy. The sensation that I experienced was indeed strange and such as I shall never forget. At one instant I felt an almost choking excess of joy, and at the next I wanted the relief of a flood of tears.

When I arrived at the spot, whither I had hastened as fast as my weak legs would carry me, I found my companions had all taken their fill. With an extreme degree of forbearance, I then satisfied myself by drinking in small quantities and at intervals of two or three minutes apart. Notwithstanding the remonstrances of prudence and, in some cases, force, many of the men had lain down and thoughtlessly swallowed large quantities of it, until they could drink no more. The effect of this was, however, neither so sudden nor bad as we had imagined. It only served to make them a little stupid and indolent for the remainder of the day.

Upon examining the place from whence we had obtained this miraculous and unexpected succour, we were equally astonished and delighted with the discovery. It was on the shore; above it the sea flowed to a depth of nearly six feet at high tide, and we could procure the water, therefore, from it only when the tide was down. The crevice from which the spring rose was in a flat rock. We filled our two kegs before the tide rose and went back again to our boats. The remainder of this day was spent in seeking for fish, crabs, birds, and anything else that fell our way that could contribute to satisfy our appetites.

We enjoyed, during that night, a most comfortable and delicious sleep, unattended with those violent cravings of hunger and thirst that had poisoned our slumbers for so many previous ones. Since the discovery of the water, too, we began to entertain different notions altogether of our situation. There was no doubt we might here depend upon a constant and ample supply of it as long as we chose to remain. And in all probability, we could manage to obtain food until the island should be visited by some vessel or until time allowed us to devise other means of leaving it. Our boats would still remain to us, and a stay here might enable us to mend, strengthen, and put them in more perfect order for the sea and get ourselves so far recruited as to be able to endure, if necessary, a more protracted voyage to the mainland. I made a silent determination in my own mind that I would myself pursue something like this plan, whatever might be the opinion of the rest, but I found no difference in the views of any of us as to this matter. We therefore concluded to remain at least four or five days. Within this time, it could be sufficiently known whether it would be advisable to make any arrangements for a more permanent abode.

December 23rd. At eleven o'clock, A.M., we again visited our spring. The tide had fallen to about a foot below it, and we were able to procure, before it rose again, about twenty gallons of water. It was at first a little brackish but soon became fresh from the constant supply from the rock and the departure of the sea. Our observations this morning tended to give us every confidence in its quantity and quality. We therefore rested perfectly easy in our minds on the subject and commenced to make further discoveries about the island.

Each man sought for his own daily living on whatsoever the mountains, the shore, or the sea could furnish him with. Every day during our stay there, the whole time was employed in roving about for food. We found, however, on the 24th, that we had picked up everything that could be got in the way of sustenance. And, much to our surprise, some of the men came in at night and complained of not having got sufficient during the day to satisfy the cravings of their stomachs. Every accessible part of the mountain contiguous to us—or within the reach of our weak enterprise—was already ransacked for birds' eggs and grass and was rifled of all that it contained, so we began to entertain serious apprehensions that we should not be able to live long here. With the view of being prepared as well as possible, should necessity at any time oblige us to quit the island, we commenced, on the 24th, to repair our boats.

We continued to work upon them all that and the succeeding day. We were enabled to do this with much facility by drawing them up and turning them over on the beach, working by spells of two or three hours at a time and then leaving off to seek for food.

We procured our water daily when the tide would leave the shore, but on the evening of the 25th, we found that a fruitless search for nourishment had not repaid us for the labours of the whole day. There was no one thing on the island upon which we could in the least degree rely except the peppergrass. The supply of that was precarious, and it was not much relished without some other food. Our situation here, therefore, now became worse than it would have been in our boats on the ocean. In the later case, we should be still making some progress towards the land while our provisions lasted, and, too, the chance of falling in with some vessel would be considerably increased. It was certain that we ought not to remain here unless we felt the strongest assurances in our own minds of sufficient sustenance, in regular supplies, that might be depended upon.

After much conversation amongst us on the subject and after again examining our navigators, it was finally concluded to set sail for Easter Island, which we found to be east-southeast from us in latitude 27° 9' south, longitude 109° 35' west. All we knew of this island was that it existed as laid down in the books. Of its extent, productions, or inhabitants, if any, we were entirely ignorant. At any rate, it was nearer by eight hundred and fifty miles to the coast and could not be worse in its productions than the one we were about to leave.

The *26th of December* was wholly employed in preparations for our departure. Our boats were hauled down to the vicinity of the spring, and our casks—and everything else that would contain water—filled with it.

There had been considerable talk between three of our companions about their remaining on this island and taking their chance both from their living on it and an escape from it. As the time at which we were to leave drew near, they made up their minds to stay behind. The rest of us could make no objection to their plan as it lessened the load of our boats and allowed us to share of the provisions. Moreover, the probability of their being able to sustain themselves on the island (being few in number) was much stronger than that of our reaching the mainland. Should we, however, ever arrive safely, it would become our duty, and we so assured them, to give information of their situation and to make every effort to procure their removal from the island.

Their names were William Wright of Barnstable, Massachusetts, Thomas Chapple of Plymouth, England, and Seth Weeks of the former place. They had begun, before we came away, to construct a sort of habitation, composed of the branches of trees. We left with them every little article that could be spared from the boats. It was their intention to build a considerable dwelling, which would protect them from the rains, as soon as time and materials could be provided.

The captain wrote letters, which were to be left on the island. These gave information as to the fate of the ship and of ourselves and stated that we had set out to reach Easter Island. Further details were added in an attempt to give notice of our misfortunes should our three fellow sufferers die there and the place afterwards ever be visited by any vessel. These letters were put in a tin case, which was enclosed in a small wooden box and nailed to a tree on the west side of the island near our landing place.

December 27th. I went, before we set sail this morning, and procured for each boat, a flat stone and two armfuls of wood, with which to make a fire in our boats, should it afterwards become necessary in the further prosecution of our voyage. We calculated we might catch a fish or a bird, and, in that case, we would be provided with the means of cooking it. Otherwise, we knew, from the intense heat of the weather, that they could not be preserved from spoiling.

By ten o'clock, A.M., the tide had risen far enough to allow our boats to float over the rocks. We made all sail and steered around the island for the purpose of making a little further observation. This would not detain us any great time and might be productive of some unexpected good fortune.

Before we started, we missed our three companions and found they had not come down, either to assist us to get off or to take any kind of leave of us. I walked up the beach towards their rude dwelling and informed them that we were then about to set sail and should probably never see them more. They seemed to be very much affected, and one of them shed tears. They wished us to write to their relations, should Providence safely direct us again to our homes, but said little else. They had every confidence in being able to procure a subsistence there as long as they remained. Finding them ill at heart about taking any leave of us, I hastily bid them good-bye, hoped they would do well, and came away. They followed me with their eyes until I was out of sight, and I never saw more of them.

On the northwest side of the island we perceived a fine white beach, on which we imagined we might land and, in a short time, ascertain if any further useful discoveries could be effected or if any addition could be made to our stock of provisions. Having set ashore five or six of the men for this purpose, the rest of us shoved off the boats and commenced fishing. We saw a number of sharks, but all efforts to take them proved ineffectual, and we got but a few small fish, about the size of mackerel, which we divided amongst us. In this business we were occupied until six o'clock in the afternoon, when the men returned to the shore from their search in the mountains. They brought with them a few birds.

We again set sail and steered directly for Easter Island. During that night—after we had got quite clear of the land—we had a fine strong breeze from the northwest. We kept our fires going, cooked our fish and birds, and felt our situation as comfortable as could be expected. We continued on our course, consuming our provisions and water as sparingly as possible, without any material incident. . . .

On the 3ʳᵈ of January we experienced heavy squalls from the west-southwest, accompanied with dreadful thunder and lightning that threw a gloomy and cheerless aspect over the ocean and incited a recurrence of some of those heavy and desponding moments that we had before experienced. We commenced from Ducie Island to keep a regular reckoning, by which, on the fourth of January, we found we had got to the southward of Easter Island. With the wind prevailing

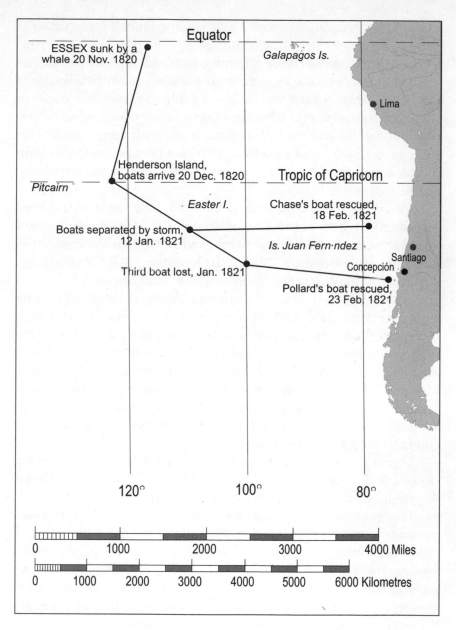

Equator

ESSEX sunk by a
whale 20 Nov. 1820

Galapagos Is.

Lima

Henderson Island,
boats arrive 20 Dec. 1820

Tropic of Capricorn

Pitcairn

Easter I.

Chase's boat rescued,
18 Feb. 1821

Boats separated by storm,
12 Jan. 1821

Is. Juan Fern·ndez

Santiago

Third boat lost, Jan. 1821

Concepción

Pollard's boat rescued,
23 Feb. 1821

120°   100°   80°

0   1000   2000   3000   4000 Miles

0   1000   2000   3000   4000   5000   6000 Kilometres

The voyage of the *Essex*

east-northeast, we should not be able to get on to the eastward so as to reach it.

Our birds and fish were all now consumed, and we had begun again on our short allowance of bread. It was necessary in this state of things to change our determination of going to Easter Island and to shape our course in some other direction where the wind would allow of our going. We had but little hesitation in concluding, therefore, to steer for the Juan Fernández Islands, which lay east-southeast from us some two thousand five hundred miles. We bent our course accordingly towards them.

For the two succeeding days we had very light winds and suffered excessively from the intense heat of the sun. The 7th of January brought us a change of wind to the northward, and at twelve o'clock we found ourselves in latitude 30° 18′ south, longitude 117° 29′ west. We continued to make what progress we could to the eastward.

January 10th. Mathew P. Joy, the second mate, had suffered debility from the privations we had experienced, much beyond any of the rest of us. On the 8th, he was removed to the captain's boat, under the impression that he would be more comfortable there and that more attention and pains could be bestowed in nursing and endeavouring to comfort him. This day being calm, he manifested a desire to be taken back again. But at four o'clock in the afternoon—having been, according to his wishes, placed in his own boat—he died very suddenly after his removal.

On the *11th*, at six o'clock in the morning, we sewed him up in his clothes, tied a large stone to his feet, and having brought all the boats to, consigned him in a solemn manner to the ocean.

This man did not die of absolute starvation, although his end was no doubt very much hastened by his sufferings. He had a weak and sickly constitution and had complained of being unwell the whole voyage. It was an incident, however, which threw a gloom over our feelings for many days. In consequence of his death, one man from the captain's boat was placed in the boat from which he died to supply his place. We then stood again away on our course.

On the *12th of January* we had the wind from the northwest, which commenced in the morning and came on to blow before night a perfect gale. We were obliged to take in all sail and to run before the winds. Flashes of lightning were quick and vivid, and the rain came down in cataracts. As, however, the gale blew us fairly on our course and as our speed had been great during the day, we derived, I may say, even pleasure from the uncomfortableness and fury of the storm. But we were apprehensive that, in the darkness of this night, we should be separated and made arrangements for each boat to keep to an east-southeast course all night.

About eleven o'clock—my boat being ahead a short distance of the others—I turned my head back, as I was in the habit of doing every minute, and neither of the others was to be seen. It was blowing and raining at this time as if the heavens were separating, and I knew not hardly at the moment what to do. I hove my boat to the wind and lay drifting about an hour, expecting every moment that they would come up with me. Not seeing anything of them, I put away again and stood on the course agreed upon, with strong hopes that daylight would enable me to discover them again.

When the morning dawned, in vain did we look over every part of the ocean for our companions. They were gone! And we saw no more of them afterwards. By my observation we separated in latitude 32° 16' south, longitude 112° 20' west.

It was folly to repine at the circumstance. It could neither be remedied, nor could sorrow secure their return. But it was impossible to prevent ourselves from feeling all the poignancy and bitterness that characterizes the separation of men who have long suffered in each other's company and whose interests and feelings fate had so closely linked together. . . .

The *14th of January* proved another very squally and rainy day. We had now been nineteen days from the island and had only made a distance of about nine hundred miles. Necessity began to whisper to us that a still further reduction of our allowance must take place or else we must abandon altogether the hopes of reaching the land and rely wholly on the chance of being taken up by a vessel.

How to reduce the daily quantity of food with any regard for life itself was a question of the utmost consequence. Upon our first leaving the wreck, the demands of the stomach had been circumscribed to the smallest possible measure. Subsequently, before reaching the island, there had been a diminution in this already pitiable ration of nearly one half, and it was now, from a reasonable calculation, necessary to curtail even that at least one half again, which must, in a short time, reduce us to mere skeletons again.

We had a full allowance of water, but it only served to contribute to our debility, as our bodies derived only the scanty support which an ounce and a half of bread for each man afforded. It required a great effort to bring matters to this dreadful alternative: either to feed our bodies—and our hopes—a little longer or, in the agonies of hunger, to seize upon or devour our provisions and then coolly to await the approach of death.

We were as yet just able to move about in our boat and to slowly perform the necessary labours appertaining to her. But we were fast wasting away with the relaxing effects of the water, and we daily almost perished under the torrid rays of a meridian sun, to escape from which, we would lie down in the bottom of the boat, cover ourselves over with the sails, and abandon her to the mercy of the waves. Upon attempting to rise again, the blood would rush into the head, and an intoxicating blindness would come over us—almost to occasion our suddenly falling down again. A slight interest was still kept up in our minds by the distant hopes of yet meeting with the other boats, but it was never realized.

An accident occurred at night, which gave me a great cause of uneasiness and led me to an unpleasant rumination upon the probable consequences of a repetition of it. I had lain down in the boat without taking the usual precaution of securing the lid of the provision chest, when one of the men awoke me and informed me that one of his companions had taken some bread from it.

I felt at the moment the highest indignation and resentment at such conduct in any of our crew. I immediately took my pistol in my hand and charged the man, if he had taken bread, to give it up without the least hesitation or I should instantly shoot him! He became at once very much alarmed and, trembling, confessed the fact, pleading the hard necessity that urged him to it. He appeared to be very penitent for his crime and earnestly swore that he would never be guilty of it again. I could not find it in my soul to extend towards him the least severity on this account, however much, according to the strict imposition which we felt upon ourselves, it might demand. This was the first infraction; and the security of our lives and our hopes of redemption from our sufferings loudly called for a prompt and signal punishment, but every humane feeling of nature plead in his behalf. He was permitted to escape with the solemn injunction that a repetition of the same offense would cost him his life.

I had almost determined upon this occurrence to divide our provisions and give to each man his share of the whole stock. I should have done so in the height of my resentment had it not been for the reflection that some might, by imprudence, be tempted to consume it all at once and bring on a premature weakness or starvation. This would of course disable them for the duties of the boat and reduce our chances of safety and deliverance.

On the *15th of January*, at night, a very large shark was observed swimming about us in a most ravenous manner. He made attempts every now and then upon different parts of the boat, as if he would devour the very wood with hunger. Several times he came and snapped at the steering oar and even at the sternpost. We tried in vain to stab him with a lance, but we were so weak as to be unable to make any impression upon his hard skin. He was so much larger than an ordinary shark and manifested such a fearless malignity as to make us afraid of him. Our utmost efforts, which were at first directed to kill him for prey, became in the end self-defense. Baffled, however, in all his hungry attempts upon us, he shortly made off.

The night of *January 18th* was a despairing time in our sufferings. Our minds were wrought up to the highest pitch of dread and apprehension for our fate, and in them all was dark, gloomy, and confused. About eight o'clock, the terrible noise of whale spouts near us sounded in our ears. We could distinctly hear the furious thrashing of their tails in the water, and our weak minds pictured their appalling and hideous aspects. One of my companions, a black man, took an immediate fright and solicited me to take out the oars and to endeavour to get away from them. I consented to his using any means for that purpose, but, alas, it was wholly out of our power to raise a single arm in our own defense. Two or three of the whales came down near us and went swiftly off across our stern, blowing and spouting at a terrible rate; however, after an hour or two they disappeared, and we saw no more of them.

January 20th. The black man, Richard Peterson, manifested today symptoms of a speedy dissolution. For the last three days he had been lying, utterly dispirited and broken down, between the seats in the boat, without being able to do the least duty or hardly to place his hand to his head. This morning he had made up his mind to die rather than to endure further misery. He refused his allowance of bread, said he was sensible of his approaching end and was perfectly ready to die. In a few minutes he became speechless. The breath appeared to be leaving his body without producing the least pain. At four o'clock he was gone.

I had, two days previously, conversations with him on the subject of religion, on which he reasoned very sensibly and with much composure. He begged me to let his wife know his fate if ever I reached home in safety. The next morning we committed him to the sea, in latitude 35° 07' south, longitude 105° 46' west.

The wind prevailed to the eastward until the *24th of January*, when it again fell calm. We were now in a most wretched and sinking state of debility, hardly able to crawl around the boat and possessing but strength enough to convey our scanty morsel to our mouths. . . .

One ounce and a half of bread, which was to serve us all day, was in some cases greedily devoured, as if life was to continue but another moment. At other times, it was hoarded up and eaten crumb by crumb, at regular intervals during the day, as if it was to last us forever. To add to our calamities, boils began to break out upon us, and our imaginations shortly became as diseased as our bodies.

I lay down at night to catch a few moments of oblivious sleep, and immediately my starving fancy was at work. I dreamt of being placed near a splendid and rich repast, where there was everything that the most finicky appetite could desire, and I contemplated the moment in which we were to commence to eat with enraptured feelings of delight. Just as I was about to partake of it, I suddenly awoke to the cold realities of my miserable situation. Nothing could have oppressed me so much. It set such a longing frenzy for victuals in my mind that I felt as if I could have wished the dream to continue forever, as if I never might have awoke from it. I cast a sort of vacant stare about the boat until my eyes rested upon a bit of tough cowhide, which was fastened to one of the oars. I eagerly seized it and commenced to chew it, but there was no substance in it, and it only served to fatigue my weak jaws and add to my bodily pains.

My fellow sufferers murmured very much the whole time and continued to press me continually with questions upon the probability of our reaching land again. I kept constantly rallying my spirits to enable me to afford them comfort. I encouraged them to bear up against all evils and—if we must perish—to die in our own cause and not weakly distrust the providence of the Almighty by giving ourselves up to despair. I reasoned with them and told them that we would not die sooner by keeping up our hopes and that the dreadful sacrifices and privations we endured were to preserve us from death. These were not to be put in competition with the price with which we set upon our lives, or with their value to our families. It was, besides, unmanly to repine at what neither admitted of alleviation nor cure. Withal, it was our solemn duty to recognize in our calamities an overruling Divinity, by Whose mercy we might be suddenly snatched from peril. We must rely upon Him alone.

The three following days, the 25th, 26th, and 27th, were not distinguished by any particular circumstances. The wind still prevailed in the eastward and, by its obduracy, almost tore the very hopes of our hearts away. It was impossible to silence the rebellious repinings of our nature at witnessing such a succession of hard fortune against us. It was our cruel lot not to have had one bright anticipation realized—nor one wish of our thirsting souls gratified. We had, at the end of these three days, been urged to the southward as far as latitude 36°, into a chilly region where rains and squalls prevailed. We now calculated to tack and stand back to the northward. After much labour, we got our boat about, and so great was the fatigue attending this small exertion of our bodies that we all gave up for a moment and abandoned her to her own course. Not one of us had now strength sufficient to steer or, indeed, to make one single effort towards getting the sails properly trimmed to enable us to make any headway. After an hour or two of rest, during which the horrors of our situation came upon us with a despairing force and effect, we made a sudden effort and got our sails into such a disposition that the boat would steer herself. We then threw ourselves down, awaiting the issue of time to bring us relief or to take us from the scene of our troubles. We could now do nothing more. Strength and spirits were totally gone. . . .

January 28th. Our spirits this morning were hardly sufficient to allow of our enjoying a change of the wind, which took place to the westward. It has nearly become indifferent to us from what quarter it blew. Nothing but the slight chance of meeting with a vessel remained to us now. It was this narrow comfort alone that prevented me from lying down at once to die. Only fourteen days' stinted allowance of provisions remained. It was absolutely necessary, however, to increase the quantity of it to enable us to live five days longer. We therefore partook of it as pinching necessity demanded and gave ourselves wholly up to the guidance and disposal of our Creator.

During the *29th* and *30th of January* the wind continued west, and we made considerable progress until the *31st*, when it again came from ahead and prostrated all our hopes. On the *1st of February* it changed again to the westward and on the *2nd* and *3rd* blew to the eastward. It was light and variable until the *8th of February*.

Our sufferings were now drawing to a close. A terrible death appeared shortly to await us. Hunger became violent and outrageous, and we prepared for a speedy release from our troubles. Our speech and reason were both considerably impaired, and we were reduced at this time to being certainly the most helpless and wretched of the whole human race.

Isaac Cole, one of our crew, had the day before this, in a fit of despair, thrown himself down in the boat, determined to calmly wait there for death. It was obvious that he had no chance. All was dark, he said, in his mind. Not a single ray of hope was left for him to dwell upon, and it was folly and madness to be struggling against what appeared so palpably to be our fixed and settled destiny. I remonstrated with him as effectually as the weakness both of my body and my understanding would allow. What I said appeared, for a moment, to have a considerable effect. He made a powerful and sudden effort, half rose up, crawled forward and hoisted the jib, and firmly and loudly cried that he would not give up, that he would live as long as the rest of us.

But, alas, this effort was but the hectic fever of the moment, and he shortly again relapsed into a state of melancholy and despair. This day his reason was attacked, and about nine o'clock in the morning, he became a most miserable spectacle of madness. He spoke incoherently about everything, calling loudly for a napkin and water, and then—lying stupidly and senselessly down in the boat again—closed his hollow eyes, as if in death.

About ten o'clock, we suddenly perceived that he had become speechless. We got him, as well as we were able, upon a board, which was placed on one of the seats of the boat, and after covering him up with some old clothes, we left him to his fate.

He lay in the greatest pain and apparent misery, groaning piteously until four o'clock in the afternoon, when he died in the most horrid and frightful convulsions I ever witnessed. We kept his corpse all night. In the morning my two companions began, as a matter of course, to make preparations to dispose of it in the sea when, having reflected on the subject all night, I addressed them on the painful subject of keeping the body for food! Our provisions could not possibly last us beyond three days. Within this time it was not in any degree probable that we should find relief from our sufferings, and, accordingly, hunger would at last drive us to the necessity of casting lots. It was without any objection agreed to, and we set to work as fast as we were able to prepare the body so as to prevent its spoiling. We separated the limbs from the body and cut all the flesh from the bones, after which we opened the body, took out the heart, closed it again—sewing it up as decently as we could—and then committed it to the sea.

We now first commenced to satisfy the immediate cravings of nature from the heart, which we eagerly devoured. We then ate sparingly of a few pieces of the flesh, after which we hung up the remainder, cut in thin strips, about the boat to dry in the sun. We made a fire and roasted some of it to serve us during the next day.

In this manner did we dispose of our fellow sufferer, the painful recollection of which brings to mind, at this moment, some of the most disagreeable and revolting ideas that it is capable of conceiving. We knew not then to whose lot it would fall next either to die or to be shot and eaten like the poor wretch we had just dispatched. Humanity must shudder at the dreadful recital. I have no language to paint the anguish of our souls in this dreadful dilemma.

The next morning, the *10th of February*, we found that the flesh had become tainted and had turned a greenish colour. We concluded to make a fire and cook it at once to prevent its becoming so putrid as not to be eatable at all. We, accordingly, did so and, by that means, preserved it for six or seven days longer. Our bread during the time remained untouched. As that would not be liable to spoil, we placed it carefully aside for the last moments of our trial.

About three o'clock this afternoon, *February 10th*, a strong breeze set in from the northwest, and we made very good progress, considering that we were compelled to steer the boat by the sails alone. This wind continued until the *13th*, when it changed again ahead.

We contrived to keep soul and body together by sparingly partaking of our flesh, which was cut up in small pieces and eaten with salt water. By the *14th*, our bodies became so far recruited as to enable us to make a few attempts at guiding our boat again with the oar. By each taking his turn, we managed to steer it and make a tolerably good course.

On the *15th* our flesh was all consumed. We were driven to the last morsel of bread, consisting of two cakes. Our limbs had, for the last two days, swelled very much and now began to pain us most excessively. We were still, as near as we could judge, three hundred miles from land, with but three days of our allowance on hand. The hope of a continuation of the wind, which came out of the west this morning, was the only comfort and solace that remained to us. So strong had our desires at last become in respect to the wind that a high fever and a longing had set in our veins, which nothing but its continuation could satisfy. Matters with us were now at their height. All hope was cast upon the breeze, and we tremblingly and fearfully awaited its progress and the dreadful development of our destiny.

On the *17th*, in the afternoon, a heavy cloud appeared to be setting down in an east by north direction from us, which, in my view, indicated the vicinity of some land. This I took for the island of Más Afuera. I concluded it could be no other; and immediately upon this reflection, the life blood began to flow again briskly in my veins. I told my companions that I was well convinced it was land, and, if so, we should in all probability reach it before two days more.

My words appeared to comfort my companions much. By repeated assurances of the favourable appearance of things, their spirits acquired even a degree of elasticity that was truly astonishing. The dark features of our distress began now to diminish a little and the countenance, even amid the gloomy bodings of our hard lot, to assume a much fresher hue. We directed our course for the cloud, and our progress that night was extremely good.

The next morning, before daylight, Thomas Nickerson—a boy about fifteen years of age and one of my two companions who had thus far survived with me—lay down after having bailed the boat, drew a piece of canvas over himself, and cried out that he then wished to die immediately. I saw that he had given up, and I attempted to speak a few words of comfort and encouragement to him. I endeavoured to persuade him that it was a great weakness, and even a wickedness to abandon a reliance upon the Almighty while the least hope and breath of life remained. But he felt unwilling to listen to any of the consolatory suggestions which I made to him, and he insisted— notwithstanding the extreme probability which I stated there was of our gaining the land before the end of two days more—upon lying down and giving himself up to despair.

A fixed look of settled and forsaken despondency came over his face. He lay for some time silent, sullen, and sorrowful. I felt at once certain that the coldness of death was fast gathering upon him. There was a sudden and unaccountable earnestness in his manner that alarmed me and made me fear that I myself might unexpectedly be overtaken by a like weaknes of nature, which would bereave me at once of both reason and life. But Providence willed it otherwise.

At about seven o'clock this morning, *February 18th*, while I was lying asleep, my companion who was steering suddenly and loudly called out: *"There's a sail!"*

I know not what was the first movement I made upon hearing such an unexpected cry. The earliest of my recollections is that immediately I stood up and gazed in a state of abstraction and ecstasy upon the blessed vision of a vessel about seven miles off from us. She was standing in the same direction with us, and the only sensation I felt at the moment was that of a violent and unaccountable impulse to fly directly towards her. I do not believe it is possible to form a just conception of the pure, strong feelings and the unmingled emotions of joy and gratitude that took possession of my mind on this occasion. The boy, too, took a sudden and animated start from his despondency and stood up to witness the probable instrument of his salvation.

Our only fear now was that she would not discover us or that we might not be able to intercept her course. However, we immediately put our boat—as well as we were able—in a direction to cut her off and found, to our great joy, that we sailed faster than she did. Upon observing us, she shortened sail and allowed us to come up to her. The captain hailed us and asked who we were.

I told him we were from a wreck, and he cried out immediately for us to come alongside the ship. I made an effort to assist myself along to the side, for the purpose of getting up, but strength failed me altogether, and I found it impossible to move a step further without help.

We must have formed at that moment, in the eyes of the captain and his crew, a most deplorable and affecting picture of suffering and misery. Our cadaverous countenances, sunken eyes, and bones just starting through the skin—with the ragged remnants of clothes stuck about our sunburnt bodies—must have produced an appearance to him affecting and revolting in the highest degree. The sailors commenced to remove us from our boat, and we were comfortably provided for in every respect. In a few minutes we were permitted to taste of a little thin food, made from tapioca, and in a few days, with prudent management, we were considerably recruited.

Our rescue vessel proved to be the brig *Indian*, Captain William Crozier of London, to whom we are indebted for every polite, friendly, and attentive disposition towards us that can possibly characterize a man of humanity and feeling. We were taken up in latitude 33° 45' south, longitude 81° 03' west. At twelve o'clock on this same day, we saw the island of Más Afuera, and on the *25th of February*, we arrived at Valparaiso in utter distress and poverty. Our wants were promptly relieved there.

Captain Pollard and the lone survivors of his boat's crew were taken up by the American whaleship *Dauphin*, Captain Zimri Coffin of Nantucket. They arrived at Valparaiso on the following *17th of March*. They had been taken up in latitude 37° south off the island of St. Mary. The third boat got separated from the captain on the 28th of January and has not been heard of since.

The names of all the survivors are as follows: Captain George Pollard, Junior, Charles Ramsdell, Owen Chase, Benjamin Lawrence, and Thomas Nickerson, all of Nantucket. There died in the captain's boat the following: Brazilla Ray of Nantucket, Owen Coffin of the same place, who was shot, and Samuel Reed, a black.

The captain relates that after being separated from us, as herein before stated, they continued to make what progress they could towards the Juan Fernández Islands as was agreed upon. But contrary winds and the extreme debility of the crew prevailed against their united exertions. He was, like ourselves, equally surprised and concerned at the separation that took place between us, but continued on his course, almost confident of meeting with us again.

On the *14th of January* the whole stock of provisions belonging to the second mate's boat was entirely exhausted. On the *25th*, the black man, Lawson Thomas, died and was eaten by his surviving companions. On the *21st*, the captain and his crew were in the like dreadful situation with respect to their provisions. On the *23rd* another coloured man, Charles Shorter, died, and his body was shared for food between the crews of both boats. On the *27th*, Isaiah Shepherd, a black man, died in the third boat, and on the *28th*, another black named Samuel Reed died out of the captain's boat. The bodies of these men constituted their only food while it lasted.

On the *28th of January*, owing to the darkness of the night and want of sufficient power to manage their boats, those of the captain and the second mate separated in latitude 35° south, longitude 100° west. On the *1st of February*, having consumed their last morsel, the captain and the three other men that remained with him were reduced to the necessity of casting lots. It fell upon Owen Coffin to die. With great fortitude and resignation, he submitted to his fate. They drew lots to see who should shoot him. He placed himself firmly to receive his death and was immediately shot by Charles Ramsdell, whose hard fortune it was to become his executioner.

On the *11th*, Brazilla Ray died. The captain and Charles Ramsdell, the only two that were then left, subsisted on the two bodies until the morning of the *23rd of February*, when they fell in with the ship *Dauphin*, as before stated, and were snatched from impending destruction.

Every assistance and attentive resource of humanity was bestowed upon them by Captain Coffin, to whom Captain Pollock acknowledged every grateful obligation. Upon making known the fact—that three of our companions had been left at Ducie Island—to the captain of the U.S. frigate *Constellation*, which lay at Valparaiso when we arrived, that officer said he should immediately take measures to have them taken off.

On the *11th of June* following, I arrived at Nantucket in the whaleship *Eagle*, Captain William H. Coffin. My family had received the most distressing account of our shipwreck and had given me up for lost. My unexpected appearance was welcomed with the most grateful obligations and acknowledgements to a beneficent Creator, who had guided me through darkness, trouble, and death, once more to the bosom of my country and friends.

FOUR YEARS IN THE ARCTIC

She was soon alongside, when the mate in command addressed us, by presuming that we had met with some misfortune and lost our ship. This being answered in the affirmative, I requested to know the name of his vessel, and expressed our wish to be taken on board. I was answered that it was the "*Isabella of Hull, once commanded by Captain Ross;*" on which I stated that I was the identical man in question, and my people the crew of the *Victory*. That the mate, who commanded this boat, was as much astonished at this information as he appeared to be, I do not doubt; while, with the usual blunderheadedness of men on such occasions, he assured me that I had been dead two years. I easily convinced him, however, that what ought to have been true, according to his estimate, was a somewhat premature conclusion; as the bear-like form of the whole set of us might have shown him, had he taken time to consider, that we were certainly not whaling gentlemen, and that we carried tolerable evidence of our being "true men, and no impostors," on our backs, and in our starved and unshaven countenances.

– from John Ross's Narrative

The Ottoman conquest of the Middle East in the mid-fifteenth century blocked the traditional land passage to Asia and ushered in the Age of Discovery as explorers searched for new maritime trade routes between Europe and the Orient. After Christopher Columbus "discovered" the Americas in 1492 and Portuguese explorer Vasco de Gama sailed eastward around Africa in 1498, Ferdinand Magellan made the passage around the Horn of South America in 1521 and reached across the Pacific to the East Indies.

Perhaps the greatest of England's early polar navigators and discoverers, William Baffin sailed in 1615 as pilot under Captain Robert Bylot in *Discovery*. Admired centuries later for his astonishingly accurate tidal and astronomical measurements, Baffin carefully charted the Hudson Strait on his first voyage. In 1617, again as pilot of *Discovery*, he navigated through the Davis Strait into Baffin Bay and discovered the straits—Lancaster, Jones, and Smith—that radiate from its head, sailing more than three hundred miles beyond Davis' furthermost northern reach, a record that remained unsurpassed until the 1850s. But Baffin's remarkable voyages also marked a limit to the frustrated hopes of discovering a Northwest Passage and his discoveries fell into doubt until Captain John Ross reconfirmed them in the course of his first voyage two centuries later.

In 1804 Lord Melville appointed the brilliant Sinologist and diplomat John Barrow to serve as second secretary to the Admiralty, a post in which Barrow flourished for forty years under eleven chief lords who served during his tenure. At the conclusion of the Napoleonic Wars, Barrow actively promoted efforts to resolve the riddle of the Northwest Passage. Buoyed by victory in Europe and the bright prospects of burgeoning Empire, the prevailing mood in Britain was optimistic as the Admiralty launched the first of a sustained series of attempts to open this vital sea route to the East. The best candidate for the expedition—the brilliant and experienced whaling captain William Scoresby—was discarded in the imperative favor of selecting a candidate from among serving British naval officers, and the choice fell to two candidates, Commander John Ross and Lieutenant William Edward Parry. Unlike Scoresby, neither had any Arctic experience, but the brusque and independently-minded Scot, John Ross, had long experience of service in the Baltic with the Swedish navy and was thus selected over Barrow's preference, the younger, more pious, and more ingratiating Parry, who was named second in command of the 1818 expedition, which set out on April 21st of that year in the *Isabella* and the *Alexander*.

Although Ross had been expected to bivouac in the Arctic and to spend two seasons there, he turned his ships around and sailed back to England in November of 1818. The expedition had recorded many scientific observations and had rediscovered the northern reaches of Baffin Bay, but Ross had failed to explore Lancaster Sound and upon his return was judged to have discovered nothing "new" of any worth, so, ultimately, Barrow had his way and Parry was entrusted with the next two voyages of exploration for the Northwest Passage (1819–20, and 1824–25, both in the *Fury* and the *Hecla*). Aided by rare favorable weather in 1819, Parry transited Lancaster Sound and pierced through Barrow Strait, advancing to Melville Island where his party wintered. The following summer, however, ice blocked significant further progress to the west and Parry, almost trapped in the ice-choked seas, was forced to turn back to England, where he and his party were greeted as heroes. In the voyage of 1824–1825, Parry sought a passage through the Prince Regent Inlet. But conditions were much harsher on this voyage than the previous. Ice impeded Parry's progress and crushed the *Fury* during the second summer, forcing Parry to abandon most of the ship's stores on Somerset Island after a desperate effort to save her. Parry narrowly escaped the grip of the ice in the *Hecla* to return empty-handed to England with the *Fury's* crew crowded aboard.

If the costly failure of Parry's second voyage had cooled the Admiralty's ardor to send out another expedition in search of a Northwest Passage, it was for John Ross an inducement to emerge from years of chaffing exile in Scotland to restore his tarnished honor. When the Admiralty quickly dismissed his proposal to take a steam-powered ship to the Arctic, Ross turned to a friend, gin-magnate Felix Booth, under whose generous sponsorship Ross's second expedition set out in *Victory* in the early summer of 1829. Despite problems with a fickle steam engine that proved more an impediment than an aid, Ross and his small party—with the blessing of superb weather—made excellent progress under sail, reaching Fury Beach on Somerset Island on August 12th. Frustrated in his first attempts to make landfall there, Ross explored Creswell Bay to the south before returning and finally managing to secure an anchorage and replenish the *Victory's* stores with those which Parry had salvaged from the wreck of the *Fury* four summers beforehand. Ross then sailed far to the south, three hundred miles beyond Parry's furthest point. But at the end of September the expedition's good fortune was transformed into a trap of stormy weather and seas suddenly choked with dangerous ice pack. Finally securing a safe harbor, Ross and his men settled in for the winter, not knowing that four winters would pass before the ice would loosen its grip and they could seek freedom.

By April of 1832, with supplies running short, Ross had concluded that his party would never be able to escape in the icebound *Victory*. His small band would have to make the arduous overland journey overland to Fury Beach where the remnant of Parry's stores would offer them a slim margin of survival and he and his men would have a chance to reach help in the three smaller boats that were there. In April of 1832 they began the effort of sledging supplies and men forward in stages, finally scuttling and abandoning the *Victory* on May 29th. Exhausted and famished, the men reached Fury Beach on July 1st, only to find the sea still blocked by ice. The ice finally cleared a month later and Ross and his men were able to make a tortured advance to the northern tip of Somerset Island, only to find further progress barred. Forced to haul up their boats at the furthest point of their advance, their only hope was to return to Fury Beach by land, survive another dreadful winter in a makeshift shelter, and again attempt to free themselves the following summer.

Selections from the final chapters of Captain John Ross' account of the four-year ordeal of his party—of their last harsh winter, of the last stages of their struggle for life, and of their suspenseful rescue—are presented as a unique record of stoicism and grim endurance. An old-school disciplinarian, aloof and sometimes at odds with his men, Ross managed to lead them to freedom against impossible odds. As it happened, it was the *Isabella*—the very ship that Ross had commanded on his ill-regarded first voyage—that rescued Ross and his men and returned them to England where they had long been given up as dead.

Although Captain John Ross would never succeed in pleasing John Barrow and others at the Admiralty, his expedition was undoubtedly a significant scientific success as well as a human triumph, and he and his men were lionized in society. He died in 1856. Roald Amundsen finally made the Northwest Passage in 1906 after a harrowing three-year voyage in the forty-seven-ton *Gjöa*.

Four Years in the Arctic

from *Narrative of a second voyage in search of a north-west passage, and of a residence in the Arctic regions during the years 1829, 1830, 1831, 1832, 1833*. By Sir John Ross . . . Including reports of . . . James Clark Ross . . . and the discovery of the northern magnetic pole. London, A. W. Webster, 1835.

Summary of September 1832: Anxious as the preceding months had been, owing to the impending prospect of our deliverance from that miserable country in which we had been so long imprisoned, and to the difficulties which had beset our attempts to extricate ourselves, the present one had passed in even greater anxiety, and had been a period of more frequent and more provoking disappointment. Yet we found some occupation for our minds, serving at least to divert our attention from the painful part of our prospects and the vexatious difficulties that were ever recurring, in the discussions among us, which, however frequent they had recently been, had now, very naturally, become more persistent and more energetic.

These also were occasionally sources of amusement, deficient as we were in all others; since we could extract this, even from the acrimony which these disputes often engendered; while we were all too intent on one great object to disagree long about the collateral circumstances under which it was to be attained. Nor was it a small advantage that these debates served to keep up our spirits: the sanguine, in the heat of their arguments, magnifying our prospects of success, as happens in all disputes, and the timid and desponding thus gaining some courage, and admitting some brighter gleams of hope, from the very speculations and anticipations which they were opposing.

Each of our three tents thus formed a kind of separate deliberative party, or a little society; in two of which, the opinions of the leader was that of his men also, while the collision of views lay thus between these different bodies. Among them, Commander Ross[1], who had always been the most sanguine, was still the leader of the hopeful, at least nearly up to this time, whatever doubts might have arisen in his mind during the after days of this attempt. The contrary opinion prevailed in the party of Mr. Thom, whose estimable qualities in all other points were not accompanied by that spirit of confidence which

[1] James Clark Ross, Ross' nephew

141

belongs in general to a period of life which my excellent friend had passed. My own tent alone was one of divided opinions; and it afforded, therefore, the greater opportunities for these discussions; while I presume I need not now say what was the extent of my own confidence. . . .

But it was my wish (I believed it my best policy) to conceal my opinions, and to interfere with none of their debates; and thus, not only to see what their several tempers were on this subject, but, as might happen, to profit by that knowledge.

These views and feelings, however, underwent some changes during the time that we were making this often doubtful and always difficult progress. Within the last days of the month, Commander Ross seemed to have more than hesitated respecting our escape; and, on the twentieth, I must needs say, with whatever regret, I began myself to question whether we should succeed in passing the barrier of ice this season; in which case, there could be no resource for us but another winter, another year, I should say, on Fury beach; if, indeed, it should be the fortune of anyone to survive after another such year as the three last.

If it was the fruitless attempt to cross the strait on the twentieth which had brought my mind to this state of feeling, the effect was not to be indulged; nor did my opinions tend in any degree to alter my resolution as to our conduct, or rather as to my own, respecting the men under my charge. While there was the remotest chance for us, it was my duty to persevere, as far and as long at least as I should be justified by the state of our provisions: since, if we should be obliged to leave our boats at the furthest point where we could succeed in placing them, we should be obliged to travel back, eighty miles, over a road so rugged that it would necessarily occupy a very long time, and induce a great consumption of our stores; which we could not afford to have increased beyond what we had actually taken, from the great labour of transport and our very limited means of carriage.

The circumstances in which we were now placed, served also to prove another point bearing essentially on my voyage of 1818, and on the discussions to which it afterwards gave rise. The fact, indeed, was but too surely proved for our safety or hopes: it would have been far better for us at present, had that been false which I had asserted to have been then true; had Barrow's strait been incapable of freezing, had it never been, and was never to be, frozen over; as had been most confidently asserted of late.

It was now frozen, or at least had hitherto been so, during the preceding winter and the present summer, even up to this time, into a solid sea, from Admiralty inlet to Croker's inlet; and this is precisely what I found it to be in 1818. I have equally little doubt, from the state of things with us during all the years of our present detention, that this had been its condition during the whole period; while there are even proofs of this, in the endeavours of the whalers to penetrate into Lancaster strait, and in the failures which they experienced.

. . . Thence it was, that when we arrived off Lancaster sound on the thirty-first of August, the pack of ice was still to the northward of it; while that on the south side was, beyond all doubt, in the same state that we now found it, forming a solid unbroken mass, stretching from side to side of the strait, which neither ship nor boat could penetrate.

During the last days of our detention in this place, when, in addition to what we believed the impossibility of succeeding in our attempt to leave this country, it had further become doubtful whether the state of the ice would allow us to return to Fury beach, or even to surmount a small part of the way to this only hope that remained for us, our situation had become truly serious, not simply critical. We had fixed on the twenty-fifth of September for our departure, should the sledges then be ready, and, from that date we had but ten days' provisions left, at half allowance, while we had not fuel enough remaining to melt the snow which would be required for our consumption of water. Thus did our arrival at Batty bay turn out to be a most providential circumstance, as there were, from this point, butthirty-two miles of direct distance remaining; a line which all the intri-cacies and obstructions of the route could well increase to more than forty.

At this time it was, that we began to experience the greatest sufferings we had yet endured from the cold. We had been unable to carry with us our usual quantity of clothes and of canvas, so that we were most in want of protection from the weather when we were least able to bear up against its severity. There was not now the employment that would have aided us to resist it, by keeping us in action; and perhaps, still worse, the diminution of our hopes during the latter days of this month tended to diminish that energy of the system by which, assuredly, the animal heat is maintained. Be all this as it may, we were really very cold, and very miserable; and from what I have formerly said of my own constitution, I have reason to believe, that whatever my own sufferings may have been, every one of the party was much more miserably cold than myself. The prospect before us, in the case of being obliged to return, was even worse; unless indeed the excess of our labours in the expected journey, with the conviction that there was an object, and a home, such as that was, in view, should enable us to accomplish this undertaking.

During the latter part of this month our success in procuring foxes and ptarmigans had been considerable; and while our whole party was not so large as to prevent this supply from being of real use, so did it form a valuable addition, both in quantity and quality, to our much too scanty stock of provisions. There was great reason to dread the effect of a narrowed diet on the men: not merely on their health or strength, but on their very lives. All of us had already suffered from this at various times; but the chances of irremediable evil were increasing every day.

A review of the weather showed this to have been the coldest September which we had recorded: a fact which I attributed to the permanence and proximity of the great bodies of ice and snow which surrounded us, and especially to the total want of that open sea which has always such influence on the temperature. This month had been noted for the tranquillity of the winds, and thence was there no cause adequate to the disruption of the ice. The whole land also, ever since the middle of August, had been entirely covered with snow, so that, but for the appearance of the sun, every thing bore the aspect of deep winter.

Summary of October 1832: The month of October in this year surpassed all others for cold and stormy weather; there being only six days moderate. Our journey from Batty bay, which was accomplished in four days, was exceedingly laborious, and from the nature of the weather, very trying to all the men; but had we been obliged to walk all the way from our furthest position, the journey would have been fatal to some, if not to all of us, since we should have been overtaken by the storm of the ninth. We therefore felt very thankful that we had been so mercifully permitted to reach even this cold and dreary spot in safety.

Having constructed our house previously was also a very providential circumstance; for, defective as it was, it could not have been so nearly well done at this season; and indeed before it could have been done at all, we must have suffered severely; but what we had most reason to be thankful for is the store of provisions still left, now sufficient to last and maintain us for another season; and when we reflected on the various circumstances which have as it were

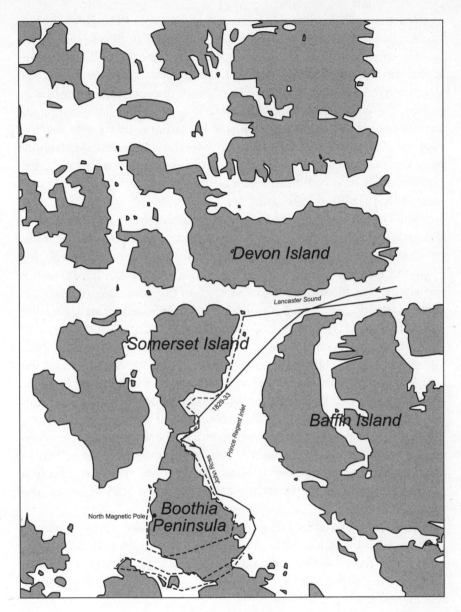

John Ross and James Clark Ross, 1929-33

exerted themselves to prolong our lives, we cannot but offer up our humble acknowledgements to the Great Disposer of events.

First, I may enumerate the loss of the *Fury*, by which accident the stores and provisions were left: next, the mutiny of the *John's* crew, for if that ship had come with us, we intended to have cleared Fury beach: thirdly, the engine boilers, without which, we might have got so far that we could not have returned: fourthly, the *Fury's* boats, after having been carried off in the storms of the winter; having been cast on shore near the same place, without any material damage: and lastly, the construction of a habitation in summer, to which we were now mercifully permitted to return.

Mr. Thom now inspected and took an account of the remains of the provisions; namely, of the flour, sugar, soups, peas, vegetables, pickles, and lemon-juice, which were in abundance; though we regretted to find, that of the present preserved meats, there was not more than would suffice for our voyage in the boats during the next season, together with half a pound additional on Sundays, and the same on Thursdays.

With respect to the present rations, the men were allowed, alternately, pea-soup, with one made of carrots and turnips, out of the stores of the *Fury*. Instead of bread, which we could not now finish to a sufficient extent, they were provided with dumplings of flour and water, and they had no reason to be dissatisfied with this compulsory substitute. They were, indeed, sufficiently fed, since it was observed that they had become in much better condition since our return to this place. Our present allowance in meat, indeed, was a pound in a day: while it was settled that the short rations would begin on the first of November.

The storms of this month, by breaking up the ice in Prince Regent's inlet, and driving it down Baffin's bay, must have been of great service; but the low temperature was against us. Taylor, Laughy, and J. Wood, were on the sick list. We began to keep regular watch, and register the thermometer every two hours.

Summary of November 1832: This month had been still more remarkable than the preceding, for the constant succession of storms by which it had been distinguished, and for being the only November on record in which the thermometer never rose above zero. The maximum was 4° minus, and the mean temperature not less than 19½° below that of the November in the last year; while it was 8° lower than that of the year before, and 15½° lower than in the November of 1824, at Port

Bowen. It was, however, higher than at Melville island, in 1819; though it must be remarked that this is in $2\frac{1}{2}°$ of latitude further north

The open water had been seen to a great extent during the gales of this month. It was with much difficulty that we succeeded in finishing our habitation. . . . During this very severe month, the men, not having clothing to withstand the cold, could seldom work in the open air; but we at length succeeded in making our house tolerably comfortable, so that the temperature inside was about 45°, excepting near the enclosing walls, where it was, of course, below the freezing point; as were our cabins. The men had each a bed place with a canvas bottom, and a thrummed mat for a bed; while in addition to a blanket each, we were about to make mats as further coverings.

Our system of feeding could not be changed, for want of means, whatever we might have wished; but the men did not seem to suffer, and there was no one on the sick list but Taylor, the lame mate, and Thomas, the carpenter; our prospects had not, indeed, been brightened by the aspect of the weather in this month; but we were all in endurable spirits, and the thankful were contented with the advantages which we enjoyed.

Summary of December 1832: In the course of this month it blew hard during most days, and always from the north and north-west; in consequence of which the ice was kept in violent motion. Open water was seen through all the month; and, on the last day of the year, it was visible from the beach as far as the eye could trace to the north-north-east.

The mean temperature of the month had been 1° below any on record; and the cold was very severely felt by us in our frozen habitation; but by increasing the mass of ice and snow on the outside, and by flooring the house, we made it more comfortable. Half a dozen foxes were taken, and afforded us an excellent meal on Sundays and on Christmas-day; which was the first that we had spent without tasting spirits or wine: these luxuries having been now utterly ex-hausted, as they had long been set apart for those periods of regale, which a seaman does not easily resign, and ought not to be allowed to forget.

The aurora borealis had been seen but seldom, and was inconspicuous, while its position was generally opposed to that of the sun. But to end with the summary of this month, the weather, variable and severe as it had been, became calm and clear, though cold, and thus did we terminate the month of December, and the year 1832.

Summary of January 1833: This month began and continued for ten days, with such severity that it promised to be the coldest on record. It improved, however, about the middle, so that the mean temperature was 30° minus, while the extremes were minus 4° and minus 44°. Nevertheless, our habitation was very cold and miserable; while, on attempting to warm ourselves on one side, we were frozen on the opposite, and were otherwise more than enough wearied, from the want of books or other occupation, and the impossibility of taking exercise out of doors. The crew, with the exceptions formerly noticed, were not ailing: but, of the carpenter's recovery, there was no hope.

. . . The chief event was the death of the carpenter, Thomas; which, apart from any regret for a worthy and useful man, the more painful when we looked round on all, saw the decided illness of some, and could not easily avoid anticipating what our own fate might be, was a very serious loss; since his assistance could scarcely fail to be required hereafter, in the reparation of the boats, and in such other matters that belonged to his profession. Respecting himself, I need only note the excellent character he had acquired, in the navy, before he joined us: but, to compensate any pain that might have been felt under the impression that this expedition might have been fatal to him, we knew that his constitution had been much impaired by long service, especially on the American lakes and in the Burmese war. His age was forty-eight; and at that time of life, a seaman who has served much is an aged man, if he does not chance to be worn out.

My own condition, from the state of ancient wounds, brought into troublesome action by that tendency to scurvy which displayed itself in no other very marked way, was, at this time, somewhat threatening. I had now, indeed, some reason to suppose that I might not be ultimately able to surmount all the present circumstances; in which case, I know not that my anxiety for the fate of those who might not have very well guided themselves when I was no longer present to aid them, was not much greater than any thing which I felt on my own account.

The state of the ice could not have been worse than it was at the end of this month, and the hills were entirely covered with snow. It was so deep about the place of our compulsory residence, that our miserable abode was almost hidden by it, like the snow hut of an Esquimaux in winter. . . .

Summary of March 1833: The first eight days of March were unusually severe: the change on the ninth was great and sudden, but did not prove durable. The mean temperature thus became 20°, as the extremes had been from minus 45° to plus 5°. The gales were exceedingly severe, and the last, which was just before the equinox, continued during four days.

The men had, therefore, as in the preceding month, been extremely confined; and thus the impossibility of talking exercise, added to a want of sufficient employment, short allowance of food, and the inevitable lowness of spirits produced by the unbroken sight of this dull, melancholy, uniform, waste of snow and ice, combined to reduce us all to a state of very indifferent health. Mr. Thom was ill, my old wounds were very troublesome, and two of the seamen were so far gone in the scurvy, that we were afraid they would not recover.

On this account more than any other, we had reason to lament our ill success in shooting; as it was long, too, ere we could hope for the arrival of the summer birds, to allow us to add some fresh meat to our diet. We had taken but three foxes and two hares in the whole month; which, as food, amounted to nothing.

We were indeed all very weary of this miserable home. It had been a welcome one when we first reached it; because it was a contrast to what had been much worse. It had received us, fatigued, shelterless, and half-starved, and it at least promised us comparative peace and rest. But the novelty of this feeling had long been worn out; and, for a long time now, the days had been almost without variation or mark; duller than its predecessor, and the night returning only to tell us that another such day would come to-morrow. . . . If those of the least active minds dozed away their time in the waking stupefaction which such a state of things produces, they were the most fortunate of the party. Those among us, who had the enviable talent of sleeping at all times, where they were anxious or not, fared best.

. . . Another month would pass in the daily approaching prospect of moving: within one more, we might be in motion; and if June must still be a term of struggle and hopes, the month of July might find us in Baffin's bay.

Summary of April 1833: The last month was, on the whole, mild, being never less than 26° minus, nor higher than 19° plus; and the mean temperature was 4°, being four degrees above that at Port Bowen, and seven above that at *Victory* harbour in the same month of the last year.

We had succeeded in getting all of our provisions forward, containing our supply from the first of July to the end of September, and were thus eight miles, or a quarter of the distance, advanced towards the place of the boats in Batty bay. The transportation of them onwards to that depot was calculated to be work enough for the next month, because the parties would be compelled to travel the same ground eight times, so as to make the distance 256 miles.

The fat of the bears which we had killed was an addition of some moment to our food, as the skins had their own value. Five grouse had been killed; but not a snow bunting had yet been seen. One fox only had been taken.

The men were better, except one of the scorbutic patients, John Wood, who appeared to be in a hopeless state. The sun had produced a visible effect on the snow, which was now disappearing from the tops of the hills.

Summary of May 1833: The mean temperature of this month was lower by seven degrees than that at Port Bowen in 1824; it was 11° plus, and the extremes plus 25° and minus 3°. There had been no appearance of a thaw; the ice in the offing was as bad as ever, and the two or three gulls, with a few snow buntings that we saw, without one grouse, were but feeble signs of an advancing summer.

The fatigues of the men, of men and officers, since no one was exempted, were very great in the last twenty days of the month which our ever renewed travelling occupied; yet they had not materially suffered, though the sick continued no better.

Our allowance of provisions was as low as before, and the mode of distribution into meals the same; while the night had been made our day. The quantity of provisions that we had secured thus far on our road to the expected liberation, was sufficient to last us, on a two-thirds allowance, until the first of October

Summary of June 1833: In the beginning of June the prospect was exceedingly unfavourable, as the weather was very cold, and the temperature lower than in the preceding ones at the same period. It however improved, though there was very little rain during the time, and much snow. The extremes were 45° plus and 16° plus, and the mean plus 35°.

We had advanced the tents and some stores to the second position forwards; which, though but thirty miles off, required more than a hundred miles of travelling, from the necessity of returning to bring up the loads which we could not carry on to their places in any other manner. We were still, however, encumbered by the sick, who could not walk at all; while, unfortunately, they were the three heaviest men in the crew. Some others could barely walk, but could give no assistance in drawing the sledges. It was well that some appeared in good health; while all were now in hopes of a speedy embarkation, and of an ultimate escape from the miserable abode of people who had, on the whole, been sufficiently miserable in all ways.

(July 1 to 4) The wind and weather were variable during the first four days of July, but generally cold, with snow and sleet, while the thermometer at night scarcely ever rose above the freezing point. Our preserved meat was expended; and we had here, now, no other fresh animal food than what we could produce by our own guns; which was not much as yet, since it consisted but of a few ducks and dovekies. Some spare grates were made for the house, and the roof was repaired and strengthened, in case we should be obliged to return to it for the ensuing winter; though somewhat at a loss to know how we were to subsist under such an unfortunate event.

(July 5 & 6) A quantity of flannel cartridges were given to the men for repairing their clothes before encountering the journey to Batty bay. An avalanche of ice from the cliffs, intermixed with rocks and water, was a novel sight, and, in this dearth of events, would have been interesting, even had it been far less splendid as a spectacle. Falling into the sea, it carried all before it; breaking the flat ice to a great distance, and showing us, had that been now necessary, the manner in which the icebergs are now found to be covered with fragments of rock and layers of earth.

(July 7) The shooting of fifty dovekies yesterday gave the men a good Sunday's dinner; and the last divine service we trusted ever to attend in this house, was performed. It was the commencement of a farewell which all hoped would be eternal; but every one must answer for the feelings under which he, for the expected last time, repeated the Lord's prayer, and heard himself dismissed in those words which promise, those who deserve it, that peace which passes all understanding. . . .

(July 8) On Monday, every thing was ready, and we too were as prepared as we were anxious to quit this dreary place, as we hoped, for ever. Yet, with those hopes, there were mingled many fears; enough to render it still but too doubtful in all our minds whether we might not yet be compelled to return; to return once more to despair, and perhaps, to return but to die. . . . Scarcely the feeling of a farewell, for

hope or regret, for pain or for pleasure, was in any mind, when we coldly departed in the evening with our three sledges, to encounter such fate as Providence might have in store for us.

The sick, who formed our great difficulty, bore the first journey well, and we reached our first station before mid-day. It was a fine day, and the warmest that had yet occurred; the temperature being 48°. In the afternoon, at three, we proceeded again, with infinite toil, through nearly impassable way, which were rendered more difficult to us by the care which the sick required: and so hard was the labour, that even here, and at night, we were obliged to work in our shirts. We gained but two miles by midnight, and were glad to rest.

(July 10) We recommenced with all the baggage, labouring through ways as bad, or worse, under a sun that was occasionally very hot; and at nine, reached the third position, at the cascade, which was now pouring abundantly into a pool filled with kittiwakes; where we procured some sorrel. We found that the bears had upset a cask full of skins which we had left here, but they could not contrive to open it.

(July 11) On the next day we brought forward the sick, whom we could not move together with the baggage, and then proceeded to the third position, after a very fatiguing journey, backwards and forwards, of twenty-four miles. (July 12) We had lately obtained a good supply of dovekies, and could now afford every one a good breakfast; which was not less necessary than agreeable, emaciated as most of us were, and nevertheless compelled to endure this constant labour. In the afternoon, the road on the shore being better, we contrived to take most of our stores, the sick included: but it was not, finally, till after many difficulties in avoiding and traversing bad ice, that we reached the boats in Batty bay, at eight in the morning.

We found that the bears and foxes had committed considerable depredations on our stores, by destroying a cask of bread, some oil, and some sugar, and also all the leather shoes and boots they could find. The weather was very fine, and the dovekies being numerous, we killed some for our provision. Even at midnight the thermometer was now 48°: it was a great revolution in the weather, and it had been a sudden one; unexpected, but not undue.

(July 13) Two light sledges to-day brought up the few things which we had been obliged to leave at the last place, together with some sorrel for the sick; while we obtained thirty dovekies. (July 14) Sunday was made a day of rest. They who walked found the land quite destitute of vegetation, and a considerable river running into the head of the bay. *(July 15)* On the following day the ice was examined from the hills, but was not yet breaking in the offing: the weather being calm and fine, but sometimes foggy. The men were employed in repairing the boats, and in preparations for embarking. *(July 16)* The ice moved on the sixteenth; but the large creek was still filled, and impassable. *(July 17 to 19)* On the next two days it rained almost constantly, and we were prisoners. About a hundred dovekies were killed, so that our supply of fresh meat was respectable, if not great.

(July 21 to 30) On Sunday the ice was reported to be broken up in the offing; but after three days, without any thing material to note, except the killing of fifty dovekies, it remained close packed on the shore, so that it was impossible for us to move. The weather, from this time, continued variable, with occasional rain and wind, together with fogs, till the thirtieth; as the only events worth noticing, were the improvement of the sick, and the killing of some more birds for our table.

(July 31) We had now seen the ice leave the shore at last, but had yesterday been prevented from embarking, by a heavy fog. This ending in rain and sleet, with an adverse east wind, on the last morning of the month, we did not load the boats until mid-day; but as it proved, in vain, since it came to blow and rain so heavily all the afternoon and evening, that it was impossible to embark. In every way it was desirable to quit this pace; as the stones had now begun to fall from the cliffs, in consequence of which two men experienced severe contusions, and one narrowly escaped with his life. Thus ended July.

Summary of July 1833: Of that month, any summary is superseded by the preceding journal; it is almost sufficient to note that the mean temperature had been 36°, and the extremes 28° and 50° plus. It had not been an unfavourable one to our prospects, on the whole, while we had no right to expect an open sea in these regions at so early a period, far less in a strait which had exhibited such perseverance in preserving its ice through the whole summer, during the preceding years. That the sick had improved was a very consoling circumstance; while our situation was, at least, one of joint exertion and hope.

(August 1 to 15, 1833) Between the first and the fifteenth of August, the changes of the wind and the vacillations in the nature of the

weather were such as I often recorded during the past two; while the general result is all that is here worthy of notice. The prevailing nature of the former was north-easterly: and the consequence was, to block up the shore with ice, and to keep us closely imprisoned to our beach and our boats. On the third, indeed, we made an attempt to move round the southern point of the bay: but being unable to effect this, and finding the blockade of this headland so heavy that the bay must open sooner, so as to give us notice where we might possibly pass it, we returned, as there was nothing to gain by this project.

But even this fruitless labour was not without its use. The result of it was, to do something: and, to do, even what was useless, was to keep up the spirits and hopes of the people, as it also interrupted that uniformity of idle wakefulness which led them to brood over their present condition, and to indulge in evil anticipations. The Highland squire who makes Boswell haul on the backstay in a gale of wind, displays more knowledge than a landsman has any right to possess.

I know not what we should have done, what would have "become of us," as the phrase is, had we not made work when we ceased to find it. "The men," as they are called, are not much given to thinking, it is certain; though seamen of the present day (and I am sorry to say it), think much more than they did in the days of my junior service, and, most assuredly and certainly, are "all the worse" for it. Let my fraternity in command say whether this be true or not; and they are the bold men who will so say, despite of the paltry, fantastical, and pretending, ultra philanthropy of these days of ruinous folly. But that is an over serious matter to discuss at present. "An idle man is a pillow for the devil," says a Spanish or Italian proverb: it was not good that our men should have been pillowed in this manner: better was it that they should work themselves into utter weariness, that they should so hunger as to think only of their stomachs, fall asleep and dream of nothing but a better dinner, as they awoke to hope and labour for it, and that their sleep should be, not on the pillow of the proverb, but on a couch of snow, sufficient to impede all reflections but the wish for a better bed after a better supper, and the gnawing desire of more and better on the following day.

The shooting of waterfowl furnished indeed some occupation to those who were worthy of being trusted with powder and shot; but I believe the best occupation, to a set of such starved wretches as we were, was to eat the game, not to shoot it. Every morning now rose on the hopes of a good supper: if that came, it was more than welcome; and when it did not, why then there was the chance of one to-morrow.

I do not say that the supper which was missed was equivalent to the one that was eaten; since hope or expectation will not, more than wishing, fill a man's stomach; but it is certain that the sick recovered rapidly, and the well improved in strength; nor could I doubt that their present state of mind was, in this, scarcely less efficacious than the broiled ducks and dovekie sea-pies.

To look out from the top of a hill, for the state of the ice, was another occupation for anyone that chose; and it was exercise, while it served to waste the time. . . . The day of relief might be delayed, but it was long yet before it would be time to fear that it was not to arrive; while, in every change of a breeze, in every shower of rain, and in every movement of the ice, however minute, there was sufficient to maintain hope, and to render all anxious for the to-morrow . . . .

(August 14) It was on the fourteenth day that hope became anxiety, when a lane of water was for the first time seen, leading to the northward; and not many, I believe, slept, under the anticipations of what the next day might bring. *(August 15)* On this, all were employed in cutting the ice which obstructed the shore, as early as four o'clock in the morning; and the tide having risen soon after, with a fine westerly breeze, we launched the boats, embarked the stores and the sick, and, at eight o'clock, were under way.

We really were under way at last; and it was our business to forget that we had been in the same circumstances, the year before, in the same place; to feel that the time for exertion was now come, and those exertions to be at length rewarded; to exchange hope for certainty, and to see, in the mind's eye, the whole strait open before us, and our little fleet sailing with a fair wind through that bay which was now, in our views, England and home.

We soon rounded the north cape of Batty bay, and, finding a lane of water, crossed Elwin's bay at midnight; *(August 16)* reaching, on the sixteenth, that spot to the north of it where we had pitched our tents on the twenty-eighth of August in the preceding year. I know not if all were here quite free of recollections to dampen our new hopes. The difference in time was but twelve days; and should those days pass as they had done in the former, it might still be our fate to return to our last winter's home, and there to end our toils as it was but too easy to anticipate; the first whose fortune it should be, in a frozen grave, and the last in the maws of bears and foxes.

We found here no passage to the eastward, but the lane of water still extended to the north; so that our stay was of no longer duration than was indispensable for rest. As we proceeded, the open water increased in breadth; and, at eight in the evening, we reached our former position at the north-eastern cape of America. A view from the hill here, showed that the ice to the northward and north-eastward was in such a state as to admit of sailing through it; but as it blew too hard to venture among it in the night, we pitched our tents for rest.

(August 17) At three in the morning we embarked once more, leaving an additional note of our proceedings, in the same place where the former was concealed. It was calm, and we held on to the eastward by rowing, until, at noon, we reached the edge of the packed ice, through many streams of floating pieces; when we found that its extremity was but a mile to the northward. A southerly breeze then springing up, enabled us to round it: when, finding the water open, we stood on through it, and reached the eastern shore of the strait at three in the afternoon. In a few hours we had at length effected that for which we had formerly waited in vain so many days, and which, it is likely, could not have been effected in any of the years that we had been imprisoned in this country.

Accustomed as we were to the ice, to its caprices, and to its sudden and unexpected alterations, it was a change like that of magic, to find that solid mass of ocean . . . suddenly converted into water; navigable, and navigable to us, who had almost forgotten what it was to float at freedom on the seas. It was at times scarcely to be believed: and he who dozed to awake again, had for a moment to renew the conviction that he was at length a seaman on his own element, that his boat once more rose on the waves beneath him, and that when the winds blew, it obeyed his will and his hand.

Thus we ran quickly along the shore as the breeze increased; and passing Eardly point, were at length compelled, by the rising of this breeze to a gale accompanied by hard squalls, to take shelter on a beach twelve miles west of Cape York; having made, on this day, a run of seventy-two miles.

(August 18) The wind moderating, and it at length becoming calm, we were obliged, in the morning, to take to the oars; and finding no ice to obstruct us, rowed along to the eastward, and by midnight rested for a short time at the cape to the east of Admiralty inlet. *(August 19)* On the next day, the weather being the same, we were halfway between this place and that termed Navy-board inlet, by eight in the morning, when, the men being exhausted with nearly twenty hours' rowing,

we stopped on the beach and pitched our tents. The weather had not yet become warm, clear as the water might be; since the night temperature had never exceeded 35°, nor that of the day 40°.

We were soon driven from this exposed place by the coming on of an easterly wind; and thus, taking once more to the oars, we rowed along among icebergs, till we arrived at an excellent harbour, receiving a considerable stream, where we were protected by these heavy masses, while we could, if necessary, haul the boats into a pool at the mouth of the river. We had thus gained five miles more; and being six or seven to the west of Navy-board inlet, were within eighty of Possession bay.

(*August 20*) It began to blow hard last night with a north-east wind, and a heavy sea, which continued this day; blocking us up completely, but allowing us to haul up the boats for repair.

(*August 22*) It had become prudent to reduce ourselves, once more, to a two-thirds allowance; (*August 23 & 24*) and thus we were imprisoned on the twenty-third and twenty-fourth, by a continuance of the gale, with fog and rain; the thermometer falling to 29°; a degree of cold which was severely felt by the sick people.

(*August 25*) The wind at length abated, and the sea came down, so that we launched the boats; and it being by that time calm, we rowed to the eastward across navy-board inlet, passing through several streams of ice; when, the men being exhausted by twelve hours' labour, we found a harbour after a progress of ten miles, and pitched our tents at the mouth of another river; there resting, and repairing the boats, which were not in the best condition.

(*August 26*) At four in the morning, when all were asleep, the look-out man, David Wood, thought he discovered a sail in the offing, and immediately informed Commander Ross, who, by means of his glass, soon saw that it was, in reality, a ship. All hands were immediately out of their tents and on the beach discussing her rig, quality, and course; though there were still some despairers who maintained that it was only an iceberg.

No time was however lost: the boats were launched, and signals made by burning wet powder; when, completing our embarkation, we left our little harbour at six o'clock. Our progress was tedious, owing to alternate calms, and light airs blowing in every direction;

yet we made our way towards the vessel, and had it remained calm where she was, should soon have been alongside. Unluckily, a breeze just then sprang up, and she made all sail to the south-eastward; by which means the boat that was foremost was soon left astern, while the other two were steering more to the eastward with the hope of cutting her off.

About ten o'clock in the morning we saw another sail to the northward, which appeared to be lying in for her boats; thinking, at one time, when she hove to, that she had seen us. That, however, proved not to be the case, as she soon bore up under all sail. In no longer time it was apparent that she was fast leaving us; and it was the most anxious moment, that we had yet experienced, to find that we were near to no less than two ships, either of which would have put an end to all our fears and all our toils, and that we should probably reach neither.

It was necessary, however, to keep up the courage of the men, by assuring them, from time to time, that we were coming up with her; when, most fortunately, it fell calm, and we really gained so fast, that, at eleven o'clock, we saw her heave to with all sails aback, and lower down a boat, which rowed immediately towards our own.

She was soon alongside, when the mate in command addressed us, by presuming that we had met with some misfortune and lost our ship. This being answered in the affirmative, I requested to know the name of his vessel, and expressed our wish to be taken on board. I was answered that it was the "*Isabella of Hull*, once commanded by Captain Ross;" on which I stated that I was the identical man in question, and my people the crew of the *Victory*. That the mate, who commanded this boat, was as much astonished at this information as he appeared to be, I do not doubt; while, with the usual blunder-headedness of men on such occasions, he assured me that I had been dead two years. I easily convinced him, however, that what ought to have been true, according to his estimate, was a somewhat premature conclusion; as the bear-like form of the whole set of us might have shown him, had he taken time to consider, that we were certainly not whaling gentlemen, and that we carried tolerable evidence of our being "true men, and no impostors," on our backs, and in our starved and unshaven countenances. A hearty congratulation followed of course, in the true seaman style, and, after a few natural inquiries, he added that the Isabella was commanded by Captain Humphreys; when he immediately went off in his boat to communicate his information on board; repeating that we had long been given up as lost, not by them alone, but by all England.

Though we had not been supported by our names and characters, we should not the less have claimed, from charity, the attentions that we received, for never was seen a more miserable-looking set of wretches; while, that we were but a repulsive-looking people, none of us could doubt. . . . Unshaven since I know not when, dirty, dressed in the rags of wild beasts instead of the tatters of civilization, and starved to the very bones, our gaunt and grim looks, when contrasted with those of the well-dressed and well-fed men around us, made us all feel, I believe for the first time, what we really were, as well as what we seemed to others. Poverty is without half its mark, unless it be contrasted with wealth: and what we might have known to be true in the past days, we had forgotten to think of, till we were thus reminded of what we truly were . . . .

But the ludicrous soon took place of all other feelings; in such a crowd and such confusion, all serious thought was impossible, while the new buoyancy of our spirits made us abundantly willing to be amused by the scene which now opened. Every man was hungry and was to be fed, all were ragged and were to be clothed, there was not one to whom washing was not indispensable, nor one whom his beard did not deprive of all English semblance. All, every thing, too, was to be done at once; it was washing, dressing, shaving, eating, all intermingled, it was all the materials of each jumbled together; while, in the midst of all, there were interminable questions to be asked and answered on all sides; the adventures of the *Victory*, our own escapes, the politics of England, and the news which was now four years old. But all subsided into peace at last. The sick were accommodated, the seamen disposed of, and all was done, for all of us, which care and kindness could perform. Night at length brought quiet and serious thoughts; and I trust there was not one man among us who did not then express, where it was due, his gratitude for that interposition which had raised us all from a despair which none could now forget, and had brought us from the very borders of a not distant grave, to life and friends and civilization.

Long accustomed, however, to a cold bed on the hard snow or the bare rock, few could sleep amid the comforts of our new accommodations. I was myself compelled to leave the bed which had been kindly assigned me, and take my abode in a chair for the night, nor did it fare much better with the rest. It was for time to reconcile us to this sudden and violent change, to break through what had become habit, and to inure us once more to the usages of our former days.

1890 & 1931
BLACK ELK SPEAKS

A thunder being nation I am, I have said.
    A thunder being nation I am, I have said.
    You shall live.
    You shall live.
    You shall live.
    You shall live.

After their defeat in the Indian Wars of 1876–77, the tribes of the Teton Sioux lost their ancestral lands in the Black Hills of South Dakota and the Powder River country of Wyoming and Montana. Although the great chieftain Sitting Bull escaped into Canada with a large group, most of the Teton Sioux were corralled into a great reservation of lands—then regarded as worthless by their white conquerors—between the 103rd meridian and the Missouri River in South Dakota. In the years of imposed treaties and broken promises that followed, these Sioux suffered the loss of their freedom and their noble way of life, sinking into abject poverty as the great herds of Plains buffalo upon which they depended were slaughtered and pressures from white settlers and government officials mounted.

Unwelcome in Canada, Sitting Bull returned to the United States in the summer of 1881 at the head of a starving band of survivors. He surrendered to the authorities and was imprisoned. But his prominence as the greatest living Sioux chieftain could not be repressed and he was released less than two years later. Sitting Bull firmly resisted the relentless efforts of United States authorities to manipulate the Sioux to sign away the lands granted to them by treaty, but on August 8, 1888, government commissioners finally induced the fractured, confused, and dispirited tribes to agree to the dissolution of the Great Sioux Reservation into small, isolated parcels of land.

By the autumn of 1890 the Sioux were reduced to subsistence agriculture on poor land, and their survival almost wholly depended on government aid. It was at this time that a Sioux named Kicking Bear came to a skeptical Sitting Bull with news of a new religion that promised salvation to the suffering tribes. Essentially a native adaptation of the Christian faith spread by the white missionaries, this was the Ghost Dance religion of the Paiute Messiah Wovoko. This religion encouraged its desperate adherents to invoke, through frenzied dancing and singing, the springtide return of the Great Spirit, the return of abundant game, of life and youth and health to all who in the living memory of those Native Americans had so terribly suffered or perished—and promised that in this renewal the white man and all troubles would disappear.

Although Sitting Bull did not believe in the resurrection of the dead, he saw no harm in the new religion's much-needed message of nonviolence and hope, so he invited Kicking Bear to teach his people this new Ghost Dance, which, to the bewilderment and alarm of government officials, had already spread like wildfire among Native Americans throughout the entire West. Government officials quickly agreed that this troublesome "ghost dancing" must be stopped. Authorities were quick to expel Kicking Bear from the reservation, but did not take further action for fear of stirring up fresh trouble. By late autumn, however, the dancing and singing had spread throughout the scattered Sioux settlements, as more and more Indians dropped all other activities to participate in the Ghost Dance's exorcism of hopelessness and its promise of resurrection.

Troops were finally brought up, and government authorities set plans into motion to repress the Ghost Dance, blindly targeting Sitting Bull as one of its principal "fomenters." On December 15th, forty-three Indian agents surrounded Sitting Bull's cabin with a warrant for his arrest. The proud chief placidly offered himself into custody, but a swarm of protesting ghost dancers surrounded the Lakota Indian police. The situation soon spun out of control. Sitting Bull was shot and killed and a wild melee broke out, the Indian police saved only by the timely arrival of a troop of cavalry.

The tragic murder of their great leader would at any other time have stirred a general revolt, but the Sioux ghost dancers, their sorrow and their anger assuaged with the promise of forthcoming resurrection, scattered through the cold of the oncoming winter to the safety of other Ghost Dance encampments, many heading toward Pine Ridge to gather at the encampment of Red Cloud, the last remaining of the great Sioux chieftains. One of these bands was that of Big Foot, who, suffering from pneumonia, was likewise leading his band to Pine Ridge. When elements of the U.S. Seventh Cavalry—General Custer's former command—surrounded Big Foot's band of 230 women and children and 120 men, the ailing chief surrendered peacefully to the horse soldiers who led the Indians to the cavalry encampment at

Wounded Knee Creek. There the Indians were held for the night, surrounded by guards to prevent any escape, with rapid-firing Hotchkiss guns placed on a hill over the encampment to assure this.

The following morning of a clear winter day, December 29, 1890, Colonel Forsyth, the commanding officer of the Seventh Cavalry, ordered the Indians to surrender their rifles and all other arms. After the weary Sioux complied, Colonel Forsyth, still unsatisfied, ordered his troopers to verify this, which they did in a rough manner, manhandling the Indians and ransacking their ragged teepees. Two rifles were discovered, one a new Winchester belonging to a nearly deaf Indian called Black Coyote, who, although protesting that he had paid a fortune for the weapon, was in the process of surrendering it when an impatient trooper grabbed it from him and it went off. The report of the gun was answered by roaring fusillades of bullets from the Seventh Cavalry's rapid firing carbines, almost instantly supplemented by the Hotchkiss guns, each of which spat more than fifty heavy metal projectiles per minute. When the firing lulled, Big Foot and more than 150 of his band lay dead in the blood-drenched snow. Almost as many crawled or ran panic-stricken down the gully of Wounded Knee Creek. Of the Indians who managed to flee, another 150 perished from wounds and in the skirmishes that followed. The Seventh Cavalry also suffered heavy losses on that sad day, mostly from their own guns. After sunset, under the approach of a harsh prairie blizzard, only fifty-one of Big Foot's band—most of them wounded—finally arrived at Pine Ridge.

More than forty years later, poet and scholar John G. Neihardt arrived at Pine Ridge to speak with surviving ghost dancers. When he met the Oglala Holy Man, Black Elk, he encountered not only someone who could tell him about the Messiah movement, but also a Sioux who had been gifted with a great Vision, and who had living memories of Sioux life on the Great Plains, of Custer's defeat at Little Big Horn, and of the massacre at Wounded Knee Creek. Neihardt's meeting with Black Elk resulted in one of the great spiritual autobiographies of American literature; Black Elk Speaks, from which Black Elk's account of the events leading to the Wounded Knee Massacre and of his role in it is here reprinted along with Neihardt's moving epilogue.

Black Elk's story is a story of survival—not merely the survival of suffering and deprivation and of bullets—but of a Holy Man whose life spanned the life and death of a vanished civilization, and whose faith and courage impart to us the precious living spirit of his people.

Black Elk Speaks:
Being the Life Story of a Holy Man of the Oglala Sioux

by Black Elk, as told through John G. Neihardt

Chapter 23: Bad Trouble Coming

While these things were happening, the summer (1890) was getting old. I did not then know all that was going on at other places, but some things I heard, and much more I heard later.

When Good Thunder and Kicking Bear came back in the spring from seeing the Wanekia, the Wasichus at Pine Ridge put them in prison awhile, and then let them go. This showed the Wasichus were afraid of something. In the Moon of Black Cherries (August) many people were dancing at No Water's Camp on Clay Creek, and the agent came and told them to stop dancing. They would not stop, and they said they would fight for their religion if they had to do it. The agent went away, and they kept on dancing. They called him Young-Man-Afraid-of-Lakotas.

Later, I heard that the Brules were dancing over east of us; and then I heard that Big Foot's people were dancing on the Good River reservation; also that Kicking Bear had gone to Sitting Bull's camp on Grand River, and that the people were dancing there too. Word came to us that the Indians were beginning to dance everywhere.

The people were hungry and in despair, and many believed in the good new world that was coming. The Wasichus gave us less than half the beef cattle they promised us in the treaty, and these cattle were very poor. For a while our people would not take the cattle, because there were so few of them and they were so poor. But afterwhile they had to take them or starve to death. So we got more lies than cattle, and we could not eat lies. When the agent told the people to quit dancing, their hearts were bad.

From the dancing on Wounded Knee I went over to the Brules, who were camping on Cut Meat Creek at this time, and I took with me six shirts like those I had seen the twelve men wearing in my vision, and six dresses like the twelve women wore. I gave these to the Brules and they made others for themselves.

We danced there, and another vision came to me. I saw a Flaming Rainbow, like the one I had seen in my first great vision. Below the rainbow was a tepee made of cloud. Over me there was a spotted eagle soaring, and he said to me: "Remember this." That was all I saw and heard.

I have thought much about this since, and I have thought that this was where I made my great mistake. I had had a very great vision, and I should have depended only upon that to guide me to the good. But I followed the lesser visions that had come to me while dancing on Wounded Knee Creek. The vision of the Flaming Rainbow was to warn me, maybe; and I did not understand. I did not depend upon the great vision as I should have done; I depended upon the two sticks that I had seen in the lesser vision. It is hard to follow one great vision in this world of darkness and of many changing shadows. Among those shadows men get lost.

When I came back from the Brules, the weather was getting cold. Many of the Brules came along when I came back, and joined the Ogalalas in the dancing on Wounded Knee. We heard that there were soldiers at Pine Ridge and that others were coming all the time. Then one morning we heard that the soldiers were marching toward us, so we broke camp and moved west to Grass Creek. From there we went to White Clay and camped awhile and danced.

There came to us Fire Thunder, Red Wound and Young American Horse with a message from the soldiers that this matter of the ghost dance must be looked into, and that there should be rulings over it; and that they did not mean to take the dance away from us. But could we believe anything the Wasichus ever said to us? They spoke with forked tongues.

We moved in closer to Pine Ridge and camped. Many soldiers were there now, and what were they there for?

There was a big meeting with the agent, but I did not go to hear. He made a ruling that we could dance three days every moon, and the rest of the time we should go and make a living for ourselves somehow. He did not say how we could do that. But the people agreed to this.

The next day, while I was sitting in a tepee with Good Thunder, a policeman came to us and said: "I was not sent here, but I came for your good to tell you what I have heard—that they are going to arrest you two."

Good Thunder thought we ought to go to the Brules, who had a big camp on Wounded Knee below Manderson. So that evening we saddled and started. We came through Pepper Creek and White Horse Creek to Wounded Knee and followed it down to the Brule camp. They were glad to see us.

In the morning the crier went around and called a meeting. I spoke to the Brules, and this is what I said: "My relatives, there is a certain thing that we have done. From that certain sacred thing, we have had visions. In those visions we have seen, and also we have heard, that our relatives who have gone before us are in the Other World that has been revealed to us, and that we too shall go there. They are right now with the Wanekia. If the Wasichus want to fight us, let them do it. Have in your minds a strong desire, and take courage. We must depend upon the departed ones who are in the new world that is coming."

More Brules came there from Porcupine and Medicine Root creeks, and we all broke camp, moving down the Wounded Knee to Smoky Earth River (the White). There a Black Robe (Catholic Priest) came and tried to coax us to return. Our people told him that Wasichu promises were no good; that everything they had promised was a lie. Only a few Ogalalas turned back with the Black Robe. He was a good man and he was badly wounded that winter in the butchering of Big Foot's band. He was a very good man, and not like the other Wasichus.[1] From Smoky Earth River we moved to High Pockets' place southwest of the Top of the Badlands.[2] While we were there, American Horse and Fast Thunder came to us. They were both chiefs, and they came to bring us in to Pine Ridge. We had to obey. The Brules would not obey and tried to keep us from going. They struck us, and there was quite a struggle for a while; but we went anyway, because we had to go. Kicking Bear stayed with the Brules that time, but he came in to Pine Ridge a little later. A very few of the Brules went along with us.

We camped on White River, then on White Clay, then on Cheyenne Creek north of Pine Ridge. Most of the Ogalalas were camping near there too.

It was about this time that bad news came to us from the north. We heard that some policemen from Standing Rock had gone to arrest Sitting Bull on Grand River, and that he would not let them take him; so there was a fight, and they killed him.

It was now near the end of the Moon of Popping Trees, and I was twenty-seven years old (December, 1890). We heard that Big Foot was coming down from the Badlands with nearly four hundred people. Some of these were from Sitting Bull's band. They had run away when Sitting Bull was killed, and joined Big Foot on Good River. There were only about a hundred warriors in this band, and all the others were women and children and some old men. They were all starving and

[1] This was Father Craft.
[2] Cuny Table, a high plateau in the midst of the Badlands.

freezing, and Big Foot was so sick that they had to bring him along in a pony drag.[3] They had all run away to hide in the Badlands, and they were coming in now because they were starving and freezing. When they crossed Smoky Earth River, they followed up Medicine Root Creek to its head. Soldiers were over there looking for them. The soldiers had everything and were not freezing and starving. Near Porcupine Butte the soldiers came up to the Big Foots, and they surrendered and went along with the soldiers to Wounded Knee Creek where the Brenan store is now.

It was in the evening when we heard that the Big Foots were camped over there with the soldiers, about fifteen miles by the old road from where we were. It was the next morning (December 29, 1890) that something terrible happened.

Chapter 24: The Butchering at Wounded Knee
That evening before it happened, I went in to Pine Ridge and heard these things, and while I was there, soldiers started for where the Big Foots were. These made about five hundred soldiers that were there next morning. When I saw them starting I felt that something terrible was going to happen. That night I could hardly sleep at all. I walked around most of the night.

In the morning I went out after my horses, and while I was out I heard shooting off toward the east, and I knew from the sound that it must be wagon-guns (cannon) going off. The sounds went right through my body, and I felt that something terrible would happen. When I reached camp with the horses, a man rode up to me and said: "Hey-hey-hey! The people that are coming are fired on! I know it!"

I saddled up my buckskin and put on my sacred shirt. It was one I had made to be worn by no one but myself. It had a spotted eagle outstretched on the back of it, and the daybreak star was on the left shoulder, because when facing south that shoulder is toward the east. Across the breast, from the left shoulder to the right hip, was the flaming rainbow, and there was another rainbow around the neck, like a necklace, with a star at the bottom. At each shoulder, elbow, and wrist was an eagle feather; and over the whole shirt were red streaks of lightning. You will see that this was from my great vision, and you will know how it protected me that day.

I painted my face all red, and in my hair I put one eagle feather for the One Above.

It did not take me long to get ready, for I could still hear the

[3] He was very ill with pneumonia.

shooting over there.

I started out alone on the old road that ran across the hills to Wounded Knee. I had no gun. I carried only the sacred bow of the west that I had seen in my great vision. I had gone only a little way when a band of young men came galloping after me. The first two who came up were Loves War and Iron Wasichu. I asked what they were going to do, and they said they were just going to see where the shooting was. Then others were coming up, and some older men.

We rode fast, and there were about twenty of us now. The shooting was getting louder. A horseback from over there came galloping very fast toward us, and he said: "Hey-hey-hey! They have murdered him!" Then he whipped his horse and rode away faster toward Pine Ridge. In a little while we had come to the top of the ridge where, looking to the east, you can see for the first time the monument and the burying ground on the little hill where the church is. That is where the terrible thing started. Just south of the burying ground on the little hill a deep dry gulch runs about east and west, very crooked, and it rises westward to nearly the top of the ridge where we were. It had no name, but the Wasichus sometimes call it Battle Creek now. We stopped on the ridge not far from the head of the dry gulch. Wagon guns were still going off over there on the little hill, and they were going off again where they hit along the gulch. There was much shooting down yonder, and there were many cries, and we could see cavalrymen scattered over the hills ahead of us. Cavalrymen were riding along the gulch and shooting into it, where the women and children were running away and trying to hide in the gullies and the stunted pines.

A little way ahead of us, just below the head of the dry gulch, there were some women and children who were huddled under a clay bank, and some cavalrymen were there pointing guns at them.

We stopped back behind the ridge, and I said to the others: "Take courage. These are our relatives. We will try to get them back." Then we all sang a song which went like this:

A thunder being nation I am, I have said.
A thunder being nation I am, I have said.
You shall live.
You shall live.
You shall live.
You shall live.

Then I rode over the ridge and the others after me, and we were crying: "Take courage! It is time to fight!" The soldiers who were guarding our relatives shot at us and then ran away fast, and some more cavalrymen on the other side of the gulch did too. We got our relatives and sent them across the bridge to the northwest where they would be safe.

I had no gun, and when we were charging, I just held the sacred bow out in front of me with my right hand. The bullets did not hit us at all.

We found a little baby lying all alone near the head of the gulch. I could not pick her up just then, but I got her later and some of my people adopted her. I just wrapped her up tighter in a shawl that was around her and left her there. It was a safe place, and I had other work to do.

The soldiers had run eastward over the hills where there were some more soldiers, and they were off their horses and lying down. I told the others to stay back, and I charged upon them holding the sacred bow out toward them with my right hand. They all shot at me, and I could hear bullets all around me, but I ran my horse right close to them, and then swung around. Some soldiers across the gulch began shooting at me too, but I got back to the others and was not hurt at all.

By now many other Lakotas, who had heard the shooting, were coming up from Pine Ridge, and we all charged on the soldiers. They ran eastward toward where the trouble began. We followed down along the dry gulch, and what we saw was terrible. Dead and wounded women and children and little babies were scattered all along there where they had been trying to run away. The soldiers had followed along the gulch, as they ran, and murdered them in there. Sometimes they were in heaps because they had huddled together, and some were scattered all along. Sometimes bunches of them had been killed and torn to pieces where the wagon guns hit them. I saw a little baby trying to suck its mother, but she was bloody and dead.

There were two little boys at one place in this gulch. They had guns and they had been killing soldiers all by themselves. We could see the soldiers they had killed. The boys were all alone there, and they were not hurt. These were very brave little boys.

When we drove the soldiers back, they dug themselves in, and we were not enough people to drive them out from there. In the evening they marched off up Wounded Knee Creek, and then we saw all that they had done there.

Men and women and children were heaped and scattered all over the flat at the bottom of the little hill where the soldiers had their wagon-guns, and westward up the dry gulch all the way to the high ridge, the dead women and children and babies were scattered.

When I saw this I wished that I had died too, but I was not sorry for the women and children. It was better for them to be happy in the other world, and I wanted to be there too. But before I went there I wanted to have revenge. I thought there might be a day, and we should have revenge.

After the soldiers marched away, I heard from my friend, Dog Chief, how the trouble started, and he was right there by Yellow Bird when it happened. This is the way it was:

In the morning the soldiers began to take all the guns away from the Big Foots, who were camped in the flat below the little hill where the monument and burying ground are now. The people had stacked most of their guns, and even their knives, by the tepee where Big Foot was lying sick. Soldiers were on the little hill and all around, and there were soldiers across the dry gulch to the south and over east along Wounded Knee Creek too. The people were nearly surrounded, and the wagon-guns were pointing at them.

Some had not yet given up their guns, and so the soldiers were searching all the tepees, throwing things around and poking into everything. There was a man called Yellow Bird, and he and another man were standing in front of the tepee where Big Foot was lying sick. They had white sheets around and over them, with eyeholes to look through, and they had guns under these. An officer came to search them. He took the other man's gun, and then started to take Yellow Bird's. But Yellow Bird would not let go. He wrestled with the officer, and while they were wrestling, the gun went off and killed the officer. Wasichus and some others have said he meant to do this, but Dog Chief was standing right there, and he told me it was not so. As soon as the gun went off, Dog Chief told me, an officer shot and killed Big Foot who was lying sick inside the tepee.

Then suddenly nobody knew what was happening, except that the soldiers were all shooting and the wagon-guns began going off right in among the people.

Many were shot down right there. The women and children ran into the gulch and up west, dropping all the time, for the soldiers shot them as they ran. There were only about a hundred warriors and there were nearly five hundred soldiers. The warriors rushed to where they had piled their guns and knives. They fought soldiers with only their hands until they got their guns.

Dog Chief saw Yellow Bird run into a tepee with his gun, and from there he killed soldiers until the tepee caught fire. Then he died full of bullets.

It was a good winter day when all this happened. The sun was shining. But after the soldiers marched away from their dirty work, a heavy snow began to fall. The wind came up in the night. There was a big blizzard, and it grew very cold. The snow drifted deep in the crooked gulch, and it was one long grave of butchered women and children and babies, who had never done any harm and were only trying to run away.

Chapter 25: The End of the Dream

After the soldiers marched away, Red Crow and I started back toward Pine Ridge together, and I took the little baby that I told you about. Red Crow had one too.

We were going back to Pine Ridge, because we thought there was peace back home; but it was not so. While we were gone, there was a fight around the Agency, and our people had all gone away. They had gone away so fast that they left all the tepees standing.

It was nearly dark when we passed north of Pine Ridge where the hospital is now, and some soldiers shot at us, but did not hit us. We rode into the camp, and it was all empty. We were very hungry because we had not eaten anything since early morning, so we peeped into the tepees until we saw where there was a pot with papa (dried meat) cooked in it. We sat down in there and began to eat. While we were doing this, the soldiers shot at the tepee, and a bullet struck right between Red Crow and me. It threw dust in the soup, but we kept right on eating until we had our fill. Then we took the babies and got on our horses and rode away. If that bullet had only killed me, then I could have died with papa in my mouth.

The people had fled down Clay Creek, and we followed their trail. It was dark now, and late in the night we came to where they were camped without any tepees. They were just sitting by little fires, and the snow was beginning to blow. We rode in among them and I heard my mother's voice. She was singing a death song for me, because she felt sure I had died over there. She was so glad to see me that she cried and cried.

Women who had milk fed the little babies that Red Crow and I brought with us.

I think nobody but the little children slept any that night. The snow blew and we had no tepees.

When it was getting light, a war party went out and I went along; but this time I took a gun with me. When I started out the day before to Wounded Knee, I took only my sacred bow, which was not made to shoot with, because I was a little in doubt about the Wanekia religion at that time, and I did not really want to kill anybody because of it.

But I did not feel like that any more. After what I had seen over there, I wanted revenge; I wanted to kill.

We crossed White Clay Creek and followed it up, keeping on the west side. Soon we could hear many guns going off. So we struck west, following a ridge to where the fight was. It was close to the Mission, and there are many bullets in the Mission yet.

From this ridge we could see that the Lakotas were on both sides of the creek and were shooting at soldiers who were coming down the creek. As we looked down, we saw a little ravine, and across this was a big hill. We crossed and rode up the hillside.

They were fighting right there, and a Lakota cried to me: "Black Elk, this is the kind of a day in which to do something great!" I answered: "How!"[1]

Then I got off my horse and rubbed earth on myself, to show the Powers that I was nothing without their help. Then I took my rifle, got on my horse and galloped up to the top of the hill. Right below me the soldiers were shooting, and my people called out to me not to go down there; that there were some good shots among the soldiers and I should get killed for nothing.

But I remembered my great vision, the part where the geese of the north appeared. I depended upon their power. Stretching out my arms with my gun in the right hand, like a goose soaring when it flies low to turn in a change of weather, I made the sound the geese make—br-r-r-p, br-r-r-p, br-r-r-p; and, doing this, I charged. The soldiers saw, and began shooting fast at me. I kept right on with my buckskin running, shot in their faces when I was near, then swung wide and rode back up the hill.

All this time the bullets were buzzing around me and I was not touched. I was not even afraid. It was like being in a dream about shooting. But just as I had reached the very top of the hill, suddenly it was like waking up, and I was afraid. I dropped my arms and quit making the goose cry. Just as I did this, I felt something strike my belt as though some one had hit me there with the back of an ax. I nearly fell out of my saddle, but I managed to hold on, and rode over the hill.

An old man by the name of Protector was there, and he ran up and held me, for now I was falling off my horse. I will show you where the bullet struck me sidewise across the belly here (showing a long

[1] Signifying assent.

deep scar on the abdomen). My insides were coming out. Protector tore up a blanket in strips and bound it around me so that my insides would stay in. By now I was crazy to kill, and I said to Protector: "Help me on my horse! Let me go over there. It is a good day to die, so I will go over there!" But Protector said: "No, young nephew! You must not die to-day. That would be foolish. Your people need you. There may be a better day to die." He lifted me into my saddle and led my horse away down hill. Then I began to feel very sick.

By now it looked as though the soldiers would be wiped out, and the Lakotas were fighting harder; but I heard that, after I left, the black Wasichu soldiers came, and the Lakotas had to retreat.

There were many of our children in the Mission, and the sisters and priests were taking care of them. I heard there were sisters and priests right in the battle helping wounded people and praying.

There was a man by the name of Little Soldier who took charge of me and brought me to where our people were camped. While we were over at the Mission Fight, they had fled to the O-ona-gazhee[2] and were camped on top of it where the women and children would be safe from soldiers. Old Hollow Horn was there. He was a very powerful bear medicine man, and he came over to heal my wound. In three days I could walk, but I kept a piece of blanket tied around my belly.

It was now nearly the middle of the Moon of Frost in the Tepee (January). We heard that soldiers were on Smoky Earth River and were coming to attack us in the O-ona-gazhee. They were near Black Feather's place. So a party of about sixty of us started on the war-path to find them. My mother tried to keep me at home, because, although I could walk and ride a horse, my wound was not all healed yet. But I would not stay; for, after what I had seen at Wounded Knee, I wanted a chance to kill soldiers.

We rode down Grass Creek, Smoky Earth, and crossed, riding down stream. Soon from the top of a little hill we saw wagons and cavalry guarding them. The soldiers were making a corral of their wagons and getting ready to fight. We got off our horses and went behind some hills to a little knoll, where we crept up to look at the camp. Some soldiers were bringing harnessed horses down to a little creek to water, and I said to the others: "If you will stay here and shoot at the soldiers, I will charge over there and get some good horses." They knew of my power, so they did this, and I charged on my buckskin while the others kept shooting. I got seven of the horses;

[2] Sheltering place, an elevated plateau in the Badlands, with precipitous sides, and inaccessible save by one narrow neck of land easily defended.

but when I started back with these, all the soldiers saw me and began shooting. They killed two of my horses, but I brought five back safe and was not hit. When I was out of range, I caught up a fine bald-faced bay and turned my buckskin loose. Then I drove the others back to our party.

By now more cavalry were coming up the river, a big bunch of them, and there was some hard fighting for a while, because there were not enough of us. We were fighting and retreating, and all at once I saw Red Willow on foot running. He called to me: "Cousin, my horse is killed!" So I caught up a soldier's horse that was dragging a rope and brought it to Red Willow while the soldiers were shooting fast at me. Just then, for a little while, I was a wanekia[3] myself. In this fight Long Bear and another man, whose name I have forgotten, were badly wounded; but we saved them and carried them along with us. The soldiers did not follow us far into the Badlands, and when it was night we rode back with our wounded to the O-ona-gazhee.

We wanted a much bigger war-party so that we could meet the soldiers and get revenge. But this was hard, because the people were not all of the same mind, and they were hungry and cold. We had a meeting there, and were all ready to go out with more warriors, when Afraid-of-His-Horses came over from Pine Ridge to make peace with Red Cloud, who was with us there.

Our party wanted to go out and fight anyway, but Red Cloud made a speech to us something like this: "Brothers, this is a very hard winter. The women and children are starving and freezing. If this were summer, I would say to keep on fighting to the end. But we cannot do this. We must think of the women and children and that it is very bad for them. So we must make peace, and I will see that nobody is hurt by the soldiers."

The people agreed to this, for it was true. So we broke camp next day and went down from the O-ona-gazhee to Pine Ridge, and many, many Lakotas were already there. Also, there were many, many soldiers. They stood in two lines with their guns held in front of them as we went through to where we camped.

And so it was all over.

I did not know then how much was ended. When I look back now from this high hill of my old age, I can still see the butchered women and children lying heaped and scattered all along the crooked gulch as plain as when I saw them with eyes still young. And I can see that something else died there in the bloody mud, and was buried in the

[3] A "make-live," savior.

blizzard. A people's dream died there. It was a beautiful dream.

And I, to whom so great a vision was given in my youth, —you see me now a pitiful old man who has done nothing, for the nation's hoop is broken and scattered. There is no center any longer, and the sacred tree is dead.

AUTHOR'S POSTSCRIPT

After the conclusion of the narrative, Black Elk and our party were sitting at the north edge of Cuny Table, looking off across the Badlands ("the beauty and the strangeness of the earth," as the old man expressed it). Pointing at Harney Peak that loomed black above the far sky-rim, Black Elk said: "There, when I was young, the spirits took me in my vision to the center of the earth and showed me all the good things in the sacred hoop of the world. I wish I could stand up there in the flesh before I die, for there is something I want to say to the Six Grandfathers."

So the trip to Harney Peak was arranged, and a few days later we were there. On the way up to the summit, Black Elk remarked to his son, Ben: "Something should happen to-day. If I have any power left, the thunder beings of the west should hear me when I send a voice, and there should be at least a little thunder and a little rain." What happened is, of course, related to Wasichu readers as being merely a more or less striking coincidence. It was a bright and cloudless day, and after we had reached the summit the sky was perfectly clear. It was a season of drouth, one of the worst in the memory of the old men. The sky remained clear until about the conclusion of the ceremony.

"Right over there," said Black Elk, indicating a point of rock, "is where I stood in my vision, but the hoop of the world about me was different, for what I saw was in the spirit."

Having dressed and painted himself as he was in his great vision, he faced the west, holding the sacred pipe before him in his right hand. Then he sent forth a voice; and a thin, pathetic voice it seemed in that vast space around us:

"Hey-a-a-hey! Hey-a-a-hey! Hey-a-a-hey! Hey-a-a-hey! Grandfather, Great Spirit, once more behold me on earth and lean to hear my feeble voice. You lived first, and you are older than all need, older than all prayer. All things belong to you—the two-leggeds, the four-leggeds, the wings of the air and all green things that live. You have set the powers of the four quarters to cross each other. The good road and the road of difficulties you have made to cross; and where they cross, the place is holy. Day in and day out, forever, you are the life of things.

"Therefore I am sending a voice, Great Spirit, my Grandfather, forgetting nothing you have made, the stars of the universe and the grasses of the earth.

"You have said to me, when I was still young and could hope, that in difficulty I should send a voice four times, once for each quarter of the earth, and you would hear me.

"To-day I send a voice for a people in despair.

"You have given me a sacred pipe, and through this I should make my offering. You see it now.

"From the west, you have given me the cup of living water and the sacred bow, the power to make live and to destroy. You have given me a sacred wind and the herb from where the white giant lives—the cleansing power and the healing. The daybreak star and the pipe, you have given from the east; and from the south, the nation's sacred hoop and the tree that was to bloom. To the center of the world you have taken me and showed the goodness and the beauty and the strangeness of the greening earth, the only mother—and there the spirit shapes of things, as they should be, you have shown to me and I have seen. At the center of this sacred hoop you have said that I should make the tree to bloom.

"With tears running, O Great Spirit, Great Spirit, my Grandfather—with running tears I must say now that the tree has never bloomed. A pitiful old man, you see me here, and I have fallen away and have done nothing. Here at the center of the world, where you took me when I was young and taught me; here, old, I stand, and the tree is withered, Grandfather, my Grandfather!

"Again, and maybe the last time on this earth, I recall the great vision you sent me. It may be that some little root of the sacred tree still lives. Nourish it then, that it may leaf and bloom and fill with singing birds. Hear me, not for myself, but for my people; I am old. Hear me that they may once more go back into the sacred hoop and find the good red road, the shielding tree!"

We who listened now noted that thin clouds had gathered about us. A scant chill rain began to fall and there was low, muttering thunder without lightning. With tears running down his cheeks, the old man raised his voice to a thin high wail, and chanted: "In sorrow I am sending a feeble voice, O Six Powers of the World. Hear me in my sorrow, for I may never call again. O make my people live!"

For some minutes the old man stood silent, with face uplifted, weeping in the drizzling rain.

In a little while the sky was clear again.

1911
MAWSON'S TRIAL

There, exhausted, weak and chilled, hanging freely in space and slowly turning round as the rope twisted one way and the other, I felt that I had done my utmost and failed, that I had no more strength to try again and that all was over except the passing. It was to be a miserable and slow end and I reflected with disappointment that there was in my pocket no antidote to speed matters; but there always remained the alternative to slipping from the harness. There on the brink of the great Beyond I well remember how I looked forward to the peace of the great release—how almost excited I was at the prospect of the unknown to be unveiled. From those flights of mind I came back to earth, and remembering how providence had miraculously brought me so far, felt that nothing was impossible and determined to act up to Service's lines: "Just have one more try—it's dead easy to die, / It's the keeping-on-living that's hard."

– Sir Douglas Mawson

The heroic era of Antarctic exploration unfolded in the first two decades of the twentieth century. Men of Robert F. Scott's British *Discovery* Expedition (1901–1904) penetrated deep into the continent from their base on Ross Island. On December 30, 1902, Scott, with Ernest Shackleton and E.A. Wilson, reached 82°27'S on the Ross Ice Shelf, the point of furthest advance in their effort to sledge to the South Pole at 90°S. Under Shackleton's command, the subsequent British *Nimrod* Expedition (1907–1909) was even more successful. On January 9, 1909, Shackleton led a group of five to 88°23'S—within ninety-seven miles of the prize. One week later, on January 16, 1909, another team from Shackleton's *Nimrod* group—the twenty-six year old British-born Australian Douglas Mawson and T.W.E. David— reached the south magnetic pole at 72°25'S, 155°16'E. Roald Amundsen and members of his Norwegian expedition, aided by their skillful skiing and their dog-teams, were the first to reach the South Pole, on December 14, 1911, followed a month later, on January 17, 1912, by Scott and members of the British *Terra Nova* Expedition (1910–1913). Although Amundsen and his team were spared severe hardships in making it back to their base, Scott and his men were caught in a blizzard and perished only a short march from safety.

Young Douglas Mawson had proven his skills and determination as an Antarctic explorer in Shackleton's *Nimrod* Expedition, so during a visit to England early in 1910, he discussed joining the prestigious *Terra Nova* Expedition with its leader Robert F. Scott, who eagerly encouraged his participation. After consulting with Shackleton, however, Mawson decided instead to set out on December 2, 1911 on the stout old wooden ship *Aurora* as leader of the first Australasian expedition, whose purpose was to chart almost two thousand miles of Antarctica's virtually unexplored coastline. After a hazardous voyage, Mawson and his men established their main base camp on the Adélie Land coast of Commonwealth Bay in January 1912, constructing a hut there which they named "Home of the Blizzard" because of savage winds gusting up to two hundred miles per hour that howled around the site. There they passed the stormy months of winter, preparing to set out with the break in the weather that would come with the Antarctic spring and summer.

Having divided his command into several task forces, Mawson set out into terrible weather on November 10, 1912 with Swiss scientist and mountaineer Dr. Xavier Mertz and Lieutenant Belgrave Ninnis of Britain's Royal Fusiliers—and teams of superb Greenland dogs to pull their three sledges. In the five weeks that followed, Mawson's group advanced more than three hundred miles, by the end of November, crossing the vast crevasse-ridden Mertz Glacier and then attacking the almost impossibly rugged chaos of the Ninnis Glacier. Fighting difficult terrain, bad light, and appalling weather, with winds often gusting above sixty miles per hour, Mawson and his colleagues nevertheless managed to map the coastline, collect geological samples, photograph the terrain, and—despite all the hardships they had to endure—maintain high morale. A vicious blizzard on December 6th halted progress until December 9th when the men dug themselves and the dogs out of the snow and continued onward.

On December 13th the men discarded the third sledge, and, as a precaution, teamed the strongest dogs and loaded most of the expedition's remaining food supply on Ninnis' sledge, which would follow the sledge handled by Mawson, in turn advancing behind Mertz, who was on skis in the lead to inspect the terrain for dangerous crevasses. Disaster struck on December 14th. Mertz waved a warning that he had located a crevasse hidden beneath the snow. Mawson's team and sledge dashed safely across the fragile snow bridge without realizing the danger, but Ninnis and his sledge and dogs suddenly disappeared from Mertz's horrified view. When Mawson looked behind for his friend, only the bleak landscape met his unbelieving and searching eyes. Mawson and Mertz rushed terrified to the edge of the bottomless crevasse. All they could see, on a ledge some one hundred and fifty feet below, was one of the dogs, its back obviously broken, crying as it struggled to right itself. Mawson and Mertz had not even the length of rope necessary to reach the crippled dog, which soon fell silent and still. After more than three hours of frantic calling out into the abyss, they set their minds to the question of their own survival.

The tragedy of losing Ninnis was compounded by the grim situation in which Mawson and Mertz were now caught. Almost all of their food, their tent and spare clothing, and other vital supplies had plunged with Ninnis, their best dogs and the sledge into nothingness. With barely more than a week of rations left, and nothing at all for their six remaining dogs, Mawson and Mertz were stranded in the bleak and hostile Antarctic landscape—more than three hundred miles from the safety of their main base. In the succeeding days of difficult marching—twenty-seven miles on one day, then twenty, then eighteen, then eleven miles and less were covered—the famished dogs lost all strength and one by one were killed for food. Though of little nutritive value, the bitter sinew and muscle tissue carved from their emaciated frames was an indispensable supplement to the meager provisions remaining to Mawson and Mertz. Weakened almost to delirium with hunger—with Mertz also suffering from dysentery and other complaints—they continued their struggle to advance through difficult and worsening conditions, when any further progress was brought to a halt by a blizzard and then by Mertz's final collapse.

Early in the morning hours of January 8, 1913 Mertz was "accepted into *the peace that passeth all understanding*."

It is on this morning that we began our selection. Mawson—exhausted, emaciated and sickened, his feet and skin severely damaged—was confronted with the task of moving on alone. He did not know that toxic levels of vitamin A that he and Mertz had ingested from the livers of their dogs had undoubtedly helped kill Mertz and had poisoned him as well. Mawson struggled to adapt his gear to the changed situation, cutting the last remaining sledge down to a manageable size and casting aside anything that was not absolutely essential. Blizzard conditions delayed his departure until the beautifully sunny 11th of January when he finally set out to reach base camp across more than one hundred miles of treacherous terrain. Six days of strenuous and painful effort followed. Mawson had advanced twenty-five miles by the fateful day of January 17th—when he twice found himself precariously suspended in his harness at the end of a rope over an unfathomable abyss, and with superhuman effort he managed to escape the grasp of certain death.

Yet two weeks more of determined struggle—and almost sixty miles more across forbidding landscapes—would pass before Mawson miraculously came upon supplies that a search party had set out for him at a rendez-vous point not far from his final destination. He had missed his comrades by only five hours, but they had left precise directions to the next point of safety, Aladdin's Cave, a supply depot dug into the ice a little more than five miles out from the main base. Held up by blizzards and difficulty crossing icy terrain with makeshift crampons, Mawson finally reached the shelter of Aladdin's Cave on the evening of February 1st. He was most fortunate in this, for upon his arrival a raging blizzard struck, lasting until February 8th when he marched the last several miles to base camp. There he was reunited with his comrades—in joy for his own survival and in sorrow at the loss of Ninnis and Mertz—after an epic journey that can justly be called the greatest achievement of solo survival in the annals of polar exploration.

Douglas Mawson survived his extreme trial for one reason only: he never gave up. After Mertz's death, he refused the seductive temptation simply to remain in his sleeping bag and accept burial beneath the blizzard snows. Time and again he refused death and continued on, without doubt assisted by the favor of chance, but chance critically supported by his own supreme determination and the application of all his skills in confronting relentless mortal dangers. Returning to Adelaide a year after his ordeal, Mawson was knighted for his scientific accomplishments, married, and resumed his academic career—just as Ernest Shackleton was setting out in *Endurance* in the prelude to the noble closing act of the heroic age of Antarctic exploration. Fifteen years later, in 1929, and then again in 1931, Mawson led expeditions to Antarctica—both times on Scott's famous Dundee-constructed *Discovery*—to research marine life and oceanography. Professor Mawson spent the remaining years of his life in the warm glow of family and friends and the honors he had earned, in his teaching of geology and his devotion to the conservation of the natural world. He died peacefully in 1958, at the age of seventy-six, the last surviving leader of the heroic age of Antarctic exploration.

Mawson's Trial

from *The Home of the Blizzard* by Sir Douglas Mawson

Alone

"Then on the shore of the wide world I stand alone."– Keats

Outside the bowl of chaos was brimming with drift-snow and as I lay in the sleeping-bag beside my dead companion I wondered how, in such conditions, I would manage to break and pitch camp single-handed. There appeared to be little hope of reaching the Hut, still one hundred miles away. It was easy to sleep in the bag, and the weather was cruel outside. But inaction is hard to bear and I braced myself together determined to put up a good fight.

Failing to reach the Hut, it would be something done if I managed to get to some prominent point likely to catch the eye of a search-party, where a cairn might be erected and our diaries cached. So I commenced to modify the sledge and camping gear to meet fresh requirements.

The sky remained clouded, but the wind fell off to a calm which lasted several hours. I took the opportunity to set to work on the sledge, sawing it in halves with a pocket tool and discarding the rear section. A mast was made out of one of the rails no longer required, and a spar was cut from the other. Finally, the load was cut down to a minimum by the elimination of all but the barest necessities, the abandoned articles including, sad to relate, all that remained of the exposed photographic films.

Late that evening, the 8th, I took the body of Mertz, still toggled up in his bag, outside the tent, piled snow blocks around it and raised a rough cross made of the two discarded halves of the sledge runners. On January 9 the weather was overcast and fairly thick drift was flying in a gale of wind, reaching about fifty miles an hour. As certain matters still required attention and my chances of re-erecting the tent were rather doubtful, if I decided to move on, the start was delayed.

Part of the time that day was occupied with cutting up a waterproof clothes-bag and Mertz's Burberry jacket and sewing them together to form a sail. Before retiring to rest in the evening I read through the burial service and put the finishing touches on the grave.

January 10 arrived in a turmoil of wind and thick drift. The start was still further delayed. I spent part of the time in reckoning up the food remaining and in cooking the rest of the dog meat, this latter operation serving the good object of lightening the load, in that the kerosene for the purpose was consumed there and then and had not to be dragged forward for subsequent use. Late in the afternoon the wind fell and the sun peered amongst the clouds just as I was in the middle of a long job riveting and lashing the broken shovel.

The next day, January 11, a beautiful, calm day of sunshine, I set out over a good surface with a slight down grade.

From the start my feet felt curiously lumpy and sore. They had become so painful after a mile of walking that I decided to examine them on the spot, sitting in the lee of the sledge in brilliant sunshine. I had not had my socks off for some days for, while lying in camp, it had not seemed necessary. On taking off the third and inner pair of socks the sight of my feet gave me quite a shock, for the thickened skin of the soles had separated in each case as a complete layer, and abundant watery fluid had escaped saturating the sock. The new skin beneath was very much abraded and raw. Several of my toes had commenced to blacken and fester near the tips and the nails were puffed and loose.

I began to wonder if there was ever to be a day without some special disappointment. However, there was nothing to be done but make the best of it. I smeared the new skin and the raw surfaces with lanoline, of which there was fortunately a good store, and then with the aid of bandages bound the old skin casts back in place, for these were comfortable and soft in contact with the abraded surface. Over the bandages were slipped six pairs of thick woollen socks, then fur boots and finally crampon over-shoes. The latter, having large stiff soles, spread the weight nicely and saved my feet from the jagged ice encountered shortly afterwards.

So glorious was it to feel the sun on one's skin after being without it for so long that I next removed most of my clothing and bathed my body in the rays until my flesh fairly tingled—a wonderful sensation which spread throughout my whole person, and made me feel stronger and happier.

Then on I went, treading rather like a cat on wet ground endeavouring to save my feet from pain. By 5:30 P.M. I was quite worn out—nerve-worn—though having covered but six and a quarter miles. Had it not been a delightful evening I should not have found strength to erect the tent.

The day following passed in a howling blizzard and I could do nothing but attend to my feet and other raw patches, festering fingernails and inflamed frost-bitten nose. Fortunately there was a good supply of bandages and antiseptic. The tent, spread about with dressings and the meagre surgical appliances at hand, was suggestive of a casualty hospital.

Towards noon the following day, January 13, the wind subsided and the snow cleared off. It turned out a beautifully fine afternoon. Soon after I had got moving the slope increased, unfolding a fine view of the Mertz Glacier ahead. My heart leapt with joy, for all was like a map before me and I knew that over the hazy blue ice ridge in the far distance lay the Hut. I was heading to traverse the depression of the glacier ahead at a point many miles above our crossing of the outward journey and some few miles below gigantic ice cascades. My first impulse was to turn away to the west and avoid crossing the fifteen miles of hideously broken ice that choked the valley before me, but on second thought, in view of the very limited quantity of food left, the right thing seemed to be to make an air-line for the Hut and chance what lay between. Accordingly, having taken an observation of the sun for position and selected what appeared to be the clearest route across the valley, I started downhill. The névé gave way to rough blue ice and even wide crevasses made their appearance. The rough ice jarred my feet terribly and altogether it was a most painful march. So unendurable did it become that, finding a bridged crevasse extending my way, I decided to march along the snow bridge and risk an accident. It was from fifteen to twenty feet wide and well packed with winter snow. The march continued along it down slopes for over a mile with great satisfaction as far as my feet were concerned. Eventually it became irregular and broke up, but others took its place and served as well; in this way the march was made possible. At 8 P.M. after covering a distance of nearly six miles a final halt for the day was made.

About 11 P.M. as the sun skimmed behind the ice slopes to the south I was startled by loud reports like heavy gun shots. They commenced up the valley to the south and trailed away down the southern side of the glacier towards the sea. The fusillade of shots rang out without interruption for about half an hour, then all was silent. It was hard to believe it was not caused by some human agency, but I learnt that it was due to the cracking of the glacier ice.

A high wind which blew on the morning of the 14th diminished in strength by noon and allowed me to get away. The sun came out so warm that the rough ice surface underfoot was covered with a film of water and in some places small trickles ran away to disappear into crevasses.

Though the course was downhill, the sledge required a good deal of pulling owing to the wet runners. At 9 P.M., after travelling five miles, I pitched camp in the bed of the glacier. From about 9:30 P.M. until 11 P.M. "cannonading" continued like that heard the previous evening.

January 15—the date on which all the sledging parties were due at the Hut! It was overcast and snowing early in the day, but in a few hours the sun broke out and shone warmly. The travelling was so heavy over a soft snowy surface, partly melting, that I gave up, after one mile, and camped.

At 7 P.M. the surface had not improved, the sky was thickly obscured and snow fell. At 10 P.M. a heavy snowstorm was in progress, and, since there were many crevasses in the vicinity, I resolved to wait. On the 16th at 2 A.M. the snow was falling as thick as ever, but at 5 A.M. the atmosphere lightened and the sun appeared. Camp was broken without delay. A favourable breeze sprang up, and with sail set I managed to proceed in short stages through the deep newly-fallen blanket of snow. It clung in lumps to the runners, which had to be scraped frequently. Riven ice ridges as much as eighty feet in height passed on either hand. Occasionally I got a start as a foot or a leg sank through into space, but, on the whole, all went unexpectedly well for several miles. Then the sun disappeared and the disabilities of a snow-blind light had to be faced.

After laboriously toiling up one long slope, I had just taken a few paces over the crest, with the sledge running freely behind, when it dawned on me that the surface fell away unusually steeply. A glance ahead, even in that uncertain light, flashed the truth upon me—I was on a snow cornice, rimming the brink of a great blue chasm like a quarry, the yawning mouth of an immense and partly filled crevasse. Already the sledge was gaining speed as it slid past me towards the gaping hole below. Mechanically, I bedded my feet firmly in the snow and, exerting every effort, was just able to take the weight and hold up the sledge as it reached the very brink of the abyss. There must have been an interval of quite a minute during which I held my ground without being able to make it budge. It seemed an interminable time; I found myself reckoning the odds as to who would win, the sledge or I. Then it slowly came my way, and the imminent danger was passed.

The day's march was an extremely heavy five miles; so before turning in I treated myself to an extra supper of jelly soup made from dog sinews. I thought at the time that the acute enjoyment of eating compensated in some measure for the sufferings of starvation.

January 17 was another day of overcast sky and steady falling snow. Everything from below one's feet to the sky above was one uniform ghostly glare. The irregularities in the surfaces not obliterated by the deep soft snow blended harmoniously in colour and in the absence of the shadows faded into invisibility. These were most unsuitable conditions for the crossing of such a dangerous crevassed valley, but delay meant a reduction of the ration and that was out of the question, so nothing remained but to go on.

A start was made at 8 A.M. and the pulling proved easier than on the previous day. Some two miles had been negotiated in safety when an event occurred which, but for a miracle, would have terminated the story then and there. Never have I come so near to an end; never has anyone more miraculously escaped.

I was hauling the sledge through deep snow up a fairly steep slope when my feet broke through into a crevasse. Fortunately as I fell I caught my weight with my arms on the ledge and did not plunge in further than the thighs. The outline of the crevasse did not show through the blanket of snow on the surface, but an idea of the trend was obtained with a stick. I decided to try a crossing about fifty yards further along, hoping that there it would be better bridged. Alas! It took an unexpected turn catching me unawares. This time I shot through the centre of the bridge in a flash, but the latter part of the fall was decelerated by the friction of the harness ropes which, as the sledge ran up, sawed back into the thick compact snow forming the margin of the lid. Having seen my comrades perish in diverse ways and having lost hope of ever reaching the Hut, I had already many times speculated on what the end would be like. So it happened that as I fell through into the crevasse the thought "so this is the end" blazed up in my mind, for it was to be expected that the next moment the sledge would follow through, crash on my head and all go to the unseen bottom. But the unexpected happened and the sledge held, the deep snow acting as a brake.

In the moment that elapsed before the rope ceased to descend, delaying the issue, a great regret swept through my mind, namely; that after having stinted myself so assiduously in order to save food, I should pass on now to eternity without the satisfaction of what remained—to such an extent does food take possession of one under such circumstances. Realizing that the sledge was holding I began to look around. The crevasse was somewhat over six feet wide and sheer walled, descending into blue depths below. My clothes, which, with a view to ventilation, had been but loosely secured were now stuffed with snow broken from the roof, and very chilly it was. Above at the other end of the fourteen-foot rope, was the daylight seen through the hole in the lid.

In my weak condition, the prospect of climbing out seemed very poor indeed, but in a few moments the struggle was begun. A great effort brought a knot in the rope within my grasp, and, after a moment's rest, I was able to draw myself up and reach another, and, at length, hauled my body onto the overhanging snow-lid. Then, when all appeared to be well and before I could get to quite solid ground, a further section of the lid gave way, precipitating me once more to the full length of the rope.

There, exhausted, weak and chilled, hanging freely in space and slowly turning round as the rope twisted one way and the other, I felt that I had done my utmost and failed, that I had no more strength to try again and that all was over except the passing. It was to be a miserable and slow end and I reflected with disappointment that there was in my pocket no antidote to speed matters; but there always remained the alternative of slipping from the harness. There on the brink of the great Beyond I well remember how I looked forward to the peace of the great release—how almost excited I was at the prospect of the unknown to be unveiled. From those flights of mind I came back to earth, and remembering how Providence had miraculously brought me so far, felt that nothing was impossible and determined to act up to Service's lines:

"Just have one more try—it's dead easy to die,
It's the keeping-on-living that's hard."

My strength was fast ebbing; in a few minutes it would be too late. It was the occasion for a supreme attempt. Fired by the passion that burns the blood in the act of strife, new power seemed to come as I applied myself to one last tremendous effort. The struggle occupied some time, but I slowly worked upward to the surface. This time emerging feet first, still clinging to the rope, I pushed myself out extended at full length on the lid and then shuffled safely on to the solid ground at the side. Then came the reaction from the great nerve strain and lying there alongside the sledge my mind faded into a blank.

When consciousness returned it was a full hour or two later, for I was partly covered with newly fallen snow and numb with the cold. I took at least three hours to erect the tent, get things snugly inside and clear the snow from my clothes. Between each movement, almost, I had to rest. Then reclining in luxury in the sleeping-bag I ate a little food and thought matters over. It was a time when the mood of the Persian philosopher appealed to me:

> "Unborn To-morrow and dead Yesterday,
> Why fret about them if To-day be sweet?"

I was confronted with this problem: whether it was better to enjoy life for a few days, sleeping and eating my fill until the provisions gave out, or to "plug on" again in hunger with the prospect of plunging at any moment into eternity without the supreme satisfaction and pleasure of the food. While thus cogitating an idea presented itself which greatly improved the prospects and clinched the decision to go ahead. It was to construct a ladder from a length of alpine rope that remained; one end was to be secured to the bow of the sledge and the other carried over my shoulder and loosely attached to the sledge harness. Thus if I fell into a crevasse again, provided the sledge was not also engulfed, it would be easy for me, even though weakened by starvation, to scramble out by the ladder.

Notwithstanding the possibilities of the rope-ladder, I could not sleep properly, for my nerves had been overtaxed. All night long considerable wind and drift continued.

On the 18th it was overcast and light snow falling; very dispiriting conditions after the experience of the day before, but I resolved to go ahead and leave the rest to Providence.

My feet and legs, as they wallowed through the deep snow, occasionally broke through into space. Then I went right under, but the sledge held up and the ladder proved "trumps." A few minutes later I was down again, but emerged once more without much exertion, though half-smothered with snow. Faintness overcame me and I stopped to camp, though only a short distance had been covered.

All around there was a leaden glare and the prospect was most unpromising. The sun had not shown up for several days and I was eager for it, not only that it might illuminate the landscape, but for its cheerful influence and life-giving energy. A few days previously my condition had been improving, but now it was relapsing.

During the night of the 18th loud booming noises, sharp cracks and muffled growls issued from the neighbouring crevasses and kept waking me up. At times one could feel a vibration accompanying the growling sounds, and I concluded that the ice was in rapid motion.

The sun at last appeared on the 19th, and the march was resumed by 8:30 A.M. The whole surface, now effectively lighted up, was seen to be a network of ice-rifts and crevasses, some of the latter very wide. Along one after another of these, I dragged the sledge in search of a spot where the snow bridge appeared to be firm. Then I would plunge across at a run risking the consequences.

After a march of three hours safer ground was reached. On ahead, leading to the rising slopes on the far side of the glacier, was a nearly level ice plain dotted over with beehive-shaped eminences usually not more than a few feet in height. Once on this comparatively safe wind-swept surface I became over-reliant and in consequence sank several times into narrow fissures.

At length the glacier was crossed and the tent pitched on a snowy slope under beetling, crevassed crags which rose sheer from the valley-level some five hundred feet. I had never dared expect to get so far and now that it was an accomplished fact I was intoxicated with joy. Somewhat to the right could be traced out a good path, apparently free from pitfalls, leading upwards to the plateau which still remained to be crossed. This entailed a rise of some three thousand feet and led me to reconsider the lightening of the load on the sledge. The length of alpine rope was abandoned as also were finnesko-crampons and sundry pairs of worn finnesko and socks. The sledge was overhauled and sundry repairs effected, finishing up by treating the runners to a coat of water-proofing composition to cause them to glide more freely on moist snow.

January 20 was a wretched overcast day and not at all improved by considerable wind and light drift. In desperation a start was made at 2 P.M. and, though nothing was visible beyond a few yards distant, I kept a steady course uphill and, assisted by the wind, covered two and a half miles as the day's work.

The next day, though windy, was sunny and a stretch of three miles of steep rise was negotiated. All that night and until noon on the 22nd wind and drift prevailed, but the afternoon came gloriously sunny. Away to the north beyond Aurora Peak was a splendid view of the sea at Buchanan Bay. It was like meeting an old friend and I longed to be down near it. That evening six more miles had been covered, but I felt very weak and weary. My feet were now much improved and the old skin-casts after shrivelling up a good deal had been thrown away. However, prolonged starvation aided by the unwholesomeness of the dog meat was taking the toll in other ways. My nails still continued to fester and numerous boils on my face and body required daily attention. The personal overhaul necessary each day on camping and before starting consumed much valuable time.

During the early hours of the 23rd the sun was visible, but about 8 A.M. the clouds sagged low, the wind rose and everything became blotted out in a swirl of drifting snow.

I wandered through it for several hours, the sledge capsizing at times owing to the strength of the wind. It was not possible to keep an accurate course, for even the wind changed direction as the day wore on. Underfoot there was soft snow which I found comfortable for my sore feet, but which made the sledge drag heavily at times.

When a halt was made at 4 P.M. to pitch camp I reckoned that the distance covered in a straight line was but three and a half miles. Then followed a long and difficult task erecting the tent in the wind. It proved a protracted operation. When the outside was finished off satisfactorily the inside was discovered to be filled with drift snow and had to be dug out. Everything was stuffed with soft damp snow including the sleeping-bag, and it took a rare time to put things right. By this time I was doing a good deal of "thinking out aloud" which, by the way, seemed to give some sort of consolation.

High wind and dense snow persisted throughout the 24th and a good five and a half miles were made. I was able to sit on the sledge much of the time and the wind and the good sail did the work. I was quite done up when at last the tent was up and everything snug for the night.

Torrents of snow fell throughout the 25th and it sizzled and rattled against the tent under the influence of a gale of wind. After the trying experience of the previous two days I did not feel well enough to go on. As the hours went by the snow piled higher, bulging in the sides of the small, odd-shaped tent until it weighed down upon the sleeping-bag and left practically no room at all. The threshing of the seething drift was no longer audible. I was buried indeed! The coffin shape of the bag lent a more realistic touch to the circumstances. With such a weight above there was no certainty that I would be able to get out when the time came to move. So, though the weather was just as bad on the 26th, I determined to struggle out and try another stage. It was a long and laborious work reaching the daylight from beneath the flattened tent and digging everything free. Then some hot food was prepared of which I was in much need. Only four or five pounds of food remained now and there was no guarantee that the weather would clear in the near future, so the position was most anxious. At that time the skin was coming off my hands which were the last parts of my body to peel. A moulting of the hair followed the peeling of the skin. Irregular tufts of beard came out and there was a general shedding of hair from my head, so much so that at each camp thereabouts the snowy floor of the tent was noticeably darkened.

There was no need of a sail on the 26th. The wind, blowing from behind, caught the sledge and drove it along so that, though over a soft surface of snow, the travelling was rapid. The snow came down in the form of large pellets and rattled as it struck the sledge. For one in so poor a condition it was a very trying day, blindly struggling through the whirl of the seething snow; after covering nine miles and erecting the tent I was thoroughly done up. The night was far spent before I had cleared the snow out of my clothes, sleeping-bag, etc.: cooked some food and given myself the necessary medical attention. As the 27th was just such another day as the 26th I decided to rest further to recuperate from the exertions of the previous day.

By the morning of January 28 the wind had moderated considerably, but the sky remained overcast and snow continued to fall. It was a difficult matter getting out of the tent and a long job excavating it, for the packed snow had piled up within a few inches of the peak. There was no sign of the sledge which with the harness and spars had all to be prospected for and dug out. It appeared that since pitching the tent the whole level of the country had been raised a uniform three feet by a stratum of snow packed so densely that in walking over it but little impression was left.

Soon after the start the sun gleamed out and the weather improved. The three-thousand-foot crest of the plateau had been crossed and I was bearing down rapidly on Commonwealth Bay, the vicinity of which was indicated by a dark water-sky on the north-west horizon. The evening turned out beautifully fine and my spirits rose to a high pitch, for I felt for the first time that there was a really good chance of making the Hut. To increase the excitement Madigan Nunatak showed up a black speck away to the right front. Eight good miles were covered that afternoon. The change in the weather had come most opportunely, for there now remained only about twenty small chips of cooked dog meat in addition to half a pound of raisins and a few ounces of chocolate which I had kept carefully guarded for emergencies.

However, the wind and drift got up in the night and the start next morning was made in disappointing weather. When five miles on the way another miracle happened.

I was travelling along on an even down grade and was wondering how long the two pounds of food which remained would last, when something dark loomed through the haze of the drift a short distance away to the right. All sorts of possibilities raced through my mind as I headed the sledge for it. The unexpected had happened—in thick weather I had run fairly into a cairn of snow blocks erected by McLean, Hodgeman and Hurley, who had been out searching for my party. On the top of the mound, outlined in black bunting, was a bag of food, left on the chance that it might be picked up by us. In a tin was a note stating the bearing and distance of the mound from Aladdin's Cave (E. 30° S., distance twenty-three miles), and mentioning that the ship had arrived at the Hut and was waiting, and had brought the news that Amundsen had reached the Pole, and that Scott was remaining another year in Antarctica.

It certainly was remarkably good fortune that I had come upon the depot of food; a few hundred yards to either side and it would have been lost to sight in the drift. On reading the note carefully I found that I had just missed by six hours what would have been crowning good luck, for it appeared that the search party had left the mound at 8 a.m. that very day (January 29). It was about 2 P.M. when I reached it. Thus, during the night of the 28th our camps had been only some five miles apart.

Hauling down the bag of food I tore it open in the lee of the cairn and in my greed scattered the contents about on the ground. Having partaken heartily of frozen pemmican, I stuffed my pocket, bundled the rest into a bag on the sledge and started off in high glee, stimulated in body and mind. As I left the depot there appeared to be nothing on earth that could prevent me reaching the Hut within a couple of days, but a fresh obstacle with which I had not reckoned was to arise and cause further delay, leading to far-reaching results.

It happened that after several hours' march the surface changed from snow to polished névé and then to slippery ice. I could scarcely keep on my feet at all, falling every few moments and bruising my emaciated self until I expected to see my bones burst through the clothes. How I regretted having abandoned those crampons after crossing the Mertz Glacier; shod with them, all would be easy.

With nothing but finnesko on the feet, to walk over such a sloping surface would have been difficult enough in the wind without any other hindrance; with the sledge sidling down the slope and tugging at one, it was quite impossible. I found that I had made too far to the east and to reach Aladdin's cave had unfortunately to strike across the wind. Before giving up, I even tried crawling on my hands and knees. However, the day's run, fourteen miles, was by no means a poor one.

Having erected the tent I set to work to improvise crampons. With this object in view the theodolite case was cut up, providing two flat pieces of wood in which were struck as many screws and nails as could be procured by dismantling the sledgemeter and the theodolite itself. In the repair-bag there were still a few ice-nails which at this time were of great use.

Late the next day, the wind, which had risen in the night, fell off and a start was made westwards over the ice slopes with the pieces of nail-studded wood lashed to my feet. A glorious expanse of sea lay to the north and several recognizable points on the coast were clearly in view to east and west.

The crampons were not a complete success for they gradually broke up, lasting only a distance of six miles. Then the wind increased and I got into difficulties by the sledge sidling into a narrow crevasse. It was held up by the boom at the foot of the mast. It took some time to extract and the wind continued to rise, so there was nothing for it but to pitch camp.

Further attempts at making crampons were more handicapped than ever, for the best materials available had been utilized already. However, from the remnants of the first pair and anything else that could be pressed into the service, a second pair was evolved of the nature of wooden-soled finnesko with spikes. This work took an interminable time, for the tools and appliances available were almost all contained in a small pocket knife that had belonged to Mertz. Besides a blade it was furnished with a spike, a gimlet and a screw-driver.

A blizzard was in full career on January 31 and I spent all day and most of the night on the crampons. On February 1 the wind and drift had subsided late in the afternoon, and I got under way expecting great things from the new crampons. The beacon marking Aladdin's Cave was clearly visible as a black dot on the ice slopes to the west.

At 7 P.M. that haven within the ice was attained. It took but a few moments to dig away the snow and throw back the canvas flap sealing the entrance. A moment later I slid down inside, arriving amidst familiar surroundings. Something unusual in one corner caught the eye—three oranges and a pineapple—circumstantial evidence of the arrival of the *Aurora*.

The improvised crampons had given way and were squeezing my feet painfully. I rummaged about amongst a pile of food-bags hoping to find some crampons or leather boots, but was disappointed, so there was nothing left but to repair the damaged ones. That done and a drink of hot milk having been prepared I packed up to make a start for the Hut. On climbing out of the cave imagine my disappointment at finding a strong wind and draft had risen. To have attempted the descent of the five and a half miles of steep ice slope to the Hut with such inadequate and fragile crampons, weak as I still was, would have been only as a last resort. So I camped in the comfortable cave and hoped for better weather next day.

But the blizzard droned on night and day for over a week with never a break. Think of my feelings as I sat within the cave, so near and yet so far from the Hut, impatient and anxious, ready to spring out and take the trail at a moment's notice. Improvements to the crampons kept me busy for a time; then, as there were a couple of old boxes lying about, I set to work and constructed a second emergency pair in case the others should break up during the descent. I tried the makeshift crampons on the ice outside, but was disappointed to find that they had not sufficient grip to face the wind, so had to abandon the idea of attempting the descent during the continuance of the blizzard. Nevertheless, by February 8 my anxiety as to what was happening at the Hut reached such a pitch that I resolved to try the passage in spite of everything, having worked out a plan whereby I was to sit on the sledge and sail down as far as possible.

Whilst these preparations were in progress the wind slackened. At last the longed for event was to be realized. I snatched a hasty meal and set off. Before a couple of miles had been covered the wind had fallen off altogether, and after that it was gloriously calm and clear.

I had reached within one and a half miles of the Hut and there was no sign of the *Aurora* lying in the offing. I was comforted with the thought that she might still be at the anchorage and have swung inshore so as to be hidden under the ice cliffs. But even as I gazed about seeking for a clue, a speck on the northwest horizon caught my eye and my hopes went down. It looked like a distant ship—Was it the *Aurora*? Well, what matter! The long journey was at an end—a terrible chapter of my life was concluded!

Then the rocks around winter quarters began to come into view; part of the basin of the Boat Harbor appeared, and lo! there were human figures! They almost seemed unreal—was it all a dream? No, indeed, for after a brief moment one of them observed me and waved an arm—I replied—there was a commotion and they all ran towards the Hut. Then they were lost, hidden by the crest of the first steep slope. It almost seemed to me that they had run away to hide.

Minutes passed as I slowly descended trailing the sledge. Then a head rose over the brow of the hill and there was Bickerton, breathless after a long run uphill. I expect for a while he wondered which of us it was. Soon we had shaken hands and he knew all in a few brief words, I for my part learning that the ship had left earlier that very day. Madigan, McLean, Bage and Hodgeman arrived, and then a newcomer, Jeffryes. Five men had remained behind to make a search for our party, and Jeffryes was a new wireless operator landed from the *Aurora*.

My heart was deeply touched by the devotion of these men who thus faced a second year of the rigours and extreme discomfort of the Adelie Land blizzard.

For myself that wonderful occasion was robbed of complete joy by the absence of my two gallant companions, and as we descended to the Hut there were moist eyes amongst the little party as they learnt of the fate of Ninnis and Mertz.

We were soon at the Hut, where I found that full preparations had been made for wintering a second year. The weather was calm and the ship was not more than eighty miles away, so I decided to recall her by wireless. The masts at the Hut had been re-erected during the summer, and on board the *Aurora* Hannam was provided with a wireless receiving set. Jeffryes had arranged with Hannam to call up at 8, 9 and 10 P.M. for several evenings while the *Aurora* was within wireless range, in case there was any news of my party. A message recalling the ship was therefore sent off and repeated at frequent intervals till past midnight.

Next morning there was a forty-mile wind, but the *Aurora* was in view away across Commonwealth Bay to the west. She had returned in response to the call and was steaming up and down, waiting for the wind to moderate.

We immediately set to work getting all the records, instruments and personal gear ready to be taken down to the Boat Harbour in anticipation of calm weather during the day.

The wind chose to continue and towards evening was in the sixties, while the barometer fell. The sea was so heavy that the motor-boat could never have lived through it.

That evening Jeffryes sent out another message, which we learned afterwards was not received, in which the alternative course was offered to Captain Davis of either remaining until calm weather supervened or of leaving at once for the Western Base. I felt that the decision should be left to him, as he could appreciate exactly the situation of the Western Base and what the ship could be expected to do amid the ice at that season of the year.

The wintering of Wild's party on the floating ice through a second year would be fraught with such danger for their safety that it was to be avoided at all costs.

On the morning of the 10th there was no sign of the ship and evidently Captain Davis had decided to wait no longer, knowing that further delay would endanger the chances of picking up the eight men on the shelf ice far away to the west. At such a critical moment determination, fearless and swift, was necessary, and, in coming to his momentous decision Captain Davis acted well and for the best interests of the Expedition.

A long voyage lay before the *Aurora*, through fifteen hundred miles of ice-strewn sea, swept by intermittent blizzards and shrouded now at midnight in darkness. Indeed, it was by no means certain that it would be possible to reach them, for the pack-ice off Queen Mary Land was known to be exceptionally heavy.

The long Antarctic winter was fast approaching and we turned to meet it with resolution, knowing that the early summer of the same year would bring relief.

1915–1916
ENDURANCE & COURAGE:
SHACKLETON'S HEROIC JOURNEY

The rope could not be recovered. We had flung down the adze from the top of the fall, and also the logbook wrapped in one of our blouses. That was all we brought, except our wet clothes, from the Antarctic, which a year and a half before we had entered with well-found ship, full equipment and high hopes. That was all of tangible things; but in memories we were rich. We had pierced the veneer of outside things. We had seen God in His splendors; we had heard the text that Nature renders. We had reached the naked soul of man.

– Sir Ernest Henry Shackleton

The virtues of high adventure drew Irish born and educated Ernest Henry Shackleton to the sea, first as a merchantman, then as an officer in the Royal Navy Reserve, and ultimately as an Antarctic explorer. Joining Robert Falcon Scott's *Discovery* Expedition in 1901, Shackleton, with Scott and Robert Wilson, reached 82°16'33" S on a sledge journey across the Ross Ice Shelf in the summer of 1903, but the punishing demands of this journey had so threatened his health that soon afterwards he departed to convalesce in England. Five years later Shackleton returned on the *Nimrod*, in command of the British Antarctic Expedition (1907–1909). When his ship could not penetrate the pack ice to reach the Edward VII peninsula, where he had first intended to establish his base, the expedition wintered on Ross Island. The next summer Shackleton led a sledging party to within a scant one hundred miles of the South Pole, but with supplies running low and his team at the limits of their strength he had to make the heartrending decision to turn back.

By the time Shackleton again set out for the Antarctic—in command of the British Imperial Trans-Antarctic Expedition (1914–16)—both Amundsen (December 14, 1911) and Scott (January 17, 1912) had reached the South Pole. Shackleton did not abandon his ambition to lead a party there, but conceived a journey even more grand and daring—which he proclaimed in the expedition prospectus as *the last great Polar journey that can be made*—to reach the South Pole from a base on the Weddell Sea and then to continue across the frozen continent to an ultimate destination on McMurdo Sound. Once again the harsh Antarctic would thwart Shackleton's first ambitions, but would impel him on a journey that was to be a supreme test of his leadership and of his family's motto: *By endurance we shall conquer.*

When Shackleton and the three-hundred ton, Norwegian-built *Endurance* reached the island of South Georgia in early November of 1914, whalers there reported unprecedented pack ice in the Weddell Sea just beyond. Shackleton delayed departure for a month. Although the dangerous conditions had not noticeably improved, *Endurance* finally set out on December 5, 1914 with her crew of twenty-seven handpicked men, a stowaway, and sixty-nine superb Canadian sledge dogs. Encountering the first pack ice on December 7th, *Endurance* beat her way forward for the next six weeks, dodging dangerous ice and ramming through it when necessary, under the direction of her experienced and determined captain, Frank Worsley. The high-spirited men aboard *Endurance* were confident that their sturdy ship would reach her destination, Vahsel Bay, on the Caird coast of Antarctica. But this was not to be.

On January 18, 1915, only one day out from Vahsel Bay, a dense field of pack ice forced *Endurance* to a halt. Rather than risking the ship in stoking its powerful steam engines to batter a path through the ice, Shackleton and Worsley decided to wait for an opening, but the ice tightened around the ship overnight and a northeasterly gale compressed the pack against the nearby shore, gripping *Endurance* ever more tightly in a trap from which it soon became clear there could be no escape until the renewed thaw of the austral spring nine months later. By the end of that February the crew had effectively transformed *Endurance* into a winter station. The dogs were moved off the ship and comfortably housed in "dogloos" constructed of blocks of hewn ice. For the next ten months the crew remained aboard the ship, helplessly drifting with the Weddell Sea pack ice. Under Shackleton's leadership good spirits prevailed among the crew and officers, and the men were snug enough in their quarters to be well protected from the howling winds and freezing temperatures of the Antarctic winter.

Thaw came with the Antarctic spring and with the thaw fresh dangers that proved fatal to *Endurance.* Late in the night of October 15, 1915, the ice around the ship split apart with a thunderous clap and she floated free. The crew hastily raised sail and *Endurance* advanced almost one hundred yards before becoming lodged between two ridges of ice with icebergs ahead blocking any further advance.

Now vulnerable to the movements of huge sheets of ice, *Endurance* heeled to a 30° Port List on October 18th. On October 24th the ice again attacked the damaged ship, with heavy pressure ridges jamming into her sternward quarter, heaving *Endurance* onto her port side and crushing her against the ice floe. On the 27th of October the men were forced to abandon *Endurance*. Over the next few days they built their "Ocean Camp" on the ice floe, salvaging all that they could from the wreck. By November 8th the ice had driven all but scant twisted ruins of her remains into the frigid ocean. On November 21st, at 5 P.M., she disappeared forever.

Now, more than a year after their departure from South Georgia, the men of *Endurance* were imprisoned on a floe in a sea of ice—with three lifeboats, their dogs, and the supplies that they had managed to salvage from their vanished ship. Knowing that the lifeboats were their sole lifelines, the men spent the next weeks refitting them for the inevitable voyage that lay ahead and mounting them on sledges to transport them across the ice in search of open waters. After a midsummer's Christmas feast on December 22nd, the expedition set out the next day. With great difficulty they advanced eight miles over a chaotic terrain of broken and tumbled ice, only to realize on the fifth day of a cruel and sodden March that the wind had pushed them back almost to their starting point. Retreating and shifting camps in search of a stable surface amidst melting and colliding ice floes, the men finally established a relatively secure site for "Patience Camp," where, on January 14, 1916, they were obliged to shoot twenty-seven of their beloved dogs. Week after week passed, with openings in the ice appearing then rapidly closing. Although the men managed to stretch their provisions with penguin and seal and dog meat, by the end of March their supplies had run dangerously low, and with the Antarctic summer drawn to an end, no passage of escape had yet appeared. On March 30th, the men shot the last of their faithful dogs.

Finally, on Sunday, April 9, 1916, after 156 days on the ice, Shackleton ordered the men to the three boats—the *James Caird*, the *Dudley Docker*, and the *Stancomb-Wills*. After a full day of hard rowing and fresh dangers averted, the men found themselves on a small ice floe heaving in the open ocean. In the middle of that first night their tiny island camp cracked in half, but all men were recovered and the boats were again launched the following morning into winds which mounted to blizzard force, lashing freezing gusts at the men in the worn and sodden remnants of their clothing. That night the utterly exhausted men of *Endurance* camped apprehensively on an ice floe

only twenty yards wide, to confront—on the morning of April 11th—
huge ocean swells jammed with icebergs bearing down upon their
precarious position. Early that afternoon an opening appeared in the
water. The men quickly launched their boats and spent five agonizing
days facing the brutal elements along with their own utter exhaustion,
hunger, thirst, and seasickness. Lost in the shifting winds and currents,
many of the men had surrendered to delirium and were nearing death
when at last by chance and good fortune, at dawn on April 14th, land
was sighted—Elephant Island, some thirty miles distant. Struggling
with their last desperate energies, the men brought the three boats to
within ten miles of salvation by late that afternoon—only to encounter
strong winds and currents, which held them at bay for one more night
on a blizzard-swept sea. The next day—seven days out from "Patience
Camp"—the men of *Endurance* reached the forlorn shore of storm-
blasted Elephant Island, with all hands alive.

His crew had reached safety, but Shackleton knew that they would
never be rescued from the bleak South Shetland Island, so he selected
five men—Worsley, Crean, McNish, McCarthy, and Vincent—all eager
volunteers and excellent sailors—to join him on an impossible voyage
to seek help—across 800 miles of the earth's most treacherous ocean—
from the whaling stations on South Georgia Island. While carpenter
McNish fitted out the largest of the three lifeboats—the *James Caird*—
for the journey, Shackleton worked to assure the lives of the twenty-
two men whom he would leave behind under the capable leadership
of Frank Wild, the expedition's second-in-command. On April 24, 1916,
the 22½ foot *James Caird* and its heroic crew disappeared behind the
waves off Elephant Island, at the start of a miraculous voyage that
was to last for seventeen harrowing days, at the seventh day of which
we open our selection from Shackleton's account.

But for the truthful and modest sobriety of Shackleton's prose,
the reader might take his story as a parody of the virtues celebrated in
a Victorian boy's novel: of unflinching courage and resourcefulness,
the sheer force of will, and selfless dedication to the welfare of one's
comrades in the face of mortal dangers. Utterly devoid of unmanly
vainglory, Shackleton's narrative bears plain testimony to these
qualities, which assured the survival of himself and his men, and he
does not fail to add a measure of wonder and piety. After suffering
seventeen days through tortured seas, it was both a miracle and a
tribute to the navigational skills of Captain Worsley that the six men
of the *James Caird* finally made a difficult landing on South Georgia
Island on May 10, 1916. After ten days of recuperation from their

unprecedented ocean voyage, it was no less a miracle and no less a tribute to courage, determination and skill that Shackleton, Worsley, and Crean marched twenty-two miles across the uncharted glaciers and mountains of the South Georgia interior—their only tools a carpenter's adze, fifty feet of rope, and a compass—to reach the whaling station at Stromness only thirty-six hours later on the afternoon of May 20, 1916.

Ice and storms frustrated Shackleton's first three attempts to rescue the men he had left on Elephant Island. Finally, aboard the Chilean tug Yelcho, he reached them on August 30, 1916. Although three men of A. E. Mackintosh's supporting Ross Sea party, which had sailed in *Aurora*, had perished after laying down depots for the use of the aborted trans-Antarctic mission, all the men of the Weddell Sea party had survived. On October 8, 1916 the men of *Endurance* dispersed. Although the expedition had failed, the survival of its members would always be remembered in the annals of polar exploration as a noble triumph of the human spirit. Shackleton returned to South Georgia in 1922 at the head of a new Antarctic expedition. Exhausted, he died there at Grytviken before setting out. Overlooking the harbor, his modest grave is a place of pilgrimage and a sober monument to masterful leadership and steadfast courage.

SHIP'S MANIFEST OF THE ENDURANCE-WEDDELL SEA PARTY

Sir Ernest Shackleton, Leader (Boss); **Frank Wild**, 2nd in Command (Frankie); **Frank Worsley**, Ship's Captain (Skipper): **Lionel Greenstreet**, First Officer (Horace); **Hubert T. Hudson**, Navigator (Buddha); **Thomas Crean**, Second Officer (Tom); **Alfred Cheetham**, Third Officer (Alf); **Louis Rickinson**, First Engineer (Rickey); **A. J. Kerr**, Second Engineer (Krasky); **Dr. James A. McIlroy**, Surgeon (Mickey); **Dr. Alexander H. Macklin**, Surgeon (Mack); **Robert S. Clark**, Biologist (Bob); **Leonard D. A. Hussey**, Meteorologist (Uzbird); **James M. Wordie**, Geologist (Jock); **Reginald W. James**, Physicist (Jimmy); **George E. Marston**, Artist (Putty); **Thomas Orde-Lees**, Motor Expert (The Colonel); **James Francis Hurley**, Photographer (The Prince); **Henry McNish**, Carpenter (Chips); **Charles Green**, Cook (Dough-balls); **Perce Blackborow**, Stowaway, later Steward (Blackie); **John Vincent**, Able Seaman (Bo'sun); **Timothy McCarthy**, Able Seaman (Tim); **Walter E. How**, Able Seaman (Hownow); **William Bakewell**, Able Seaman (Bakie);**Thomas McLeod**, Able Seaman (Stornoway); **William Stevenson**, Fireman (Steve); **Ernest Holness**, Fireman (Holie).

Shackleton's Heroic Journey

from *South: The Story of Shackleton's 1914-1917 Expedition*
by Sir Ernest Henry Shackleton

The End of the Boat Journey

During the afternoon the wind freshened to a good stiff breeze, and the *James Caird* made satisfactory progress. I had not realized until the sunlight came how small our boat really was. So low in the water were we that each succeeding swell cut off our view of the skyline. At one moment the consciousness of the forces arrayed against us would be almost overwhelming, and then hope and confidence would rise again as our boat rose to a wave and tossed aside the crest in a sparkling shower. My gun and some cartridges were stowed aboard the boat as a precaution against a shortage of food, but we were not disposed to destroy our little neighbours, the Cape pigeons, even for the sake of fresh meat. We might have shot an albatross, but the wandering king of the ocean aroused in us something of the feeling that inspired, too late, the Ancient Mariner.

The eighth, ninth and tenth days of the voyage had few features worthy of special note. The wind blew hard during these days, and the strain of navigating the boat was unceasing, but we kept on advancing towards our goal and felt that we were going to succeed. We still suffered severely from the cold, for our vitality was declining owing to shortage of food, exposure, and the necessity of maintaining our cramped positions day and night. I found that it was now absolutely necessary to prepare hot milk for all hands during the night, in order to sustain life until dawn. This involved an increased drain upon our small supply of matches, and our supply already was very small indeed. One of the memories which comes to me of those days is of Crean singing at the tiller. He always sang while he was steering, but nobody ever discovered what the song was.

On the tenth night Worsley could not straighten his body after his spell at the tiller. He was thoroughly cramped, and we had to drag him beneath the decking and massage him before he could unbend himself and get into a sleeping-bag.

A hard north-westerly gale came up on the eleventh day (May 5th), and in the late afternoon it shifted to the south-west. The sky was overcast and occasional snow-squalls added to the discomfort produced by a tremendous cross-sea—the worst, I thought, which we had encountered. At midnight I was at the tiller, and suddenly noticed a line of clear sky between the south and south-west. I called to the other men that the sky was clearing, and then, a moment later, realised that what I had seen was not a rift in the clouds but the white crest of an enormous wave.

During twenty-six years' experience of the ocean in all its moods I had never seen a wave so gigantic. It was a mighty upheaval of the ocean, a thing quite apart from the big white-capped seas which had been our tireless enemies for many days. I shouted, "For God's sake, hold on! It's got us!" Then came a moment of suspense which seemed to last for hours. We felt our boat lifted and flung forward like a cork in breaking surf. We were in a seething chaos of tortured water; but somehow the boat lived through it, half-full of water, sagging to the dead weight and shuddering under the blow. We bailed with the energy of men fighting for life, flinging the water over the sides with every receptacle which came into our hands; and after ten minutes of uncertainty we felt the boat renew her life beneath us. She floated again, and ceased to lurch drunkenly as though dazed by the attack of the sea. Earnestly we hoped that never again should we encounter such a wave.

The conditions of the boat, uncomfortable before, were made worse by this deluge of water. All our gear was thoroughly wet again, and our cooking-stove was floating about in the bottom of the boat. Not until 3 a.m., when we were all chilled to the limit of endurance, did we manage to get the stove alight and to make ourselves hot drinks. The carpenter was suffering particularly, but he showed grit and spirit. Vincent, however, had collapsed, and for the past week had ceased to be an active member of the crew.

On the following day (May 6th) the weather improved, and we got a glimpse of the sun. Worsely's observation showed that we were not more than 100 miles from the north-west corner of South Georgia. Two more days, with a favourable wind, and we should sight the promised land. I hoped that there would be no delay, as our supply of water was running very low. The hot drink at night was essential, but I decided that the daily allowance of water must be cut down to half a pint per man. Our lumps of ice had gone some days before; we were dependent upon the water which we had brought from Elephant Island, and our thirst was increased by the fact that we were at this time using the brackish water in the breaker which had been slightly stove in when the boat was being loaded. Some sea-water had entered it.

Thirst took possession of us, but I dared not permit the allowance of water to be increased, because an unfavourable wind might have driven us away from the island and have lengthened our voyage by several days. Lack of water is always the most severe privation which men can be condemned to endure, and we found that the salt water in our clothing and the salt spray which lashed our faces made our thirst quickly grow to a burning pain. I had to be very firm in refusing to allow any one to anticipate the morrow's allowance, which sometimes I was begged to do.

I had altered the course to the east so as to make sure of striking the island, which would have been impossible to regain if we had run past the northern end. The course was laid on our scrap of chart for a point some thirty miles down the coast. That day and the following day passed for us in a sort of nightmare. Our mouths were dry and our tongues were swollen. The wind was still strong and the heavy sea forced us to navigate carefully. But any thought of our peril from the waves was buried beneath the consciousness of our raging thirst. The bright moments were those when we each received our one mug of hot milk during the long, bitter watches of the night.

Things were bad for us in those days, but the end was approaching. The morning of May 8th broke thick and stormy, with squalls from the north-west. We searched the waters ahead for a sign of land, and, although we searched in vain, we were cheered by a sense that the goal was near. About 10 A.M. we passed a little bit of kelp, a glad signal of the proximity of land. An hour later we saw two shags sitting on a big mass of kelp, and we knew then that we must be within ten or fifteen miles of the shore. These birds are as sure an indication of the proximity of land as a lighthouse is, for they never venture far to sea.

We gazed ahead with increasing eagerness, and at 12:30 P.M., through a rift in the clouds, McCarthy caught a glimpse of the black cliffs of South Georgia, just fourteen days after our departure from Elephant Island. It was a glad moment. Thirst-ridden, chilled, and weak as we were, happiness irradiated us. The job was nearly done. We stood in towards the shore to look for a landing-place, and presently we could see the green tussock-grass on the ledges above the surf-beaten rocks. Ahead of us, and to the south, blind rollers showed the presence of uncharted reefs along the coast. The rocky coast appeared to descend sheer to the sea. Our need of water and rest was almost desperate, but to have attempted a landing at that time would have been suicidal.

Night was approaching and the weather indications were

unfavourable. We could do nothing but haul off until the following morning, so we stood away on the starboard tack until we had made what appeared to be a safe offing. Then we hove to in the high westerly swell. The hours passed slowly as we waited the dawn; our thirst was a torment and we could scarcely touch our food, the cold seemed to strike right through our weakened bodies.

At 5 A.M. the wind shifted to the northwest, and quickly increased to one of the worst hurricanes any of us had ever experienced. A great cross-sea was running and the wind simply shrieked as it converted the whole seascape into a haze of driving spray. Down into the valleys, up to tossing heights, straining until her seams opened, swung our little boat, brave still but labouring heavily. We knew that the wind and set of the sea were driving us ashore, but we could do nothing.

The dawn revealed a storm-torn ocean, and the morning passed without bringing us a sight of the land; but at 1 P.M., through a rift in the flying mists, we got a glimpse of the huge crags of the island and realised that our position had become desperate. We were on a dead lee shore, and we could gauge our approach to the unseen cliffs by the roar of the breakwaters against the sheer walls of rock. I ordered the double-reefed mainsail to be set in the hope that we might claw off, and this attempt increased the strain upon the boat.

The *James Caird* was bumping heavily, the water was pouring in everywhere. Our thirst was forgotten in the realisation of our imminent danger, as we bailed unceasingly and from time to time adjusted our weights; occasional glimpses showed that the shore was nearer.

I knew that Annewkow Island lay to the south of us, but our small and badly marked chart showed uncertain reefs in the passage between the island and the mainland, and I dared not trust it, though, as a last resort, we could try to lie under the lee of the island.

The afternoon wore away as we edged down the coast, and the approach of evening found us still some distance from Annewkow Island; dimly in the twilight we could see a snow-capped mountain looming above us. The chance of surviving the night seemed small, and I think that most of us felt that the end was very near. Just after 6 P.M., as the boat was in the yeasty backwash from the seas flung from this iron-bound coast, just when things looked their worst, they changed for the best; so thin is the line which divides success from failure.

The wind suddenly shifted, and we were free once more to make an offing. Almost as soon as the gale eased, the pin which locked the mast to the thwart fell out. Throughout the hurricane it must have been on the point of doing this, and if it had nothing could have saved us. The mast would have snapped like a carrot. Our backstays had carried away once before, when iced up, and were not too strongly fastened. We were thankful indeed for the mercy which had held the pin in its place during the hurricane.

We stood off shore again, tired almost to the point of apathy. Our water had long been finished. The last was about a pint of hairy liquid, which we strained through a bit of gauze from the medicine chest. The pangs of thirst attacked us with redoubled intensity, and I felt that at almost any risk we must make a landing on the following day. The night wore on. We were very tired and longed for day. When at last dawn came there was hardly any wind, but a high cross-sea was running. We made slow progress towards the shore.

About 8 A.M. the wind backed to the north-west and threatened another blow. In the meantime we had sighted a big indentation which I thought must be King Haakon Bay, and I decided that we must land there. We set the bows of the boat towards the bay, and ran before the freshening gale. Soon we had angry reefs on either side. Great glaciers came down to the sea and offered no landing-place. The sea spouted on the reefs and thundered against the shore. About noon we sighted a line of jagged reef, like blackened teeth, which seemed to bar the entrance to the bay. Inside, fairly smooth water stretched eight or nine miles to the head of the bay.

A gap in the reef appeared, and we made for it, but the fates had another rebuff for us. The wind shifted and blew from the east right out of the bay. We could see the way through the reef, but we could not approach it directly. That afternoon we bore up, tacking five times in the strong wind. The last tack enabled us to get through, and at last we were in the wide mouth of the bay.

Dusk was approaching. A small cove, with a boulder-strewn beach guarded by a reef, made a break in the cliffs on the south side of the bay, and we turned in that direction. I stood in the bows, and directed the steering as we ran through the kelp and made the passage of the reef. The entrance was so narrow that we had to take in the oars, and the swell was piling itself right over the reef into the cove. But in a minute or two we were inside, and in the gathering darkness the *James Caird* ran in on a swell and touched the beach.

I sprang ashore with the short painter, and held on when the boat went out with the backward surge. When the boat came in again three men got ashore and held the painter while I climbed some rocks with another line. A slip on the wet rocks 20 feet up nearly closed my part of the story, just when we were achieving safety. A jagged piece of rock held me and also sorely bruised me. I, however, made fast the line, and in a few minutes we were all safe on the beach, with the boat floating in the surging water just off the shore.

We heard a gurgling sound which was sweet music in our ears, and, peering round, we found a stream of fresh water almost at our feet. A moment later we were down on our knees drinking the pure, ice-cold water in long draughts which put new life in us. It was a splendid moment.

King Haakon Bay

Our next task was to get the stores and ballast out of the boat so that we might secure her for the night, and having taken out the stores and gear and ballast, we tried to pull the empty boat up the beach. By this effort we discovered how weak we were, for our united strength was not enough to get the *James Caird* clear of the water. Time after time we pulled together but without avail, and I saw that we must have food and rest before we beached the boat.

We made fast a line to a heavy boulder, and set a watch to fend the boat off the rocks of the beach. Then I sent Crean round to the left side of the cove, about thirty yards away, where I had noticed a little cave as we were running in. He could not see much in the darkness, but reported that the place certainly promised some shelter. We carried the sleeping-bags round and found a mere hollow in the rock-face, with a shingle floor sloping at a steep angle to the sea. There we prepared a hot meal, and when the food was finished I ordered the men to turn in. I took the first watch beside the *James Caird*, which was still afloat in the tossing water just off the beach.

Fending the boat off the rocks in the darkness was awkward work, and during the next few hours I laboured to keep her clear of the beach. Occasionally I had to rush into the seething water. Then, as a wave receded, I let the boat out on the alpine rope so as to avoid a sudden jerk. The *James Caird* could only be dimly seen in the cove, where the high black cliffs made the darkness almost complete, and the strain upon one's attention was great.

After several hours had passed my desire for sleep became irresistible and I called Crean. While he was taking charge of the boat she got adrift, and we had some anxious moments; but fortunately she went across towards the cave and we secured her unharmed. I arranged for one-hour watches during the remainder of the night, and then took Crean's place among the sleeping men.

The sea went down in the early hours of the morning (May 11th), and, having braced ourselves with another meal, we again started to get the boat ashore. We waited for Byron's "great ninth wave," and when it lifted the *James Caird* in we held her, and, by dint of great exertion, worked her round broadside to the sea. Inch by inch we dragged her up until we reached the tussock-grass and knew that the boat was above high-water mark. The completion of this task removed our immediate anxieties, and we were free to examine our surroundings and plan the next move. The day was bright and clear.

King Haakon Bay is an eight-mile sound penetrating the coast of South Georgia in an easterly direction. The northern and southern sides of the sound were formed by steep mountain-ranges, their flanks being furrowed by mighty glaciers. It was obvious that our way inland from the cove was barred, and that we must sail to the head of the sound. Several magnificent peaks and crags gazed out across their snowy domains to the sparkling waters of the sound.

Our cove lay a little inside the southern headland of King Haakon Bay. A narrow break in the cliffs, which were about 100 feet high, formed the entrance to the cove. Our cave was a recess in the cliff on the left-hand of the beach. The rocky face of the cliff was undercut at this point, and the shingle thrown up by the waves formed a steep slope, which we reduced to about one in six by scraping the stones away from inside. Later we strewed the rough floor with the dead, nearly dry leaves of the tussock-grass, and thus formed a slightly soft bed for our sleeping-bags.

Water had trickled down the face of the cliff and formed long icicles, which hung down in front of the cave to the length of about 15 feet. These icicles provided shelter, and when we had spread our sails below them, with the assistance of the oars, we had quarters which, under the circumstances, were reasonably comfortable. The camp at least was dry, and we moved our gear there with confidence. We also built a fireplace and arranged our sleeping-bags and blankets around it. The cave was about 8 feet deep and 12 feet wide at the entrance.

. . . Crean and I climbed the tussock slope behind the beach, and reached the top of a headland overlooking the sound. There we found the nests of albatrosses, and to our delight the nests contained young birds. The fledglings were fat and lusty, and we had no hesitation in deciding that some of them must die at an early age.

At this stage our most pressing anxiety was about fuel. We had rations for ten more days, and we knew now that we could get birds for food; but if we were to have hot meals fuel must be secured. Our store of petroleum was running low, and it was necessary to keep some of it for the overland journey which lay before us. A sea-elephant or a seal would have provided fuel as well as food, but we could not see a sign of either. During the morning we started a fire in the cave with wood from the top sides of the boat, and, in spite of the dense smoke, we enjoyed the warmth and the splendid stew which Crean, who was cook for the day, provided for us.

Four young albatrosses went into the pot, with a Bovril ration for thickening. The flesh was white and succulent, and the bones, not fully formed, almost melted in our mouths. That was a memorable meal. Afterwards we dried our tobacco in the embers of the fire and smoked contentedly, but an attempt to dry our soaked clothes was not successful. Until we could secure blubber or driftwood we could not afford to have a fire except for cooking.

The final stage of the journey was still before us. I realized that the condition of the party generally, and of McNeish and Vincent in particular, would prevent us putting to sea again except under the pressure of absolute necessity. I also doubted if our boat in its weakened condition could weather the island. By sea we were still 150 miles away from Stromness Whaling Station.

The alternative was to attempt the crossing of the island. If we could not get over we must try to get food and fuel enough to keep us through the winter, but such a task was almost hopeless. On Elephant Island were twenty-two men whose plight was worse than ours, and who were waiting the relief which we alone could secure for them. Somehow or other we had got to push on, though several days must elapse before our strength would be sufficiently recovered for us to row or sail the last nine miles up to the head of the bay. In the meantime we could make what preparations were possible.

Shortly before midnight a gale sprang up suddenly from the north-east, with rain and sleet showers, and when daylight came the temperature was the highest we had experienced for several months.

Our party spent a quiet day, attending to clothing and gear, checking stores, eating and resting. We had previously discovered that when we were landing from the boat on May 10th we had lost the rudder. The *James Caird* had been bumping heavily astern as we scrambled ashore, and evidently the rudder had then been knocked off. A careful search of the beach and rocks failed to reveal the missing rudder, and this was a serious loss, even if the voyage to the sound could be made in good weather.

In the afternoon Crean and McCarthy brought down six young

albatrosses, so we were well supplied with fresh food. The air temperature on that night was probably not lower than 38° or 40° Fahr., and the unaccustomed warmth made us quite uncomfortable in our sleeping quarters. The ice in the cove was rearing and crashing on the beach, but with firm land beneath our feet the noise of it did not trouble us.

The bay was still filled with ice on the morning of Saturday, May 13th, but the tide took it all away in the afternoon. Then a strange thing happened. The rudder, with all the broad Atlantic to sail in, came bobbing back into our cove. Nearer and nearer it came as we waited anxiously on the shore, oars in hand; and at last we were able to seize it. Surely a remarkable salvage!

The day was bright and clear; our clothes were drying and our strength was returning. In the afternoon we began to prepare the *James Caird* for the journey to the head of King Haakon Bay. During the morning of this day (May 13th) Worsley and I tramped across the hills in a north-easterly direction for the purpose of getting a view of the sound, and possibly gathering useful information for the next stage of our journey. It was exhausting work, but after covering about two and a half miles in two hours we were able to look east up the bay. We, however, could not see very much of the country which we should have to cross in order to reach the whaling station on the other side of the island. Some gentoo penguins and a young sea-elephant which we found were killed by Worsley.

When we got back to the cave, tired and hungry, we found a splendid meal of stewed albatross chicken waiting for us. We had carried a quantity of blubber and the sea-elephant's liver in our blouses, and produced our treasures as a surprise for the men. Rough climbing on the way back had nearly persuaded us to throw the stuff away, but we held on and had our reward at the camp.

The long bay had been a magnificent sight, even to eyes which had dwelt long enough on grandeur and were hungry for the familiar things of every-day life. Its green-blue waters were being beaten to fury by the gale. The mountains peered through the mists, and between them huge glaciers poured down from the great ice-slopes which lay behind. We counted twelve glaciers, and every few minutes we heard the great roar caused by masses of ice calving from the parent streams.

On May 14th we made our preparations for an early start on the following day, should the weather hold fair. All hands were recovering from the chafing caused by our wet clothes during the boat journey. We paid our last visit to the nests of the albatrosses. Each nest consisted

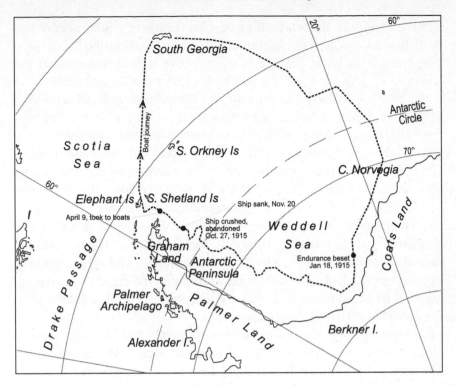

of a mound over a foot high of tussock-grass, roots and a little earth. The albatross lays one egg, and very rarely two. We did not enjoy attacking these birds, but our hunger was so great that each time we killed one we felt a little less remorseful.

May 15th was a great day. We made our hoosh at 7:30 A.M., and then loaded up the boat and gave her a flying launch down the steep beach into the surf. A gusty north-westerly wind was blowing, but the *James Caird* headed to the sea as if anxious to face the battle of the waves once more. As we sailed merrily up the bay the sun broke through the mists and made the tossing waters sparkle around us. We were a curious-looking party on that bright morning, but we were feeling happy.

The wind blew fresh and strong, and a small sea broke on the coast as we advanced. We had hoped to find sea-elephants on the upper beaches, and our expectations were realised. As we neared the head of the bay we heard the roar of the bulls, and soon afterwards we saw their great unwieldy forms lying on a shelving beach towards the bay-head.

We rounded a high, glacier-worn bluff on the north side, and soon after noon we ran the boat ashore on a low beach of sand and pebbles, with tussock-grass growing above high-water mark. Hundreds of sea-elephants were lying about, enough to provide food and blubber for years and years. Our landing-place was about a mile and a half west of the north-east corner of the bay. Just east of us was a glacier-snout ending on the beach but giving a passage towards the head of the bay, except at high-water or when a very heavy surf was running.

A cold rain had begun to fall, and as quickly as possible we hauled the *James Caird* up above high-water mark, and turned her over just to the east side of the bluff. The spot was separated from the mountain side by a low bank, rising 20 or 30 feet above sea-level.

We soon converted the boat into a very comfortable cabin *à la* Peggotty, turfing it round with tussocks. One side of the *James Caird* rested on stones so as to afford a low entrance, and when we had finished she looked as if she had grown there. A sea-elephant provided us with fuel and meat, and that evening found a well-fed and fairly contented party in Peggotty Camp.

Our camp, as I have said, lay on the north side of King Haakon Bay near the head. The path towards the whaling stations led round the seaward end of the snouted glacier on the east side of the camp, and up a snow-slope which seemed to lead to a pass in the great Allard-yce range, which forms the main backbone of South Georgia. The range dipped opposite the bay into a well-defined pass from east to west.

I planned to climb to the pass, and then be guided by the configuration of the country in the selection of a route eastward to Stromness Bay, where the whaling stations were established in the minor bays, Leith, Husvik and Stromness. On Tuesday, May 16th, the weather was bad, and we stayed under the boat nearly all day. The quarters were cramped but gave full protection from the weather, and we regarded our little cabin with much satisfaction, abundant meals adding to our contentment.

A fresh breeze was blowing on the following morning, with misty squalls, sleet and rain. I took Worsley with me on a pioneer journey to the west for the purpose of examining the country to be crossed at the beginning of the overland journey. We went round the seaward end of the snouted glacier, and tramped about a mile, crossing some big ridges of scree and moraines on our way. We found good going for a sledge as far as the north-east corner of the bay, but a snow squall obscured the view and we did not get much information regarding the conditions farther on. I had satisfied myself, however, that we could reach a good snow-slope leading apparently to the inland ice.

Worsley reckoned from the chart that the distance from our camp to Husvik was seventeen geographical miles, but we could not expect to follow a direct line. The carpenter started to make a sledge for the overland journey, but the materials at his disposal were limited in quantity and scarcely suitable in quality.

We overhauled our gear on Thursday, May 18th, and hauled our sledge to the lower edge of the snouted glacier. The sledge proved heavy and cumbrous, and I realised that three men would be unable to manage it amid the snow-plains, glaciers and peaks of the interior. Worsley and Crean were coming with me, and, after consultation, we decided to leave the sleeping-bags behind and make the journey in very light marching order.

We decided to take three days' provisions for each man in the form of sledging ration and biscuit, the Primus lamp filled with oil, the small cooker, the carpenter's adze (for use as an ice-ax), and the alpine rope, which made a total length of 50 feet when knotted, and would help us to lower ourselves down steep slopes or cross crevassed glaciers.

We had two boxes of matches left, one full and the other partially used. We decided to leave the full box at the camp and to take the second box, which contained forty-eight matches. I was unfortunate as regards foot-gear, as I had given away my heavy boots on the floe, and only had a lighter pair in poor condition. The carpenter helped me by putting several screws into the sole of each boot with the object of providing a grip on the ice. The screws came out of the *James Caird*.

We turned in early that night, but troubled thoughts kept me from sleeping. The task before the overland party would in all probability be heavy, and we were going to leave a weak party behind us in the camp. Vincent was still in the same condition and could not march. McNeish was pretty well broken up. These two men could not manage for themselves, and I had to leave McCarthy to look after them. Should we fail to reach the whaling station McCarthy might have a difficult task.

We had a very scanty knowledge of the interior, for no man had ever penetrated from the coast of South Georgia at any point, and I knew that the whalers regarded the country as inaccessible.

At 2 A.M. on the Friday morning we turned out, and an hour later our hoosh was ready. The full moon was shining in a practically cloudless sky, and we made a start as soon as we had eaten our meal. Our first difficulty was to get round the edge of the snouted glacier, which had points like fingers projecting into the sea. The waves were reaching the points of these fingers, and we had to rush from one recess to another when the waters receded. We soon reached the east side of the glacier, and began to ascend a snow-slope, heading due east on the last lap of our long trail.

The snow-surface was disappointing, and as we sank over our ankles at each step our progress was slow. After two hours' steady climbing we were 2,500 feet above sea level, and the bright moonlight showed us that the interior was tremendously broken. High peaks, impassable cliffs, steep snow-slopes, and sharply descending glaciers could be seen in all directions, with stretches of snow-plain overlaying the ice-sheet of the interior. The slope which we were ascending mounted to a ridge, and our course lay direct to the top. The moon, which was a good friend to us, threw a long shadow at one point and told us that the surface was broken in our path. Thus warned we avoided a huge hole capable of swallowing an army. The bay was now about three miles way.

I had hoped to get a view of the country ahead of us from the top of this slope, but as the surface became more level a thick fog drifted down. Under these conditions we roped ourselves together as a precaution against holes, crevasses and precipices, and I broke trail through the soft snow. With almost the full length of the rope between myself and the last man we could steer an approximately straight course, for if I veered to the right or left when marching into the blank wall of fog, the last man on the rope could shout a direction. So, like a ship with its "port," "starboard," "steady," we tramped through the fog for the next two hours.

Then, as daylight came, the fog partially lifted, and, from a height of about 3,000 feet, we looked down on what seemed to be a huge frozen lake, with its farther shores still obscured by fog. We halted there to eat a bit of biscuit, and to discuss whether we would go down and cross the flat surface of the lake or keep on the ridge we had already reached. I decided to go down, as the lake lay on our course. After an hour's fairly easy travel through the snow we began to meet crevasses, which showed that we were on a glacier. Later on the fog lifted completely and then we saw that our lake stretched to the horizon, and suddenly we realized that we were looking down upon the open sea on the east coast of the island.

Evidently we were at the top of Possession Bay, and the island at that point could not be more than five miles across from the head of King Haakon Bay. Our rough chart was inaccurate, and there was nothing for it but to start up the glacier again. That was about seven o'clock, and in two hours we had more than recovered our lost ground.

We regained the ridge and then struck south-east, for the chart showed that two more bays indented the coast before Stromness. It was comforting to know that we should have the eastern water in sight during our journey, although we could see that there was no way around the shore-line owing to steep cliffs and glaciers.

Men lived in houses lit by electric light on the east coast. News of the outside world awaited us there, and, above all, the coast meant for us the means of rescuing the twenty-two men left on Elephant Island.

Across South Georgia

The sun rose with every appearance of a fine day; we were travelling over a gently rising plateau, and at the end of an hour we found ourselves becoming uncomfortably hot. After passing an area of crevasses we paused for our first meal. We dug a hole in the snow about 3 feet deep and put the Primus into it. The hot hoosh was soon eaten, and we plodded on towards a sharp ridge between two of the peaks which lay ahead of us. By 11 a.m. we were almost at the crest. The slope became precipitous, and we had to cut steps as we advanced. For this purpose the adze proved an excellent instrument. At last I stood upon the razorback, while the other men held the rope and waited for news. The outlook was disappointing. I looked down a sheer precipice to a chaos of crumpled ice 1,500 feet below. There was no way down for us. The country to the east was a great snow upland, sloping upward for seven or eight miles to a height of over 4,000 feet. To the north it fell away steeply in glaciers into the bays, and to the south it was broken by huge outfalls from the inland ice-sheet. Our path lay between the glaciers and the outfalls, but first we had to descend from the ridge on which we were standing.

Cutting steps with the adze we moved in a lateral direction round the base of a dolomite, but the same precipice confronted us. Away to the north-east there appeared to be a snow-slope which might give a path to the lower country, and so we retraced our steps down the long slope which had taken us three hours to climb. In an hour we were at the bottom, but we were beginning to feel the strain of unaccustomed marching.

Skirting the base of the mountain above us, we came to a gigantic gully, a mile and a half long and 1,000 feet deep. This gully was semi-circular in form, and ended in a gentle incline. We passed through it, and at the far end we had another meal and short rest. This was at 12:30 P.M. Refreshed by our steaming Bovril ration we started once more for the crest, and after another weary climb we reached the top.

The same precipice lay below, and my eyes searched vainly for a way down. The snow, loosened by the hot sun, was now in a treacherous condition, and, looking back, we could see that a fog was rolling up behind us and meeting in the valleys another fog which was coming up from the east. This was a plain warning that we must get down to lower levels before we were enveloped.

The ridge was studded with peaks, which prevented us from getting a clear view either to the right or left, and I had to decide that our course lay back the way which we had come. It was of the utmost importance for us to get down into the next valley before dark. We were up 4,500 feet and the night temperature at that elevation would be very low. The afternoon was wearing on, and the fog was rolling up ominously from the west. We had neither tent nor sleeping-bags, and our clothes were terribly weather-worn.

In the distance, down the valley below us, we could see tussock-grass close to the shore, and if we could get down we might possibly dig out a hole in one of the lower snow-banks, line it with dry grass, and make ourselves fairly comfortable for the night. Back we went, and presently reached the top of another ridge in the fading light. After a glance over the top I turned to the anxious faces of the men behind me and said, "Come on, boys." Within a minute they stood beside me on the ice-ridge, the surface of which fell away at a sharp incline before us but merged into a snow-slope.

We could not see the bottom, and the possibility of the slope ending in a sheer fall occurred to us, but the fog which was creeping up behind us allowed no time for hesitation. At first we descended slowly, cutting steps in the hard snow, then the surface became softer, indicating that the gradient was less severe There could be no turning back now, so we unroped and slid in the fashion of youthful days. When we stopped on a snow-bank at the foot of the slope we found that we had descended at least 900 feet in two or three minutes. We looked back and saw the grey fingers of the fog appearing on the ridge. But we had escaped.

The country to the east was an ascending snow upland dividing the glaciers of the north coast from the outfalls of the south. From the top we had seen that our course lay between two huge masses of crevasses, and we thought that the road ahead was clear. This belief and the increasing cold made us abandon the idea of camping. At 6 P.M. we had another meal, and then we started up the long, gentle ascent. Night was upon us, and for an hour we plodded on in almost complete darkness, watching warily for signs of crevasses. But about

8 P.M. the full moon rose ahead of us and made a silver pathway for our feet. Onwards and upwards through soft snow we marched, resting occasionally on hard patches. By midnight we were again at an elevation of 4,000 feet. Still we were following the light, for as the moon swung round towards the north-east our path curved in that direction. The friendly moon seemed to pilot our weary feet. We could have had no better guide.

Midnight found us approaching the edge of a great snow-field, and a gentle slope lured our all-too-willing feet in that direction. At the base of the slope we thought that Stromness Bay lay. After we had descended about 300 feet a thin wind began to attack us. We had been on the march for over twenty hours, only halting for occasional meals. After 1 A.M. we cut a pit in the snow, piled up loose snow around it, and again started the Primus. Worsley and Crean sang their old songs when the Primus was going merrily. Laughter was in our hearts, though not on our parched and cracked lips.

Within half an hour we were away again, still downward to the coast. We now felt almost sure that we were above Stromness Bay, and joyfully pointed out various landmarks revealed by the light of the moon, whose friendly face was by this time cloud-swept. Our high hopes were soon shattered. Crevasses warned us that we were on another glacier, and presently we looked down almost to the seaward edge of the great riven ice-mass. I knew that there was no glacier in Stromness and realised that this must be Fortuna Glacier. The disappointment was severe. Back we turned and tramped up the glacier again, working at a tangent to the south-east. We were very tired.

At 5 A.M. we were at the foot of the rocky spurs of the range. The wind blowing down from the heights was chilling us, and we decided to get under the lee of a rock and rest. We put our sticks and the adze on the snow, sat down on them as close to one another as possible, and put our arms round each other. I thought that in this way we might keep warm and have half-an-hour's rest. Within a minute my two companions were fast asleep, and I realised how disastrous it would be if we all slumbered together, for sleep under such conditions merges into death. So after five minutes I awoke them and gave the word for a fresh start. So stiff were we that for the first 300 yards or so we marched with our knees bent.

A jagged line of peaks with a gap like a broken tooth confronted us. This was the ridge which runs in a southerly direction from Fortuna Bay, and our course to Stromness lay across it. A very steep slope led up to the ridge and an icy wind burst through the gap. With anxious hearts as well as with weary bodies we went through the gap at 6 a.m. Had the farther slope proved impassable our situation would have been almost desperate; but the worst was turning to the best for us.

The twisted, wave-like rock formations of Husvik Harbour appeared right ahead of us in the opening of dawn. Without a word we shook hands with one another. To our minds the journey was over, though really twelve miles of difficult country had still to be crossed. A gentle snow-slope descended at our feet towards a valley which separated our ridge from the hills immediately behind Husvik, and as we stood gazing Worsley said solemnly, "Boss, it looks too good to be true!"

Down we went, to be checked presently by water 2,500 feet below. We could see the little wave-ripples on the black beach, penguins strutting, and dark objects like seals lolling on the sand. This was an eastern arm of Fortuna Bay, separated by the ridge from the arm we had seen below us during the night.

The slope which we were traversing seemed to end in a precipice above the beach. But our revived spirits were not to be damped by any difficulties on the last stage of our journey, and cheerfully we camped for breakfast. While breakfast was being prepared, I climbed the ridge above us to secure an extended view of the country below; and at 6:30 A.M. I thought I heard the sound of a steam-whistle. I dared not be certain, but I knew that the men at the whaling stations would be called from their beds about that time.

Descending again to the camp I told the others, and in intense excitement we watched the chronometer for seven o'clock, when the whalers would be summoned to work. Right to the minute the steam-whistle came clearly to us, and never had any one of us heard sweeter music. It was the first sound created by outside human agency which had come to our ears since December 1914. That whistle told us that men were near, that ships were ready, and that very soon we should be on our way back to Elephant Island to rescue the men waiting there. It was a moment hard to describe. Pain and aches, boat journeys, marches, hunger and fatigue were forgotten, only the perfect contentment which comes from work accomplished remained.

My examination of the country before us had not provided definite information, so I put the situation before Worsley and Crean. Our obvious course lay down a snow-slope in the direction of Husvik. "Boys," I said, "this snow-slope seems to end in a precipice, but perhaps there is no precipice. If we don't go down we shall have to make a detour of at least five miles before we reach level going. What shall it be?" They both replied at once, "Try the slope." So again we started downwards.

We abandoned the Primus lamp, now empty, and carried with us one ration and a biscuit each. Deep snow clogged our feet, but after descending about 500 feet we thought that we saw our way clear ahead. A steep gradient of blue ice was the next obstacle. Worsley and Crean got a firm footing in a hole excavated with the adze, and then lowered me as I cut steps until the full 50 feet of our alpine rope was out. Then I made a hole big enough for the three of us, and the other two men came down the steps. In this laborious fashion we spent two hours descending about 500 feet. Halfway down we had to strike laboriously to the left, for we noticed that the fragments of ice loosened by the adze were taking a leap into space at the bottom of the slope. At last, and very thankfully, we got off the steep ice at a point where some rocks protruded, and then we could see that there was a perilous precipice directly below the point where we had started to cut the steps.

A slide down a slippery slope, with the adze going ahead, completed this descent, and, incidentally, still further damaged our much-tried trousers. When we arrived at the bottom we were not more than 1,500 feet above the sea. The slope was comparatively easy, and presently we came to patches of tussock-grass, and a few minutes later we reached the sandy beach. At our best speed we went along the beach to another rising ridge of tussock, and here we saw the first evidence of the proximity of man. A recently killed seal was lying there, and presently we saw several other bodies bearing the marks of bullet-wounds. Later I heard that men from Stromness go around by boat to Fortuna Bay to shoot seals.

By noon we were well up the slope on the other side of the bay, and half an hour later we were on a flat plateau, with one more ridge to cross before we descended into Husvik. I was leading when I suddenly found myself up to my knees in water and quickly sinking deeper through the snow-crust. I flung myself down and called to the others to do the same, so that our weight should be distributed on the treacherous surface. We were on top of a small lake, snow covered. After lying still for a few moments we rose and walked delicately, like Agag, for 200 yards, until a rise in the surface showed us that we were clear of the lake.

At 1:30 P.M. we climbed round a final ridge and saw a little steamer, a whaling boat, entering the bay, 2,500 feet below. A few moments later the masts of a sailing ship lying at a wharf came in sight. Minute

figures moving to and fro caught our gaze, and then we saw the sheds
and factory of Stromness Whaling Station. Once more we paused and
shook one another warmly by the hand.

Cautiously we started down the slope which led to warmth and
comfort, but the last lap of the journey was extraordinarily difficult.
Vainly we sought a safe, or reasonably safe, way down the steep ice-
clad mountain side. The sole possible pathway seemed to be a channel
cut by water running from the upland. Down through icy water we
followed the course of this stream. We were wet to the waist, shivering,
cold and tired.

Presently our ears detected an unwelcome sound which might
under other conditions have been musical. It was the splashing of a
waterfall, and we were at the wrong end. When we reached the top of
this fall we peered over cautiously and discovered that there was a
drop of 25 or 30 feet, with impassable ice-cliffs on both sides. To go up
again was, in our utterly wearied condition, scarcely thinkable. The
way down was through the waterfall itself.

With some difficulty we made fast one end of our rope to a boulder,
and then Worsley and I lowered Crean, who was the heaviest man.
He disappeared altogether in the falling water and came out gasping
at the bottom. I went next, sliding down the rope, and Worsley, who
was the lightest and nimblest of us, followed. At the bottom of the fall
we again stood on dry land.

The rope could not be recovered. We had flung down the adze
from the top of the fall, and also the log-book wrapped in one of our
blouses. That was all we brought, except our wet clothes, from the
Antarctic, which a year and a half before we had entered with well-
found ship, full equipment and high hopes. That was all of tangible
things; but in memories we were rich. We had pierced the veneer of
outside things. We had seen God in His splendours; we had heard the
text that Nature renders. We had reached the naked soul of man.

Shivering with cold, yet with hearts light and happy, we set off
towards the whaling station, now not more than a mile and a half
distant. The difficulties of the journey lay behind us. The thought that
there might be women at the station made us painfully conscious of
our uncivilized appearance, and we tried to straighten ourselves out
a bit. Our beards were long and our hair was matted. We were
unwashed, and the garments which we had worn for nearly a year
without a change were tattered and stained. Three more unpleasant-
looking ruffians could scarcely be imagined. Worsley produced several
safety-pins from some corner of his garments, and made some

temporary repairs which really emphasized his disrepair.

Down we hurried, and when quite close to the station we met two small boys ten or twelve years old. I asked them where the manager's house was, and they did not answer. They gave us one most informing look and then they ran from us as fast as their legs would carry them.

We reached the outskirts of the station and passed through the "digesting house," which was dark inside. Emerging at the other end we met an old man who gave us no time to ask any question. He hurried away. This greeting was not friendly. Then we came to the wharf, where the man in charge stuck to his station. I asked him if Mr. Sørlle (the manager) was in the house.

"Yes," he said as he stared at us.

"We would like to see him," said I.

"Who are you?" he asked.

"We have lost our ship and come over the island," I replied.

"You have come over the island?" he said, in a tone of entire disbelief.

Then he went towards the manager's house and we followed him. I learned afterwards that he said to Mr. Sørlle: "There are three funny-looking men outside, who say that they have come over the island and they know you. I have left them outside." A very necessary precaution from his point of view.

Mr. Sørlle came to the door and said, "Well?"

"Don't you know me?" I said.

"I know your voice," he replied doubtfully. "You're the mate of the *Daisy*."

"My name is Shackleton," I said.

Immediately he put out his hand and said, "Come in. Come in."

"Tell me, when was the war over?" I asked.

"The war is not over," he answered. "Millions are being killed. Europe is mad. The world is mad."

Mr. Sørlle's hospitality had no bounds. He would scarcely let us wait to remove our freezing boots before he took us into his house, and gave us seats in a warm and comfortable room. We were not fit to sit in any one's house until we had washed and put on clean clothes, but the kindness of the station manager was proof even against the unpleasantness of being in a room with us. He gave us coffee and cakes in the Norwegian fashion, and then showed us upstairs to the bath-room, where we shed our rags and scrubbed ourselves luxuriously.

Mr. Sørlle's kindness did not end with his personal care to us.

While we were washing he gave orders for one of the whaling vessels to be prepared at once, so that it might leave that night to pick up the other three men on the other side of the island. Soon we were clean again, and then we put on delightful new clothes supplied from the station stores and got rid of our superfluous hair. Then came a splendid meal, while Mr. Sørlle told us the arrangements he had made, and we discussed plans for the rescue of the main party on Elephant Island.

I arranged that Worsley should go with the relief ship to show the exact spot where the carpenter and his two companions were camped, while I began to prepare for the relief of the party on Elephant Island. The whaling vessel that was going round to King Haakon Bay was expected back on the Monday morning, and was to call at Grytviken Harbour, the port from which we sailed in December, 1914, in order that the magistrate resident there might be informed of the fate of the *Endurance*. It was also possible that letters were awaiting us there.

Worsley went aboard the whaler at ten o'clock that night; and on the next day the relief ship entered King Haakon Bay and Worsley reached Peggotty Camp in a boat. The three men were delighted beyond measure to be relieved, but they did not recognise Worsley, who had left them a hairy, dirty ruffian and returned spruce and shaven.

Within a few minutes the whalers had moved our bits of gear into their boat. They towed off the *James Caird*, and, having hoisted her to the deck of their ship, they started on the return voyage. They entered Stromness Bay at dusk on Monday afternoon, and the men of the whaling station mustered on the beach to receive the rescued party, and also to examine the boat which we had navigated across 800 miles of the stormy ocean they knew so well.

When I look back at those days I do not doubt that Providence guided us, not only across those snowfields, but also across the stormy white sea which separated Elephant Island from our landing place on South Georgia. I know that during that long march of thirty-six hours over the unnamed mountains and glaciers of South Georgia it often seemed to me that we were four, not three. And Worsley and Crean had the same idea. One feels "the dearth of human words, the roughness of mortal speech," in trying to describe intangible things, but a record of our journeys would be incomplete without reference to a subject very near to our hearts.

1935 –1936
SAINT-EXUPÉRY: PRISONER OF THE SANDS

Water, thou hast no taste, no color, no odor; canst not be defined, art relished while ever mysterious. Not necessary to life, but rather life itself, thou fillest us with a gratification that exceeds the delight of the senses. By thy might, there return into us treasures that we had abandoned. By thy grace, there are released in us all the dried-up runnels of our heart. Of the riches that exist in the world, thou art the rarest and also the most delicate . . . .

– Antoine de Saint-Exupéry

Born in 1900 into a privileged milieu of ancestral nobility, Antoine de Saint-Exupéry lived his adult life in exile from the happy idyll of his childhood. He grew up to be a bear-like man with a captivating smile, a tall and somewhat ungainly aristocrat, alternately spendthrift and impoverished, hardworking and marked by fears of personal failure, who gave himself over to a lyrical life unmoved by conventional ambition yet punctuated with heroic moments of adventure and danger. The visions of his poetic soul ultimately produced such remarkable works as *Wisdom of the Sands* (posthumously, 1948), the universally beloved "children's" classic *The Little Prince* (1943), and *Wind, Sand, and Stars* (1940) from which this chapter of *Survivors* is drawn.

Finding his calling as a pilot after World War I, Saint-Exupéry logged hundreds of hours of flying time with the military near Casablanca. In 1925 he became a pilot for Aéropostale. He flew the mails over North Africa for three years, surviving several close brushes with death before becoming director of the Cap Juby airfield at Rio de Oro in the remote Spanish Sahara. In 1929 Saint-Exupéry became director of airmail services for Aéropostale in Argentina. He performed this task with verve and dedication, for which he received the princely annual salary of 225,000 francs.

In the spring of 1935 *Paris-Soir* offered Saint-Exupéry a lucrative opportunity to travel to Moscow as a special correspondent. He arrived in time to report on the May Day celebration in Red Square and telephoned a series of brilliant dispatches before returning to Paris in June. Although he now had ample opportunity to make a substantial living as a journalist, he again took to the air, this time in his own airplane, a handsomely designed state-of-the-art variable-pitch propeller-driven Renault. In November Saint-Exupéry flew his new Caudron-Simoun beyond the French frontier on a lecture tour of the Eastern Mediterranean.

Troubles awaited Saint-Exupéry and his wife Consuelo when they returned to Paris in late November. The lecture proceeds of the Mediterranean tour had barely covered expenses. Saint-Exupéry was once again homeless and penniless, but he was not without concerned friends. They decided that he should compete for the generous cash prize of 150,000 francs that the French Air Ministry was then offering to any pilot who could post the best flight time between Paris and Saigon before the end of the year. Although not yet fitted out for such a "raid," Saint-Exupéry's fast and powerful Caudron-Simoun was the ideal aircraft for the contest. The aircraft was overhauled, map and compass bearings were prepared, and Saint-Exupéry negotiated an advance payment from the Paris newspaper *L'Intransigeant* for his account of the adventure.

On December 16th André Japy reached Saigon in just under ninety-nine hours. Weary from lack of sleep, Saint-Exupéry left Le Bourget at 7:01 P.M. on Sunday, December 29, 1935 with his flight mechanic André Prévot. Even based on Saint-Exupéry's estimation that his powerful Caudron-Simoun could make the flight in less than eighty hours, there was no margin for error. Critically, Saint-Exupéry had decided to travel without a radio, ostensibly in order to reduce weight in the plane and thus carry more fuel. Flying into a headwind in the early morning hours of December 30th, Saint-Exupéry became unsure of his position as his plane cut through towering banks of cumulus clouds. Shortly before 2:45 A.M., thinking that he by then had crossed the Nile, he descended, pitching his craft into a pebble-covered slope of sand on a plateau in the Libyan Desert—at a speed of 170 miles per hour. Leaving a trail of wreckage, the plane violently ploughed a grove two hundred and fifty yards long into the stony surface before coming to an abrupt halt in a bed of sand. Although badly shaken, Saint-Exupéry and Prévot miraculously emerged unscathed from the wreckage. Amazed to be still alive, the exhausted airmen decided that there was nothing better to do first than to take refuge in sleep and in dreams.

Waking with the sun, Saint-Exupéry and Prévot were completely disoriented. In which direction lay escape from the ring of desert that imprisoned them? In fact more than 100 miles west of Cairo, they half-believed that they had crossed the Nile, and their first instinct was to march westward to its waters, but they soon turned to the east, into the sun, in "the direction of life." They encountered only desert before turning back on their tracks to the site of the crash where they lit a bonfire in the forlorn hope of being spotted by rescuers who surely were searching for them across an impossibly vast expanse of desert.

With the next dawn, Saint-Exupéry left Prévot beside the wreckage and wandered alone into the desert, where—foreshadowing the appearance of the wise fox of the *Little Prince*—he encountered the tracks of the fennec, a small desert sand fox, upon whom he meditated before his mind dipped into the dizzy lucidities and the initial deliriums of severe thirst. With twilight came a return to his senses as Saint-Exupéry turned back to the plane—a bonfire ignited by his worried companion guiding him—where Prévot awaited him. It is here that our excerpt begins.

On the third day the men left the plane, determined to march to the end, choosing, without reason or hope, the only path—to the east-north-east—that promised salvation. And salvation they found at the last extremity, when they encountered a Bedouin caravan on the morning of their fourth day in the desert. By the next morning word that Saint-Exupéry had reached safety had spread to Paris, where his disappearance had dominated all the front pages and where family and friends had been gathered in a vigil of worry and grief. Telegrams were exchanged with loved ones, and Saint-Exupéry was deluged with notes of congratulation and relief. A failure that had almost become a tragedy was overnight transformed into a triumph, which Saint-Exupéry celebrated with an endless round of toasts and lavish meals.

Celebrity and celebration had hardly quieted when it was again ignited by the appearance in *L'Intransigeant*—in six installments between the 30th of January and the 4th of February—of Saint-Exupéry's own account of his desert ordeal, which the public received with wild enthusiasm. Slightly condensed, these articles—*Prison de Sable*—were published three years later to enormous popular acclaim in *Terre des Hommes* (1939), awarded the French Academy's prestigious *Grand Prix du Roman* that year and named the winner of the *National Book Award* in the United States upon its publication there as *Wind, Sand, and Stars* (1940), from which Saint-Exupéry's *Prisoner of the Sands* is here reprinted in Lewis Galantière's excellent original translation.

The fine literary qualities of Saint-Exupéry's poetry-infused prose certainly deserved its enthusiastic popular and critical reception. This account of desert survival offers a rare immediacy in its honest detailing of the inner reality of a man confronted with death, its dissection of the effects of extreme thirst and delirium, and its revelation of the determination to live for the sake of others.

The few remaining years of Saint-Exupéry's life were rich and filled with many fresh achievements. Pressed to repay his many debts, he accepted numerous assignments as a journalist, including the wrenching task of producing a series of dispatches from war-torn Spain. He later flew for France in the disastrous days of Nazi conquest in the spring of 1940. From exile in the United States, Saint-Exupéry subsequently took refuge in his writing, producing, among other works, *Flight to Arras* (1942) and the universally loved classic *Le Petit Prince* (1943).

On July 31, 1944, Saint-Exupéry took off for the last time, from an airfield in Sardinia, for a flight over Southern France. After so many adventures on earth, he was never seen again ... but he had survived the desert and had earned a rare immortality in the human heart.

Prisoner of the Sands

from *Wind, Sand and Stars* by Antoine de Saint Exupéry

I had been walking two hours when I saw the flames of the bonfire that Prévot, frightened by my long absence, had sent up. They mattered very little to me now.

Another hour of trudging. Five hundred yards away. A hundred yards. Fifty yards.

"Good Lord!"

Amazement stopped me in my tracks. Joy surged up and filled my heart with its violence. In the firelight stood Prévot, talking to two Arabs who were leaning against the motor. He had not noticed me, for he was too full of his own joy. If only I had sat still and waited with him! I should have been saved already. Exultantly I called out:

"Hi! Hi!"

The two Bedouins gave a start and stared at me. Prévot left them standing and came forward to meet me. I opened my arms to him. He caught me by the elbow. Did he think I was keeling over? I said:

"At last, eh?"

"What do you mean?"

"The Arabs!"

"What Arabs?"

"Those Arabs there, with you."

Prévot looked at me queerly, and when he spoke I felt as if he was very reluctantly confiding a great secret to me:

"There are no Arabs here."

This time I know I am going to cry.

A man can go nineteen hours without water, and what have we drunk since last night? A few drops of dew at dawn. But the northeast wind is still blowing, still slowing up the process of our evaporation. To it, also, we owe the continued accumulation of high clouds. If only they would drift straight overhead and break into rain! But it never rains in the desert.

"Look here, Prévot. Let's rip up one of the parachutes and spread the sections out on the ground, weighed down with stones. If the wind stays in the same quarter till morning, they'll catch the dew and we can wring them out into one of the tanks."

We spread six triangular sections of parachute under the stars, and Prévot unhooked a fuel tank. This was as much as we could do for ourselves till dawn. But, miracle of miracles! Prévot had come upon an orange while working over the tank. We shared it, and though it was little enough to men who could have used a few gallons of sweet water, still I was overcome with relief.

Stretched out beside the fire I looked at the glowing fruit and said to myself that men did not know what an orange was. "Here we are, condemned to death," I said to myself, "and still the certainty of dying cannot compare with the pleasure I am feeling. The joy I take from this half of an orange which I am holding in my hand is one of the greatest joys I have ever known.

I lay flat on my back, sucking my orange and counting the shooting stars. Here I was, for one minute infinitely happy. "Nobody can know anything of the world in which the individual moves and has his being," I reflected. "There is no guessing it. Only the man locked up in it can know what it is."

For the first time I understood the cigarette and glass of rum that are handed to the criminal about to be executed. I used to think that for a man to accept these wretched gifts at the foot of the gallows was beneath human dignity. Now I was learning that he took pleasure from them. People thought him courageous when he smiled as he smoked or drank. I knew now that he smiled because the taste gave him pleasure. People could not see that his perspective had changed, and that for him the last hour of his life was a life in itself.

We collected an enormous quantity of water—perhaps as much as two quarts. Never again would we be thirsty! We were saved; we had a liquid to drink!

I dipped my tin cup into the tank and brought up a beautifully yellow-green liquid the first mouthful of which nauseated me so that despite my thirst I had to catch my breath before swallowing it. I would have swallowed mud, I swear; but this taste of poisonous metal cut keener than thirst.

I glanced at Prévot and saw him going round and round with his eyes fixed to the ground as if looking for something. Suddenly he leaned forward and began to vomit without interrupting his spinning. Half a minute later it was my turn. I was seized by such convulsions that I went down on my knees and dug my fingers into the sand while I puked. Neither of us spoke, and for a quarter of an hour we remained thus shaken, bringing up nothing but a little bile.

After a time it passed and all I felt was vague, distant nausea. But our last hope had fled. Whether our bad luck was due to a sizing on the parachute or to the magnesium lining of the tank, I never found out. Certain it was that we needed either another set of cloths or another receptacle.

Well, it was broad daylight and time we were on our way. This time we should strike out as fast as we could, leave this cursed plateau, and tramp till we dropped in our tracks. That was what Guillaumet had done in the Andes. I had been thinking of him all the day before and had determined to follow his example. I should do violence to the pilot's unwritten law, which is to stick by the ship; but I was sure no one would be along to look for us here.

Once again we discovered that it was not we who were shipwrecked, not we but those who were waiting for news of us, those who were alarmed by our silence, were already torn with grief by some atrocious and fantastic report. We could not but strive towards them. Guillaumet had done it, had scrambled towards his lost ones. To do so is a universal impulse.

"If I were alone in the world," Prévot said, "I'd lie down right here. Damned if I wouldn't.

East-northeast we tramped. If we had in fact crossed the Nile, each step was leading us deeper and deeper into the desert.

I don't remember anything about that day. I remember only my haste. I was hurrying desperately towards something—towards some finality. I remember also that I walked with my eyes to the ground, for the mirages were more than I could bear. From time to time we would correct our course by the compass, and now and again we would lie down to catch our breath. I remember having flung away my waterproof, which I had held onto as covering for the night. That is as much as I recall about the day. Of what happened when the chill of evening came, I remember more. But during the day I had simply turned to sand and was a being without mind.

When the sun set we decided to make camp. Oh, I knew as well as anybody that we should push on, that this one waterless night would finish us off. But we had brought along the bits of parachute, and if the poison was not in the sizing, we might get a sip of water next morning. Once again we spread our trap for the dew under the stars. But the sky in the north was cloudless. The wind no longer had the same taste on the lip. It had moved into another quarter. Something was rustling against us, but this time it seemed to be the desert itself. The wild beast was stalking us, had us in its power. I could feel its breath in my face, could feel it lick my face and hands. Suppose I walked on: at the best I could do five or six miles more. Remember that in three days I had covered one hundred miles, practically without water.

And then, just as we stopped, Prévot said:

"I swear to you I see a lake!"

"You're crazy."

"Have you ever heard of a mirage after sunset?" he challenged.

I didn't seem able to answer him. I had long ago given up believing my own eyes. Perhaps it was not a mirage; but in that case it was a hallucination. How could Prévot go on believing? But he was stubborn about it.

"It's only twenty minutes off. I'll go have a look."

His mulishness got on my nerves.

"Go ahead!" I shouted. "Take your little constitutional. Nothing better for a man. But let me tell you, if your lake exists it is salt. And whether it's salt or not, it's a devil of a way off. And besides, there is no damn lake!"

Prévot was already on his way, his eyes glassy. I knew the strength of these irresistible obsessions. I was thinking: "There are somnambulists who walk straight into locomotives." And I knew that Prévot would not come back. He would be seized by the vertigo of empty space and would be unable to turn back. And then he would keel over. He somewhere, and I somewhere else. Not that it was important.

Thinking thus, it struck me that this mood of resignation was doing me no good. Once when I was half drowned I had let myself go like this. Lying now flat on my face on the stony ground, I took this occasion to write a letter for posthumous delivery. It gave me a chance, also, to take stock of myself again. I tried to bring up a little saliva: how long was it since I had spit? No saliva. If I kept my mouth closed, a kind of glue sealed my lips together. It dried on the outside of the lips and formed a hard crust. However, I found I was still able to swallow, and I bethought me that I was still not seeing a blinding light in my eyes. Once I was treated to that radiant spectacle I might know that the end was a couple of hours away.

Night fell. The moon had swollen since I last saw it. Prévot was still not back. I stretched out on my back and turned these few data over in my mind. A familiar impression came over me, and I tried to seize it. I was . . . I was . . . I was at sea. I was on a ship going to South America and was stretched out, exactly like this, on the boat deck.

The tip of the mast was swaying to and fro, very slowly, among the stars. That mast was missing tonight, but again I was at sea, bound for a port I was to make without raising a finger. Slave-traders had flung me on this ship.

I thought of Prévot who still was not back. Not once had I heard him complain. That was a good thing. To hear him whine would have been unbearable. Prévot was a man.

What was that! Five hundred yards ahead of me I could see the light of his lamp. He had lost his way. I had no lamp with which to signal back. I stood up and shouted, but he could not hear me.

A second lamp, and then a third! God in Heaven! It was a search party and it was me they were hunting!

"Hi! Hi!" I shouted.

But they had not heard me. The three lamps were still signaling me.

"Tonight I am sane," I said to myself. "I am relaxed. I am not out of my head. Those are certainly three lamps and they are about five hundred yards off." I stared at them and shouted again, and again I gathered that they could not hear me.

Then, for the first and only time, I was really seized with panic. I could still run, I thought. "Wait! Wait!" I screamed. They seemed to be turning away from me, going off, hunting me elsewhere! And I stood tottering, tottering on the brink of life when there were arms out there ready to catch me! I shouted and screamed again and again.

They had heard me! An answering shout had come. I was strangling, suffocating, but I ran on, shouting as I ran, until I saw Prévot and keeled over.

When I could speak again I said: "Whew! When I saw those lights . . . "

"What lights?"

God in Heaven, it was true! He was alone!

This time I was beyond despair. I was filled with a sort of dumb fury.

"What about your lake?" I rasped.

"As fast as I moved towards it, it moved back. I walked after it for about half an hour. Then it seemed still too far away, so I came back. But I am positive, now, that it is a lake."

"You're crazy. Absolutely crazy. Why did you do it? Tell me. Why? What had he done? Why had he done it? I was ready to weep with indignation, yet I scarcely knew why I was so indignant. Prévot mumbled his excuse:

"I felt I had to find some water. You . . . your lips were awfully pale."

Well! My anger died within me. I passed my hand over my forehead as if I were waking out of sleep. I was suddenly sad. I said:

"There was no mistake about it. I saw them as clearly as I see you now. Three lights there were. I tell you, Prévot, I saw them!"

Prévot made no comment.

"Well," he said finally, "I guess we're in a bad way."

In this air devoid of moisture the soil is swift to give off its temperature. It was already very cold. I stood up and stamped about. But soon a violent fit of trembling came over me. My dehydrated blood was moving sluggishly and I was pierced by a freezing chill which was not merely the chill of night. My teeth were chattering and my whole body had begun to twitch. My hand shook so that I could not hold an electric torch. I who had never been sensitive to cold was about to die of cold. What a strange effect thirst can have!

Somewhere, tired of carrying it in the sun, I had let my waterproof drop. Now the wind was growing bitter and I was learning that in the desert there is no place of refuge. The desert is as smooth as marble. By day it throws no shadow; by night it hands you over naked to the wind. Not a tree, not a hedge, not a rock behind which I could seek shelter. The wind was charging me like a troop of cavalry across open country. I turned and twisted to escape it: I lay down, stood up, lay down again, and still I was exposed to its freezing lash. I had no strength to run from the assassin and under the sabre-stroke I tumbled to my knees, my head between my hands.

A little later I pieced these bits together and remembered that I had struggled to my feet and had started to walk on, shivering as I went. I had started forward wondering where I was and then I had heard Prévot. His shouting had jolted me into consciousness.

I went backwards towards him, still trembling from head to foot— quivering with the attack of hiccups that was convulsing my whole body. To myself I said: "It isn't the cold. It's something else. It's the end." The simple fact was that I hadn't enough water in me. I had tramped too far yesterday and the day before when I was off by myself, and I was dehydrated.

The thought of dying of the cold hurt me. I preferred the phantoms of my mind, the cross, the trees, the lamps. At least they would have killed me by enchantment. But to be whipped to death like a slave! Confound it! Down on my knees again! We had with us a little store of medicines—a hundred grams of ninety per cent alcohol, the same of pure ether, and a small bottle of iodine. I tried to swallow a little of the ether: it was like swallowing a knife. Then I tried the alcohol: it contracted my gullet. I dug a pit in the sand, lay down in it, and flung handfuls of sand over me until all but my face was buried in it.

Prévot was able to collect a few twigs, and he lit a fire which soon burnt itself out. He wouldn't bury himself in the sand, but preferred to stamp round and round in a circle. That was foolish.

My throat stayed shut, and though I knew that was a bad sign, I felt better. I felt calm. I felt a peace that was beyond all hope. Once more, despite myself, I was journeying, trussed up on the deck of my slave-ship under the stars. It seemed to me that I was perhaps not in such a bad pass after all.

So long as I lay absolutely motionless, I no longer felt the cold. This allowed me to forget my body buried in the sand. I said to myself that I would not budge an inch, and would therefore never suffer again. As a matter of fact, we really suffer very little. Back of all these torments there is the orchestration of fatigue or of delirium, and we live on in a kind of picture-book, a slightly cruel fairy-tale.

A little while ago the wind had been after me with whip and spur, and I was running in circles like a frightened fox. After that came a time when I couldn't breathe. A great knee was crushing in my chest. A knee. I was writhing in vain to free myself from the weight of the angel who had overthrown me. There had not been a moment when I was alone in this desert. But now I had ceased to believe in my surroundings; I have withdrawn into myself, have shut my eyes, have not so much as batted an eyelid. I have the feeling that this torrent of visions is sweeping me away to a tranquil dream: so rivers cease their turbulence in the embrace of the sea.

Farewell, eyes that I loved! Do not blame me if the human body cannot go three days without water. I should never have believed that man was so truly the prisoner of the springs and freshets. I had no idea that our self-sufficiency was so circumscribed. We take it for granted that a man is able to stride straight out into the world. We believe that man is free. We never see the cord that binds him to wells and fountains, that umbilical cord by which he is tied to the womb of the world. Let man take but one step too many . . . and the cord snaps.

Apart from your suffering, I have no regrets. All in all, it has been a good life. If I got free of this I should start right in again. A man cannot live a decent life in cities, and I need to feel myself live. I am not thinking of aviation. The airplane is a means, not an end. One doesn't risk one's life for a plane any more than a farmer ploughs for the sake of the plough. But the airplane is a means of getting away from towns and their bookkeeping and coming to grips with reality. Flying is a man's job and its worries are a man's worries. A pilot's business is with the wind, with the stars, with night, with sand, with the sea. He strives to outwit the forces of nature. He stares in expectancy for the coming of dawn the way a gardener awaits the coming of spring. He looks forward to port as to a promised land, and truth for him is what lives in the stars.

I have nothing to complain of. For three days I have tramped the desert, have known the pangs of thirst, have followed false scents in the sand, have pinned my faith on the dew. I have struggled to rejoin my kind, whose very existence on earth I had forgotten. These are the cares of men alive in every fibre, and I cannot help thinking them more important than the fretful choosing of a nightclub in which to spend the evening. Compare this one life with the other, and all things considered this is a luxury! I have no regrets. I have gambled and lost. It was all in the day's work. At least I have had the unforgettable taste of the sea on my lips.

I am not talking about living dangerously. Such words are meaningless to me. The toreador does not stir me to enthusiasm. It is not danger that I love. I know what I love. It is life.

The sky seemed to me faintly bright. I drew up one arm through the sand. There was a bit of the torn parachute within reach, and I ran my hand over it. It was bone dry. Let's see. Dew falls at dawn. Here was dawn risen and no moisture on the cloth. My mind was befuddled and I heard myself say: "There is a dry heart here, a dry heart that cannot know the relief of tears."

I scrambled to my feet. "We're off, Prévot," I said. "Our throats are still open. Get along, man!"

The wind that shrivels up a man in nineteen hours was now blowing out of the west. My gullet was not yet shut, but it was hard and painful and I could feel that there was a rasp in it. Soon that cough would begin that I had been told about and was now expecting. My tongue was becoming a nuisance. But most serious of all, I was beginning to see shining spots before my eyes. When those spots changed into flames, I should simply lie down.

The first morning hours were cool and we took advantage of them to get on at a good pace. We knew that once the sun was high there would be no more walking for us. We no longer had the right to sweat. Certainly not to stop and catch our breath. This coolness was merely the coolness of low humidity. The prevailing wind was coming from the desert, and under its soft and treacherous caress the blood was being dried out of us.

Our first day's nourishment had been a few grapes. In the next three days each of us ate half an orange and a bit of cake. If we had had anything left now, we couldn't have eaten it because we had no saliva with which to masticate it. But I had stopped being hungry. Thirsty I was, yes, and it seemed to me that I was suffering less from thirst itself than from the effects of thirst. Gullet hard. Tongue like plaster-of-Paris. A rasping in the throat. A horrible taste in the mouth. All these sensations were new to me, and though I believed water could rid me of them, nothing in my memory associated them with water. Thirst had become more and more a disease and less and less a craving. I began to realize that the thought of water and fruit was now less agonizing than it had been. I was forgetting the radiance of the orange, just as I was forgetting the eyes under the hat-brim. Perhaps I was forgetting everything.

We had sat down after all, but it could not be for long. Nevertheless it was impossible to go five hundred yards without our legs giving way. To stretch out on the sand would be marvelous—but it could not be.

The landscape had begun to change. Rocky places grew rarer and the sand was now firm beneath our feet. A mile ahead stood dunes and on those dunes we could see a scrubby vegetation. At least this sand was preferable to the steely surface over which we had been trudging. This was the golden desert. This might have been the Sahara. It was in a sense my country.

Two hundred yards had now become our limit, but we had determined to carry on until we reached the vegetation. Better than that we could not hope to do. A week later, when we went back over our traces in a car to have a look at the *Simoon*, I measured this last lap and found that it was just short of fifty miles. All told we had done one hundred and twenty-four miles.

The previous day I had tramped without hope. Today the word "hope" had grown meaningless. Today we were tramping simply because we were tramping. Probably oxen work for the same reason. Yesterday I had dreamed of a paradise of orange trees. Today I would not give a button for paradise; I did not believe oranges existed. When I thought about myself I found in me nothing but a heart squeezed dry. I was tottering but emotionless. I felt no distress whatever, and in a way I regretted it; misery would have seemed to me as sweet as water. I might then have felt sorry for myself and commiserated with myself as with a friend. But I had not a friend left on earth.

Later, when we were rescued, seeing our burnt-out eyes men thought we must have called aloud and wept and suffered. But cries of despair, misery, sobbing grief are a kind of wealth, and we possessed no wealth. When a young girl is disappointed in love she weeps and knows sorrow. Sorrow is one of the vibrations that prove the fact of living. I felt no sorrow. I was the desert. I could no longer bring up a little saliva; neither could I any longer summon those moving visions towards which I should have loved to stretch forth arms. The sun had dried up the spring of tears in me.

And yet, what was that? A ripple of hope went through me like a faint breeze over a lake. What was this sign that had awakened my instinct before knocking on the door of my consciousness? Nothing had changed, and yet everything was changed. This sheet of sand, these low hummocks and sparse tufts of verdure that had been a landscape, were now become a stage setting. Thus far the stage was empty, but the scene was set. I looked at Prévot. The same astonishing thing had happened to him as to me, but he was as far from guessing its significance as I was.

I swear to you that something is about to happen. I swear that life has sprung in this desert. I swear that this emptiness, this stillness, has suddenly become more stirring than a tumult on a public square. "Prévot! Footprints! We are saved!"

We had wandered from the trail of the human species; we had cast ourselves forth from the tribe; we had found ourselves alone on earth and forgotten by the universal migration; and here, imprinted in the sand, were the divine and naked feet of man!

"Look, Prévot, here two men stood together and then separated."

"Here a camel knelt."

"Here . . . "

But it was not true that we were already saved. It was not enough to squat down and wait. Before long we should be past saving. Once the cough has begun, the progress made by thirst is swift.

Still. I believed in that caravan swaying somewhere in the desert, heavy with its cargo of treasure.

We went on. Suddenly I heard a cock crow. I remembered what Guillaumet had told me: "Towards the end I heard cocks crowing in the Andes. And I heard the railway train." The instant the cock crowed I thought of Guillaumet and I said to myself: "First it was my eyes that played tricks on me. I suppose this is another of the effects of thirst. Probably my ears have merely held out longer than my eyes."

But Prévot grabbed my arm:

"Did you hear that?"

"What?"

"The cock."

"Why . . . why, yes, I did."

To myself I said: "Fool! Get it through your head! This means life!"

I had one last hallucination—three dogs chasing one another. Prévot looked, but could not see them. However, both of us waved our arms at a Bedouin. Both of us shouted with all the breath in our bodies, and laughed for happiness.

But our voices could not carry for thirty yards. The Bedouin on his slow-moving camel had come into view from behind a dune and now he was moving slowly out of sight. The man was probably the only Arab in this desert, sent by a demon to materialize and vanish before the eyes of us who could not run.

We saw in profile on the dune another Arab. We shouted, but our shouts were whispers. We waved our arms and it seemed to us that they must fill the sky with monstrous signals. Still the Bedouin stared with averted face away from us.

At last, slowly, slowly he began a right angle turn in our direction. At the very second when he came face to face with us, I thought, the curtain would come down. At the very second when his eyes met ours, thirst would vanish and by this man would death and the mirages be wiped out. Let this man but make a quarter-turn left and the world is changed. Let him but bring his torso round, but sweep the scene with a glance, and like a god he can create life.

The miracle had come to pass. He was walking towards us over the sand like a god over the waves.

The Arab looked at us without a word. He placed his hands upon our shoulders and we obeyed him: we stretched out upon the sand. Race, language, religion were forgotten. There was only this humble nomad with the hands of an archangel on our shoulders.

Face to the sand, we waited. When the water came, we drank like calves with our faces in the basin, and with a greediness which alarmed the Bedouin so that from time to time he pulled us back. But as soon as his hand fell away from us we plunged our faces anew into the water.

Water, thou hast no taste, no color, no odor; canst not be defined, art relished while ever mysterious. Not necessary to life, but rather life itself, thou fillest us with a gratification that exceeds the delight of the senses. By thy might, there return into us treasures that we had abandoned. By thy grace, there are released in us all the dried-up runnels of our heart. Of the riches that exist in the world, thou art the rarest and also the most delicate—thou so pure within the bowels of the earth! A man may die of thirst lying beside a magnesian spring. He may die within reach of a salt lake. He may die though he hold in his hand a jug of dew, if it be inhabited by evil salts. For thou, water, art a proud divinity, allowing no alteration, no foreignness in thy being. And the joy that thou spreadest is an infinitely simple joy.

You, Bedouin of Libya who saved our lives, though you will dwell forever in my memory yet I shall never be able to recapture your features. You are Humanity and your face comes into my mind simply as man incarnate. You, our beloved fellowman, did not know who we might be, and yet you recognized us without fail. And I, in my turn, shall recognize you in the faces of all mankind. You came towards me in an aureole of charity and magnanimity bearing the gift of water. All my friends and all my enemies marched towards me in your person. It did not seem to me that you were rescuing me; rather did it seem that you were forgiving me. And I felt I had no enemy left in all the world.

This is the end of my story. Lifted on to a camel, we went on for three hours. Then, broken with weariness, we asked to be set down at a camp while the cameleers went on ahead for help. Toward six in the evening a car manned by armed Bedouins came to fetch us. A half-hour later we were set down at the house of a Swiss engineer named Raccaud who was operating a soda factory beside saline deposits in the desert. He was unforgettably kind to us. By midnight we were in Cairo.

I awoke between white sheets. Through the curtains came the rays of a sun that was no longer an enemy. I spread butter and honey on my bread. I smiled. I recaptured the savor of my childhood and all its marvels. And I read and re-read the telegram from those dearest to me in all the world whose three words had shattered me:

"So terribly happy!"

THE SINKING OF THE USS SQUALUS AND THE RESCUE OF ITS SURVIVORS

The USS *Squalus* (SS-192) was the eleventh of a new class of American submarines. Larger than earlier models, this diesel-electric powered submarine, designed for speed and extended range, was built at the Portsmouth Navy Yard, New Hampshire, where it was commissioned on March 1, 1939. Seven weeks later, with a crew of fifty-nine under the command of Lieutenant Oliver Naquin, the *Squalus* set out from Portsmouth early in the morning of May 23rd to test an emergency dive. From its maximum surface cruising speed of 16 knots, the submarine was to submerge to fifty feet within sixty seconds. The test dive off the Isle of Shoals seemed to go perfectly at first, but a catastrophic valve failure flooded the rear compartments of the submarine, and it plunged at a steep angle stern down to the bottom. It came to rest on its keel at an angle of eleven degrees in freezing waters sixty fathoms (240 feet) beneath the surface, with a complete loss of power and lights, and the loss of almost half its crew.

Under the steady command of Lieutenant Naquin, the crew responded with disciplined professionalism to the sudden sinking of their submarine, acting instantly to seal off its separate compartments to avoid further flooding, and, in the faint glow of emergency hand lanterns, quickly shutting valves to control jets of water and oil. Of the crew of fifty-nine, twenty-three in the control room and ten in the forward torpedo room had survived, but there was no communication with the twenty-six crew members in the after battery room and the two engine rooms, and it was probable that they had perished. Five of the survivors were moved from the control room to the forward torpedo compartment. Saltwater, which could mix with battery acid and form deadly chlorine gas, was leaking into the forward battery, so this compartment, located between the control room and the forward torpedo room, had to be left abandoned. A foot of water and oil had accumulated at the aft bulkhead of the control room. In the pump room below, a slow leak had developed.

Soon after the sinking, Lieutenant Naquin ordered the launch of a telephone buoy and the firing of rockets, the smoke of the sixth of which was fortunately spotted by a lookout on the *Squalus'* sister sub, the USS *Sculpin*, which immediately navigated to the site and picked up the telephone buoy. Communication was established, but soon afterward the telephone cable snapped. Aboard the *Squalus* the crew was calm and quiet. To conserve oxygen, conversation was strictly limited to essential communication. Momsen Lungs were distributed to the crew, and their use was briefly reviewed, in case the men had to evacuate the submarine and rise to the surface with the Lung to sustain them. Wet and cold, the survivors waited. At noon they were issued rations of canned fruit. The increasing toxicity of the air induced drowsiness. Carbon dioxide absorbent was spread in the control room and the forward torpedo compartment early in the afternoon. The submariners did have a reserve of oxygen in pressurized canisters. This was held in reserve until evening, when some was bled into the stale atmosphere. A second meal—of tomatoes, beans, and fruit—was issued at 6:00 P.M.

Submerged and stranded on the bottom, in the dark, wet, and cold, the crew bravely endured the hours of suspenseful terror. In the black silence they thought of their companions who had perished in the dive, and of their loved ones ashore. They knew that no one had ever been rescued from such a depth. But discipline didn't falter, and spirits rose the next morning at the sound of rescue ships above.

The navy rapidly mobilized a rescue operation under the direction of the legendary submariner, and innovator of naval undersea rescue, Commander Charles B. Momsen, "the Swede." Late in the morning of May 24th, less than twenty-seven hours after the sinking of the *Squalus,* the USS *Falcon* lowered the McCann rescue chamber—a new version of a diving bell invented by Momsen. Such a rescue had never before been accomplished, but the rescue chamber performed perfectly, and over the next 13 hours, all thirty-three survivors were plucked from the stricken submarine.

Our narrative of this tragic disaster is drawn from three accounts. The first two, describing the sinking itself, are from the report of Lieutenant W.T. Doyle, the submarine's chief diving officer, accompanied by excerpts from the official report to Lieutenant Naquin of Harold C. Preble, the civilian naval architect who was aboard through all the dark hours of the harrowing experience. The account of the actual rescue is from the text of a lecture delivered on October 6, 1939 by Momsen. In their spare and grave tones, all of these accounts of survival and rescue bear testimony to the courage and resolution of survivors and rescuers alike, and form a particularly proud chapter in the history of the United States Navy.

The Rescue of USS Squalus

Part One

The Sinking of the USS *SQUALUS*
Statement of Lieutenant W. T. Doyle, U.S.N; USS *Squalus*
Survivor; Source: Biographical files, Operational Archives,
Naval Historical Center with excerpts from: Harold C. Preble,
Naval Architect, Portsmouth Navy Yard, report to Lieutenant
O. F. Naquin, U.S.N., Commanding Officer, USS *SQUALUS.*

Lieut Doyle: Word was passed "Rig ship for dive" at 0800 DST on 23
May [1939]. At this time I took my usual position at the diving control
station in the control room and proceeded to check the trim of the
Squalus while awaiting the first reports from compartments that they
were rigged for the dive. The man stationed at the phones in the control
room reported each compartment to me as each compartment
completed its rig, whereupon that particular compartment was
checked off on the rigging board provided for the purpose, at the
diving station. The compartments forward of the control room were
checked by Lieut. (jg) Nichols and the compartments aft of the control
room were checked by Ens. Patterson. In addition to the reports by
telephone, as each individual compartment completed its "rig for
dive," Lt. Nichols and Ensign Patterson personally reported to me
that their portion of the ship was rigged for dive.

It was approximately 0825 before the ship was rigged, whereupon
the word was passed "submerged trial crew take stations." Shortly
thereafter word was passed "Observers to take station," since the trial
board procedure was going to be rehearsed and all data was to be
recorded as on actual trials. At the diving station all main ballast
kingstons were operated to check their operation. Following this, all
main ballast vents were operated to test them and also to vent all
pressure therefrom. Two 2800-pound air banks were cut into the air
manifold. The stern planes were tested both by power and by hand.
All indicator lights at the hydraulic manifold were indicating properly.
Word was then given to the bridge at approximately 0830 "Ship rigged
for dive, with the exception of engine exhaust valves, engine and hull
inductions, radio antenna trunk, bow planes, and conning tower
hatch." Word then came from the bridge to rig out bow planes, which

were then rigged out and tested. The diving message was sent and the radio antenna trunk secured. Word was passed "standby to dive," which was relayed by the control room talker to all compartments.

The dive was to be a quick dive from four main engines, with no main ballast kingstons or vents open, until the first diving alarm was sounded. At the sounding of the first diving alarm all main ballast kingstons were opened, followed immediately by opening vents on bow buoyancy, #1 main ballast, #2 main ballast, and safety tanks. Bow and stern planes were put on hard dive. About 10 seconds later the indicator lights showed the conning tower hatch closed and the four main engine outboard exhaust valves closed. Telephone reports from the forward and after engine rooms came simultaneously, that all engines were stopped and valves closed. The hull and engine inductions were then closed immediately and indicated such on the indicator board. The air manifold man bled air into the boat until there was a pressure indicated on the barometer. At this time I held up two fingers as the signal for the second diving alarm and at the same time opened the vents on #3 and #4 main ballast tanks. As the C[ommanding] O[fficer] entered the control room, I reported "pressure in the boat, green board" and proceeded to take the vessel down to 63 feet. The main motors were now driving the vessel at the one-hour, 1280 spec. gravity rate and when I last looked at the revolution indicators they were indicating 220 r.p.m. The dive took on the attitude of an excellent one and as we approached 40 feet and closed all vents. Our maximum diving angle was 9°, and at 45 feet I began to ease the angle off. I kept a close watch on the indicator light board, since I wanted to be ready in all respects to blow in case our high speed drove the vessel down too deep. The hull opening indicators continued green at all times, and both the kingston and vent indicators showed green.

As we approached 50 feet . . . I ordered all diving angle taken off and to level off at 63 feet. The C.O. had been standing alongside me up to this point and as we began to level off he walked to his station at the periscope. We had just commenced leveling off when a telephone report came that the after engine room was flooding. I immediately ordered "blow main ballast," followed immediately by "blow safety and bow buoyancy." Another air bank was cut in on the manifold shortly after this.

Harold Preble: Realizing that we needed more H[igh] P[ressure] air than two banks, I knew then that the only thing to do was to cut in another bank. I wedged myself between the chart desk and the H.P.

air manifold, sitting on the desk, and took the handle for opening up H.P. air banks and started cutting in another bank. While I was doing this I felt a sudden terrific increase in pressure and while I was in this position, trying to open this bank, I was struck on the back with a volume of water coming in the ventilation line directly over me, driving my head and shoulders down. This same volume of water knocked down the trim manifold man and he, in turn, fell on me. While in this position I saw them close the door into the after battery room. Water was then flowing through this door. The man closing the starboard bulkhead ventilation valve over the door to after battery seemed to be experiencing considerable trouble in closing this valve as water continued to come. Emergency lights went out when Gainor pulled the battery switches. The vessel in going to the bottom assumed more of a down angle by the stern and I should judge it to be approximately 45°. We struck the bottom easily and finally settled at 11° up by the bow. A hydraulic line up over the steering gear spurted a considerable amount of oil in the control room and after the oil there was heard a hissing sound of air from the same line.

At 80 feet it seemed as though our downward progress had stopped and we had about 14 up angle, but this angle suddenly increased until the bubble was lost and without a definite sensation of going down we settled at 206 feet. Blowing of ballast was stopped when it was certain that no water was left to be blown. Light and power was lost simultaneously with settling on the bottom. Up until the time lights went out, the lights on the indicator board showed no change over their original status at the start of the dive. Emergency lights were lit, but shortly after went out, after which, Gainor reported that he had pulled the disconnected switches in the forward battery tank. Means of further lightening the vessel were discussed and it was decided that the after trim tank was the only tank which would be blown to effect any change. This tank was blown as dry as possible without any change in the vessel's position. Further expenditure of air was not deemed advisable at this time, as it was considered possible that we might aid salvage attempts in getting the vessel to the surface.

Lieut. Doyle: All men were equipped with "lungs" and a review of their operation held. Cans of CO_2 absorbent were made ready, and the oxygen system was tested up to the Schrader valve connections in the conning tower. A red rocket was fired from the signal ejector and hourly from then on until the [USS] *Sculpin* was heard. The telephone buoy was released from the forward torpedo room. Telephone communications was possible forward, but no communications could be gotten with the after section. Slugs of oil were blown out of the toilet bowl periodically to augment the smoke rockets. At no time did any sound come from aft to indicate that there was life there. The crew was instructed to move about as little as possible and aside from getting food, replacing flashlights, replenishing the air or tapping signals, there was little movement.

Soon after settling on the bottom the relief valve on the hydraulic system lifted and oil discharged therefrom. Salt water finally took the place of the oil which indicated a break in the hydraulic system. The forward battery room was investigated and found to be very warm but no indications of chlorine gas. Chlorine gas was present when the 18 men in the control room proceeded to the forward torpedo room after the first [rescue chamber] bell trip left the vessel.

During the emergency and the entire time we were on the bottom, all hands exhibited coolness and precision in carrying out the duties of their stations. Orders of the Commanding Officer were carried out promptly and efficiently. In spite of the low temperature and cramped quarters there were no complaints. A finer quality or higher spirited group of men, than those on the *Squalus*, will never be surpassed.

Harold Preble: Throughout the time of this extreme emergency the officers and men on the ship acted as if the same emergency arose on every dive undertaken by the ship. There was absolutely no excitement. Captain Naquin, his officers and men were very cool and I cannot think of one single detail that was left undone. The Commanding Officer, officers and men, from my observations while operating with them, knew their ship very well. In my estimation, Gainor's quickness in noting the high rate of discharge and his bravery in entering the battery tank and pulling the switches to prevent fire in the forward battery can by no means be overlooked.

USS *Squalus* (SS-192)

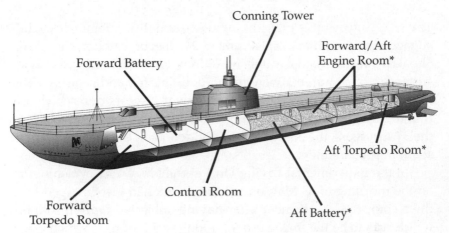

Conning Tower

Forward/Aft
Engine Room*

Forward Battery

Aft Torpedo Room*

Forward
Torpedo Room

Control Room

Aft Battery*

Shaded areas represent the flooded compartments.

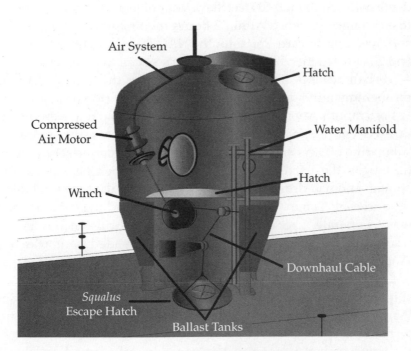

Air System

Hatch

Compressed
Air Motor

Water Manifold

Hatch

Winch

Squalus
Escape Hatch

Downhaul Cable

Ballast Tanks

The McCann Rescue Bell

Artwork courtesy of the Office of Naval Research, Department of the Navy

Part Two

Rescue of the USS *Squalus* by Commander Charles B. Momsen, U.S.N. (Excerpted from a lecture delivered on 6 Oct. 1939)

The USS *Squalus* [SS-192], the newest model of submarine, while engaged in preliminary trials, sunk in 243 feet of water off the Isles of Shoals in North Atlantic waters on 23 May 1939. On 24 May, the living survivors, 33 in number were rescued, uninjured and healthy. [This was] the concluding chapter of the story of 12 years of research and training by the Navy after the tragic loss of the *S-4* [SS-109] in 1927. In the 33 survivors, the Navy paid a "dividend" on the time and money spent in preparedness.

In the Experimental Diving Unit at the Navy Yard, Washington, on the morning of 23 May, one of the divers had just emerged from the recompression chamber after having subjected himself to a test which was to be the final check of a long series of tests which established a new conception of decompression for divers. . . . A telephone call from Commander Lockwood in Operations of the Navy Department said briefly these grim words "*Squalus* is down off Isles of Shoals, depth between 200 and 400 feet, have your divers and equipment ready to leave immediately." Within 2 hours the first group was in the air and speeding toward Portsmouth, N.H. By midnight the 5 officers and 20 enlisted men had arrived at the scene of the accident.

I shall never be able to record the various thoughts that flashed through my mind during that 150-mile-an-hour ride through the air to Portsmouth. My memory went back to the first lung experiments, thrills of ten years ago, to the long and tedious years spent in training submarine officers and enlisted men of the submarine service to use the lung; to the first diving bell, the cranky open bell that would dump and fall and half drown us if we were not careful, of the final design produced by Commander Allen R. McCann and the comfort that it was to operate. I recalled the hundreds of thrills encountered in training and developing this device. The dreaded hour was here! Would the dreams of the experimenter come true or would some quirk of fate cross up the plans and thus destroy all of this work? How many shipmates were waiting for the answer? What were they thinking? Were they too deep? Would the crude helium apparatus work if they were too deep for air diving?

Upon arrival I reported to Rear Admiral Cyrus W. Cole, the Commandant of the Navy Yard, Portsmouth, N.H., who was in charge at the scene of the accident. He was in the *Sculpin* [SS-191], a sister ship of the *Squalus*. The wind was blowing briskly and the seas were choppy. It was nearly midnight. After giving me the facts, he said "I will appoint you to take charge of the diving operations."

The *Squalus* was lying in 243 feet of water, slight list to port, down by the stern a few degrees. She was flooded aft up to the control room, which meant the after battery compartment, forward engine room, after engine room, and after torpedo room were probably flooded.

Thirty-three of her crew were alive in the forward compartments, but all telephones to the after compartments were silent. The *Squalus* had dived about 9 A.M., on the 23rd. After leveling off at periscope depth a sudden rush of air was felt and immediately after, water was observed to be pouring in through the engine induction lines. Attempts to surface failed and the stern sunk out of control. When at an angle of nearly 60 degrees she hit bottom, the bow settled down to rest. The marker buoy in the forward torpedo room was released and picked up by the *Sculpin*. The telephone in the marker buoy was manned.

While the Captain of the *Sculpin*, Lt.Cdr. Wilkin, was talking to the Captain of the *Squalus*, Lieutenant Naquin, the cable parted and conversation had to be continued by the laborious process of hammering code signals on the hull. Obviously the power system had failed which meant that some sea water had leaked into the forward battery. This introduced the danger of chlorine gas. It was later learned that this was true, and that lungs were broken out and distributed to all survivors, for protection against gas and for escape if such action was decided upon.

The Captain reported all hands comfortable, but cold; pressure in the compartments was about 12.5 pounds above atmospheric; hand lanterns were being used for light air, clear of chlorine gas and excessive CO_2 in the control room and torpedo room; battery compartment closed off except for the passage—(It lies between the two).

The USS *Falcon* [ASR-2], one of the Navy Rescue vessels, Lieutenant G. A. Sharp, U.S.N., commanding, was on her way from New London with the rescue chamber and would arrive shortly after daybreak on the 24th.

We told the Captain of the *Squalus* to rest as easily as possible, that the pressure in the compartments would not injure the men and that the *Falcon* would arrive about 6 A.M. with the rescue chamber.

We kept in contact with Lt. Naquin, bearing in mind that delay meant danger if escape by use of "lungs" must be attempted. Escape by this means would become necessary if some developments made it dangerous for the men to remain in the compartments. This was a delicate situation, for delay in attempting escape might reduce the chances for successful operation of the lung because of the reduced strength of the men caused by gas, exposure, lack of sleep, and hunger. On the other hand, rescue by the rescue chamber is safer, and there is less chance of losing men.

Wind and sea were increasing, when the *Falcon* arrived, four anchors were dropped in a square about 1500 feet on a side, and she moored in the center near the *Squalus*. Some difficulty was experienced in getting the *Falcon* in position because of the dragging of the windward anchors. She was finally hauled as near to the correct position as we dared about noon and rescue operations commenced.

During the previous night the wreck had been snagged with a grapnel [grapple] by the [harbor tug] *Penacook* [YT-6] and it was the line to this grapnel (21-thread manila) that was used for sending down our first diver. We were not sure that the grapnel was attached to the wreck and if it was attached just where it might be located. This was worse than drawing to an inside straight. My first diver was a second class Boatswain's Mate on the *Falcon*, Sibitzky, over six feet tall and about 200 pounds of the Navy's best brawn. We dressed him in his 200 pounds of equipment and sent him down. Lady Luck smiled on us for he landed on deck and excitedly reported "I see the capstan." What more could we ask for? Our diver was within 6 feet of the hatch that we wanted to get into. We had filled that inside straight. He reported that the broken cable of the marker buoy lay across the hatch. This, he was able to move clear.

... The forward and after hatches of our submarines are fitted for attaching the rescue chamber. They have a flat doughnut shaped plate welded to the hatch combing upon which the bottom of the chamber rests and a bail over the center of the hatch to which the haul down wire must be attached by the diver.

We made ready the end of the downhaul wire and slid it down the descending line to the diver. He got the end and promptly lost it so that we had to haul it up again and send it down a second time. This time he shackled it into the bail and was ready to come up.

Eleven years ago (1928) the first diving bells for rescuing men from submarines were designed by the Bureau of Construction and Repair, Navy Department. A curious quirk of circumstances led up to this incident. While in command of the submarine *S-1* [SS-105], in 1926, I wrote to the Bureau of Construction and Repair and recommended the adoption of a diving bell for the purposes of rescuing entrapped personnel from submarines. The *S-1* carried the only submarine airplane hanger in the Navy, and I completed tests with a new type of plane during my tours of duty. This hanger was a tank 20 feet long and 6 feet in diameter. When I was relieved of command of the *S-1*, I went to the Navy Department, Bureau of Construction and Repair, for duty in the Submarine section. There I found my letter about the diving bell, unanswered. A short time later I handled a letter from the new Commanding Officer of the *S-1*, stating that the airplane tank was of no further use, requesting authority to remove it, and requesting disposition. I felt opportunity knocking and prepared a reply to send it to New York there to be cut in half and used to make two diving bells for experimental purposes.

In the meantime the *S-4* was lost with all hands and the Navy was very much "on the spot" because of the loss of lives that might have been saved. The pressure of this incident forced favorable action on the diving bell project. After nearly two years of experimentation full of highly interesting results, the final bell was evolved and christened a "rescue chamber."

Upon completion of two years ashore in the Bureau, I was sent to sea in the reconditioned *S-4* to carry out practical experiments and training with the rescue chambers for all of our rescue vessels. In the meantime, I had been perfecting the lung for individual escape and the training of submarine personnel in its use went hand in hand with the training of personnel to handle the rescue chambers.

I have left the survivors waiting, but felt that some background for the introduction of the now famous rescue chamber was needed. This apparatus is a pear-shaped steel chamber, the big end uppermost, seven feet at the greatest diameter and ten feet high. It is divided into an upper closed compartment and a lower open compartment by a horizontal bulkhead which has a water-tight hatch in its middle. Surrounding the lower compartment is a ballast tank of a capacity just equal to that of the lower compartment. Inside the lower compartment is a reel with 400 feet of $1/_2$" steel wire on it. The reel is operated by a shaft leading into the upper compartment. The shaft is rotated by an air motor. On the bottom edge of the lower compartment a rubber gasket is embedded into a circular groove, so that when the chamber is brought into contact with a flat surface (the hatch ring), a watertight joint may be effected with the application of pressure. Attached to the upper compartment is an air supply and an atmospheric exhaust hose, wire wound for strength. Also electric cables for telephone and light are attached. A wire pendant for hoisting and lowering is shackled into a padeye on top. This wire is also used for retrieving the chamber in case of emergency.

To return to the rescue operations, two experienced operators, Harmon and Mihalowski, both divers from the *Falcon* entered the upper compartment and the chamber was lowered over the side. The end of the haul down wire had been unreeled and attached to the hatch by Sibitzky. With the lower compartment flooded, the ballast tank full and auxiliary cans full of water, the chamber floated with several hundred pounds of positive buoyancy. The auxiliary cans, 14 in number are carried in the upper compartment and are dumped as passengers enter so that the proper buoyancy will be maintained. Extra blankets, flashlight, hot soup, sandwiches and extra CO_2 absorbent were taken aboard for delivery to the submarine.

Harmon reported ready and I told him to go down. He turned on the air motor and as the wire was taken in the chamber crept along the surface about one hundred feet from the point where it was lowered into the water. Then it gradually submerged looking like some sea monster as it sank from sight. Progress was reported continuously until finally the report "Hatch is in sight." Taking it slowly they hauled the chamber down until it was resting on the flat seat surrounding the hatch. The wire leading through a centrally located fair lead to the hatch bail, also centrally located, causes the gasket to come into contact with the seat evenly. The ballast tank is then flooded from sea and the lower compartment emptied by admitting compressed air. The seal of the gasket to the hatch is then accomplished by suddenly releasing the compressed air in the lower compartment through the hose leading to the atmosphere. Harmon reported the seal made and the hatch leading to the lower compartment opened. Bear in mind that the upper compartment is under atmospheric pressure. Thus the sea exerts an enormous pressure on the gasket and the joint is absolutely watertight. The seating pressure in this case was about 175 tons. Four steel bolts were then attached to the hatch rings as a safety measure and the submarine hatch was opened. This was opened slowly so that such pressure that was in the submarine could be equalized with that in the chamber. Each move could be followed by listening on the telephone. When the submarine hatch was finally opened the dull thud of the hatch falling open was a thrill I cannot describe. Not a shout or cheer came over the phone. A few "wise cracks" such as "why the delay," "where in the hell are the napkins." The men had been trained and this was just like a drill. I ordered them to dump 1000 pounds of water from the auxiliary cans and load seven passengers. I wanted to make four trips, 7, 8, 9, and 9 in order to bring up the 33 survivors. I wanted to see how she carried the load with each trip, so planned on increasing the number by 1 each trip.

Harmon reported 7 passengers loaded, designated by the submarine's skipper, Lieutenant Naquin. Next he reported "hatch closed" and "ready to come up." I ordered him to "unbolt, flood lower compartment, and blow the ballast tank." This done, he reported "Seal broken, coming up." The air motor, in reverse, unreeling wire, chugged away and there gradually rising to the surface by its own buoyancy came the first load of lucky men, almost a routine drill for us but in the eyes of the outside world a miracle. We tried to appear calm and maybe others were but to me this was the most exciting moment of my life. 11 years of preparation, combating skepticism, and constructing imaginary disasters, all telescoped into one moment, who could remain calm?

The chamber appeared first a green splotch beneath the surface and she was hauled alongside. The top hatch was opened and the 7 lucky men removed. I changed the operators for each trip.

Soon the second trip was made, and when the chamber returned to the surface with eight passengers it looked so heavy that I felt that it would not be safe to carry nine on the third trip. This was a blow for each trip meant greater risk; the weather might get too rough, the anchors drag—in fact any one of a dozen things might happen. However, it looked risky and I made my decision. Five trips I announced, and told Lt. Naquin to send up 8 in the third trip.

They were loading the 3rd bunch when Commander Sackett rushed aft to tell me that by mistake 9 men had been brought up in the 2nd trip. I felt a genuine relief and immediately told Naquin to send 9 the 3rd trip, leaving 8 for that eventful 4th trip. How fortunate this was, we did not realize at the time. The 4th trip was made to the bottom. The last eight including the Captain, traditionally the last to leave his ship, were loaded. All were secured and the return trip started. All of a sudden she stopped! McDonald, the operator said "The wire is jammed on the reel." Loose turns had allowed the hauling part of the wire to slip between the turns on the reel and jam. This emergency had been provided for and I told him we would heave on the retrieving wire and help clear it. While hauling on this wire, it started to strand, strands parted like fire crackers. We stopped hauling just before the last strand parted. This emergency had not been provided for. It was almost dark by now and the wind and sea were no better. In order to save what wire was left I told McDonald to flood his ballast tank slowly and I would lower the chamber to the bottom. This was done and fortunately there was enough slack in the downhaul wire to permit the chamber to reach the ocean bottom without turning over. It was necessary to send down a diver to detach the haul down wire from the hatch bail. Squire, a big 200-pounder from the Experimental Diving Unit at Washington, was designated to do this. He was dressed, went down in the dark, and reported that the wire was too taught to unshackle. We had to send him a pair of wire cutters. With these he cut the wire. This was a fine job and could have been done only by an expert diver and one who has lots of power in his arms.

The next step was to attach a new retrieving wire to the chamber. Duncan and then Clayton attempted to take a new wire down, but the darkness proved to be too much of a handicap. We used a lamp, but the extra cable fouled and we found ourselves in a serious situation with a diver fouled in the wire, the most dangerous kind of fouling in the diving business. We finally managed to get Clayton up and then I changed the plan and decided to use the stranded wire and have the chamber brought to the surface. I told McDonald to blow the ballast tank a little at a time, in fact 3 seconds each time I gave the word. In the meanwhile, I had about 10 men hauling on the wire by hand. The strand would hold this amount of hauling. If we could pull the wire up until the stranded portion was on deck, we could then get a secure hold on the good part of the wire. At last we had the chamber light enough to haul it in by hand and we hauled it to the surface where the last of the survivors were rescued after a trying wait of four and a half hours. All survivors were in excellent condition and not even a cold developed from their exposure of nearly 40 hours.

The next diver to go down was Lt. J. K. Morrison. He took the descending line aft to the after torpedo room hatch. This was a long hard dive. Morrison did the job but the pressure nearly got him. Diving on air to such depths is extremely hazardous because the compressed nitrogen of the air acts more or less as an anesthetic. Only the greatest will power and determination will see the diver through. Diver Baker then went down and attached the haul down wire to the after hatch. Strange to say, he too lost the wire once before he made it fast.

Badders and Mihalowski then went down in the rescue chamber to see if there was anyone alive in the after end of the submarine. This brought back the sad but not surprising word that all was flooded and no signs of life. Thus the rescue operations were completed, with 33 lives saved and 26 lost.

1942
ESCAPE FROM COLDITZ

Over the Swiss frontier we came to very deep snowdrifts through which we stumbled and sometimes sank, having to drag each other to our feet. Ahead were neither huts nor frontier guards, nothing to point the way to safety. At this point the territory of Switzerland is a narrow appendix forming a no-man's land before the first Swiss village is reached. Three hundred yards to the east a single lamp flickered ominously. We dared not approach it. We could not be sure that it did not shine in a German frontier post. We had to march due south on an accurate compass bearing to avoid blundering back into the enemy. Striving to maintain our reason after the nightmare of our escape, we stopped every few steps to check our bearings.
— Airey Neave, *They Have Their Exits*

G irded with sheer walls of massive stone, medieval Colditz Castle looms forbiddingly 250 feet above the Mulde River. Isolated in the heart of Germany, about thirty miles to the southwest of the Saxon capital of Leipzig and four hundred miles from the nearest neutral border, it was here—in the Third Reich's most secure military prison—that the most talented and inveterate escape artists among Allied officers were interned as prisoners-of-war between 1940 and 1945. Belgian, Dutch, French, Polish, Serbian, and British, these prisoners both worked together and competed among themselves to see which national group could best confound their Wehrmacht guardians and score the most impressive tally of escapes. The Colditz *Sonderlager* was designed to confine two hundred high-risk prisoners, although at given times many more were held there—always well outnumbered by their guards—under a sophisticated regimen of maximum security.

In the course of the war, more than 300 prisoners escaped the rigorously guarded confines of Colditz in approximately 130 episodes marked by a kaleidoscopic range of methods and styles, ingenuity and resourcefulness, clever disguise and deception, virtuosic technique, bribery, and outrageous daring. But breaching the castle walls was only the first stage of a long and hazardous journey to the

safety of the distant frontier. All but thirty-two of the escapees—
fourteen French, eight British, nine Dutch, and one Polish—were
recaptured and returned to endure solitary confinement before being
allowed to resume "normal" life and, in many cases, launching fresh
escape schemes. English Lieutenant Michael Sinclair—called "the
greatest escaper" by Colditz security chief Reinhold Eiger—made
seven attempts to gain freedom. In the late summer of 1943,
convincingly disguised as an impressively mustachioed German
Sergeant-Major, he almost succeeded but was caught by an alert sentry
and was shot and wounded in the ensuing scuffle. Sinclair survived
and attempted two more escapes, but was shot dead in his last attempt
on September 25, 1944. The Germans buried Sinclair with full military
honors in the prison cemetery.

On his third effort to escape, Lieutenant Airey Neave was the first
British officer to break out of Colditz Castle and make the "Home
Run" to freedom in Switzerland. Born in 1916, this Eton-bred Merton
College Oxonian had launched a career in law before enlisting in the
British Army at the outbreak of World War II. Wounded and captured
at Calais in 1940, Neave escaped his first POW camp into the
countryside of Poland before being recaptured and interned at Colditz.
In his first try to escape the *Sonderlager* on August 28, 1941, Neave
audaciously attempted to stroll through the castle prison's front gate,
disguised as a German guard in a uniform dyed Wehrmacht green
and impeccably retailored from an RAF tunic. He managed to pass
two sentries before his mannerisms betrayed him at the last moment
and he was forced to surrender to a crowd of soldiers. Neave never
ceased plotting escape and soon after this episode he concocted a new
plan. Aided by the legendary British escape-master Pat Reid, this
minutely prepared plan was executed on the night of January 5–6,
1942. Neave and the cool-headed Dutch Lieutenant Tony Luteyn,
skillfully disguised as German officers, were the first of two pairs of
escapees to make a tortured exit from the prison, first dropping into
an empty room through a cleverly concealed hole cut into the camp
theater floor—where Neave had starred in a crudely humorous
performance that very evening. They then made their way through a
corridor over the main gate of the prisoners' yard to an attic above the
German guardroom. With Reid's expert help picking the locks that
stood in their way, the men succeeded in passing through the briefly
unoccupied guardroom and strolled through the courtyard and out
the main gate before scaling an unguarded wall in the darkness to
avoiding the checkpoint at the final gate.

This suspenseful story of escape and subsequent flight to safety in Switzerland is from *They Have Their Exits,* Airey Neave's own account of his daring exploits in wartime Germany. After their ingenious escape from the castle, Neave and Luteyn, disguised in the denim of Dutch electrical workers in transit, faced a formidable series of challenges and threats. They succeeded in their desperate effort with cool aplomb through various close encounters with their enemies and narrow escapes, their tracks finally fortuitously covered by a fresh fall of snow, before ultimately, utterly exhausted, they reached freedom. Alerted to watch for "Dutch electrical workers" with confusing papers, German authorities captured the pair of escapees who followed in the wake of Neave and Luteyn, but ten months later Pat Reid and three other British officers succeeded in an escape even more bold. Indeed, with each fresh escape from Colditz, prison security was tightened in the ongoing contest between prisoners and their guards. The Allied liberation of the *Sonderlager* in April 1945 forestalled the launching of the last method of flight, literally by means of a glider plane—patiently fashioned by British prisoners from mattress covers, wooden shutters, and mud—concealed behind a false wall high in a castle attic.

Upon his return to England in 1942, Neave was assigned to the organization of MI-9, the British intelligence department charged with laying out "ratlines" to assist the escape of Allied personnel and POWs from Occupied Europe. After the war Neave participated in the Nuremburg trials of Nazi war criminals before entering British politics with his election to Parliament as a Conservative in 1951 and serving in a series of junior government posts. Allied with Margaret Thatcher in deposing Conservative Party leader Edward Heath in 1975, the trusted counselor to the prime-minister-to-be was placed in charge of her private office. Designated to become Secretary of State for troubled Northern Ireland when the Conservatives assumed power under Thatcher in 1979, the survivor of Colditz Castle did not survive the bomb that shattered his car, severed his legs and rendered his corpse unrecognizable as he was departing the House of Commons on May 30, 1979. Though his assassination has been attributed to the Irish National Liberation Army (INLA), a radical offshoot of the IRA, the matter remains unresolved to this day.

Escape from Colditz

from *They Have Their Exits* by Airey Neave

A sentry led me from the courtyard, and as we passed under the gateways along the route of my ill-fated attempt I saw a new white wooden barrier across the road at the final exit. The sentry grinned at me and said,

"They put this here because of you."

I paid no attention to him. I was not interested in the new white barrier. I was concentrating furiously on something I had seen in the wall of the moat-bridge. Looking over it I had seen the moat below, its dry bed filled with heavy stones half-hidden by grass. Down each side of its bank there ran a roughly paved pathway. Steps led from a gap in the wall of the bridge and joined the pathway as it swept steeply down into the moat. Up through the grass of the far bank went the pathway until it vanished near the married quarters of the prison staff at the edge of the park. In the space in the wall of the moat-bridge where the steps began, a little wicket-gate stood half open.

I could hardly contain my excitement. The sentry hearing me crow with delight, turned in surprise. He did not know that I had seen a way of freedom. If I could cross the moat-bridge and reach the Park, escape was possible. On the far side of the moat there was no longer barbed wire, but palings which overlooked the steep slope of trees leading to the Park below. The married quarters, a building on the far bank, represented danger, but once the escaper had climbed the palings he would be sheltered by the trees at night. There remained the ancient stone wall of the Park, twelve feet high and thick with moss. . . .

The camp theatre was a great room on the second floor of the building adjoining the gates of the inner courtyard. In this building senior officers of the Allied Nations were quartered. Here lived a French General, a Polish Admiral, and a Polish General with senior British officers. Connecting this building with the guard-house was the mysterious Bridge of Sighs. What lay behind those tiny dusty windows above the gateway? Was there a passageway leading to the attic on the upper floor of the guard-house? At either end of the bridge the rooms which led to it were locked and barred and doors bricked up. Roaming like inquisitive children around some mysterious mansion in the hours of daylight, we came excitedly upon the secret.

There was a passageway. *The way to it lay under the floor of the theatre where a rough dais was raised to form a stage. . . .*

Beneath the stage the searchers found space enough to crawl and slowly sawed away the floorboards with stolen implements making a square hole in the ceiling of the passage below. To disguise this hole Reid made an ingenious mask known as "Shovewood." Then, with the usual rope of mattress covers tied to one of the supports of the stage, he climbed down into the sealed passage. Facing him was a locked door leading to the gate-bridge. He picked the lock and, walking softly in slippered feet through the musty air, he came to a further door on the far side of the bridge. It opened without difficulty, revealing steps into an attic above the guard-house. On the floor beneath was the German Officers' Mess and up the stairs into this gloomy place came the hoarse laughter of Hauptmann Priem and the tinkle of glasses.

Pat Reid proposed that teams of two, one British and one Dutch officer should attempt to escape disguised as German officers. He selected John Hyde-Thomson and myself and we both set to work to make the uniforms. My friends were not enthusiastic. The failure of other attempts had disheartened them. They did not believe that even in a German uniform would it be possible to get past the guard-room, and there were disheartening though friendly comments. . . .

. . . It seemed to me that if two men in German officers' uniforms were to descend the stairs from the attic and emerge from the guard-house door through the passage which the door of the actual guard-room opened, their appearance would not be questioned by the sentry outside. What more natural than that two officers, after visiting the mess above, should appear from the guard-room door walking towards the Kommandantur? From the moment that the passage was discovered, I concentrated every thought on how to fool the sentry who was posted outside the guard-room. If the man were cold and bored with duty on a winter's night, would his numbed brain suspect two officers coming from his own guard-house?

A pantomime produced by British officers in a prison camp is always pathetic. No amount of ingenuity exercised by stage managers and costume makers can conceal its futility. Senior officers with large moustaches appear half-naked as chorus girls in brassiers and ballet skirts of paper. Good-looking officers appear as leading ladies and rougher customers as red-nosed comedians. Although such an occupation keeps the prisoners from brooding on their fate, the actual performances are ghastly. On only one occasion do I remember seeing any real acting, that was in a sensitive performance of *Journey's End at Spangenburg* produced by Michael Langham of the Black Watch.

During preparations for the guard-house escape, I was able to write and produce a section of the pantomime, which was a three-act sketch entitled "The Mystery of Wombat College." The principal character in this episode was Dr. Calomel, an unpleasant headmaster.

I decided to play the part of Dr. Calomel myself. I created the part of a leering headmaster with heavy black brows resembling Groucho Marx. My costume consisted of a gown and a mortar-board made of black paper, and a pair of steel-rimmed spectacles. . . .

As the weeks passed in rehearsal, I searched for a new and more authentic German uniform. My first and most valuable acquisition was a long, green uniform overcoat of an officer of the Netherlands Home Army. There were in the camp upwards of sixty officers of the Dutch Forces, who, rather than take an oath of allegiance to Hitler, had resolved to spend the war in captivity. All of them were men of high character who spoke good English and German. Most of the officers were of the Netherlands East Indies Army, whose uniform was a shade of jungle green and unsuitable for my purpose. The pre-war Home Army, however, had blue-green uniforms, whose colour could easily pass at night for field grey.

The Dutch and the British had early come to an agreement upon escape matters. Since the Dutch officers spoke German they were allowed to take part in British schemes and share the store of aids to escape. They also volunteered to hand over pieces of their uniform for the escape from the guard-house. The final plan agreed on envisaged the escape of two parties of bogus German officers at an interval of twenty-four hours. The first party would consist of Lieutenant Toni Luteyn of the Netherlands East Indies Army and myself. The second would consist of John Hyde-Thomson and Lieutenant Donkers of the Netherlands East Indies Army.

A bogus German uniform had to be most carefully hidden, for the enemy made constant searches of the room where I slept and of all my belongings. I was obliged to keep the precious Dutch overcoat rolled in some sacking under the floor boards beneath a "mask." If this hiding place were suspected another would have to be found.

Such was the talent in the camp that I had no difficulty in discovering officers who could convert the Dutch material into a very passable German officer's overcoat. The epaulettes, normally of woven silver braid, were made from thick linoleum cut from the floor of the

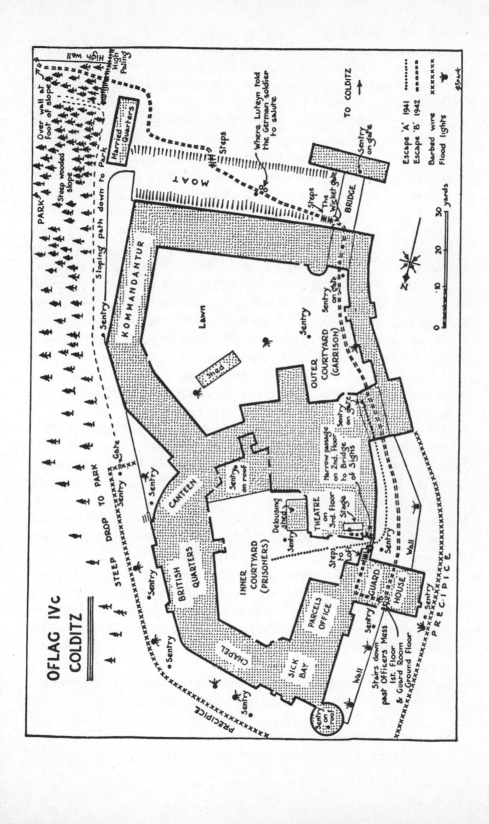

bathroom, painted silver and sewn to the shoulders.

I had decided to promote myself to the rank of Ober-leutnant and to take on the identity of an infantry officer named Schwartz. It was therefore necessary to provide small gold stars to denote that rank. These were fashioned from wood, cut with a penknife by Scarlet O'Hara and painted gold. Although the Germans, after several discoveries of imitation uniforms, stopped supplies of silver and gold paint to the canteen, a quantity had been saved and carefully stored. The epaulettes were finished with a gold numeral to denote an infantry regiment. There remained only the collar of the overcoat and the buttons. A dark green collar was cut from green baize material. The buttons were of lead from lavatory piping poured into skilful moulds made by the Dutch. My belt on this occasion was of cardboard painted brown from a box of water colours, and with a fine imitation revolver holster of cardboard filled with newspaper. My disguise was nearly complete.

Much of this faithful work was done for me by Squadron Leader Brian Paddon, D.S.O., D.F.C. Paddon was the most ingenious mind among escapers of my experience. He eclipsed even Scarlet O'Hara in the picking of locks and making of keys. Obsessed by such technicalities, he amassed a vast hoard of implements many of which he absentmindedly carried in his pockets. At nightfall he could be seen making the rounds of his private hiding-places or testing the strength of ancient locks. His long face bore an expression of morose determination as he haunted the more mysterious corners of the castle. His persevering nature was rewarded by a brilliantly successful exploit. He was returned to Stalag XXa to stand his court-martial for insulting the German Feldwebel who had thrown Forbes and myself into the dungeons at the end of our escape in Poland. As the court was due to assemble, Paddon broke out of his cell and after many adventures reached the safety of neutral Sweden in 1942.

Through that icy December, I rehearsed the part of Dr. Calomel by day and collected the parts of my uniform by night. On several occasions precious pieces met with disaster. Epaulettes of linoleum and badges carelessly left about were found and confiscated. Often tragedies came thick and fast. John Hyde-Thomson sat on his German hat crushing the carefully poised brim; there was a shortage of lead piping from the lavatories; the prisoners were banned from the theatre for several days for stealing a workman's coat.

Undeterred, we hastened our preparations in a running fight with the searching guards.

Toni Luteyn, my Dutch companion, was playing the drums in the camp orchestra which accompanied the musical part of "Ballet Nonsense." Since we were both occupied in the theatre we were able to transfer our disguises in Red Cross boxes underneath the stage. I rehearsed the coarse absurdities of Wombat College, wondering how long it would be before the Germans decided to look beneath the stage. It was bitterly cold and snow lay on the ground for many days as the time for the opening of the pantomime drew near. I had hoped to combine my escape with my appearance in the part of Dr. Calomel. This was a situation which appealed not only to my sense of humour, but it had its merits as a plan to deceive the Germans. If officers from the camp staff were present at the final performance a day or two before Christmas, Luteyn and I would be able to crawl under the stage before the finale. Then, under cover of deafening music above, we would descend to the passageway by the sheet rope carrying our uniforms in boxes. We would then remove our theatre costumes and dress ourselves as German officers. The thought of disappearing under the stage in the costume of Dr. Calomel and reappearing in German uniform outside the guard-house delighted me.

This ambitious, if sensational, plan proved impossible. When the curtain was due to rise at the beginning of the show, which was announced for three nightly performances, our German uniforms were not complete. We had suffered severe losses of material and our papers as foreign workers were unfinished. These documents were vital to success. We had planned to remove the German uniform overcoats and caps when we were outside the Park walls and bury them in the woods. Underneath the overcoats we were to be disguised as Dutch workers for the journey through enemy territory.

. . . On the morning of 5th January, 1942, Luteyn and I were ready to escape. We held a conference with Pat Reid and Hank Wardle and decided to try immediately after the nine o'clock *Appel* that evening. Our compasses, maps and a small bundle of notes were ready for hiding inside our bodies. The uniforms were now intact beneath the stage and our civilian clothes had so far escaped detection in their "hide." In a moment of supreme confidence, I collected the addresses of relatives of my companions. Then flushed and excited, I lay down to sleep throughout the afternoon and early evening.

A few minutes before nine I went down to the courtyard, when the snow was falling lightly. The turrets cast long shadows in the light of the moon and the steep walls enfolded me for what I believed to be the last time. There was once more the eternal sound of hundreds of men taking their meagre exercise in clogs. I stood waiting for the

Appel, eyeing the Dutch contingent where Luteyn was waiting ready to join me. We wore cardboard leggings painted with black polish. I wore my usual combination of battledress and sweater, and my Army boots, being brown, were also darkened with black polish. Underneath I had my 'civilian clothes' with a pair of R.A.F. trousers. I had an over-powering sense that this was my last evening in the castle. The certainty grew with every minute, making me composed and determined.

There was a sharp order of dismissal and mingling with the dispersing prisoners, Pat Reid, 'Hank' Wardle, Luteyn and I hurried quickly into the senior officers' quarters. In the darkness of the theatre, we felt our way beneath the stage, then carefully prised up the loose floorboards. Pat Reid lifted the trap called "Shovewood" which, on its under-side was whitewashed, disguising the hole in the ceiling of the passage below. I could see the strong, determined lines on his face as he worked in the glow of a cigarette-lighter. The trap removed, the mattress-cover rope was let down through the hole in the ceiling. Cautiously we climbed down, holding the boxes of uniforms, and landed with soft bumps on the floor of the passage.

The bright lights from the courtyard shone through the cobwebbed windows in the outer wall of the passage. Treading softly in our socks we reached the door of the gate-bridge. Pat Reid, shining his lighter on the lock, swiftly picked it. It opened without a sound for he had oiled the hinges earlier in the week. We were in the half-light of a narrow corridor. We walked quietly across it and stopped at the door that led to the guard-house.

The German uniform overcoats were unpacked in silence and we put them over our workmen's clothes, leaving our battledress in the boxes. As we pulled on our boots there was no sound except the grating of Pat Reid's wire searching in the lock. A minute passed, and suddenly came fear and exasperation. The door would not open. Beneath our feet we could hear the creaking of the gates and the voices of sentries changing guard. We stood motionless, fully dressed as German officers, and waited with pounding hearts. Pat Reid spoke in a hoarse whisper,

"I'm afraid I can't get it open!"

He continued turning the wire in the lock. I could hear the wire rasping against the rusty metal as he tried again and again to open it. The minutes passed in terrible suspense. Through the cobwebbed window I could see the snow falling. I folded my arms and waited. Suddenly there was the noise of old hinges creaking. A quick snap and the door swung open, showing us the dim interior of the attic.

"Good luck," said Pat Reid, and shook hands.

We waited till the door was locked behind us and we could no longer hear his muffled steps. Then we crept carefully to the top of stone spiral stairs at an open door on the other side of the attic. A wireless in the guard-room on the ground floor was playing organ music. It was the moment to go down, for the music was loud. We walked quickly down the first flight of stairs, past the door of the officers' mess on the first floor where a light showed beneath. We waited, then stepped confidently down through darkness, into the passage beside the guard-room. The guard-room door was half-open, and I caught a glimpse of German uniforms inside, as we marched smartly into the blinding whiteness of the snow under the arc lights. The testing time had come. I strode through the snow trying to look like a Prussian. There stood the sentry, the fallen snow covering his cap and shoulders, stamping his feet, just as I had pictured him. He saluted promptly, but he stared at us, and as our backs were turned I felt him watching. We walked on beneath the first archway and passed the second sentry without incident. Then, between the first and second archways, two under-officers talking loudly came from the Kommandantur. They began to march behind us. I felt Luteyn grow tense beside me. I clasped my hands behind my back with an air of unconcern. I might have been casually pacing an English parade ground. In a moment of excitement I had forgotten my part. "March with our hands at your sides, you bloody fool," came a fierce sharp whisper from my companion.

Again I saw the bicycles near the clock tower. Could they be ridden fast in this thick snow? We passed beneath the tower, saluted by the sentry, and came to the fateful wicket-gate. As Luteyn opened it I watched the under-officers, their heads bowed to the driving snow, march on across the moat bridge. Down we went into the moat, stumbling and slipping, until we reached its bed. A soldier came towards us from the married quarters. He reached us, stopped and stared deliberately. I hesitated for a moment ready to run, but Luteyn turned on him quickly and in faultless German said crossly, "Why do you not salute?"

The soldier gaped. He saluted still looking doubtful and began to walk up the side of the moat towards the wicket-gate. We did not look back but hastened up to the path on the far side, and, passing the married quarters, came to the high oak paling which bordered the pathway above the park. We were still within the faint glare of searchlights. Every moment that we stayed on the pathway was dangerous. Lifting ourselves quickly over the paling, we landed in thick snow among the tangle of trees. My cardboard belt was torn and broke and with it into the darkness vanished the holster.

Groping among the trees we struggled through frozen leaves down the steep bank and made for the outer stone wall. It was five minutes before we were at the bottom of the slope. Helped by Luteyn, I found a foothold in the stones of the wall and sat astride the coping. The wall, descending steeply with the tree-covered slope, was shrouded in snow and ice. Each time that I tried to pull Luteyn on top, I lost my foothold and slid backwards through the steep angle of the wall. Then with numbed hands, I caught him beneath the armpits and, after great efforts, hoisted him up beside me. For a minute we sat breathless in the cold air clinging to the coping, and then jumped a distance of twelve feet. We fell heavily on the hard ground in the woods outside the castle grounds. I was bruised and shaken and frightened. I stood leaning against a tree looking at Luteyn. Another minute passed in the falling snow.

"Let's go," I said, and we began to climb towards the east seeking the direction of Leisnig, a small town six miles away.

At ten o'clock the snow was falling less thickly and the moon showed us a way through the trees as we continued to climb towards the road to Leisnig. Beyond the trees we stumbled over frozen fields with hearts uplifted. The headlights of a car, yellow in the bright moonlight, turned in our direction. We lay flat in the snowdrifts till the lights swung towards the east. As we felt the hard surface of the road, I turned up the collar of my dark blue jacket against the cold. I had left the warm green overcoat behind me buried with the rest of the uniform beneath a pile of leaves and snow. The blue jacket was made from an officer's uniform of the Chasseurs Alpins. Shorn of silver galons and badges it became a rough workman's coat of serviceable cloth. . . .

On my head I wore a ski cap made of blanket and my Royal Air Force trousers were now turned down over my Army boots. From this moment Luteyn and I were Dutch electrical workers with papers permitting us to change our place of occupation from Leipzig to Ulm in South-Western Germany. Leipzig was twenty-two miles from the castle. We planned to reach it by walking the six miles to Leisnig, and there to take an early workman's train. Foreign workers, it was said, were numerous in Leipzig and some were to be transferred to the south.

We had no papers for the journey to Leipzig. Success depended on our safe arrival at the main station for the south. Pausing a while beside the road, we recovered money, maps and papers from the containers concealed in our bodies and then trudged smartly along the road. After two hours we passed a row of cottages close to Leisnig and came to what appeared to be a barracks. A faint light shone from the entrance gate and in the moonlight we saw a sentry. We stopped, turned from the road, and floundered through deep snow towards a belt of trees on higher ground. We stood there, sheltering among the trees against the sharp winds of the night. The ingenious Dutch officers in Colditz had acquired by bribery a timetable of the trains from Leisnig to Leipzig. We therefore knew that the first workmen's train was due to start at five o'clock. Three hours passed. It was too cold to talk. We waited silently for the train, looking towards the town and listening to the sound of shunting on the railway. . . .

There was no one at the station so we walked away to the outskirts of the town unnoticed.

When the train was due we came slowly back to the entrance of the station where a small group of German working people had collected at the gate. As is the custom, the travellers were not allowed on the platform until the train was due to start. We stood silently aside from the others sheltering from the cold beside a wooden hut. When it was nearly five o'clock the doors opened, and the crowd surged forward to the ticket office. We followed in their wake and Luteyn, who spoke the best German, stopped at the *guichet* and bought two workmen's tickets to Leipzig. I followed him on to the platform where we stood apart from the others, men and women carrying small baskets or bags of tools.

The orange front light of an engine appeared. It was a scene of true romance. Here were we, escaped enemy prisoners of war, standing on the platform of the little station, mingling with ordinary people travelling to their daily work. The train, puffing with determination through the snow, halted and we climbed into a wooden carriage.

We were herded together in the semi-darkness of air-raid precautions. The warmth inside the carriage covered the windows with moisture so that I could hardly see the dawn. I bowed my head and dozed beside an old, and evil-smelling market-woman. Suddenly I was awakened by a sharp kick on my shins and looked up in fear. I met the half-smiling eyes of Luteyn. He sat hunched in a short tight overcoat, his ski cap on one side. Then I realised that I must have been talking English in my sleep. No one had noticed or even listened to my murmurs. I watched the thin, strained faces of the working-men as they dozed shoulder to shoulder, and saw the dawn slowly appear through the sweaty windows.

I felt ashamed that Luteyn was more alert and awake. He was strongly-built with humorous grey eyes and long dark hair. He was a strong and buoyant character whose life was spent in laughter and good fellowship. Yet he had a Dutch quality of thoroughness which made him a great escaper. He had staying power and resourcefulness and his great advantage lay in his superior knowledge of Germany and its language, so that he could take each fence with boldness and aplomb. He had a gay, attractive manner of speaking which disarmed the enemy and saved us both in the many dangerous situations which were to follow. For my part, rebellious by temperament though I was, I found him easy to work with and we seldom argued with each other. At six o'clock we drew in to the great station of Leipzig. The travellers, woken by shrill whistles, began to yawn and swear in low exhausted voices. We looked around us and followed the crowd towards a barrier where we gave up our tickets. There came upon me a sense of alarm and bewilderment. It was twenty months since I had seen the outside world, except for my adventures in the wild desolate country of Poland. Here, among the silent crowds of people moving in the dim light of the station, I was aghast at my helplessness. I felt like a peasant come for the first time to a city, unable to comprehend the paraphernalia of civilisation.

We wandered timidly round the station watching the indicators for a train to Ulm and found that no train left until 10.30 in the evening. It slowly dawned on us that we must stay in Leipzig with nowhere to shelter or sleep for many hours. We tried to find refreshment. Entering a tea-room we ordered coffee, supplied with a small envelope of saccharine. This was all we could obtain, for every other article of food required coupons. The coffee warmed us as we looked shyly at each other, smiling a little, and not daring to speak in any language. After paying for our coffee, we wandered to a waiting-room crowded with travellers, mostly poor, who sat among their luggage and children, silent and obedient. I looked at these victims of Hitler's war and felt a great pity. The hopelessness in their faces brought a stark realisation of suffering. We had heard rumours of their plight in the camp, they were now confirmed beyond our belief. Musing I took from my pocket a huge bar of Red Cross chocolate and began to eat. A young woman with fierce hysterical eyes, gazed at the chocolate as if she had seen a ghost. I stared back at her uncomprehending. She spoke to an old woman beside her and they looked at me in anger. Immediately the crowd near us began to talk in threatening whispers. I heard the word tchokalade many times. Luteyn turned to me and frowned angrily. Slowly realising the danger of my position, I put the chocolate back in my pocket. I had committed a terrible blunder. Chocolate had been unknown to working Germans for many months. Goering himself may well have tasted little. We British prisoners were well supplied. To sit eating this forbidden delicacy in the waiting-room of a great station made one not only an object of envy but of deep suspicion. We rose awkwardly and walked out of the waiting room into the town.

Leipzig at nine in the morning on January the 6th, 1942. The snow was cleared from the streets and there was a distant hum of traffic in the sunshine. Military vehicles sped by us filled with hard-looking men in steel helmets who ignored the civilians. The sidewalks were a mass of field-grey and the mauve-blue of the Luftwaffe. We stared into the shop windows, gazing like children at expensive dresses and furs. Around us stiff, bourgeois, young men in uniform tapped their smart black boots on the pavement, as they stood before the shops. Blonde girls, in short skirts, looked up at the soldiers with fiercely possessive blue eyes and clutched them tightly.

We entered a big emporium and moved among bright lights and dance music and tinsel finery. We watched the people strolling by the counters. The Germans were young, confident and hopeful and we, mere beggars with a few bars of precious chocolate, had only our own high courage between us and the enemy on every side. Only a few sad civilians of an older generation, shabby and worn, crept among the counters like wraiths. The Nazi Revolution of Destruction was at hand.

We were bitterly disappointed to see no sign of bombing, yet the civilians looked hungry and unhappy. We threaded our way through the crowd and came to a square of gardens where a few old men and women walked in the sunshine with their dachshunds. I could read memories in their worn faces and their hatred of Hitler's New Order. I sat beside Luteyn on a seat watching their slow, hopeless perambulation among the snowbound flower beds and shrubs. For me the months of imprisonment were gone and past. I was a detached spectator watching Life go by. New sights and sounds, fresh and clear, came to me after the darkness of prison. Elderly business men and lawyers with brief cases under their arms marched past muttering sombrely to each other. A girl left the procession of Life and sat beside me.

She was young and blonde and plainly of the working class. She looked at me sharply as she sat on the wooden seat. She wore a torn overcoat and her short tight skirt was above her bare knees. She looked down at her shoes with ersatz wooden heels and kicked at a heap of snow. Her mouth was set in a hard determined line. I struggled to look at her calmly but with an inwardly beating heart. Her prominent blue eyes had ruthlessness.

"Good morning," she said.

I dared not answer or risk conversation. She pouted!

"You are unsociable, my friend."

I turned to see Luteyn had already risen from the seat and was walking slowly away. I followed him in dismay and embarrassment and, for a moment, turned towards the girl. She was looking hard at us. I felt her blue eyes watching, deep with suspicion and annoyance. We hurried away and wandered along the streets of Leipzig till it was noon.

A cinema in enemy territory is a fine hiding place for the fugitive. After a lunch of *ersatz* coffee we came to a cheap stuffy cinema at the bottom of an arcade. Luteyn bought the tickets. Our small stock of German marks was enough for only the cheapest seats. We stood, obediently waiting for the performance, regimented by a commissionaire. In a few minutes, we took our seat among German soldiers and sailors and their girls and waited for the curtain, and, as the lights went out, a tall young German officer came in alone and sat next to me.

We saw first on the programme a news-film of events in Libya. Rommel, standing beside a staff car in the desert, talking decisively; then excellent shots of panzers in action and a British plane being shot down. Close ups followed of a British pilot taken prisoner by the Germans and waving encouragement to his friends still fighting in the air. In my excitement I clutched the seat in front of me and was rewarded by the occupant turning round with a harsh whisper of protest.

The feelings of a prisoner who for many months has been shut out from the war and accustomed only to the crudest enemy propaganda, are hard to describe. I could have wept from joy. At least the war was not yet lost. In the next part of the news-film there came a most shattering revelation. The scene was set in a Russian winter. Up a long snow-bound hill German soldiers struggled against the blizzard, dragging guns and vehicles. There were photographs of frozen bodies and men's limbs swollen to unrecognisable size with frost-bite. If Goebbels wanted to impress the Germans with the sufferings of their troops to inspire them to greater sacrifices at home, he hid no detail of their hardships.

There was a shocked silence when the news-film came to an end.

The lights went up in the shabby hall while martial music played from a cracked loud-speaker. Young men and girls chanted Nazi songs and around us their clear voices sounded in perfect harmony. Only the old people were glum and quiet. The music changed to

"We are marching against England!"

For a moment I caught my companion's eye and, with a faint grin on our faces, Luteyn and I sang loudly with the rest.

... From the cinema we walked again into the blackout of the city. The moon had not yet risen and only the soft whiteness of the snow guided us through public gardens to the main station. Often at corners of the streets we caught the faint reflection of a policeman's polished helmet and edged away among the crowds or dodged the trams to cross the street.

We came again to the station waiting-room and sat there, tired and cold and anxious. The numerous passengers in the waiting-room, many poor and infirm, assembled for the night trains. Then came the men in uniform, elbowing all the civilians aside. I watched them closely. The bullying S.S. men, the clod-like infantrymen, and the pale, and spectacled administrative clerks. All in uniform, they tramped over the gloomy station like locusts, demanding refreshment or newspapers or anything they wanted. Such is total war.

Luteyn bought the tickets to Ulm. We had decided to change there and, if all went well, to take tickets to the Swiss frontier. At the barrier of the platform for the train to the south, military police stood to check the soldiers but there seemed no control of civilians. We waited beside the train before it started, preferring to find standing room than risk conversation in a compartment. As it began to move we climbed the steps of a carriage and stood in the corridor.

The compartment opposite was occupied by a single figure in the uniform of the S.S. I could see the man as we stood outside, a great ape-like person with a heavy jaw. His uniform was new and spotless and he crossed his legs which were in fine black boots as he read a newspaper with screaming red and black headlines. I caught only the word "Rommel." So that he should not watch us, we moved into the shadow at the end of the corridor and looked into the darkness where only a few pin-points of light showed the effective blackout of the city. The train jolted over the points and gathered speed with piercing whistles. Above its rattle I heard the door of the compartment open, and turning my head saw the big S.S. man standing in the doorway.

His hands were on each side of the entrance door and he spoke to us in a soft voice.

"Are you Jews?"

"Certainly not. We are Dutch," replied Luteyn.

"Good. Come in and sit here. This compartment was reserved, but my friends are not coming."

We took our seats beside the big man who spoke very slowly to us, using simple phrases. His friendliness alarmed me.

"Where are you travelling?"

"To Ulm."

"Why?"

"We are Dutch electrical workers transferred there from Leipzig."

Luteyn was doing the talking. He had his genuine Dutch passport ready to produce in an emergency. Then the man turned to me and his stupid eyes examined my face, searching for something he did not understand.

"You are Dutch, too?"

"Yes."

"How are things in Holland?"

"We have not been there for some months. We have been in Leipzig since the summer."

It was Luteyn who spoke. The S.S. man turned to me.

"I am going to Munich," he said unexpectedly. "Then I go to Vienna for a conference."

We nodded politely and the conversation stopped. Men and women passengers were walking up and down the corridor and were soon invited into the reserved compartment. They bowed respectfully to the high S.S. officer, took their seats and gave our shabby clothes a scornful stare.

There was no further conversation about Holland. I was glad of this. My sole visit to that country had been the journey in the barge up the River Waal to Germany as a prisoner in 1940. As soon as the passengers began to snore, Luteyn stayed awake according to our arrangement and I slept for a few hours until his turn came to sleep. I was awakened by a loud tapping on the glass of the door and two military policemen looked in. They checked the passes of the soldiers and even scrutinised the documents of the S.S. officer. They stopped for a moment to stare at our queerly tailored clothes. I wondered for a moment whether they would recognise the colour of R.A.F. trousers, but the S.S. officer intervened importantly.

"These are foreign workers (*fremdarbeiter*). Dutch," he said with conviction.

The military police hesitated, then turned away as if suspicious civilians were nothing to do with their department. Now it was Luteyn's turn to sleep and I listened to the endless rattle of the express as we passed through Plauen and Hof and sped southwards into Bavaria. Lifting the blind, I glimpsed the snow outside or studied the sleeping faces in the dim light of the compartment. Towards four in the morning the train began to slow and came to a halt amid the sounds of a large station. I woke Luteyn, rose and stretched my limbs, and walked over to the doorway. In the gloom there was shouting and the bustle of passengers. I leant out of the window and saw on a sign before me the word "Regensburg."

It was here that we were due to change for the train to Ulm and we stepped on to the platform in the sharp cold.

"Good-bye, Dutchmen," said the S.S. man pompously from inside the compartment.

We went into a waiting-room and sat down at a table. Passengers with their luggage came with us, and promptly fell asleep with their heads resting on the tables. Opposite, a man in railway police uniform stared at us in unfriendly fashion. We did not wait for him to speak but walked out again on to the platform and entered the booking-hall. We sat on the floor with other travellers leaning against a wooden partition. A man and a girl smelling of spiced sausages and garlic lay near us in a close embrace.

. . . At nine on the second morning of the escape the train drew into Ulm and we left it, making our way towards the booking office. Luteyn calmly asked the girl for two tickets to Singen on the Swiss frontier. She frowned and my heart began to sink. She asked for papers and we showed our papers to her.

"I must fetch the railway police. Stay here."

We did not wish to run away, hoping that our papers would satisfy them. A fat, red-faced railway policeman in his dark blue uniform asked us why we wished to go to the frontier zone. Luteyn explained that we were due to begin work in Ulm on the morrow and wished to spend a short vacation. The policeman, looking baffled, released us and we started to leave the station, walking across the big square in front. There was a shout behind us.

"Come back, gentlemen! I want to speak to you again."

The policeman took us to a place in the goods-yard where a thin, tight-lipped German railway police lieutenant sat at a desk. He examined our false papers with bewilderment. It appeared to me that the writing on it did not make sense to him. I could hardly stop myself from laughing as he lifted them to the light, looking, no doubt, for water marks. He was, however, impressed by Luteyn's Dutch passport and there seemed no inkling in his mind that we were escaped prisoners of war.

"I don't understand these men at all," he said helplessly. "Take them to the Labour Office. I wish someone would control these foreign workers more efficiently."

We walked across the square outside the station escorted by another policeman with a revolver. We chatted gaily in German, complimenting the man on the beauties of the town of Ulm. He was flattered and asked us about our own country of Holland. So much did we win his confidence that when we reached the State Labour Office, where men in brown uniforms with spades stood guard at the entrance, he bade us walk up the steps on our own, saying he would wait for us. His parting words were:

"You speak good German. Go and report to the office on the first floor and I shall wait for you here."

Smiling to ourselves and hardly able to believe our good fortune, we climbed to the top floor of the building and it was not long before we discovered some stairs on the far side from the entrance. Hurrying down them we left by another door. Avoiding the policeman and the guards with spades, we made for the back streets of Ulm, and Luteyn bought a map of the surrounding country in a small shop.

The cold had now become intense and, walking beyond the suburbs of Ulm, we left the snow-capped roofs of the university town behind us and hurried towards the town of Laupheim. It was nearly dusk when we reached the market-square and, asking the way to the station, we took tickets to Stockach, a village as near to the Swiss frontier as we dared to go. The country folk on the platform watched us in silence as we sat upon a bench sleepily waiting for the train. When it arrived we entered a wooden compartment too tired to be able to take turns to stay awake. The train jolted on into the night. We wakened only at the sound of a halt, and after passing the village of Pfullendorf we reached Stockach about nine in the evening.

Of Stockach I only remember white cottages in the moonlight and a doubtful station master watching us as we walked into the hills hoping to reach the frontier town of Singen when the moon went down and the frontier was in darkness. The road began to rise steeply through the forests and great banks of snow were on either side of us. Even by two o'clock in the morning we still had many miles to go, struggling along the icy road as the moon began to wane. The road slowly descended towards Singen.

It seemed hopeless to try to cross the frontier that night and we determined to look for somewhere to hide until the following evening. At five o'clock on the morning of January 8th, we were still moving towards Singen. Lights showed ahead of us in the roadway and to our tired eyes they seemed welcoming and kind. Then the figures of four men appeared. They were woodcutters walking to work from Singen. They hailed us and we wished them good morning. Something about us surprised them.

"Are you Poles?" said one of them.

"Yes," replied Luteyn.

"I don't believe it," said another. "Poles are not allowed out of their camp at five in the morning."

Evidently there was a Polish labour camp in the neighbourhood. The four woodcutters looked startled and undecided. As for me, I was near to surrender. My feet seemed to be frozen in my boots as if in blocks of ice. I hardly cared that we had come so far only to be recaptured. I could only think of warm fires and beds.

"Go, Hans, fetch the police," said the oldest woodcutter. The man called Hans who wheeled a bicycle, mounted it and rode off towards Singen. The remainder confronted us uncertainly. They did not try to detain us but stood irresolute and dumb. We suddenly realised that they were frightened of us. Without a word we dashed to the side of the road and into the forest, running in the snow until we sank exhausted. My breath came painfully and my head began to swim. I could not look at the whiteness around me without pain. We rose to our feet after a minute and began to move across a clearing. There was no sign of the woodcutters. As I walked there came over me a kind of delirium between sleep and waking. I thought that I was on some parade ground in England. I felt a figure beside me and turned to see my old Colonel marching in the snow in his uniform and field boots. I spoke to him and addressed him respectfully.

"What the hell?" said Luteyn.

"It's all right," I said ashamed.

Luteyn grunted impatiently, and a few paces across the clearing we came to a large wooden hut surrounded by a fence. There was the outline of a pathway, shrubs and flower beds in the snow, and beside the hut were beehives. We walked up to the hut and tried the doors which were all locked, but a small window in the wall was open. We lifted ourselves in and staggered crazily around the hut in the faint light of dawn. There was no sound of life. We found a kitchen and

two rooms in one of which there was a bed. Tired and faint, we lay
together on the bed in the intense cold and with an old blanket over
us fell into a deep sleep, not waking until the afternoon.

When we awoke there had been another heavy fall of snow which
luckily concealed our footsteps leading to the hut. From outside it
seemed that we could hear the far-off sound of dogs and we got ready
to escape into the woods. But as the hours passed no one came in
sight and the sound of barking grew faint. Searching the hut, we found
in one corner of the kitchen, spades and shovels, and hanging behind
the door, two long white coats evidently used by the bee keeper.

According to our map we were in the middle of a forest, two or
three miles from Singen. We planned, therefore, to leave the hut at
dusk and walk along the road to the town. West of the town and to
the south lay woods through which ran the road and railway line to
Schaffhausen in Switzerland. At some points the road formed the
frontier between Switzerland and Germany.

Shortly before five o'clock on .this afternoon of the eighth of
January, we shouldered spades, and carrying the two white coats under
our arms we cut through the forest to the road to Singen. For more
than a mile we saw no one on the road, then the lights of bicycles
came towards us and a voice called "Halt." In the glow of the bicycle
lamps I could see two boys in the uniform of the Hitler Youth, each
armed with truncheons. I felt no fear of them. Refreshed by sleep, I
was determined they should not stop us. The boys spoke in a hectoring
fashion.

"What are your names and where are you going?"

"We are Westphalian working in the neighbourhood and we are
going back to our lodgings in Singen," said the resourceful Luteyn.
This was a good choice of disguise for the Dutch accent resembles
that of the Westphalians. The boys seemed doubtful.

"What is wrong?" I said trying to imitate Luteyn's accent.

"We have been told to look for two British prisoners who have
escaped and are thought to be trying to cross the frontier tonight."

We both laughed.

"They won't get far," said Luteyn, it is much too cold for prisoners
of war!"

The boys laughed uncertainly and rode off towards Singen and as
we reached the town they turned again and came towards us. One
said to the other:

"There are the Westphalians."

As this conversation was taking place in the road I reflected that these boys alone stood between us and freedom. Afterwards I asked Luteyn what was in his mind.

"For me to kill one with my spade and you the other," he said, "what did you intend to do?"

"Exactly the same."

We passed through Singen in the black-out, without incident, and skirting a great dark mound which seemed to be a slag heap we set off southwards through the wood, marching upon a compass bearing to the frontier. At two o'clock in the morning on the ninth of January we crossed the railway to Schaffhausen about two miles north of a point where the road forms the frontier. It was a fine, cold night and the moon was full. Wrapping ourselves in the white bee-keepers coats for camouflage, we slowly advanced until we could see a gap in the trees and lights of cars passing along the road ahead. Not far to the east were voices and lanterns and what appeared to be a frontier post. For an hour we crouched in a ditch beside the road and watched a sentry pacing up and down only forty yards away. Here we ate the remainder of our chocolate and swallowed a few mouthfuls of snow. Black clouds began to hide the moon and the cold increased with a rising wind. I watched the German buttoning the collar of his overcoat and saw him move towards the sentry-box beside the frontier barrier. Before us across the road was a smooth plain of snow surrounded by distant trees. Beyond this few hundred yards of open No Man's Land was freedom. At half-past four in the morning the sentry turned away from us. I could no longer hear his footsteps against the wind.

"Do you agree to cross now?" said Luteyn.

"This is the moment," I whispered.

We crawled from the ditch and across the road still dressed in our white coats. We continued crawling across the field in front of us, ploughing on hands and knees through the deep snow. After what seemed an eternity we rose to our feet, and surged forward into Switzerland.

Over the Swiss frontier, we came to very deep snowdrifts through which we stumbled and sometimes sank, having to drag each other to our feet. Ahead were neither huts nor frontier guards, nothing to point the way to safety. At this point the territory of Switzerland is a narrow appendix forming a no-man's land before the first Swiss village is reached. Three hundred yards to the east a single lamp flickered ominously. We dared not approach it. We could not be sure that it did not shine in a German frontier post. We had to march due south on an accurate compass bearing to avoid blundering back into the enemy. Striving to maintain our reason after the nightmare of our escape, we stopped every few steps to check our bearings.

So tired were my limbs that I could hardly lift my feet. My boots were weighed down with ice. Often we were both waist-deep in snow. Sometimes neither of us could go further and for minutes lay panting and cursing.

Luteyn, so calm and resourceful through these perilous days, began to talk despairingly in Dutch and seemed to be wandering in his mind. I pulled him from a deep drift where only his ski cap showed against that cruel whiteness. Then it was my turn to flounder, helpless and distraught, murmuring with a last attempt at humour that Patriotism was not enough.

It was an hour before we had travelled a quarter of a mile and found ourselves on higher ground. There came to us the sound of cow bells, and a clock chimed the hour of five in sweet tones. Under our feet we felt with unspeakable relief the welcome surface of a road. Suddenly, there were shadowy walls on either side. There was a row of small farmhouses and cow sheds. A single question tortured us. Were we in Switzerland? The buildings, faintly discerned, began to form a street with a church tower at its farthest end. The snow crunched loudly beneath our feet as we went by bounds from doorway to doorway watching and listening in terrible anxiety. I saw a blurred whiteness against the wall of a barn and I lit my petrol lighter. Pushing aside the snow, I could see an advertisement for a circus. There were elephants and tigers in gay colours and a ring-master with long moustaches. And then, with pounding heart, I sought the place of the performance. It was Schaffhausen, and we were at the Swiss village of Ramsen. We had come through!

1943
KAZIK: THE WARSAW GHETTO REBELLION
& THE ESCAPE OF THE REMNANT

... A sudden calm surrounded me. I felt so good among the ruins of the Ghetto, near the corpses that were dear to me, that I wanted to stay and wait for dawn, for the Germans to come, to kill some of them and then die. My life passed dizzily before my eyes, like film. I saw myself fall in battle as the last Jew in the Warsaw Ghetto. I felt I was on the border between sanity and madness.

With a superhuman effort, I wrenched myself free of thoughts of suicide and decided to return to the sewers. The closer I got to the manhole cover, the brighter were the searchlights in the area because the German position was close to the entrance of the Ghetto. I crawled the last part of the way and finally managed to slither into the sewer. I went down and closed the cover. "Let's go! There's nobody there!" The shout leaped out of my mouth. It wasn't my voice, it wasn't a human voice: it was aimed at Ryszek and the sewer workers who were waiting for me.

– Kazik (Simha Rotem), *Memoirs of a Ghetto Fighter*

Despite the severe impact of economic depression and the politically motivated anti-Semitism and persecution of Polish Jews after World War I, Warsaw was a vibrant center of Jewish life and culture until the invading armies of Nazi Germany shattered Poland in September of 1939. Within a year the Nazi authorities had confined Warsaw's 360,000 Jews into a small quarter of the city, which the Nazis sealed behind a ten-foot high wall on November 15, 1940. With a flood of Jewish war refugees forced into the 3.5 square miles within the walls, the Ghetto population swelled to almost 460,000 by the spring of 1941. Horrendously overcrowded and impoverished, tens of thousands perished of disease and starvation as the Jews of Warsaw struggled to maintain a semblance of civil society and merely to survive.

The mass deportation of Jews from the Warsaw Ghetto began on July 22, 1942. In the seven weeks that followed, the Nazi regime packed almost 300,000 Ghetto Jews into railcars for "resettlement in the East." Only those Jews who held an *Ausweis* (a special employment pass) were exempted. Those who resisted deportation were shot in the streets. The real destination of the deportees was the nearby death camp at Treblinka where they were murdered. When the deportations were halted on September 13th less than 55,000 Jews remained in the Warsaw Ghetto. More than 30,000 of these were workers with *Ausweis*. Some 20,000 others—the "wildcats"—had hidden to evade deportation and had no legal status. Approximately 8,000 Jews had escaped to "Aryan" Warsaw.

On July 28th, when it had become clear that the deportations would continue, young men and women from Jewish pioneer youth groups gathered to discuss how to resist the Nazis. While there was some talk of fleeing from Warsaw altogether, they ultimately agreed that it was their duty to remain in the Ghetto to defend their people and to die with them. With nothing more than raw courage, determined intelligence, and two pistols, they formed the seed group of the Jewish Fighting Organization—the *Zydowska Organizacja Bojowa*, ZOB—which was formally organized three months later on October 20, 1942. Even as the deportations continued unabated, the young Jewish resisters began to develop a network to coordinate resistance, move people and funds, and smuggle arms into the Ghetto. On August 20th they attempted to assassinate Jozef Szerynski, the head of the detested Jewish Police, and set fire to a Nazi warehouse filled with pillaged Jewish property. The bullet to Szerynski's head did not kill him, but it sent a message, which the ZOB fatally delivered to more than a dozen Jewish police officers and collaborators in the months that followed.

After the first week of deportations any remaining semblance of private-sector economy and civil society in the Warsaw Ghetto collapsed. By the time mass deportations came to a stop in mid-September, the Ghetto had essentially been transformed into a mass labor camp. Reduced in size, the Ghetto was divided into four separate enclaves. More than half the remaining population was concentrated in the Central Ghetto, the heart of Warsaw's traditional Jewish quarter, which remained a focal point of Jewish life and resistance through the autumn of 1942 and into the winter and spring of the following year. The remnants of the *Judenrat* and the Jewish Police were quartered there along with most of the Jewish laborers who were transported each day to work outside the Ghetto walls. Most of the "wildcats" also lived in the Central Ghetto. There were few "shops" (forced labor factories) in this enclave. During the last months, the most important work site there was the *Werterfassung*, an enormous SS facility engaged in the task of sorting, appraising, and liquidating the mountains of Jewish property that the Nazis had pillaged from the Ghetto's emptied buildings. Approximately 20,000 Jewish workers were quartered in housing attached to "shops" in an enclave bounded by Leszno, Nowolipki, Smocza, and Karmelipka Streets. Four thousand additional workers were quartered in an enclave called the Brushmakers' Shop, which was centered along Franciskánska Street. Another 2,000 workers were isolated in "Little Többens." No movement was permitted through the abandoned wastelands of vacant housing that separated these enclaves, but people dared to dart through the haunted shadows to maintain contact with each other.

Hideous news of the death camps filtered throughout the Ghetto during the last cruel months of 1942, as the young fighters of the ZOB struggled to organize resistance. The tortured people of the Ghetto gradually woke from the numbed bewilderment and utter despair and grief that had gripped them throughout the nightmare period of the deportations. A spirit of resistance and a thirst for revenge deepened within the surviving Ghetto population. By the onset of winter the people of the Ghetto were desperately preparing hidden shelters and underground bunkers in which to take refuge during the final liquidation. Everyone knew that this was coming, but the heavy Nazi incursion into the Ghetto on January 18, 1943—with the goal of removing a quota of 8,000 Jews—came as a surprise. The day began normally with workers reporting to the "shops" and lining up to be transported to work sites outside the walls. When it quickly became apparent that the Nazis were launching an *Aktion*, everyone fled to their hiding places, but many were caught and many were shot dead in the streets as the Nazis indiscriminately rounded up approximately 3,000 people, many of them documented workers. For the first time encountering fierce armed resistance—which on this occasion arose spontaneously from scattered groups—the Nazis were afraid to pursue the Jews into their places of hiding, although many of these were still flimsy and vulnerable and their occupants almost entirely unarmed. When the *Aktion* came to an end after four appalling days, the Nazis had captured approximately 5,000 Jews for transport to murder.

Jewish resistance in the Ghetto lifted the spirits of the surviving population, whose hopeless hopes were further raised when news reached them of the German defeat at Stalingrad. The courageous fight of the Ghetto Jews also raised their standing among the Polish population and strengthened their tenuous ties to the Polish resistance from whom at last, at least for a brief time, some little help would be forthcoming. Desperately pressed on the Eastern Front, the Nazis were paralyzed in debate over what course they next should take, either to liquidate the Ghetto completely and immediately or to attempt to maintain war-production from its factories. In the meantime the Jews of the Warsaw Ghetto applied all their ingenuity in redoubled efforts to construct secure bunkers and to arm themselves for the final battle. That terrible battle, when it came, was to last for almost a month, during which all but a few of the remaining survivors of the Ghetto would be finally extinguished in a ferocious inferno of fire, bombardment, and poison gas.

Thirty-eight years later, at the Kibbutz Lohamei Ha-Gettaot in Israel, Simha Rotem reluctantly dictated the story of his experiences as Kazik—a nineteen-year-old ZOB fighter—in the battle that began on April 19, 1943 and ended when Kazik led the last survivors of the Mila 18 command bunker through the sewers to safety. It is this story that is presented here to be read with care and always to be remembered.

In the Ranks of the ZOB

from *Memiors of a Warsaw Ghetto Fighter*

by Kazik (Simha Roten)

In Battle, under the command of Hanoch Gutman

We knew the day we would start shooting wasn't far off. When my turn came to stand guard, I would sit at the observation post, as required by ZOB discipline, and various thoughts would go through my mind: Wouldn't it be better to go out and attack the Germans, to shoot and kill them? The observation post was connected to the base by an alarm bell. I was on edge, impatient; something urged me to "pull the trigger." I played with the gun I had just gotten—a WIS, a Polish revolver. I rolled a grenade or a Molotov cocktail in my hand. In training, especially in quick draw and escape, I was good; but I was fed up with pointless exercises.

From where I stood, I could see the street. It was different than it had been a month before, and certainly than it had been a year earlier. Before the war I wasn't familiar with that area. I had almost never been in a crowded Jewish quarter. I felt stifled and as if my hands were tied; the observation post was cramped. Hanoch Gutman's group at Walowa Street 6 (the corner of Swietojerska Street 34) numbered ten fighters, including four girls. As in the other fighting groups in the Brushmakers' Area, there was a sense of expectation; we hadn't yet opened fire on the enemy.

We had heard the couriers' reports about the clashes with Germans and the other events of the previous day in the Central Ghetto. With their own eyes they had seen Germans killed. The news excited me even more: I wanted to get into the action! It wasn't long before it came: the Brushmakers' Area was surrounded by gendarmes and Ukrainian mercenaries. I stood on a balcony facing Walowa Street. Germans and Ukrainians were visible beyond the wall. From time to time they shot at our windows, just for fun, while we had orders to hold our fire.

On April 19, at four in the morning, we saw German soldiers crossing the Nalewki intersection on their way to the Central Ghetto, walking in an endless procession. Behind them were tanks, armored vehicles, light cannons, and hundreds of Waffen-SS [combat] units on motorcycles. "They look like they're going to war," I said to Zippora, my companion at the post. Suddenly I felt how very weak we were. What force did we have against an army, against tanks and armored vehicles? We had nothing but pistols and grenades. I didn't get depressed. Finally, the time came to settle accounts with them. Sounds of rifle and machine gun fire and grenade explosions reached us from the Central Ghetto. We distinguished between one shot and another: "That's a German, that's ours," we would determine. "Here, that's our mine, our grenade." Calm prevailed for a day in our area. At dusk came a letter from the Többens-Schultz factory calling on everyone to come to work, "since there won't be any aktsia in the Brushmakers' Area." At dusk we left our positions, left scouts in the observation post, and went to the unit base. We had been in a state of readiness for several days, but now we made high-level preparations: everyone held the weapons and supplies he had been issued.

As I said, we had planted a large quantity of explosives near the Brushmakers' gate, under the street. One day after the Germans began liquidating the Ghetto—on April 20—as I stood at the observation post near the gate, I suddenly saw an SS unit approaching. With one hand I pushed the alarm button, and with the other grabbed the fuse to the explosives. At that moment my commander, Hanoch, burst in, snatched the fuse out of my hand, and, after waiting a few seconds, exploded the mine. I was nailed to the spot, almost paralyzed—a tremendous explosion! I had a fervent desire to see it with my own eyes. And I did see: crushed bodies of soldiers, limbs flying, cobblestones and fences crumbling, complete chaos. I saw and I didn't believe: German soldiers screaming in panicky flight, leaving their wounded behind. I pulled out one grenade and then another and tossed them. My comrades were also shooting and firing at them. We weren't marksmen but we did hit some. The Germans took off. But they came back later, fearful, their fingers on their triggers. They didn't walk, they ran next to the walls. We let the first group of six pass—a shame to waste ammunition on a small group. Then we burst out, with two homemade grenades, ten Molotov cocktails, and pistols in our hands. "Shlomek—the gasoline!" I shouted to one of my comrades, and hurled a grenade at the Germans. We threw the Molotov cocktails at them and they burst into flames, so we shot at the fire. A waste of the only grenade we had, and we retreated up the street, taking a position with the rest of the fighters. Quiet prevailed.

The Germans ran away, but they came back half an hour later. We welcomed them with Molotov cocktails and grenades. One of the

Germans, seeing a girl at the post, called out in amazement: "Hans, look! A woman!" and started shooting at her. But she didn't retreat. Protecting themselves with a strong fire cover, the Germans began withdrawing. One of our fighters, who had taken a position in the attic, poured shots onto the Germans near the walls, in spite of the heavy fire coming from there, and killed six of them. In the yard of a large building fronting on Swietojerska and Walowa streets, Dr. Laus, one of the leaders of the Brushmakers' Area, appeared with two Germans in uniform. They were waving rifles as a sign that their intentions were peaceful. As they went from house to house, Dr. Laus called on the Fighting Organization to put down its weapons within fifteen minutes. We replied with shooting. One of the Germans was killed. Dr. Laus ran away.

Some time later, the Germans returned carrying stretchers, and gathered up their wounded. We took advantage of the lull to leap to another position. The enemy began using automatic weapons, machine guns and flame throwers. They avoided coming into the Ghetto in orderly files and adopted the tactics of fighting in a populated area. Now the real siege began: the sounds of all kinds of weapons blended together—cannons, machine guns, mortars, light weapons. We all held our positions and the enemy was invisible. Despair! There was nobody to fight! The Germans took positions outside the wall and poured hellfire onto us. Suddenly, flames surrounded the building: flames and stifling smoke forced us to leave our positions. Three men covered our retreat; when we found there was nothing more we could do in the Brushmakers' Area, we decided to withdraw.

There was no advance plan for withdrawal, and not knowing what direction to turn made our situation difficult. In the chaos, I went to scout out a retreat route. I took this job because I looked Aryan, and I was wearing an SS uniform that allowed me to move around in the daytime. But there was a danger that fighters in other groups, seeing me from a distance, would think I really was an SS man and would open fire on me. As I searched, I came on a bunker at Swietojerska Street 34. When I started down, the people in the bunker saw first my boots and then my SS coat, and started screaming. I had trouble calming them down in time. We didn't think the bunker was a fit place for our group and we continued searching until we found another, well-built bunker, completely underground, whose inhabitants agreed to take us. After we gathered the whole group in that bunker, we started looking for the other two groups of the organization, with whom we had lost contact. We wanted to turn this bunker into a gathering point for all the fighting groups in the Brushmakers' Area. Gradually, the groups began to assemble.

As commander of the mission, I had to appoint people to scout. This wasn't hard, since they volunteered. We went to search for our comrades. On the way, we came on some Germans but didn't get into battle with them. A few times we tried in vain to make contact with the other groups. As we retreated, Marek Edelman, Hanoch Gutman, and I went to scout the way to the new position on Franciszkanska Street. I saw houses burning. Panicky Jews ran out, straight into the German line of fire. I tried to ignore what I saw. I clung to my mission— to find a safe and quick way to rescue my companions. Then we came on the body of Michal Klepfisz. Michal was an engineer, our "operations man"; with the help of comrades, he had set up a small "factory" to make Molotov cocktails. It was he who had made and planted the mine that had exploded a short while before. We didn't find his revolver on him; the Germans had certainly taken it. Before then, after the first battle, my friend Shlomo Shuster and I noticed two Jews trying to get out of the Ghetto. When we stopped them, we found documents proving that they were Gestapo agents. We took the documents from them and sent them off, figuring that the Germans would destroy them and that it would be too bad to waste our bullets on them.

Finally, we met our two groups, who were also looking for us. We gathered all of them, eighty to a hundred members of the ZOB, in the bunker at Swietojerska 34. The people of the bunker welcomed us warmly. These "ordinary Jews" wanted to join our ranks, but unfortunately we didn't have enough weapons. The echoes of explosions and the constant rumble of machine gun fire reached us. All night long we were busy cleaning our weapons, checking the bullets and the grenade fuses: Finally, we imposed a short rest on ourselves. In the evening, a few comrades went out to bring back Michal's body and to dig a grave for him in one of the courtyards. We dug in silence. Night fell and, between isolated shots, a momentary silence descended on the Ghetto.

To the Central Ghetto
All day long patrols of the Jewish Fighting Organization covered the Brushmakers' Area, but the Germans kept out of sight. At dusk, people whose bunkers had been burned down began streaming to us; many had been burned alive. The area was engulfed in flames. The

organization hadn't prepared bunkers, since that ran counter to its purpose; and those that were prepared had been built by private initiative. Some were well built, others were hastily thrown together at the last minute. With the fire rampaging through every house in the Ghetto, the situation in the bunkers became untenable. Our bunker was filled with smoke, and when we were forced to leave it, we decided to make our way to the Central Ghetto. We assembled in the courtyard before we left, standing in straight rows. I shall never forget the picture of the gathering: it was night, but the flames made it bright as day. Everything all around was on fire, walls were crashing down. We had to go through burning shops, with flames surrounding us on all sides. The heat was unbearable. Slivers of glass in the yards were melted.

We put wet cloths on our faces. Our goal was to get to Franciszkanska Street 20. We only had to cross the street. Nothing seems easier, but the wall along Bonifraterska Street at the intersection, as well as the wall separating the Brushmakers' Area from no-man's-land, had been destroyed. We were exposed to the patrols of Latvians, Ukrainians, and Germans lying in wait for us at the breaches in the wall. It was possible to reach the Central Ghetto only through one gap. Despite the danger, we succeeded and only one group, with which we lost contact, failed. Shlomo Shuster and I served as guides. The members jumped through the gap after they got a signal from us.

We knew that a German tank had been set on fire in the Central Ghetto and that dozens of Germans had been killed in the uprising. Our losses were few. In the first three days the Germans didn't take a single Jew out of the buildings. After their attempts to penetrate the Ghetto had failed, they decided to spare themselves casualties by destroying it from outside with cannon and aerial bombings. A few days later the Ghetto was totally destroyed. Those who survived continued living in bunkers. Apparently the Germans concluded there weren't many Jews left in the Ghetto and decided it was safe to enter during the day. At night they were careful and stayed outside: control of the Ghetto was in the hands of the ZOB, and we could walk around among the ruins, without fear. So all communications operations between the groups, provisioning, and searching for survivors or bodies took place at night.

I was in charge of reconnaissance, visited all the positions, and had a chance to meet all the members of the organization who were there. In the Central Ghetto, we gathered in the "Gepner" bunker, underneath the central food supply warehouses at Franciszkanska 22. When we got there, the bunker—a big cellar—was already overfull.

The stifling heat was unbearable; people behaved like complete lunatics, ready to steal food from one another at gunpoint. We weren't surprised by the almost friendly reception we received, because when only a handful of Jews were left in the Ghetto, everyone finally understood—unfortunately too late—that the fighters weren't the "enemies of the people."

We went out to search for food in empty bunkers and cellars. Once we went down to a cellar whose walls emitted waves of heat. My companions and I found ourselves walking on a kind of soft, light ground, like feathers. It was ash with scorched bodies lying in it. In a corner we came on a barrel of honey. We dipped our hands in it and it was almost boiling. We licked that honey until we got sick. At night we continued our reconnaissance patrols. The "streets" were nothing but rows of smoldering ruins. It was hard to cross them without stepping on charred bodies. Once I came on a heap of bodies and heard a child's weeping. As I approached, I saw a woman's dead body hugging a living infant. I stood still a moment and then went on walking.

One night, before dawn on a Friday, a reconnaissance patrol went out to contact fighting groups in the Central Ghetto. Two men went toward Gesia Street, Jurek and I turned toward Nalewki. The street was full of corpses, and to avoid trampling on them we had to leap from place to place. At Nalewki 36 we came on a group of fighters commanded by Lutek. From that moment, constant contact was renewed with the command of the Fighting Organization and all the groups. At that time no planned activities were being carried out except for skirmishes with patrols. Three days later we were forced to leave that bunker, which had served as a base for our sorties. We moved to no-man's-land but had to leave there too because of the flames and the stifling smoke. The situation in the bunkers was depressing, hopeless—no air, no water, and no food. One day passed and another, and on the tenth day of the aktsia the Ghetto was burned down.

In this dreadful situation, unable to continue the war for lack of weapons, unable to engage the enemy in battle since they no longer came into the Ghetto, we had the idea of getting our people out to the city in order to continue fighting there. On April 29 the command staff—Mordechai Anielewicz, Zivia Lubetkin, Michael Rosenfeld, and Hirsh Berlinski—met to discuss the situation. We had no delusions about the future of the burning Ghetto. They decided to send messengers to the Aryan side, to the representative of the Fighting Organization, Antek, who had been there for two weeks.

After eleven or twelve days of battle, most of the fighters were still alive. The Germans continued destroying the Ghetto from outside, with artillery bombardments and air attacks; finally, sappers were sent to set fires and explode every cellar and bunker. In this situation, we couldn't get into a battle with them anyway, and it was only a question of time until we would all be buried alive under the debris. The command staff therefore decided to find a way to rescue the fighters who could still be saved so they could continue fighting the Germans under other conditions. At first an experiment was made: a small group would make contact with Antek and get advice about smuggling the rest of the fighters out of the Ghetto. But the attempt to send emissaries failed and several members were killed. Tuvia Borzykowski was in one of these groups. He was lucky and survived after his group was attacked by a German patrol. Hella Schüpper was in the second group. Other attempts also failed, but I can't remember who took part in them.

TO THE SEWERS: RESCUE OF THE REMNANT
Mission to the Aryan Side

Despite these failures, the command staff decided to send Zygmunt Fryderych, a Bundist, and me to make another attempt to contact our companions on the Aryan side. We used the tunnel dug by the Jewish Military Union (the Revisionists), which we had discovered on one of our expeditions to seek a way out of the Ghetto. Before the uprising the local commanders of the two organizations had made contact to coordinate future operations. During the uprising we heard that there had been a fierce battle between the Revisionist Military Union and the Germans and that the Jewish fighters had decided to cross to the Aryan side in coordination with the Polish underground (a faction of the AK). Later we learned that they had fled through that tunnel under Bonifraterska Street. The Ghetto wall divided the street in the middle: the odd numbers were inside the Ghetto and the even numbers were on the Aryan side.

We assembled a few items we might need on the Aryan side, things like a shirt and sweater. We had no identity papers. Hochberg and Lolek accompanied us to the entrance. We said good-bye, descended into the tunnel—and there we were on the Aryan side. We hid in an attic until morning because we had to familiarize ourselves with the area. Moreover, it was better not to walk around outside after curfew. At dawn we went downstairs and peeked outside. Clear signs of battle remained in the courtyard. All of a sudden we were surprised by a Christian Pole who appeared in one of the doorways. I immediately began a story I made up on the spot: the two of us had gotten stuck with the Jews in the Ghetto; we had gone to deal in clothes and were caught in the uprising; only now had we somehow managed to get out. The man was convinced, congratulated us on escaping from the Ghetto, and even told us how to get out of the building without running into the nearby German patrol, whose function, he said, was to guard the Ghetto from outside. He also told us that a group of armed Jews from the Ghetto had been holed up in his house not long before. They had been caught in the building by the Gestapo and the SS, and there had been a fight, whose "results you can still see," he said, pointing to the yard and the rooms. Indeed, we did see bodies on the roof, bullet cases, holes in the walls—confirmation of the event. According to him, a few of the group had made off in a car apparently provided by "outsiders."

Later I learned that these were indeed members of the Revisionist group, who had used the tunnel when they decided to leave the Ghetto and go to the Aryan side. Zygmunt and I followed the man's instructions and avoided the gap in one of the walls. We were on our way to Krzyzanowski Street 44, to the apartment of Anna Wachalska and her sister, Marysia Sawicka. We hadn't gone far when we were joined by a group of blackmailers who had immediately recognized that we were Jews and who tried to extort whatever we had. We didn't have anything valuable and I realized that unless we got rid of them, they would turn us over to the Germans. I glanced around and thought quickly. As I looked, a truck passing by in the street came into my field of vision. At once we ran and climbed on from behind. By the time the blackmailers understood what was going on, we were far away. The truck picked up speed as we hung on. At the corner it slowed down, and we jumped off unhurt and moved on to our destination.

Walking swiftly and strenuously—we were weak after several days without food—we reached Anna's house and rang the doorbell. Anna, the widow of a PPS (Polska Partia Socjalistyczna, or Polish Socialist party) activist, knew Zygmunt well and greeted us warmly. Zygmunt introduced me and we were joined by Marysia Sawicka. The women suggested we wash and change our clothes. This was my first shower since April 18, an opportunity not only to wash my body but also to restore my soul. When I went into the bright bathroom, covered with white tiles, and was given soap and a fragrant towel—it was like a dream. It was hard for me to believe that, just a few hours before, I had been in another world, between the crumbling walls of the Ghetto, where everything beyond the walls seemed inaccessible. We shaved and washed and put on the clothes we were given, which belonged to a relative, Stefan Szewerski. We were invited to the dining room, to a table covered with a white cloth, loaded with food: an abundance of bread, sausages, and even vodka.

The welcome of the two women whom I had just met dazzled me, but I didn't forget why we had come. That very day, or perhaps the next, their cousin Stefan sent us to Feigl Peltel, who lived under the assumed name of Wladka at Barakowa Street 2. Wladka was the courier of the Bund on the Aryan side of Warsaw. Her apartment became a base of operations to rescue the fighters left behind in the Ghetto. We wanted to get in touch immediately with Antek, the ZOB representative on the Aryan side. He showed up that afternoon with Franya Beatus, his courier, and Tadek (Tuvia Shayngut). We reported on the situation in the Ghetto, speaking in disjointed fragments, piling details on top of one another. We named every person who had been killed. We described the deployment of the fighting groups, told of the systematic destruction and the hopelessness of the situation. (Later I learned that after she heard our report, Franya Beatus committed suicide. She had done her job loyally and effectively. Antek didn't talk much about her afterward, but when he did, it was with great praise.)

Our discussion focused on how to save our comrades. In my naiveté I had thought ways could be found immediately. But it soon became apparent that "nobody was standing and waiting for us on the Aryan side" and that if we wanted to rescue anybody, we would have to do it ourselves. That was the message I absorbed clearly. We agreed that, given the circumstances, each of us—using his or her contacts—would try to do something to rescue the fighters in the Ghetto. We learned that, aside from those present, we could get help from Stefan Szewerski, our hostess, Kostek, and Stefan Pokropek. We agreed on methods of communication and set another meeting in the near future. We already understood that our essential problems were: how to get back into the Ghetto; how to bring the fighters out; where to house and hide them afterward; and how to transport them.

The solution was to make contact with the sewer workers, who knew their way around the labyrinthinc, complex system and could lead us back to the Ghetto on a route we could also use to remove those who had survived. At this point all of us—using our connections on the Aryan side—went to look for vehicles to transport the fighters (if we managed to get them out) and to search for guides to the sewers. We knew that the destruction in the Ghetto was continuing, that every moment was crucial. We met every day to consult and report on our efforts. . . .

One evening, after a day of running around, I returned to Wladka's apartment once again empty-handed. It was dark and through the window, in the distance, I saw the burning Ghetto. In despair, I went over everything I had done since we had left the Ghetto; I kept asking myself if I had done everything I could. Unfortunately, we had no one to rely on except ourselves. In my innocence I had thought that by getting out of the Ghetto I had accomplished the essence of my mission; and now I was shocked to find that this wasn't so and that we were still at the very beginning. . . .

In our searches, we were helped by Tadek Shayngut, of Ha-Shomer Ha-Tza'ir, who was already on the Aryan side; by Krzaczek of the PPR (the Polish Workers' party); and also by the "King of the Blackmailers" (the "Shmaltsovniks"), famous as the leader of the gangs who extorted money from Jews and who helped us—naturally, for a stiff sum. Stefan, the nephew of Anna Wachalska and Maria Sawicka, also helped us. Gradually a plan to get the fighters out of the Ghetto took shape. We needed an exit base where we could descend into the sewers; a guide from the sewer workers; and transportation to take the fighters from the sewer opening to the forest, where they would join in a group of comrades who had left the Ghetto through the tunnel to Ogrodowa Street and had been living in the forest since the end of April.

A week later we were prepared to put the plan into action. Krzaczek and Tadek agreed to provide vehicles; they ordered trucks to move furniture to the house next to the sewer exit on Prosta Street. The base from which we would go down to the sewers would be the apartment of the King of the Blackmailers, as he was called on the Aryan side. The king and his "aides" weren't supposed to know we were rescuing Jews, so we concocted this story for them: "A group of Polish Christians went into the Ghetto before the uprising and got stuck there. We are acting on behalf of the AK, and since we now know exactly where the group is, we plan to send men into the Ghetto to get them out."

On the night of May 7, 1943, an advance group went to the Ghetto. To our great disappointment, they soon returned because the sewers were blocked. Moreover, the Germans posted at the sewer exits tossed grenades in and sprayed the sewer with bullets whenever they heard the echo of footsteps. The next night another group was formed, under my command. . . .

To and from the Ghetto in the Sewers

We set out on May 8. Tadek and Kostek remained outside. The two sewer workers, Ryszek, and I went in and turned toward the Ghetto. It was ten o'clock at night and pitch-dark in the sewers, where there was neither day nor night. Before we descended into the sewer, the King of the Blackmailers had begun to suspect I was a Jew and to doubt the truth of the story about rescuing Christians. I had asked him to postpone his investigation of this issue until I came back. We started walking: the sewer workers first, with me behind. The central sewer in Warsaw is about two meters high and the sewage streams in a mighty flow. There is one more difficulty: the side channels are small and we sometimes had to crawl on our bellies to get through them. It was no pleasure to flounder in excrement, to smell the stench, but we had no choice. The walking itself went on too long. The guides changed their minds from time to time and threatened to desert us. I gave them drinks; sometimes I cajoled them and sometimes I browbeat them and threatened them with my gun—and thus we advanced. At a certain moment the two men said, "That's it, we're inside the Ghetto." I climbed the iron ladder in the wall of the sewer. Ryszek stayed below to keep the guides from taking off. I lifted the manhole cover and found that we really were in the Ghetto, a few meters away from the gate on Zamenhof Street, between Stawki and Nis. It was two o'clock in the morning.

Zamenhof Street was lighted by a searchlight from Dzika Street. I had to crawl on my belly to Muranowska Street. I had the addresses of a few of our fighting groups. First I made my way to the supply cellar on Franciszkanska Street, where I had left for the Aryan side. I entered the yard but found only the ruins of the shelter. Apparently the Germans had discovered it. Among the ruins I found two men and a woman, not human beings but ghosts. The woman was moaning because her leg was broken. I wanted to take them with me to the Aryan side, but they didn't have the strength to stand up. They told me the ZOB had fought a battle here with a few dozen Germans. It was the battle in which my friend Abraham Eiger had been killed and seventeen-year-old Shlomek Shuster had shown amazing courage.

I left these poor people to their fate and went to Franciszkanska Street 22. I didn't recognize the bunkers in the yard. I signaled with my flashlight, called to the comrades, gave our passwords. Suddenly a woman's voice rose from the ruins to lead me to where our comrades were hiding. She told me her leg was broken and asked me to look for her in the heap of debris. I walked around for about half an hour, trying to follow her voice, but it came from a different place every time, as if in a mirage. I sensed that time was running out. I stopped searching. In despair, I rushed to Nalewki, Mila, and Zamenhof streets, but I didn't find anyone anywhere. The Ghetto had been completely burned down. Piles of corpses rolled around in the streets, in the yards, and among the heaps of ruins.

A sudden calm surrounded me. I felt so good among the ruins of the Ghetto, near the corpses that were dear to me, that I wanted to stay and wait for dawn, for the Germans to come, to kill some of them and then die. My life passed dizzily before my eyes, like a film. I saw myself fall in battle as the last Jew in the Warsaw Ghetto. I felt I was on the border between sanity and madness.

With a superhuman effort, I wrenched myself free of thoughts of suicide and decided to return to the sewers. The closer I got to the manhole cover, the brighter were the searchlights in the area because the German position was close to the entrance of the Ghetto. I crawled the last part of the way and finally managed to slither into the sewer. I went down and closed the cover. "Let's go! There's nobody there!" The shout leaped out of my mouth. It wasn't my voice, it wasn't a human voice: it was aimed at Ryszek and the sewer workers who were waiting for me.

We started back. As we walked I signaled with my flashlight, in case someone remained hiding here. Suddenly I heard a noise in a side sewer. I thought I could make out a flickering light. Were they Germans or Jews? My nerves were stretched to the limit, my finger caressed the trigger of my revolver. I was ready to shoot, but something stopped me. I waited and repeated the password of the organization. The tension mounted. From the side sewer a group of ten fighters suddenly burst out. For a moment we were petrified. Was this a dream? Everyone wanted to hug me. A few minutes later I knew we had arrived only one day late. ...

On the spot, I sent two of that group back to the Ghetto to round up the remnants of the fighters and bring them to the sewer. One of them was my best friend, Shlomo Shuster, my comrade-in-arms in the Brushmakers' Area; we had been inseparable until I left for the Aryan side. I gave the fighters clear instructions: "When you come back from the Ghetto, stay together in the sewer, as close as possible to the exit." I emphasized that they were absolutely not to disperse into the side sewers. I promised to lead the way and even to post fighters to guide them at junctions where they might get lost. On the way our comrades told what had happened to them and described the eight days I had been out of the Ghetto. The shelter at Mila 18 had not been discovered until the day of May 8. The bunker had been surrounded and when the Germans had found the ventilating slits, they had poured poison gas into them. Almost a hundred members of the Jewish Fighting Organization had been gathered in the bunker, led by Mordechai Anielewicz, the commander. Hungry, broken, hopeless, some of the fighters had committed suicide; others had tried to break out and had fallen dead at the entrance to the bunker.

Before leaving the sewer, I once more briefed those who remained below. Over and over I emphasized the need to keep from scattering and to maintain total silence so as not to be discovered. Finally, I promised to make contact in the afternoon, before curfew. We kept walking, as the water came up to our waist.

Then Ryszek and I climbed out of the sewers. Tadek and Krzaczek were waiting for us at the home of the "King of the Blackmailers." We changed clothes and went to our comrades to report on the situation. We decided that Tadek and I would contact the fighters in the sewers at dusk. Krzaczek was assigned to get hold of a vehicle to take the fighters to the forest. We agreed to meet the next day, May 10, right after curfew, at the manhole cover and to take out the fighters gathered below.

At the Manhole on Prosta Street

At five o'clock the next morning we were standing at the manhole cover on Prosta Street, waiting for Tadek and the trucks Krzaczek was supposed to obtain. He was to call a moving company to send a truck to take some furniture to a house near the manhole. We were to force the driver at gunpoint to take the fighters coming out of the sewer to their destination. Tadek worked with Krzaczek to get the truck. By nine o'clock no one had come back, and there was no truck either. It was very dangerous to bring the comrades out of the sewer at that hour. On the other hand, if we didn't bring them out soon, we were condemning them to death. So I decided we had to get them out that day whenever we could. It would have been good to have an armed cover during the exit, but unfortunately we didn't.

Another hour passed before the truck arrived with Kostek, and other "Aryan-looking" fellows: Jurek, Ryszek, and Wacek. We surrounded the manhole cover because, at the corner of Zelazna Street, about a hundred meters away, was the German-Ukrainian guard, the guard of the "small Ghetto." We opened the manhole cover. I didn't recognize any of those coming out: figures from another world, ghosts, yet I knew every one of them! I covered the exit, Krzaczek sat in the driver's seat, the rest of us helped the fighters out of the sewer. Meanwhile, Israel Kanal, the commander of the Central Ghetto, shouted to me from the truck, "Kazik, is there cover here?" And I yelled back, "Everybody around," pointing to the big group of onlookers gathered at the manhole cover. One of them joked, "The cats are coming out."

Meanwhile, I came on a Polish police officer on his way to the German guard. I went up to him and politely but firmly explained that this was an operation of the Polish underground and that he would do better to go back where he came from and pretend he hadn't seen a thing. The man obeyed without a word. We went on taking the people out. More than half an hour passed—complete victory. Terrified, I continued walking around in the crowd of onlookers, which increased by the minute. Suddenly I noticed that they had stopped taking people out of the sewers. I rushed to the manhole cover to find out what had happened. "It looks like there aren't any more fighters down there," Ryszek said to me. I bent down into the sewer and roared, "Anybody inside?" Not a sound. I ordered the manhole cover closed, and as I went to the driver's cab, I told Krzaczek we had to move. In the back of the truck were more than thirty comrades. I got in. As the truck began to move, Zivia ordered me to stop because several comrades were still left in a side sewer. I refused. I said I was the commander of the operation and that it wouldn't be right or wise to delay because the Germans were close and were liable to show up any minute. I added that the truck was completely full; another truck which had been ordered hadn't come. After we took those people to the forest, we'd come back and try to find those who were left.

We went on to Lomianki Forest. I remained standing in the truck. Krzaczek was sitting next to the driver. We had to pass through the whole city and cross the bridge over the Wisla. From time to time I ordered preparations in case we were stopped by German patrols. When we got to the bridge, I saw that vehicles were being stopped and searched by the Germans. At the last minute Krzaczek ordered the driver to turn around, which he did with a screech. We tried our luck on another bridge and succeeded in crossing without incident. When we got to the forest, where there was a group of fighters from the Többens-Schultz Area, Zivia came up and said she wanted to shoot me. I replied, "No problem. We can settle our accounts immediately. I'll shoot you and you'll shoot me and we'll be even."

Zivia was angry and tense. She told me that Shlomek and Adolf had been sent to call the comrades in the side sewer as soon as the manhole cover had been removed, and had promised to wait for them. I couldn't help or comfort Zivia. The night before I had dropped a note into the sewer telling everyone to be ready to leave before dawn the next day. I had carefully explained to Shlomek that he was not to scatter the people, and I had also gotten confirmation that all of them were ready to be evacuated. I fell into a depression. I had to stay in Lomianki with the comrades and escort them to a safe place, since nobody wanted to stay with them, despite my request. So we agreed they'd go back where we came out and see what could still be done. Many years have passed. Much has been told and written about that group coming out from the sewers. Later I discussed it with Marek Edelman, who was one of those rescued. He was walking next to Zivia. When they came to the manhole cover, the two of them went from the end of the group to the head of the line, where they had to make the decisions. They received the note I had dropped telling them of the postponement of the escape till the next day because we hadn't yet found trucks. Marek told me, "I was the one who promised Shlomek and Adolf when they went to look for the 'lost' group in the junctions of the sewer that we wouldn't leave without them. While Zivia said, 'I promised them.' " And I have told how furious she was when I ordered the truck to move.

It's hard to know why they delayed. The real story was lost with them when they were killed.

Ryszek, Jurek, and Wacek returned to town in the truck. They went to rescue the rest of the group, in the hope that they had reached the manhole cover on Prosta Street. I waited for them to come back—one hour, two hours, three hours. No one returned. I started worrying; every minute that passed increased the anxiety gnawing at me. I decided I had to do something. I left the forest for Warsaw. As I passed near Bank Square, from the tram I saw people gathering on the street. Impelled by some instinct, I jumped off the moving tram and made my way through the crowd. Then I saw Ryszek lying dead on the pavement. Not far from him I saw Jurek, also killed. Germans and police were crowded in the square.

I mingled with the crowd and listened. Apparently, some Jews had burst out of the sewer. The German guard had been no more than a hundred meters from the manhole, and when they had sensed something suspicious, they had approached and opened fire. They had shot those coming up to the street as well as those inside the sewer. There had been a struggle and every last one of the Jews had been killed.

Later, we heard more: a Polish woman who had seen Jurek and

Ryszek in the first rescue operation identified them when they returned from the forest to the manhole cover and turned them over to the Germans. The two were shot on the spot.

Obviously, I had to get away immediately, since I was liable to be identified as one of those walking around in charge of things. And I did get away before the Germans spotted me.

The next day I met Antek, told him about the incident with Zivia, and listed the names of the fighters we had rescued. I said that Zivia was among them, and I sensed that it was hard for him to believe it. We made an appointment for the next day to go to Lomianki to visit our comrades. The rules of caution sometimes prevented us from making quick contact. Frequently, each of us had to make serious decisions on our own. We went to Lomianki the next day as planned. We took food for our comrades and made our way without incident. At the edge of the forest we came on an advance guard of fighters, who led us in. We spent several hours with the fighters and, after meeting the surviving command staff of the organization and Antek, we returned to Warsaw at dusk.

1944
SURVIVAL IN AUSCHWITZ: THE DROWNED AND THE SAVED

... there is a vast category of prisoners, not initially favoured by fate, who fight merely with their own strength to survive. One has to fight against the current; to battle every day and every hour against exhaustion, hunger, cold and the resulting inertia; to resist enemies and have no pity for rivals; to sharpen one's wits, build up one's patience, strengthen one's will-power. Or else, to throttle all dignity and kill all conscience, to climb down into the arena as a beast against other beasts, to let oneself be guided by those unsuspected subterranean forces which sustain families and individuals in cruel times. Many were the ways devised and put into effect by us in order not to die: as many as there are different human characters. All implied a weakening struggle of one against all, and a by no means small sum of aberrations and compromises. Survival without renunciation of any part of one's own moral world – apart from powerful and direct interventions by fortune – was conceded only to very few superior individuals, made of the stuff of martyrs and saints.

– Primo Levi from
The Drowned and the Saved in *Survival in Auschwitz*

P rimo Levi carved out of himself the moral strength to speak with unflinching clarity of the unspeakable evil of the Nazi labor-extermination camps at Auschwitz, to bear the testimony of his own experiences on behalf of the millions who perished there and on behalf of those few who survived. Levi's stark scientific dissection of the grotesque realities of Auschwitz hollows deep wells of horror, humility, and grief within his readers. It is from within these depths that Levi calls upon us to join our hearts in memory to the millions of hearts that were extinguished there.

Of Jewish ancestry, Primo Levi was born in 1919 into a secular middle-class family in the Northern Italian industrial city of Turin. A brilliant student, in 1941 he graduated summa cum laude with a degree in chemistry from the University of Turin. Despite anti-Jewish laws, he found employment with a Swiss pharmaceutical firm in Milan, where he lived a relatively normal life until he joined the Partisan Resistance to the Fascists in the late summer of 1943. Captured in December of that year, he avowed his Jewish origins and was sent to the vast detention camp at Carpi-Fossoli near Modena. After this camp fell under SS control, Levi was deported to Auschwitz with 650 Italian Jews on February 22, 1944. After a cruel four-day journey the transport train arrived at Auschwitz, and more than five hundred of these Jews—children, the infirm, men and women middle-aged or older—were marched away and engulfed in the darkness of night, never again to be seen. Levi was among the ninety-six men and twenty-nine women who were selected for work details. Of this group, only twenty-three are known to have survived. In his preface to *Survival in Auschwitz* Levi ironically writes of his own survival: "It was my good fortune to be deported to Auschwitz only in 1944, that is, after the German Government had decided, owing to the growing scarcity of labour, to lengthen the average lifespan of the prisoners destined for elimination; it conceded noticeable improvements in the camp routine and temporarily suspended killings at the whim of individuals."

"Good fortune" was an indispensable element of survival at Auschwitz. Any prisoner who was not exterminated immediately was fortunate. Primo Levi was indeed fortunate to have arrived at Auschwitz "only in 1944" to endure "only" eleven months of its nightmarish horrors and "only" eleven months of extreme privation before his deliverance from evil. An accomplished chemist, he was indeed fortunate to be assigned to the laboratory of the Buna-Monowitz camp (Auschwitz III) where he was precariously shielded from the killing labor in which so many tens of thousands of others were enslaved. Levi was indeed fortunate that camp authorities for a time frowned upon the indiscriminate murder of prisoners upon whose skills the German war machine depended. Levi was even more fortunate to be stricken with scarlet fever and left to die in January 1945 when the approaching Russians forced the Germans to abandon Auschwitz, evacuating 58,000 prisoners who were still able to walk and executing many of them along the line of retreat. The Germans certainly intended to kill everyone left in the camps, but fierce Allied air raids and the quickening Russian advance hastened their departure before this final work was done. Of the eight hundred prisoners confined in the sick bays of Buna-Monowitz, all but a scant hundred would die in the days that followed.

But if "good fortune" was certainly an indispensable element of survival at Auschwitz, pure physical resilience and qualities of personal character, good or evil or mixed, were also imperative. Doomed to death were the *Muselmänner* of Auschwitz, those who were weak and had not the strength to resist, those who could not adapt to the bewildering and dehumanizing insanity of the camps, those who, starved and worked to death, were ultimately drained even of complaint and pain and despair and shifted cadaverously and glassy-eyed to their end. This was the fate of the vast majority of prisoners who had been "fortunate" not to be immediately exterminated upon their arrival. Others adapted more successfully to the death in life at Auschwitz. While some quickly descended into criminal bestiality, more gifted individuals were able to navigate on the margins of life and morality, maintaining a wolfish independence in the savage world into which the tide of Nazi evil had swept them.

One of these survivors was Primo Levi, who due to his "good fortune" had just a little more to cling to than others. He arrived at Auschwitz a vigorous, deeply intelligent young man of twenty-four. His academic training afforded him not only the survival platform of his skills, but also an alert mind trained in scientific observation. For Levi "the Lager was pre-eminently a gigantic biological and social experiment" as well as the arena of his desperate personal struggle to survive. And the key to that survival was Levi's maintenance of his independent spirit, which he exercised through his acute capacities to communicate with other prisoners and to learn from them, as he observed with clinical detachment their behaviors and adaptation to an utterly irrational landscape of death. Among the subjects of his observations were three men: the natural "prominent" Alfred L., formerly a leading figure in Europe's chemical industry, who managed to win and coldly retain a sinecure in the camp; the atavistically brutish criminal Elias, who found an apparent happiness there; and the exquisitely educated and "eminently civilized" Henri, who icily made his way with a manipulative armory of tools that included "sympathy" and "compassion." Any reader who so wishes may judge these three men, whom Levi describes in this chapter *The Drowned and the Saved*, from Levi's first book *Sequesto è un huomo*, first published in Italy in 1947 and subsequently published in English under the titles *If This is a Man* and *Survival in Auschwitz*.

After the liberation of Auschwitz on January 27, 1945, Primo Levi, wasted and weakened with fever, remained bedridden for a month before ultimately making his way home to Turin in the course of an incredible nine-month odyssey through war-ravaged Poland, Byelorussia, and Central Europe. Astonished to find his home intact, his family whole, and himself alive, Levi spoke endlessly of his passage through the inferno of Auschwitz. Safe at last, he felt a profound and grief-ridden guilt not uncommon among survivors of the Holocaust. Motivated by this grief and this guilt and by his deeply felt duty to bear witness, he recorded the truth of his experiences in the first book *Se questo è un huomo* and went on to become one of the greatest of Italy's post-war writers. Levi remained at the home of his birth until his tragic and controversial death on April 11, 1987.

> You who live safe
> In your warm houses,
> You who find, returning in the evening,
> Hot food and friendly faces:
>> Consider if this is a man
>> Who works in the mud
>> Who does not know peace
>> Who fights for a scrap of bread
>> Who dies because of a yes or a no.
>> Consider if this is a woman,
>> Without hair and without name
>> With no more strength to remember,
>> Her eyes empty and her womb cold
>> Like a frog in winter.
> Meditate that this came about:
> I commend these words to you.
> Carve them in your hearts
> At home, in the street,
> Going to bed, rising;
> Repeat them to your children,
>> Or your house may fall apart,
>> May illness impede you,
>> May your children turn their faces from you.

> – from *Se questro è un huomo*
> (*If This is a Man / Survival in Auschwitz*)

The Drowned and the Saved

from *If This is a Man / Survival in Auschwitz*

by Primo Levi

What we have so far said and will say concerns the ambiguous life of the Lager. In our days many men have lived in this cruel manner, crushed against the bottom, but each for a relatively short period; so that we can perhaps ask ourselves if it is necessary or good to retain any memory of this exceptional human state.

To this question we feel that we have to reply in the affirmative. We are in fact convinced that no human experience is without meaning or unworthy of analysis, and that fundamental values, even if they are not positive, can be deduced from this particular world which we are describing. We would also like to consider that the Lager was preeminently a gigantic biological and social experiment.

Thousands of individuals, differing in age, condition, origin, language, culture and customs, are enclosed within barbed wire: there they live a regular, controlled life which is identical for all and inadequate to all needs, and which is more rigorous than any experimenter could have set up to establish what is essential and what adventitious to the conduct of the human animal in the struggle for life.

We do not believe in the most obvious and facile deduction: that man is fundamentally brutal, egoistic and stupid in his conduct once every civilized institution is taken away, and that the Häftling is consequently nothing but a man without inhibitions. We believe, rather, that the only conclusion to be drawn is that in the face of driving necessity and physical disabilities many social habits and instincts are reduced to silence.

But another fact seems to us worthy of attention: there comes to light the existence of two particularly well differentiated categories among men—the saved and the drowned. Other pairs of opposites (the good and the bad, the wise and the foolish, the cowards and the courageous, the unlucky and the fortunate) are considerably less distinct, they seem less essential, and above all they allow for more numerous and complex intermediary gradations.

This division is much less evident in ordinary life; for there it rarely

happens that a man loses himself. A man is normally not alone, and
in his rise or fall is tied to the destinies of his neighbours; so that it is
exceptional for anyone to acquire unlimited power, or to fall by a
succession of defeats into utter ruin. Moreover, everyone is normally
in possession of such spiritual, physical and even financial resources
that the probabilities of a shipwreck, of total inadequacy in the face of
life, are relatively small. And one must take into account a definite
cushioning effect exercised both by the law, and by the moral sense
which constitutes a self-imposed law; for a country is considered the
more civilized the more the wisdom and efficiency of its laws hinder
a weak man from becoming too weak or a powerful one too powerful.

But in the Lager things are different: here the struggle to survive
is without respite, because everyone is desperately and ferociously
alone. If some Null Achtzehn vacillates, he will find no one to extend
a helping hand; on the contrary, someone will knock him aside, because
it is in no one's interest that there will be one more 'muselman'*
dragging himself to work every day; and if someone, by a miracle of
savage patience and cunning, finds a new method of avoiding the
hardest work, a new art which yields him an ounce of bread, he will
try to keep his method secret, and he will be esteemed and respected
for this, and will derive from it an exclusive, personal benefit; he will
become stronger and so will be feared, and who is feared is, ipso facto,
a candidate for survival.

In history and in life one sometimes seems to glimpse a ferocious
law which states: 'to he that has, will be given; from he that has not,
will be taken away'. In the Lager, where man is alone and where the
struggle for life is reduced to its primordial mechanism, this unjust
law is openly in force, is recognized by all. With the adaptable, the
strong and astute individuals, even the leaders willingly keep contact,
sometimes even friendly contact, because they hope later to perhaps
derive some benefit. But with the muselmans, the men in decay, it is
not even worth speaking, because one knows already that they will
complain and will speak about what they used to eat at home. Even
less worthwhile is it to make friends with them, because they have no
distinguished acquaintances in camp, they do not gain any extra
rations, they do not work in profitable Kommandos and they know
no secret method of organizing. And in any case, one knows that they
are only here on a visit, that in a few weeks nothing will remain of
them but a handful of ashes in some near-by field and a crossed-out

*This word 'Muselmann,' I do not know why, was used by the old ones of the
camp to describe the weak, the inept, those doomed to selection.

number on a register. Although engulfed and swept along without rest by the innumerable crowd of those similar to them, they suffer and drag themselves along in an opaque intimate solitude, and in solitude they die or disappear, without leaving a trace in anyone's memory.

The result of this pitiless process of natural selection could be read in the statistics of Lager population movements. At Auschwitz, in 1944, of the old Jewish prisoners (we will not speak of the others here, as their condition was different), *'kleine Nummer'*, low numbers less than 150,000, only a few hundred had survived; not one was an ordinary Häftling, vegetating in the ordinary Kommandos, and subsisting on the normal ration. There remained only the doctors, tailors, shoemakers, musicians, cooks, young attractive homosexuals, friends or compatriots of some authority in the camp; or they were particularly pitiless, vigorous and inhuman individuals, installed (following an investiture by the SS command, which showed itself in such choices to possess satanic knowledge of human beings) in the posts of Kapos, *Blockältester,* etc.; or finally, those who, without fulfilling particular functions, had always succeeded through their astuteness and energy in successfully organizing, gaining in this way, besides material advantages and reputation, the indulgence and esteem of the powerful people in the camp. Whosoever does not know how to become an 'Organisator', 'Kombinator', 'Prominent' (the savage eloquence of these words!) soon becomes a 'musselman'. In life, a third way exists, and is in fact the rule; it does not exist in the concentration camp.

To sink is the easiest of matters; it is enough to carry out all the orders one receives, to eat only the ration, to observe the discipline of the work and the camp. Experience showed that only exceptionally could one survive more than three months in this way. All the muselmans who finished in the gas chambers have the same story, or more exactly, have no story; they followed the slope down to the bottom, like streams that run down to the sea. On their entry into the camp, through basic incapacity, or by misfortune, or through some banal incident, they are overcome before they can adapt themselves; they are beaten by time, they do not begin to learn German, to disentangle the infernal knot of laws and prohibitions until their body is already in decay, and nothing can save them from selections or from death by exhaustion. Their life is short, but their number is endless; they, the *Muselmänner*, the drowned, form the backbone of the camp, an anonymous mass, continually renewed and always identical, of non-men who march and labour in silence, the divine spark dead within them, already too empty to really suffer. One hesitates to call them living: one hesitates to call their death death, in the face of which they have no fear, as they are too tired to understand.

They crowd my memory with their faceless presences, and if I could enclose all the evil of our time in one image, I would choose this image which is familiar to me: an emaciated man, with head dropped and shoulders curved, on whose face and in whose eyes not a trace of a thought is to be seen.

If the drowned have no story, and single and broad is the path to perdition, the paths to salvation are many, difficult and improbable. The most traveled road, as we have stated, is the *'Prominenz'*. *'Prominenten'* is the name for the camp officials, from the Häftling-director (*Lagerältester*) to the Kapos, the cooks, the nurses, the night-guards, even to the hut-sweepers and to the *Scheissminister* and *Bademeister* (superintendents of the latrines and showers). We are more particularly interested in the Jewish prominents, because while the others are automatically invested with offices as they enter the camp in virtue of their natural supremacy, the Jews have to plot and struggle hard to gain them.

The Jewish prominents form a sad and notable human phenomenon. In them converge present, past and atavistic sufferings, and the tradition of hostility towards the stranger makes of them monsters of asociality and insensitivity.

They are the typical product of the structure of the German Lager: if one offers a position of privilege to a few individuals in a state of slavery, exacting in exchange the betrayal of a natural solidarity with their comrades, there will certainly be someone who will accept. He will be withdrawn from the common law and will become untouchable; the more power that he is given, the more he will be consequently hateful and hated. When he is given the command of a group of unfortunates, with the right of life or death over them, he will be cruel and tyrannical, because he will understand that if he is not sufficiently so, someone else, judged more suitable, will take over his post. Moreover, his capacity for hatred, unfulfilled in the direction of the oppressors, will double back, beyond all reason, on the oppressed; and he will only be satisfied when he has unloaded on to his underlings the injury received from above.

We are aware that this is very distant from the picture that is usually given of the oppressed who unite, if not in resistance, at least in suffering. We do not deny that this may be possible when oppression does not pass a certain limit, or perhaps when the oppressor, through inexperience or magnanimity, tolerates or favours it. But we state that in our days, in all countries in which a foreign people have set foot as invaders, an analogous position of rivalry and hatred among the subjected has been brought about; and this, like many other ruffian characteristics, could be experienced in the Lager in the light of particularly cruel evidence.

About the non-Jewish prominents there is less to say, although they were far and away the most numerous (no 'Aryan' Häftling was without a post, however modest). That they were stolid and bestial is natural when one thinks that the majority were ordinary criminals, chosen from the German prisons for the very purpose of their employment as superintendents of the camps for Jews; and we maintain that it was a very apt choice, because we refuse to believe that the squalid human specimens whom we saw at work were an average example, not of Germans in general, but even of German prisoners in particular. It is difficult to explain how in Auschwitz the political German, Polish and Russian prominents rivalled the ordinary convicts in brutality. But it is known that in Germany the qualification of political crime also applied to such acts as clandestine trade, illicit relations with Jewish women, theft from Party officials. The 'real' politicals lived and died in other camps, with names now sadly famous, in notoriously hard conditions, which, however, in many aspects differed from those described here.

But besides the officials in the strict sense of the word, there is a vast category of prisoners, not initially favoured by fate, who fight merely with their own strength to survive. One has to fight against the current; to battle every day and every hour against exhaustion, hunger, cold and the resulting inertia; to resist enemies and have no pity for rivals; to sharpen one's wits, build up one's patience, strengthen one's will-power. Or else, to throttle all dignity and kill all conscience, to climb down into the arena as a beast against other beasts, to let oneself be guided by those unsuspected subterranean forces which sustain families and individuals in cruel times. Many were the ways devised and put into effect by us in order not to die: as many as there are different human characters. All implied a weakening struggle of one against all, and a by no means small sum of aberrations and compromises. Survival without renunciation of any part of one's own moral world—apart from powerful and direct interventions by fortune —was conceded only to very few superior individuals, made of the stuff of martyrs and saints.

We will try to show in how many ways it was possible to reach salvation with the stories of Schepschel, Alfred L., Elias and Henri.

Schepschel has been living in the Lager for four years. He has seen the death of tens of thousands of those like him, beginning with the pogrom which had driven him from his village in Galicia. He had a wife and five children and a prosperous business as a saddler, but for a long time now he has grown accustomed to thinking of himself only as a sack which needs periodic refilling. Schepschel is not very robust, nor very courageous, nor very wicked; he is not even particularly astute, nor has he ever found a method which allows him a little respite, but he is reduced to small and occasional expedients, 'kombinacje' as they are called here.

Every now and again he steals a broom in Buna and sells it to the *Blockältester*; when he manages to set aside a little bread-capital, he hires the tools of the cobbler in the Block, his compatriot, and works on his own account for a few hours; he knows how to make braces with interlaced electric wires. Sigi told me that he has seen him during the midday interval singing and dancing in front of the hut of the Slovak workers, who sometimes reward him with the remainders of their soup.

This said, one would be inclined to think of Schepschel with indulgent sympathy, as of a poor wretch who retains only a humble and elementary desire to live, and who bravely carries on his small struggle not to give way. But Schepschel was no exception, and when the opportunity showed itself, he did not hesitate to have Moischl, his accomplice in a theft from the kitchen, condemned to a flogging, in the mistaken hope of gaining favour in the eyes of the *Blockältester* and furthering his candidature for the position of *Kesselwäscher*, 'vat-washer'.

The story of engineer Alfred L. shows among other things how vain is the myth of original equality among men.

In his own country L. was the director of an extremely important factory of chemical products, and his name was (and is) well-known in industrial circles throughout Europe. He was a robust man of about fifty; I do not know how he had been arrested, but he entered the camp like all others: naked, alone and unknown. When I knew him he was very wasted away, but still showed on his face the signs of a disciplined and methodical energy; at that time, his privileges were limited to the daily cleaning of the Polish workers' pots; this work, which he had gained in some manner as his exclusive monopoly, yielded him half a ladleful of soup per day. Certainly it was not enough to satisfy his hunger; nevertheless, no one had ever heard him complain. In fact, the few words that he let slip implied imposing secret resources, a solid and fruitful 'organization'.

This was confirmed by his appearance. L. had a 'line': with his hands and face always perfectly clean, he had the rare self-denial to wash his shirt every fortnight, without waiting for the bi-monthly change (we would like to point out here that to wash a shirt meant finding soap, time and space in the over-crowded washroom; adapting oneself to carefully keep watch on the wet shirt without losing attention for a moment, and to put it on, naturally still wet, in the silence-hour when the lists are turned out); he owned a pair of wooden shoes to go to the shower, and even his striped suit was singularly adapted to his appearance, clean and new. L. had acquired in practice the whole appearance of a prominent considerably before becoming one; only a long time after did I find out that L. was able to earn all this show of prosperity with incredible tenacity, paying for his individual acquisitions and services with bread from his own ration, so imposing upon himself a regime of supplementary privations.

His plan was a long-term one, which is all the more notable as conceived in an environment dominated by a mentality of the provisional; and L. carried it out with rigid inner discipline, without pity for himself or—with greater reason—for comrades, who crossed his path. L. knew that the step was short from being judged powerful to effectively becoming so, and that everywhere, and especially in the midst of the general levelling of the Lager, a respectable appearance is the best guarantee of being respected. He took every care not to be confused with the mass; he worked with stubborn duty, even occasionally admonishing his lazy comrades in a persuasive and deprecatory tone of voice; he avoided the daily struggle for the best place in the queue for the ration, and prepared to take the first ration, notoriously the most liquid, every day, so as to be noticed by his *Blockältester* for his discipline. To complete the separation, he always behaved in his relations with his comrades with the maximum courtesy compatible with his egotism, which was absolute.

When the Chemical Kommando was formed, as will be described, L. knew that his hour had struck: he needed no more than his spruce suit and his emaciated and shaved face in the midst of the flock of his sordid and slovenly colleagues to at once convince both Kapo and *Arbeitsdienst* that he was one of the genuinely saved, a potential prominent; so that (to he who has, shall be given) he was without hesitation appointed 'specialist', nominated technical head of the Kommando, and taken on by the Direction of the Buna as analyst in the laboratory of the styrene department. He was subsequently appointed to examine all the new intake to the Chemical Kommando, to judge their professional ability; which he always did with extreme severity, especially when faced with those in whom he smelled possible future rivals.

I do not know how his story continued; but I feel it is quite probable that he managed to escape death, and today is still living his cold life of the determined and joyless dominator.

Elias Lindzin, 141565, one day rained into the Chemical Kommando. He was a dwarf, not more than five feet high, but I have never seen muscles like his. When he is naked you can see every muscle taut under his skin, like a poised animal; his body, enlarged without alteration of proportions, would serve as a good model for a Hercules: but you must not look at his head.

Under his scalp, the skull sutures stand out immoderately. The cranium is massive and gives the impression of being made of metal or stone; the limit of his shaven hair shows up barely a finger's width above his eyebrows. The nose, the chin, the forehead, the cheekbones are hard and compact, the whole face looks like a battering ram, an instrument made for butting. A sense of bestial vigour emanates from his body.

To see Elias work is a disconcerting spectacle; the Polish *Meister*, even the Germans sometimes stop to admire Elias at work. Nothing seems impossible to him. While we barely carry one sack of cement, Elias carries two, then three, then four, keeping them balanced no one knows how, and while he hurries along on his short, squat legs, he makes faces under the load, he laughs, curses, shouts and sings without pause, as if he had lungs made of bronze. Despite his wooden shoes Elias climbs like a monkey on to the scaffolding and runs safely on cross-beams poised over nothing; he carries six bricks at a time balanced on his head; he knows how to make a spoon from a piece of tin, and a knife from a scrap of steel; he finds dry paper, wood and coal everywhere and knows how to start a fire: in a few moments even in the rain. He is a tailor, a carpenter, a cobbler, a barber; he can spit incredible distances; he sings in a not unpleasant bass voice. Polish and Yiddish songs never heard before; he can ingest ten, fifteen, twenty pints of soup without vomiting and without having diarrhæa and begin work again immediately after. He knows how to make a big, hump come out between his shoulders, and goes around the hut, bow-legged and mimicking, shouting and declaiming incomprehensibly, to the joy of the Prominents of the camp. I saw him fight a Pole a whole head taller than him and knock him down with a blow of his cranium into the stomach, as powerful and accurate as a catapult. I never saw him rest, I never saw him quiet or still, I never saw him injured or ill.

Of his life as a free man, no one knows anything; and in any case, to imagine Elias as a free man requires a great effort of fantasy and induction; he only speaks Polish, and the surly and deformed Yiddish of Warsaw; besides it is impossible to keep him to a coherent conversation. He might be twenty or forty years old; he usually says that he is thirty-three, and that he has begot seventeen children—which is not unlikely. He talks continuously on the most varied of subjects; always in a resounding voice, in an oratorical manner, with the violent mimicry of the deranged; as if he was always talking to a dense crowd—and as is natural, he never lacks a public. Those who understand his language drink up his declamations, shaking with laughter; they pat him enthusiastically on the back—a back as hard as iron—inciting him to continue; while he, fierce and frowning, whirls around like a wild animal in the circle of his audience, apostrophizing now one, now another of them; he suddenly grabs hold of one by the chest with his small hooked paw, irresistibly drags him to himself, vomits into his face an incomprehensible invective, then throws him back like a piece of wood, and amidst the applause and laughter, with his arms reaching up to the heavens like some little prophetic monster, continues his raging and crazy speech.

His fame as an exceptional worker spread quite soon, and by the absurd law of the Lager, from then on he practically ceased to work. His help was requested directly by the *Meister* only for such work as required skill and special vigour. Apart from these services he insolently and violently supervised our daily, flat exhaustion, frequently disappearing on mysterious visits and adventures in who knows what recesses of the yard, from which he returned with large bulges in his pockets and often with his stomach visibly full.

Elias is naturally and innocently a thief: in this he shows the instinctive astuteness of wild animals. He is never caught in the act because he only steals when there is a good chance; but when this chance comes Elias steals as fatally and foreseeably as a stone drops. Apart from the fact that it is difficult to surprise him, it is obvious that it would be of no use punishing him for his thefts: to him they imply a vital act like breathing or sleeping.

We can now ask who is this man Elias. If he is a madman, incomprehensible and para-human, who ended in the Lager by chance. If he is an atavism, different from our modern world, and better adapted to the primordial conditions of camp life. Or if he is perhaps a product of the camp itself, what we will all become if we do not die in the camp, and if the camp itself does not end first.

There is some truth in all three suppositions. Elias has survived the destruction from outside, because he is physically indestructible; he has resisted the annihilation from within because he is insane. So, in the first place, he is a survivor: he is the most adaptable, the human type most suited to this way of living

If Elias regains his liberty he will be confined to the fringes of human society, in a prison or a lunatic asylum. But here in the Lager there are no criminals nor madmen; no criminals because there is no moral law to contravene, no madmen because we are wholly devoid of free will, as our every action is, in time and place, the only conceivable one.

In the Lager Elias prospers and is triumphant. He is a good worker and a good organizer, and for this double reason, he is safe from selections and respected by both leaders and comrades. For those who have no sound inner resources, for those who do not know how to draw from their own consciences of sufficient force to cling to life, the only road to salvation leads to Elias: to insanity and to deceitful bestiality. All the other roads are dead-ends.

This said, one might perhaps be tempted to draw conclusions, and perhaps even rules for our daily life. Are there not all around us some Eliases, more or less in embryo? Do we not see individuals living without purpose, lacking all forms of self-control and conscience, who live not *in spite of* these defects, but like Elias precisely because of them?

The question is serious, but will not be further discussed as we want these to be stories of the Lager, while much has already been written on man outside the Lager. But one thing we would like to add: Elias, as far as we could judge from outside, and as far as the phrase can have meaning, was probably a happy person.

Henri, on the other hand, is eminently civilized and sane, and possesses a complete and organic theory on the ways to survive in Lager. He is only twenty-two, he is extremely intelligent, speaks French, German, English and Russian, has an excellent scientific and classical culture.

His brother died in Buna last winter, and since then Henri has cut off every tie of affection; he has closed himself up, as if in armour, and fights to live without distraction with all the resources that he can derive from his quick intellect and his refined education. According to Henri's theory, there are three methods open to man to escape extermination which still allow him to retain the name of man: organization, pity and theft. He himself practises all three. There is no better strategist than Henri in seducing ('cultivating' he says) the English POWs. In his hands they become real geese with golden eggs— if you remember that in exchange for a single English cigarette you can make enough in the Lager not to starve for a day. Henri was once seen in the act of eating a real hard-boiled egg.

The traffic in products of English origin is Henri's monopoly, and this is all a matter of organization; but his instrument of penetration, with the English and with others, is pity. Henri has the delicate and subtly perverse body and face of Sodoma's San Sebastian: his eyes are deep and profound, he has no beard yet, he moves with a natural languid elegance (although when necessary he knows how to run and jump like a cat, while the capacity of his stomach is little inferior to that of Elias). Henri is perfectly aware of his natural gifts and exploits them with the cold competence of a physicist using a scientific instrument: the results are surprising. Basically it is a question of a discovery: Henri has discovered that pity, being a primary and instinctive sentiment, grows quite well if ably cultivated, particularly in the primitive minds of the brutes who command us, those very brutes who have no scruples about beating us up without a reason, or treading our faces into the ground; nor has the great practical importance of the discovery escaped him, and upon it he has built up his personal trade.

As the ichneumon paralyses the great hairy caterpillar, wounding it in its only vulnerable ganglion, so Henri at a glance sizes up the subject, 'son type'; he speaks to him briefly, to each with the appropriate language, and the 'type' is conquered: he listens with increasing sympathy, he is moved by the fate of this unfortunate young man, and not much time is needed before he begins to yield returns.

There is no heart so hardened that Henri cannot breach it if he sets himself to it seriously. In the Lager, and in Buna as well, his protectors are very numerous: English soldiers, French, Ukrainian, Polish civilian workers: German 'politicals'; at least four Blockältester, a cook, even an SS man. But his favourite field is Ka-Be: Henri has free entry into Ka-Be; Doctor Citron and Doctor Weiss are more than his protectors, they are his friends and take him in whenever he wants and with the diagnosis he wants. This takes place especially immediately before selections, and in the periods of the most laborious work: 'hibernation', as he says.

Possessing such conspicuous friendships, it is natural that Henri is rarely reduced to the third method, theft; on the other hand, he naturally does not talk much about this subject.

It is very pleasant to talk to Henri in moments of rest. It is also useful: there is nothing in the camp that he does not know and about which he has not reasoned in his close and coherent manner. Of his conquests, he speaks with educated modesty, as of prey of little worth, but he digresses willingly into an explanation of the calculation which led him to approach Hans asking him about his son at the front, and Otto instead showing him the scars on his shins.

To speak with Henri is useful and pleasant: one sometimes also feels him warm and near; communication, even affection seems possible. One seems to glimpse, behind his uncommon personality, a human soul, sorrowful and aware of itself. But the next moment his sad smile freezes into a cold grimace which seems studied at the mirror; Henri politely excuses himself ('... *j'ai quelque chose à faire,*' ... '*j'ai quelqu'un à voir*') and here he is again, intent on his hunt and his struggle; hard and distant, enclosed in armour, the enemy of all, inhumanly cunning and incomprehensible like the Serpent in Genesis.

From all my talks with Henri, even the most cordial, I have always left with a slight taste of defeat; of also having been, somehow inadvertently, not a man to him, but an instrument in his hands. I know that Henri is living today. I would give much to know his life as a free man, but I do not want to see him again.

1946-1947
THESIGER IN THE DESERT:
RETURN TO SALALA

It is a bitter, desiccated land which knows nothing of gentleness or ease. Yet men have lived there since earliest times. Passing generations have left fire-blackened stones at camping sites, a few faint tracks polished on the gravel plains. Elsewhere the winds wipe out their footprints. Men live there because it is the world into which they were born; the life they lead is the life their forefathers led before them; they accept hardships and privations; they know no other way.
> – Wilfred Thesiger, Prologue to *Arabian Sands*

In the tradition and style of the great explorers of the eighteenth and nineteenth centuries, the legendary Sir Wilfred Thesiger ranks among the greatest of the twentieth. In his classic works *Arabian Sands* and *The Marsh Arabs*, Thesiger is a fluent and inspiring chronicler of regions largely unknown to European eyes and a passionate defender of ancient ways and cultures on the verge of extinction.

Born into the upper class in 1910 at the British Legation in Addis Ababa (Abyssinia)—where his father was Minister—"Billy" Thesiger was raised within the hierarchical world of class and empire. Young Billy grew up with a sure sense of his Englishness but with a deep respect for the exotic cultures to which he was early exposed. At the Legation he learned to ride and shoot—passions that would so mark his later life. This happy time ended in 1919 when his family was recalled to England, and where Billy's father died soon thereafter. While firmly invested in the values of his class, the young man who advanced from Eton to Magdalen College, Oxford in 1929 was infused with dreams of adventure and faraway peoples and places, nurtured by his own memories and the works of authors such as John Buchan, Joseph Conrad, Rider Haggard, Rudyard Kipling, and T.E. Lawrence.

Thesiger spent four productive years at Oxford, interrupted for a term in the autumn of 1930 when Haile Selassie personally invited the young undergraduate—in honor of his deceased father—to join the luminaries of the British royal delegation at his coronation as Emperor of Abyssinia. In 1934 he was appointed Assistant District Commissioner of Darfur Province in British-administered Sudan. It was during this posting at Kutum that he mastered the art of camel riding, first savored the way of life of the Bedu, and first learned to love the desert and its spiritual splendors. But these passions for exploration, adventure and hunting distracted him from the devoted study of Law and Arabic required of civil service officers. Failing his examinations and uninterested in a bureaucratic career, Thesiger requested a remote posting as a contract District Commissioner.

Returning to the Sudan at the outbreak of World War II, he served as an officer in the newly formed Sudan Defence Force, fighting to expel the Italians from Abyssinia. After the restoration of Haile Selassie to his throne, Thesiger was called to Cairo where he boldly suggested that he could be useful against theVichy French in Syria. Commissioned as a regular army major, he organized Druze resistance in the Trans-Jordan before joining the elite Special Air Services Regiment with whom he saw action in the campaign against Rommel.

Now, a seasoned soldier, fluent in Arabic and at ease with the Islamic world, Thesiger prepared to further explore Southern Arabia. A British-sponsored Locust survey—with the indispensable authorization of King Abd al Aziz Ibn-Saud—provided a opportunity to venture into the harsh and alien landscapes of the mysterious *Rub' al Khali*, the "Empty Quarter". The largest sand desert on the earth, in the summers its sands can reach scorching temperatures of up to 175° F. In 1930 Bertram Thomas crossed the Empty Quarter by camel, followed three months later Harry St. John Philby—while they were the only Europeans ever to have achieved this—vast expanses between Yemen and Oman remained untouched by Westerners. Thesiger, determined to make his mark, arrived at Salala on the south Arabian coast on October 15, 1945.

Thesiger negotiated with the *Wali* (local governor) at Salala for a retinue of Bait Kathir tribesmen to accompany him through the lawless territory that lay before Mughshin. When they set out, he dressed as they dressed, ready to observe his companions with perception and respect, and prepared to learn from them, living with them on their terms. It astonished the aristocratic Thesiger that his companions looked on him as an *inferior*, and he was grateful that Bertram Thomas had made a good impression on the Bedu fifteen years before. It was in his character to aspire to make an even better impression, as he lived side by side with the Bait Kathir. Showing the same patience and goodwill that Bertram before him had, he learned the value of their ways as he shared their daily existence. It was also on this first journey that Thesiger met men of the Rashid tribe, a thoroughbred race of hardened survivors, who over hundreds of years had adapted to life in the desert sands. One of these, the young Salim bin Kabina, would be the companion of all Thesiger's desert travels for the next five years.

Reaching drought-stricken Mughshin too late in the season to venture into the Empty Quarter, Thesiger parted with his companions. He eventually reached London where he delivered a mangled collection of insect specimens and reported his findings. When questions about the conditions in the western sands of the Empty Quarter arose, Thesiger leapt at the opportunity to return to the desert, declaring himself ready to investigate. Unfortunately, the Sultan of Oman had strictly forbidden access to the mountain interior—for the Imam, a fanatic religious leader who really ruled this region, was fiercely opposed to any European penetration. Thesiger felt that he could manage the journey, if access again could be arranged as far as Mughshin and the southern sands immediately to its north. This agreed, he set out again for Salala, arriving there on October 16, 1946.

Giving no indication that he planned to go far beyond Mughshin, Thesiger assembled an escort of Bait Kathir. He also enlisted a group of the desert-hardened Rashid, arranging to rendezvous ten days later at Shisur. Well provisioned for the journey, he departed Salala with twenty-four Bait Kathir tribesmen. Almost all of them had traveled with him the previous year—and now clearly accepted him more as one of them as they advanced into the barren, stony terrain of the interior. As planned, Amair, bin Kabina and five other Rashid met this group at Shisur and the enlarged party departed on November 9th.

At Mughshin, one of the Rashid suffered a broken leg, and most of his fellow tribesmen felt obliged to remain behind to protect him. After a division of provisions that left the desert attack party with the barest supply of food for the journey ahead, they set out on November 24th with two Rashid-and eight Bait Kathir.

As the party had moved north toward Ramlat al Ghafa, the leader of the Bait Kathir, already aware that Thesiger planned to go beyond where he had been authorized to travel, became more alarmed when they were told of Saudi soldiers arresting trespassers in Dhafara. Unwilling to go further—especially in the company of a Christian— most of the Bait Kathir turned back. Thesiger was left to his perilous destiny in the sands—accompanied by two men of the Bait Kathir, Mabkhaut and the town-bred Musallim bin Tafl, and by two Rashid, young Salim bin Kabina and the experienced Muhammad al Auf, the only one among them who had actually crossed the sands.

Into the heart of the Empty Quarter marched the five men and their six camels, their caravan dwarfed by the infinite wilderness of sand. As the desert marchers reached the point of no return, their lives depended entirely on al Auf, who proved himself a capable guide, finding passages for them over the Urug al Shaiba, where centuries of winds had whipped the sands into towering dunes, five to nine hundred feet high. Finally, close to collapse after two weeks of hunger, thirst and the bitter chill of the desert nights, al Auf led them to the Khaba well in the territory of Dhafara. Ahead was a strand of green with villages mysteriously tucked among the dunes—the oasis of Liwa—where fresh provisions could be purchased. It is here that our selection from *Arabian Sands* begins.

Exhausted and starving, their camels terribly depleted, the men had illegally entered Dhafara, and Thesiger above all had to remain hidden from local tribesmen on watch for raiders and other intruders. When bin Kabina and bin Hanna returned to the camp days later, bringing only a supply of sand-encrusted dates and a little ground wheat, the situation appeared dire. In front of the weary band was a desperate journey of more than 500 miles through dangerous country infested with hostile Duru tribesmen. Only from the relative safety at Bai could they hope to rendezvous with a party of Bait Kathir and travel onward towards the Indian Ocean and on to Salala.

How Thesiger survived is perhaps best understood in the custom of *rabia*, or companion, which he describes. In the desert, the bond between fellow travelers surpasses that of tribe or family, as complete cooperation is requisite for survival. So the English aristocrat-adventurer became less a paymaster to his companions and more truly a man of the desert. In extending desert hospitality, sometimes reluctantly, he in turn received it in full measure when most needed. Coming to fully appreciate Bedu generosity, Bedu asceticism, and Bedu appetite, suffering on equal terms with his companions he adapted to the harsh extremes of the desert and the Bedu way of life. Surely it was as a man transformed, as a brother who had faithfully been protected by his brothers of the desert, that Thesiger finally returned to Salala on the 23rd of February 1947, after a journey of 1,500 miles, almost four months to the day after his departure. It was a triumphal return. The town was crowded with tribesmen, the sultan was there, and the Wali greeted Thesiger with a great feast in a tent by the sea.

From the crucible of this experience, Thesiger lived richly on. Returning regularly to England, he never ceased exploration, continuing his life of adventure for more than four decades during which he walked more than 100,000 miles. Thesiger's works are a lasting legacy that reveals, defends, and preserves landscapes and peoples that too often have not survived the blessings of modernity.

Return to Salala

from *Arabian Sands*
by Wilfred Thesiger

To avoid crossing more sand we return
over the gravel plains of Oman, a long detour made difficult
by the distrust of the tribes and our lack of food

We were across the Empty Quarter, but we still had to return to Salala. We could not go back the way we had come. The only possible route was through Oman.

I tried to work out our position on a map which showed Mughshin and Abu Dhabi but nothing else, except from hearsay. It was difficult to plot our course with no firm surface larger than my notebook on which to work. Bin Kabina held the map while the others sat and watched, and all of them distracted me with questions. They could never follow a map unless it was orientated, though curiously enough they could understand a photograph even when they held it upside down. I estimated that we should have between five hundred and six hundred miles to travel before we could rejoin Tamtaim and the rest of the Bait Kathir on the southern coast, and then a further two hundred miles to reach Salala. I asked al Auf about water and he said, 'Don't worry about that, there are plenty of wells ahead of us. It is food which is going to be our trouble.' We went over to the saddle-bags and Musallim measured out the flour. There were nine mugfuls left—about seven pounds.

While we were doing this, Hamad came back, bringing with him another Rashid, called Jadid. 'Another mouth to feed', I thought as soon as I saw him. Bin Kabina made coffee for them, and we then discussed our plans. Hamad assured us that we should be able to buy plenty of food in Liwa, enlarging on what we should find there – flour and rice and dates and coffee and sugar – but he added that it would take us three, perhaps four, days to get there. I said wryly, 'We shall be as hungry as the camels', and al Auf grunted, 'Yes, but the sons of Adam cannot endure like camels.' Hamad, questioned by Mabkhaut and Musallim, said that as long as we remained to the south of Liwa we should be outside the range of the fighting on the coast, and insisted that all the tribes in the south, whether they were Awamir, Manasir, or Bani Yas, were on good terms with the Rashid. He said, 'It will be different when you reach Oman. There the Duru are our enemies. There is no good in any of the Duru. You will have to be careful while you are among them for they are a treacherous race.' Al Auf laughed and quoted, 'He died of snake-bite', a well-known expression for Duru treachery.

He was tracing patterns on the sand with his camel-stick, smoothing them out and starting again. He looked up and said thoughtfully; 'The difficulty is Umbarak [Thesiger]. No one must know he is here. If the Arabs hear that there is a Christian in the sands they will talk of nothing else, and the news will soon be all round the place. Then Ibn Saud's tax-collectors will hear of it and they will arrest us all and take us off to Ibn Jalawi in the Hasa. God preserve us from that. I know Ibn Jalawi. He is a tyrant, utterly without mercy. Anyway, we don't want the news about Umbarak to get ahead of us among the Duru. We shall never get through the country if it does. If we meet any Arabs we had better say that we are Rashid from the Hadhramaut, travelling to Abu Dhabi to fight for the Al bu Falah. Umbarak can be an Arab from Aden.'

Turning to me, he said, 'Keep quiet if we meet anyone. Just answer their salutations, and, what is more, from now on you must ride all the time. Any Arab who came across your monstrous footprints would certainly follow them to find out who on earth you were.' He got up to fetch the camel, saying, 'We had better be off.' . . .

. . . The past three days had been an ordeal, worse for the others than for me, since, but for me, they could have ridden to the nearest tents and fed. However, we had not suffered the final agony of doubt. We had known that the others would return and bring us food. We had thought of this food, talked of this food, dreamt of this food. A feast of rich and savoury meat, the reward of our endurance. Now all we had was this. Some wizened dates, coated with sand, and a mess of boiled grain. There was not even enough of it. We had to get back across Arabia, travelling secretly, and we had enough food for ten days if we were economical. I had eaten tonight, but I was starving. I wondered how much longer I should be able to face this fare. We *must* get more food. Al Auf said, 'We must get hold of a camel and eat that', and I thought of living for a month on sun-dried camel's meat and nothing else. Hamad suggested that we should lie up near Ibri in the Wadi el Ain, and send a party into Ibri to buy food. He said, 'It is one of the biggest towns in Oman. You will get everything you want there.' With difficulty I refrained from pointing out that he had said this of Liwa.

Musallim interrupted and said that we could not possibly go into the Duru country; the Duru had heard about my visit to Mughshin last year and had warned the Bait Kathir not to bring any Christians into their territory. Al Auf asked him impatiently where in that case he did propose to go. They started to wrangle. I joined in and reminded Musallim that we had always planned to return through the Duru country. Excitedly he turned towards me and, flogging the ground with his camel-stick to give emphasis to his words, shouted: 'Go through it? Yes, if we must, quickly and secretly, but through the uninhabited country near the sands. We never agreed to hang about in the Duru country, nor to go near Ibri. By God, it is madness! Don't you know that there is one of the Imam's governors there. He is the Riqaishi. Have you never heard of the Riqaishi? What do you suppose he will do if he hears there is a Christian in his country? He hates all infidels. I have been there. Listen, Umbarak, I know him. God help you, Umbarak, if he gets hold of you. Don't think that Oman is like the desert here. It is a settled country—villages and towns, and the Imam rules it all through his governors, and the worst of them all is the Riqaishi. The Duru, yes; Bedu like ourselves; our enemies, but we might smuggle you quickly through their land. But hang about there —no; and to go near Ibri would be madness. Do you hear? The first people who saw you, Umbarak, would go straight off and tell the Riqaishi.'

. . . Eventually we agreed that we must get food from Ibri and that meanwhile we would buy a camel from the Rashid who were ahead of us in the Rabadh, so that we should have an extra camel with us to eat if we were in trouble. Hamad said, 'You must conceal the fact that Umbarak is a Christian.' Mabkhaut suggested that I should pretend that I was a *saiyid* from the Hadhramaut, since no one would ever mistake me for a Bedu. I protested, 'That is no good; as a *saiyid* I should get involved in religious discussions. I should certainly be expected to pray, which I don't know how to do; they would probably even expect me to lead their prayers. A nice mess I should make of that.' The others laughed and agreed that this suggestion would not work. I said, 'While we are in the sands here I had better be an Aden townsman who has been living with the tribes and is now on his way to Abu Dhabi. When we get to Oman I will say I am a Syrian who has been visiting Riyadh and that I am now on my way to Salala.' Bin Kabina asked, 'What is a Syrian?' and I said, 'If you don't know what a Syrian is I don't suppose the Duru will either. Certainly they will never have seen one.'

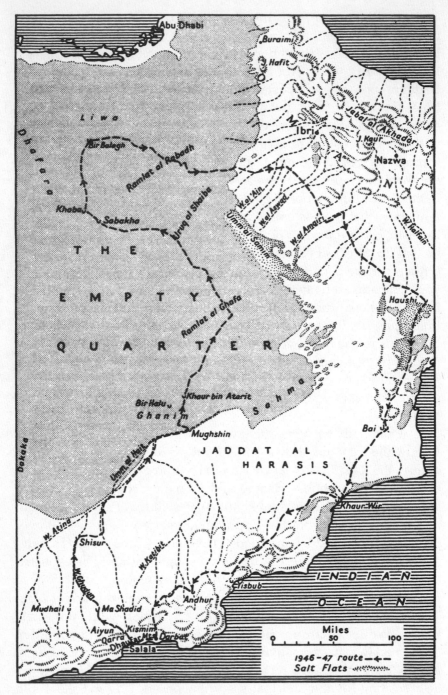

The Empty Quarter

. . . Among these people arguments frequently become impassioned, but usually the excitement dies away as quickly as it arises. Men who were screaming at each other, ready apparently to resort to violence, will sit happily together a short while later drinking coffee. As a rule Bedu do not nurse a grievance, but if they think that their personal honour has been slighted they immediately become vindictive, bent on vengeance. Strike a Bedu and he will kill you either then or later. It is easy for strangers to give offence without meaning to do so. I once put my hand on the back of bin Kabina's neck and he turned on me and asked furiously if I took him for a slave. I had no idea that I had done anything wrong.

Hamad now volunteered to accompany us as far as Ibri, an offer which we gladly accepted since he knew the Sands and the present distribution of the tribes. He said that we had better keep along the southern edge of Liwa, where the country was at present empty. Normally the salt-flats south of Liwa were filled with camel herds belonging to the Manasir, but recently they had been raided by a force from Dibai and had suffered losses. Now most of the Manasir were assembled farther to the west . . . bin Kabina asked if we should find anything for them on our route. He said, 'The wretched animals don't deserve any more starvation. It has made me miserable to watch their suffering.' Hamad assured him that we should find enough for them during the next few days and plenty as soon as we reached Rabadh. We therefore agreed to his suggestion.

We ate some dates, and Jadid then went back while the rest of us set off in an easterly direction, the mist still thick about us. I hoped we should not stumble on some Arab encampment. The mist did not lift for another two hours.

The dunes ran from west to east so that we were travelling easily. They consisted of great massifs similar to the *qaid* which I had seen in Ghanim, but there they were linked together to form parallel dune chains about three hundred feet in height, the broad valleys between them being covered with bright-green salt-bushes. We passed several palm groves and a few small settlements of dilapidated huts made, as bin Kabina had described, from matting and palm fronds. They were all abandoned.

At midday, while we were eating more of our revolting dates, two Arabs accompanied by a saluki appeared on a distant dune. They stood and watched us, so al Auf went over to them. They shouted to him not to come any nearer, and when he called back that he wanted 'the news' they answered that they had none and wanted none of his and threatened that they would shoot if he came any closer. They watched us for a while and then made off.

We travelled slowly to rest our camels and reached the Rabadh sands five days after leaving Balagh. Sometimes we saw camels. It did not seem to matter how far off they were; my companions were apparently always able to distinguish if they were in milk. They would say 'There are camels', and point to some dots on a dune a mile or more away. After a further scrutiny they would agree that one or more were in milk. We would then ride over to them, for travellers in the desert may milk any camels they encounter. . . . Once we passed a dozen camels tended by a woman with two small children. Al Auf said, 'Let's get a drink', and we rode over to them. He jumped from his camel, greeted the woman, a wizened old thing bundled up in black cloth turned green with age, took the bowl which she handed him, and went towards the camels. She shrilled at her sons, 'Hurry! Hurry! Fetch the red one. Fetch the two-year-old. God take you, child! Hurry! Fetch the red one. Fetch the two-year-old. Welcome! Welcome! Welcome to the guests!' Al Auf handed us the bowl and in turn we squatted down to drink, for no Arab drinks standing, while the old woman asked us where we were going. We answered that we were going to fight for the Al bu Falah and she exclaimed, 'God give you victory!'

On another occasion we came upon a small encampment of Manasir. Hamad insisted that we must go over to them, or we should arouse their suspicions since they had already seen us. We were on foot at the time and I suggested that they should leave the camels to graze and that I should herd them until they returned. After some argument they agreed. I knew that they wanted milk, and I should have liked a drink myself, but it seemed stupid to run the risk of detection. When they returned, bin Kabina grinned whenever he looked at me, so I asked him what the joke was. He said, 'The Manasir gave us milk but insisted that we should fetch you, saying, "Why do you leave your companion without milk?" Al Auf explained that you were our slave, but they still insisted that we should fetch you.' I knew that among Bedu even a slave is considered as a travelling companion, entitled to the same treatment as the rest of the party. Bin Kabina went on, 'Finally al Auf said, "Oh! he is half-witted. Leave him where he is", and the Manasir insisted no more.' Mabkhaut said, 'True, they said no more, but they looked at us a bit oddly.'

Next morning while we were leading our camels down a steep

dune face I was suddenly conscious of a low vibrant hum, which grew in volume until it sounded as though an aeroplane were flying low over our heads. The frightened camels plunged about, tugging their head-ropes and looking back at the slope above us. The sound ceased when we reached the bottom. This was 'the singing of the sands'. The Arabs describe it as roaring, which is perhaps a more descriptive word. During the five years that I was in these parts I only heard it half a dozen times. It is caused, I think, by one layer of sand slipping over another. Once I was standing on a dune-crest and the sound started as soon as I stepped on to the steep face. I found on this occasion that I could start it or stop it at will by stepping on or off this slip-face.

Near Rabadh, Musallim suddenly jumped off his camel, pushed his arm into a shallow burrow, and pulled out a hare. I asked him how he knew it was there, and he said that he had seen its track going in and none coming out. The afternoon dragged on until we reached the expanse of small contiguous dunes which give these sands the name of Rabadh. There was adequate grazing, so we stopped on their edge. We decided to eat the rest of our flour, and Musallim conjured three onions and some spices out of his saddle-bags. We sat round in a hungry circle watching bin Kabina cooking the hare, and offering advice. Anticipation mounted, for it was more than a month since we had eaten meat, except for the hare that al Auf had killed near the Uruq al Shaiba. We sampled the soup and decided to let it stew just a little longer. Then bin Kabina looked up and groaned, 'God! Guests!'

Coming across the sands towards us were three Arabs. Hamad said, 'They are Bakhit, and Umbarak, and Salim, the children of Mia', and to me, 'They are Rashid.' We greeted them, asked the news, made coffee for them, and then Musallim and bin Kabina dished up the hare and the bread and set it before them, saying with every appearance of sincerity that they were our guests, that God had brought them, that today was a blessed day, and a number of similar remarks. They asked us to join them but we refused, repeating that they were our guests. I hoped that I did not look as murderous as I felt while I joined the others in assuring them that God had brought them on this auspicious occasion. When they had finished, bin Kabina put a sticky lump of dates in a dish and called us over to feed.

Feeling thoroughly ill-tempered I lay down to sleep, but this was impossible. The others, excited by this meeting with their fellow-tribesmen, talked incessantly within a few yards of my head. I wondered irritably why Bedu must always shout. Gradually I relaxed. I tried the old spell of asking myself, 'Would I really wish to be anywhere else?' and having decided that I would not, I felt better. I pondered on this desert hospitality and, compared it with our own. I remembered other encampments where I had slept, small tents on which I had happened in the Syrian desert and where I had spent the night. Gaunt men in rags and hungry-looking children had greeted me, and bade me welcome with the sonorous phrases of the desert. Later they had set a great dish before me, rice heaped round a sheep which they had slaughtered, over which my host poured liquid golden butter until it flowed down on to the sand; and when I had protested, saying, 'Enough! Enough!', had answered that I was a hundred times welcome. Their lavish hospitality had always made me uncomfortable, for I had known that as a result of it they would go hungry for days. Yet when I left them they had almost convinced me that I had done them a kindness by staying with them.

My thoughts were interrupted by the raised voices of my companions. . . . It is characteristic of Bedu to do things by extremes, to be either wildly generous or unbelievably mean, very patient or almost hysterically excitable, to be incredibly brave or to panic for no apparent reason. Ascetic by nature, they derive satisfaction from the bare simplicity of their lives and scorn the amenities which others would judge essential. Although, on the rare occasions that offer, they eat enormously, I have never met a Bedu who was greedy. Continent for months on end, not one of them, even the most austere, would regard celibacy as a virtue. They want sons, and consider that women are provided by God for the satisfaction of men. Deliberately to refrain from using them would be not only unnatural but also ridiculous, and Bedu are very susceptible to ridicule. Yet an Arab will use his sister's name as his battle-cry, and Glubb has suggested that the medieval conception of chivalry came to Europe from the Arabs at the time of the Crusades. Bedu set great score by human dignity, and most of them would prefer to watch a man die rather than see him humiliated. Always reserved in front of strangers and accustomed on formal occasions to sit for hours motionless and in silence, they are a garrulous, lighthearted race. But, at the instigation of religious zealots, they can become uncompromisingly puritanical, quick to frown on all amusement, regarding song and music as a sin and laughter as unseemly. Probably no other people, either as a race or as individuals, combine so many conflicting qualities in such an extreme degree.

I was dimly conscious of their voices until nearly dawn.

In the morning Bakhit pressed us to come to his tent, saying, 'I will give you fat and meat', the conventional way of saying that he would kill a camel for us. We were tempted, for we were very hungry, but Hamad said that it would be wiser not to go there, for the sands in which Bakhit was camped were full of Arabs. We told Bakhit that we wished to buy a camel, and he said he would fetch one and meet us next day at an abandoned well farther to the east. He met us there a little before sunset. He had with him an old camel, a *hazmia*, black-coated and in good condition, which had been bred in the sands. There were long strips of skin hanging from the soles of her feet. Al Auf said she would not be able to travel far on the gravel plains in the Duru country, but Mabkhaut answered that we could take her along with us until her feet wore through and then kill her. He bought her after a little haggling.

The next morning we saw some tents, and Hamad said. 'I don't know who they are', so we bore off to the right in order to pass wide of them; but a man came out from among them and ran across the sand towards us shouting, 'Stop! Stop!' As he came near, Hamad said, 'It is all right. He is Salim, old Muhammad's son.'

We greeted him and he said, 'Why do you pass by my tent? Come, I will give you fat and meat.' I protested instinctively, but he silenced me by saying, 'If you do not come to my tent I shall divorce my wife.' This was the divorce oath, which he was bound to obey if we refused. He took my camel's rein and led her towards the tents. An old man came forward and greeted us. He had a long white beard, kindly eyes, and a gentle voice. He walked very upright, as do all the Bedu. Hamad said, 'This is old Muhammad.' The two tents were very small, less than three yards long and four feet high, and were half-filled with saddles and other gear. An old woman, a younger woman, and three children, one of them a small naked child with a running nose and his thumb in his mouth, watched us as we unloaded. The women were dressed in dark-blue robes, and were unveiled. The younger one was very pretty. Salim called to al Auf and together they went off across the dunes. They came back later with a young camel, which they slaughtered behind the tents.

Meanwhile the old man had made coffee and set out dates for us to eat. Hamad said, 'He is the Christian.' The old man asked, 'Is he the Christian who travelled last year with bin al Kamam and the Rashid to the Hadhramaut?' and after Hamad had assented he turned to me and said, 'A thousand welcomes.' It had not taken long for this news to arrive, although here we were near the Persian Gulf, far from the Hadhramaut; but I was not surprised. I knew how interested Bedu always are in 'the news', how concerned to get the latest information

about their kinsmen, about raids and tribal movements and grazing.
I knew from experience how far they would go out of their way to ask
for news. I had realized that it was the chance of getting this as much
as the craving for milk that had tantalized my companions during the
past days when we had seen and avoided distant tents. They hated
travelling through inhabited country without knowing exactly what
was happening around them.

'What is "the news"?' It is the question which follows every
encounter in the desert even between strangers. Given a chance the
Bedu will gossip for hours as they had done last night, and nothing is
too trivial for them to recount. There is no reticence in the desert. If a
man distinguishes himself he knows that his fame will be widespread;
if he disgraces himself he knows that the story of his shame will
inevitably be heard in every encampment. It is this fear of public opinion which enforces at all times the rigid conventions of the desert. The
consciousness that they are always before an audience makes many
of their actions theatrical. Glubb once told me of a Bedu sheikh who
was known as 'The Host of the Wolves', because whenever he heard a
wolf howl round his tent he ordered his son to take a goat out in the
desert, saying he would have no one call on him for dinner in vain.

It was late in the afternoon when Salim spread a rug in front of us,
and placed on it a large tray covered with rice. He lifted joints of meat
from the cauldron and put them on this, ladled soup over the rice,
and finally tipped a dishful of butter over it. He then poured water
over our outstretched hands. Old Muhammad invited us to eat, but
refused our invitation to join us. He stood and watched us, saying,
'Eat! Eat! You are hungry. You are tired. You have come a long way.
Eat!' He shouted to Salim to bring more butter, although we protested
that there was enough already, and taking the dish from Salim's hand
poured it over the rice. Gorged at last, we licked our fingers and rose
together muttering 'God requite you.'. . . He and his father urged us
to remain with them at least for another day to rest ourselves and our
camels, and we willingly agreed. They brought us milk at sunset and
we drank till we could drink no more. As each of us handed back the
bowl from which he had drunk, he said, 'God bless her!', a blessing
on the camel who had given the milk. Bakhit and Umbarak turned up
next morning, saying that they had expected to find us here. Bakhit
was anxious to accompany us to Ibri, where he wished to buy rice and
coffee with the money we had given him for the camel. He was afraid
to go alone because of the enmity between the Rashid and the Duru.

All the tribes between the Hadhramaut and Oman belong to one or other of two rival factions, known today as Ghafari and Hanawi. The names themselves date back only as far as a civil war in Oman at the beginning of the eighteenth century, but the division between the tribes which these names denote is very ancient and probably originated in the difference between tribes of Adnan and Qahtan origin. The Duru were Ghafaris, while the Rashid, who were descended from Qahtan, were Hanawis. To travel safely among the Duru we needed a *rabia* or companion, who could frank us through their territory. He could be either from the Duru or from some other tribe entitled by tribal custom to give his travelling companions protection among the Duru while they were in his company. A *rabia* took an oath: 'You are my companions and your safety, both of your blood and of your possessions, is in my face.' Members of the same party were responsible for each other's safety, and were expected to fight if necessary in each other's defence, even against their own tribes or families. If one of the party was killed, all the party were involved in the ensuing blood-feud. No tribe would be likely to attack a party which was accompanied by a tribesman from a powerful tribe to which they were allied, but a *rabia* could belong to a small and insignificant tribe and still give protection. The question of how and where each tribe could give protection was complicated. It often amused my companions to argue hypothetical cases as we rode along, and their arguments sometimes became so involved that I was reminded of lawyers disputing. Our present difficulty was that we should have to penetrate into the Duru territory without a *rabia* and hope to find one when we arrived there. At present the Rashid and the Duru were not at war, but there was no love lost between them.

Three days later we camped on the eastern edge of the Sands among some scattered thorn-bushes, and the following day we rode for seven hours across a flat plain, whose gravel surface was overspread with fragments of limestone. Ahead of us a yellow haze hung like a dirty curtain across the horizon. We camped in the evening on a sandy watercourse, among some *ghaf* trees. There was a large package of dates in the fork of one of these, left there by its owner in perfect confidence that no one would touch it. A sunset we saw some goats in the distance; but no one came near us. During the night a wolf howled round our camp; it as one of the eeriest sounds I have ever heard.

At dawn I saw a great mountain to the east and Hamad told me that it was Jabal Kaur near Ibri. Later the haze thickened again and hid it from our sight . . . In the afternoon the young herdsman, whose name was Ali, led us to his encampment two miles away. Here the Wadi al Ain, the largest of the three great wadis which run down from the Oman mountains into the desert to the west, consisted not of a single dry river-bed, but of several smaller watercourses separated by banks of gravel and drifts of sand. The trees and shrubs that grew here were parched with drought but, even so, they made a pleasant change after the bare gravel plain which we had just crossed.

There were no tents or huts at Ali's encampment. He and his family were living under two large acacias on which they hung their household utensils. They had evidently been here for a long time, since the two brush wood pens in which they put their goats at night were thickly carpeted with droppings. There were two women, both of them veiled, a half-witted boy of fourteen, and three small children. We unsaddled a short distance away from this encampment, in a grove of ghaf trees which had been lopped and mutilated to provide grazing for the goats and camels. Ali slaughtered a goat for us, and in the evening brought over a good meal of meat, bread, and dates. He was accompanied by a slave who was spending the night here. Ali agreed to take some of my party to Ibri, although the slave disconcerted us by saying that there had been trouble there a few days earlier between the townsfolk and a party of Rashid. Ali asked me if I was going to Ibri, but I said that I had been suffering from fever and would remain here to rest. Al Auf had told him already that I was from Syria, that I had recently been at Riyadh, and that I was now on my way to Salala. We agreed that bin Kabina and Musallim should remain with me while the others went to Ibri. Ali promised that when he returned from Ibri he would come with us to the Wadi al Amairi, where he could find us another *rabia* to take us through the rest of the Duru country.

The party going to Ibri left in the morning; Ali said that they would be back in five days' time. In the afternoon his father, who was called Staiyun, arrived with a nephew called Muhammad. Staiyun was a kindly, simple old man with a wrinkled face and humorous eyes. . . . They were pleasant, lazy days. Staiyun fed us on bread, dates, and milk and spent most of his time with us. The more I saw of the old man the more I liked him . . . I determined that I would come back and visit Umm al Samim and that I would try to penetrate into the mountains which were ruled by the Imam. It was interesting to collect from old Staiyun the information I should require to enable me to do this journey: about the tribes and their alliances, the different sheikhs and their rivalries, the Imam's government and where and how it worked, and about wells and the distances that lay between them.

But for the present I should be satisfied if I arrived at Bai without mishap and without delay; already I was worried for five days and then six had passed and still there was no news of my companions.

Staiyun was anxious about his son as a result of the recent trouble in Ibri, and he urged me to go there. He said that if they were in difficulties I could intervene with Muhammad al Riqaishi, the Governor, or even go and see the Imam in Nazwa on their behalf. On the seventh day I decided that I must go in the morning with Staiyun to Ibri. There I should stand revealed as a Christian, and from what I had heard of the Riqaishi and the Imam this would not be pleasant; nor would my intervention help my companions if they were in trouble, but there was nothing else for me to do. It was a great relief when they arrived at sunset. All was well. They pretended that the way was farther than they had expected, but I knew that they had dallied in Ibri enjoying themselves, and I did not blame them.

Next day Hamad and Bakhit returned to their homes, and after Staiyun had fetched Muhammad the rest of us camped on the far side of the wadi. It took us eight hours to reach the Wadi al Aswad and two more long days to reach the Amairi. It was difficult to get the observations which I required for my mapping, and impossible to take photographs while Muhammad was with us. He inquired from the others why I did not pray, and they said that Syrians were evidently lax about their religion.

The Amairi was another large wadi with many trees and bushes. Muhammad took us to the encampment of a man called Rai, who belonged to the small tribe of the Afar, and arranged with him that he should take us to the Wahiba country. The Wahiba are Hanawis and are enemies of the Duru, and none of the Duru could escort us into their country. But the Afar are accepted as *rabia* by both the Duru and the Wahiba. Muhammad went back next day, but we remained for four days, since we had a long way still ahead of us and Rai said that there would be little grazing for the camels once we left the Amairi. Here there had been no recent rain and the trees were in leaf. There were many Duru in the wadi, with herds of camels, flocks of sheep and goats, and numerous donkeys. That night I told Rai who I was, since Musallim said that there was no necessity to keep my identity a secret from him. He looked at me and said. 'You would not have got here if the Duru had known who you were', and he warned me to tell no one else. From our camp I could see the long range of Jabal al Akhadar, the Green Mountain, which lies behind Muscat. It rises to ten thousand feet and was still unexplored. I could see other and nearer mountains, none of which were marked on my map. What was shown was guesswork. The Wadi al Ain, for instance, was marked as flowing into the sea near Abu Dhabi. I was more than ever determined to come back and explore this country properly. . . .

We set off once more. Each interminable, empty day ended at sunset and started again at dawn. The others ate dates before we started, but I could no longer face their sticky sweetness, and I fasted till the evening meal. Hour after hour my camel shuffled forward, moving, it seemed, always up a slight incline towards an indeterminable horizon, and nowhere in all that glaring emptiness of gravel plain and colourless sky was there anything upon which my eyes could focus. I would notice some dots, think that perhaps they were far-off camels, only to realize a few strides farther on that they were stones immediately beneath our feet. I marvelled how Rai kept his direction, especially when the sun was overhead. I knew that camels will never walk straight; my own animal edged off the whole time to the right towards her homeland and I had to tap her back with my stick, a constant source of irritation. Rai and the others talked continuously and seemingly paid no attention to where they were going, and yet when at intervals I checked our course with my compass it never varied more than a few degrees. We reached the well at Haushi near the southern coast six days after leaving the Amairi. For the past two days it had been grievous to watch the limping agony of the *hazmia*. There was nothing here for the camels to eat but the shoots of leafless thorn bushes growing in occasional watercourses. The *hazmia* could not even feed. She was accustomed to the grazing of the Sands, and her tender gums could not chew this woody fare. She was becoming thin. Al Auf eyed her and said, 'When we do kill her she won't be worth eating.' We murdered her the evening we got to Haushi. We cut the meat into strips and hung it on bushes to dry, and put the marrowbones into the sac of her stomach, which we tied up with a strip of her skin and buried in the sands, lighting a fire on top of it. Next day when we uncovered it, there was a blood-streaked mess floating among the empty bones, which Mabkhaut poured into an empty goatskin. Bedu yearn hungrily for fats, but I dreamt of fruit, of bunches of grapes, and whiteheart cherries. We had hidden ourselves away among sand-dunes but two Wahiba found us there. They were, however, delightful old men, courteous and welcoming, who had not come looking for meat but seeking news and entertainment. They fetched us milk and then spent the night with us. We fed at sunset, eating till we could eat no more. The meat smelt rank and was very tough, the soup was greasy and of a curious flavour, but it was a wonderful meal after all these hungry weeks. Replete at last, I lay on the sand while the old men mumbled reminiscences through toothless gums and the nearby camels belched and chewed the cud.

We spent the next day there drying the meat, and then set off westwards for Bai.

Once more we rode across an empty land, but now it was not only empty, it was dead. Shallow depressions in the limestone floor held sloughs of glutinous black mud, crusted with scabs of salt and sand, like putrescent patches on a carcase rotting in the sun. We rode for seven and eight and nine hours a day, without a stop, and it was dreary work. Conversation died with the passing hours and boredom mounted within me like a dull ache of pain. We muffled our faces against the parching wind, screwed up our eyes against the glare which stabbed into our heads. The flies we had brought with us from our butchers' work at Haushi clustered black upon our backs and heads. If I made a sudden movement they were thick about my face in a noisy questing cloud. I rode along, my body swaying backwards and forwards, backwards and forwards, to the camel's stride, a ceaseless strain upon my back which from long practice I no longer felt. I watched the sun's slow progress and longed for evening. As the sun sank into the haze it became an orange disc without heat or brilliance. I looked at it through my field-glasses and saw the sun-spots like black holes in its surface. It disappeared while still a span above the horizon, vanishing in a yellow sky that was without a cloud.

We reached Bai five days after leaving Haushi. Seeing camels in the distance, Mabkhaut said, 'That is bin Turkia's camel and there is bin Anauf's.' We approached a ridge and suddenly a small figure showed up upon it. It was bin Anauf. 'They come! They come! he screamed, and raced down the slope. Old Tamtaim appeared, hobbling towards us. I slid stiffly from my camel and greeted them. The old man flung his arms about me, with tears running down his face, too moved to be coherent. Bitter had been his wrath when the Bait Kathir returned from Ramlat al Ghafia. He said they had brought black shame upon his tribe by deserting me. We led our camels over to their camping place and there exchanged the formal greetings and 'the news.' It was 31 January. I had parted from them at Mughshin on 24 November. It seemed like two years. . . . My anxieties and difficulties were now over, but we still had far to go before we reached Salala.

We rode across the flatness of the Jaddat al Harasis, long marches of eight and even ten hours a day. We were like a small army, for many Harasis and Mahra travelled with us, going to Salala to visit the sultan of Muscat, who had recently arrived there. I was as glad now to be back in this friendly crowd as I had been to escape from it at Mughshin. I delighted in the surging rhythm of this mass of camels, the slapping shuffle of their feet, the shouted talk, and the songs which stirred the blood of men and beasts so that they drove forward with quickened pace. And there was life here. Gazelle grazed among the flat-topped acacia bushes, and once we saw a distant herd of oryx looking very white against the dark gravel of the plain. There were lizards, about eighteen inches in length, which scuttled across the ground. They had disc-shaped tails, and in consequence the Arabs called them 'The Father of the Dollar'. I asked if they ate them, but they declared that they were unlawful; I knew that they would eat other lizards which resembled them except for their tails. But, anyway, there was no need now for us to eat lizard-meat. Every day we fed on gazelles, and twice Musallim shot an oryx.

. . . We had sent word into Salala, and next morning the Wali rode out to meet us accompanied by a crowd of townsfolk and Bedu. There were many Rashid with him, some of them old friends, others I had not yet met, among these bin Kalut who had accompanied Bertram Thomas. With him were the Rashid we had left at Mughshin, who told us that Mahsin had recovered and was in Salala.

The Wali feasted us in a tent beside the sea, and in the afternoon we went to the R.A.F. camp. My companions insisted on a triumphal entry, so we rode into the camp firing off our rifles, while ahead of us some Bait Kathir danced and sang, brandishing their daggers.

1950
MAURICE HERZOG'S ANNAPURNA

I felt as though I were plunging into something new and quite abnormal. I had the strangest and most vivid impressions, such as I had never before known in the mountains. There was something unnatural in the way I saw Lachenal and everything around us. I smiled to myself at the paltriness of our efforts, for I could stand apart and watch myself making these efforts. But all sense of exertion was gone, as though there were no longer any gravity. This diaphanous landscape, this quintessence of purity—these were not the mountains I knew: they were the mountains of my dreams.

– Maurice Herzog

T he conquest of the supreme peaks of the Himalaya—fourteen of which soar above 8,000 meters—has long inspired and inspires today the dreams and ambitions of mountaineers and adventurers. From the end of the nineteenth century until the eve of World War II, scores of expeditions from many nations explored the Himalaya and a score of these had striven—and failed—to reach the summits of the highest mountains . . . although climbers did reach an altitude of 8,580 meters (28,150 feet) on Everest in 1924. After World War II access to the Himalaya was impossible through closed-off Tibet, and for several years the peaks of Nepal—"the roof of the world"— were open only to the French, who had won exclusive access to them from Nepal's maharajah.

For the war-scarred people of France the conquest of the Himalaya quickly became a great national cause. The French government supplied substantial funding and material resources for a first expedition, while an enthusiastic public, climbing associations, and a web of commercial interests provided additional support. It was decided at the outset that all profits that the expedition might generate—from books, films, or other commercial enterprises—would be dedicated to the support of subsequent expeditions. With funding assured and plans underway, the French Alpine Club enlisted a crack team of France's best mountaineers—Jean Couzy, Louis Lachenal, Gaston Rébuffat, Marcel Schatz, and Lionel Terray. The Club selected medical

and other personnel to support this team and placed the entire
expedition under the authority of thirty-one year old Maurice Herzog.

Arriving in Nepal with tons of supplies and equipment, the French
climbers engaged the services of nine Sherpas and almost two hundred
and fifty porters. With maps that were both inaccurate and incomplete,
and no direct knowledge of the terrain, the expedition spent eight
precious weeks reconnoitering the high mountains before finally
designating the summit of Annapurna as its goal, and establishing at
5,100 meters the first of five camps on the mountain's north face. Well
conditioned to the high attitudes through weeks of arduous
reconnaissance, the French climbing teams and the experienced
Sherpas pushed up the forbidding mountain in determined and
carefully orchestrated activity as they prepared to attack its summit,
probing and unlocking the mountain's defenses as they moved vital
supplies up from base camp to position them at Camp II and beyond
at Camps III and IV, and, ultimately, to Camp V, at 7,300 meters, within
striking distance of the ultimate prize.

Accompanied by the Sherpas Sarki and Ang-Tharkey, Herzog and
Lachenal passed Rébuffat and Terray as they struggled down from
Camp III on June 1st. Threatened with frostbite, and reporting terrible
weather and extreme cold, the seasoned climbers were skeptical that
the expedition would ever reach its goal. Determined to continue,
Herzog and Lachenal—aided by a break in the weather, the Sherpas,
and the work that Rébuffat and Terray had already accomplished—
advanced up the mountain. On the afternoon of June 2nd they hewed
a precarious perch out of the ice and snow of a steep mountain slope
and set up Camp V. After a hideous and sleepless night there, the
climbers set out grimly into the brilliantly fine and freezing dawn of
July 3, 1950. They ascended painfully by dreamlike step through a
fantastic, utterly alien, and unforgiving universe. At 2 p.m., eight hours
later, incredulous, joyful, a savage wind tearing at them, Maurice
Herzog and Louis Lachenal reached the icy summit—8,091 meters,
26,545 feet—the mountain plunging downward to unfathomable
depths only feet away from them. It was a glorious moment, and a
moment of extreme danger for the two severely diminished men.

Above 7,000 meters, the atmosphere is charged with barely a third
of the oxygen that it contains at lower altitudes. Blood thickens in the
veins. Everything moves slowly. Due to poor circulation the extremities
of the body are more vulnerable to freezing. Even the strongest mind
functions only haltingly. There was almost no conversation between
the climbers as they struggled toward the summit that morning, but

Lachenal, intensely suffering from severe frostbite, did ask Herzog what he would do if he decided to turn back. When Herzog affirmed his determination to reach the summit, alone if he must, Lachenal, despite his suffering and his grave and well-justified fears, declared that he would not abandon him.

Some controversy has emerged in recent years around the team's triumphant summit of Annapurna. Why did Herzog and Lachenal make their ascent without bottled oxygen? Should they have turned back? Who deserves what credit? It is clear that Herzog put his own life and that of his colleague at extreme risk in his determination to reach their goal. But a high price had already been paid to bring that goal so closely within reach, and Herzog, his own mind seized in the ecstasy of the moment, could not, would not let that prize slip through their frozen grasp. It is clearly evident in Herzog's account that he was carried away by the emotion of their achievement and wanted to linger on the summit, while Lachenal, aware of the extreme danger to their lives, desperately urged immediate retreat.

Drawn from Maurice Herzog's brilliantly evocative *Annapurna*, the selection presented here opens as the climbers began their descent from the summit and relates the harrowing hours and days that followed. Lachenal was the first to plunge back, followed at some distance by Herzog. As storm clouds gathered and mists shrouded the mountain, the two men separately made their ways to the refuge of Camp V. Herzog was the first to arrive. His hands and feet frozen into wood, he was still intoxicated with the emotion of triumph and his hold on reality was tenuous at best.

If Gaston Rébuffat and Lionel Terray had not made their way up to Camp V and cleared space there for a second tent, if they had not been there to greet and care for Herzog, how could he have survived the stormy night that was to come? If Terray and Rébuffat had not heard the desperate cries of Lachenal—who had taken a terrible fall and was stranded helpless more than one hundred meters below the camp—and Terray then had not retrieved him with such devoted bravery and skill, would not Lachenal surely have perished, exposed and helpless on the mountainside? If Terray had not spent the entire night in one storm-buffeted tent with Lachenal, and Rébuffat in the other with Herzog, each desperately working to beat life back into the severely damaged limbs of their comrades and to restore their strength, would either Herzog or Lachenal have had any capacity to affront the raging blizzard the following morning and continue their descent through further dangers that awaited them before safety and the merest possibility of sustaining their lives?

The four men lost their way in the winds and swirling mists and driving snow of June 4th. Fiercely determined Rébuffat and powerful and resourceful Terray guided their crippled comrades through the storm but they could not find the refuge of the camp below. If the four men had not miraculously found a natural shelter for the night, could they have survived? If Marcel Schatz had not the following morning come to the aid of the four men, by then all severely crippled or snow-blinded, could they have survived the perils that yet awaited them? Ultimately, it was devotion to each other that saved the two, then four men stricken by the mortal dangers of the mountain of their dreams. Ultimately, the victory of reaching the wind-torn summit of Annapurna belonged to them all, and through them, to all of us. And this cannot be diminished by disputes many decades later, when all are gone but one.

Annapurna

by Maurice Herzog

Lachenal was already far below; he had reached the foot of the couloir. I hurried down in his tracks. I went as fast as I could, but it was dangerous going. At every step one had to take care that the snow did not break away beneath one's weight. Lachenal, going faster than I thought he was capable of, was now on the long traverse. It was my turn to cross the area of mixed rock and snow. At last I reached the foot of the rock-band. I had hurried and I was out of breath. I undid my sack. What had I been going to do? I couldn't say.

"My gloves!"

Before I had time to bend over, I saw them slide and roll. They went further and further straight down the slope. I remained where I was, quite stunned. I watched them rolling down slowly, with no appearance of stopping. The movement of those gloves was engraved in my sight as something irredeemable, against which I was powerless. The consequences might be most serious. What was I to do?

"Quickly down to Camp V."

Rébuffat and Terray would be there. My concern dissolved like magic. I now had a fixed objective again: to reach the camp. Never for a minute did it occur to me to use as gloves the socks which I always carry in reserve for just such a mishap as this.

On I went, trying to catch up with Lachenal. It had been two o'clock when we reached the summit; we had started out at six in the morning, but I had to admit that I had lost all sense of time. I felt as if I were running, whereas in actual fact I was walking normally, perhaps rather slowly, and I had to keep stopping to get my breath. The sky was now covered with clouds, everything had become gray and dirty-looking. An icy wind sprang up, boding no good. We must push on! But where was Lachenal? I spotted him a couple of hundred yards away, looking as if he was never going to stop. And I had thought he was in indifferent form!

The clouds grew thicker and came right down over us; the wind blew stronger, but I did not suffer from the cold. Perhaps the descent had restored my circulation. Should I be able to find the tents in the mist? I watched the rib ending in the beak-like point which overlooked the camp. It was gradually swallowed up by the clouds, but I was able to make out the spearhead rib lower down. If the mist should thicken I would make straight for that rib and follow it down, and in this way I would be bound to come upon the tent.

Lachenal disappeared from time to time, and then the mist was so thick that I lost sight of him altogether. I kept going at the same speed, as fast as my breathing would allow.

The slope was now steeper; a few patches of bare ice followed the smooth stretches of snow. A good sign—I was nearing the camp. How difficult to find one's way in thick mist! I kept the course which I had set by the steepest angle of the slope. The ground was broken; with my crampons I went straight down walls of bare ice. There were some patches ahead—a few more steps. It was the camp all right, but there were *two tents!*

So Rébuffat and Terray had come up. What a mercy! I should be able to tell them that we had been successful, that we were returning from the top. How thrilled they would be!

I got there, dropping down from above. The platform had been extended, and the two tents were facing each other. I tripped over one of the guy-ropes of the first tent; there was movement inside, they had heard me. Rébuffat and Terray put their heads out.

"We've made it. We're back from Annapurna!"

Chapter XIV: The Crevasse
Rébuffat and Terray received the news with great excitement.

"But what about Biscante?" asked Terray anxiously.

"He won't be long. He was just in front of me! What a day—started out at six this morning—didn't stop . . . got up at last."

Words failed me. I had so much to say. The sight of familiar faces dispelled the strange feeling that I had experienced since morning, and I became, once more, just a mountaineer.

Terray, who was speechless with delight, wrung my hands. Then the smile vanished from his face: "Maurice—your hands!" There was an uneasy silence. I had forgotten that I had lost my gloves: my fingers were violet and white and hard as wood. The other two started at them in dismay—they realized the full seriousness of the injury. But, still blissfully floating on a sea of joy remote from reality, I leaned over toward Terray and said confidentially, "You're in such splendid form, and you've done so marvelously, it's absolutely tragic you didn't come up there with us!"

"What I did was for the Expedition, my dear Maurice, and anyway you've got up, and that's a victory for the whole lot of us."

I nearly burst with happiness. How could I tell him all that his answer meant to me? The rapture I had felt on the summit, which might have seemed a purely personal, egotistical emotion, had been transformed by his words into a complete and perfect joy with no shadow upon it. His answer proved that this victory was not just one man's achievement, a matter for personal pride; no—and Terray was the first to understand this—it was a victory for us all, a victory for mankind itself.

"Hi! Help! Help!"

"Biscante!" exclaimed the others.

Still half intoxicated and remote from reality I had heard nothing. Terray felt a chill at his heart, and his thoughts flew to his partner on so many unforgettable climbs; together they had so often skirted death, and won so many splendid victories. Putting his head out, and seeing Lachenal clinging to the slope a hundred yards lower down, he dressed in frantic haste.

Out he went. But the slope was bare now; Lachenal had disappeared. Terray was horribly frightened, and he could only utter unintelligible cries. It was a ghastly moment for him. A violent wind sent the mist tearing by. Under the stress of emotion Terray had not realized how it falsified distances.

"Biscante! Biscante!"

He had spotted him, through a rift in the mist, lying on the slope much lower down than he had thought. Terray set his teeth, and glissaded down like a madman. How would he be able to brake without crampons, on the wind-hardened snow? But Terray was a first-class skier, and with a jump turn he stopped beside Lachenal, who was suffering from concussion after his tremendous fall. In a state of collapse, with no ice axe, balaclava, or gloves, and only one crampon, he gazed vacantly around him.

"My feet are frostbitten. Take me down . . . take me down, so that Oudot can see to me."

"It can't be done," said Terray sorrowfully. "Can't you see we're in the middle of a storm . . . It'll be dark soon."

But Lachenal was obsessed by the fear of amputation. With a gesture of despair he tore the axe out of Terray's hands and tried to force his way down; but soon saw the futility of his action and resolved to climb up to the camp. While Terray cut steps without stopping, Lachenal, ravaged and exhausted as he was, dragged himself along on all fours.

Meanwhile I had gone into Rébuffat's tent. He was appalled at the sight of my hands and, as rather incoherently I told him what we had done, he took a piece of rope and began flicking my fingers. Then he took off my boots with great difficulty for my feet were swollen, and beat my feet and rubbed me. We soon heard Terray giving Lachenal the same treatment in the other tent.

For our comrades it was a tragic moment: Annapurna was conquered, and the first eight-thousander had been climbed. Every one of us had been ready to sacrifice everything for this. Yet, as they looked at our feet and hands, what can Terray and Rébuffat have felt?

Outside the storm howled and the snow was still falling. The mist grew thick and darkness came. As on the previous night we had to cling to the poles to prevent the tents being carried away by the wind. The only two air mattresses were given to Lachenal and myself while Terray and Rébuffat both sat on ropes, rucksacks, and provisions to keep themselves off the snow. They rubbed, slapped and beat us with a rope. Sometimes the blows fell on the living flesh, and howls arose from both tents. Rébuffat persevered; it was essential to continue painful as it was. Gradually life returned to my feet as well as to my hands, and circulation started again. Lachenal, too, found that feeling was returning.

Now Terray summoned up the energy to prepare some hot drinks. He called to Rébuffat that he would pass him a mug, so two hands stretched out towards each other between the two tents and were instantly covered with snow. The liquid was boiling through scarcely more than 60° centigrade (140° Fahrenheit). I swallowed it greedily and felt infinitely better.

The night was absolute hell. Frightful onslaughts of wind battered us incessantly, while the never-ceasing snow piled up on the tents.

Now and again I heard voices from next door—it was Terray massaging Lachenal with admirable perseverance, only stopping to ply him with hot drinks. In our tent Rébuffat was quite worn out, but satisfied that warmth was returning to my limbs.

Lying half unconscious I was scarcely aware of the passage of time. There were moments when I was able to see our situation in its true dramatic light, but the rest of the time I was plunged in an inexplicable stupor with no thought for the consequences of our victory.

As the night wore on the snow lay heavier on the tent, and once again I had the frightful feeling of being slowly and silently asphyxiated. I tried, with all the strength of which I was capable, to push off with both forearms the mass that was crushing me. These fearful exertions left me gasping for breath and I fell back into the same exhausted state. It was much worse than the previous night.

"Rébuffat! Gaston! Gaston!"

I recognized Terray's voice.

"Time to be off!"

I heard the sounds without grasping their meaning. Was it light already? I was not in the least surprised that the other two had given up all thought of going to the top, and I did not at all grasp the measure of their sacrifice.

Outside the storm redoubled in violence. The tent shook and the fabric flapped alarmingly. It had usually been fine in the mornings: did this mean the monsoon was upon us? We knew it was not far off—could this be its first onslaught?

"Gaston! Are you ready?" Terray called again.

"One minute," answered Rébuffat. He did not have an easy job: he had to put my boots on and do everything to get me ready. I let myself be handled like a baby. In the other tent Terray finished dressing Lachenal whose feet were still swollen and would not fit into his boots. So Terray gave him his own, which were bigger. To get Lachenal's on to his own feet he had to make slits in them. As a precaution he put a sleeping bag and some food into his sack and shouted to us to do the same. Were his words lost in the storm? Or were we too intent on leaving this hellish place to listen to his instructions?

Lachenal and Terray were already outside.

"We're going down!" they shouted.

Then Rébuffat tied me on the rope and we went out. There were only two ice axes for the four of us, so Rébuffat and Terray took them as a matter of course. For a moment as we left the two tents of Camp V, I felt childishly ashamed at leaving all this good equipment behind. Already the first rope seemed a long way down below us. We were blinded by the squalls of snow and we could not hear each other a yard away. We had both put on our *cagoules*, for it was very cold. The snow was apt to slide and the rope often came in useful.

Ahead of us the other two were losing no time. Lachenal went first and, safeguarded by Terray, he forced the pace in his anxiety to get down. There were no tracks to show us the way, but it was engraved on all our minds—straight down the slope for 400 yards then traverse to the left for 150 to 200 yards to get to Camp IV. The snow was thinning and the wind less violent. Was it going to clear? We hardly dared to hope so. A wall of seracs brought us up short.

"It's to the left," I said, "I remember perfectly."

Somebody else thought it was to the right. We started going down again. The wind had dropped completely, but the snow fell in big flakes. The mist was thick, and, not to lose each other, we walked in line: I was third and I could barely see Lachenal who was first. It was impossible to recognize any of the pitches. We were all experienced enough mountaineers to know that even on familiar ground it is easy to make mistakes in such weather. Distances are deceptive; one cannot tell whether one is going up or down. We kept colliding with hummocks, which we had taken for hollows. The mist, the falling snowflakes, the carpet of snow, all merged into the same whitish tone and confused our vision. The towering outlines of the seracs took on fantastic shapes and seemed to move slowly around us.

Our situation was not desperate; we were certainly not lost. We would have to go lower down; the traverse must begin further on—I remembered the serac which served as a milestone. The snow stuck to our *cagoules*, and turned us into white phantoms noiselessly flitting a-gainst a background equally white. We began to sink in dreadfully, and there is nothing worse for bodies already on the edge of exhaustion.

Were we too high or too low? No one could tell. Perhaps we had better try slanting over to the left! The snow was in a dangerous condition, but we did not seem to realize it. We were forced to admit that we were not on the right route, so we retraced our steps and climbed up above the serac which overhung us. No doubt, we decided, we should be on the right level now. With Rébuffat leading, we went back over the way which had cost us such an effort. I followed him jerkily, saying nothing, and determined to go on to the end. If Rébuffat had fallen I could never have held him.

We went doggedly on from one serac to another. Each time we thought we had recognized the right route, and each time there was a fresh disappointment. If only the mist would lift, if only the snow would stop for a second! On the slope it seemed to be growing deeper every minute. Only Terray and Rébuffat were capable of breaking the trail and they relieved each other at regular intervals, without a word and without a second's hesitation.

I admired that determination of Rébuffat's for which he is so justly famed. He did not intend to die! With the strength of desperation and at the price of super-human effort he forged ahead. The slowness of his progress would have dismayed even the most obstinate climber, but he would not give up, and in the end the mountain yielded in the face of his perseverance. . . .

We were well and truly lost.

The weather did not seem likely to improve. A minute ago we had still had ideas about which way to go—now we had none. This way or that . . . We went on at random to allow for the chance of a miracle which appeared increasingly unlikely. The instinct of self-preservation in the two fit members of the party alternated with a hopelessness which made them completely irresponsible. Each in turn did the maddest things: Terray traversed the steep and avalanchy slopes with one crampon badly adjusted. He and Rébuffat performed incredible feats of balance without the least slip . . . .

We had eaten nothing since the day before, and we had been on the go the whole time, but men's resources of energy in face of death are inexhaustible. When the end seems imminent, there still remain reserves, though it needs tremendous will power to call them up. . . .

"We must find a crevasse."

"We can't stay here all night!"

"A hole—it's the only thing."

"We'll all die in it."

Night had suddenly fallen and it was essential to come to a decision without wasting another minute; if we remained on the slope, we should be dead before morning. We would have to bivouac. What the conditions would be like, we could guess, for we all knew what it meant to bivouac above 23,000 feet.

With his axe Terray began to dig a hole. Lachenal went over to a snow-filled crevasse a few yards further on, then suddenly let out a yell and disappeared before our eyes. We stood helpless: should we, or rather Terray and Rébuffat, have enough strength for all the maneuvers with the rope that would be needed to get him out? The crevasse was completely blocked up save for the one little hole which Lachenal had fallen through.

"Lachenal!" called Terray.

A voice, muffled by many thicknesses of ice and snow, came up to us. It was impossible to make out what it was saying.

"Lachenal!"

Terray jerked the rope violently; this time we could hear.

"I'm here!"

"Anything broken?"

"No! It'll do for the night! Come along."

This shelter was heaven-sent. None of us would have had the strength to dig a hole big enough to protect the lot of us from the wind. Without hesitation Terray let himself drop into the crevasse, and a loud "Come on!" told us he had arrived safely. In my turn I let myself go: it was a regular toboggan-slide. I shot down a sort of twisting tunnel, very steep, and about thirty feet long. I came out at great speed into the opening beyond and was literally hurled to the bottom of the crevasse. We let Rébuffat know he could come by giving a tug on the rope.

The intense cold of this minute grotto shriveled us up, the enclosing walls of ice were damp and the floor a carpet of fresh snow; by huddling together there was just room for the four of us. Icicles hung from the ceiling and we broke some of them off to make more headroom and kept little bits to suck—it was a long time since we had had anything to drink.

That was our shelter for the night. At least we should be protected from the wind, and the temperature would remain fairly even, though the damp was extremely unpleasant. We settled ourselves in the dark as best we could. As always in a bivouac we took off our boots; without this precaution the constriction would cause immediate frostbite. Terray unrolled the sleeping bag which he had had the foresight to bring, and settled himself in relative comfort. We put on everything warm that we had, and to avoid contact with the snow I sat on the movie camera. We huddled close up to each other, in our search for a hypothetical position in which the warmth of our bodies could be combined without loss, but we couldn't keep still for a second.

We did not open our mouths—signs were less of an effort than words. Every man withdrew into himself and took refuge in his own inner world. Terray massaged Lachenal's feet; Rébuffat felt his feet freezing too, but he had sufficient strength to rub them himself. I remained motionless, unseeing. My feet and hands went on freezing, but what could be done? I attempted to forget suffering by withdrawing into myself, trying to forget the passing of time, trying not to feel the devouring and numbing cold which insidiously gained upon us.

Terray shared his sleeping bag with Lachenal, putting his feet and hands inside the precious eiderdown. At the same time he went on rubbing.

Anyhow the frostbite won't spread further, he was thinking.

None of us could make any movement without upsetting the others, and the positions we had taken up with such care were continually being altered so that we had to start all over again. This kept us busy. Rébuffat persevered with his rubbing and complained of his feet; like Terray he was thinking: We mustn't look beyond tomorrow—afterwards we'll see. But he was not blind to the fact that "afterwards" was one big question-mark.

Terray generously tried to give me part of his sleeping bag. He had understood the seriousness of my condition, and knew why it was that I said nothing and remained quite passive; he realized that I had abandoned all hope for myself. He massaged me for nearly two hours; his feet, too, might have frozen, but he didn't appear to give the matter a thought. I found new courage simply in contemplating his unselfishness; he was doing so much to help me that it would have been ungrateful of me not to go on struggling to live. Though my heart was like a lump of ice itself, I was astonished to feel no pain. Everything material about me seemed to have dropped away. I seemed to be quite clear in my thoughts and yet I floated in a kind of peaceful happiness. There was still a breath of life in me, but it dwindled steadily as the hours went by. Terray's massage no longer had any effect upon me. All was over, I thought. Wasn't this cavern the most beautiful grave I could hope for? Death caused me no grief, no regret—I smiled at the thought.

After hours of torpor a voice mumbled "Daylight!"

This made some impression on the others. I only felt surprised—I had not thought that daylight would penetrate so far down.

"Too early to start," said Rébuffat.

A ghastly light spread through our grotto and we could just vaguely make out the shapes of each other's heads. A queer noise from a long way off came down to us—a sort of prolonged hiss. The noise increased. Suddenly I was buried, blinded, smothered beneath an avalanche of new snow. The icy snow spread over the cavern, finding its way through every gap in our clothing. I ducked my head between my knees and covered myself with both arms. The snow flowed on and on. There was a terrible silence. We were not completely buried, but there was snow everywhere. We got up, taking care not to bang our heads against the ceiling of ice, and tried to shake ourselves. We were all in our stockinged feet in the snow. The first thing to do was to find our boots.

Rébuffat and Terray began to search, and realized at once that they were blind. Yesterday they had taken off their glasses to lead us down and now they were paying for it. Lachenal was the fist to lay hands upon a pair of boots. He tried to put them on, but they were Rébuffat's. Rébuffat attempted to climb up the chute down which we had come yesterday, and which the avalanche had followed in its turn.

"Hi, Gaston! What's the weather like?" called up Terray.

"Can't see a thing. It's blowing hard."

We were all still groping for our things. Terray found his boots and put them on awkwardly, unable to see what he was doing. Lachenal helped him, but he was all on the edge and fearfully impatient, in striking contrast to my immobility. Terray then went up the icy channel, puffing and blowing, and at least reached the outer world. He was met by terrible gusts of wind that cut right through him and lashed his face.

Bad weather, he said to himself, this time it's the end. We're lost . . . we'll never come through.

At the bottom of the crevasse there were still two of us looking for our boots. Lachenal poked fiercely with an ice axe. I was calmer and tried to proceed more rationally. We extracted crampons and an axe in turn from the snow, but still no boots.

Well—so this cavern was to be our last resting place! There was very little room—we were bent double and got in each other's way. Lachenal decided to go out without his boots. He called frantically, hauled himself up on the rope, trying to get a hold or to wiggle his way up, digging his toes into the snow walls. Terray from outside pulled as hard as he could. I watched him go; he gathered speed and disappeared.

When he emerged from the opening he saw the sky was clear and blue, and he began to run like a madman, shrieking, "It's fine, it's fine!"

I set to work again to search the cave. The boots *had* to be found, or Lachenal and I were done for. On all fours, with nothing on my hands or feet I raked the snow, stirring it around this way and that, hoping every second to come upon something hard. I was no longer capable of thinking—I reacted like an animal fighting for its life.

I found the boot! The other was tied to it—a pair! Having ransacked the whole cave I at last found the other pair. But in spite of all my efforts I could not find the movie camera, and gave up in despair. There was no question of putting my boots on—my hands were like lumps of wood and I could hold nothing in my fingers; my feet were very swollen—I should never be able to get boots on them. I twisted the rope around the boots as well as I could and called up the chute: "Lionel . . . Boots!"

There was no answer, but he must have heard for with a jerk the precious boots shot up. Soon after the rope came down again. My turn. I wound the rope around me. I could not pull it tighter so I made a whole series of little knots. Their combined strength, I hoped, would be enough to hold me. I had no strength to shout again; I gave a great tug on the rope, and Terray understood.

At the first step I had to kick a notch in the hard snow for my toes. Further on I expected to be able to get up more easily by wedging myself across the runnel. I wriggled up a few yards like this and then I tried to dig my hands and my feet into the wall. My hands were stiff and hard right up to the wrists and my feet had no feeling up to the ankles, the joints were inflexible and this hampered me greatly.

Somehow or other I succeeded in working my way up, while Terray pulled so hard he nearly choked me. I began to see more distinctly and so knew that I must be nearing the opening. Often I fell back, but I clung on and wedged myself in again as best I could. My heart was bursting and I was forced to rest. A fresh wave of energy enabled me to crawl to the top. I pulled myself out by clutching Terray's legs; he was just about all in and I was in the last stages of exhaustion. Terray was close to me and I whispered:

"Lionel . . . I'm dying!"

He supported me and helped me away from the crevasse. Lachenal and Rébuffat were sitting in the snow a few yards away. The instant Lionel let go of me I sank down and dragged myself along on all fours. The weather was perfect. Quantities of snow had fallen the day before and the mountains were resplendent. Never had I seen them look so beautiful—our last day would be magnificent.

Rébuffat and Terray were completely blind; as he came along with me Terray knocked into things and I had to direct him. Rébuffat, too, could not move a step without guidance. It was terrifying to be blind when there was danger all around. Lachenal's frozen feet affected his nervous system. His behavior was disquieting—he was possessed by the most fantastic ideas:

"I tell you we must go down . . . down there . . ."

"You've nothing on your feet!"

"Don't worry about that."

"You're off your head. The way's not there . . . it's to the left!"

He was already standing up; he wanted to go straight down to the bottom of the glacier. Terray held him back, made him sit down, and though he couldn't see, helped Lachenal put his boots on.

Behind them I was living in my own private dream. I knew the end was near, but it was the end that all mountaineers wish for—an end in keeping with their ruling passion. I was consciously grateful to the mountains for being so beautiful for me that day, and as awed by their silence as if I had been in church. I was in no pain, and had no worry. My utter calmness was alarming. Terray came staggering towards me, and I told him: "It's all over for me. Go on . . . you have a chance . . . you must take it . . . over to the left . . . that's the way."

I felt better after telling him that. But Terray would have none of it: "We'll help you. If we get away, so will you."

At this moment Lachenal shouted: "Help! Help!"

Obviously he didn't know what he was doing . . . Or did he? He was the only one of the four of us who could see Camp II down below. Perhaps his calls would be heard. They were shrieks of despair, reminding me tragically of some climbers lost in the Mont Blanc massif whom I had endeavored to save. Now it was our turn. The impression was vivid: we were lost.

I joined in with the others: "One . . . Two . . . Three . . . *Help!* One

... Two ... Three *Help!*" We tried to shout together, but without much success; our voices could not have carried more than ten feet. The noise I made was more of a whisper than a shout. Terray insisted that I should put my boots on, but my hands were dead. Neither Rébuffat nor Terray, who were unable to see, could help much, so I said to Lachenal: "Come and help me to put my boots on."

"Don't be silly, we must go down!"

And off he went once again in the wrong direction, straight down. I was not in the least angry with him; he had been sorely tried by the altitude and by everything he had gone through.

Terray resolutely got out his knife, and with fumbling hands slit the uppers of my boots back and front. Split in two like this I could get them on, but it was not easy and I had to make several attempts. Soon I lost heart—what was the use of it anyway since I was going to stay where I was? But Terray pulled violently and suddenly he succeeded. He laced up my now gigantic boots, missing half the hooks. I was ready now. But how was I going to walk with my stiff joints?

"To the left, Lionel!"

"You're crazy, Maurice," said Lachenal, "it's to the right, straight down."

Terray did not know what to think of these conflicting views. He had not given up like me, he was going to fight; but what, at the moment, could he do? The three of them discussed which way to go. I remained sitting in the snow. Gradually my mind lost grip—why should I struggle? I would just let myself drift. I saw pictures of shady slopes, peaceful paths, there was a scent of resin. It was pleasant—I was going to die in my own mountains. My body had no feeling—everything was frozen.

"Aah ... aah!"

Was it a groan or a call? I gathered my strength for one cry: "They're coming!" The others heard me and shouted for joy. What a miraculous apparition! "Schatz ... it's Schatz!"

Barely two hundred yards away Marcel Schatz, waist-deep in snow, was coming slowly towards us like a boat on the surface of the slope. I found this vision of a strong and invincible deliverer inexpressibly moving. I expected everything of him. The shock was violent, and quite shattered me. Death clutched at me and I gave myself up.

When I came to again the wish to live retuned and I experienced a violent revulsion of feeling. All was not lost! As Schatz came nearer my eyes never left him for a second—twenty yards—ten yards—he came straight towards me Why? Without a word he leaned over me, held me close, hugged me, and his warm breath revived me.

1953
K2: THE SAVAGE MOUNTAIN

We had the feeling that matters were beyond our control. We seemed to be puppets pulled by a string, as if things were fated to happen in a certain way, do what we would, and nothing in the world could change them. Under the circumstances this fatalism, caused no doubt by the series of accidents of the past few days, was almost comforting, for we did not lose strength through nervous worry. We were doing our best. If that wasn't good enough, there was nothing else we could do to change things. What would be would be.

– Robert H. Bates

Second only to Everest's 29,028 feet (8,848 meters), K2 thrusts up from its granite base to a menacing peak of ice-covered limestone, which soars to a height of 28,250 feet (8,611 meters) above the wild borderland between China and Kashmir-Jammu. Many mountaineers regard K2—the second of thirty-five mountains in the Himalaya Karakoram Range—to be a climbing challenge even more daunting than Everest. Above fifteen thousand feet, K2 is sheathed in snow and ice throughout the year, and freezing temperatures, high winds, and sudden storms protect its summit.

Between 1902 and 1939, five attempts to reach the summit failed. In 1902 a European team reached only 6,600 meters. In 1909 an Italian team led by the Duke of Abruzzi launched a better prepared and more determined assault on the mountain, but after two attempts failed to reach higher than 6,666 meters. The Italians returned to K2 in 1929 but were unprepared to mount a serious attack on its summit. Then, in 1938, the American Alpine Club launched an expedition under the leadership of experienced climber Dr. Charles S. Houston, who two years earlier had participated in the conquest of Nanda Devi. Supported by an excellent team, in turn aided by skilled Sherpas, lead climbers Houston and Petzoldt reached the foot of the summit pyramid—Petzoldt pushing beyond to a point estimated at more than 7,900 meters—but, after being the first to challenge the summit, they decided to turn back. The controversial and ill-fated Second American Expedition, led in 1939 by the superb German-American climber Fritz

Wiessner, reached within 300 meters of the summit but ended in tragedy when the expedition's supporting organization collapsed in the lower base camps, leaving climber Dudley Wolfe perilously isolated at Camp VII. No trace was ever found of Wolfe or of the three Sherpas who bravely set out in an attempt to bring him down from the mountain.

After World War II and the political upheaval that followed, mountaineering resumed in the Karakoram with a third American expedition, led again by Charles Houston, who, with another veteran of the 1938 expedition, Robert H. Bates, as co-leader, selected six experienced men to join them in the climbing team that set out to conquer K2 in the summer of 1953: George Bell, Robert Craig, Art Gilkey, Dee Molenaar, Peter K. Schoening, and Tony Streather. Forged into a close-knit team, these highly skilled climbers planned their expedition with the greatest detail and care. Drawing important lessons from the accumulated wisdom and experiences of previous attempts to overcome K2's defenses, they laid out a series of well-supplied camps as they approached the 28,250-foot summit of the world's highest unconquered mountain. They were well aware that ultimate success rested largely in the hands of fate and the weather.

With the help of Hunza carriers, the expedition established Base Camp at 5,000 meters at the foot of the Abruzzi-spur on June 19th, and worked to set up and supply advance camps for the next three weeks, mostly at the same sites that had been chosen in the 1938 and 1939 expeditions. They enjoyed good weather during this period, but in mid-July the weather turned and storm winds pounded at the mountain, halting any further advance for several days. By August 1st, all eight men had reached Camp VIII at 7,750 meters, each of them appearing to be in excellent condition to mount the final stage of their assault on the summit, when once again the weather turned and the team had to remain huddled in their tents, day after day, night after night, to endure howling winds and blizzards of snow. On account of their excellent planning, the team had ten days of supplies on hand, enough to sustain them until the storm passed. Only needing two or three more days of good weather to reach their goal, the team chose two rope teams to attack the summit as soon as conditions permitted. But the storm did not abate, and, on August 4th, Art Gilkey was stricken with a crippling and potentially fatal case of thrombophlebitis. As Gilkey's condition deteriorated and their supplies ran low, the team was faced with the impossible task of bringing their crippled comrade off the mountain in the midst of the still raging storm. By August 10th, where we open our selection from the account of Robert Bates, the situation had become critical. With no break in the weather, and George Bell showing the first signs of frostbite, the team had no choice but to retreat from Camp VIII in a stark struggle to survive.

It is nothing less than a miracle that any of the eight men survived the dangers against which they relentlessly struggled in the five desperate days that followed. But it is a miracle that could have never happened without the margins for survival provided by the team's excellent planning and skills, and, above all, by the practiced experience of each team member, which enabled these men to make their perilous descent in vicious weather, and to survive an accident, which would have swept five of them off the face of the mountain in an instant but for the quick-thinking actions of experienced belayer Peter K. Schoening. Although the mountain quickly claimed Art Gilkey, the team never abandoned their stricken comrade, nor at any time did the stronger among them abandon the weaker, as, roped together, they fought to reach the safety of base camp, step by treacherous step.

Robert Bates' account of the team's harrowing descent is a classic of mountaineering literature and a classic of the literature of survival. Bates' narrative directly and truthfully testifies to qualities of loyalty, determination, and endurance of men plunged into a struggle to maintain their very sanity under the most extreme stress and in the most extreme conditions. Crippled and beyond the last reserves of their strength, the survivors finally reached the goal of their retreat, Camp II, and the food, warmth, and kindly succor of their Sherpas. Though the Third American Expedition had failed to reach the summit of K2, the climbing team had attained summits of human nobility and endurance that will ever remain as inspirations to mountaineers everywhere. And K2 was conquered the following year.

K2: *The Savage Mountain*

by Robert H. Bates and Charles S. Houston

The Accident

We all knew now that some of us might never get down the mountain alive. Each had long recognized the near impossibility of evacuating an injured man from the upper ledges of K2. We had told one another that "if somebody broke a leg, you never could get him down the mountain," but now that we were faced with Gilkey's helplessness, we realized that we *had* to get him down. We didn't know how, but we knew we had to do it.

Schoening in particular, and also Bob Craig and Dee Molenaar, had done a lot of mountain rescue work, and the rest of us placed great confidence in their faith that somehow we could get our casualty to Base Camp. Gilkey's high morale and his confidence in us was a great boost to our spirits and we faced the job ahead with strong determination. When on the morning of August 10 Charlie Houston thrust his shoulders through the tunnel entrance of the tent where Schoening, Streather, and I, shoulder rubbing shoulder, had tossed during the long night hours, we spoke almost in unison: "How is he?"

"We've got to take him down," said the doctor. "His other leg has a clot now and he can't last long *here*."

The wind was hammering the tent fabric so hard that we had to yell at one another. Drifts of fine powder snow were sifting in through a strained seam in the tent vestibule, though we had done our best to keep the shelter airtight, and we could feel the whole tent vibrate as gusts stretched the fabric to the utmost.

"What? Move in this storm?" said someone.

"We've got to," said Houston. "He'll soon be dead if we don't get him down."

Nothing needed saying after that, for we knew what this decision meant. All of us had fought mountain storms before, but we had never seen anything like the duration and violence of this furious wind and snow that was still battering us. We all knew the story of the storm on Nanga Parbat in 1934, when nine members of a German expedition had died of exhaustion while battling the wind and snow. Willy Merkl, Uli Wieland, and Willi Welzenbach had been famous mountaineers, but a storm had exhausted them and killed them one by one. Here on K2 we had not only the storm to fight but the steepest part of the mountain, and we were trying to bring down these precipitous slopes a crippled companion as well!

We all realized that our adventure had now become grim, for the odds against getting Art down were obvious, and our own position was getting more critical all the time. While Houston and Schoening were easing Art out of his tent into the storm, the rest of us began packing light loads to take down. We would need one tent in case of emergency, and we took the Gerry tent, our lightest one. We also might need a stove and pot, and some meat bars, chocolate, or quick-energy food that needed no cooking. Often the effects of altitude so weaken one's determination that doing nothing becomes a positive pleasure, but this was no time for lethargy, and as we moved purposefully out of the tents into the stinging blasts of snow, we knew that we had to move fast, while fingers and toes still had feeling. Little was spoken. Each of us realized that he was beginning the most dangerous day's work of his lifetime.

Gilkey seemed in no pain as we wrapped him in the smashed tent, put his feet in a rucksack, and tied nylon ropes to him in such a way that they cradled him. Four ropes, tied to this cradle, could be held by one man ahead, one man behind, and one on either side. We had already put on all our warm clothing—sweaters, wool jackets, down jackets, and nylon parkas—and stripped our packs to the minimum. As we worked, the disabled man watched the preparations silently. He was an experienced mountaineer and realized what all of us were up against. But he knew also that we would never leave him, and that we would bring him down safely if it were humanly possible. Art's cap was pulled down over his face, which looked drawn and bluish-gray, but he gave a wan smile whenever someone asked, "How is it going?"

"Just fine," he would say. "Just fine." And his mouth would smile. He never showed a moment's fear or the slightest lack of confidence, but he realized of course that he had been stricken by something that was likely to be fatal, that his condition was getting worse, and that he was 9,000 feet above Base Camp in a terrible monsoon storm. The nearest tent, at Camp VI, was 2,000 feet below. He knew that we could not carry him down the tricky route we had come up, and that we must go only where we could lower him. Even in perfect weather with all men in top physical condition, the task might prove impossible—yet Art Gilkey could smile, and his smile gave us strength.

While we were adjusting the tow ropes, Schoening and Molenaar strapped on their crampons and disappeared into the storm. They were to find the best route past the dangerous avalanche slope that had blocked us a few days before, and to go along to the Camp VII cache to get a climbing rope that was strung on the ice slope just above. It would be useful in the descent. After their departure Houston called Base Camp on the walkie-talkie and told Ata-Ullah our plans. "It's pretty desperate, Ata," he said grimly, "but we can't wait. We're starting down now. We'll call you at three o'clock."

Each man took his place on a rope tied to Gilkey and for a couple of hundred yards we lunged hard at the tow ropes to pull Art through the knee-deep drifts of powder snow; then gravity took over and we had to hold back just as strongly to keep our helpless 185-pound load from plunging into the abyss. The steep slope we were on disappeared below us into nothingness. Was there a cliff there, a jumping-off place? We strained our eyes peering into the storm, but we could not wait for clearing weather. Instead we had to depend on Schoening and Molenaar, who had gone ahead to scout out the way. As we descended, Craig and Bell pulled the front ropes, one on each side, and Houston directed operations from a point immediately behind Gilkey, while Streather and I anchored the rope higher up. Gradually we worked our way to a rock ridge, climbed down alongside it, and then began to lower Gilkey down a steep snow slope leading to a snow chute and an ice gully below. This route was not the one we would have taken had Gilkey been able to walk, but now we had no choice: we could go only where we could lower our companion, and we had faith that the two men ahead would find a route down. Once we were well started, return to Camp VIII would be impossible for any of us.

The wind and cold seeped insidiously through our layers of warm clothing so that by the end of the third hour none of us had feeling in his toes any longer, and grotesque icicles hung from our eyebrows, beards, and mustaches. Goggles froze over and we continually raised them on our foreheads in order to see how to handle the rope. Moving the sick man was frightfully slow. We had to belay one another as well as Gilkey, and our numb fingers would not move quickly. Somehow, when we got to the steepest pitch, however, someone managed to tie two 120-foot nylon ropes together and we started to lower Gilkey down, down in the only direction the slope would permit. Houston and I, braced on the storm-swept ridge, backs to the wind, could feel the terrible gusts trying to hurl us off the rocks. We could not see where we were lowering Art, but we could hear faint shouts from Schoening and Molenaar, who were out of sight below. As we slowly payed out the coils of rope, thankful that they were of nylon and would not freeze in kinks, Bob Craig unroped from us and climbed down alongside the injured man to direct the descent. Soon he was completely obscured, too, but Streather climbed down to where he could see Craig's arm signals, yet still see us, and so we belayers had communication with Craig and Gilkey and knew whether to lower or to hold the rope. Alternately we anchored and payed out line until we were nearly frozen, and our arms were strained when Tony Streather, whom we could barely see, turned and shouted, "Hold tight! They're being carried down in an avalanche!"

We held. Our anchorage was good and the ropes stretched taut. For a moment snow flurries blotted out everything, and then we could hear a muffled shout from Streather. "They're still there!" The rope had broken loose a wind-slab avalanche of powder snow that had roared down over both men, blotting them from sight. Craig clung to the rope to Gilkey, and held on to it for his life. The pull of the hissing particles must have been terrible, but the avalanche was of unconsolidated snow. The falling powder slithered out of sight and down off the side of the mountain, where it must have kept falling long after we could hear it. When it was gone, Craig still clung to the rope, gray and very chilled. Both men were safe. The grim descent continued.

Schoening and Molenaar, who were not far from Camp VII, soon were able to reach Gilkey, but it seemed like hours to the four of us on the icy rocks of the wind-swept ridge before they shouted up that they had him strongly belayed "on the edge of a cliff," and we could climb down. Stiffly we shifted from our frozen positions, and climbed clumsily down the steep, crumbly rocks to the snow chute above the ice gully. Houston and I were on one rope, Bell and Streather on the other. All were so cold, so near exhaustion, that moving down over dangerous, snow-covered ice stretched us to the limit. Through the murk of blowing snow we saw Schoening standing in front of a large, rounded rock that had become frozen onto a narrow ledge. His ice ax was thrust deep into the snow above the rock, and the rope with which he held Art Gilkey was looped tightly around the shaft of the ax. The sick man was at the edge of a 20-foot cliff, beneath which we could glimpse the ice gully dropping off steeply into the storm toward the Godwin-Austen Glacier nearly 2 miles below.

. . . The problem now was not to get Gilkey down, but to swing him across the steep ice slope to the ice shelf at Camp VII. Our plan was to get a firm anchorage and then pendulum him across, but unfortunately the ice near him was too hard for axes to be driven in and the slope was relentlessly steep.

Even during the best weather conditions the maneuver would have been dangerous, and our position at that moment I shall never forget. Schoening was belaying Gilkey, who hung 60 feet below him, suspended against the sharply angled ice. On the same level as Gilkey, and 40 feet across from him, five of us, facing into the stinging, drifting snow, were searching for a place where we could stand and anchor the rope to Gilkey as we pulled him across the ice in the direction of Craig on the ice shelf. With our spiked crampons biting the hard ice, Streather, Houston, Molenaar, and I stood close together. Bell and Streather were roped together, Houston and I were on a rope together—and Molenaar had just "tied in" to a loose rope to Gilkey. He had done this when Craig had unroped and gone over to the ice shelf to rest, and it was Molenaar's precaution that saved us all. For George Bell, who was some 60 feet above us, began to descend a delicate stretch of hard ice in order to help with Gilkey's ropes. At that moment, what we had all been dreading occurred. Something threw Bell off balance and he fell.

I never saw Bell fall, but to my horror I saw Streather being dragged off the slope and making desperate efforts to jam the pick of his ax into the ice and stop. Streather had been standing above the rope from Houston to me. In almost the same instant I saw Houston swept off, and though I turned and lunged at the hard ice with the point of my ax, a terrible jerk ripped me from my hold and threw me backward headfirst down the slope.

This is it! I thought as I landed heavily on my pack. There was nothing I could do now. We had done our best, but our best wasn't good enough. This was the end. Since nobody was on the rope with Houston and me, there was no one else to hold us, and I knew that nothing could stop us now. On the slope below, no rock jutted on which the rope between us could catch. Only thousands of feet of empty space separated us from the glacier below. It was like falling off a slanting Empire State Building six times as high as the real one.

Thrown violently backward, with the hood of my down jacket jammed over my eyes, I had a feeling of unreality, of detachment. The future was beyond my control. All I knew was that I landed on my pack with great force, bouncing faster and faster, bumping over rocks in great thumps. The next bound I expected to take me over the cliff in a terrible drop that would finish it all, when, by a miracle, I stopped sliding.

I was on my back with my hood over my eyes and my head a yard below my feet. My arms, stretched over my head, were so completely tangled with the taut rope that I could not loosen them. I was helpless, and when I tried to move, I realized that I was balanced on the crest of some rocks and that a change of position might throw me off the edge. The rope had apparently snagged on a projection—though how and where I couldn't imagine—but it might not be securely caught. Whether it was firmly held, whether anyone else was alive, I did not know, but I didn't need to wait. Almost immediately I heard a groan coming from nearly on top of me. "Get me loose," I called, and immediately I felt the pressure of a leg braced against my shoulder and the rope was pulled off my arms.

Grabbing a rock, I swung my head around. Dee Molenaar and I were clinging to a rocky outcrop at the side of a steep ice slope, studded with rocks, about 150 to 200 feet below the place where we had been working on the ropes to Gilkey. Blood from Dee's nose trickled across his mustache and beard, and he looked badly shaken. My rope was tight to someone or something above, and I heard a distant yell, "Get your weight off the rope!" Fifty feet higher, through a mist of blowing snow, I could see Tony Streather staggering to his feet, a tangle of ropes still tight about his waist. Below me I heard a cry, "My hands are freezing!" and, looking down, to my amazement I saw George Bell, who seconds before had been 60 feet above me. Now about 60 feet *below*, he was climbing up over the edge of nothingness. He wore neither pack nor glasses and was staggering up over the steep rocks, obviously dazed, with his hands held out grotesquely in front of him. His mittens had been ripped off in the fall, and already the color of his hands had turned an ugly fish-belly white. If his hands were badly frozen, of course, we might never be able to get him down off the mountain.

Turning to Molenaar, I thrust my pack into his arms. Most of the lashing had ripped loose and the walkie-talkie radio, which had been on top, was gone; my sleeping bag was half off, held by a single twist of line. Without sleeping bags we were unlikely to survive the night, no matter how we tried! Since Molenaar wore no pack, I imagined that his sleeping bag had also been torn off in the fall. Whether or not the tent someone had been carrying had survived the fall, I didn't know. "For God's sake, hold this," I yelled above the wind, placing my load in Molenaar's arms. (For all I knew, mine was the only sleeping bag to survive the fall, and we must not lose it now.) The loose pack was awkward to hold securely while we were standing on

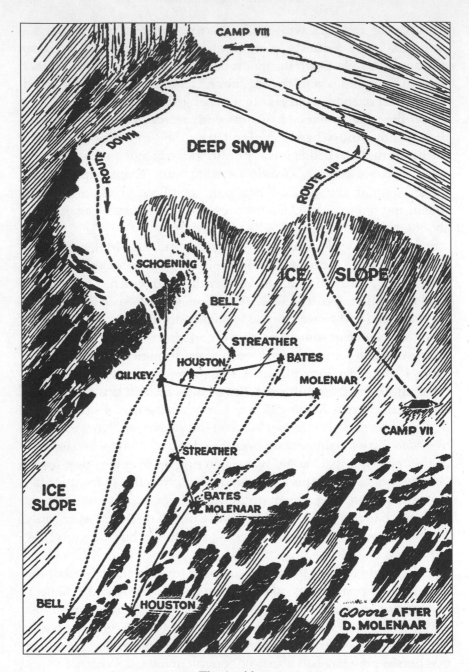

The Accident

such steep rock, but Molenaar grasped it and I unroped and started to climb shakily down to meet Bell. As I climbed down, I wondered about the ropes that had saved us. They were snagged to something up above, but the driving snow kept us from seeing what was holding them. Luckily I had a spare pair of dry, loosely woven Indian mitts in the pouch pocket of my parka, and when I reached Bell, whose face was gray and haggard, I helped him to put them on. Already his fingers were so stiff with cold that he couldn't move them, but balancing on projections of rock on the steep slope, we struggled to save his hands and finally forced the big white mittens past his stiff thumbs and down over his wrists.

Bell's fall had ended with him suspended over the edge of a ledge, below which the slope dropped away precipitously for thousands of feet. The weight of his pack pulled him head down, and he had lost it while trying to get right side up and back over the ledge. While Bell crouched down, working desperately to warm his hands under his parka, I left him, for Molenaar and I had seen a crumpled figure lying below a 30-foot cliff on a narrow shelf that seemed projecting over utter blankness below. It was Houston. Somehow a rope to him was snagged high above us, too. Climbing unsteadily but cautiously, for I was not roped and felt shaken by the fall, I worked my way down the steep rocks and across to the ledge. Houston was unconscious, but his eyes opened as I touched his shoulder. When he staggered to his feet, I felt relief it is impossible to describe.

"Where are we?" he asked. "What are we doing here?"

He was obviously hurt. His eyes did not focus and he appeared to be suffering from a concussion. Again and again I tried to persuade him to climb up the cliff, while Molenaar anchored the rope still attached to him from above. He didn't understand. "Where are we?" he kept saying, for my replies did not mean anything to him in his confused state.

The wind and blowing snow were searing our faces. We were all near exhaustion and in danger of crippling frostbite. If we were to survive, we had to get shelter at once, or we would be so numbed by exposure that we could not protect ourselves. What had happened in that Nanga Parbat storm which had taken so many men was a grim reminder. All of us working together did not now have strength enough to pull or carry Houston up the steep rock and snow to the ice ledge, 150 feet above, which we had called Camp VII.

"Charlie," I said with the greatest intensity, looking directly into his eyes, "if you ever want to see Dorcas and Penny again [his wife and daughter], climb up there *right now!*"

Somehow this demand penetrated to his brain, for, with a frightened look and without a word, he turned and, belayed by Molenaar, fairly swarmed up the snowy rocks of the cliffs. Instinct and years of climbing helped him now in his confused condition, for he climbed brilliantly up to Molenaar. I followed more slowly because, being fully conscious, I had great respect for this steep rock wall, and with great care I pulled myself up over the snow-covered slabs. When I reached Molenaar, he was looking puzzled and very unhappy as he tried to answer Houston's repeated question, "What are we doing here?"

The Bivouac

When I reached Molenaar, I still did not know what had caused the near disaster or how all five of us who fell had been saved. Up above, through the murk of blinding snow, I caught glimpses of Art Gilkey, anchored where he had been before the fall, but now Bob Craig was near him. Tony Streather, in a direct line above me, seemed to be untangling himself from a confused snarl of nylon climbing ropes, one of which led down to me.

Much later I learned the sequence of events that had put us in this position and marveled even more at our escape. Fortunately for us all, Schoening is an expert belayer, and his skill and quick thinking saved our lives. Later he told us how he did it.

By the time I returned to Molenaar and Houston, it was clear that through some miracle every climber was still able to move under his own power, but our exposure to the wind-driven snow was chilling us dangerously; we had to move fast to take shelter before we became too numb to set up a tent or became so crippled by frostbite that we would never be able to continue the descent. Since Molenaar's leg hurt and he didn't feel like moving much, I took Charlie Houston's rope and began climbing slowly up toward the ice ledge at Camp VII. I couldn't hurry, to save my life. Houston was obviously confused, but by instinct he climbed well and did what was asked. I hadn't climbed far when Tony Streather threw me a rope-end, and then Bob Craig returned from anchoring Art Gilkey and he and Streather took over the task of escorting Houston to the ledge. Craig had not seen the fall, but had looked up suddenly and been horrified to see the slope bare except for Schoening and Gilkey and a solitary ice ax with its pick end jabbed into the ice. At that moment a cloud of snow had blown across the ice, blotting out everything. When it cleared, Schoening, whose tight grip on the rope was freezing his hands, called to Craig to help him to anchor Gilkey. The sick man had not fallen, and he lay suspended against the ice as he had been at the time of the accident. He was probably the warmest of us all, but we could not continue to move him until the injured were cared for and we had more manpower to help get him across the slope.

When Craig reached him, Art handed over his ice ax, which he had retained for use in the descent. To make a secure anchorage was not easy, and Craig, still exhausted from his struggle against the avalanche, was not secured by anyone while he did it, but he skillfully found firm snow and drove in Art's ice ax right up to the head. He told the sick man that we would return for him as soon as we had a tent up. Gilkey understood. Not until then, when Craig had an ice ax firmly embedded, could Pete Schoening release his grip—which had held six men!—and begin to warm his freezing hands. Craig had not been involved in the accident, but all the rest of us owed our lives to Schoening's skill, courage, and technique.

Fortunately the tent had not been in one of the lost packs, but as I started to unroll it, the wind threatened to sweep it off the mountain. Craig and I were trying to wrestle the corners of the tent into position when Streather, who had now anchored Gilkey with a second ice ax, joined us to help pin the flapping edges under loose rocks till we could get anchorage for the guy ropes. The slope was so steep that the outer third of the tent was off the ledge and overhanging, so that it was impossible to keep the wind from sucking under the tent and trying to tear it away.

We were fortunate that this was our smallest two-man tent, for it held the ledge better than a wider one. . . . Finally we tied the front guy rope to a rock piton and lashed the inside corners as well as we could to projecting rocks. When Bob Craig later pounded in a Bernays ice piton, we felt somewhat safer, though the nylon shroud line attached to it didn't look too strong and the outer section of the tent bulged out over the slope. If someone inside forgot how precariously the tent was poised and leaned against the outer wall, we knew that the fabric would probably tear or the whole tent pull loose from the little ledge, and with everyone in it roll down the mountain into space.

The moment the tent was up, we moved Bell and Houston inside, where they would be under shelter and their weight would be useful in anchoring the tent. Molenaar at this point joined them to help take care of Houston, for Dee by now had lashed my loose pack together and carried it to the ledge. His left thigh hurt and he had a cracked rib.

While these men were trying to warm themselves in the tent, the rest of us began to hack another platform in the ice for Schoening's bivouac tent, which had previously been cached on the ledge as a safeguard for Streather and me on the day when we climbed from Camp VI to Camp VIII. The tent was meant for one person or in an emergency two, but if we could get it up, we meant to use it for three men to huddle inside.

At this moment Peter Schoening climbed down to us and declared laconically, "My hands are freezing." He too crawled in the tent to try to save his hands. All of us were still too busy to find out how Schoening had held us, for it seemed as if we would never get a platform flat enough or wide enough to pitch the bivouac tent. All our strength and energy went into chipping out an ice platform, for we had to get shelter from the bitter blast for everyone; but when we did get an uneven floor carved out, the wind whipped the fabric violently. It was like working in the slipstream behind an airplane as it taxied across the snow, spraying stinging particles behind. Finally Pete crawled out to help us insert the poles and we fastened the tent insecurely to rocks and pitons near the shelf of ice. It too overhung in an alarming manner.

The moment the bivouac tent went up, three of us prepared to go back for Art Gilkey. He was only 150 feet away, but a low rib of rock hid the ice gully where we had left him suspended from the two widely separated ice axes, each firmly thrust into the snow. Gilkey had called to us a couple of times while we were desperately hacking at the slope to make a platform for the bivouac tents, but the severity of the storm and the position of the gully made it impossible to distinguish words. Gilkey sounded as if he were shouting encouragement, but the wind blurred his words, as it must have muffled our answering shouts to him. He knew that we were making a shelter and would come for him as soon as we could.

About ten minutes after Gilkey's last shout, Streather, Craig, and I roped up and began to cross the slope to reach the injured man and move him somehow to the ice ledge where we now had two small tents. We knew that moving him even this short distance would take every bit of strength we had left, and we roped together carefully and braced ourselves for the effort.

. . . Streather and I had had our snow glasses off most of the day, because snow had frozen over the lenses, turning them almost to blinders. Apparently we had developed a touch of snow blindness, because we now seemed to be seeing everything through a very light mist. This mist was hard to distinguish from blowing snow, and we seemed to be moving in a dream. Fortunately, the wind had dropped as we reached the rock rib and looked into the gully where Art had been left suspended. What we saw there I shall never forget. The whole slope was bare of life. Art Gilkey was gone!

Our sick comrade, who had called out to us a few minutes before, had disappeared. Even the two ice axes used to anchor him safely had been torn loose. The white, windswept ice against which he had been resting showed no sign that anyone had been there. It was as if the hand of God had swept him away.

The shock stunned us. Blowing snow stung our faces as we silently stared and stared, but the slope remained empty. Something about it had changed, however, for there seemed to be a groove on the lower part of the slope that had not been there before. A snow or ice avalanche must have swept the sick man away scant minutes before we came to get him. As Craig and I belayed Streather out onto the center of the gully, he looked down past his cramponed feet to where the slope disappeared into the storm below. We called and shouted, but all of us knew that there would be no answer. Nobody could slide off that slope out of sight and remain alive. Dazed and incredulous, we turned and plodded back to the tents.

Gilkey's death, though anticipated for other reasons, was a violent shock. He had been very close to us, and we could not forget his many kindnesses to each of us in the past weeks. We had admired him and loved him. But too many immediate problems faced us to permit brooding over our loss now. Several men were injured. Whether they were in condition to climb down the mountain without help, we didn't know; nor did we know whether we could get them down if they could not walk. We could never leave anybody, but our struggle to lower Art Gilkey had shown us that to get a helpless man down the upper slopes of K2 under storm conditions required more strength and manpower than we now had. The route down from Camp VII to Camp VI would be longer and infinitely more difficult for rescue work than anything we had yet descended.

At Schoening's request, I moved into the Gerry tent alongside Houston. Four of us were now crowded into this little shelter with our backs to the ice slope and our feet resting lightly on the one-third of the tent which bellied out and overhung the slope. Luckily we had an air mattress, and once this was inflated and worked under the men inside, it gave some insulation from the cold. I opened my sleeping bag and placed the outer bag under our feet on the droopy side of the tent, while the inner half I wrapped around Houston, who was in a state of shock.

By this time the sky was darkening, but to our great relief the wind had dropped. We wore all our clothes and though they were damp we were not too cold, yet the night was a ghastly experience. George Bell, his hands and feet frozen, had jammed his great bulk into one end of the little Gerry tent. He cannot see well without glasses, and the pair he was wearing and the spare pair in his pack had disappeared in the fall. That night he must have realized the effort that would be required of him next day, for the steepest part of the route lay immediately below our ledge, and it would be impossible for us to carry him if he could not climb down. At the opposite end of the tent lay Dee Molenaar, a deep cut stiffening his left thigh and a bruised or cracked rib making his breathing painful. What was he thinking during the long hours of darkness I don't know, but he insisted on covering up Houston in his down jacket, even though he himself was lying exposed just inside the doorway of the tent.

Between Molenaar and Bell were Houston and I. Charlie Houston is usually bursting with energy, and if he had had his normal strength that night he would have been far too powerful for us. At first he was in a state of shock, but he soon stopped shivering and began to ask question after question, "Where are we?" "Where is Pete?" "How is Art?" Some things he seemed to understand, but he would ask the same questions again and again. A dozen times at least during the night he would ask, ""How's Pete?" I would say, "He's all right," but Charlie wouldn't believe me. Then I would call across to the tiny bivouac tent, which was swelled to bursting by the three men inside, "Hey, Pete, tell Charlie you're all right."

Pete Schoening would call out, "I'm fine Charlie. Don't worry about me."

"Oh, that's fine; that's fine," Charlie would say, and for a moment he would be quiet. Then again he would say solicitously, "How's Tony?" and the rigmarole would begin all over again. We were touched by his anxiety about us but we were more concerned about him.

During the fall Houston had evidently struck his forehead against a rock, causing a concussion and a hemorrhage which blurred the vision in his right eye. Another blow had given him a painful chest injury, which so affected his breathing that any deep breath was painful. In his confused state he thought that the pain in his chest when he breathed was caused by lack of oxygen in the tent, and so he tried to remedy the situation by clawing a hole in the fabric. Then, to keep from breathing deeply, he would take short breaths, faster and faster, until he would slump over unconscious and breathe normally until he became conscious again. When he became unconscious, we would shift position and try to get more comfortable, for the moment he was conscious he would become active again and we would have to restrain him.

Somehow—I still don't know how—the three men crammed into the bivouac tent, which was just as precariously pitched, were able to make tea and pass it in to us occasionally. There wasn't a great deal, but those swallows of tea were a godsend. They helped us to keep awake. Molenaar even opened the tent door to humor Charlie, but he still wanted to cut a hole in the tent. "I know about these things," he would say "I have studied them. We'll all be dead in three minutes if you won't let me cut a hole in the tent." And again his breathing would speed up tremendously and he would collapse.

The night seemed unbearably long, but at least we could converse with those in the other tent and the tea cheered us. During the long darkness we asked each man about his injuries and each man told a compressed story of what had happened to him in the fall. Schoening wasn't saying much, but we kept calling over to him, "How did you do it, Pete?"

"What kind of belay do you have?"

"If you can stop five men at 25,000 feet, how many could you stop at 15,000?"

Pete's story was brief. "Well, I was lucky," he said. "My ice ax was driven into the snow and braced against the upper side of that big boulder frozen in the ice. The rope passed around the ax to where I stood in front of the boulder, and went around my body, so that the force was widely distributed. Of course I was belaying Art anyway, and when I saw George slip and then Tony and the others pulled off, I swung weight onto the head of the ax and held on as the rope slid a bit. The force must have come in a series of shocks. The strain on me was not too great, but at the ice ax that seven-sixteenth-inch nylon rope stretched until it looked like a quarter-inch line, and I was scared stiff the boulder would be pulled loose. If that happened, the ax, which was braced against it, would go, too, and we would be lost. For minutes, it seemed, the rope was taut as a bowstring. Snow squalls blotted out everything below, and I couldn't tell what was happening. My hands were freezing, but of course I could not let go. Then the air cleared a bit and I yelled to Bob Craig, who was over at Camp VII, to come and anchor Art. By the time he reached him, most of the weight was off the rope, and from below I could hear someone calling, 'Charlie's hurt.' Once Art was secured, I came down to thaw out."

This simple story failed to stress the remarkable fact that one man had held five men who slid 150 to 300 feet down a 45-degree slope and that he had done it at nearly 25,000 feet, where the mere job of survival absorbs most of the strength of a man. Such magnificent belay work has rarely been recorded in mountaineering anywhere. Nor have I read of any other climbing miracle when three separate ropes fouled together to save the lives of five men. Bad luck had forced us to move in storm and had placed us where the fall had swept us off, but good luck, the resilience of nylon rope, and a remarkable tangle had saved our lives.

When the long hours finally wore away and the first rays of daylight came, a dour gray sky showed that more storm was coming fast. Silent, haggard, exhausted, we waited until Bob Craig had first made some tea and then cooked a little cereal. We had only one pot. During the night someone had placed the other pot outside the door of the crowded tent and it had immediately slid off the mountain. At the first light Houston crawled to the door and thrust out his shoulders. He seemed astonished that he didn't find more oxygen or easier breathing outside the tent. The morning air was raw and we were sore and weary. Everyone's eyes looked dead. But there was no question about the next move. We had to go down.

From Camp VII to Camp II

During the long hours of darkness we had had much to think about, and in the morning we soberly assessed our situation. Art Gilkey, who had camped here so cheerfully a few days before, was gone. Houston seemed physically able to climb but he was weak and still out of his head, had a chest injury, and couldn't reason. Whether he had internal injuries we didn't know. George Bell was an almost greater worry. His hands were covered with frostbite blisters and his feet were blotched with deeper frostbite. He wasn't sure that he could get his swollen feet into his boots again. In addition he could not see well without his glasses. Whether he and Houston could climb down, we didn't know, but we realized that we didn't have the manpower to carry them if they couldn't.

Schoening's chest seemed better during the night, but it was still a potential cause for worry. Fortunately, his hands, which he had nipped when he held the fall, had not suffered damage and did not give him trouble. Molenaar had a cracked rib and a cut on his thigh which would slow him down, but his morale was good and he was anxious to get started. Craig, too, looked exhausted, but the early morning light showed him to be obviously in better shape than he had been the evening before. Tony Streather, who with Craig and Schoening had been brewing tea for us during the night, looked more himself than anyone did.

. . . Schoening and Craig wanted to take Houston down, for he was still suffering from the concussion, and we were all very worried about how he would climb. If he stopped climbing, if he decided to act independently or if he slipped, he might bring disaster to the teammates whom he would have risked anything to save. We knew that this day's descent was the most dangerous we faced. If we could get the whole party down to Camp VI, there was a good chance that we would all get safely off the mountain. Accordingly, when everyone's crampons were on, Houston was tied carefully into the middle of Craig's and Schoening's rope and they started to climb carefully down over the snow-covered slabs. Schoening, whose ability at belaying had been established for all time, went last and anchored the rope. Those of us who were to follow on the second rope watched breathlessly as the three started down. We knew how close to exhaustion everyone was, and we worried over whether Houston would be able to climb. As we watched, he started off all right, but after going 20 feet he sat down in the middle of a steep snow patch, put his chin in his hand, and looked around as if to say, "What are we doing here?" Schoening looked perplexed. After a few moments he shook the rope and called down, "Come on, Charlie. Let's go!" And Charlie, still looking bewildered, got up and continued to climb down.

Perhaps this was a good time to have no inhibitions, for we were faced with a problem similar to climbing down a wind-swept, steeply slanted house roof, 1,700 feet long, with snow and ice covering many of the slates. The exposure was so severe that any slip would be hard to check and might pull the whole rope of men down off the mountain. We knew that we were physically exhausted and climbing under conditions that would have been extremely dangerous even when we were at our strongest. Each one of us had to climb with all the strength and skill he possessed. No one could slip.

The first rope had descended 100 yards and all were making good progress when the rest of us turned our backs on Camp VII and started to descend the relentlessly steep slopes. The storm clouds had risen a little, but the wind was sweeping great plumes of snow whirling across the rock slabs. Footing was dreadfully uncertain, and since Streather seemed strong, we had him go first. Next went Bell, whose uncertain steps because of his missing glasses and his frostbitten hands and feet were alarming, and finally came Molenaar and I. Molenaar's leg was bothering him but he kept as sound a belay as he could on Bell, and obviously did everything he could to secure me when I moved down behind him. We had moved down only a couple of rope lengths when we saw 100 feet to our right an ice ax sticking into the snow at a crazy angle. Molenaar made a careful traverse across the snow to reach it. It was Houston's ax, which had disappeared in the fall, and we quickly handed it over to Bell, whose ax had also vanished in his headlong plunge down the slope. This chance find helped Bell tremendously, for now with the ax he could probe places where he could not see clearly; but to watch George lean out over the slope and tap around with the tip of the ax was anything but reassuring . . . Under these conditions Bell's poise and steady climbing, despite his handicaps, were magnificent. He knew that his own life and ours were at stake, for we were all so near exhaustion that a slip could easily drag all four of us thousands of feet in a fall. And if Bell reached the point where he could not walk, we might be too weak to get him down.

In the back of our minds was the terrible lesson of the fatal storm on Nanga Parbat. We had more food on K2 than the Germans had had, but that wouldn't help if we couldn't reach it. Our feet and hands were numb as we cleared away the snow to find handholds and footholds. . . . Here, in an utter maelstrom of wind and whirling snow, we had to take off our crampons to climb down the smooth, steeply angled rock. We were already cold and as we eyed the slabs, which were here too steep for snow to cling, we faced a wind that was eddying furiously up the mountain directly at us. I have seldom been so cold.

With numb fingers we got George Bell's crampons off, pulled off our own, and then Streather climbed over the edge and disappeared. . . . I still had confidence that we would get down that cliff, and on down to Camp VI. I wasn't going to worry, but I was terribly anxious to get all of us under shelter so we could start work to save our feet.

One at a time we moved down across the steep slabs, along the ridge and down another fixed rope on the other side. Here, on loose rocks precariously poised, we had a brief respite from the wind. Our strength was ebbing fast, and Molenaar, who had belayed so well above, was now climbing entirely on reserve strength and hardly able to take care of himself. At 200 feet from camp, Streather, the strongest man on our rope, climbed 20 feet down the wrong place and had to climb back. Reascending cost him frightful effort! Ahead was one more slippery traverse, but no one slipped, and after descending a shallow gully we stepped down almost onto the tents of Camp VI.

The others were already there when we arrived. They had found both tents full of snow, one of them right up to the top, for a couple of small rocks had fallen and made slits in one, and faulty closure of a zipper had provided a tiny opening in the other. Through these small entrances the driving monsoon winds had forced powder snow until the tents were drifted full.

Fortunately for us on the second rope, the others had just finished clearing out the powder snow when we arrived, and they had started a stove. As we climbed into these tents, the most blessed sense of relief came over us. We had come down safely. We had passed the worst part of the route. Here were shelter and food. No matter how exhausted we were now, we had faith that we could get down.

Uncomfortable though we were, the next hours in camp seemed by contrast to be almost luxury. Charlie Houston seemed far more himself. Schoening and Craig reported that he had climbed extraordinarily well for a man in his condition, only occasionally sitting down in the most unexpected places and looking around as if to wonder what he was doing there. All of us looked years older than when we had been here before, but there was a confidence in our voices that had not been there that morning. Nobody made optimistic statements, but morale had improved.

While snow was melting for tea, we blew up the air mattresses which had not been abandoned above, arranged some 1939 sleeping bags we had found there, and took off our boots to work on our feet. My toes had no sensation, but neither did anyone else's, and I was glad to remember that my feet had not hindered my climbing down. Since the tent Houston and I were sharing stood in the lee of the other, and our tent had no holes that let in the wind, we called in George Bell to trade places with Bob Craig and move into the warmer tent. Bell's feet were a great worry to us now, for they were in the most dangerous condition of all. George shouted, "Okay," and started to crawl across the space between the tents. As he did so, he saw a little bag about 15 inches long and 8 inches high in the passage between the tents.

"Where did that come from?" he called, and without waiting for an answer he picked it up and pushed it into our tent ahead of him.

"Why, Tony found it about 1,000 feet below Camp VII," I said. "He thinks it's something of Art's. I haven't looked at it yet, but I'm going to take it to his family."

"It isn't Art's," said George huskily. "It's mine. It was in my pack when I lost it in the fall."

Eagerly he pulled at the zipper, drew it open, and began to fumble frantically inside. And now, to our utter amazement, George let out a gasp of joy and pulled forth his spare pair of eyeglasses—unbroken! What the discovery did for Bell's morale we couldn't tell, but his delight did us all a lot of good. . . .

All the way down, of course, we had been looking for Art Gilkey's body, but we never found it. We did see, however, a tangle of ropes and a broken ice ax about 1,000 feet below the ice gully where we had last seen him. The wooden shaft of the ax, broken in its fall down the mountain, had jammed between two rocks. Our friend must have had an instant and merciful death, the swift death that is the best kind, before his body was swallowed forever beneath the snows of the Karakoram.

That evening at six o'clock Charlie Houston was so far recovered that he could use the spare walkie-talkie, which was at Camp VI, to call Colonel Ata-Ullah at Base Camp. The emotion and relief in that good man's voice when he learned that we were alive was tremendous. "Thank God," he said, and for a moment or two he said little more. He had listened constantly since we had failed to keep our schedule with him at three o'clock the day before, and by now had practically given us up for dead. Next day he was planning to search the glaciers for us, and then, when weather permitted, climb as high as he could to look for us before accepting the fact that we were lost. He had told his fears to the Hunzas, and together they had had a mournful time. That night at Camp VI we had a magnificent dinner of tomato soup, canned ham, rice, and cups and cups of tea, but darkness overtook us before the cups were cleaned and the sleeping bags arranged. Pushing aside the stove and dishes, Houston and I fell asleep almost before we could pull ourselves into the two parts of my sleeping bag, for Houston's bag, of course, had disappeared in the fall. Drugged as I was by exhaustion, my sleep was fitful, however, for Houston was out of his head again and all night long he kept getting out of the inner half of the sleeping bag, which he was using, and crawling about the tent. He was most anxious not to waken me and kept steadily apologizing for the trouble he was causing. "If I can just get out of this warehouse," he would say, "everything will be all right." Then, as best I could in the darkness, I would find the opening to his sleeping bag and try to get him inside. The next thing I knew, I would be awakened again by Houston crawling around the foot of my sleeping bag. "I'm terribly sorry to bother you," he would say. "If I can only get out of this warehouse. . . .

Next morning the storm had increased in violence and we were apprehensive about starting down to Camp V for fear that Geroge Bell would extend the damage already done to his feet. We were deeply worried about his condition. We feared that he might reach the point where he could not walk, and we hated to think what would happen then, for in our exhausted state and with a storm raging we could not carry anybody, let alone our biggest man, down along the ridges below. Since food and gasoline were short at Camp VI we were anxious to move some men down, and Schoening and Streather took advantage of a lull in the storm to push their way down to the next camp, but the lull ended and the rest of us stayed behind. Supplies of fuel were low and that night we went to bed with a cold supper and the realization that we had to start down again next day. Bell was now the main problem, for Houston was gaining strength and clarity of thought with remarkable rapidity.

August 13 was cold and windy with light snow falling, much like the day we had moved down to Camp VI. Craig and Molenaar had had a cold night in the torn tent, and after cold meat bars for breakfast, they pulled on their packs and started down. Putting George Bell in the torn tent for shelter, Houston and I began trying to free the bottom of the tent we were in from ice, for it was necessary for us to carry down one tent, and the other one was ripped. Our tent had become iced-in during previous use, and our hands became frightfully cold as we hacked at the ice and pulled at the knots. Meanwhile the wind was getting at the tent Craig and Molenaar had emptied, so that by the time we had freed the tent that was to go down, the wind had torn the other one from end to end with Bell in it, and the whole fabric began to shred apart as we huddled in it to try to bring back sensation to our nipped fingers. Then, swinging on heavy packs, we started down to Camp V.

To our delight, Bell climbed steadily and safely. The route from VI to V was normally not particularly difficult, but with fresh snow on the rocks some of the route was dangerously coated with loose snow, especially in one gully. Here Houston did a fine job of anchoring the rope as I went ahead, He seemed almost his old self as we moved down onto a tiny scree slope and around a corner into Camp V. Craig and Molenaar were already there, and they made way for us to move in where Schoening and Streather pumped the stove to a red-hot roar and poured cup after cup of orange juice–flavored tea down our still dehydrated throats. They had battled the storm the day before and had been glad to reach camp safely.

Our descent was going well now and the storm had let up a bit, but there was no indication that another frightful blow wasn't on the way. "If we can only get below House's Chimney," someone said, "it will take mighty bad weather to hold us back after that." We were still going on reserve energy and it was now about two-thirty in the afternoon, but the thought of putting the last major barrier behind us spurred us on. Normally we would climb from Camp V to the top of House's Chimney in five minutes, and from there look down on the tents of Camp IV almost directly beneath.

Now it took over an hour of the hardest work to get to the top of the chimney. Craig and Molenaar, who went ahead, shouted up to watch out for the ice, for everything was glazed over and there was great danger of a slip's pulling a whole rope of men off the mountain. We had heavier loads now, Houston especially, and we concentrated grimly on crossing this dangerously exposed section safely. Even so, Houston and I had a number of unpleasant moments and cut many steps before we climbed to the base of the A-frame and looked down the fixed rope Craig and Molenaar had set up in House's Chimney. And 150 feet below us we could see them working on the tents at Camp IV.

The hour was late enough so that not a moment could be wasted if we were to make the descent before dark. Houston insisted on belaying each man down in turn, and then we began to lower the packs to Schoening, who had climbed up the snow slope across from the foot of the chimney and made himself a platform there. These operations took time, for each pack had to be well secured, and it was almost dark when I climbed down the chimney and, guided by Schoening, crossed the ice steps to the rock outcrop from which we had hoisted loads three weeks earlier. Houston had been first man up the chimney and he wanted to be the last man down it, but it was nearly pitch-black by the time he left the tiny platform where he had been crouching so long and backed off the plunging cliff into space. Such a tangle of old and new ropes hung in the chimney that in the blackness the terrible thought swept over him that he was hanging on the wrong rope! Swinging out over this sheer cliff with the awesome gulf below is an impressive experience at any time, but it was doubly so to Houston, as with numb hands he launched himself out over the blackness, hoping that the rope was the right one and that it would reach the line of steps cut in the snow at the bottom.

The rope held, and Schoening was soon helping to guide Houston across the slope. A few minutes later we were all at the tent platforms of Camp IV, too tired to do more than swallow some tea, eat a cold meat bar for energy, and climb into our sleeping bags. Having House's Chimney behind us was a boost to our determination to get the whole party down safely. That night Molenaar, Houston, and I shared one tent, and I remember rubbing and rubbing to try to get feeling back into my toes. They didn't hurt and they weren't swollen, but try as I would, I couldn't bring back any sensation to some of my toes. Still, the chimney, which had been long in our thoughts, was now behind us and we lay down scarcely conscious of the dampness of the half sleeping bag each of us was using.

When another gray dawn broke on August 14, gaunt, hollow-eyed men began to stumble out onto the slippery scree to collect pieces of ice to melt. Craig's feet were very painful but George Bell was an even greater worry, for he was now going on nerve alone. This morning his feet were so swollen that he couldn't get his boots on no matter how hard he struggled, and at last he was forced to slit the boots with a knife in order to pull them on. These openings wouldn't increase his protection against further cold damage, but at least they would permit him to climb down with something on his feet.

This time Streather and I started down ahead to find and improve the route if possible. We found powder snow masking loose rocks and making part of our upward route unusable. Worse still, most of our fixed ropes were completely buried and we had to hack and hack to cut steps in smooth ice that covered slopes we had descended with ease before. Cutting steps straight down is arduous work, and both Streather and I were feeling the strain of the past few days. A couple of hundred yards above Camp III, we checked a slip before it got started, and then Schoening took over the lead to give us a rest and began cutting the last of the steps needed to get to camp.

How rich the air seemed! We had descended the equivalent of five Eiffel Towers, or ten Washington Monuments, below Camp VIII, and that part of the mountain already seemed impossibly remote. New York and home by contrast seemed almost around the corner. But we were not down by any means. Storm clouds shrouded the slopes above us, and we knew that if the ice we had met just above Camp III plastered the route to Camp II, the next part of the descent would be especially dangerous, for the continuous strain was having its effect on all of us.

Camp III was well stocked with food, and since the wind had dropped, we made a solid lunch there. Like starving men, we gulped down date bars with almonds in them, chunks of Gruyère cheese, dried apricots, biscuits, and chocolate. We mixed a can of concentrated orange juice with snow, beat the icy mixture with a spoon until it grew mushy, and then took turns gulping great spoonfuls. Our bodies sorely needed replenishing with hot food and sleep, but Camp II was calling to us, for we knew that our faithful Hunzas would be there. Also, it was imperative that Bell waste no time in getting as low as possible, for we realized that before long, no matter how much nerve he had, he would be unable to walk on his frozen feet.

Ice over the rocks would make the route below Camp III very dangerous, and while we were pondering whether to descend or wait until the next day, Schoening moved down to the traverse across the first gully and found not ice but firm snow. We were much impressed, for we had expected more of the ice we had found just above. Morale soared. We even added to our packs a few items that had been left in duffel bags at Camp III, and then continued the descent.

This time Houston, Bell, and Schoening went first on one rope; Streather and I followed; and Craig and Molenaar brought up the rear. More than ever we were determined not to slip, and despite the need for one delicate maneuver after another, no one fell. Luckily the ice was not so bad as we had feared, and we gained confidence as we climbed down. The mountain took one parting shot at us, however, for just before Schoening, Bell, and Houston turned off the main slope into the shelter of a safe gully, a rock plummeting with great speed and noise from high on the mountain whizzed within a few feet of their heads.

Streather had the walkie-talkie, and exactly at six o'clock he tried to call Ata-Ullah. There was no flat place near us. Actually at exactly six I was standing on one foot traversing a steep rock wall, and didn't dare to move for fear of dislodging Streather, who was in an only slightly more secure position with one hand on the walkie-talkie. We hoped to tell Ata-Ullah to send porters next day to the glacier near Camp I to help Bell down, but Ata couldn't hear us and Streather finally folded in the radial aerial and went on.

As we started down the last couloir (gully) toward Camp II, we could hear the Hunzas shouting, and as we stepped onto the last snow slope, Ghulam, Vilyati, and Hidayat, roped together with what looked like a string, swarmed out onto the steep slope and embraced us with tears rolling down their cheeks. It was an overwhelming welcome and almost too much for us in more ways than one, for we were clinging to small holds and standing at the top of a steep couloir which fell away 1,500 feet to the glacier below. Such a position is not suited to an uninhibited heart-to-heart embrace!

Our packs were taken from us and these hardy frontiersmen, with tears streaking their cheeks, handed us down from rock to rock as if afraid that at the last moment we would collapse. As each one of us reached Camp II, where sleeping bags had been laid out on the rocks for us to sit on, each Hunza in turn with great emotion embraced each one of us. The storm had ebbed away, the wind had dropped, and the first stars we had seen for weeks were glittering in the night sky as Craig and Molenaar climbed down the last rock pitch above camp. Our feeling of relief and luxury at that moment is too great to describe. The ship had been saved; the lost, found. Every man who had started down from the dreadful bivouac at Camp VII had reached the safety of Camp II and the protection of our Hunzas. That evening was one of the sweetest any of us will ever spend, for a sense of supreme peacefulness enveloped us. Yet we were sad, too. We talked about Art Gilkey, and the Hunzas cried and prayed in unison for him. They wanted to know what had happened and how we had forced our way down through the storm.

And slowly as we lay there on sleeping bags with our boots off in the warm, rich air, with a stove roaring cheerily *in the open* at our feet, we began to return to life. First the Hunzas fed us rice cooked in milk; then, with three stoves burning, we started on tea. Fuel and fire were plentiful here, and we made the most of it. Stacks of the flat pancakes called *chupattis* were cooked and pot after pot of tea and milk was brought over to us as we lay talking, relaxing, rubbing our feet, too emotionally stirred to go to bed. And all this while, kindly Hunza hands were kneading our tired muscles as only Asiatics can, bringing us back to life. At that heartwarming moment differences of race and language meant nothing. We and the Hunzas by the light of a flickering flare shared a great emotional experience as we talked and talked. Those who also have faced hardship and danger can appreciate our emotions and the bond between us all as we lay there. Then, after hours of delicious rest, we hoisted ourselves to our feet, staggered to our tents, and crawled gratefully into our sleeping bags. We had done it.

1967-1973
JOHN McCAIN: PRISONER OF WAR

It's an awful thing, solitary. It crushes your spirit and weakens your resistance more effectively than any other form of mistreatment. Having no one else to rely on, to share confidences with, to seek counsel from, you begin to doubt your judgment and your courage. But you eventually adjust to solitary, as you can to almost any hardship, by devising various methods to keep your mind off your troubles and greedily grasping any opportunity for human contact.

John Sidney McCain III's story of survival—during five and a half harrowing years in North Vietnamese prisoner of war camps—has inspired people throughout the world, regardless of the views they may hold of the wider conflict in which he and many millions of other souls were caught up. Speaking directly to us in an unvarnished colloquial voice, his deeply felt story is both a testament of personal courage and almost unfathomable strength and an affirmation of the human bonds—with fellow prisoners—that were crucial to his emergence from his ordeal. The sources of John McCain's personal strength—in his upbringing and the formation of his character in traditions of integrity, duty, honor, and love of country—are revealed in his family memoir *Faith of My Fathers*, from which two chapters follow. In this excerpt the qualities of McCain's character glow through his fiercely honest account of the day-to-day realities of his first years as a prisoner of war, the experience of which forged his character into tempered steel and stirred his heart with an intense devotion to "causes greater than oneself."

Indeed, strong character was to be expected from the grandson and son of two four-star admirals—the first American family to be honored with this distinction—John S. McCain, Sr., who led the formidable aircraft carrier task force of the Third Fleet in the Pacific theater during World War II, and John S. McCain, Jr., who commanded all U.S. forces in the Pacific during the Vietnam conflict. But the personal qualities of John S. McCain III would not be fully tested and revealed until the Vietnam War, when he faced a prolonged struggle for life after his plane was shot down and he violently parachuted, gravely wounded, into Truc Bach Lake in central Hanoi and was dragged half alive from the water into the midst of a furious crowd.

Born in the Panama Canal Zone in 1936, John McCain III was raised and schooled in Northern Virginia. High-spirited, fun-loving, and not altogether devoted to his studies, the young McCain graduated with small distinction from the United States Naval Academy in 1958 to embark upon a twenty-two year career as a naval aviator. In late 1966 McCain was assigned to fly an A-4 Skyhawk from the deck of the USS *Forrestal* stationed in the Tonkin Gulf. The thirty-one-year-old pilot had successfully made five sorties over North Vietnam when disaster struck. After careful preflight checks, just before eleven A.M. on the morning of July 29, 1967, his flight canopy tightly shut, McCain was in the cockpit of his A-4, third in line for takeoff from the *Forrestal's* deck, when a six-foot Zuni missile misfired from a neighboring F-4 Phantom hit the two hundred gallon belly fuel tank of his plane, igniting an enormous explosion and fireball and knocking loose onto the carrier deck two of the A-4's thousand-pound bombs. McCain miraculously escaped, leaping from his plane, rolling through the jet-fuel fire, and managing to extinguish the flames consuming his flight suit. The pilot in the A-4 next to McCain's also jumped from his plane into the fire, his flight suit bursting into flame. McCain was rushing to his aid when the raging deck fire ignited one of the thousand-pound bombs, setting off an inferno of violent explosions and raging fires, which the crew of the *Forrestal* finally brought under control after a desperate twenty-four hour struggle.

Soon after his narrow survival of the *Forrestal* disaster, McCain volunteered for flight duty aboard the USS *Oriskany*. Like the *Forrestal*, the *Oriskany* was stationed in the Tonkin Gulf, and, like the *Forrestal*, it had suffered an enormous fire, but one that had been more quickly brought under control—with no explosions of ordinance, but with the loss of forty-four men. On September 30, 1967, McCain joined an A-4 attack squadron aboard the *Oriskany*. Called the *Saints*, this squadron had suffered severe losses since the inception in 1965 of bombing raids—*Operation Rolling Thunder*—over heavily defended North Vietnam. In 1967 alone, a third of the *Saints* were either killed or captured. And it was John McCain III's fate to be among these, on his twenty-third sortie over North Vietnam, and his first over the North Vietnamese capital. On October 26, 1967, McCain was on a bombing run 3,500 feet above Hanoi, in a sky filled and blackened with intensely bursting antiaircraft fire, when an alarm in his cockpit alerted him that he was under SAM attack. Instead of immediately taking evasive action to avoid the missile hurtling at his plane, McCain hesitated for the few seconds it took to release his bombs on target. As he was pulling into a steep climb to escape, the SAM ripped into the right wing of his agile A-4.

McCain's compelling account of what followed is a remarkable story of courage, strength, and endurance, as the severely wounded pilot survived neglect, torture, near starvation, and the barest medical care before being thrown among fellow prisoners to die. This was followed by more than two years of solitary confinement which imposed bitter challenges on his weakened body and mind. That he was offered any medical treatment at all was almost certainly due to the fact that his North Vietnamese captors hoped to derive some propaganda value from McCain, after they realized that he was the son of a powerful American admiral. But McCain disappointed any hopes that he could be used for propaganda purposes, just as he was later to refuse the early release that the North Vietnamese offered to him, or any other special treatment as a prisoner of war. Most important to McCain's survival through the years of his captivity— more important even than his innate physical resilience and his strength of character—were the solidarity and the faith that he kept with fellow American POWs, and they with him. It was this, and only this, that kept him alive.

Released from North Vietnamese captivity in 1973, John McCain continued his service as a naval aviator until 1981. Elected to the U.S. House of Representatives in 1982, he has since served the people of Arizona and the United States through three terms in the United States Senate. A genuine American hero, he lifted the hopes of millions of Americans in his campaign for the American presidency in 2000. With the satisfactions and accomplishments of a brilliant career already behind him, the happiness of a rich family life, and his love of his desert home in beautiful Arizona, one might think that John McCain III would be content to fade away, but one believes that the lessons deeply burned into him during the years of his captivity will encourage him to continue to serve, and to strive better to serve, "causes greater than oneself."

Prisoner of War

from *Faith of My Fathers*

by John McCain with Mark Salter

I knew I was hit. My A-4, traveling at about 550 miles an hour, was violently spiraling to earth. In this predicament, a pilot's training takes over. I didn't feel fear or any more excitement than I had already experienced during the run, my adrenaline surging as I dodged SAMs and flak to reach the target. I didn't think, "Gee, I'm hit—what now?" I reacted automatically the moment I took the hit and saw that my wing was gone. I radioed, "I'm hit," reached up, and pulled the ejection seat handle.

I struck part of the airplane, breaking my left arm, my right arm in three places, and my right knee, and I was briefly knocked unconscious by the force of the ejection. Witnesses said my chute had barely opened before I plunged into the shallow water of Truc Bach Lake. I landed in the middle of the lake, in the middle of the city, in the middle of the day. An escape attempt would have been challenging. I came to when I hit the water. Wearing about fifty pounds of gear, I touched the bottom of the shallow lake and kicked off with my good leg. I did not feel any pain as I broke the surface, and I didn't understand why I couldn't move my arms to pull the toggle on my life vest. I sank to the bottom again. When I broke the surface the second time I managed to inflate my life vest by pulling the toggle with my teeth. Then I blacked out again.

When I came to the second time, I was being hauled ashore on two bamboo poles by a group of about twenty angry Vietnamese. A crowd of several hundred Vietnamese gathered around me as I lay dazed before them, shouting wildly at me, stripping my clothes off, spitting on me, kicking and striking me repeatedly. When they had finished removing my gear and clothes, I felt a sharp pain in my right knee. I looked down and saw that my right foot was resting next to my left knee, at a ninety-degree angle. I cried out, "My God, my leg." Someone smashed a rifle butt into my shoulder, breaking it. Someone else stuck a bayonet in my ankle and groin. A woman, who may have been a nurse, began yelling at the crowd, and managed to dissuade them from further harming me. She then applied bamboo splints to my leg and right arm.

It was with some relief that I noticed an army truck arrive on the scene to take me away from this group of aggrieved citizens who seemed intent on killing me. Before they put me in the truck, the woman who had stopped the crowd from killing me held a cup of tea to my lips while photographers recorded the act. The soldiers then placed me on a stretcher, loaded me into the truck, and drove me a few blocks to an ocher-colored, trapezoid-shaped stone structure that occupied two city blocks in the center of downtown Hanoi.

I was brought in through enormous steel gates, above which was painted the legend "Maison Centrale." I had been shot down a short walk's distance from the French-built prison, Hoa Lo, which the POWs had named "the Hanoi Hilton." As the massive steel doors loudly clanked shut behind me, I felt a deeper dread than I have ever felt since.

They took me into an empty cell, in a part of the prison we called the Desert Inn, set me down on the floor still in the stretcher, stripped to my underwear, and placed a blanket over me. For the next few days I drifted in and out of consciousness. When awake, I was periodically taken to another room for interrogation. My interrogators accused me of being a war criminal and demanded military information, what kind of aircraft I had flown, future targets, and other particulars of that sort. In exchange I would receive medical treatment.

I thought they were bluffing, and refused to provide any information beyond my name, rank, serial number, and date of birth. They knocked me around a little to force my cooperation, and I began to feel sharp pains in my fractured limbs. I blacked out after the first few blows. I thought if I could hold out like this for a few days, they would relent and take me to a hospital.

For four days I was taken back and forth to different rooms. Unable to use my arms, I was fed twice a day by a guard. I vomited after the meals, unable to hold down anything but a little tea. I remember being desperately thirsty all the time, but I could drink only when the guard was present for my twice-daily feedings.

On about the fourth day, I realized my condition had become more serious. I was feverish, and was losing consciousness more often and for longer periods. I was lying in my own vomit, as well as my other bodily wastes. Two guards entered my cell and pulled the blanket down to examine my leg. I saw that my knee had become grossly swollen and discolored. I remembered a fellow pilot at Meridian who had broken his femur ejecting from his plane. His blood had pooled in his leg, and he had gone into shock and died. I realized the same thing was happening to me, and I pleaded for a doctor.

The two guards left to find the camp officer, who spoke some English. He was short and fat, with a strangely wandering right eye that was clouded white by a cataract. The POWs called him "Bug." He was a mean son of a bitch.

Desperate, I tried to bargain with him. "Take me to the hospital and I'll give you the information you want." I didn't intend to keep my word, reasoning that after my injuries had been treated, I would be strong enough to deal with the consequences of not holding up my end of the bargain.

Bug left without replying, but returned a short while later with a medic, a man the POWs called Zorba. Zorba squatted down and took my pulse. He turned to Bug, shook his head, and uttered a few words.

"Are you going to take me to the hospital?" I asked.

"No," he replied. "It's too late."

I appealed, "Take me to the hospital and I'll get well."

"It's too late," he repeated.

He and the doctor left my cell, and panic that my death was approaching briefly overtook me.

There were few amputees among the POWs who survived their imprisonment. The Vietnamese usually refused treatment to the seriously injured. I don't know whether they were negligent for purposes of cost efficiency, reasoning that Americans, unused to unsanitary conditions, were likely to develop fatal infections following an amputation, or if they refused us treatment simply because they hated us. Whatever the reason, a lot of men died who shouldn't have, the victims of genuine war crimes.

I lapsed into unconsciousness a few minutes after Bug and Zorba left me to my fate, a condition that blessedly relieved me of the terrible dread I was feeling. I was awakened a short while later when an excited Bug rushed into my cell and shouted, "Your father is a big admiral. Now we take you to the hospital."

God bless my father.

My parents were in London when I was shot down. They were dressing for a dinner party when my father received a telephone call saying that my plane had been shot down over Hanoi. My father informed my mother what had happened. They kept their dinner engagement, never mentioning to any of the other guests the distressing news they had just learned.

When they returned home, my father got a call from his boss, Admiral

Tom Moorer, Chief of Naval Operations. Admiral Moorer was a friend and had decided to break the sad news to my father himself. "Jack, we don't think he survived."

My parents then called Carol, who had already been notified of my shootdown by the Navy. My mother told her to prepare for the worst: that I was dead, and they would have to find a way to accept that. My father, very matter-of-factly, said, "I don't think we have to."

After speaking with Carol, my parents placed calls to my sister and brother to break the bad news to them. Joe was working as a reporter for the *San Diego Tribune* at the time. He knew something was wrong when he answered the phone and both our parents were on the line.

Without any preliminaries, my mother said: "Honey, Johnny's been shot down."

"What happened?"

"He was hit by a missile and went down."

My brother's question hung in the air unanswered for a moment until my father explained: "His wingman saw his plane explode. They don't think he got out."

Joe began to cry, and then asked my father, "What do we do now?" He recalled my father answering in a soft, sad voice, "Pray for him, my boy."

The next day, October 28, Johnny Apple wrote a story that appeared on the front page of the *New York Times:* ADM. MCCAIN'S SON, *FORRESTAL* SURVIVOR, IS MISSING IN RAID.

I was moved by stretcher to a hospital in central Hanoi. As I was being moved, I again lapsed into unconsciousness. I came to a couple of days later and found myself lying in a filthy room, about twenty by twenty feet, lousy with mosquitoes and rats. Every time it rained, an inch of mud and water would pool on the floor. I was given blood and glucose, and several shots. After several more days passed, during which I was frequently unconscious, I began to recover my wits. Other than the transfusion and shots, I received no treatment for my injuries. No one had even bothered to wash the grime off me.

Once my condition had stabilized, my interrogators resumed their work. Demands for military information were accompanied by threats to terminate my medical treatment if I did not cooperate. Eventually, I gave them my ship's name and squadron number, and confirmed that my target had been the power plant. Pressed for more useful information, I gave the names of the Green Bay Packers' offensive line, and said they were members of my squadron. When asked to identify future targets, I simply recited the names of a number of North Vietnamese cities that had already been bombed.

I was occasionally beaten when I declined to give any more information. The beatings were of short duration, because I let out a hair-raising scream whenever they occurred. My interrogators appeared concerned that hospital personnel might object. I also suspected that my treatment was less harsh than might be accorded other prisoners. This I attributed to my father's position, and the propaganda value the Vietnamese placed on possessing me, injured but alive. Later, my suspicion was confirmed when I heard accounts of other POWs' experiences during their first interrogations. They had endured far worse than I had, and had withstood the cruelest torture imaginable.

Although I rarely saw a doctor or a nurse, I did have a constant companion, a teenage boy who was assigned to guard me. He had a book that he read at my bedside every day. In the book was a picture of an old man with a rifle sitting on the fuselage of a downed F-105. He would show me the picture, point to himself, and then slap me. I still could not feed myself, so the boy would spoon-feed me a bowl of noodles with some gristle in it. The gristle was hard to chew. He would jam three of four spoonfuls in my mouth before I could chew and swallow any of it. Unable to force any more into my mouth, he would finish the bowl himself. I got three or four spoonfuls of food twice a day. After a while I really didn't give a damn, although I tried to eat as much as I could before the boy took his share.

After about a week in the hospital, a Vietnamese officer we called Chihuahua informed me that a visiting Frenchman had asked to look in on me, and had volunteered to carry a message back to my family. I was willing to see him, assuming at the time that my family probably believed I was dead.

As I later learned, the Vietnamese, always delighted when a propaganda opportunity presented itself, had already announced my capture, and helpfully supplied quotes from the repentant war criminal commending the Vietnamese people's strong morale and observing that the war was turning against the United States. And in an English-language commentary broadcast over the Voice of Vietnam, entitled "From the Pacific to Truc Bach Lake," Hanoi accused Lyndon Johnson and me of staining my family's honor.

"Adding to the ever longer list of American pilots captured over North Vietnam was a series of newcomers. John Sidney McCain was one of them. Who is he? A U.S. carrier navy lieutenant commander. Last Thursday, 26 October, he took off from the carrier *Oriskany* for a raiding mission against Hanoi City. Unfortunately for him, the jet plane he piloted was one of ten knocked out of Hanoi's sky. He tried in vain to evade the deadly accurate barrage of fire of this city. A surface-to-air missile shot down his jet on the spot. He bailed out and was captured on the surface of Truc Bach Lake right in the heart of the DRV capital. What were the feats of arms which McCain achieved? Foreign correspondents in Hanoi saw with their own eyes civilian dwelling houses destroyed and Hanoi's women, old folks and children killed by steel-pellet bombs dropped from McCain's aircraft and those of his colleagues.

Lt. Com. John Sidney McCain nearly perished in the conflagration that swept the flight deck of the U.S. carrier *Forrestal* last July. He also narrowly escaped death in Haiphong the Sunday before last but this time what must happen has happened. There is no future in it.

McCain was married in 1965 and has a ten-month-old daughter. Surely he also loves his wife and child. Then why did he fly here dropping bombs on the necks of the Vietnamese women and children?

The killing he was ordered to do in Vietnam has aroused indignation among the world's peoples. What glory had he brought by his job to his father, Admiral John S. McCain Jr., commander in chief of U.S. Naval Forces in Europe? His grandfather, Admiral John S. McCain, commander of all aircraft carriers in the Pacific in World War II, participated in a just war against the Japanese forces. But nowadays, Lt. Com. McCain is participating in an unjust war, the most unpopular one in U.S. history and mankind's history, too. This is Johnson's war to enslave the Vietnamese people.

From the Pacific to Truc Bach Lake, McCain has brought no reputation for his family in the United States. The one who is smearing McCain's family honor is also smearing the honor of Washington's United States of America. He is Lyndon B. Johnson."

Prior to the Frenchman's arrival, I was rolled into a treatment room, where a doctor tried to set my broken right arm. For what seemed like an eternity, he manipulated my arm, without benefit of anesthesia, trying to set the three fractures. Blessedly, the pain at its most acute rendered me unconscious. Finally abandoning the effort, he slapped a large and heavy chest cast on me, an act I can hardly credit as considerate on the part of my captors. The cast did not have a cotton lining, and the rough plaster painfully rubbed against my skin. Over time, it wore two holes in the back of my arm down to the bone. My other arm was left untreated.

Exhausted and encased from my waist to my neck in a wet plaster cast, I was rolled into a large, clean room and placed in a nice white bed. The room contained six beds, each protected by a mosquito net. I asked if this was to be my new room, and was told that it was.

A few minutes later, a Vietnamese officer, a Major Nguyen Bai, paid me a visit, accompanied by Chihuahua. He was the commandant of the entire prison system, a dapper, educated man whom the POWs had nicknamed "the Cat." The Cat informed me that the Frenchman who would arrive shortly was a television journalist, and that I should tell him everything I had told my interrogators. Surprised, I told the Cat I didn't want to be filmed.

"You need two operations on your leg, and if you don't talk to him, then we will take your cast off and you won't get any operations," he threatened. "You will say you are grateful to the Vietnamese people, and that you are sorry for your crimes, or we will send you back to the camp."

I assured him that I would say nothing of the kind, but believing that the Cat would send me back to Hoa Lo, and worrying that I could not endure the truck ride back, I agreed to see the Frenchman.

A few minutes later, François Chalais entered the room with two cameramen. He questioned me for several minutes, asking about my shootdown, my squadron, the nature of my injuries, and my father. I repeated the same information about my ship and squadron and told him I was being treated well by the doctors, who had promised to operate on my leg. Off camera, the Cat and Chihuahua were visibly displeased with my answers. Chihuahua demanded that I say more.

"I have no more to say about it," I replied.

Both Vietnamese insisted that I express gratitude for the lenient and humane treatment I had received. I refused, and when they pressed me, Chalais said, "I think what he told me is sufficient."

Chalais then inquired about the quality of the food I was getting, and I responded, "It's not like Paris, but I eat it." Finally, Chalais asked if I had a message for my family.

"I would just like to tell my wife that I'm going to get well. I love her, and hope to see her soon. I'd appreciate it if you'd tell her that. That's all I have to say."

Chihuahua told me to say that I could receive letters and pictures from home. "No," I replied. A visibly agitated Cat demanded that I say on camera how much I wanted the war to end so I could go home. Again, Chalais stepped in to help me, saying very firmly that he was satisfied with my answer, and that the interview was over. I appreciated his help.

Although I had resisted giving my interrogators any useful information and had greatly irritated the Cat by refusing his demands during the interview, I should not have given out information about my ship and squadron, and I regret very much having done so. The information was of no real use to the Vietnamese, but the Code of Conduct for American Prisoners of War orders us to refrain from providing any information beyond our name, rank, and serial number. When Chalais had left, the Cat admonished me for my "bad attitude" and told me I wouldn't receive any more operations. I was taken back to my old room.

Carol went to see Chalais after he returned to Paris, and he gave her a copy of the film, which was shown in the States on the CBS evening news a short time later.

My parents saw it before it was broadcast nationally. A public affairs officer, Herbert Hetu, who worked for my father when my father was the Navy chief in Europe, had a friend who was a producer at CBS. His friend informed him that CBS had the film of my interview, and he offered to screen it for my parents. Hetu and my parents were in New York at the time. My father was scheduled to give a speech on the emerging strength of the Soviet Navy to the prestigious Overseas Press Club. It was an important and much-anticipated speech that he had been preparing for weeks.

Hetu viewed the film and decided not to show it to my father before he delivered his speech, fearing it would "uncork him." Instead, he persuaded his friend at CBS to hold the film until the morning, when my parents could view it. He then contacted my father's personal aide and told him: "After the speech, get with the admiral and tell him about this film. They're going to hold it and we'll take him over to CBS tomorrow. I'm sure he'll want to see it."

Hetu accompanied my parents to CBS the next day. He remembered my father reacting very emotionally to the film. "We took him over with Mrs. McCain, and I think I said to the admiral, 'I think you and Mrs. McCain ought to see this by yourselves. You don't want anybody else in there.' So that's the way they watched it, and it was a very emotional piece of film. . . . I think Admiral McCain and his wife looked at the film twice. His reaction afterward was very emotional, but he never talked to us about it. Some things are just too painful for words."

It was hard not to see how pleased the Vietnamese were to have captured an admiral's son, and I knew that my father's identity was directly related to my survival. Often during my hospital stay I received visits from high-ranking officials. Some observed me for a few minutes and then left without asking any questions. Others would converse idly with me, asking only a few innocuous questions. During one visit, I was told to meet with a visiting Cuban delegation. When I refused, they did not force the issue, either out of concern for my condition or because they were worried about what I might say. One evening, General Vo Nguyen Giap, minister of defense and hero of Dien Bien Phu, paid me a visit. He stared at me wordlessly for a minute, then left.

Bug arrived one day and had me listen to a tape of a POW denouncing America's involvement in the war. The POW was a Marine, a veteran who had flown in the Korean War. The vigor with which he criticized the United States surprised me. His language did not seem stilted, nor did his tone sound forced.

Bug told me he wanted me to make a similar statement. I told him I didn't want to say such things.

He told me I shouldn't be afraid to speak openly about the war, that there was nothing to be ashamed of or to fear.

"I don't feel that way about the war," I replied, and was threatened for what seemed like the hundredth time with a warning that I would be denied an operation because of my "bad attitude."

In early December, they operated on my leg. The Vietnamese filmed the operation. I haven't a clue why. Regrettably, the operation wasn't much of a success. The doctors severed all the ligaments on one side of my knee, which has never fully recovered. After the war, thanks to the work of a kind and talented physical therapist, my knee regained much of its mobility—enough, anyway, for me to return to flight status for a time. But today, when I am tired or when the weather is inclement, my knee stiffens in pain, and I pick up a trace of my old limp.

They decided to discharge me later that December. I had been in the hospital about six weeks. I was in bad shape. I had a high fever and suffered from dysentery. I had lost about fifty pounds and weighed barely a hundred. I was still in my chest cast, and my leg hurt like hell.

On the brighter side, at my request, the Vietnamese were taking me to another prison camp. Bug had entered my room one day and abruptly announced, "The doctors say you are not getting better."

The accusatory tone he used to relay this all too obvious diagnosis implied that I was somehow responsible for my condition and had deliberately tried to embarrass the Vietnamese medical establishment by refusing to recover.

"Put me with other Americans," I responded, "and I'll get better."

Bug said nothing in reply. He just looked at me briefly with the expression he used to convey his disdain for an inferior enemy, then withdrew from the room.

That evening I was blindfolded, placed in the back of a truck, and driven to a truck repair facility that had been converted into a prison a few years earlier. It was situated in what had once been the gardens of the mayor of Hanoi's official residence. The Americans held there called it "the Plantation."

To my great relief, I was placed in a cell in a building we called "the Gun Shed" with two other prisoners, both Air Force majors, George "Bud" Day and Norris Overly. I could have asked for no better companions. There has never been a doubt in my mind that Bud Day and Norris Overly saved my life.

Bud and Norris later told me that their first impression of me, emaciated, bug-eyed, and bright with fever, was of a man at the threshold of death. They thought the Vietnamese expected me to die and had placed me in their care to escape the blame when I failed to recover.

Despite my poor condition, I was overjoyed to be in the company of Americans. I had by this time been a prisoner of war for two months, and I hadn't even caught a glimpse of another American.

I was frail, but voluble. I wouldn't stop talking all through that first day with Bud and Norris, explaining my shootdown, describing my treatment since capture, inquiring about their experiences, and asking for all the details of the prison system and for information about other prisoners.

Bud and Norris accommodated me to the best of their ability, and were the soul of kindness as they eased my way to what they believed was my imminent death. Bud had been seriously injured when he ejected. Like me, he had broken his right arm in three places and had torn the ligaments in his knee—the left knee in his case. After his capture near the DMZ, he had attempted an escape, and had nearly reached an American airfield when he was recaptured. He was brutally tortured for his efforts, and for subsequently resisting his captors' every entreaty for information.

First held in a prison in Vinh before making the 150-mile trip north to Hanoi, Bud had experienced early the full measure of the mistreatment that would be his fate for nearly six years. His captors had looped rope around his shoulders, tightened it until his shoulders were nearly touching, and then hung him by the arms from the rafter of the torture room, tearing his shoulders apart. Left in this condition for hours, Bud never acceded to the Vietnamese demands for military information. They had to refracture his broken right arm and threaten to break the other before Bud gave them anything at all. He was a tough man, a fierce resister, whose example was an inspiration to every man who served with him. For his heroic escape attempt, he received the Medal of Honor, one of only three POWs in Vietnam to receive the nation's highest award.

Because of his injuries, Bud was unable to help with my physical care. Norris shouldered most of the responsibility. A gentle, uncomplaining guy, he cleaned me up, fed me, helped me onto the bucket that served as our toilet, and massaged my leg. Thanks to his tireless ministration, and to the restorative effect Bud and Norris's company had on my morale, I began to recover.

I slept a lot those first weeks, eighteen to twenty hours a day. Little by little, I grew stronger. A little more than a week after I had been consigned to his care, Norris had me on my feet and helped me to stand for a few moments. From then on, I could feel my strength return more rapidly each day. Soon I was able to stand unaided, and even maneuver around my cell on a pair of crutches.

In early January, we were relocated to another end of the camp, a place we called "the Corn Crib." We had neighbors in the cells on either side of ours, and for the first time we managed to establish communications with fellow POWs. Our methods were crude, yelling to each other whenever the turnkeys were absent, and leaving notes written in cigarette ash in a washroom drain. It would be some time before we devised more sophisticated and secure communication methods.

One day a young English-speaking officer escorted a group of older, obviously senior party members into our cell. Their privileged status was evident in the quality of their attire, which, although perhaps not elegant by Western standards, was far better than that worn by most Vietnamese of our acquaintance.

For a few moments after entering, the entire group just stared at me. Finally, the young officer began asking me questions in English, translating my answers for the assembled dignitaries.

"How many corporations does your family own?"

Puzzled by the question, I looked at him for a moment before asking, "What do you mean?"

"How many corporations does your family own? Your father is a big admiral. He must have many companies that work with your government."

Laughing at the absurd premise of the question, I replied, "You've got to be putting me on. My father is a military officer whose income is confined to his military salary."

When my answer had been translated, the crowd of high-ranking officials, all of whom had thrived in a system of government infamously riddled with corruption, smiled and nodded at each other, dismissing my protest as unimaginative propaganda. In their experience, admirals and generals got rich. Surely in a country as wealthy and undisciplined as the United States, military officers used their influence to profit themselves and their families.

Around that time, we began to notice that the Vietnamese were showing us unusual leniency. Our diet improved a little. For a few days we received large bunches of bananas. The Cat would often visit us and inquire about our health and how we were getting along.

No one invested much effort in interrogating us or getting us to make propaganda statements. Once we were instructed to write summaries of our military histories. We invented all the details. Mine contained references to service in Antarctica and as the naval attaché in Oslo, two places, I am sorry to say, I had never visited.

We were suspicious of the Vietnamese's motives, as we doubted that they had begun to take seriously their public commitments to a policy of humane treatment of prisoners. But initially we were at a loss to figure out their purpose.

We weren't in the dark for long. One evening in early February, Norris told us that the Vietnamese were considering releasing him along with two other prisoners. For a couple of weeks, the Vietnamese had regularly interrogated Norris. Unbeknownst to us, they had been quizzing Norris to determine whether he was willing and suitable to be included in their first grant of "amnesty." Bud advised him to reject the offer. The Code of Conduct obliged us to refuse release before those who had been captured earlier had been released.

The next day, Norris was removed from our cell. The day of his release, February 16, I was carried on a stretcher with Bud walking beside me to a room where we were to bid Norris good-bye. A crew was filming the departure ceremony. Bud asked if he had been required to make any propaganda statement or do anything else he might later on regret. Norris said that he had not, and we let the matter drop.

Some of the prisoners were pretty hard on Norris and the other two prisoners for taking early release. Norris had taken very good care of me. He had saved my life. I thought him a good man then, as I do today. I feared he had made a mistake, but I couldn't stand in judgment of him. I thought too well of him, and owed him too much to stand between him and his freedom. I wished him well as he departed, carrying a letter from me to Carol in his pocket.

Solitary

Bud and I remained roommates for about another month. When the Vietnamese observed that I could get around on my crutches, they moved Bud to another cell. In April 1968, Bud was relocated to another prison, and I was moved into another building, the largest cell-block in the camp, "the Warehouse." I cannot adequately describe how sorry I was to part company with my friend and inspiration. Up until then, I don't believe I had ever relied on any other person for emotional and physical support to the extent I had relied on Bud.

Although I could manage to hobble around on my crutches, I was still in poor shape. My arms had not yet healed, and I couldn't pick up or carry anything. I was still suffering from dysentery, a chronic ailment throughout most of my years in prison, and I weighed little more than a hundred pounds. The dysentery caused me considerable discomfort. Food and water would pass immediately through me, and sharp pains in my stomach made sleeping difficult. I was chronically fatigued and generally weak from my inability to retain nourishment. Bud, whose injuries were nearly as debilitating as mine, helped me enormously by building my confidence in my eventual recovery. He joked often about our condition, and got me to laugh about it as well. When other POWs teased us as they observed us hobbling along to the showers, no one laughed harder than Bud.

Bud had an indomitable will to survive with his reputation intact, and he strengthened my will to live. The only sustenance I had in those early days I took from the example of his abiding moral and physical courage. Bud was taken to a prison, "the Zoo," where the conditions and the cruelty of camp authorities made the Plantation seem like a resort. He would suffer terribly there, confronting the full force of man's inhumanity to man. But he was a tough, self-assured, and amazingly determined man, and he bore all his trials with an unshakable faith that he was a better man than his enemies. I was distraught when he left, but better prepared to endure my fate thanks to the months of his unflagging encouragement. I bid good-bye to him warmly, trying not to betray the sadness I felt to see him go. I would remain in solitary confinement for over two years.

It's an awful thing, solitary. It crushes your spirit and weakens your resistance more effectively than any other form of mistreatment. Having no one else to rely on, to share confidences with, to seek counsel from, you begin to doubt your judgment and your courage. But you eventually adjust to solitary, as you can to almost any hardship, by devising various methods to keep your mind off your troubles and greedily grasping any opportunity for human contact.

The first few weeks are the hardest. The onset of despair is immediate, and it is a formidable foe. You have to fight it with any means necessary, all the while trying to bridle the methods you devise to combat loneliness and prevent them from robbing your senses.

I tried to memorize the names of POWs, the names and personal details of guards and interrogators, and the details of my environment. I devised other memory games to keep my faculties sound. For days I tried to remember the names of all the pilots in my squadron and our sister squadron. I also prayed more often and more fervently than I ever had as a free man.

Many prisoners spent their hours exercising their minds by concentrating on an academic discipline or hobby they were proficient in. I knew men who mentally designed buildings and airplanes. I knew others who spent days and weeks working out complicated math formulas. I reconstructed from memory books and movies I had once enjoyed. I tried to compose books and plays of my own, often acting out sequences in the quiet solitude of my cell. Anyone who had observed my amateur theatrics might have challenged the exercise's beneficial effect on my mental stability.

I had to carefully guard against my fantasies becoming so consuming that they took me permanently to a place in my mind from which I might fail to return. On several occasions I became terribly annoyed when a guard entered my cell to take me to the bath or to bring me my food and disrupted some flight of fantasy where the imagined comforts were so attractive that I could not easily bear to be deprived of them. Sadly, I knew of a few men in prison who had grown so content in their imaginary worlds that they preferred solitary confinement and turned down the offer of a roommate. Eventually, they stopped communicating with the rest of us.

For long stretches of every day, I would watch the activities in camp through a crack in my door, grateful to witness any unusual or

amusing moment that broke the usual monotony of prison administration. As I began to settle into my routine, I came to appreciate the
POW adage "The days and hours are very long, but the weeks and
months pass quickly."

Solitary also put me in a pretty surly mood, and I would resist
depression by hollering insults at my guards, resorting to the
belligerence that I had relied on earlier in my life when obliged to
suffer one indignity or another. Resisting, being uncooperative and a
general pain in the ass, proved, as it had in the past, to be a morale
booster for me.

Hypochondria is a malady that commonly afflicts prisoners held
in solitary confinement. A man becomes extremely conscious of his
physical condition and can worry excessively over every ailment that
plagues him. After Bud and I were separated, I struggled to resist
concern bordering on paranoia that my injuries and poor health would
eventually prove mortal.

I received nothing in the way of medical treatment. Three or four
times a year, Zorba, the prison medic, would drop by for a brief visit.
After a quick visual appraisal of my condition he would leave me
with the exhortation to eat more and exercise. That I often could not
keep down the little food allowed me after the guards had taken their
share did not strike Zorba as paradoxical. Nor did Zorba bother to
explain how I might manage to exercise given my disabling injuries
and the narrow confines of my cell. I was routinely refused permission
to spend a few minutes a day out of doors where I might have had the
space necessary to concoct some half-assed exercise regimen.

I did try, despite my challenging circumstances and uncooperative
guards, to build up my strength. In the summer of 1968, I attempted
to do push-ups, but lacked the strength to raise myself once from my
cell floor. I was able to perform a single standing push-up off the wall,
but the experience was so painful that it only served to exacerbate my
concern about my condition.

By late summer in 1969, my dysentery had eased. The strength
I gained from holding down my food enabled me to begin exercising my leg. Whenever possible, I limped around my cell on my stiff
leg, and I was greatly cheered when I noticed the limb slowly
becoming stronger.

My arms were another matter. Over a period of two years, I began
to regain some use of them, but even then exercise occasionally resulted
in my arms' total immobility for a period that could last up to a month.
After I returned to the States, an orthopedic surgeon informed me

that because the fracture in my left arm had not been set, using my arm as much as I had during my imprisonment had worn a new socket in my left shoulder.

In the last two years of my captivity, prisoners were quartered together in large cells. Because of the improvement in our food and living conditions, I was strong enough to perform a rigorous daily exercise routine. Lopsided push-ups and a form of running in place that resembled hopping more than it did running gave my daily workout a comical aspect. But in addition to endlessly amusing my roommates, the routine considerably strengthened both my mental and physical reserves.

Left alone to act as my own physician, I made diagnoses that were occasionally closer to hysterical than practical. Among its many unattractive effects, dysentery often causes rather severe hemorrhoids. When this affliction visited me, I became morose, brooding about its implications for my survival. After some time, it finally occurred to me that I had never heard of a single person whose hemorrhoids had proved fatal. When this latest infirmity disappeared after a couple of months, I made a mental note to stop acting like an old man who stayed in bed all day fussing about his angina.

There is little doubt that solitary confinement causes some mental deterioration in even the most resilient personalities. When in 1970 my period of solitary confinement was finally ended, I was overwhelmed by the compulsion to talk nonstop, face-to-face with my obliging new cellmate. I ran my mouth ceaselessly for four days. My cellmate, John Finely, who had once been held in solitary himself and understood my exuberant reaction to his company, listened intently, frequently nodding his head in assent to my rhetorical points even though he could not possibly have taken in more than a fraction of my rambling dialogue.

I have observed this phenomenon in many other men when they were released from solitary. One of the more amusing spectacles in prison is the sight of two men, both just released from solitary, talking their heads off simultaneously, neither one listening to the other, both absolutely enraptured by the sound of their voices. Most "solos" settled down after spending a few days with a roommate and recovered the strength and confidence of men who were sound in both mind and body.

We had a saying in prison: "Steady strain." The point of the remark was to remind us to keep a close watch on our emotions, not to let them rise and fall with circumstances that were out of our control. We tried hard to avoid seizing on any small change in our treatment as an indication of an approaching change in our fortunes.

We called some POWs "gastro politicians," because their spirits soared every time they found a carrot in their soup. "Look at this. They're fattening us up," they would declare. "We must be going home." And when no omen appeared in the next day's meal, the gastro politician's irrational exuberance of the previous day would disappear, and he would sink into an equally irrational despondency, lamenting, "We're never getting out of here."

Most of the prisoners considered it unhealthy to allow themselves to interpret our circumstances like tea leaf readers divining some secret purpose in the most unremarkable event. Prison was enough of a psychological strain without riding an emotional roller coaster of our own creation. Once you began investing meals or an unexpectedly civil word from a guard with greater meaning than it merited, you might begin to pay attention to the promises or threats of your captors. That was the surest way to lose your resolve or even your mind.

"Steady strain, buddy, steady strain," we cautioned each other whenever we began to take a short view of our lives. It was best to take the long view. We would get home when we got home. There wasn't anything we could do to hasten that day's arrival. Until then we had to manage our hardships as best we could, and hope that when we did get home we would have been a credit to ourselves and to the country.

When you're left alone with your thoughts for years, it's hard not to reflect on how better you could have spent your time as a free man. I had more than a normal share of regrets, but regret for choosing the career that had landed me in this place was not among them.

I regretted I hadn't read more books so I could keep my mind better occupied in solitary. I regretted much of the foolishness that had characterized my youth, seeing in it, at last, its obvious insignificance. I regretted I hadn't worked harder at the Academy, believing that had I done so, I might have been better prepared for the trial I now faced.

My regrets were never so severe that they made me despondent, but I did experience remorse to an extent I had never known in the past, an emotion that helped mature me. I gained the insight, common to many people in life-threatening circumstances, that the trivial pleasures of life and human vanity were transient and insignificant. And I resolved that when I regained my freedom, I would seize opportunities to spend what remained of my life in more important pursuits.

"All that's beautiful drifts away / Like the waters," lament Yeats's old men. Except, I discovered, love and honor. If you valued them, and held them strongly, love and honor would endure undiminished by the passing of time and the most determined assault on your dignity. And to hold on to love and honor I needed to be part of a fraternity. I was not as strong a man as I had once believed myself to be.

Of all the activities I devised to survive solitary confinement with my wits and strength intact, nothing was more beneficial than communicating with other prisoners. It was, simply, a matter of life and death.

Fortunately, the Vietnamese—although they went to extraordinary lengths to prevent it—couldn't stop all communication among prisoners. Through flashed hand signals when we were moved about, tap codes on the wall, notes hidden in washroom drains, and holding our enamel drinking cups up to the wall with our shirts wrapped around them and speaking through them, we were able to communicate with each other. The whole prison system became a complex information network, POWs busily trafficking in details about each other's circumstances and news from home that would arrive with every new addition to our ranks.

The tap code was a simple device. The signal to communicate was the old rhythm "shave and a haircut," and the response, "two bits," was given if the coast was clear. We divided the alphabet into five columns of five letters each. The letter K was dropped. A, F, L, Q, and V were the key letters. Tap once for the five letters in the A column, twice for F, three times for L, and so on. After indicating the column, pause for a beat, then tap one through five times to indicate the right letter. My name would be tapped 3-2,1-3,1-3, 1-1, 2-4, 3-3.

It was an easy system to teach the uninitiated, and new guys would usually be communicating like veterans within a few days. We became so proficient at it that in time we could communicate as efficiently by tapping as we could by speaking through our drinking cups. But I preferred, whenever circumstances allowed, to speak to my neighbors. The sound of the human voice, unappreciated in an open society's noisy clutter of spoken words, was an emblem of humanity to a man held at length in solitary confinement, an elegant and poignant affirmation that we possessed a divine spark that our enemies could not extinguish.

The punishment for communicating could be severe, and a few POWs, having been caught and beaten for their efforts, had their spirits broken as their bodies were battered. Terrified of a return trip to the punishment room, they would lie still in their cells when their com-

rades tried to tap them up on the wall. Very few would remain uncom-
municative for long. To suffer all this alone was less tolerable than
torture. Withdrawing in silence from the fellowship of other Americans
and the doggedly preserved cohesion of an American military unit
was to us the approach of death. Almost all would recover their
strength in a few days and answer the summons to rejoin the living.

In October 1968, I heard the guards bring a new prisoner into the
camp and lock him into the cell behind mine. Ernie Brace was a
decorated former Marine who had flown over a hundred combat
missions in the Korean War. He had been accused of deserting the
scene of an aircraft accident, court-martialed, and discharged
dishonorably from the service. Determined to restore his good name,
he had volunteered as a civilian pilot to fly supply missions in Laos
for the United States Agency for International Development, and,
when asked, to secretly supply CIA-supported military units in the
Laotian jungle.

During one such operation, Communist insurgents, the Pathet Lao,
overran the small airstrip where he had just landed and captured him.
His captors handed him over to soldiers in the North Vietnamese
Army, who marched him to a remote outpost near Dien Bien Phu. He
was imprisoned for three years in a bamboo cage with his arms and
legs bound. He attempted three escapes. He was brutally tortured,
held in leg stocks, and tethered to a stake by a rope around his neck.
After his last failed escape attempt, the Vietnamese buried him in a
pit up to his neck and left him there for a week.

In 1968, he was brought to Hanoi. Uncertain whether the United
States government was aware he had been captured alive, he was
greatly relieved to realize that he was now in the company of American
POWs whose captivity was known to our government.

When the commotion in the cell behind me died down as the
guards left Ernie alone in his new home, I tried to tap him up on the
wall. In terrible shape, and fearful that the knocks he heard in the cell
next door were made by Vietnamese trying to entrap him in an
attempted violation of the prohibition against communicating, he
made no response. For days I tried in vain to talk to him.

Finally, he tapped back, a faint but audible "two bits." I put my
drinking cup to the wall and spoke directly to my new neighbor.

"Do you have a drinking cup?"

No response.

"Tap twice if you have a drinking cup and once if you don't."

No response.

"I'm talking through my cup. Do you have a drinking cup? If you have a cup, wrap your shirt around it, hold it up to the wall, and talk to me."

No response.

"You want to communicate, don't you?"

No response.

I continued at some length, vainly trying to get him to talk to me. But as he had just been given a drinking cup, his suspicion that he was being set up by the Vietnamese intensified as I urged him to make illicit use of it.

A few days later, the possibility that he could talk with another American for the first time in three years overrode his understandable caution. When I asked him if he had a cup, he tapped twice for yes.

"I'm Lieutenant Commander John McCain. I was shot down over Hanoi in 1967. Who are you?"

"My name is Ernie Brace," came the response.

"Are you Air Force? Navy? Marine?"

"My name is Ernie Brace."

"Where were you shot down?"

"My name is Ernie Brace."

To my every query, Ernie could only manage to say his name before he broke down. I could hear him crying. After his long, awful years in the jungle, the sound of an American voice, carrying with it the promise of fraternity with men who would share his struggle, had overwhelmed him.

It took some time before Ernie could keep his composure long enough to engage in informative conversation. But once he did, he became a tireless talker, hungry for all information about his new circumstances and eager to provide me with all the details of his capture and captivity.

I was somewhat surprised to learn he was a civilian. I assumed he was CIA, but refrained from asking him. As a civilian, Ernie was under no obligation to adhere to the Code of Conduct. The United States expected him not to betray any highly sensitive information, the disclosure of which would endanger the lives of other Americans. But other than that, he was not required to show any fidelity to his country and her cause beyond the demands of his own conscience. But Ernie's conscience demanded much from him. He kept our code faithfully. When the Vietnamese offered to release him, he declined, insisting that others captured before him be released first. No one I knew in prison, Army, Navy, Marine, or Air Force officer, had greater loyalty to his country or derived more courage from his sense of honor. It was an honor to serve with him.

Incongruous though it must seem, early on, POWs could be better informed about the circumstances of other prisons and the men held there than we were about the population of our own camp. Many cells at the Plantation were uninhabited when I first came there, and we had a hard time establishing a camp-wide communications network. Some prisoners were located in other buildings or in cells some distance away and separated by empty rooms from mine. Most of our senior officers at the Plantation were kept in isolated cells. They were out of reach of our tapping, and we did not walk by their cells when we were taken to the washroom and the interrogation room.

New arrivals who had been placed in cells within my communications bloc brought us information about the men held at Hoa Lo, the Zoo, and other prisons in and around Hanoi. But we often puzzled over the identity of men held a short distance from us in different parts of the camp. A tough resister, Ted Guy, an Air Force colonel, was living in a different building. Unable to communicate with him, the men in my block assumed for several months that the senior officer nearest to us, Dick Stratton, a Navy commander, was the senior ranking officer for the whole camp. Ernie Brace informed us of our error. He had learned about Colonel Guy's presence in our ranks in a conversation with another POW.

There were about eighty Americans held at the Plantation during my first years in prison. Eventually I would come to know many of the men at the Plantation. Keeping an ever-lengthening account of the men we learned were prisoners was the solemn responsibility of every POW. We would fall asleep at night while silently chanting the names on the list. Knowing the men in my prison and being known by them was my best assurance of returning home. Communicating not only affirmed our humanity. It kept us alive.

1970
EXPLOSION ON APOLLO 13

Manned exploration of space is a dangerous business conducted at the extreme limits of human ingenuity and technology. Over the past four decades, more than four hundred individuals have ventured into space, and eighteen have perished there. The first tragedy of America's space program occurred on the ground, not in the sky. During a test countdown of the first manned Apollo mission on January 27, 1967 a fire flared in the oxygen-rich Command Module and quickly incinerated the three astronauts trapped inside. This tragedy, and the shattering loss of the shuttles *Challenger* and *Columbia* and their crews, have reminded us that spaceflight is anything but routine, and has reaffirmed our grateful admiration of those who face its dangers with willing courage. Just as the Apollo program was not halted with the loss of the crew of its first manned mission, the two remaining space shuttles —the *Atlantis* and the *Discovery*—will again venture into outer space, and new programs of exploration and discovery will be launched in the years to come, as man continues to reach to the stars.

After the tragic Apollo fire, three unmanned Apollo test flights were successfully conducted before manned missions were resumed with *Apollo 7* (October 1968) whose three-man crew tested the Command Module (CM) while orbiting the earth 163 times, *Apollo 8* (December 1968) which successfully orbited the moon ten times, and *Apollo 9* (March 1969) which tested the Lunar Module (LM) in earth orbit. During the mission of *Apollo 10* (May 1969) two astronauts transferred to the LM and descended to an orbit 14,300 meters above the surface of the moon. Launched two months later, *Apollo 11* reached the moon with astronauts Neil Armstrong, Edwin E. "Buzz" Aldrin, and Michael Collins. Armstrong and Aldrin landed on the lunar surface at 8:17 P.M. GMT on July 20, 1969 and remained there for twenty-one hours and thirty-six minutes before returning to the CM for the journey back to earth. The following November *Apollo 12* seconded this historic success with its own lunar landing and safe return.

The third in a continuing series of manned voyages to the surface of the moon, *Apollo 13* lifted from pad 39A at the Kennedy Space Center on April 11, 1970. Under the command of the exceptionally experienced and capable NASA astronaut James A. Lovell, Jr., with John L. Swigert, Jr. as pilot of the CM *Odyssey* and Fred W. Haise, Jr., the LM *Aquarius* pilot, the mission of *Apollo 13* is a study in success—and survival— coolly and skillfully engineered out of catastrophic failure. Two hundred thousand miles from earth, their flight path adjusted to attain lunar orbit, *Apollo 13* was experiencing a nearly flawless mission. A few minutes after the crew had concluded an *"Odyssey* to Earth" television broadcast, CM pilot Jack Swigert switched on the fans to stir oxygen tanks numbers 1 and 2 in the Command Service Module (CSM). During preflight procedures wires inside troublesome oxygen tank number 2 had overheated with resulting damage to their Teflon insulation. These wires shorted, igniting a fire inside the tank, raising tank pressure and causing the tank to explode seconds later. A sharp bang and a vibration were immediately noticed inside the Command Module where indicators blinked alarms that were also noted at Mission Control in Houston. As the minutes passed the gravity of the situation became apparent. The explosion had also damaged oxygen tank number 1 and gutted a large section of the CSM. Threatened with the loss of all oxygen stores, the CSM propulsion system, and vital supplies of water and electrical power, the crew was forced to power down the CM *Odyssey* and transfer to the LM which was to be their "lifeboat" for the long and uncertain journey around the moon and back to the outer atmosphere of the earth.

Not long after the crew's return to the safety of earth, James A. Lovell composed the succinct account of disaster and the subsequent struggle for survival that is presented here. Working closely with Mission Control, the three *Apollo 13* astronauts resolved a cascading series of problems that had never been anticipated and whose solutions had never been modeled. Adapting to the unforeseeable exigencies of the life-or-death situation, they successfully managed severely constrained life-support resources, and resolved delicate and fateful issues of navigation in a spirit of discipline and responsibility, self-confidence and teamwork, resilience, and even tough humor, that are all signature values of the men and women of America's space program. Lovell's account certainly reflects all of these values that proved essential to the survival of the crew of *Apollo 13,* whose mission—much more than a "successful failure"—remains a point of high honor in humanity's continuing quest for a bright future. After the so nearly fatal voyage of *Apollo 13,* the astronauts of *Apollo* missions 14, 15, 16, and 17 successfully landed men on the moon.

"Houston, we've had a problem."

by James A. Lovell

Since Apollo 13 many people have asked me, "Did you have suicide pills on board?" We didn't, and I never heard of such a thing in the eleven years I spent as an astronaut and NASA executive.

I did, of course, occasionally think of the possibility that the spacecraft explosion might maroon us in an enormous orbit about the Earth—a sort of perpetual monument to the space program. But Jack Swigert, Fred Haise, and I never talked about that fate during our perilous flight. I guess we were too busy struggling for survival.

Survive we did, but it was close. Our mission was a failure but I like to think it was a successful failure.

Apollo 13, scheduled to be the third lunar landing, was launched at 1313 Houston time on Saturday, April 11, 1970; I had never felt more confident. On my three previous missions, I had already logged 572 hours in space, beginning with Gemini 7, when Frank Borman and I stayed up 14 days—a record not equaled until Skylab.

Looking back, I realize I should have been alerted by several omens that occurred in the final stages of the Apollo 13 preparation. First, our command module pilot, Ken Mattingly, with whom Haise and I had trained for nearly two years, turned out to have no immunity to German measles (a minor disease the backup LM pilot, Charlie Duke, had inadvertently exposed us to). I argued to keep Ken, who was one of the most conscientious, hardest working of all the astronauts. In my argument to Dr. Paine, the NASA Administrator, I said, "Measles aren't that bad, and if Ken came down with them, it would be on the way home, which is a quiet part of the mission. From my experience as command module pilot on Apollo 8, I know Fred and I could bring the spacecraft home alone if we had to." "Besides," I said, "Ken doesn't have the measles now, and he may never get them." (Five years later, he still hadn't.)

Dr. Paine said no; the risk was too great. So I said in that case we'd be happy to accept Jack Swigert, the backup CMP, a good man (as indeed he proved to be, though he had only two days of prime-crew training).

The second omen came in ground tests before launch, which indicated the possibility of a poorly insulated supercritical helium tank in the LM's descent stage. So we modified the flight plan to enter the LM three hours early, in order to obtain an onboard readout of helium tank pressure. This proved to be lucky for us because it gave us a chance to shake down this odd-shaped spacecraft that was to hold our destiny in its spidery hands. It also meant the LM controllers were in Mission Control when they would be needed most.

Then there was the No.2 oxygen tank, serial number 10024X-TA0009. This tank had been installed in the service module of Apollo 10, but was removed for modification (and was damaged in the process of removal). I have to congratulate Tom Stafford, John Young, and Gene Cernan, the lucky dogs, for getting rid of it.

This tank was fixed, tested at the factory, installed in our service module, and tested again during the Countdown Demonstration Test at the Kennedy Space Center beginning March 16, 1970. The tanks normally are emptied to about half full, and No.1 behaved all right. But No.2 dropped to only 92 percent of capacity. Gaseous oxygen at 80 psi was applied through the vent line to expel the liquid oxygen, but to no avail. An interim discrepancy report was written, and on March 27, two weeks before launch, detanking operations were resumed. No.1 again emptied normally, but its idiot twin did not. After a conference with the contractor and NASA personnel, the test director decided to "boil off" the remaining oxygen in No.2 by using the electrical heater within the tank. The technique worked, but it took eight hours of 65-volt DC power from the ground-support equipment to dissipate the oxygen.

With the wisdom of hindsight, I should have said, "Hold it. Wait a second. I'm riding on this spacecraft. Just go out and replace that tank." But the truth is, I went along, and I must share the responsibility with many, many others for the $375 million failure of Apollo 13. On just about every space flight we have had some sort of failure, but in this case, it was an accumulation of human errors and technical anomalies that doomed Apollo 13.

At five and a half minutes after liftoff, Swigert, Haise, and I felt a little vibration. Then the center engine of the S-II stage shut down two minutes early. This caused the remaining four engines to burn 34 seconds longer than planned, and the S-IVB third stage had to burn nine seconds longer to put us in orbit. No problem: the S-IVB had plenty of fuel.

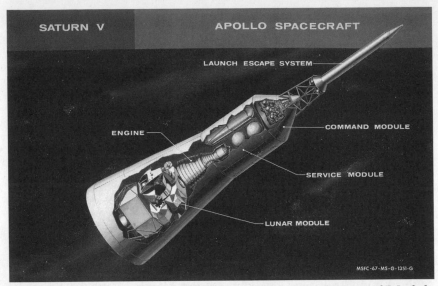

LAUNCH ESCAPE SYSTEM

COMMAND MODULE

ENGINE

SERVICE MODULE

LUNAR MODULE

MSFC-67-MS-G-1351-G

This cutaway illustration of the Saturn V shows the Command Module (CM) atop the Service Module (SM) and the Lunar Module (LM) within its adapter. The CM was crammed with some of the most complex equipment ever sent into space at the time. The three astronaut couches were surrounded by instrument panels, navigation gear, radios, life-support systems, and small engines to keep it stable during reentry. The entire cone, 11 feet long and 13 feet in diameter, was protected by a charring heat shield. The 6.5 ton CM was all that was finally left of the 3,000-ton Saturn V vehicle that lifted off on the journey to the Moon.

The severely damaged Service Module after final separation from the Command Module prior to re-entry.

Artwork courtesy of NASA.

The first two days we ran into a couple of minor surprises, but generally Apollo 13 was looking like the smoothest flight of the program. At 46 hours 43 minutes Joe Kerwin, the CapCom on duty, said, "The spacecraft is in real good shape as far as we are concerned. We're bored to tears down here." It was the last time anyone would mention boredom for a long time.

At 55 hours 46 minutes, as we finished a 49-minute TV broadcast showing how comfortably we lived and worked in weightlessness, I pronounced the benediction: "This is the crew of Apollo 13 wishing everybody there a nice evening, and we're just about ready to close out our inspection of Aquarius (the LM) and get back for a pleasant evening in Odyssey (the CM). Good night."

On the tapes I sound mellow and benign, or some might say fat, dumb, and happy. A pleasant evening, indeed! Nine minutes later the roof fell in; rather, oxygen tank No. 2 blew up, causing No. 1 tank also to fail. We came to the slow conclusion that our normal supply of electricity, light, and water was lost, and we were about 200,000 miles from Earth. We did not even have power to gimbal the engine so we could begin an immediate return to Earth.

The message came in the form of a sharp bang and vibration. Jack Swigert saw a warning light that accompanied the bang, and said, "Houston, we've had a problem here." I came on and told the ground that it was a main B bus undervolt. The time was 2108 hours on April 13.

Next, the warning lights told us we had lost two of our three fuel cells, which were our prime source of electricity. Our first thoughts were ones of disappointment, since mission rules forbade a lunar landing with only one fuel cell.

With warning lights blinking on, I checked our situation; the quantity and pressure gauges for the two oxygen tanks gave me cause for concern. One tank appeared to be completely empty, and there were indications that the oxygen in the second tank was rapidly being depleted. Were these just instrument malfunctions? I was soon to find out.

Thirteen minutes after the explosion, I happened to look out of the left-hand window, and saw the final evidence pointing toward potential catastrophe. "We are venting something out into the—into space," I reported to Houston. Jack Lousma, the CapCom replied, "Roger, we copy you venting." I said, "It's a gas of some sort."

It was a gas—oxygen—escaping at a high rate from our second, and last, oxygen tank. I am told that some amateur astronomers on top of a building in Houston could actually see the expanding sphere of gas around the spacecraft.

Arranging for Survival

The knot tightened in my stomach, and all regrets about not landing on the Moon vanished. Now it was strictly a case of survival. The first thing we did, even before we discovered the oxygen leak, was to try to close the hatch between the CM and the LM. We reacted spontaneously, like submarine crews, closing the hatches to limit the amount of flooding. First Jack and then I tried to lock the reluctant hatch, but the stubborn lid wouldn't stay shut! Exasperated, and realizing that we didn't have a cabin leak, we strapped the hatch to the CM couch. In retrospect, it was a good thing that we kept the tunnel open, because Fred and I would soon have to make a quick trip to the LM in our fight for survival. It is interesting to note that days later, just before we jettisoned the LM, when the hatch had to be closed and locked, Jack did it—easy as pie. That's the kind of flight it was.

The pressure in the No. 1 oxygen tank continued to drift downward, passing 300 psi, now heading toward 200 psi. Months later, after the accident investigation was complete, it was determined that, when No. 2 tank blew up, it either ruptured a line on the No. 1 tank, or caused one of the valves to leak. When the pressure reached 200 psi, it was obvious that we were going to lose all oxygen, which meant that the last fuel cell would also die. At 1 hour and 29 seconds after the bang, Jack Lousma, then CapCom, said after instructions from Flight Director Glynn Lunney: "It is slowly going to zero, and we are starting to think about the LM lifeboat." Swigert replied, "That's what we have been thinking about too."

A lot has been written about using the LM as a lifeboat after the CM has become disabled. There are documents to prove that the lifeboat theory was discussed just before the Lunar Orbit Rendezvous mode was chosen in 1962. Other references go back to 1963, but by 1964 a study at the Manned Spacecraft Center concluded: "The LM [as lifeboat] . . . was finally dropped, because no single reasonable CSM failure could be identified that would prohibit use of the SPS." Naturally, I'm glad that view didn't prevail, and I'm thankful that by the time of Apollo 10, the first lunar mission carrying the LM, the LM as a lifeboat was again being discussed. Fred Haise, fortunately, held the reputation as the top astronaut expert on the LM—after spending fourteen months at the Grumman plant on Long Island, where the LM was built. Fred says: "I never heard of the LM being used in the sense that we used it. We had procedures, and we had trained to use it as a backup propulsion device, the rationale being that the thing we were really covering was the failure of the command module's main engine, the SPS engine. In that case, we would have used combinations of the LM descent engine, and in some cases, for some lunar aborts, the ascent engine as well. But we never really thought and planned, and obviously, we didn't have the procedures to cover a case where the command module would end up fully powered down."

To get Apollo 13 home would require a lot of innovation. Most of the material written about our mission describes the ground-based activities, and I certainly agree that without the splendid people in Mission Control, and their backups, we'd still be up there.

They faced a formidable task. Completely new procedures had to be written and tested in the simulator before being passed up to us. The navigation problem was also theirs: essentially how, when, and in what attitude to burn the LM descent engine to provide a quick return home. They were always aware of our safety, as exemplified by the jury-rig fix of our environmental system to reduce the carbon dioxide level.

However, I would be remiss not to state that it really was the teamwork between the ground and flight crew that resulted in a successful return. I was blessed with two shipmates who were very knowledgeable about their spacecraft systems. And the disabled service module forced me to relearn quickly how to control spacecraft attitude from the LM, a task that became more difficult when we turned off the attitude indicator.

Fifteen Minutes of Power Left
With only 15 minutes of power left in the CM, CapCom told us to make our way into the LM. Fred and I quickly floated through the tunnel, leaving Jack to perform the last chores in our forlorn and pitiful CM that had seemed such a happy home less than two hours earlier. Fred said something that strikes me as funny as I read it now: "Didn't think I'd be back so soon." But nothing seemed funny in real time on that 13th of April 1970.

There were many, many things to do. In the first place, did we have enough consumables to get home? Fred started calculating, keeping in mind that the LM was built for only a 45-hour lifetime, and we had to stretch that to 90. He had some data from previous LMs in his book—average rates of water usage related to amperage level, rate of water needed for cooling. It turned out that we had enough oxygen. The full LM descent tank alone would suffice, and in addition, there were two ascent-engine oxygen tanks, and two backpacks whose oxygen supply would never be used on the lunar surface. Two emergency bottles on top of those packs had six or seven pounds each in them. (At LM jettison, just before reentry, 28.5 pounds of oxygen remained, more than half of what we started with.)

We had 2181 ampere-hours in the LM batteries. We thought that was enough if we turned off every electrical power device not absolutely necessary. We could not count on the precious CM batteries, because they would be needed for reentry after the LM was cast off. In fact, the ground carefully worked out a procedure where we charged the CM batteries with LM power. As it turned out, we reduced our energy consumption to a fifth of normal, which resulted in our having 20 percent of our LM electrical power left when we jettisoned Aquarius. We did have one electrical heart-stopper during the mission. One of the CM batteries vented with such force that it momentarily dropped off the line. We knew we were finished if we permanently lost that battery.

Water was the real problem. Fred figured that we would run out of water about five hours before we got back to Earth, which was calculated at around 151 hours. But even there, Fred had an ace in the hole. He knew we had a data point from Apollo 11, which had not sent its LM ascent stage crashing into the Moon, as subsequent missions did. An engineering test on the vehicle showed that its mechanisms could survive seven or eight hours in space without water-cooling, until the guidance system rebelled at this enforced toasting. But we did conserve water. We cut down to six ounces each per day, a fifth of normal intake, and used fruit juices; we ate hot dogs and other wet-pack foods when we ate at all. (We lost hot water with the accident and dehydratable food is not palatable with cold water.) Somehow, one doesn't get very thirsty in space and we became quite dehydrated. I set one record that stood up throughout Apollo: I lost fourteen pounds, and our crew set another by losing a total of 31.5 pounds, nearly 50 percent more than any other crew. Those stringent measures resulted in our finishing with 28.2 pounds of water, about 9 percent of the total.

Fred had figured that we had enough lithium hydroxide canisters, which remove carbon dioxide from the spacecraft. There were four cartridges from the LM, and four from the backpacks, counting backups. But he forgot that there would be three of us in the LM instead of the normal two. The LM was designed to support two men for two days. Now it was being asked to care for three men nearly four days.

A Square Peg in a Round Hole
We would have died of the exhaust from our own lungs if Mission

Control hadn't come up with a marvelous fix. The trouble was the square lithium hydroxide canisters from the CM would not fit the round openings of those in the LM environmental system. After a day and a half in the LM a warning light showed us that the carbon dioxide had built up to a dangerous level, but the ground was ready. They had thought up a way to attach a CM canister to the LM system by using plastic bags, cardboard, and tape—all materials we had on board. Jack and I put it together: just like building a model airplane. The contraption wasn't very handsome, but it worked. It was a great improvisation—and a fine example of cooperation between ground and space.

The big question was, "How do we get back safely to Earth?" The LM navigation system wasn't designed to help us in this situation. Before the explosion, at 30 hours and 40 minutes, we had made the normal midcourse correction, which would take us out of a free-return-to-Earth trajectory and put us on our lunar landing course. Now we had to get back on that free-return course. The ground-computed 35-second burn, by an engine designed to land us on the Moon, accomplished that objective 5 hours after the explosion.

As we approached the Moon, the ground informed us that we would have to use the LM descent engine a second time; this time a long 5-minute burn to speed up our return home. The maneuver was to take place 2 hours after rounding the far side of the Moon, and I was busy running down the procedures we were to use. Suddenly, I noticed that Swigert and Haise had their cameras out and were busy photographing the lunar surface. I looked at them incredulously and said, "If we don't make this next maneuver correctly, you won't get your pictures developed!" They said, "Well, you've been here before and we haven't." Actually, some of the pictures these tourists took turned out to be very useful.

It was about this time that I said, "Boys, take a good look at the Moon. It's going to be a long time before anybody gets up here again." Later on I was accused of sabotaging Apollo; poor Dr. Paine had to explain that I didn't really mean it, and the space program would go on. The Senate Space Committee asked me about it a week after we got back. Actually, I didn't mean that remark to be public. (I later learned that, unknown to us, we had had a hot mike for about 45 minutes.) Nonetheless, it was 9 months before Apollo 14 was launched.

We had many crises on Apollo 13, but the biggest heart-stopper has hardly been noticed, partly because the transcription released to the press was garbled, and partly because there wasn't much point in talking about a crisis that had been averted earlier. It occurred prior to the second maneuver I mentioned earlier; we called it P.C.+2 (pericynthian 2 hours).

We had transferred the CM platform alignment to the LM, but we had to make sure that this alignment was accurate before we made the long P.C. + 2 burn. Ordinarily it is simple to look through the sextant device, called the Alignment Optical Telescope, find a suitable navigation star, and with the help of our computer verify the guidance platform's alignment. But traveling with us was a swarm of debris from the ruptured service module. The sunlight glinting on these bits of junk—I called them false stars—made it impossible to sight a real star.

So what to do? If we couldn't verify the accuracy of the alignment, we didn't have a way to make an accurate burn, or to align the CM platform for reentry. In other words, the ground would have no accurate way to tell us the correct attitude to make the proper maneuvers to return home.

A genius in Mission Control came up with the idea of using the Sun to check the accuracy of our alignment. No amount of debris could blot out that star! Its large diameter could result in considerable error, but nobody had a better plan.

I rotated the spacecraft to the attitude Houston had requested. If our alignment was accurate, the Sun would be centered in the sextant.

When I looked through the AOT, the Sun just had to be there. It really had to be. And it was. At 73:46 hours the air-to-ground transcript sounds like a song from "My Fair Lady":

Lovell: O.K. We got it. I think we got it. What diameter was it?

Haise: Yes. It's coming back in. Just a second.

Lovell: Yes, yaw's coming back in. Just about it.

Haise: Yaw is in ...

Lovell: What have you got?

Haise: Upper right corner of the Sun ...

Lovell: We've got it!

If we raised our voices, I submit it was justified.

I'm told the cheer of the year went up in Mission Control. Flight Director Gerald Griffin, a man not easily shaken, recalls: "Some years later I went back to the log and looked up that mission. My writing was almost illegible I was so damned nervous. And I remember the exhilaration running through me: My God, that's the last hurdle—if we can do that, I know we can make it. It was funny, because only the people involved knew how important it was to have that platform properly aligned." Yet Gerry Griffin barely mentioned the alignment in his change-of-shift briefing—"That check turned out real well" is all he said an hour after his penmanship failed him Neither did we, as crew members, refer to it as a crisis in our press conference nor in later articles.

The alignment with the Sun proved to be less than a half a degree off. Hallelujah. Now we knew we could do the 5-minute P.C. + 2 burn with assurance, and that would cut the total time of our voyage to about 142 hours. We weren't exactly home free: we had a dead service module, a command module with no power, and a lunar module that was a wonderful vehicle to travel home in, but unfortunately didn't have a heat shield required to enter the Earth's atmosphere. But all we needed now was a continuation of the expertise we seemed blessed with, plus a little luck.

Tired, Hungry, Wet, Cold, Dehydrated

The ground, anxious not to disturb our homeward trajectory, told us not to dump any waste material overboard. What to do with urine taxed our ingenuity. There were three bags in the command module; we found six little ones in the LM, then we connected a PLSS condensate tank to a long hose and finally we used two large bags designed to drain remaining water out of the PLSS's after the first lunar EVA. I'm glad we got home when we did, because we were just about out of ideas for stowage.

A most remarkable achievement of Mission Control was quickly developing procedures for powering up the CM after its long cold sleep. They wrote the documents for this innovation in three days, instead of the usual three months. We found the CM a cold, clammy tin can when we started to power up. The walls, ceiling, floor, wire harnesses, and panels were all covered with droplets of water. We suspected conditions were the same behind the panels. The chances of short circuits caused us apprehension, to say the least. But thanks to the safeguards built into the command module after the disastrous fire in January 1967, no arcing took place. The droplets furnished one sensation as we decelerated in the atmosphere: it rained inside the CM.

Four hours before landing, we shed the service module; Mission Control had insisted on retaining it until then because everyone feared what the cold of space might do to the unsheltered CM heat shield. I'm glad we weren't able to see the SM earlier. With one whole panel missing, and wreckage hanging out, it was a sorry mess as it drifted away.

Three hours later we parted with faithful Aquarius, rather rudely, because we blasted it loose with pressure in the tunnel in order to make sure it completely cleared. Then we splashed down gently in the Pacific Ocean near Samoa, a beautiful landing in a blue-ink ocean on a lovely, lovely planet.

Nobody believes me, but during this six-day odyssey we had no idea what an impression Apollo 13 made on the people of Earth. We never dreamed a billion people were following us on television and radio, and reading about us in banner headlines of every newspaper published. We still missed the point on board the carrier *Iwo Jima*, which picked us up, because the sailors had been as remote from the media as we were. Only when we reached Honolulu did we comprehend our impact: where we found President Nixon and Dr. Paine to meet us, along with my wife Marilyn, Fred's wife Mary (who being pregnant, also had a doctor along just in case), and bachelor Jack's parents, in lieu of his usual airline stewardesses.

In case you are wondering about the cause of it all, I refer you to the report of the Apollo 13 Review Board, issued after an intensive investigation. In 1965 the CM had undergone many improvements, which included raising the permissible voltage to the heaters in the oxygen tanks from 28 to 65 volts DC. Unfortunately, the thermostatic switches on these heaters weren't modified to suit the change. During one final test on the launch pad, the heaters were on for a long period of time. "This subjected the wiring in the vicinity of the heaters to very high temperatures (1000°F), which have been subsequently shown to severely degrade Teflon insulation . . . the thermostatic switches started to open while powered by 65 volts DC and were probably welded shut." Furthermore, other warning signs during testing went unheeded and the tank, damaged from 8 hours overheating, was a potential bomb the next time it was filled with oxygen. That bomb exploded on April 13, 1970—200,000 miles from Earth.

1972
SURVIVE THE SAVAGE SEA

If these poor bloody seamen couldn't rescue us, then we would have to make it on our own and to hell with them. We would survive without them, yes, and that was the word from now on, "survival," not "rescue," or "help," or dependence of any kind, just survival. I felt the strength flooding through me, lifting me from the depression of disappointment to a state of almost cheerful abandon. I felt the bitter aggression of the predator fill my mind. This was not our environment and the beasts around us would eat us if we failed. We would carve a place for ourselves amongst them; they had millions of years of adaptation on their side, but we had brains and some tools. We would live for three months or six months from the sea if necessary, but "We would get these boys to land" as Lyn had said and we would do it ourselves if there was no other way. From that instant on, I became a savage.

– Dougal Robertson, *Survive the Savage Sea*

In the autumn of 1970 Scottish-born Dougal Robertson and his wife Lyn were in the fifteenth year of their pursuit of an idyllic country life on a modest English dairy farm, where they were raising a fine family of four spirited children: nine-year-old twin boys Neil and Sandy, fifteen-year-old Douglas, and sixteen-year-old Anne. Twenty-one months later Dougal and Lyn Robertson, with their sons and a bright twenty-two-year-old Welshman named Robin Williams, were stranded on an inflatable life raft in the midst of the Pacific Ocean, in tow behind a tiny dinghy. With almost no food and water and almost no equipment, the six castaways survived thirty-eight days on the open ocean before a Japanese tuna boat picked them up within days reach of the coast of Central America.

It all began in the course of a playful early autumn Sunday of family togetherness, and a brief respite from the unrelenting labor of the farm, with the Robertson family gathered for tea in the parents' farmhouse bedroom. After touching on a variety of topics, the family conversation focused on the Round the World yacht race as Dougal explained the exhilaration and rigors of life at sea to his intently listening wife and children. Suddenly young Neil burst forth with a lighthearted question, "Daddy's a sailor, why can't we go round the world?" To which Lyn replied, "What a lovely idea! Let's buy a boat and sail around the world!" This was a radical departure from the rural life in which the forty-six-year-old Dougal and his wife had invested so much effort, but it struck a deep chord within them. Dougal had served for twelve years in Britain's Merchant Marine and had earned a Foreign Going Master Mariner's Certificate. He and Lyn had sailed together in the waters off Hong Kong before taking up life on the farm. Toughened by the labor of rural life and experienced in its practical arts, the Robertson family was certainly fit to adapt to the challenges of a life at sea, and Lyn's extensive experience as a State Registered Nurse added reassuring skills to the mix. Most importantly, the parents decided, the experience of circumnavigating the globe would immeasurably broaden the horizons of their children.

In the weeks that followed Dougal and Lyn sold their farm and livestock, and purchased the forty-three-foot, nineteen-ton *Lucette* in Malta, where they had the fifty-year-old schooner carefully surveyed and thoroughly refitted before sailing it to Falmouth, England through the stormy November waters of the Bay of Biscay. The Robertsons laid over in Falmouth for two months to accustom the family to life aboard *Lucette* and to make additional repairs, replacing the schooner's Biscay storm-shattered boom, freshening her caulking, and re-stitching her sails. Setting out into Northerly winds in late January of 1971, the family met their first test at sea only six days later when Dougal and young Douglas steered the *Lucette* to safety through a sixty-mile-per-hour gale in the treacherously churning waters off the Cape Finisterre coast of Northwest Spain. After a brief respite in Lisbon, the Robertsons made a fair-weather passage to the Canary Islands, took on fresh stores, and sailed forth across the stormy Atlantic Ocean to the Windward Islands of the Caribbean. Now all experienced mariners, they passed month after pleasant month sailing from one beautiful island to the next and then to the Bahamas before taking refuge in Miami during the hurricane season.

It was while they were laid over in Miami that the Robertsons purchased the nine-foot fibreglass dinghy that only months later would be their lifeboat. With the dinghy *Ednamair* securely positioned on *Lucette's* deck, the Robertsons set out again in February of 1972—this time without their daughter Anne, who had decided to remain behind in Nassau. They sailed to Jamaica, where they celebrated Douglas's eighteenth birthday at the 7,400-foot summit of Blue

Mountain, and then voyaged onward to Panama, where Robin Williams joined them for the trip through the Panama Canal and the thousand-mile voyage to the Galapagos Islands and across the Pacific Ocean to the Marquesas islands three thousand miles beyond.

The days spent cruising among the Galapagos Islands and exploring their fascinating ecologies were deeply satisfying to the Robertsons and their young Welsh guest, but, as they readied to set sail across the vast expanse of ocean that lay between them and their next destination, a feeling of unease was apparent among them. On July 13, 1972, the *Lucette* was anchored under graying skies in a cove of the westernmost island of the Galapagos, Fernandina, whose forlorn aspect had inspired some feelings of depression and anxiety in the voyagers. Lyn objected to setting out on the thirteenth, but Dougal, Douglas, and Robin were all anxiously impatient to set out immediately, and so, late that afternoon, the *Lucette* cleared the headland of Fernandina's Cape Espinosa on what were to be her last days of sailing.

Shortly before ten o'clock on the morning of June 15th, attacking killer whales violently breached the *Lucette's* hull. Within little more than a minute the gallant *Lucette* dipped gracefully beneath the waves. In that desperate flash of time, the Robertsons miraculously managed to free the dinghy, inflate the life raft, and secure the lives of all aboard, but they were now adrift in the open ocean, two hundred miles down current and downwind from the Galapagos, with no hope of returning to safety there, with food and water at hand barely sufficient for a few days. The passages selected for *Survivors* from Dougal Robertson's starkly brilliant *Survive the Savage Sea* tell the story of how the family wrested life from thirst and starvation, severe exposure and exhaustion, stormy seas and murderous sharks. Twice unnoticed by passing ships, they relied upon themselves. Perilously balancing six souls in the nine-foot *Ednamair* after the loss of their inflatable life raft, they seized upon every resource within themselves and from the very ocean that at every moment threatened to engulf them as they made an incredible voyage towards the shores of Central America. And in their struggle their greatest resource was clearly the profound love of two parents fiercely determined "to get these boys to land."

Survive the Savage Sea

by Dougal Robertson

First day: We sat on the salvaged pieces of flotsam lying on the raft floor, our faces a pale bilious colour under the bright yellow canopy, and stared at each other, the shock of the last few minutes gradually seeping through to our consciousness. Neil, his teddy bears gone, sobbed in accompaniment to Sandy's hiccup cry, while Lyn repeated the Lord's Prayer, then, comforting them, sang the hymn 'For those in peril on the Sea'. Douglas and Robin watched at the doors of the canopy to retrieve any useful pieces of debris which might float within reach and gazed with dumb longing at the distant five-gallon water container, bobbing its polystyrene lightness ever further away from us in the steady trade wind. The dinghy

Ednamair wallowed, swamped, near-by with a line attached to it from the raft and our eyes travelled over and beyond to the heaving undulations of the horizon, already searching for a rescue ship even while knowing there would not be one. Our eyes travelled fruitlessly across the limitless waste of sea and sky, then once more ranged over the scattering debris. Of the killer whales which had so recently shattered our very existence, there was no sign. Lyn's sewing basket floated close and it was brought aboard followed by a couple of empty boxes, the canvas raft cover, and a plastic cup.

I leaned across to Neil and put my arm round him, 'It's alright now, son, we're safe and the whales have gone.' He looked at me reproachfully. 'We're not crying 'cos we're frightened,' he sobbed, 'we're crying 'cos Lucy's gone.' Lyn gazed at me over their heads, her eyes filling with tears. 'Me too,' she said, and after a moment added, 'I suppose we'd better find out how we stand.' . . . .

We cleared a space on the floor and opened the survival kit, which was part of the raft's equipment, and was contained in a three-foot-long polythene cylinder; slowly we took stock:

Vitamin fortified bread and glucose for ten men for two days.

Eighteen pints of water, eight flares (two parachute, six hand).

One bailer, two large fish-hooks, two small, one spinner and trace and a twenty-five pound breaking strain fishing line.

A patent knife which would not puncture the raft (or anything else for that matter), a signal mirror, torch, first-aid box, two sea anchors, instruction book, bellows, and three paddles.

In addition to this there was the bag of a dozen onions which I had given to Sandy, to which Lyn had added a one-pound tin of biscuits and a bottle containing about half a pound of glucose sweets, ten oranges and six lemons. How long would this have to last us? As I looked round our meagre stores my heart sank and it must have shown on my face for Lyn put her hand on mine; 'We must get these boys to land,' she said quietly. 'If we do nothing else with our lives, we must get them to land!' I looked at her and nodded, 'Of course, we'll make it!' The answer came from my heart but my head was telling me a different story. We were over two hundred miles down wind and current from the Galapagos Islands. To try to row the small dinghy into two hundred miles of rough ocean weather was an impossible journey even if it was tried by only two of us in an attempt to seek help for the others left behind in the raft. The fact that the current was against us as well only put the seal of hopelessness on the idea. There was no way back.

The Marquesas Islands lay two thousand eight hundred miles to the west but we had compass or means of finding our position; if, by some miraculous feat of endurance, one of us made the distance the chance of striking an island were remote.

The coast of Central America, more than a thousand miles to the north-east, lay on the other side of the windless Doldrums, that dread area of calms and squalls which had inspired Coleridge's

Water, water, everywhere,
And all the boards did shrink;
Water, water, everywhere,
Nor any drop to drink.

I was a Master Mariner, I thought ruefully, not an ancient one, and could count on no ghostly crew to get me out of this dilemma!

What were our chances if we followed the textbook answer, 'Stay put and wait for rescue?' In the first place we wouldn't be missed for at least five weeks and if a search was made, where would they start looking in three thousand miles of ocean? In the second place the chance of seeing a passing vessel in this area was extremely remote and could be discounted completely, for of the two possible shipping routes from Panama to Tahiti and New Zealand, one lay four hundred miles to the south and the other three hundred miles to the north. Looking at the food, I estimated that six of us might live for ten days

and since we could expect no rain in this area for at least six months,
apart from an odd shower, our chances of survival beyond ten days
were doubtful indeed. It seemed to me that we stood a very good
chance of becoming one of Robin's statistics.

My struggle to reach a decision, gloomy whichever way I looked
at it, showed on my face, and Lyn leaned forward. 'Tell us how we
stand,' she said, looking round, 'we want to know the truth.' They all
nodded, 'What chance have we?' I could not tell them I thought they
were going to die so I slowly spelled out the alternatives, and then
suddenly I knew there was only one course open to us; we must sail
with the trade winds to the Doldrums four hundred miles to the north.
We stood a thin chance of reaching land but the only possible shipping
route lay in that direction, our only possible chance of rain water in
any quantity lay in that direction even if it was four hundred miles
away, and our only possible chance of reaching land lay in that
direction, however small that chance might be. We would work and
fight for our lives at least; better than dying in idleness! 'We must get
these boys to land,' Lyn had said. I felt the reality of the decision lifting
the hopelessness from my shoulders and looked around; five pairs of
eyes watched me as I spoke, Lyn once again with her arms round the
twins, Douglas and Robin each at their lookout posts watching for
any useful debris that might come within reach. 'We have no
alternative,' I said, 'we'll stay here for twenty-four hours to see if any
other wreckage appears, then we must head north and hope to find
rain in the Doldrums.' I looked round, 'We might also find an easterly
current here which will help us to the coast of Central America, if
we've not been picked up by then.' The lifting of my depression
communicated and as I talked of the problems and privations which
confronted us, I saw the resolve harden on Douglas's face. Robin
nodded and fired a question about shipping lanes, Lyn smiled at me,
not caring that I was offering her torture from thirst, starvation and
probably death if we were not rescued, just so long as we had a
working chance. The twins dried their tears and eyed the sweets; we
were in business again.

With one of the sea anchors streamed we set to work, clearing the
raft floor of the debris we had collected: the huge genoa sail, two
hundred feet of nylon fishing line (breaking strain one hundred
pounds), three gallons of petrol, two oars, two empty boxes. Lyn's
sewing basket was a treasure beyond wealth for not only did it contain
the usual threads and needles, but also two scalpel blades, four knitting
needles, a blanket pin, hat pin, three plastic bags, a ball of string,

buttons, tinfoil, a shoehorn, two small plastic cups, two plastic boxes, two small envelopes of dried yeast, a piece of copper wire one foot long, some elastic, a bottle of soluble aspirin, a pencil, and a biro pen. (What else could one possibly expect to find in a sewing basket!) We also had a half pint of copal varnish, a very sodden edition of a West Indies pilotage book, and one cracked and saturated smoke flare. My watch, a twenty-year-old Rolex Oyster, gave us the time and the first-aid box contained artery forceps and scissors, but otherwise we had no compass, no charts, no instruments of any kind in fact, that would aid our navigation or measure our distance run.

We stowed the mountain of debris as best we could then set to work, our first task being to strip out the long luff wire from the genoa so that it could be used to join the dinghy to the raft. It was at this point that we met our first real drawback for first Robin, then Neil started being seasick, the undulating motion of the raft in the high swell and breaking seas finding them unable to settle to the strange movement. Lyn administered seasick pills from the first-aid box as soon as she thought the boys able to retain them, but they had already lost precious quantities of body fluid. Lyn and I continued to work on the sail while Douglas checked and re-stowed the rations and equipment. In one of the raft pockets he found two sponges and plugs, with a repair kit for holes, but the glue had completely dried out, rendering the repair kit useless. In another pocket he found the instruction book which gave little intelligent information on how to preserve one's life in mid-ocean, but gave a lot of superfluous jargon about morale, leadership, and rescue, finishing up with the two most sensible words in the whole book in capital letters, GOOD LUCK!! (The exclamation marks are mine.)

At last we freed the luff wire, about forty feet long and covered with white plastic, then set about cutting a sail for the dinghy, after which we could use the surplus for sheets and covers for warmth at night, since we were all clad in swimming shorts and shirts with the exception of Lyn, who was wearing a nylon housecoat. The wire would make an excellent tow rope for the dinghy and I fastened it to the outside of the raft to give us a little more space in which to settle down for the night. As evening drew in we had one biscuit and a sip of water, one orange between six, and a glucose sweet each, generally speaking a pretty sumptuous banquet in the light of things to come, but meagre enough rations for us at that time . . . .

. . . as darkness fell we curled round the boxes and tins, legs and bodies overlapping in places, and tried to rest. The raft was still plunging and lifting in the long fifteen-feet-high swells, while the shorter crested waves, built up under the force of the local winds, surged heavily around us, causing the raft to jerk into the troughs as she brought up sharply on the sea anchor. As we turned and twisted around seeking ease for our aching limbs, we began to experience curious bumps and sharp nudges through the inflated floor of the raft; at first I thought something sharp had wedged under the raft and worried lest it should puncture the flotation chambers, then I heard Lyn give a faint shriek as she too was nudged from below. Douglas, on lookout, said that he could see large fish swimming under the raft, dorado, he thought, and they seemed to be after some smaller fish close under the raft floor.

The bumps and. nudges occurred at frequent intervals as the dorado performed their endless gyrations under the raft, often several times in the space of a minute. The severity of the bump depended on the speed and angle of the dorado's impact but generally speaking they were mild compared with the blows from sharks, and quite distinctive from the hard bump of a turtle's shell under the floor which we were to experience later. Turtles were also to bite us through the floor of the raft (no doubt an endearing courtship practice) but never hard enough to penetrate the double skin, although they were probably responsible for the leaks which developed in the air chambers of which the raft floor was composed, destroying the buffered effect which the air chambers rendered against the assaults of the fish. There didn't seem to be any shortage of fish around, I thought hopefully; perhaps we wouldn't find it so difficult to supplement our rations after all, but none the less the experience of being poked sharply in the sit-upon when drowsing, or worse, bitten on sit-upon while asleep, was quite startling and we never became accustomed to these assaults during our occupation of the raft . . . .

. . . I glanced over to where Neil lay asleep, his limbs entangled under Sandy's and on top of Lyn's; he was a very loving child, with unorthodox views and a stubborn streak of determination which would stand him in good stead in the days to come. Lyn was worried about his seasickness for his young body would not stand up to the loss of fluid as well as Robin's. Douglas grunted as a dorado collided with the raft under him—'We'll have to do something about these fish, Dad,' he mumbled, half asleep, 'like catching them.'

'Two o'clock!' I jerked awake from my doze to see Robin bending towards me in the darkness. 'Aye aye! Everything alright?' I crawled across to the doorway to take over the watch; the stars twinkled brightly in the arch of darkness beyond the sweep of the sea. Robin gagged at the water; 'No ships,' he muttered and crawled to his place beside Douglas. I peeped round the canopy of the raft at the dinghy; the *Ednamair* lay disconsolately awash at the end of her painter, her white gunwhale just visible above the surface of the water. She was helping the sea anchor, I supposed, but we'd have to bail her out first thing in the morning. . . .

The water exploded as a thirty-pound dorado leapt high in the air after a flying fish, landing with a slap on its side in a shower of luminescence. I glanced down to where several large fish swam under the raft, constantly rising to skim the underside of the raft's edge, sometimes hitting it a heavy blow with their high jutting foreheads. Douglas was right, we should have to do something about these fish!

Second day: The long night paled into the beautiful dawn sky of the South Pacific; slowly we collected our scattered wits for already our dreams of being elsewhere than on the raft had taken on the vivid reality of hallucination. Wretched with cramp and discomfort it had been such simple solution to go next door and there I would find my childhood bed, so clear in every forgotten detail, waiting for me.

I looked across at Lyn, rubbing the cramp out of the twins' legs. 'We'll see to the *Ednamair* after breakfast'; I looked hopefully at the water jar, but it was nearly empty. We had emptied the glucose sweets out of their glass jar so that it could be used to hold drinking water as it was decanted from the tin, for although we had discussed the issue of equal rations of water (there wasn't enough to do that) we had decided simply to pass the jar round, each person limiting him or herself to the minimum needed to carry on; at the same time, the visible water level in the jar enabled everyone to see there was no cheating. Breakfast consisted of one quarter-ounce biscuit, a piece of onion and a sip of water, except for Robin and Neil who could not eat and were with difficulty persuaded to take some extra water with a seasick pill. We had used two pints of water in one day between six, hardly a maintenance ration under a tropic sun, which I remembered had been placed as high as two pints per person per day! We ate slowly, savouring each taste of onion and biscuit with a new appreciation and, although we hardly felt as if we had breakfasted on bacon and eggs, we were still sufficiently shocked at our altered circumstances not to feel hunger.

Breakfast over, Lyn, with Sandy helping, sorted out the various pieces of sail which were to be used for bedding, chatting quietly all the while to Neil and Robin. Douglas and I went to the door of the raft and, pulling the dinghy alongside, first attempted to bail it out as it lay swamped, but the waves filled it as fast as we bailed. We turned its stern towards us and, lifting slowly, allowed the bow to submerge, then when we could lift it no higher, I called 'Let go!' The dinghy flopped back in the water with three inches of freeboard, we bailed desperately with small bailers, then Douglas took one of the wooden boxes and with massive scoops bailed enough water out to allow him to board the dinghy and bail it dry. We were all cheered by the sight of little *Ednamair* afloat again, and with a cry of delight Douglas held up his Timex watch; it had been lying in the bottom of the dinghy all this time and was still going! He also found what was to prove our most valuable possession, the stainless-steel kitchen knife which I had thrown in after the fruit.

After a segment of orange each for elevenses we loaded the oars, a paddle, the empty boxes, the petrol can, the hundred-foot raft painter, and the piece of the genoa designated for the dinghy sail, then climbing into the dinghy started work on the jury rig that was to turn the *Ednamair* into a tugboat for our first stage of the journey north. Douglas, in the meantime, helped Lyn to reorganise the inside of the raft now that there was much more room, and topped up the flotation chambers with air. I rigged one oar in the mast step with appropriate fore and back stays . . . then cutting notches in the raft paddle, bent the head of the sail on to it to form a square sail. I had previously taken the precaution of making the luff wire, shackled to the towing straps of the raft, fast to the ringbolt in the bow of the dinghy, in case the nylon painter had frayed. I had decided the dinghy would have to perform her function of towing by proceeding stern first, for her cutaway stern could not be exposed to the overtaking waves without danger of swamping. The paddle was made fast to the top of the oar, and the sail foot secured to the two ends of the other oar, placed athwartships across the rowlock sockets. A violent jerk sent me sprawling into the bottom of the boat and I realised that we were operational. . . .

Ednamair was now straining at the leash so I called to Douglas to trip the sea anchor and haul it aboard; the time was two o'clock in the afternoon and we had started our voyage to the Doldrums, and, I shuddered at the thought of the alternative, rain. I estimated our position at Latitude 1° South and Longitude 94°40' West or, more accurately, two hundred miles west of Cape Espinosa.

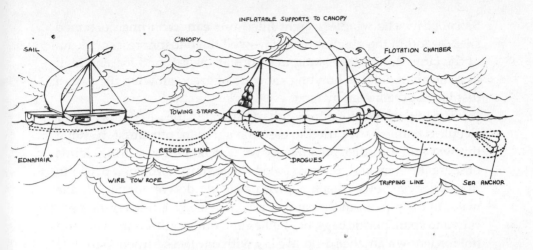

Ednamair towing raft with sea anchor streamed

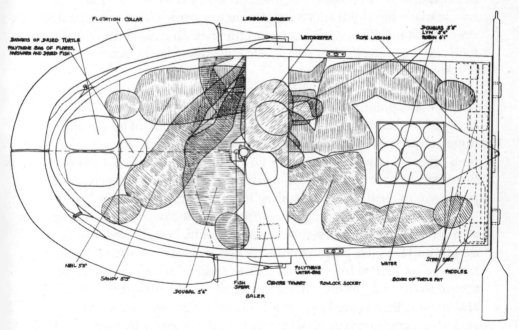

Disposition of bodies at night in *Ednamair*

Artwork courtesy of Sheridan House Publishers

Seventh day: The windless night filled our ears with unaccustomed silence, and in the quiet of the calm swell the phosphorescent gleam of the large dorado, streaking from under the raft and leaping high into the air, to land in bursting showers of green glowing fire, was a display not often seen by men.

The foul dryness of our mouths aggravated the discomfort of our sleepless bodies as we tried to ease the agony of our thirst, twisting this way and that, then breathlessly we watched the gathering clouds obscure the stars and as dawn paled the eastern horizon, it began to rain, a heavy shower this time, with a steady downpour. Slowly the water in the pipe from the canopy ran clear and we filled our empty cans and spare plastic bags, our bellies and our mouths until we could not force down another drop. We lay with our faces turned to the sky and let the pure fresh water cleanse the salt from our beards and hair; suddenly everything had changed from the shadow of the spectre of death to the joyful prospect of life, and all by a shower of rain. We would make the Doldrums now! We lay uncaring, chewing strips of dorado and revelling in the absence of thirst, talking excitedly of good food and watching the bulging plastic bags swing lazily from the roof of the canopy. We had water!

Douglas, lazily watching the dispersing clouds, suddenly sat up with a start, pointing excitedly. 'A ship! A ship! It's a ship!' We all crowded to the door of the raft, staring in the direction of his pointing finger; a cargo vessel of about six thousand tons was approaching us on a course that would bring her within three miles of us. I felt my heart pound against my ribs. 'Get out the flares,' I said hoarsely, 'and pass them to me in the dinghy, they'll see us better from there.'

Three miles was a fair distance, but on a dull day like this, against a background of rain they should see us easily. I clambered into the dinghy and Douglas passed me the rockets and hand flares; my hands trembled as I ripped open a parachute rocket flare and, with mute appeal to the thing to fire, struck the igniter on the fuse. It spluttered and hissed, then roared off on a trajectory high above the raft, its pinkish magnesium flare slowly spiralling downwards leaving a trail of smoke in the sky. They couldn't fail to see it. I waited a moment or two watching for the ship to alter course, then struck a hand flare, holding it high above my head. The blinding red light was hot to hold and I pointed it away from the wind to ease my hand, the red embers of the flare dropping into the dinghy; as it went out I struck another, smoke from the first now a rising plume in the sky; surely they must see that. I waited a little, my hands trembling. 'This chance might not come again,' I said, anxious faces crowding the door of the raft, 'I'm going to use our last rocket flare and one more hand flare.' We watched tensely as the second rocket flare soared and spiralled its gleaming distress message high above us; desperately I struck the third hand flare and held it high, standing on the thwart and holding on to the mast. 'Look, look, you bastards!' I shouted. 'Set fire to the sail!' Lyn's voice. I stuck the flare to the sail but it only melted. The ship sailed on, slowly disappearing behind a rain shower, and when she reappeared her hull was half obscured by the horizon, five miles distant and disappearing fast. The time was eleven o'clock. My shoulders drooped. 'We daren't use another,' I said. 'They won't see it now and we have to keep something for the next one.' We had three hand flares left. Lyn smiled cheerfully. 'It says in the instruction book that the first one probably wouldn't see us,' she said slowly, 'and I'd already told the twins not to expect anything.' She gathered the twins to her, comfortingly. We stared at the dwindling speck on the horizon and felt so lonely that it hurt. 'I'm sorry lads,' I felt very tired. 'We used to consider that one of the more important tenets of good seamanship was "Keep a good Lookout". That lot seem to be pretty poor seamen!'

Our position was 3° North and 240 miles west of Espinosa (almost 95°20' W) on Wednesday 21 June, midsummer's day, on the route from Panama to the Marquesas; the ship was westbound. I surveyed the empty flare cartons bitterly, and the one smoke flare which was damaged and wouldn't work, and something happened to me in that instant, that for me changed the whole aspect of our predicament. If these poor bloody seamen couldn't rescue us, then we would have to make it on our own and to hell with them. We would survive without them, yes, and that was the word from now on, 'survival', not 'rescue', or 'help', or dependence of any kind, just survival. I felt the strength flooding through me, lifting me from the depression of disappointment to a state of almost cheerful abandon. I felt the bitter aggression of the predator fill my mind. This was not our environment and the beasts around us would eat us if we failed. We would carve a place for ourselves amongst them; they had millions of years of adaptation on their side, but we had brains and some tools. We would live for three months or six months from the sea if necessary, but 'We would get these boys to land' as Lyn had said and we would do it ourselves if there was no other way. From that instant on, I became a savage.

We lunched on dry fish, a half biscuit and a tiny piece of glucose each to cheer us up, followed by a good mouthful of water, after which

I returned to the *Ednamair* to clear up the debris of empty cases and burnt powder. When I returned to the raft I said: 'From now on we have a new password; we forget words like rescue for we can expect none, and think of existence only in terms of survival.' Lyn nodded immediately. 'What's the password for today?' she called to the twins—'Survival' they echoed, and they seemed to understand that it was no longer a question of 'if' we would reach land, but 'when'. Robin seemed to regard our change of attitude with mild indifference, but in Douglas's eyes I could see that the shadow of the ship's passing would haunt him for the rest of his days.

The wind rose from the south again after the passage of rain and I decided to stream the sea anchor, to hold the raft in the shipping route, for forty-eight hours. I was tempted to carry straight on but rescue is, after all, part of the survival exercise and I would at least pay lip service to the ordinary practices of seamen. In two days the current would have carried us beyond the shipping lane and we could then proceed on our voyage to the coast. The sea anchor streamed and the sail reefed, I had just returned to the raft when an excited call from Sandy, watching the sea anchor's mushroom trailing behind us, brought us to the after door of the raft. A huge hammerhead shark glided six feet below, its wicked eye leering up at us. Towards late afternoon we felt an unusually hard bump on the raft floor, unlike the quick thrust of the striking dorado, and poking our heads out of the stern door of the raft we found ourselves gazing at the large scaly head of a turtle, protruding eyes set above a nasty-looking beak, surveying us with a dispassionate unblinking scrutiny. The day before I would have said, 'Leave it, we can't manage that,' but now things were different. 'We'll have this one' I said. 'Let's get it aboard the dinghy.' The turtle's flippers had become entangled in the sea anchor line, so first passing rope from the dinghy under the raft, we made it fast to one of the back flippers, then, carefully avoiding the searching beak, freed the turtle from the sea anchor rope and towed it around the raft to the *Ednamair*. I scrambled on to the dinghy and pulled the now struggling turtle alongside, reaching down to grasp the back flippers. I twisted the turtle round until its back was next to the dinghy and heaved. It was surprisingly heavy and as it came aboard, the dinghy tilted alarmingly. I threw my weight to the other side to trim her, then with bump and a thrashing of claws the reptile lay on its back in the bottom of the dinghy, all eighty pounds of it. I put my thumbs up to the twins and Douglas watching from the raft, and they cheered excitedly.

Now for the difficult bit. I looked at the armoured amphibian with a farmer's eye; where to cut to reach the artery? I had helped to slaughter a few pigs and lambs and had a pretty good idea how to tackle this one. I grasped the pointed knife in my right hand and, putting a foot on each of the front flippers, held its beak with my left hand, then plunged the knife into the leathery skin of the neck, deep into the spinal column, then with quick, outward strokes of the knife to right and left I cut both vein and artery. Deep red blood spurted into the bottom of the dinghy and gradually, beak and flippers ceased thrashing as the beast died. Apart from a few minor scratches I was unscathed, as in the gathering dusk I washed the blood from my hands into the bottom of the dinghy, careful not to spill any in the water. I didn't want to bring any inquisitive sharks around, especially our hammerheaded friend, until we had started moving again, for if they suspected that the blood came from the raft they would probably attack the inflatable with disastrous consequences. Excitedly we discussed this addition to our larder. Lyn had heard from someone that turtle livers were inedible so we decided to discard the offal rather than risk illness. Twenty-four hours previously I would not have had the stomach for such a bloody business but the laws of survival applied and the first principle, 'The fittest survive, the weakest go to the wall', had now become our way of life. We would struggle and endure and if our reflexes were not as swift as the animals and fish around us, we had cunning, and we would improve with practice . . . .

The wind steadily increased during the evening and the sea became noisy about the raft again. Inside, bodies twisted and turned restlessly seeking a comfortable position, for only the twins were small enough to lie down full length on the floor. Water slopped around the depressions made by hip-bones and elbows in the inflated rubber flooring and the sound of the watchkeeper blowing up the rotation chambers became just another sound in the night to those who tried to rest. To the watchkeeper, it was an exhausting routine of bailing and blowing which left the mouth sore, the hands cramped and the tiny pimples, forerunners of salt water boils, stinging on hands, feet, legs, arms and buttocks. We sometimes found time to look around for ships! *Eighth day:* As dawn broke and we awoke again to the realisation that the ship had not seen us, Lyn called from her watchkeeping at the doorway: 'What's the password for the day?' The answer 'Survival' came with surprising vigour from us all and we set about the morning chores of mopping up and drying bedding with a cheerfulness scarcely appropriate to our desperate situation. I went over to *Ednamair* to dress the turtle. It took me an hour and a half to remove the belly shell, sawing and hacking with the knife blade which grew blunter as the shell seemed to grow thicker; finally with a bit of undercutting, I managed to lift the shell off and set about extracting the meat. The turtle has a poor killing out ratio, about twenty-five per cent to thirty per cent, and has its joints in the most inaccessible places. It took me another hour to hack out the shoulder meat and that surrounding the back flipper bones. I opened the stomach and found, to my delight, a golden cascade of a hundred or so yellow egg yolks awaiting collection. I cut some meat from the shoulder piece and then with a couple of dozen eggs in a dish returned to the aft for breakfast where all waited curiously for their first taste of turtle meat . . . .

Neil grinned and sank his teeth into a piece of steak. 'Good' was all he said, and we all fell with a will. We swallowed the egg yolks, bursting them like yellow plums inside our mouths and allowing their creamy richness to permeate our taste buds, enjoying the flavour of the raw food as only starving people can. Robin declined the eggs—too rich for him—but chewed vigorously at the tender meat declaring that he enjoyed his steaks done 'rare'. Douglas, Lyn and Sandy, after some initial distaste, chewed at the pieces of meat with increasing interest as rejection of the idea of raw meat gave way to acceptance of the taste of it. We washed it down with a draught of water and lay back and reflected on our good fortune. If we could catch turtles, and rain, we would survive alright; I thought of the fish spear; with turtles and dorado, we'd be wealthy!

    After discussing the day's work with Douglas and Robin, I returned to the dinghy and carefully skinned the flippers, head (Douglas wanted it for a souvenir) and neck, and loosened the offal from the shell ready to tip over the side when we started moving again. Next, the meat was cut from the bones and then divided into small pieces which were laid out across the thwart to dry in the sun. We had about twenty pounds of meat and bone altogether, and *Ednamair* looked like a slaughter-house, but there were also the dorado strips, now nearly dry again after their wetting and tasting very pleasantly too! The huge turtle shell lay in the bottom of the dinghy, like a small bath, and I tried to imagine uses to which it could be put. My primary thought was that I would be able to use a piece to arm the spear but the knife was too blunt to be of use in shaping the barbs and the shell itself would be too brittle when dried out, and not hard enough if it was kept wet. With the meat nicely drying my return to the raft with another meal was hailed with interest and lunch time found us happily gnawing bones. With the inside of the raft shaped like a cave, it was not difficult to imagine that we had dropped a few thousand years in time, for not only did we look like cave dwellers, I, at least, felt like one.

Fifteenth day: I watched the cloud develop slowly and drift across the night sky, blotting out the stars one by one. Was it another occluded front? I watched the fish surge out from under the raft, touched one as I tried to grab it, then, the memory of the shark strong in my mind, drew back. I bailed and blew until Lyn took over; I pointed to the thickening cloud: 'Maybe we'll get something to drink out of that.'

It rained at dawn, beautiful gorgeous rain. We saved three and a half gallons and drank our fill besides; the wind, from the south, freshened a little and as the weather cleared we lay back and enjoyed the sensation of being without thirst, bailing and blowing unheeded for the moment. We talked of the ship that didn't see us, for that had happened after the last rain, and argued whether it would have seen us better if it had been night time. The twins were talking when Douglas, on watch, his voice desperate with dismay, called: 'Dad, the dinghy's gone!' I was across the raft in an instant. I looked at the broken end of wire trailing in the water,) the broken line beside it. The dinghy was sixty yards away, sailing still and our lives were sailing away with it; I was the fastest swimmer, no time for goodbyes, to hell with sharks; the thoughts ran through my head as I was diving through the door, my arms flailing into a racing crawl even as I hit the water. I heard Lyn cry out but there was no time for talk. Could I swim faster than the dinghy could sail, that was the point; I glanced at it as I lifted my head to breathe, the sail had collapsed as the dinghy yawed, I moved my arms faster, kicked harder, would the sharks let me, that was another point; my belly crawled as I thought of the sharks, my arms moved faster still; I glanced again, only thirty yards to go but she was sailing again, I felt no fatigue, no cramped muscles, my body felt like a machine as I thrashed my way through the sea only one thought now in mind, the dinghy or us. Then I was there; with a quick heave I flipped over the stern of the dinghy to safety, reached up and tore down the sail before my knees buckled and I lay across the thwart trembling and gasping for breath, my heart pounding like a hammer. I lifted my arm and waved to the raft, now two hundred yards away, then slowly I untied the paddle from the sail and paddled back to the raft; it took nearly half an hour. The long shapes of two sharks circled curiously twenty feet down; they must have had breakfast . . . .

On my return to the raft we tested the wire and found it frayed under the plastic in two places, broke it, rejoined it and in doing so, made it short enough to fasten a large nylon rope between the raft and the dinghy as a reserve, after which we rigged up a sea anchor which would automatically trip if the *Ednamair* broke away from the craft again, and stop her from sailing away. We had not only closed the stable door this time, we'd hobbled the horse as well! I didn't relish a repeat performance of that swim; not ever . . . .

Our noon position of 5°15' North and 250 miles west of Espinosa put us inside the official limits of the Doldrums; we had made the rain area in fifteen days. I solemnly reflected that if we had stayed at sea anchor where *Lucette* sank and hoped for rescue, we should have been dead by now. We had travelled about four hundred miles, about seven hundred to go, and had as much, if not more, food and water than when we started. Our condition was much worse it was true, but I hoped that the increase in our water supply would help to put that right; we could not hope for an improvement otherwise until we left the raft. I still had strong misgivings about our ability to fit into *Ednamair* along with the necessary equipment. We had had only about six inches of freeboard when we had been all aboard in the Galapagos; six inches wasn't much in the middle of the Pacific with sharks about, and even if I managed to save flotation pieces from the raft it would be very difficult to support the dinghy with them. We couldn't afford to be swamped, not even once, for our water and stores would be ruined even if we saved ourselves.

As I listed in my thoughts the items we required to take into the dinghy with us, my mind boggled at the thought of trying to fit us in as well, so I stopped thinking about it and decided to start immediately on a propaganda campaign concerning the absolute necessity for instant obedience when we took to the dinghy in order to keep the correct trim. Rain had begun falling again and it settled to a steady downpour throughout the night. We would need canopy over the dinghy to keep the rain out rather than catch it if this was the sort of weather we could expect. I was glad the Ancient Mariner was wrong, just the same!

Twenty-fourth day: The steady scrape of the bailing cups went on through the night. Side by side, Robin and I knelt under the yellow sheet of raft canopy, our knees flattened against the fibreglass, our heads against the thwart as we threw the water over the side. The steady beat of the rain on our capes only served to lull our senses, and sleep, which would not come to my resting body, tried hard to take me unawares now. I felt Robin lean against me as he, too, dozed in exhausted slumber, then he would jerk awake again to the tyranny of the bailing cup. We could no longer feel any pain, our hands and limbs felt soaked to the bone, our skins were a crumpled mess of nerveless wrinkles, we shivered and bailed and sang songs, any songs, to keep our circulation going, and when we were too tired to sing, Lyn pummelled and rubbed our insensitive bodies to life again, but the scrape and splash of the bailing cups went on through the unrelenting downpour of rain, our hopes, our fears, our thirst, our despair, all forgotten in the emotionless limbo of anaesthesia by exhaustion.

Dawn came to us, a grey witness in the eastern sky; Robin was asleep as his kneeling body sagged sideways against the dinghy, the bailing cup still clutched in his hand, while Lyn knelt asleep against the stern seat, her body close to mine for warmth. My arm still moved in the motion of bailing until I realised that it had stopped raining and so sank into grateful oblivion. Death could have come to us too at this moment, without our knowledge or any resistance to its coming.

Douglas had taken over the steering as the southerly breeze strengthened during the morning. The rain still spotted and there was no sign of a break in the clouds yet. I awoke in mid-morning and checked the fastenings on the flotation collar, for one end had come adrift. While I seldom slept above an hour at any time, the boys suffered much from lack of sleep, their haggard faces belying their assurances that they were getting enough rest. We now ate without tasting our food, and drank water as an obligation to the dried turtle, rather than as a blessing from the sky. Our daydreams had switched from ice cream and fruit to hot stews, porridge, steak and kidney puddings, hotpots and casseroles. The dishes steamed fragrantly in our imaginations and as we described their smallest details to each other we almost tasted the succulent gravies as we chewed our meagre rations.

The dried meat was rapidly being used up since the hanging meat had grown a slimy film and was so unpalatable that I threw it overboard for fear of poisoning. Sickness of any description was a hazard we could do well without; but it seemed that with the bountiful supply of fresh water, our appetites had grown, so rations of the dried turtle were severely reduced in case our larder should become empty before the next catch. The clouds thinned towards noon and the sun finally broke through in the early afternoon. We greeted him like a long-lost friend, almost as welcome as the rain had been a week before, and spread soaked items of equipment to dry on the thwarts. Most of the first-aid kit was ruined beyond salvation, and my logbook, quite saturated, was spread carefully to dry.

At 7°40' North, 230 miles west of Cape Espinosa (95 14' W) our noon position placed us approximately halfway to land... the sky had again darkened and we decided to snatch what rest we could in the day time if we were required to work all night. Our hearts sank as we prepared for another miserable night but the rain, when it came, was light and intermittent, almost a drizzle, requiring the services of one bailer and then only occasionally. Normal watches were resumed and we lay down to pass the night in dry discomfort, something of a luxury. The disposition of our bodies at night had found the most suitable arrangement to be Neil and Sandy lying lengthways in the bow with myself in a U-shape across the dingy just forward of the centre thwart. The water cans were transferred from under the stern seat into the big wooden box and this was kept lashed forward of the stern seat, allowing a sleeper to lie on each side of it (sideways only of course). The watchkeeper kept watch from the centre thwart, and all dry stores and food were kept under the bow canopy right forward where they were reasonably dry . . . .

Twenty-ninth day: We made good headway in the gentle westerly breeze throughout the night, with the sea anchor tripped and *Ednamair* making over a knot to the east-north-east. The rising sun guided our daylight progress and the business of survival resumed its daily routine. I had barely started work on my gaff when, looking down into the sea past the flashing blue, green and gold of the dorado, I spotted the brown shape of a shark, but it was the first small one I had seen since my short-lived love affair with the one on the raft. This one was catchable too. We had caught a flying fish in the night, a very small one, so I put it on the large hook and weighting the line heavily I cast well out to clear the scavenger fish. My baited hook drifted down past the shark and at first I thought he was going to ignore it but after it came to rest he turned and nosed towards it. Douglas, stretched across the dinghy in my usual place beside the thwart, called: 'What're you doing, Dad?' 'Catching a shark,' I said calmly, watching the shark nose a little closer. 'You're bloody mad,' Douglas said, sitting up quickly; Robin, too, was sitting up apprehensively and Lyn said 'You mustn't'' 'Good old Dad,' said Neil and Sandy from the bows. 'I'm having him,' I said watching tensely now, as the shark reached the bait; the moment I felt him touch I would have to strike, for if he got the nylon line between his teeth he would bite through it like butter. I was going to try to get the steel shank of the hook between his jaws. He was over it now, I felt the contact with tingling fingers and struck swiftly, the line exploded in action, he was hooked!

He fought with alternate periods of listless acquiescence and galvanic action, twisting and plunging savagely to rid himself of the hook. I was afraid of the line breaking but I feared more the arrival of a larger shark which would attack the hooked one. Slowly, foot by foot, he came to the surface, the line cutting deep into the heel of my hand. Lyn sat ready in the stern, paddle in hand. The shark broke surface, struggled savagely and plunged deeply. I had to let him go, he was still too strong, but he was a nice five-footer. A Mako shark, Douglas said (he was our shark expert) and I'd hooked him in the eye! Back up he came. 'We'll have him this time,' I grunted, my hands aching. 'Be ready to take the line, Robin.. . I'm going to grab his tail and pull him in that way.' Excitement rose high in the dinghy; Robin and Lyn looked a bit uncomfortable at being given the biting end to look after, but were determined to do their best. (I knew he would break free if I tried to haul him in head first by the line.)

The shark surfaced again; gingerly Robin took the line from my hand as I quickly leaned over and grabbed the shark's tail. 'Trim!' I shouted and Douglas leaned out on the other side of the dinghy. The harsh skin gave me a good grip, and with a quick pull the shark lay over the gunwhale. 'Lift its head in now!' I kept a firm grip on the tail as Robin lifted the struggling fish inboard with the line. Lyn rammed the paddle into the gaping jaws and they clamped shut on it. Knife in hand I leaned forward and stabbed it through the other eye; the shark struggled then lay still. Giving Douglas the tail to hold, I stabbed the knife into the slits of the gills behind the head, sawing away at the tough skin until finally the head was severed. 'Right, you can let go now!' I felt like Bruce after Bannockburn. We had turned the tables on our most feared enemy; sharks would not eat Robertsons, Robertsons would eat sharks! Quickly I gutted out the liver and heart: a solid thirty-five to forty pounds of fish with very little waste apart from the head. We breakfasted on the liver and heart, then Robin chewed the head, watching carefully for the razor-sharp teeth while I cut strips of white flesh from the almost boneless carcase. It was tougher than the dorado but juicier and we chewed the moist strips of shark meat with great relish.

Our larder now began to look good; long strips of shark swung from the forestay where the remains of the turtle meat had dried nicely.

I cut out the jaw bone from the shark's head while Lyn and the twins cleaned the spinal column. We had lost all our Indian necklaces from the San Blas Islands, the most valued of which were the shark's teeth and backbone necklaces. Now we had the raw materials to hand and time to spare to make our own!

Our noon position of 7°50' North and 160 miles west of Espinosa showed our better progress and though the weather had become overcast and unsuitable for drying the shark meat, at least it afforded us a little shade from the hot sun.

. . . As we watched the pieces of shark swinging against the clearing sky in the evening we felt some satisfaction that with the turtle meat already in store we had enough food to last us for a week, plus some of the emergency rations which were reserved for the children's 'little supper' before they went to rest.

Thirty-fifth day: We watched with unbelief as the darkness of cloud grew in the southern sky, the great piling cumulus rising to the archway of heaven itself to blot out the stars. We felt the pores of our mouths tingle with the stress of anticipation as the saliva failed to generate in our too dry gums. I passed the jar round. 'Sippers only, till we know for sure.' The dawn brought rain. An hour of nice, heavy, beautiful rain. We filled the containers, tins and plastic bag (Robin's privilege) then filled our shrunken stomachs to uncomfortable distension . . . .

Our noon position of 8°10' North, 115 miles west of Espinosa showed little progress and with rain once more in the offing my thoughts turned to rowing again We needed more food reserves, particularly turtle, and a bigger water storage capacity. My eye went to the flotation collar and as a matter of routine, I leaned over to check the fastenings; the tiny spurt of water from under the rope prompted me to investigate further; it was half full of water again from a hole chafed in the other end from the one I had previously repaired. After the collar had been inspected, we established the presence of not one hole but five, two in the middle and three in the valve end. After untying and emptying the tube I lay back to rest and try to think my way out of this one. I could not see any possibility of repairing the holes, but with no flotation collar, we were living on the razor's edge, with no support for us or the dinghy if we were swamped in rough weather. I looked at the holes again and sat awhile, racking my brains to find the answer. There was none, except the possibility of trapping some air in the sleeve by bending the tube over and lashing it in the middle as well as the end, and I didn't have any suitable line left except the fishing line. I suddenly had a better idea. 'Hand me the knife,' I called to Douglas. With quick strokes I cut the tube in half where the two holes had been. I now had two pieces five feet long. I fastened the piece with the good end to the centre thwart, open end up, and lashed it in position. 'This,' I said, 'is our reserve water tank; it'll hold about seven gallons and as soon as we have it washed and half filled, we'll start rowing!' I looked at the other piece. If we were swamped, it was big enough to support the weaker swimmers while Douglas and I got the dinghy afloat again, and the fishing line would not be needed anyway until we reached the coast . . . .

As the twilight deepened into night, the faint breeze from the south ruffled the surface of the sea and I warned the watchkeepers to be on the alert for squalls later on. With no flotation collar, rough weather could mean the end for us. Only Douglas and I shared the full import of this knowledge; I felt it would be an unnecessary burden to the others to labour the point.

Thirty-sixth day: Slowly the wind rose from the south. At first it was a fine gentle breeze, then blew with increasing force until the breaking tips of the waves gleamed in the darkness.

As *Ednamair* pitched and yawed, shipping more and more water over the midships section, I set Douglas steering her into the waves while I opened the sea anchor out and adjusted the trim of the dinghy to keep a high, weather side. The squalls strengthened and Douglas and I stood watch on watch, helping the tiny boat through the violence of the rising seas. Lyn and Robin were still unable to steer so that they took over the bailing when necessary. I felt uncomfortable without the assurance of the flotation collar and prepared a strangle cord on the water sleeve to enable me to make it into an airtight float very swiftly if an emergency arose . . . .

Each day had now acquired a built-in objective in that we had to try to gain as much as possible over our reserves of stores and water until there would be enough in stock to get us to the coast. I looked upon each turtle as the last, each fish as the one before I lost the hook, by an error in strike. It only needed a six-inch mistake to make the difference between a dynamic pull of about eighty pounds and one of hundred and eighty with the consequent breaking of the unevenly tensioned lines, and I knew that sooner or later it had to happen.

Lyn washed and mended our clothes, which now had the

appearance of some aboriginal garb. . . . Robin and I had beards with unkempt moustaches which hung over our upper lips; salt water boils and scars covered our arms, legs and buttocks and were scattered on other parts of our anatomy, intermingled with clawmarks from turtles, as well as cuts and scratches from other sources. The adults were not desperately thin but the twins, Neil in particular, had become very emaciated. Knee cramps troubled us from time to time, but generally speaking, apart from Sandy who had a slight bronchial cough which Lyn's expert ear had detected the day previously (for she had a constant fear of a static pneumonia developing in our cramped situation), we were in better physical condition than when we had abandoned the raft. Many of our sores had healed and our bodies were functioning again. We were eating and drinking more, and our ability to gnaw bones and suck nutrition from them increased with our knowledge of the easiest ways to attack them. We were no longer just surviving, but were improving in our physical condition. As I looked around at our little company, only Neil gave me cause for worry for his thin physique made it difficult to determine whether he was improving or not, and though he was a most imaginative child, he seldom complained unless in real physical pain. Lyn was careful to see that his supplementary diet was kept as high as possible, and I scraped bone marrow to add to the twins' turtle 'soup' (a. mixture of pieces of dried turtle, meat juice, water, eggs when available, and fresh or dried fish).

Our thirty-sixth day ended much as it had started; wet, cold and windy, seas slopping into *Ednamair* as she bounced in the steep short waves, the bailers familiar scrape and splash, and the helmsman hunched on the stern and peering at each wave to determine its potential danger to our craft . . . .

Thirty-eighth day: . . . I planned to land another two dorado that morning, one for eating immediately, to save the turtle steak for drying, and the other to increase our already good stocks of dried fish. I angled the gaff towards two likely bull dorado of rather a large size, then a large female shot close above the hook; I struck swiftly and missed, but at that instant a small bull of about fifteen pounds followed the female's track and my hook sank into it in a perfect strike! The fish flew into the dinghy with unerring precision and it was secured and killed in the space of seconds. Feeling very pleased with ourselves, we admired the high forehead of the bull while I made some adjustments to the nylon lines which weren't taking the strain evenly, then I told Douglas to gut it and keep the offal. I had noticed that although the dorado didn't eat the offal, they gathered round curiously as the scavenger fish fought over it. I had the idea a good fish could be taken unawares at this time, so I had Robin throw some offal over just ahead of the gaff. The scavenger fish rushed in, a boil of foam as they fought over the scraps, while the dorado swooped close by. I chose a twenty-five pound female dorado and struck.

The hook gave, then with a ripping sound the lines snapped one after the other, and the gaff went light. I looked swiftly at Douglas but he was pulling in the reserve line slowly. 'Didn't feel a thing,' he said. My initial reaction was one of extreme dejection; that fish had gone with our last big hook, no more fresh dorado. The nylon must have been cracked and I failed to notice; the tensions of the lines had been different too or they would have broken together; the disturbed water had probably distorted my aim, but it was no use being wise now, there wasn't another hook to be wise with. My spirits picked up a little as I realised that our stocks of dorado exceeded those of turtle meat and we had enough of both now to get us to the coast, even if we caught no more fresh turtle to supplement our rations. I still had another small hook to use for inshore fishing if that should be necessary, and if we felt like a taste of fresh fish I could always try a stab at another scavenger fish; we had been fattening them up for a while now, with our regular dumpings of turtle and fish offal.

Noon position 8°21' North and 85 miles west of Espinosa, twelve miles nearer land, was not a great boost to our morale but I pointed out that throughout all the time we had been adrift we had either been becalmed or the wind had been favourable. There hadn't been a day yet when I had had to record an adverse run. The calming seas also indicated that we might soon be able to row although the heavy cross swell would have to diminish a little too before that would be possible.

. . . I chopped up some dried turtle meat for tea, and Lyn put it with a little wet fish to soak in meat juice. She spread the dry sheets for the twins under the canopy, then prepared their little supper as we started to talk of Dougal's Kitchen and if it should have a wine licence. As we pondered the delights of Gaelic coffee, my eye, looking past the sail, caught sight of something that wasn't sea. I stopped talking and stared; the others all looked at me. 'A ship,' I said. 'There's a ship and it's coming towards us!' I could hardly believe it but it seemed solid enough. 'Keep still now!' In the sudden surge of excitement, everyone wanted to see. 'Trim her! We mustn't capsize now!' All sank back to their places.

I felt my voice tremble as I told them that I was going to stand on the thwart and hold a flare above the sail. They trimmed the dinghy as I stood on the thwart. 'Right, hand me a flare, and remember what happened with the last ship we saw!' They suddenly fell silent in memory of that terrible despondency when our signals had been unnoticed. 'Oh God!' prayed Lyn, 'please let them see us.' I could see the ship quite clearly now, a Japanese tunny fisher. Her gray and white paint stood out clearly against the dark cross swell. 'Like a great white bird,' Lyn said to the twins, and she would pass within about a mile of us at her nearest approach. I relayed the information as they listened excitedly, the tension of not knowing, of imminent rescue, building like a tangible, touchable, unbearable unreality around me. My eye caught the outlines of two large sharks, a hundred yards to starboard. 'Watch the trim,' I warned. 'We have two man-eating sharks waiting if we capsize!' Then, 'I'm going to light the flare now, have the torch ready in case it doesn't work.'

I ripped the caps off, pulled out the striker and struck the primer. The flare smoked then sparked into life, the red glare illuminating *Ednamair* and the sea around us in the twilight. I could feel my index finger roasting under the heat of the flare and waved it to and fro to escape the searing heat radiating outwards in the calm air, then unable to bear the heat any longer, I dropped my arm, nearly scorching Lyn's face, and threw the flare high in the air. It curved in a brilliant arc and dropped into the sea. 'Hand me another, I think she's altered course!' My voice was horse with pain and excitement and I felt sick with apprehension that it might only be the ship cork-screwing in the swell, for she had made no signal that she had seen us. The second flare didn't work. I cursed it in frustrated anguish as the priming substance chipped off instead of lighting. 'The torch!' I shouted, but it wasn't needed, she had seen us, and was coming towards us.

I flopped down on the thwart. 'Our ordeal is over,' I said quietly. Lyn and the twins were crying with happiness; Douglas, with tears of joy in his eyes, hugged his mother. Robin laughed and cried at the same time, slapped me on the back and shouted 'Wonderful! We've done it. Oh! Wonderful!' I put my arms about Lyn feeling the tears stinging my own eyes: 'We'll get these boys to land after all.' As we shared our happiness and watched the fishing boat close with us, death could have taken me quite easily just then, for I knew that I would never experience another such pinnacle of contentment.

1972
ALIVE: AIRCRASH IN THE ANDES

. . . The last discovery in their search for new tastes and new sources of food were the brains of the bodies which they had hitherto discarded. Canessa had told them that, while they might not be of particular nutritional value, they contained glucose which would give them energy; he had been the first to take a head, cut the skin across the forehead, pull back the scalp, and crack open the skull with the ax. The brains were then divided up and eaten while still frozen or used to make the sauce for a stew; the liver, intestine, muscle, fat, heart, and kidneys, either cooked or uncooked, were cut up into little pieces and mixed with the brains. In this way the food tasted better and was easier to eat.

– Piers Paul Read, Alive

On Thursday, October 12, 1972 a chartered Uruguayan Air Force Fairchild F-227 took off from Montevideo, Uruguay for Santiago, Chile. Aboard were five crew and forty passengers, including the "first fifteen" of the 'Old Christians Club' rugby team. From prosperous backgrounds, and all Roman Catholic, most of the 'Old Christians' had already begun careers in family businesses or were pursuing professional studies, but they were also devoted to their sport and had achieved a certain renown. Between eighteen and twenty-six years in age, the young men were looking forward to an extended weekend of competition and fun in the Chilean capital. The passenger roster of the Fairchild-227 was mostly filled out with family and friends.

Bad weather in the Andes forced a layover in Mendoza, Argentina, but in the mid-afternoon of Friday, October 13th the airplane took off for the relatively short hop across the mountains. Last reporting the airplane's position over the Pass of Planchon at 3:21 P.M. and a few minutes later over the Chilean town of Curicó, the copilot had turned north for the approach to Santiago when he lost his bearings amidst towering fifteen-thousand-foot peaks. The festive atmosphere in the passenger cabin soon turned to fear when the airplane encountered severe turbulence and twice alarmingly lost hundreds of feet of altitude. Seconds later, one of the airplane's wings struck a mountain peak, the tail section was sheered off, and its white fuselage plunged into an isolated mountain valley between the Tinguiririca volcano in Chile and the Cerro Sosneado in Argentina, finally coming to rest in a bed of ice and snow at about 11,500 feet. Between October 13th and 21st, Uruguayan, Argentine, and Chilean air rescue teams vainly searched for survivors. The professionals of the Chilean Air Rescue Service accurately plotted the probable crash site, but their search yielded no trace of the Fairchild or of its passengers. It was evident that no one could long survive the severe cold at such high altitudes, where temperatures during the spring nights sometimes fell to forty degrees below zero.

Twenty-seven passengers, three of them gravely wounded, and the flight mechanic survived the bitter cold of the first night and the confused and desperate day that followed. The survivors were crammed into a twenty-foot-long and eight-foot-wide section of the shattered fuselage, which lay at a thirty-degree angle, its battered nose pointing downward into a snow-choked valley surrounded on three sides by sheer mountain walls. While some of the young men, dazed and disoriented in the crash, loitered over bottles of Mendoza wine and cigarettes, others struggled to build a barrier of seat cushions and snow at the broken end of the fuselage through which freezing winds swept into the wreck. Marcelo Pérez, the rugby captain of the "first fifteen" coordinated medical care and various tasks inside the cabin, including the all important task of determining what provisions were at hand and taking charge of their distribution: several bottles of wine and alcohol, a dozen candy bars, caramels, some dried fruits and dates, a pack of crackers, two tins of mussels, and a few small jars of jam. Frozen snow was the only source of water. Cigarettes were in relatively plentiful supply.

As early as Tuesday, October 17th there was talk among the survivors of eating the dead. This grim idea hung over them in the following days and nights of bitter cold while they vainly hoped for rescue as starvation took hold, their condition worsened, and squabbling broke out among them. On Sunday, October 22nd Marcello Pérez and Roy Harley managed to receive reports on a transistor radio that they had connected to a long wire antenna, but there was no news of any rescue efforts.

That afternoon Roberto Canessa cut twenty slivers of meat from the buttock of one of the corpses and laid them out to dry on the fuselage. Later that day he was the first to eat. Some of the others followed. The next day Pérez and Harley picked up a radio report that Chilean authorities had cancelled the search. The survivors now knew that they would have to find their own way to safety, which most of them believed lay across the mountains to the west. That very afternoon Zerbino, Turcatti, and Maspons, among the strongest in the group, headed up the steep valley, while Canessa and Fito Strauch returned to slice more meat from the first corpse. All the meat cut the day before had been eaten. Pedro Algorta likened it to a "Holy Communion" in which the dead would save the living. The acceptance of this grim nourishment, and the realization that their survival now almost certainly depended wholly upon themselves, galvanized the group into renewed activity as they worked to cover the corpses with snow to preserve them, melted snow on pieces of aluminum and funneled the water into empty wine bottles, and tried to clean and better organize the ruins of the passenger cabin.

After surviving a night of murderous cold on the mountain, Zerbino, Turcatti, and Maspons returned to the fuselage. Snow-blinded, their feet almost frostbitten, they greedily seized upon the meat offered to them. Strengthened by their new diet, the survivors went to sleep early on the Sunday, October 29th, when a fresh disaster struck. An avalanche swept down upon them, pushed aside the flimsy barrier of seat cushions at the open end of the wreck, and filled the fuselage with snow, smothering and killing eight of them. A second avalanche struck the grief-stricken survivors, now nineteen, wet, frozen and trapped in the snow buried fuselage, and threatened them with suffocation until Parrado managed to jam a steel pole through the roof of the cabin and work it to the surface to create a small airshaft. When dim gray light finally suffused the snow-inundated cabin the next morning, they managed to push their way to the surface where a blizzard was raging, forcing the nineteen young men to remain in their icy prison until the following Wednesday, November 1st, when the storm finally abated and they were able to emerge into the sun.

The survivors struggled through the first week of November and intensified their planning to mount an expedition to seek help. Concluding that only a smaller group of the fittest would have any chance of survival, they chose four among them to be "expeditionaries": Parrado and Turcatti, both strong, well-liked, and eager to go; hot-tempered Canessa, an inventive "realist" who was skeptical of success but dutifully accepted the assignment; and Vizintín, who was sufficiently strong but whose psychological resilience was less certain. On Wednesday November 15th, Canessa,

Vizintín, Parrado, and Turcatti set out down the valley to the east with hopes that their path would eventually turn westward toward Chile, but they were repelled by a terrible blizzard and were driven back to the fuselage three hours later. When Canessa, Parrado, and Vizintín set out under blue skies early in the morning two days later—an injured leg forced Turcatti to remain behind—they made speedy progress over the ice-encrusted surface. Two hours later they came upon the wreckage of the tail section, and a cornucopia of fresh clothing and even some food and cartons of cigarettes in the suitcases scattered around it. Enchanted by this wealth, the expeditionaries bivouacked at the tail before continuing on the next morning. The day began with light flurries of snow and then cleared and became quite hot, but the temperature plunged after sunset and the three expeditionaries spent a sleepless night, frozen under the glittering stars in a shelter that they had dug into the snow. Parrado wanted to go on the next day, but acceded to Canessa's insistence that such a course would be suicidal, so they trudged back up the valley and collapsed exhausted at the tail where they lingered for two days. The clothing and cigarettes salvaged from the tail did little to brighten the spirits of their fourteen remaining comrades, whose hopes for rescue, raised with their departure, they disappointed with their return on November 21st.

It is at this point in the story that we open to Piers Paul Read's scrupulously accurate account of its turning point. Read brilliantly portrays the situation at the tail and in the camp in the three weeks that led to the launching of the final expedition and the desperate climb up the mountain to a critical point of decision—a decision that led to salvation only a week later when Parrado and Canessa reached safety. Even with Parrado to guide them, helicopter rescue crews had difficulty locating the survivors on December 22, 1972, the seventy-first day of their ordeal. By December 23rd all fourteen men remaining had been lifted out of the camp. Few of them required hospitalization. Word of their miraculous survival instantly spread throughout Latin America and the world. Some of the survivors explained that they had subsisted on "cheese and wild herbs." But the world soon came to understand what they had been forced to do to remain alive. Some of the survivors asserted that their cannibalism had been an expression of the Holy Sacrament of Communion. Gently dismissing this idea, the Roman Catholic Church played an important role in world acceptance of the real nature of the "Christmas miracle" of survival in the High Andes.

Alive:
The Story of the Andes Survivors

by Piers Paul Read

November 23 was Bobby Francois's twenty-first birthday. He received as a present from his sixteen companions an extra pack of cigarettes. Meanwhile Canessa and Parrado set about the task of removing the radio from the panel of instruments which remained half buried in the pilot's chest.

. . . Canessa was the most enthusiastic about the radio. He thought it insane for any of them to risk their lives by setting off over the mountains if there was any chance that they could make contact with the outside world. The majority agreed with him, though many were more or lss skeptical about the outcome. Pedro Algorta did not think they would ever make it work, but he said nothing which might make the optimists despondent. Roy Harley himself, who was supposed to be their radio expert, was the most doubtful of all. He knew best the limits of his own expertness upon which they based their hopes— some odd afternoons fiddling around with the stereo set of a friend— and insisted repeatedly in a whining voice that this in no way qualified him to dismantle and then reassemble a VHF radio.

. . . Their departure, however, was not imminent because several of them were still struggling with the shark's-fin antenna, riveted on the roof of the plane above the pilot's cabin. They had to remove the rivets with only a screwdriver, and the task was made more difficult by twists in the metal caused by the fall of the plane.

Even when it was removed and lay on the snow beside the different parts of the radio, Canessa spent hour upon hour just staring at it and snapped at anyone who asked him what more there was to do that he was not ready to go. The others became impatient, but they were all wary of Canessa's temper. If he had not been an expeditionary—and the most inventive of the three—they might not have put up with him; as it was, they did not wish to antagonize him. All the same, his procrastination seemed unreasonable, and they began to suspect that he was protracting the experiment with the radio to postpone the moment when he might have to set off in the snow.

At last the three Strauch cousins became exasperated. They told him that he must take the radio and go. Canessa could think of no further excuse for delay, and at eight o'clock the next morning a small column assembled for the descent to the tail. First came Vizintín, loaded as usual like a packhorse; then Harley, with his hands in his pockets, and finally the two figures of Canessa and Parrado, with sticks and knapsacks like two winter sportsmen.

They set off down the mountain, and the thirteen they left behind were delighted to see them go. Not only were they spared the irritable and bullying presence of Canessa and Vizintín but also, with the four absent, they could sleep much more comfortably. Above all they could dream again that rescue was at hand.

They were in no position, however, to sit back and wait for their dreams to come true. For the first time since they had taken their decision to eat the flesh of the dead, they were running short of supplies. The problem was not that sufficient bodies did not exist but that they could not find them; those who had died in the accident and had been left outside the plane were now, as a result of the avalanche, buried deep beneath the snow. One or two still remained of those who had died in the avalanche, but they knew that quite soon they would have to find the earlier victims. It was also a consideration that those who had died in the accident would be fatter and their livers better stocked with the vitamins they all needed to survive.

They therefore set about searching for bodies. Carlitos Páez and Pedro Algorta were in charge of this operation, but all the other boys joined in. Their method was to dig a shaft down into the snow on the spot where they remembered a body had lain, but these holes would often go deep without anything coming to light. On other occasions they would be more successful, but often with frustrating consequences. It was thought, for instance, that a body lay somewhere around the entrance to the plane, and Algorta spent many days methodically digging a hole there, with steps going down into it. It was difficult work because the snow was hard and Pedro, like all the others, had grown increasingly weak, so it was something like finding gold when the piece of aluminum which acted as a shovel uncovered the fabric of what seemed to be a shirt. Pedro dug faster around the legs and feet of the body but suddenly saw, as he uncovered them, that the toenails were painted with red varnish. Instead of a boy's body he had found Liliana Methol, and in deference to Javier's feelings they had agreed not to eat her. . . .

Many of the boys felt themselves too weak to do any labor of this kind. Some had learned to live with their uselessness, but others did not admit to themselves that they made no contribution to the welfare of the group. Carlitos once rebuked Sabella for not doing any work, whereupon the enfeebled Moncho fell to digging a hole with such hysterical frenzy that those who watched him feared for his life, but his exertions only led him to collapse with exhaustion. Here indeed was a case where the spirit was willing but the flesh weak.

At the same time as the boys dug into the snow in search of the buried bodies, the corpses that they had preserved near the surface began to suffer from the stronger sun which melted the thin layer of snow which covered them. The thaw had truly set in—the level of the snow had fallen far below the roof of the Fairchild—and the sun in the middle of the day became so hot that any meat left exposed to it would quickly rot. Added, then, to the labors of digging, cutting, and snow melting was that of covering the bodies with snow and then shielding them from the sun with sheets of cardboard and plastic.

As the supplies grew short, an order went out from the cousins that there was to be no more pilfering. This edict was no more effective than most others which seek to upset an established practice. They therefore sought to make what food they had last longer by eating parts of the human body which previously they had left aside. The hands and feet, for example, had flesh beneath the skin which could be scraped off the bone. They tried, too, to eat the tongue off one corpse but could not swallow it, and one of them once ate the testicles.

On the other hand they all took to the marrow. When the last shred of meat had been scraped off a bone it would be cracked open with the ax and the marrow extracted with a piece of wire or a knife and shared. They also ate the blood clots which they found around the hearts of almost all the bodies. Their texture and taste were different from that of the flesh and fat, and by now they were sick to death of this staple diet. It was not just that their senses clamored for different tastes; their bodies too cried out for those minerals of which they had for so long been deprived—above all, for salt. And it was in obedience to these cravings that the less fastidious among the survivors began to eat those parts of the body which had started to rot. This had happened to the entrails of even those bodies which were covered with snow, and there were also the remains of previous carcasses scattered around the plane which were unprotected from the sun. Later everyone did the same.

What they would do was to take the small intestine, squeeze out its contents onto the snow, cut it into small pieces, and eat it. The taste was strong and salty. One of them tried wrapping it around a bone and roasting it in the fire. Rotten flesh, which they tried later, tasted like cheese.

The last discovery in their search for new tastes and new sources of food were the brains of the bodies which they had hitherto discarded. Canessa had told them that, while they might not be of particular nutritional value, they contained glucose which would give them energy; he had been the first to take a head, cut the skin across the forehead, pull back the scalp, and crack open the skull with the ax. The brains were then divided up and eaten while still frozen or used to make the sauce for a stew; the liver, intestine, muscle, fat, heart, and kidneys, either cooked or uncooked, were cut up into little pieces and mixed with the brains. In this way the food tasted better and was easier to eat. The only difficulty was the shortage of bowls suitable to hold it, for before this the meat had been served on plates, trays, or pieces of aluminum foil. For the stew Inciarte used a shaving bowl, while others used the top halves of skulls. Four bowls made from skulls were used in this way—and some spoons were made from bones.

The brains were inedible when putrid, so all the heads which remained from the corpses they had consumed were gathered together and buried in the snow. The snow was also combed for other parts which had previously been thrown away. Scavenging took on an added value—especially for Algorta, who was the chief scavenger among them. When he was not digging holes or helping the cousins cut up the bodies, his bent figure could be seen hobbling around the plane, poking into the snow with an iron stick. . . .

As the division between the two groups of workers and work-shy, provident and improvident, grew wider, Coche Inciarte's role became more important. By performance and inclination he was firmly in the camp of the parasites; on the other hand he was an old friend of Fito Strauch and Daniel Fernández. He also had the kind of pure and witty character that it was impossible to dislike. Whether he was coaxing Carlitos to cook on a windy day or shooting a pint of pus out of his dreadfully infected leg, he would always smile himself and make others smile at what he was doing. His condition, like Numa Turcatti's, was increasingly serious because both were reluctant to eat raw meat. Coche even became delirious at times and told the boys in all seriousness that there was a little door in the side of the plane where he slept which led out into a green valley. Yet when he announced one morning, as Rafael Echavarren had done, that he was going to die that day, no one took him seriously. Next day, when he awoke again, they all laughed at him and said, "Well, Coche, what's it like to be dead?"

Cigarettes were, as always, the chief source of tension. Those like the cousins, who had sufficient control of themselves to space their smoking and make their rations last, would find toward the end of the second day that each puff was watched by a dozen pair of envious eyes. The improvident—and Coche was among the most improvident—would exhaust their own supply the first day and then try and bum cigarettes off those who still had some. Pedro Algorta, who smoked less than the others, would move around with lowered eyes for fear of intercepting one of Coche's importuning glances, yet if he avoided them for long enough, Coche would say to him, "Pedro, when we get back to Montevideo, I'll invite you to eat some *gnocchi* at our uncle's house," at which the hungry Algorta would look up and be caught by the large, pleading, laughing eyes.

. . . Their improvidence with cigarettes reinforced a bond which had already existed between Coche and Delgado. They either bummed alone—Pancho taking some of Numa Turcatti's ration because he felt that smoking was doing him no good, while Coche tried to catch Algorta's eye—or, as we have seen, presented a common front to get an advance from Daniel Fernández. They also talked together about life in Montevideo and weekends in the country with Gaston Costemalle, who had been their mutual friend. Pancho, with his natural eloquence, described the scene of their former happiness so well that Coche would be transported away from the damp, stinking confines of the wrecked plane to the green pastures of his dairy farm. Then, when the story ended, he would suddenly find himself back in the foul reality, which would so depress him that he would sit like a corpse with glazed eyes.

Because of this, the Strauches and Daniel Fernández tried to keep Coche away from Delgado. They felt that these escapist conversations would lower his morale to such an extent that he would lose the will to survive. . . .

* * *

While these developments were taking place in the plane, the three expeditionaries and Roy Harley were in the tail. Their journey down had only taken them one and a half hours, and on the way they had found a suitcase which had belonged to Parrado's mother. They found candy inside and two bottles of Coca-Cola.

They spent the rest of that first day at the tail resting and looking through the suitcases which had appeared from under the melting snow since they were last there. Among other things Parrado found a camera loaded with film and his airline bag with the two bottles of rum and liqueur which his mother had bought in Mendoza and asked him to carry for her. Neither was broken, and they opened one of them but saved the other for the expedition they would have to make if they could not get the radio to work.

Canessa and Harley set about that task next morning. It seemed at first that it would not be difficult, because the sockets in the back of the transmitter were marked BAT and ANT to show where the wires to the batteries and antenna should be fixed. Unfortunately there were other wires whose connections were not so clear. Above all they could not make out which wires were positive and which negative, so often when they made a connection sparks flew into their eyes.

Their hopes of success were raised when Vizintín found an instruction manual for the Fairchild lying in the snow beside the tail. They looked at the index for some reference to the radio and discovered that the whole of chapter thirty-four was devoted to "Communications," but when they came to look for this section they discovered that certain pages had been torn out of the book by the wind and it was just these pages which made up the chapter they needed.

They had no choice, therefore, but to return to trial and error. It was a painstaking business, and while the others worked Parrado and Vizintín would rummage around, rifling all the baggage for a second time, or light a fire to cook the meat. Though there were only four of them, they were not exempt from the tensions which existed up in the fuselage. It irritated Roy Harley, for example, that Parrado would not give him the same ration as the others. It seemed clear that since he was on an expedition he should eat the same amount as an expeditionary. Parrado, on the other hand, held that Roy was only an auxiliary; if the radio failed he would not have to walk out through the mountains. Therefore he should eat only what was necessary to survive.

Nor would he let Roy smoke cigarettes. His reasoning was that they only had one lighter with them and they would need it for any final expedition; but it was also true that neither Parrado, Canessa, nor Vizintín smoked themselves but all were intolerably irritated by Roy's whimpering and wailing. Thus they told him that he could only smoke when they lit a fire. On one occasion, however, when Roy came to light a cigarette at the fire, Parrado, who was cooking, told him to get out of his way and come back when he had finished. But when Roy came back the fire had gone out. He was so angry that he picked up the lighter which Parrado had left on some cardboard and lit a cigarette. When the three expeditionaries saw what he had done they went for him like a pack of zealous school prefects. They cursed him and might have snatched the cigarette out of his mouth had not Canessa thought better of it and stopped them. "Leave him alone," he said to the other two. "Don't forget that Roy may be the one to save the lives of us all by getting this damned radio to work."

It was clear by the third day that they had not brought enough meat to last them the time it would take to set up the radio. Therefore Parrado and Vizintín set off for the plane again, leaving Harley and Canessa at the tail. The ascent, as before, was a thousand times more difficult than the descent had been. After reaching the top of the hillock which lay just east of the plane, Parrado was assaulted by a momentary but profound despair; instead of the fuselage and its thirteen inhabitants, there was nothing but a huge expanse of snow.

He assumed at once that there must have been another avalanche which had completely covered the plane, but he looked up and saw no signs of a fresh fall of snow on the sides of the mountains above him. He walked on and to his immense relief found the plane on the other side of the next hill.

The boys had not expected them and had no meat prepared. Also, they were all almost too weak to dig for the bodies that would have to be found if the expeditionaries were to restock their larder. Therefore Parrado and Vizintín themselves set about digging. They found a corpse from which the cousins cut meat and stuffed it into rugby socks, and after two nights up in the plane they returned to the tail.

There they found that Harley and Canessa had made all the necessary connections between battery and radio and radio and shark's-fin antenna but still could not pick up any signal on the earphones. They thought that perhaps the antenna was faulty, so they tore out strands of cable from the electrical circuits of the plane and linked them together. One end of this they tied to the tail, the other to a bag filled with stones which they placed on a rock high on the side of the mountain, making an aerial more than sixty feet long. When they connected it to the transistor radio which they had brought with them, they could pick up many radio stations in Chile, Argentina, and Uruguay. When they connected it to the Fairchild's radio, however, nothing came through at all. They therefore reconnected the transistor, found a program which played some cheerful music, and went back to work. . . .

On the transistor radio that they had attached to their antenna, the four of them heard a news bulletin in which it was announced that the search was to be resumed by a Douglas C-47 of the Uruguayan

Air Force. They received the news in different ways. Harley was ecstatic with hope and joy. Canessa too looked relieved. Vizintín showed no particular reaction, while Parrado looked almost disappointed. "Don't get too optimistic," he warned the others. "Just because they're looking again doesn't mean they'll find us."

They decided, all the same, that it would be a good idea to make a large cross in the snow by the tail, and they did so with the suitcases that lay scattered all around. By now they had almost given up hope of the radio, though Canessa still pottered with it and prevaricated about a return to the plane. Parrado and Vizintín, on the other hand, already had their minds on the expedition, for it had been decided up in the plane that if the radio failed the expeditionaries would set off straight up the mountain in obedience to the only thing of which they were sure—that Chile was to the west. Thus Vizintín removed the rest of the material which was wound around the Fairchild's heating system in the dark locker at the base of the tail which had contained the batteries. It was light and yet designed by the most technologically sophisticated industry in the world to contain heat; sewn together into a large sack, it would make an excellent sleeping bag and solve the one outstanding problem which had beset them—how to keep warm at night without the shelter of either tail or plane.

. . . The tail was in the same place the next morning, but it was clearly no longer safe. It was obvious that no more tinkering with the radio would make it work. They therefore made up their minds to return to the plane. Before they left they loaded themselves once again with cigarettes, and Harley—as an expression of all the misery and frustration he had felt in those eight days—kicked to pieces the different components of the radio they had so painstakingly put together. . . .

They reached the plane between half past six and seven in the evening. There was a cold wind blowing, with a slight flurry of snow. The thirteen had already gone inside, and they gave the expeditionaries a depressed reception.

Canessa, however, was less struck by their unfriendliness than by the desolation of the spectacle they presented. After eight days away he saw with some objectivity just how thin and haggard the bearded faces of his friends had become. He had seen too, with a fresh eye, the horror of the filthy snow strewn with gutted carcasses and split skulls, and he thought to himself that before they were rescued they must do something to tidy it up.

* * *

Toward the end of the first week in December, after fifty-six days on the mountain, two condors appeared in the sky and circled above the seventeen survivors. These two enormous birds of prey with bald necks and head, a collar of white down, and a wingspan of nine feet were the first sign of any life but their own that they had seen for eight weeks. The survivors were immediately afraid that they would descend and carry off the carrion. They would have shot at them with the revolver but were afraid that the sudden noise might cause another avalanche. . . .

It was now warm during the day; indeed, at midday it was so hot that their skin became burned and their lips were cracked and bleeding. Some of them tried to make a tent to shelter them from the sun with the poles from the hammocks and a bale of cloth that Liliana Methol had bought in Mendoza to make a dress for her daughter. They also thought it would make a useful signal to any plane that flew overhead, for this possibility was uppermost in their minds. When Roy and the expeditionaries had returned from the tail, they had told the thirteen who had stayed in the plane that they had heard on their transistor that the search had been restarted.

The boys were determined that this should not tempt the expeditionaries to abandon the idea of further expedition. They had had no high hopes for the radio and were not thrown into despair when Harley, Canessa, Parrado, and Vizintín returned, but they were impatient that the last three should leave again almost immediately. It soon became evident, however, that while the news of the C-47 in no way affected Parrado's determination to leave, it produced in Canessa a certain reluctance to risk his life on the mountainside. "It would be absurd for us to leave now," he said, "with this specially equipped plane on its way to find us. We should give them at least ten days and then, perhaps, set out. It's crazy to risk our lives if it isn't necessary."

The others were thrown into a fury by this procrastination. They had not pampered Canessa and suffered his intolerable temper for so long only to be told by him that he was not going. Nor were they so optimistic that the C-47 would find them, for they heard on the radio first that it had been forced to land in Buenos Aires, then that it had had to have its engines overhauled in Los Cerrillos. There was also the shortage of food that was upon them, for though they knew that corpses were hidden in the snow beneath them, they either could not find them or only found those they had agreed not to eat.

There was another factor too, which was their sense of pride in what they had already achieved. They had survived now for eight weeks in the most extreme and inhuman conditions. They wanted to prove that they could also escape on their own initiative. They all loved to think of the expression on the face of the first shepherd or farmer they found as he was told that the three expeditionaries were survivors from the Uruguayan Fairchild. All of them practiced in their minds the nonchalant tone they would adopt when telephoning their parents in Montevideo.

Fito's impatience was more practical. "Don't you realize," he said to Canessa, "that they aren't looking for survivors? They're looking for dead bodies. And the special equipment they talk about is photographic equipment. They take aerial photographs and then go back, develop them, study them. . . . It'll take weeks for them to find us, even if they do fly directly overhead."

This argument seemed to convince Canessa. Parrado did not need to be persuaded, and Vizintín always went along with what the other two decided. They therefore set to work to prepare the final expedition. The cousins cut flesh off the bodies not just for their daily needs but to set up a store for the journey. The others were set to sewing the insulating material from the tail into a sleeping bag. It was difficult. They ran out of thread and had to use wire from the electric circuits.

December 8 was the Feast of the Immaculate Conception. To honor the Virgin, and to persuade her to intercede for the success of their final expedition, the boys in the Fairchild decided to pray the full fifteen mysteries of the rosary. Alas, soon after they had finished five their voices grew thinner and fewer, and one by one they dropped off to sleep. They therefore made up the rest the next evening, the ninth, which was also Parrado's twenty-third birthday. It was a mildly melancholy occasion, for they had so often planned the party they would have in Montevideo. To celebrate here on the mountain, the community gave Parrado one of the Havana cigars that had been found in the tail. Parrado smoked it, but he took more pleasure from the warmth it provided than from the aroma.

On December 10, Canessa still insisted that the expedition was not ready to leave. The sleeping bag was not sewn to his satisfaction, nor had he collected together everything he would need. Yet instead of applying himself to what was still to be done, Canessa lay around "conserving his energy" or insisted on treating the boils that Roy Harley had developed on his legs. He also quarreled with the younger boys. He told Francois that at the tail Vizintín had wiped his backside on Bobby's best Lacoste T-shirt, which put Bobby into an unusual rage. He even quarreled with his great friend and admirer Alvaro Mangino, for that morning, while defecating onto a seat cover in the plane (he had diarrhea from eating putrid flesh), he told Mangino to move his leg. Mangino said that it had been cramped all night and so he would not. Canessa shouted at Mangino. Mangino cursed Canessa. Canessa lost his temper and grabbed Mangino by the hair. He was about to hit him but simply threw Alvaro back against the wall of the plane instead.

"Now you're not my friend any more," Mangino said, sobbing.

"I'm sorry," said Canessa, sitting back, his temper once more under control. "It's just that I'm feeling so ill . . . "

He was no one's friend that day. The cousins thought he was deliberately procrastinating and were especially angry with him. That night they did not keep his special place as an expeditionary, and he had to sleep by the door. The only one who had any influence on him was Parrado, and his determination was as great as it had ever been. That morning, as they lay in the plane waiting to go out, he suddenly said, "You know, if that plane flies over us, it might not see us. We should make a cross." And without waiting for anyone else to take up his idea, he went out of the plane and surveyed an area of pristine snow where a cross could be best constructed. The other boys followed him, and soon all those who could walk without pain were stamping the ground along preordained lines to make a giant cross in the snow. In the middle, where the two lines crossed, they put the upturned trash can which Vizintín had brought up on the trial expedition. They also laid out the bright yellow and green jackets of the pilots. Realizing that movement would attract a flier's attention, they drew up a plan whereby they would run in circles as soon as a plane was sighted overhead.

That night Fito Strauch went to Parrado and said that if Canessa would not leave on the expedition then he would.

"No," said Parrado. "Don't worry. I've talked to Muscles. He'll go. He must go. He's much better trained than you are. All we have to do now is finish the sleeping bag."

The next morning the Strauches rose early and set to work on the sleeping bag. They were determined that by that evening there should be no possible excuse for any further delay. But something was to happen that day which would make their threats and admonitions superfluous.

Numa Turcatti had been getting weaker every day. His health, along with that of Roy Harley and Coche Inciarte, caused the greatest concern to the two "doctors," Canessa and Zerbino. Though Numa, who was so pure in spirit, was loved by all on the plane, his closest friend before the accident had been Pancho Delgado, and it was Delgado who took it upon himself to look after him. He brought Numa's ration of food into the plane, made water for him, tried to stop him from smoking cigarettes because Canessa had said they were bad for him, and fed him little smears of toothpaste from a tube which Canessa had brought from the tail.

. . . Even with an extra ration, Numa's condition did not improve. Instead he grew weaker. As he grew weaker, he grew more listless, and as he grew more listless he bothered less about feeding himself, which in its turn made him weaker still. Like Inciarte and Sabella, Numa was intermittently delirious, but on the night of December 10 he slept peacefully. In the morning Delgado went out to sit in the sun. He had been told that Numa might die but his mind would not accept it. Later in the morning, however, Canessa came out and told him that Numa was in a coma. Delgado returned immediately to the cabin and went to the side of his friend. Numa lay there with his eyes open, but he seemed unaware of Delgado's presence. His breathing was slow and labored. Delgado knelt beside him and began to say the rosary. As he prayed, the breathing stopped . . .

Turcatti's death achieved what argument and exhortation had failed to achieve; it persuaded Canessa that they could wait no longer. Roy Harley, Coche Inciarte, and Moncho Sabella were all weak and incipiently delirious. A day's delay could mean the difference between their death and their survival. It was therefore agreed by all that the final expedition should set off the next day due west to Chile.

That evening, before he went into the plane for the last time, Parrado drew the three Strauch cousins to one side and told them that if they ran short of food they should eat the bodies of his mother and sister. "Of course I'd rather you didn't," he said, "but if it's a matter of survival, then you must."

The cousins said nothing, but the expression on their faces betrayed how moved they were by what Parrado had said to them.

* * *

At five o'clock the next morning, Canessa, Parrado, and Vizintín prepared to go. First they dressed themselves in the clothes they had picked from the baggage of the forty-five passengers and crew. Next to his skin Parrado wore a Lacoste T-shirt and a pair of long woolen woman's slacks. On top of these he wore three pairs of jeans, and on top of the T-shirt six sweaters. Next he put a woolen balaclava over his head, then the hood and shoulders that he had cut from Susana's fur coat, and finally a jacket. Under his rugby boots he wore four pairs of socks which he covered with plastic supermarket bags to keep out the wet. For his hands he had gloves; for his eyes a pair of sunglasses; and to help him climb he held an aluminum pole which he strapped to his wrist.

Vizintín also had a balaclava. He wore as many sweaters and pairs of jeans but covered them with a raincoat, and on his feet he wore a pair of Spanish boots. As before he also carried the heaviest load, including a third of the meat, packed either in a plastic bag or a rugby sock. With it there were pieces of fat, to provide energy, and liver, to give them vitamins. The whole supply was designed to last the three of them ten days.

Canessa carried the sleeping bag. To cover his body and keep it warm he had looked for woolen clothes, feeling that elemental conditions called for elemental materials. He also liked to think that each garment had something precious about it. One of the sweaters he wore had been given to him by a dear friend of his mother, another by his mother herself, and a third had been knitted for him by his *novia*, Laura Surraco. One of the pairs of trousers he wore had belonged to his closest friend, Daniel Maspons, and his belt had been given to him by Parrado with the words, "This was a present from Panchito, who was my best friend. Now you're my best friend, so you take it." Canessa accepted this gift; he also wore Abal's skiing gloves and the skiing boots which belonged to Javier Methol.

The cousins gave the expeditionaries some breakfast before they sent them on their way. The others watched in silence. No words could express what they felt at this awesome moment; they all knew that this was their last chance of survival. Then Parrado separated once again the pair of tiny red shoes that he had bought in Mendoza for his nephew. He put one in his pocket and hung the other from the hat rack in the plane. "I'll be back to get it," he said. "Don't worry."

"All right," they all said, their spirits raised high by his optimism. "And don't forget to book us rooms in the hotel in Santiago." Then they embraced, and amid cries of *Hasta luego!* the three expeditionaries set off up the mountain. . . .

They climbed up the valley, but they knew that this course took them slightly northwest and at some moment they would have to turn due west and climb directly up the mountain. The difficulty was that the slopes which encircled them looked uniformly steep and high. Canessa and Parrado began to argue about when, and how soon, they should start to climb. Vizintín, as usual, had no opinion on the subject. Eventually the two agreed. They took a reading on the plane's spherical compass and started to climb due west up the side of the valley. It was very heavy going. Not only were they faced with the steep slope, but the snow had already started to melt and even in their improvised snowshoes they sank up to their knees. The wet snow also made the cushions sodden and therefore exceptionally heavy to drag bowlegged up the mountain. But they persevered, pausing every few yards for a short rest, and by the time they stopped by an outcrop of rocks for lunch at midday they were already very high. Beneath them they could still see the Fairchild, with some of the boys sitting on the seats in the sun watching their progress.

After their meal of meat and fat, they took another short rest and then continued on their way. Their plan was to reach the top before dark, for it would be almost impossible to sleep on the steep slopes of the mountain. As they climbed, their minds were on the view they hoped to have on the other side—a view of small hills and green valleys, perhaps with a shepherd's hut or a farmhouse already in sight. As they had already found out, however, distances in the snow were deceptive, and by the time the sun went behind the mountain they were still nowhere near the top. Realizing that somehow they would have to sleep on the mountainside, they started to look for a level surface. To their growing dismay, it seemed that there was none. The mountain was almost vertical. . . .

. . . a little farther on they came to an immense boulder, beside which the wind had blown a trench in the snow. The floor of the trench was not horizontal, but the wall of snow would prevent them from slipping down the mountainside; they therefore pitched camp and climbed into the sleeping bag.

It was a perfectly clear night and the temperature had sunk to many degrees below freezing, but the sleeping bag succeeded in keeping them warm. They also ate some more meat and drank a mouthful each of the rum they had brought with them. The view from where they lay was magnificent. There spread before them a huge landscape of snow-covered mountains lit by the pale light of the moon and stars. They felt strange lying there—Canessa in the middle—half possessed by terror and despair, yet half marveling at the magnificence of this icy beauty before them.

At last they slept or slipped fitfully into semiconsciousness. The night was too cold and the ground too hard for the three to sleep well, and the first light of the morning found them all awake. When the sun came up from behind the mountains opposite them they started to climb once again—Parrado first, followed by Canessa and then Vizintín. All three were still tired and their limbs were stiff from the exertion of the day before, but they found a kind of path in the rock which seemed to lead toward the summit. . . .

The mountain had become so steep that Vizintín did not dare look down. He simply followed Canessa at a cautious distance, as Canessa followed Parrado. What frustrated them all was that each summit they saw above them turned out to be a false one, a ridge of snow or an outcrop of rocks. They stopped by one of these rocks to eat in the middle of the day, took a short rest, and then climbed on. By the middle of the afternoon they still had not reached the top of the mountain— and though they felt themselves to be near, they were afraid of making the same mistake as the night before. They therefore looked for and found a similar trench carved by the wind beside the same kind of rock and decided to stop there.

Unlike Vizintín, Canessa had not been afraid to look down as they climbed the mountain, and each time he did so he saw that line in the far distance grow more distinct and more like a road. As they sat down in the sleeping bag and waited for the sunset, he pointed it out to the others. "Do you see that line over there?" he said. "I think it's a road."

"I can't see anything," said Nando, who was nearsighted. "But whatever it is, it can't be a road because we're facing due east and Chile's to the west."

"I know Chile's to the west," said Canessa, "but I still say that it's a road. And there's no snow down there. Look, Tintin, you can see it, can't you?"

Vizintín's eyesight was not much better than Parrado's. He gazed into the distance with his small eyes. "I can just see a line, yes," he said, "but I couldn't say if it was a road or not."

"It can't be a road," said Parrado.

"There might be a mine," said Canessa. "There are copper mines right in the middle of the cordillera."

"How do you know?" asked Parrado.

"I read about it somewhere."

"It's more likely a geological fault."

There was a pause. Then Canessa said, "I think we should go back."

"Go back?" Parrado repeated.

"Yes," said Canessa. "Go back. This mountain's much too high. We'll never reach the top. With every step we take we risk our lives. ...

It's madness to go on."

"And what do we do if we go back?" asked Parrado.

"Go to that road."

"If we keep going to the west, we're sure to break our necks." Parrado sighed.

"Well, I'm going back anyway," said Canessa.

"And I'm going on," said Parrado. "If you walk to that road and find it isn't a road, then it'll be too late to try this way again. They're already short of food down there. There won't be enough for another expedition like this so we'll all be losers; we'll all stay up here in the cordillera."

They slept that night with their differences unresolved. At one point Vizintín was waked by lightning in the distance and he woke Canessa, fearing that a storm was about to break over them. But the night was still clear, there was no wind, and the two boys went back to sleep again.

The night did not weaken Parrado's determination; as soon as it was light he prepared himself to continue the climb. Canessa, however, seemed less sure that he was going to return to the Fairchild, so he made the suggestion that Parrado and Vizintín leave their knapsacks with him and climb a little farther up the mountain to see if they came to the top. Parrado accepted this idea and set off at once, with Vizintín behind him, but in his impatience to reach the summit Parrado climbed quickly and Vizintín was soon left behind.

The ascent had become exceptionally difficult. The wall of snow was almost vertical and Parrado could only proceed by digging steps for his hands and feet, which Vizintín used as he followed him. If he had slipped he would have fallen for many hundreds of feet, but this did not dismay him; the surface of the snow was so steep, and the sky above it so blue, that he knew he was approaching the summit. He was driven on by all the excitement of a mountaineer whose triumph is at hand and by his intense anxiety to see what was on the other side. As he climbed he told himself, "I'm going to see a valley, I'm going to see a river, I'm going to see green grass and trees—" and then suddenly the sheer face was no longer so steep. It fell sharply to a slight incline and then flattened out onto a level surface of some twelve feet wide before falling away on the other side. He was at the top of the mountain.

Parrado's joy at having made it lasted for only the few seconds it took him to scramble to his feet; the view before him was not of green valleys running down toward the Pacific Ocean but an endless expanse of snow-covered mountains. From where he stood, nothing blocked his view of vast cordillera, and for the first time Parrado felt that they were finished. He sank to his knees and wanted to curse and cry to heaven at the injustice, but no sound came from his mouth and as he looked up again, panting from his recent exertion in the thin air of the mountain, his momentary despair was replaced once again by a certain elation at what he had done. It was true that the view before him was of mountains, their peaks standing in ranks to the far horizon, but the very fact that he was above them showed that he had climbed one of the highest mountains in the Andes. I've climbed this mountain, he thought to himself, and I shall call it Mount Seler after my father . . .

As he studied the mountains spread out before him he came to notice that due west, to the far left of the panorama, there were two mountains whose peaks were not covered with snow. "The cordillera must end somewhere," he said to himself, "so perhaps those two are in Chile." The truth was, of course, that he knew nothing about the cordillera, but this idea renewed his optimism, and when he heard Vizintín calling him from below, he shouted down to him in a buoyant tone of voice, "Go back and fetch Muscles. Tell him it's all going to be all right. Tell him to come up and see for himself!"

When the two others set off for the summit, Canessa had sat back with the knapsacks and watched his road as it changed color in the changing light. The more he stared at it the more convinced he became that it was a road, but then in two hours Vizintín returned with the news that Parrado had reached the top and wanted Canessa to join him.

"Are you sure he's at the top?"

"Yes, quite sure."

"Did you get there?"

"No, but Nando says it's marvelous. He says everything's going to be all right."

Reluctantly Canessa got to his feet and clambered up the side of the mountain. He had left his knapsack with Vizintín, but still it took him an hour longer than it had taken Parrado. He followed the steps they had cut into the snow, and as he approached the summit he called out for his friend. He heard Parrado shout back and followed his directions until he too stood on the top of the mountain.

The effect of what he saw was the same on Canessa as it had been on Parrado. He looked aghast at the endless mountains stretching away to the west. "But we've had it," he said. "We've absolutely had it. There isn't a chance in hell of getting through all that."

"But look," said Parrado. "Look there to the west. Don't you see? To the left? Two mountains without any snow?"

"Do you mean those tits?"

"The tits. Yes."

"But they're miles away. It'll take us fifty days to get to them."

"Fifty days? Do you think so? But look there." Parrado pointed into the middle distance. "If we go down this mountain and along that valley it leads to that sort of Y. Now, one branch of the Y must lead to the tits."

Canessa followed the line of Parrado's arm, saw the valley, and saw the Y. "Maybe," he said. "But it'd still take us fifty days, and we've only enough food for ten."

"I know," said Parrado. "But I've thought of something. Why don't we send Tintin back?"

"I'm not sure he'd want to go."

"He'll go if we tell him to. Then we can keep his food." If we ration it out carefully, it should last us for twenty days."

"And after that?"

"After that we'll find some."

"I don't know," said Canessa. "I think I'd rather go back and look for that road."

"Then go back," said Parrado sharply. "Go back and find your road. But I'm going on to Chile."

They retraced their steps down the mountain, reaching Vizintín and the knapsacks around five in the afternoon. While they were away Vizintín had melted some snow, so they were able to quench their thirst before eating some more meat. As they were eating, Canessa turned to Vizintín and said, in the most casual tone of voice he could muster, "Hey, Tintin, Nando thinks it might be best if you went back to the plane. You see, it would give us more food."

"Go back?" said Vizintín, his face lighting up. "Sure. If you think so." And before either of the other two could say anything he had picked up his knapsack and was about to strap it to his back.

"Not tonight," said Canessa. "Tomorrow morning will do."

"Tomorrow morning?" said Vizintín. "Okay. Fine."

"You don't mind?"

"Mind? No. Anything you say."

"And when you get back," said Canessa, "tell the others that we've gone west. And if the plane spots you and you get rescued, please don't forget about us."

Canessa lay awake that night, by no means sure in his own mind that he would be going on with Parrado rather than returning with Vizintín. He continued to discuss the matter with Parrado under the stars, and Vizintín went to sleep to the sound of their arguing voices. But next morning, when they awoke, Canessa had made up his mind. He would go on with Parrado. They therefore took the meat from Vizintín and anything else that might be useful to them (though not the revolver, which they had always considered a dead weight) and prepared to send him on his way.

"Tell me, Muscles," said Vizintín, "is there anything . . . I mean, any part of the bodies that one *shouldn't* eat?"

"Nothing," said Canessa. "Everything has got some nutritional value."

"Even the lungs?"

"Even the lungs."

Vizintín nodded. Then he looked at Canessa again. "Look," he said. "Since you're going on and I'm going back, is there anything of mine you think you might need? Don't hesitate to say, because all our lives depend on your getting through."

"Well," said Canessa, looking Vizintín up and down and eying his equipment. "I wouldn't mind that balaclava."

"This?" said Vizintín, handling the white wool balaclava which he had on his head. "Do you mean this?"

"Yes. That."

"I . . . er . . . do you think you really need it?"

"Tintin, would I ask for it if I thought I didn't need it?"

Reluctantly Vizintín stripped off and handed over his prized balaclava. "Well, good luck," he said.

"Same to you," said Parrado. "Take care going down."

"I certainly will."

"Don't forget," said Canessa. "Tell Fito we've gone west. And if they rescue you, make them come and look for us."

"Don't worry," said Vizintín. He embraced his two companions and set off down the mountain.

Select Bibliography

Bates, Robert H.; Houston, Charles S. *K-2, The Savage Mountain: The Story Of The Third American Karakoram Expedition*. New York: McGraw-Hill, 1954.

Black Elk as told through John G. Neihardt. *Black Elk Speaks: Being the Life Story of a Holy Man of the Oglala Sioux*. Lincoln and London: Morrow, 1932.

Chase, Owen. *Narrative of the most extraordinary and distressing shipwreck of the whale-ship Essex, of Nantucket: which was attacked and finally destroyed by a large spermaceti-whale, in the Pacific Ocean: with an account of the unparalleled sufferings of the captain and crew*. New York: W.B. Gilley, 1821.

Equiano, Olaudah. *The Life of Olaudah Equiano, or Gustavus Vasa, The African, Written by Himself*. Boston: Isaac Knapp, 1837.

Herzog, Maurice. *Annapurna, First Conquest of an 8,000-meter Peak*. Translated from the French by Nea Morin and Janet Adam Smith. New York: E.P. Dutton, 1952.

Kazik (Simha Rotem). *Memoirs of a Warsaw Ghetto Fighter*. Translated from the Hebrew and edited by Barbara Harshav. New Haven and London: Yale University Press, 1994.

Levi, Primo. *Survival in Auschwitz: The Drowned and the Saved*. Translated by Stuart Woolf. New York: Orion Press, 1959.

Lovell, James A. *Houston, We've Had a Problem*, Chapter 13.1, *Apollo Expeditions to the Moon*. Edited by Edgar M. Cortright, Scientific and Technical Information Office, National Aeronautics and Space Administration. Washington, D.C. SP-350, 1975.

Mawson, Sir Douglas. *Home of the Blizzard, The Story of the Australasian Antarctic expedition, 1911-1914*. London: Heinemann, 1915.

McCain, John; Salter, Mark. *Faith of My Fathers*. New York: Random House, 1999.

Neave, Airey. *They Have Their Exits*. London: Hodder & Stoughton, 1953.

Nuñez Cabeza de Vaca, Alvar. *The journey of Alvar Nuñez Cabeza de Vaca and his companions from Florida to the Pacific, 1528-1536*. Translated from his own narrative by Fanny Bandelier. New York: A.S. Barnes, 1905.

Read, Piers Paul. *Alive: the Story of the Andes Survivors*. Philadelphia & New York: Lippincott, 1974.

Robertson, Dougal. *Survive the Savage Sea*. New York: Praeger, 1973.

Rogers, Woodes. *A cruising voyage round the world: first to the South-seas, thence to the East-Indies, and homewards by the Cape of Good Hope*. London: Printed for B. Lintot, and E. Symon, 1726.

Ross, John, Sir. *Narrative of a second voyage in search of a north-west passage, and of a residence in the Arctic regions during the years 1829, 1830, 1831, 1832, 1833*. London: A.W. Webster, 1835.

Rowlandson, Mary White. *The soveraignty & goodness of God, together, with the faithfulness of His promises displayed; being a narrative of the captivity and restauration of Mrs. Mary Rowlandson*. Cambridge, Massachusetts: Printed by Samuel Green, 1682.

Saint Exupéry, Antoine de. *Wind, Sand and Stars*. Translated by Lewis Galantière. New York: Harcourt, Brace & World, 1940.

Savigny, Jean Baptiste; Correard, Alexandre. *Narrative of a voyage to Senegal in 1816; undertaken by order of the French Government, comprising an account of the shipwreck of the Medusa, the sufferings of the crew, and the various occurrences on board the raft, in the desert of Zaara, at St. Louis*. London: Printed for Henry Colburn, Conduit-Street, 1818.

Shackleton, Ernest, Sir. *South: The Story of Shackleton's LastExpedition 1914–1917*. London: 1922.

Staden, Hans. *The True History of His Captivity*. Orig. (1557) translated and edited by A. Tootal, annotated by Richard F. Burton. London: Hakluyt Society, 1874.

Thesinger, Wilfred. *Arabian Sands: Return to Salala*. New York: E.P. Dutton, 1959.

Acknowledgments

In the course of researching selections for this book I often visited a treasure trove of human memories stored in the "e" section of an obscure corner of the fourth floor of the Mudd Library, a relatively isolated resting place in the labyrinth of libraries here at Yale. There one day I found a 1936 reissue of the 1924 Everyman edition of Sir John Franklin's *Narrative of a journey to the shores of the polar sea, in the years 1819-20-21-22*. John Franklin's account of his party's horrific march to Fort Enterprise did not make it into *Survivors*, but the book bore the library bookplate of Gertrude Stein and in the top right hand corner the distinctive red label of the Librairie Galignani, a magical bookstore in Paris where last I had the joy of working as a buyer and manager. For me this small event closed the circle within my own heart of sharing, so as I close I dedicate this effort to the booksellers past, present, and future at the Librairie Galignani, to implacable and cherished Marie, to devoted Mademoiselle Cordier, to divine Marie-Philippe, to Caroline, Nadia, and Krim, to Jean-Michel, to Tanguy, Christopher, Valerie, Tamara, Yvonne, Sylvie, Eric, Ariel and Betrand, to each and every one, named and unnamed, and to our marvelous clients, to my friends next door at Angelina, and above all, to Monsieur and Madame Jeancourt, who are the best stewards of a great tradition of bookselling. And from that rich center of my affection I also dedicate this book to Richard Meredith, Edith Kaye, and Jim Tenney, and to devoted booksellers everywhere. Of course my each and every effort is always dedicated to my own dear families and friends, and to our parents, to my dear Anne, to John, to Bob & Barbara, to Bruce & Tracy, Dan & Carol, Richard & Christina, Richard & Joann, Alec & Drika, Cyrus & Rosamond, to Will, Arina, Lisa, Catherine, Phoebe, and Mary, and to so many others who by but slight degrees of separation bind us all into one community of shared quest, discovery, joy, redemption, and love.

– J.B.L..

Chapter XIII: Records of the *Rescue and Salvage of USS* Squalus, including the statements of Harold Preble, Lieutenant W.T. Doyle and lecture by Commander Charles Momsen, courtesy of the Navy Historical Center, Department of the Navy.

Chapter XIV: Excerpt from *They Have Their Exits*, by Airey Neave , copyright © 1953 by Airey Neave. Reproduced by permission of Pen & Sword Books and the Airey Neave Trust.

Chapter XV: Excerpt from *Memoirs of a Warsaw Ghetto Fighter* by Kazik (Simha Roten), translated by and edited by Barbara Harshav, copyright © 1994 by Yale University. Reprinted by Permission of Yale University Press.

Chapter XVI: "The Drowned and the Saved", from *If this is a Man (Survival in Auschwitz)* by Primo Levi, translated by Stuart Woolf, copyrighty © 1959 by Orion Press, Inc., © 1958 by Guilio Einaudi editore S.P.A. Used by permission of Viking Penguin, a division of Penguin Group (USA) Inc.

Chapter XVII: Excerpt from "Return to Salala" from *Arabian Sands* by Wilfred Thesiger, copyright © 1959, 1983, renewed 1987 by Wilfred Thesiger. Used by permission of Viking Penguin, a division of Penguin Group (USA) Inc.

Chapter XVIII: Excerpt from *Annapurna* by Maurice Herzog, copyright © 1952 by Maurice Herzog. Reprinted by permission of Sterling Lord Literistic, Inc.

Chapter XIX: Excerpt from *K2: The Savage Mountain* by Charles S. Houston, MD and Robert H. Bates, copyright (©1954, 1979, 1997. Reprinted by permission of the Adventure Library.

Chapter XXII: Excerpt from *Survive the Savage Sea* by Dougal Robertson, copyright © 1973 by Dougal Robertson. Reprinted by Permission of Sheridan House.

Chapter XX: Reprinted from *Faith of My Fathers* by John McCain and Mark Salter, copyright © 1999 by John McCain and Mark Salter. Used by permission of Random House, Inc.

Chapter XXII: "Houston, We've Had a Problem", by James A. Lovell, from *Apollo Expeditions to the Moon,* edited by Edgar M. Cortright, reproduced courtesy of Scientific and Technical Information Office, National Aeronautics and Space Administration.

Chapter XXIII: Reprinted from *Alive: The Story of the Andes Survivors* by Piers Paul Read. Copyright © 1974 by Piers Paul Read. Reprinted by permission of HarperCollins Publishers, Inc.